EUROPE 1850–1914

PROGRESS,

PARTICIPATION AND APPREHENSION

D0198788

EUROPE 1850–1914
PROGRESS,
PARTICIPATION AND APPREHENSION

Jonathan Sperber

PEARSON
Longman

Harlow, England • London • New York • Boston • San Francisco • Toronto • Sydney • Singapore • Hong Kong
Tokyo • Seoul • Taipei • New Delhi • Cape Town • Madrid • Mexico City • Amsterdam • Munich • Paris • Milan

PEARSON EDUCATION LIMITED

Edinburgh Gate
Harlow CM20 2JE
United Kingdom
Tel: +44 (0)1279 623623
Fax: +44 (0)1279 431059
Website: www.pearsoned.co.uk

———————

First edition published in Great Britain in 2009

© Pearson Eduction Limited 2009

The right of Jonathan Sperber to be identified as author
or this work has been asserted by him in accordance
with the Copyright, Designs and Patents Act 1988.

ISBN: 978-1-4058-0134-8

British Library Cataloguing in Publication Data
A CIP catalogue record for this book can be obtained from the British Library

Library of Congress Cataloging in Publication Data
Sperber, Jonathan, 1952–
    Europe, 1850–1914 : progress, participation and apprehension / Jonathan
Sperber. — 1st ed.
       p. cm.
    Includes bibliographical references and index.
    ISBN 978-1-4058-0134-8 (pbk.)
    1. Europe—History—1848–1871.   2. Europe—History—1871–1918.   I. Title.
D359.s69 2009
940.2′88—dc22   2008024318

10 9 8 7 6 5 4 3 2 1
11   10   09

Set by 35 in 11.25/13pt Stone Print
Printed in Malaysia (CTP-KHL)

The Publisher's policy is to use paper manufactured from sustainable forests.

To the memory of my paternal grandparents, Nathan Sperber and Fanny née Dolberg, one-time loyal subjects of the Habsburg emperor Franz Joseph, and my personal link to the now-vanished world of pre-1914 Europe.

BRIEF CONTENTS

CONTENTS

LIST OF FIGURES, TABLES AND BOXES

LIST OF MAPS

PUBLISHER'S ACKNOWLEDGEMENTS

We are grateful to the following for permission to reproduce copyright material:

Tables 2.1, 2.2, 9.1 and 16.1, and Figures 2.1, 9.2, 16.2, 16.3, 16.4, 16.6 and 16.7 taken and adapted from B.R. Mitchell, *International Historical Statistics: Europe, 1750–1993*, 4th Ed, 1998, Palgrave Macmillan, reproduced with permission of Palgrave Macmillan; Figure 17.1 from S.L. Hoffman, *Civil Society*, 2006, Palgrave Macmillan, reproduced with permission of Palgrave Macmillan; Maps of Europe, the Crimean War, Italian National Unification, German National Unification, Europe in 1871, Balkans in 1878, Europe on the Eve of the First World War and Balkans Wars adapted from *THE MAKING OF THE WEST 3E*, by Lynn Hunt et al., Copyright © 2009 by Bedford/St. Martin's. Reproduced by permission of Bedford/St. Martin's.

In some instances we have been unable to trace the owners of copyright material, and we would appreciate any information that would enable us to do so.

INTRODUCTION

In contrast to the preceding period, the age of revolution, 1780–1850, and the succeeding one, 1914–45, the age of total war, the years 1850 to 1914 in European history are not a high concept era that can be summed up in one short phrase. That period stretching from the middle of the nineteenth century to the outbreak of the First World War was a more complex and diverse era, not dominated by drastic and dramatic events, but instead involving the slower and more gradual interaction of several different trends.

This book's title points to three of the more important ones. There was progress, a continual and continuous improvement over the past, in economic conditions – total output, standards of living, level of applicable technology – but also in human knowledge, especially in the sciences, and, perhaps most of all, in the attitudes and perceptions of contemporaries, their belief that material, intellectual, social and moral circumstances were engaged in a steady forward march. This belief in progress was strongest in the middle decades of the nineteenth century, and not quite so buoyant later on, but was clearly a defining characteristic of the era.

A second feature of the age was participation, whose growth was a feature of political and social life. Political life developed – admittedly, at a different pace and with different chronology in different countries – from the limited world of the old regime society of orders, where participation and involvement were determined by status at birth, religious confession and charters of privilege, to a bourgeois world of the notables, where ownership of property was the chief determinant of political influence, to an age of democratic, mass politics. There, all adult men – and, increasingly, if still in limited fashion, women as well – could at least raise a claim to participation in political decisions, finding in mass demonstrations, political leagues and mass political parties some of the ways to do so. Nationalism, whose growth was probably the single most important political trend in the period, was an ideology, an ideal and a practice of widespread participation. This growing participation was reflected in the organization of political and social life, in the steadily increasing number, membership, variety and activity of voluntary associations, one of the crucial but little known stories of this period of European history.

Yet all this progress and participation did not always leave contemporaries with the most cheerful and optimistic of feelings. Rather, confidence and optimism were shadowed by apprehension, whether in the form of artists' and intellectuals' scepticism of ideals and material realities of progress, doubts on the part of inhabitants of Asia and Africa over whether their incorporation into European empires was a sign of progress, fears of the results of political mass participation and worries about the way all these developments would feed into the diplomatic and military confrontations of the Great Powers. Judging in retrospect, some of these apprehensions were of dubious validity. Others had more substance, as the end of the entire era in the world's first total war would more than adequately demonstrate.

This book divides the history of Europe in the complex era 1850–1914 into three large chronological parts. Each part offers Europe-wide coverage, from the Urals to the Atlantic and from the Baltic to the Mediterranean, not only emphasizing common features and trends but also noting regional differences and, where relevant, the unique paths of individual countries. The first part, entitled 'The Age of Progress', covers the period 1850–75, the second, 'The Age of Uncertainty', 1870–95, and the third, 'The Age of Classical Modernism', the period 1890–1914. Each part has a distinct theme. The first describes the creation of a bourgeois socio-economic, intellectual and political world in the quarter-century or so following 1850, and outlines this world's chief characteristics. The second part describes how many of the intellectual certainties of this third quarter of the nineteenth century came into question over the following twenty to twenty-five years, often as a result of unexpected socio-economic, political and cultural changes. The upshot was a climate of uncertainty, containing tentative new departures mixed in with continuations of the previous era. In the third part there is a consideration of the decades before the First World War, a quarter-century which was both the climax of the entire post-1850 period and also the beginning of a new and different modern era reaching deep into the twentieth century and yet which seems, in today's postmodern world, increasingly distant.

The reader will observe that the boundaries of the three periods overlap somewhat, with each period ending after its successor begins. This is deliberate, making it possible to treat some developments of the 1870s, for instance, as the climax of the age of progress, and others, occurring simultaneously as the beginning of the age of uncertainty. Such a procedure is particularly helpful for a history which provides not just a wide geographic coverage but also a broad thematic one, encompassing economic, social, cultural, artistic, political and diplomatic structures and events, since turning points and lines of continuity can differ considerably from one aspect of the past to the next.

Each of the three chronological parts begins with a two-part overview and is then divided into a further six thematic chapters, one each for the economy and demography, social structures and social institutions, the arts and sciences, then three for politics – one focusing on domestic politics, one on international relations, and one on the interrelationships and dynamics of power. Although invariably addressing somewhat different issues in each of the three periods under consideration, the introductory overview and the six thematic chapters do have a consistent character and central themes.

The first half of the overview, 'The Shape of an Era', sketches the broad, central themes of the period under consideration. The second half, 'The Main Events',

offers a brief chronological summary of the most important developments in international relations and in the domestic politics of the major European countries. Students can refer to this summary as they consider the following six chapters.

The chapters dealing with the economy emphasize the causes and pace of economic growth (whose persistence was a major feature of the years 1850 to 1914), the structures of technology and market relations that helped bring about this growth, and the changing standards of living resulting from this economic growth and its often unequal distribution across the population. These chapters also includes a discussion of population movements, both migration and vital events, and their connections, or lack of them, to economic trends.

In the chapters on social structures and social institutions, central issues are the nature of social classes and social conflicts, the development of cities and urban life (another key feature of the 1850–1914 period), and the position and status of women. These chapters also include an account of voluntary associations, emphasizing the activities and influence of these groups, and their increase in numbers and membership as well as diversification of their functions. While the growth of the economy and of urban areas have been commented upon both at the time and ever since, and historians have for some time now devoted more attention to the position of women, it is only recently that the remarkable presence and importance of voluntary associations has been fully recognized as another central feature of the era.

The chapters on the arts and sciences include a discussion of the major landmarks in the history of biology, chemistry and physics, emphasizing the conceptual re-evaluations they entailed, the influence on broader intellectual life and even on popular culture of scientific innovations, and the changing institutional framework in which science was carried out. An account of the humanities and social sciences – gradually emerging as distinct scholarly disciplines – features the changing conceptions of human history, human society and the drives and motivations of human actions. Connected with this account are observations on broader intellectual trends and the position of religion within them. These chapters also provide an extensive discussion of the arts, picking up on artists' repeated and varied striving to develop new forms of expression and representation, a striving that marked a break with past artistic practices.

The first of the three chapters devoted to politics, entitled 'The Politics of the People', centres on political activities and structures within the boundaries of individual states. As the title indicates, analysis of political participation and political organization are central concerns, and discussions of the main political tendencies and the ideas of their supporters are placed in this context of participation and organization. There are also accounts of the main political currents of the period. Throughout these chapters, the growing importance and changing nature of nationalism – arguably the most important element of political life in the period – is emphasized.

The second chapter on politics, 'The Politics of the Powers', deals with international relations. Rather than a blow-by-blow narrative of diplomatic crises and

wars, this chapter focuses on the structural components of relations between the European powers. Important considerations are the changing relative strengths and weaknesses of the Great Powers, the relations between the European powers and the non-European world, the technology and organization of the armed forces and of warfare, and their influence on international relations, and, finally, the political forces influencing the shaping of foreign policy.

The third chapter on politics, 'The Dynamics of Power', deals with the interrelationship between domestic politics and international relations, as they developed over time. Since this book covers an entire continent, the reader should not expect a detailed discussion of political crises and landmarks in every European country, or every twist and turn of international affairs. Rather, this chapter traces out the main lines of development, the most important changes in political life and in the exercise of power, in chronological and narrative fashion. These accounts of change over time will contrast with the five previous chapters of each part, which consider the individual time periods as a whole.

The Conclusion provides a brief summary of the major trends of the years 1850 to 1914. It is followed by a discussion of the transitions between the preceding revolutionary era 1780–1850 and the years 1850 to 1914, and between that period and the age of total war, 1914–45, focused on the nature and extent of lines of continuity and points of rupture.

Notes to the text can be found at the end of the relevant part. An annotated English-language bibliography, emphasizing more recent writings on the relevant topics, is provided at the end of the book.

PART I

THE AGE OF PROGRESS, 1850–1875

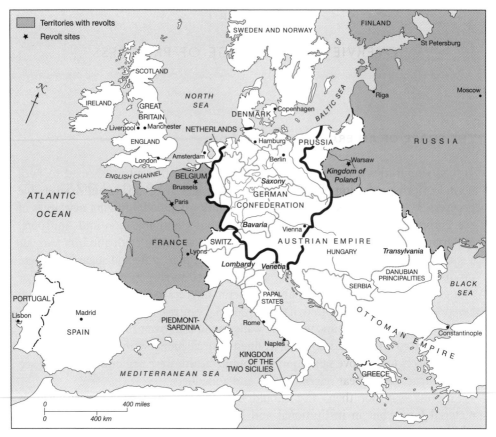

Europe in 1850

Source: From *THE MAKING OF THE WEST 3E* by Lynn Hunt et al., Copyright © 2009 by Bedford/
St. Martin's. Reproduced by permission of Bedford/St. Martin's.

CHAPTER I

OVERVIEW OF THE AGE OF PROGRESS

THE SHAPE OF AN ERA

(To contemporaries, the third quarter of the nineteenth century seemed to be a period of prosperity, improvement and reform, an age of steady and irreversible progress.)With each passing day, the rail network expanded, bringing new areas of the European continent into the circuit of rapid communication and transport. Material goods, whether manufactured ones, such as cotton cloth and iron bars, or a variety of agricultural products, including wheat, pigs, wine and sugar beet, were produced in ever greater quantities, and consumed in ever greater amounts by an ever greater portion of the population. Quiet market towns, such as Dortmund and Essen, were transformed into dynamic industrial centres. In older great cities, such as London, Paris and Vienna, medieval walls and old slum housing were demolished, to be replaced with broad boulevards lined with fashionable buildings, and ambitious projects to improve sanitation and public health were begun which would see the construction of great sewer systems and aqueducts.

Progress was not then, and should not now be, understood exclusively in material terms but in institutional and legal ways as well. Reductions in tariffs and bilateral trade treaties made trade among European countries steadily freer. Economically and socially limiting relics of a past age, including serfdom, the guild system, or legal discrimination against the Jews, were brought to an end. Elected legislatures, with constitutionally guaranteed powers, could enact new laws, making possible a politics of gradual, legal reform, in contrast to the violent, disruptive revolutionary movements that had characterized the previous sixty years. Accompanying and complementing political reforms were the actions of a whole galaxy of voluntary associations, from Masonic lodges and social clubs, to cooperatives and trade unions, from charitable and religious societies to professional and scholarly associations, whose numbers and members – both greatly expanded – energetically promoted improvements in public and private life. National groups laid claim to their rights of self-determination and, increasingly, obtained them.

Progress was an integral part of intellectual life. Primary education and, with it, the extent of literacy and other basic intellectual skills, expanded considerably. Broad advances in scientific knowledge, from the formulation of the laws of thermodynamics to the deciphering of the structure of the benzene ring, to the central scientific and intellectual accomplishment of the era, Charles Darwin's theory of evolution, demonstrated a growing understanding of the natural world, began to suggest the possibility of the application of scientific knowledge to technology and industry, and provided a powerful and influential model for all forms of intellectual enquiry. This influence extended from older forms of intellectual life, such as philosophy, to the rapidly expanding scholarly fields of history and philology and to the still nascent social sciences. Artists and novelists, following these scientific and intellectual developments, offered more exact and detailed pictures of human life, attempting to capture it as it was, rather than in idealized and distorted form. Summing up this broad picture of progress – or, perhaps more exactly, anticipating it – the British popular magazine *Household Words* proclaimed in 1850:

> Our present period recognises the progress of humanity, step by step, towards a social condition in which nobler feelings, thoughts, and actions, in concert for the good of all, instead of in general antagonism, producing a more refined and fixed condition of happiness, may be the common inheritance of great and small communities, and of all those nations of the earth who recognise and aspire to fulfil this law of human progression.[1]

In retrospect, we might want to treat this picture with a touch of suspicion, and it is not hard to find many exceptions and qualifiers to the march of progress. Prosperity was much less in evidence in the southern and eastern regions of Europe than in the British Isles or the central, northern and western portions of the continent. Even in more prosperous parts of Europe, the 1.16 million Irish and 1.1 million Germans who left their homes for North America during the 1850s and 1860s were evidently not participating in their countries' prosperity, and the people living in the slums of central Paris, cleared for the celebrated rebuilding projects of Baron Haussmann, were less than excited about losing their homes. Parliaments may have exercised their constitutional rights with vigour, but authoritarian executive powers, such as those of the French emperor Louis Napoleon Bonaparte, or the Prussian prime minister Otto von Bismarck, were vigorous too, and sometimes more than a match for parliamentarians. Revolutions and violent upheavals were fewer in the third quarter of the nineteenth century than in the second – although they did occur in southern Italy and in Spain – but the years 1853 to 1871, following almost four decades of peace among the European Great Powers, saw a revival of warfare on a scale not repeated until the outbreak of the First World War. As the outcome of these wars would painfully demonstrate, while many nations might claim the right to self-determination, only a few of them – generally those linked to the victorious armies of a Great Power – could actually exercise that right.

Yet all these exceptions should not distract our attention from the main point about the nature of the era, namely, its progress, or in other words, its steady and gradual improvement. Steady and gradual is the point here, as the positive developments were not the result of new, unprecedented changes but were a continuation of trends whose initial appearance dated from the first half of the nineteenth century. What changed in post-1850 decades was the way these characteristic features of politics, economy and society, science, scholarship and culture steadily moved towards a dominant position, found, to a greater or lesser extent, from the British Isles to the Crimea, from the Bulgarian provinces of the Ottoman Empire to the Finnish provinces of the Russian Empire, and at all places between.

THE MAIN EVENTS

Partisans of progress certainly envisaged a series of gradual improvements, but in the political sphere progress occurred in fits and starts, involved Great Power warfare and usually, although not always, stemming from this warfare, political upheaval. The ideal of smooth advance confronted a more disruptive reality.

At the very beginning of the period, in 1850, most of continental Europe was still reeling from the effects of the revolutions of 1848, which, contrary to their name, had extended well into 1849, and brought insurrection, drastic reforms and sometimes even civil war to a large area of Europe, from the Atlantic to the Carpathians and the Baltic to the Mediterranean. Although the insurgents had largely been defeated and increasingly conservative governments restored to power by 1850, there were still widespread expectations of a new round of revolution. It was only at the end of 1851, when Louis Napoleon Bonaparte, nephew of the great Napoleon and president of the French Republic, launched a successful coup making himself, first, president for life and then Emperor Napoleon III, that the mid-century revolutionary era came to a definitive end and suppression of the revolutionary events moved to the top of the political agenda.

Most of the decade of the 1850s was politically an age of repression, with constitutional government either non-existent (Russia), abolished (Austrian Empire), or present but sharply limited by conservative rule, as was the case in most of the rest of continental Europe. Switzerland, Europe's last remaining republic after France had once again become an empire, was a notable exception to this trend. Great Britain remained an offshore stronghold of liberal government ministries, civil liberties and parliamentary practice. Very much in contrast to the turbulent upheavals and mass politics of the revolutions of 1848, such political actions as took place were largely restricted to state officials, the upper classes and, sometimes, the notables, that is, the locally most influential men. The one major domestic political upheaval of the 1850s was the Spanish revolution of 1854–56, a sort of belated reprise of 1848, which ended with a resurgence of conservative political forces as the previous main event had.

Political movement in this decade came from Great Power warfare, in particular the Crimean War of 1853–56. Largely a result of Louis Napoleon Bonaparte's attempt to break the coalition of all the Great Powers against France, in existence since his uncle's final defeat in 1815, the war revolved around the Eastern Question, the future of the Ottoman Empire, the tottering Islamic realm encompassing the Balkans in south-east Europe, the Middle East and northern Africa. Provoking a Russian intervention in the Ottomans' Balkan provinces, Louis Napoleon got the British government to join him in opposing the southward expansion of Russian power, while the other Great Powers, Austria and Prussia, maintained a tortuous neutrality. The war, largely fought in the Crimean peninsula at the southern end of the Russian Empire, ended with the defeat of the Tsar's forces and a decisive weakening of the position of Russia, in 1850 the dominant power on the European continent. From the end of the Crimean War in 1856 to the end of the Franco-Prussian War in 1871, the question of which of the Great Powers would take its place was wide open.

Napoleon III certainly had his country in mind for that role, and having destroyed the coalition of forces aimed at France, he took the next step in political aggrandizement, by invading Austrian-dominated northern Italy in 1859, in league with the rulers of the northern Italian kingdom of Piedmont-Savoy. After the Franco-Piedmontese forces defeated the Austrians, the emperor designed a compromise peace which would transfer some Piedmontese territory to France, the Austrian province of Lombardy to Piedmont, and create a northern and central Italian federation. This whole settlement quickly came undone when the results of the war incited revolutionary insurrection in central Italy, and particularly in the south of the peninsula, following the invasion of the island of Sicily by the veteran revolutionary Giuseppe Garibaldi and his one thousand red-shirted followers. In the resulting upheaval, almost the entire peninsula was united under the Piedmontese dynasty as a nation-state, the Kingdom of Italy.

The 1859 war and the subsequent revolution brought the period of political repression and conservative rule in continental Europe to an end. In the following decade, three major trends – movements towards national unification, plans for political reform and a gradual return to mass politics – intersected with the diplomatic and military strategies of the Great Powers as they struggled for a dominant position in Europe. The ultimate outcomes included the only very partial realization of nationalists' aspirations, a limited victory for liberal, political reform and the failure of both radical aspirations and conservative opposition to change, and the unexpected emergence of the Kingdom of Prussia, in 1850, the smallest and weakest of the Great Powers, as the new dominant continental Power.

The Italian example of the creation of a united nation-state spurred on nationalist movements in other European countries. German nationalists campaigned aggressively for the creation of a united nation-state. Quietly and hesitantly at first, with increasing confidence and assertion as the decade went on, the many nationalist movements in the many nationalities of the Austrian Empire – among others, the Hungarians, Czechs, Poles, Slovenes and Croatians – began demanding national autonomy or even the dissolution of the empire into independent nation-states. The most dramatic example of nationalism was the Polish uprising against tsarist rule in 1863, seeking the creation of an independent nation-state, thoroughly crushed by

Russian troops. While parallel sorts of demands for independence for Ireland from the UK were less common or salient in this decade than they had been before 1850 or would be after 1880, in south-eastern Europe, nationalists in the Danubian Principalities of Moldavia and Wallachia, autonomous provinces of the Ottoman Empire, took advantage of the results of the end of the Crimean War to merge the two principalities into one state under one ruler, a step towards the future creation of an independent Romania.

Along with nationalism went the process of reform. The most striking example was in Russia, where Tsar Alexander II proclaimed the end of serfdom in 1861, a bold action which earned him the sobriquet of the 'Tsar liberator'. In central and north-ern Europe, including the German states, the Austrian Empire, the Low Countries and Scandinavia, a series of more modest reforms, including the improvement of local self-government, the abolition of the guilds and the introduction of freedom of occupation, marriage and movement, were implemented at different times in the course of the decade. In 1867, following some complicated political manoeuvring, the British parliament passed the Second Reform Act, substantially expanding the fran-chise among the male population – and there were even some MPs (not a majority) who wanted to give women the vote.

Political life was more active and contentious following 1859 than it had been in the previous decades. The various liberal political groupings were, seen on a continent-wide basis, probably the most influential, but there was also a resurgence of political radicalism in individual European countries – progressives in the German states, republicans in France, Radicals within the Liberal Party in the UK – and the first, generally somewhat feeble, attempts at the creation of labour parties. Conservatives reacted to the growth of liberal and radical movements, organizing as well, especially Catholics who foresaw a dim future for Pope Pius IX, since most of the princedom he ruled had been annexed into the Italian kingdom in 1861 and the remainder of the papal territory was under threat.

This growing political activism generally moved within the established channels of legal, constitutional procedure. Among the rare exceptions were the Spanish revolution of 1867 which inaugurated a six-year period of upheaval and civil war, ultimately ending with the creation of a constitutional monarchy, and the coup d'état of 1866 in the Danubian Principalities of Moldavia and Wallachia resulting in a new royal dynasty which would pursue more vigorously the creation of a Romanian nation-state. Ultimately, the main determinant of political outcomes would be the Great Power warfare of the 1860s.

The roots of this warfare lay in the Kingdom of Prussia, where the strength of the liberal and nationalist opposition in the early 1860s led the ruling monarch to appoint the conservative diplomat Otto von Bismarck as prime minister in 1862. Bismarck, taking a leaf from the books of other European rulers, such as Napoleon III in France or the Piedmontese dynasty in Italy, resolved to defeat the political opposition by adopting its programme of Prussian-led German national unification.

Following an initial war with Denmark over the border provinces Schleswig and Holstein in 1864, in 1866, Bismarck took on the Austrian Empire, the Prussians' main rival for control of central Europe over the previous century. Isolated from its former ally, Russia, by its neutrality in the Crimean War, weakened by its defeat by France in 1859, lacking the latest weapons and up-to-date military strategy, Austria was quickly defeated in a six weeks' war. Bismarck annexed a number of the German states that had fought on the Austrians' side and united most of the remainder into the North German Confederation, a step in the direction of a united German nation-state. The defeated Austrian government, bankrupt and near collapse, was forced to make concessions to one of the nationalist movements in the empire, establishing an autonomous Hungary and thus transforming the Austrian Empire into the Dual Monarchy of Austria-Hungary, whose governments would continue to battle the other nationalist movements until the final collapse of the regime at the end of the First World War.

Bismarck's victory was also a major defeat for the French emperor Napoleon III and his project of making France the dominant country in Europe. Between 1867 and 1870, tensions between France and the Prussian-led North German Confederation mounted steadily. Growing domestic political opposition, including election victories of supporters of a republic in France, and opponents of Prussia in the still independent states of southern Germany, added to the respective governments' inclination to consider the possibility of a military solution.

When the war between France and Prussia finally broke out in 1870, it was quickly decided in favour of the latter, quite against what contemporary experts expected. Prussian military staff work, mobilization and deployment, and battlefield command far exceeded the French. Within a month of the outbreak of hostilities, the main French armies had been defeated and the emperor himself taken prisoner. On this news, radical activists in Paris proclaimed France a republic and continued the war. Their efforts were in vain and they were forced to sue for peace within six months.

The resulting peace treaty cost France a large war indemnity and the regions of Alsace and Lorraine, which became part of the German Empire, the nation-state created in the euphoric period of military victory, by the merger of the North German Confederation with the south German states. This humiliating peace, ratified by a democratically elected French national assembly, was resisted by much of the population of Paris, under radical leadership. The insurgent government they created, the Paris Commune, later a source of socialist and communist legend, although in reality a mixture of a socialists, trade unionists, non-socialist radicals and angry French nationalists, was destroyed in a brief and bloody civil war in June 1871 by the French provisional government. The defeat of this radical uprising and the consolidation of the German Empire, successor to the Prussian kingdom as the dominant power in continental Europe, marked the end of the turbulent events of the 1860s.

POPULATION AND THE ECONOMY

Central to the understanding of the period as an age of progress was the pace of economic growth. A relatively steady and fairly rapid economic development was the major economic feature of the period. Business cycle downturns caused by harvest failures, as happened in 1816–17, 1828–32 and 1845–48, vanished from Europe after 1850. The frequent and persistent recessions of the last quarter of the century were also not present; economies of individual countries had their ups and downs, but across the continent there was just one widespread and substantial downturn, in 1857–58, followed by a good recovery.

Let us now take a closer look at this phase of economic growth. Beginning with the developments responsible for it, we will go on to consider its ramifications: the prosperity and growing consumption, the resulting changes in economic structure, and its impact on economic sectors – industry, agriculture, crafts and commerce. Finally, this chapter considers population movements and their relationship to these large economic changes.

CREATING ECONOMIC GROWTH

We can sum up the reasons for the rapid economic progress in post-1850 Europe in just one word: railways. The construction of a rail network was an important element of a major economic trend of the era, the expansion of steam-powered industrial production. Railway construction provided a major stimulus for some rapidly growing industrial sectors: the manufacture of iron and steel for the railways themselves, mechanical engineering for the construction of locomotives, and coal mining as a source of energy. Railways were also a cheap and efficient way to carry coal, a heavy and bulky commodity, so that rail transport helped to expand the market for coal, and thus for the steam-powered industrial machinery powered by coal, substantially encouraging the growth of mechanized textile mills, a major industrial sector. The replacement of charcoal with coke in iron smelting and steel manufacture was another result of the greater possibilities for the use of coal, provided by the railways.

This promotion of industry was part of a broader function of the growth of a rail network, namely the expansion of markets. By bringing commodities from distant places at rapid speeds, railways increased trade and commerce and made possible a greater economic specialization, and, with it, greater productivity and increasing

output. This process of market expansion and specialization was particularly important for European agriculture, which, in view of the growth of mechanized industry,
was no longer the leading sector of the economy, but which still employed the
majority of people and remained crucial to determining standards of living.

More broadly, this process of market expansion and specialization provided the
fundamentals for economic growth in Europe during the third quarter of the
nineteenth century. While most concentrated in the northern and western regions
of large-scale railway construction, growth was experienced across the continent, even
in such distant places as the Bulgarian (then a province of the Ottoman Empire) town
of Gabrovo, a centre of woollens manufacture. The prosperity of Gabrovo notwithstanding, the effects of this growth were more limited in southern and eastern
Europe, in Spain, southern Italy, the Balkans and the Russian Empire, where railway
construction was rudimentary or non-existent, started late, or was carried out in ways
that did not promote economic growth.

Table 2.1 offers a brief overview of the development of the rail network in Europe
during the middle decades of the nineteenth century. As can be seen, there had already
been a respectable amount of rail construction in a few European countries during
the 1840s, but the size of the rail network grew very strongly after 1850. By the mid-
1870s, every substantial town in the more affluent countries of western and central
Europe was attached to the rail network, and inhabitants of most rural areas, except
those living in mountainous regions of difficult terrain, had access to a railway line.
As the figures for Russia, Spain and Greece show, railway construction began later
and proceeded at a slower pace in the eastern and southern parts of Europe.

A comparably dramatic but also comparably regionally limited form of economic
development was the growth of the iron and steel industry. The post-1850 decades
saw rapid increases in iron and steel production, particularly in western and central
Europe, where output expanded three- to sixfold in twenty-five years. A famous
example of the expansion of steel manufacturing was the Krupp Works at Essen in
western Germany. Alfred Krupp's 'forged steel factory' counted some 80 workers

Table 2.1 Growth of the rail network in Europe, 1840–75

	Rail network (km)					
	UK	**France**	**Germany**	**Spain**	**Russia**	**Greece**
1840	2,390	410	469	0	27	0
1850	9,797	2,915	5,856	28	501	0
1860	14,603	9,167	11,089	1,649	1,626	0
1875	23,368	19,357	27,970	5,923	19,029	12

Source: B. R. Mitchell, *International Historical Statistics: Europe, 1750–1993*, 4th edn, 1998, Palgrave Macmillan,
reproduced with permission of Palgrave Macmillan.

in 1850. At the Great Exhibition, the celebrated 1851 London World's Fair, Krupp astonished contemporaries with a 2 ton block of steel, which had been forged by having all his workers stand over a mould with buckets of molten steel, and pour the steel into the mould on his command. This was very impressive, but a sort of hypertrophied craft workshop. In the early 1870s, by contrast, the Krupp Works employed 12,000 people, and was a giant industrial complex with blast furnaces, Bessemer Converters, rolling mills, coal mines, and facilities producing all manner of steel products, ranging from heavy artillery to locomotives.

The reason for this spurt in iron and steel manufacturing was a fundamental change in technology. Before 1850, the initial step in iron and steel manufacture, the reduction of iron ore to pig iron, had been carried out by heating the ore with charcoal (burnt wood) in forges. It was only in Britain that pig iron was manufactured in blast furnaces, where pig iron was heated together with coke (burnt coal). The use of coke to manufacture pig iron was cheaper, more efficient and more productive, and, oddly enough for an industrialized procedure, much better for the environment since it did not require chopping down whole forests and burning them to produce charcoal.

Before 1850, pig iron had been forged in mountainous and forested areas with a good supply of wood, such as the Haute-Marne in France, or Styria in Austria, difficult terrain to get the heavy iron ore into and the heavy pig iron and steel out of. After mid-century, production moved to the centres of coal mining, where coking coal could be had. There were a number of such centres in continental Europe that would be developed over the course of the nineteenth century – in central France, northern Spain, south-eastern and south-western Germany, the Donets Basin in Russia, and regions of Moravia and Hungary, to name just some – but the most important one was the great north-west European coalfield, running from northern France, through Belgium, into the Ruhr Basin of western Germany, where Alfred Krupp's works were located. Exploitation of this field had begun in the first half of the nineteenth century but greatly expanded after 1850 as deeper shafts were dug and much greater coal reserves were discovered. Iron ore could be shipped into a rich coalfield handily by rail and pig iron and steel shipped out the same way.

It was this revolutionary restructuring of iron and steel production that made possible the great post-1850 expansion of output, as Figure 2.1 shows. In Britain, iron was already forged with coke in the first half of the nineteenth century, so that pig iron output was very high in 1850 – indeed, higher then than any continental European country had achieved by 1875 – and almost tripled in the subsequent twenty-five years. In France and Germany, where the transition from charcoal to coke was very rapid after 1850 (similar developments in Belgium), pig iron output leapt upward, growing four- to sixfold. While Russia and Austria-Hungary were quite competitive with other continental producers in the middle of the nineteenth century, they continued to use charcoal forges to turn iron ore into pig iron, and so their iron and steel production showed, at best, very modest gains. (Iron manufacture lagged in similar ways in Spain and Sweden.) There simply was not enough wood to turn

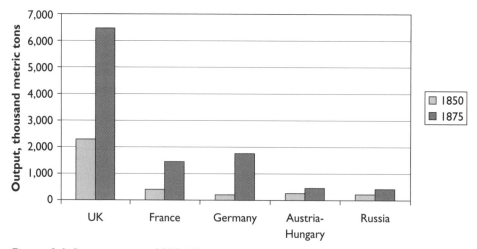

Figure 2.1 *Pig iron output, 1850–75*
Source: B. R. Mitchell, *International Historical Statistics: Europe, 1750–1993*, 4th edn, 1998, Palgrave Macmillan, reproduced with permission of Palgrave Macmillan.

into charcoal in order to expand pig iron production substantially. By contrast, coal was present in virtually unlimited amounts. The great European coalfields have been exploited for some 150–200 years, but the problem today is not so much their exhaustion as that there is no profitable use for the coal still being mined.

While the construction of a rail network and the rapid rise of mechanized steel manufacture were examples of an 'industrial revolution', the true workhorse of industrial development was textile manufacturing. More workers were employed in this sector than in any other (of the 2.4 million French industrial and craft workers in 1866, for instance, over 1.4 million worked in the textile industry); the total value of textile output exceeded that of other industrial branches and, unlike advanced iron and steel manufacture, confined, during the third quarter of the century to the British Isles and a smaller number of western and central European regions, large-scale textile production existed in a variety of forms across the European continent. In particular, textiles were a bright spot of economic development in the otherwise laggard eastern and southern reaches of Europe. Steam-powered spinning and weaving mills produced cotton textiles in Barcelona; cotton and woollens were manufactured in Reichenbach in Bohemia; silk goods in Milan and elsewhere in northern Italy; cotton and woollen textiles were woven in the upland Stara Planina region of what was then the Bulgarian province of the Ottoman Empire.

Table 2.2, recording the total number of cotton spindles, gives an overview of the progress of the mechanization of textile manufacturing since, as will be explained below, steam power in textile manufacturing began with cotton spinning. As this table suggests, the mid-nineteenth century was less of a turning point for mechanized cotton production than had been the case for railway construction or

BOX 2.1

The 'Workshop of the World'

Industrial exhibitions were first sponsored by the French revolutionary governments of the 1790s and the pattern they set – a show of national industry, arranged and financed by the state – continued for the next half-century. It was only in 1851 that such an exhibition was mounted in Great Britain, but it was of a different kind and on a fundamentally different scale. The exhibition was formally organized by a royal commission, with prominent politicians as members, and chaired by Queen Victoria's husband, Prince Albert, but both the exhibition and the commission had been devised and planned by private individuals and organizations. Funding came from businesses, particularly London financial firms. The government played no part in either the exhibition's organization or its financing. It was not just the sponsorship that was a break with past practice; in contrast to previous exhibitions, limited to one country, this would be an international one, a veritable world's fair. Yet the promotion of national industry was not neglected since, as members of the royal commission asserted, 'a particular advantage to British Industry might be derived from placing it in fair competition with that of other nations'. The sponsors' assumption that British industrial products would look good in comparison with those of other countries proved eminently justified.

British industrial superiority at this 'Great Exhibition', as the fair was known, began with the building in which the exhibition was located, the 'Crystal Palace'. A giant iron and glass structure, a sort of greenhouse on steroids, it was evidence of the superiority of British iron production. British manufacturers' stands, showing the latest locomotives, steam engines, textile production machinery, and speciality items such as the world's largest hydraulic press, a giant steam hammer or a 700 horsepower engine for the newly developed screw-type steamship propulsion, displayed advanced industrial techniques. Equally impressive were steel consumer products, including hardware, tools and razors. The contrast with the exhibits of other countries underscored British industrial supremacy. French exhibitors showed mostly high-quality craft products, such as silk, porcelain or luxury furniture, produced by hand without any mechanical power. Manufactured goods from the German states went in the opposite direction, noted as cheap but generally of low quality. Most of the other exhibits – from the Mediterranean countries, Russia, the United States, Austria and the British colonies – were raw materials and agricultural products (including the first public demonstration of the products of Australian winemaking) or imperial exotica, such as the giant Koh-i-Noor diamond and a stuffed elephant from India.

In these circumstances, it was easy to see why Great Britain acquired at the Great Exhibition the designation of the 'Workshop of the World', the globe's manufacturer. A closer look at some of the other products on display – the industrial goods at the Swiss and Belgian exhibits, the high-quality scientific instruments, manufactured in France, the giant 2 ton block of steel from the Krupp Works in Prussia, or the mass production McCormick reaper and Colt .45 revolver in the US exhibit – might have suggested some possibilities for challenges to British manufacturing supremacy. In 1851, though, these were just scattered examples of future potential; the UK ruled industrial production at least as much as Britannia ruled the waves.

Table 2.2 Growth of cotton manufacturing, 1832–77

	UK	Austria	Belgium	France	Germany	Russia	Spain	Switzerland
	Cotton spindles (thousands)							
1834	10,000	800	200	2,500	626	700	?	580
1852	20,977	1,400	400	4,500	2,235	?	?	900
1877	44,207	1,558	840	5,000	4,700	4,400*	1,865*	1,854

*1882–83.
Source: B. R. Mitchell, *International Historical Statistics: Europe, 1750–1993*, 4th edn, 1998, Palgrave Macmillan, reproduced with permission of Palgrave Macmillan.

steel manufacture. Output of cotton textiles had been increasing on a broad scale before 1850, and growth continued after mid-century, sometimes at a more rapid pace, but sometimes at a slower one – in part a result of the disruption in the supply of cotton during the 1860s due to the American Civil War. The continuing dominance of Britain in cotton textile manufacturing was even more pronounced than was the case with iron and steel products.

Table 2.2 suggests a broader point about the textile industry. Not only did mechanized output grow more slowly than was the case with iron and steel production, but textiles were characterized by the long-term coexistence of steam-, water- and human-powered production. Textiles were manufactured in steam-powered factories with hundreds of workers, but they were also made in the cottages of outworking handloom weavers. Spinning, a mechanically less complex operation than weaving, was mechanized first, so that by the 1870s, while there were still many handloom weavers in continental Europe, the yarn they wove came from mechanized spinning mills. Cotton and linen production were mechanized more rapidly than woollen – a dense and difficult fibre – and silk, a delicate fabric hard to produce by machine. Finally, textile mechanization followed the broader pattern of industrialization: universal in Great Britain, increasingly dominant in western and central Europe, much less common in the southern and eastern parts of the continent.

Iron and steel production, along with the closely associated branch of mechanical engineering (the building of iron and steel products such as steam engines, locomotives, or firearms), and textile manufacture were the primary sites of industrialization in this period. While coal mining expanded greatly, making possible the expansion of iron and steel manufacture, and steam engines were employed in mining to pump water out of deep coal shafts, mining itself was carried out by hand, as miners hacked away with picks at the coal seam. Other branches that would later be important, such as the manufacture of chemicals, were still getting started and would require future scientific advances to develop into large-scale industrial production. Most consumer goods, including food, clothing, furniture and other household goods, and paper products, were made by hand in small craft workshops or by outworkers; construction, although starting to employ industrialized products such as iron bars, was also done without powered tools. The spread of the use of steam power between 1850 and 1875 should not be exaggerated. In Great Britain, Europe's (and the world's) leader in powered industry, total horsepower in steam engines had gone from 350,000 in 1840 to 1.5 million by 1870 – an impressive advance, but very far from the 9.6 million horsepower that would be available in 1910. This post-1870 expansion of steam power was characteristic of other European countries as well, and points to the fact that the growth of industrialization in the third quarter of the nineteenth century occurred only in a few, narrowly circumscribed branches of production.[2] Given this relatively narrow scope of industrialization, a complete picture of post-1850 prosperity requires a consideration of other economic sectors.

AGRICULTURE, CRAFTS AND COMMERCE IN AN INDUSTRIAL WORLD

The quarter-century after 1850 was generally a prosperous period for agriculture in Europe. Farm prices rose, albeit modestly, but, most importantly, the sharp fluctuations in the prices of agricultural products characteristic of the first half of the century were, after one last outburst in the early and mid-1850s, increasingly smoothed out. The price of rye in Germany, the main grain grown there, offers a good example of this decline in price fluctuations. Between 1806 and 1850, the highest average yearly price for rye was almost 4.5 times the lowest. In the 1850–75 period, by contrast, the gap between low and high prices was just 2.5 times, and in the almost two decades between 1857 and 1875 the difference between lowest and highest average yearly prices was down to a factor of just 1.36. This moderation in price swings would continue until the First World War. Natural fluctuations in crop yields as a result of changing weather conditions from year to year no longer led to large price fluctuations, as they had before mid-century, because improvements in transportation and communication made the market more effective and enabled grain to be transported from areas of surplus to those of deficit. This expansion of the market due to improvement in transportation – above all due to the building of a rail network – was central to the post-1850 progress of agriculture.

The most important way this progress appeared was in the form of agricultural specialization: the cultivation, for instance, of grapes for wine. The amount of land in France planted in grapevines increased by 13 per cent between 1852 and 1874. Farmers in Languedoc, in southern France, grew grapes for a cheap wine that could now be shipped quickly to consumer markets in the northern part of the country by rail before it spoiled. The 1866 report of the committee on agriculture of the canton of Bourg-de-Visa, in Languedoc, shows how the construction of a rail network had expanded markets for farm products: 'Thirty years ago, there was no market. The landowner was forced to consume his own wine or sell it to local innkeepers.

Today, wine merchants come to the cellars to make their purchases and send it to Bordeaux, Paris, etc.'[3]

Spanish farmers did not engage in this sort of specialization, but continued to grow cereals, a difficult endeavour in the arid central and southern parts of the country. The possibilities of specialization in a variety of Mediterranean crops, from oranges to grapes for wine, to olives, remained little used. This reflected the lack of opportunities for market expansion due to the poor state of transportation. Roads were in terrible shape; there were almost no canals or navigable rivers. The rail network was built late, and was designed primarily for military and strategic purposes rather than for commercial ones. All these circumstances – existing in other parts of southern Europe, including Portugal, southern Italy and much of the Balkans – limited possibilities for agricultural development and economic growth.

Such southern regions had the additional difficulty of not being very industrialized. The process of industrialization encouraged agricultural specialization by creating large markets for specialized products. Just north of the Ruhr Basin, the rapidly growing centre of coal mining and steel manufacture in western Germany, lay the largely rural Münsterland, whose farmers specialized in pig farming. The pigs could be shipped by train to slaughterhouses and butchers in the nearby industrial area and converted into ham and sausage for the hungry coal miners and steelworkers.

This process of specialization was the primary source of increased agricultural output in the post-1850 quarter-century. The process of improving agricultural output by raising crop yields through the introduction of new systems of crop rotation – abolishing fallow, planting nitrogen-fixing crops such as alfalfa and vetch – begun in Great Britain and the Low Countries around 1750, and in continental Europe *c.*1800, certainly continued after 1850 as it had in the first half of the century. However, figures on crop yields between 1850 and 1875 suggest smaller or no increases, and in Britain, Europe's leader in crop yields, perhaps even a small decline.

The way increasing yields took a back seat to specialization encouraged by a rail-based market expansion suggests an important point about agriculture in this period. With the exception of Great Britain and the Netherlands, agriculture continued to be the economic sector employing the most people in all European countries, and, in the peripheral regions of eastern and southern Europe, it continued to be responsible for the largest share of the gross domestic product. But it was no longer the leading sector and no longer determined business cycles and total economic output. A good example of this change – one that spans the years on either side of 1850 – is the economic consequences of the potato blight. The micro-organism that attacked and destroyed the potato crop first appeared in 1845, and its effects were sharpened by the poor grain harvest of the following year. Food prices soared, leading to mass starvation in Ireland, and bringing industrial and craft activity to a screeching halt elsewhere in Europe. The resulting severe recession of 1847 was an important cause of the revolutions of 1848. The potato blight retreated after 1846 and harvests were good, so that farm prices declined very sharply over the next several years, but the blight returned in the early 1850s and food prices reached unprecedented heights by the middle of the decade. Yet, quite in contrast to ten years previously, these bad harvests did not affect the broader economy. Industrial output in steel and textiles expanded vigorously, and railway construction continued at a rapid pace. The next recession occurred in 1857–58, as farm prices were falling; its origins in industrial overproduction and problems of international finance show that the broader economy was no longer determined by agriculture.

At least some of the trends characteristic of agriculture during the third quarter of the nineteenth century could also be found in the crafts. In most European countries (the UK was an exception) there were more people employed in small workshops lacking powered machinery than in the industrial sector. Indeed, both the absolute number of craftsmen and their proportion in the workforce continued to increase. If employing fewer people than the crafts, industry did account for a steadily rising proportion of total economic output, so that the significance of craft production for the broader economy was in decline.

While rather overshadowing craft production, industrialization in this period did not harm it. Concentrated in relatively few sectors, industrial production did not compete with the vast majority of the crafts. Quite the opposite: the gradual improvement in the standard of living resulting from the progress of industrialization increased demand for craftsmen's goods and services. Potential problems and difficulties among craftsmen came from different developments, which had been ongoing since the eighteenth century. One involved the expansion of outworking, an economic arrangement in which nominally independent master craftsmen came under the domination of capitalist merchants, who provided the masters with their raw materials, purchased their output from them, and generally advanced them money to finance their production. These arrangements made master shoemakers, tailors and cabinet makers – to name three trades in which outworking was a common practice – masters in name only.

A second trend involved a polarization among master craftsmen, in which a minority of the masters developed larger businesses and employed a number of apprentices and journeymen, while the remaining majority toiled alone in their workshops, without assistance, and were often involved in outworking arrangements. Like outworking, this tendency towards polarization was on the increase in the post-1850 decades. Technological advances, such as the invention of the sewing machine, furthered these trends, making it possible for both merchant capitalists and successful master tailors to undermine the position of the other masters and their journeymen by introducing cheap female labour into the trade. In contrast to agriculture, the opportunity for market expansion and specialization through the growth of a rail network did relatively little for the crafts, since craftsmen generally sold their goods and services in very localized markets.

While these trends tended to make craftsmen the unhappy campers of the age of industrialization – although, it should be reiterated, their pre-1875 problems were largely not the result of industrialization itself – conditions in commerce, finance and services were more favourable. International trade flourished; exports from European countries increased over the period 1846–75 at a rate of 5 per cent per year, the fastest in the entire nineteenth century.[4] Domestic wholesale commerce grew considerably, reflecting the market expansion stemming from the development of a rail network. The post-1850 decades were a good period for shopkeepers (in economically less developed regions a group not entirely distinct from master craftsmen). At least part of the expansion in economic output and consumer spending passed through their hands, while potential competition in the form of larger retail enterprises, such as department stores and consumer cooperatives, a major threat to shopkeepers in the late nineteenth and early twentieth centuries, was just beginning to get under way, primarily in great metropolitan centres such as London and Paris.

For similar reasons, the market for the services offered by professionals was favourable in this period. A buoyant business climate meant more opportunities for notaries and lawyers to draw up contracts and to take legal action against parties who did not fulfil the terms of these contracts. Increasing prosperity led to higher tax receipts, enabling governments to expand the ranks of the state service. Improvements in transportation and communication offered new possibilities for gathering the news; greater affluence and more widespread education increased the market for news, so that journalists and freelance writers enjoyed better prospects than in the first half of the century.

These favourable circumstances in commerce and professional services were the result of an expansion and improvement of pre-existing structures. The picture in post-1850 financial services was one of prosperity but also of important structural innovation. Here, the key event was the founding in 1852 of the Crédit Mobilier in Paris, a joint stock or corporate bank, a financial institution whose capital came from the sale of shares of stock to the public, rather than from the private fortunes of bankers. This financial innovation made it possible to mobilize savings on a broad scale to finance industrial development and, particularly, the construction of the rail network. Over the two following decades, this new form of bank found imitators throughout Europe, from the Darmstädter Bank in Germany, to the Enskilda Bank in Stockholm, the Società Generale di Credito Mobiliare of Turin or the Bank Handlowy in Warsaw, to mention just a few examples.

There were some exceptions to this trend. In Spain, corporate banks were prohibited between 1848 and 1869, a development which limited the financing of industrialization and economic growth, and contributed to its relatively slow pace when compared with growth in western European countries further to the north. Great Britain, Europe's leader in devising innovative forms of finance since the late seventeenth century, did not adopt this new form of banking, as its privately owned banks seemed quite adequate for the needs of industry and commerce. Throughout Europe, private bankers – who continued to do a good business after 1850, even expanding their fields of enterprise to compete with corporate banks – looked with suspicion on these new competitors, regarding them as fraudulent enterprises. The spectacular bankruptcy of the Crédit Mobilier in 1867 lent some credence to these suspicions, but also showed the remarkable innovations and vigorous competition in the upper ranges of the financial sector, both a result of the rapid growth of industry and a cause of it.

PROSPERITY AND POPULATION

It is hard to see this vigorous development of agriculture, industry, commerce and services, and not think that it was all a reflection of a growing prosperity, of an increase in standards of living. Improvements were most evident in basic necessities, particularly food. One good example would be the spread of fried potatoes, after 1850. Before mid-century, street vendors in western Europe sold boiled potatoes; afterwards, their customers could afford the additional expense of oil to prepare this food in a tastier (if, by today's standards, less healthy) fashion. Statistics bear out these impressions. Evidence of improved nutrition was the decline in the proportion of conscripts rejected for military service because they were too short: in the French department of the Haute-Loire, a poor mountainous region, the proportion fell from 16 per cent at mid-century to 10 per cent in the 1870s. Admittedly, the minimum height for army service was only 156 cm, or 5 ft 2 in.

Contemporaries were likely to observe signs of prosperity in the countryside: improved housing as slate roofs replaced thatched ones, glass replaced paper in windows, and household furnishings were improved, with purchases of items such as crockery and chairs – the latter replacing backless benches, a considerable improvement in seating comfort. Markets and fairs were on the increase as was the frequenting of the taverns. Young farm women began to acquire more fashionable clothing. In Connacht, the poorest of Ireland's provinces, half the housing units in 1841 consisted of one-room mud cabins; by 1881, these wretched structures constituted just 6 per cent of houses. Peasants were also less likely to lose their nicely improved housing. Through the early 1870s in France, foreclosures on mortgages, a form of credit more prevalent in rural areas, fell by a good three-quarters from their mid-century high point.

A study of the workers in the Esslingen (a suburb of the German city of Stuttgart) industrial machinery factory suggests that growing prosperity for this group – admittedly, highly skilled and unusually well paid – involved both an increase in the consumption of basic necessities and an expansion of consumption options. By the 1860s, these workers were acquiring sofas, pocket watches, Sunday suits and other items of a modest domestic comfort and luxury. They could not afford to purchase artworks, but there were businesses that would rent them pictures to hang on their walls.

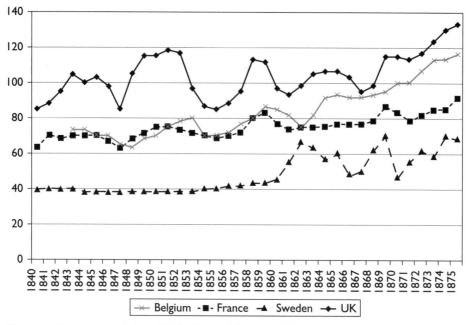

Figure 2.2 *Real wage index, 1840–75 (1860–64 = 100)*
Source: Derived from Jeffrey Williamson, 'The Evolution of Global Labor Markets since 1830', *Explorations in Economic History*, 32 (1995).

To move from these individual instances to a more general picture, Figure 2.2 shows real wage (money wages adjusted for changes in the cost of living) indices in four European countries, from 1840 to 1875. The different national series are based on a common index, which involves making some heroic assumptions about exchange rates and costs of living, so that the figures should only be seen as approximations, but the story they tell is nonetheless clear enough. Differences between countries reflected the degree of industrialization, as wages were highest in industrialized Britain, somewhat lower in Belgium and France where industry was rather less than in Britain, and lowest in the least industrialized country, Sweden. If levels of wages differed between countries, their development over time was basically the same. During the 1840s and much of the 1850s, real wages moved up and down, largely reflecting the sharp changes in food prices, then the major element in the cost of living, without showing too much of a trend. From the late 1850s onwards though, real wages steadily increased, reaching new highs by the mid-1870s as the growth of agricultural markets dampened price swings for farm products, and the additional wealth created by industrialization trickled down into workers' pockets.

One might wonder how the economic changes of the 1850s and 1860s affected movements in population. One answer, somewhat surprising, is not very much. Vital statistics showed strikingly little change in the post-1850 era. Birth rates remained consistently high, in the range of 30–45 births per thousand inhabitants per year (birth rates in France, at 25–27 per thousand, were a bit lower), three to five times the levels prevalent today in economically advanced countries. Death rates, in the range of 20–35 deaths per thousand inhabitants per year, perhaps three times today's figures, were also consistently high.

While at any one time there were definite differences between countries in these statistics – both birth and death rates were highest in the southern and eastern periphery of Europe, and lowest in the economically more developed core regions – as well as within individual countries and regions, the statistics showed very little change over time. Birth rates fluctuated a bit – lower in the 1850s, higher in the 1870s – but showed no long-term trend, either up or down. There may have been some smaller declines in the death rate, but infant mortality, the most important component of the death rate at the time, remained extremely high, of the order of 150–400 infants dying in their first year of life for each 1,000 born. This is around twenty to thirty times the levels found in affluent countries today. Pre- and post-1850 demographic patterns were similar. Differences between countries, possibly suggesting different attitudes towards birth control – birth rates in Russia were twice those in France – continued to exist, but the rates themselves did not change much in the quarter-century after 1850. Prosperity had little effect on human reproductive behaviour.

The story with another basic demographic feature – migration – was very different. The big event was the rapid and considerable expansion in overseas migration, above all to North America. While this migration had been ongoing since the sixteenth century, and had picked up some steam during the 1830s and 1840s, the 1850s marked a peak of emigration, with an estimated 3.75 million people leaving Europe for overseas destinations, above all the United States. Emigration would drop off in the 1860s, in view of the American Civil War, but grew again in the following decade. In the 1850–75 period, emigrants came almost entirely from northern and western Europe, with the UK, especially Ireland, and the German states accounting for over 90 per cent of emigrants.

This emigration on a very large scale was certainly not a reflection of prosperity, but it helped to create it. The decrease in the number of people competing for jobs in agriculture and the crafts – the two chief occupations of emigrants – put upward pressure on wages, improving conditions for those remaining in Europe. Fewer people in rural areas meant less pressure to divide farm property still further, if not actually increasing average farm size, at least helping to stem its decline. This result of emigration was most pronounced in Ireland, where massive departures following the Great Famine of 1845–49 meant that the Irish population remained below its 1840 levels down to the First World War. Standards of living of the remaining members of the rural lower classes, labourers and small tenants, steadily improved from their desolate condition. By contrast, the absence of emigration from southern and eastern Europe – which would begin on a large scale only in the 1880s – played a role in the modest or non-existent progress in popular standards of living in those regions during the quarter-century after 1850.

Thinking of migration usually brings to mind overseas travel, but many more people travelled over shorter distances. This form of migration was also steadily on the increase after 1850, as the growth of industry attracted labour and the improvement of transportation made movement physically less tedious. It was noticeably easier to travel from town to town by railway or steamboat than on foot, or even in a stagecoach. It is difficult to give figures for such internal population movement, in contrast to international ones, made up as it was of a vector sum of many different short- and medium-range moves, from rural to urban areas, from one city to another, and even from cities back to the countryside. Many scattered individual studies, based on equally scattered and diverse records, suggest two general points. Internal population movements in this period were fairly regional, with cities and industrial areas attracting migrants from 50–100 mile radius. The other is that rates of movement were increasing: more people and a greater proportion of the population were moving from place to place, with several studies suggesting about a doubling of the migration rate between the 1840s and the 1860s. Indeed, we could sum up economic developments in this period as involving increases in transportation, the market, industrialization, standards of living and population movement.

CHAPTER 3

SOCIAL STRUCTURES AND SOCIAL INSTITUTIONS

In contrast to the one main theme dominating the interpretation of economic developments in the quarter-century after 1850, social trends need to be understood as more complex, with three major areas worthy of note. One is the changing nature of urban life, as the number of people living in cities grew and the proportion of the population in urban areas increased. Another issue to be considered is the changes in the nature of labour, family and property as a result of post-1850 economic trends. Finally, the third quarter of the nineteenth century was, especially in the 1860s and 1870s, a period of rapid growth in the numbers and membership of voluntary associations, an expansion of their functions and a growing and changing influence of their activities in virtually all aspects of society.

URBAN LIFE

The quarter-century after 1850 was a period of urban growth in Europe. The proportion of the population living in urban areas increased between 1850 and the 1870s from 54 to 65 per cent in England, 25 to 32 per cent in France, 28 to 37 per cent in Prussia. There were similar, if more modest, increases in the proportion of the population living in urban areas in Sweden and the European provinces of the Russian Empire.

These overall statistical indicators were much less apparent to contemporaries than the growth of individual cities. London, by far the largest European city, grew substantially in the third quarter of the century, reaching a total population of almost 3.3 million by the early 1870s. In doing so it continued to leave its urban counterparts behind, but Paris, which had just reached the 1 million mark in the 1840s, and Berlin and Vienna, whose populations surpassed that figure in the decades after 1850, became giant cities in their own right. Yet the fastest and most dramatically growing urban areas were not these great metropolises, but smaller industrial towns. A market town of some 7,000 inhabitants in 1843, in the subsequent three decades Essen became the centre of steel manufacture in Germany and its population grew over sevenfold to almost 52,000 by 1871, while the French steel town of le Creusot tripled in size, from 8,000 in 1851 to 24,000 twenty-one years later. Industrialization had started earlier in Britain than on the European continent, so rapid post-1850 population growth connected with the beginnings of industrial production was less common, but there were examples in the UK as well, such as the north England steel town of Middlesbrough, 'this infant Hercules, the youngest child of England's enterprise', whose 1851 population of 7,400 grew more than tenfold in the next fifty years.[5]

Such rapid and considerable population growth is very difficult to imagine as the result of natural population increase, especially as death rates in urban areas were generally higher than birth rates, or only a little below them. The increase in urban population during the third quarter of the nineteenth century was only possible as the result of migration from the countryside. When we look more closely at the process of movement from country to city, we discover something surprising and revealing: the movement was not one way, and it was much larger in scope than the population increase in urban areas might lead one to think. Let us take a simple example from the city of Düsseldorf, on the east bank of the River Rhine, north of Cologne. In the first half of the nineteenth century mostly a commercial and administrative town, Düsseldorf began to develop into a centre of metalworking and steel manufacture after 1850, and its population roughly doubled between 1850 and 1870. In 1864, the city counted about 41,000 inhabitants and gained, in that year alone, 650 new ones through immigration. However, those 650 new residents were the result of 4,516 people moving to the city and 3,866 leaving it, so that the net population increase due to migration was just 8 per cent of the total movement to and from the city.[6]

Düsseldorf was not an unusual city, or 1864 an unusual year; rather, this very large population fluctuation was typical of growing urban centres of the period. People moved from the country to the city, but did not stay long in a given city, moving on to another or back to the countryside. There were seasonal movements as well. Men came from rural areas to work on construction sites during the warm seasons and returned to the country in the winter. City people went out to rural areas in the summer, when more hands were needed for the harvest. Every summer, some 20,000–30,000 Londoners, for instance, worked gathering hops in nearby Sussex and Kent, a yearly invasion, wreaking havoc in the pubs of the small town of Maidstone as they drank off the stress of their daytime labours at night. Rural–urban migration was not one-way, and moving to a city did not involve losing touch with life in the countryside – quite the opposite.

There is one more feature about this enormous population turnover that needs to be noted, namely the way it was concentrated in certain social and demographic groups. Of those 4,516 people moving to Düsseldorf in 1864, three-quarters of them were unmarried. Similar analyses of population movements carried out in other cities find that the migrants were very disproportionately young people, in the 15–30 age group, and that skilled and unskilled workers were heavily over-represented among them, while older, married people, property owners, businessmen and members of the upper classes were much less mobile. We might want to think of dynamically growing nineteenth-century cities as composed of a core of older, stable, more affluent residents, generally having families of their own, residing there over longer periods of time, surrounded by a large, lower-class, youthful, unmarried population, whose residence might well fluctuate with the seasons, would not be of very long duration, and who continued to have ties to rural areas from which they came.

While historians have investigated this feature of nineteenth-century urban life at some length, it made much less of an impact on contemporaries than did another aspect of the post-1850 scene, the process of urban redevelopment. First tried out in the largest cities, such as London and Paris, it was imitated throughout the continent over the course of the rest of the century, so that Europe's urban fabric had been quite transformed by 1900. The classic example of this work, both to contemporaries and to historians, was the large-scale rebuilding of Paris under the direction of the prefect of the Department of the Seine, Georges Haussmann (1809–91).

Haussmann's projects involved a renewal of the French capital's infrastructure. The old, narrow streets in the medieval centre of the capital were demolished; steeper slopes in the terrain were graded and a new network of broad boulevards created, along which traffic could flow more rapidly and efficiently. The new streets led to a central marketplace for agricultural products, les Halles, which improved the provisioning of the city's 1.7 million inhabitants and served in that capacity for more than a century. Elegant new residential buildings and major public structures, such as the opera house, were constructed along the boulevards.

A second aspect of infrastructure construction was the improvement in water supply and sewage disposal – matters of economic development, certainly, but of public health as well. Even before the introduction and acceptance of the germ theory of disease, contemporaries were aware of the connection between contaminated water, inadequate sewage disposal and diseases such as typhoid fever and cholera, particularly after the Europe-wide cholera epidemic of 1849. Haussmann aimed to replace the existing, insufficient and unsanitary state of water supply, in which Parisians drew their water from wells and the very polluted River Seine, with an elaborate system of aqueducts, bringing in clean water from the rural areas of the Marne Valley 80 miles away. More water for the city would mean a greater strain on its inadequate sewer system, and Haussmann presided over a considerable expansion of the city's already existing but inadequate system of liquid waste disposal.

These massive projects, carried out on a very large scale, at a rapid pace, and with remarkable technological innovations, such as night-time work under the illumination of electric arc lamps, made an equally massive impression on contemporaries. It spurred on an unparalleled construction boom: the yearly volume of construction in Paris during the 1850s and 1860s was exceeded only four times in the subsequent decades down until the outbreak of the Second World War. More than just their scale, these works seemed to exemplify the great advances of an age of progress, of the replacement of an archaic and outdated past with a healthy modern present. The literary critic Théophile Gautier offered an encomium to Parisian reconstruction in 1855, as the works were just fully getting under way:

> Modern Paris would be impossible in the Paris of the past . . . Civilization hews its large avenues through the dark labyrinths of the alleys, the squares, the dead ends of the old city; it cuts down houses as the American pioneer cuts down trees . . . The rotten walls collapse, so that from their debris can arise habitations worthy of human beings, in which health descends with fresh air and serene thought with the light of the sun.[7]

While Haussmann's work in Paris was a showcase of the era, there were large-scale projects in other major cities as well. In Vienna, the old city walls were demolished and replaced with a formal boulevard, the Ringstrasse, that became a measure of elegant urban life in central Europe. Johann Strauss the younger, the famed 'Viennese waltz king', even wrote a new score in 1862 to celebrate the event, the 'Demolition Polka'. A new sewer system was installed in London to replace the huge cesspools by the Thames, which had threatened the capital's drinking water and had caused the 'great stink' of July 1858 when the sitting of parliament had to be suspended owing to the unpleasant odours. Berlin's major renovations started somewhat later, in the 1870s, but involved waterworks and sewer projects on the same scale as those of Paris.

These examples of public works in Europe's largest cities were followed in other municipalities: urban renewal projects in France's second and third cities, Lyons and Marseilles, along the lines of Haussmann's in Paris. The Rhineland city of Cologne followed Vienna's example in demolishing its old walls and building ring boulevards; as did the municipal government of Riga, capital of the Russian Empire's Latvian province. By the 1860s, this interest in urban renewal had reached the furthest corners of Europe. Ottoman administrators of the Danube *vilayet* or province (to become part of the future Bulgaria) ordered the broadening and paving of the *çarsi* or main commercial and crafts street, the placement of gas street lamps and even the installation of public parks in provincial towns such as Pleven, Tärnovo and Plovidv.

In one respect, this Europe-wide process of urban redevelopment had a different outcome in Great Britain from that seen on the continent. The new residential construction built on the boulevards following the demolition of the older streets in Paris, and in most continental cities, was luxurious and housed a well-heeled clientele. Indeed, bourgeois tenants have continued to live in the elegant apartment houses built along Haussmann's new boulevards, from the 1850s through to the beginning of the twenty-first century, when they have been trying to fend off American property investors who want to turn their apartments into luxury condominiums. By contrast, older areas cleared in British cities were developed for railways, or for commercial and industrial purposes, but not for fashionable housing. Such housing was usually constructed on the outskirts of British cities, in suburban development, thus denot-ing a broad difference between British urban spaces, where the well-to-do typically live in the suburbs and the poor close to the centre (a state of affairs common to former British colonies in North America and the South Pacific), and continental European ones, where these residential arrangements are reversed.

All things considered, this 'Haussmannization' – as historians have come to call it – of urban space in Europe during the third quarter of the nineteenth century, was a remarkable accomplishment and exemplification in brick and stone of the dominant ideas of the age of progress. Looking back more critically, we can note some more positive and more negative features. The waterworks and sewers connected with urban renewal unquestionably had a favourable impact on public health, lessening the prevalence of water-borne infections diseases, if not eliminating them com-pletely. The last major cholera epidemics in western Europe – Naples in 1889 and 1910–11, Hamburg in 1892 – were tacit endorsements of Haussmannization, since they occurred in cities whose municipal governments were too miserly or too corrupt to create a secure water supply or effective sewer system.

The broad boulevards characteristic of urban renewal certainly helped improve traffic flow, encouraging commerce and furthering possibilities for transportation, but neither Haussmann nor his many epigones gave much thought to the relation-ship between urban planning and industry. Factories developed, largely unplanned, mostly on the outskirts of urban areas, with industrial facilities, rail spurs and working-class housing all mixed in together. The faster industry grew, the more chaotic the urban spaces around it. Finally, urban renewal replaced old, unsanitary, cramped and dark – but cheap – housing with expensive residences and non-residential construction. Poor people forced out of slums destroyed in urban redevelopment had to relocate to other lower-class areas, on the continent usu-ally on the periphery of the cities, in Britain closer to the centre, driving up rents for lower-quality housing. Since urban populations were growing in this period, due to migration from the countryside, the upshot was a chronic shortage of affordable housing for the lower classes, and a tendency towards overcrowding and the inhabit-ing of unhealthy spaces. Shanty towns emerged on the edges of particularly fast-growing cities, as was the case in Berlin at the beginning of the 1870s. But the characteristic example of bad housing was cellar rooms, dark and dank, thought by contemporaries to encourage the development of tuberculosis, although modern historians are inclined to be more sceptical of this connection. Rival British cities each suggested that the other had a greater frequency of such unhealthy cellar dwellings; social reformers in the French textile centre of Lille developed a regular tour of the industrial city's cellars, repeating it over decades with prominent guests. Increasingly, overcrowded and unhealthy working-class housing in large cities was the dark underside of the elegant boulevards, with their opera houses and luxury apart-ments, one of the most important exceptions to the rising standards of living in the age of progress.

PROPERTY, GENDER AND AN INDUSTRIAL SOCIETY

From at least the mid-eighteenth century (and earlier in some places, such as Great Britain or the Netherlands), certainly since the French Revolution of 1789, the society of orders, a social system based largely on status at birth, with different legal privileges for each status group, had been on the way out in Europe. With the abolition of serfdom in the Russian Empire and in the Danubian Principalities of Moldavia and Wallachia in 1861 and 1864, respectively, and an end to the guild system in central and northern Europe, the post-1850 decades saw the final demise of this form of society. It was replaced by a civil society of property owners, a social regime in which individuals' position depended on their ownership of property, and where the legal possibility of obtaining this property – not, of course, the resources to do so – was open to all adult men. Women's place in this society of property owners was less pronounced and typically more subordinate, although it varied from country to country depending on the respective legal codes. Speaking most generally, single adult women and widows had greater prospects for gaining property and administering it than did married ones, whose property was, in one way or another, controlled by their husbands. In a different fashion, though, women were very much involved in this society of property owners, since marital and family life was closely tied to the acquisition and intergenerational transmission of property.

A society of property owners was not a society in which every person, or even every household, owned a significant amount of property. Property ownership was widespread in many places: in rural areas and small towns of France, for instance, in western and central Germany, northern Spain, Norway, or the western and central provinces of the Austrian Empire. Workers in industrial cities of Great Britain and western Europe, by contrast, owned little or no property; agricultural labourers in southern Spain, the PoValley of northern Italy, in eastern Germany or the Austrian province of Galicia were only slightly more likely to do so. Sometimes, property ownership could take on peculiar forms, as it did in Russia following the end of serfdom, where a substantial portion of the property of the newly liberated farmers was only temporarily granted to them by their village, and was redistributed among village households at periodic intervals. For all these qualifications, the third quarter of the nineteenth century was the high point of a society centred around the ownership of, and free disposition over, property, particularly property in land, but industrial, commercial and financial assets as well.

This apotheosis of a civil society of property owners coincided with a period of vigorous economic growth, including the initiation of the process of industrialization in areas little affected by it before 1850, and the rapid expansion of pre-mid-century pioneering efforts. It also went along with an increasing urbanization, involving both the development of large cities and, particularly, of smaller industrial towns. These new economic trends began to change the nature of the civil society of property owners, even as it was becoming fully established. Such changes were felt only by a minority of the population and did not undermine this society, which persisted, in spite of even more drastic changes in the late nineteenth and early twentieth centuries, until the outbreak of the First World War; but they did represent some new departures in social structure.

One group particularly affected by the economic changes of the period was that minority of the lower classes who worked in factory industry, and whose livelihood came from their labour and not their property. This source of income transformed the relationship between having a family and earning a living. It was not so much that industrial work clearly separated family and labour. In textiles, the branch of industry employing the most people in this period, family relations permeated the workforce. Machine spinners and weavers worked with helpers, who performed tasks such as replacing the bobbins or untangling the yarn. These helpers were, very frequently, the workers' own children or nieces and nephews.

Rather, industrial labour, by making it possible to support a family, however modestly and wretchedly, without needing to own any property, changed very noticeably the relationship between property and family – admittedly a development that had its precursors, if not quite so strongly expressed, among the landless labourers and proto-industrial outworkers in Europe of the mid-eighteenth century. Farmers and craftsmen often waited until they had enough property to support a family – whether by receiving an inheritance or a pre-inheritance settlement from parents, saving up to purchase or simply renting – before marrying. This process, particularly for those from families of modest means, often involved quite painful delays and efforts, and led to a higher age at first marriage. By contrast, factory workers did not have to wait for property, since they earned their living from their labour, and so could marry and start a family earlier. Indeed, a marriage of two factory workers, as would be common in textile manufacturing regions, where women made up a large part of the factory workforce, would start fairly well off, as far as the lower classes were concerned.

Once children arrived, their prospects were less rosy, since their mother would have to take care of them and be unable to work for wages, and the earnings, even of a skilled and well-paid worker, would barely suffice to support a family. As the children grew, left school at age 12 to 14, entered the workforce and turned their wages over to their parents, the family income rose, reaching its high point. The downward slope followed quickly. Later in adolescence, the children would leave home, eventually to start families of their own. The adult male wage-earner, passing his mid-forties, would find his physical powers going, as one English metallurgical worker put it in 1879, 'after these years of his strength are past; when he is old, and grey and feeble, and capable no longer of holding his own with the best or even the average'.[8] Old age would present a prospect of unemployment, declining income and dire poverty.

In contrast, craftsmen and small farmers had their property to use in their old age, and could, in effect, bargain with it, turning it over to offspring, relatives or even strangers, in return for receiving care when their physical strength no longer sufficed. Factory labour thus created a somewhat different family life cycle from that of small proprietors: the possibility of earlier marriage and a more affluent start in life, but a more difficult end. It took a generation or two for industrial workers to experience this life cycle, before, in the last quarter of the nineteenth century, the idea of state-sponsored old-age insurance began to appear as a way of securing the end of a lifetime without property.

If factory workers of the mid-nineteenth century were beginning to experience a life cycle without even the prospect of property ownership, their contemporaries at the other end of the social scale, who owned considerable amounts of property, were also entering new, albeit very different, paths of social alignment and gender arrangements. One instance of these changes was the identity of substantial property owners. In the first half of the nineteenth century, property in Europe had been, above all, landed property, and the landed aristocracy, in much of central and eastern Europe, still buttressed by the possession of serfs and by their seigneurial privileges, was the largest possessor of such property and the leading element in society.

The rapid expansion of industry after 1850 did not entirely change this picture. The post-1850 decades were good years for agriculture and rural landowners; urban landlords also did well, as a result of the growth and development of cities. Even in Great Britain, Europe's and the world's most industrialized nation, figures from probate records persistently show that the great noble landlords were the wealthiest people in the land, followed at some distance by the bankers of the City of London, and then, again at a distance, by the merchants and manufacturers of the industrial regions in central and northern England. The dominance of the landed nobility in southern and eastern Europe, where there was no industrial development, remained solid. To be sure, the noble landlords of central and eastern Europe lost their seigneurial privileges and their serfs, but they received quite substantial compensation. The only dangers landlords' positions might face were the result of political upheaval, as occurred in the course of Italian national unification in the 1860s.

Yet if noble landlords still held first place in wealth, capitalist industrialists were coming up fast behind them. A classic example of the accumulation of wealth among industrialists was the German steel manufacturer Alfred Krupp (1812–87), known for his armaments production as the 'cannon king'. Presiding over the rise of his business, from employing 80 workers in the 1850s to over 12,000 in the 1870s, Krupp accumulated wealth at a rate quite unmatched by any noble landlord. He was offered a patent of nobility by the emperor of Germany, which he refused, preferring to remain a *Bürger*, a proud bourgeois commoner. Instead of joining the nobility, Krupp built himself a bourgeois palace, the Villa Hugel, on the banks of the Ruhr to the south of his steelworks, an enormous building that today houses an entire museum.

Krupp's rapid rise was, of course, exceptional, but it was also symbolic of the growth and development of the bourgeoisie in the third quarter of the nineteenth century.

Wealth from manufacturing, commerce and finance increased more rapidly than from other sources in this period, and the capitalists to whom it accrued became steadily more affluent and influential. In clubs, societies and associations, and in seeking marriage partners for themselves and their children, capitalists began moving away from shopkeepers and master craftsmen, while generally not having many points of contact with the nobility. Instead, they associated increasingly with academically trained professionals, with lawyers, physicians, secondary school and university teachers, or high-ranking state officials. The combination of these two social groups created a bourgeoisie, a social elite tied by the interrelated characteristics of property and education, and no longer by status at birth or by charters of privilege. Admittedly, the process of creating such a group had been ongoing for some time and, like many of the post-1850 developments, had clear precursors, particularly in Great Britain during the first half of the nineteenth century, but the rapid increase in non-landed wealth as a result of industrialization marked a major step forward in this process.

This distinct social group was also characterized by a distinct pattern of gender relations which historians have designated 'separate spheres'. Women were concerned with the home and family, bringing up children and running the household, while men were oriented towards the world outside the home, whether in their jobs and business, or in their membership in clubs and societies, and their interests in politics and public life. Both historians and contemporaries saw this division in life as typical of the upper classes but not the lower ones. The German journalist and folklorist Wilhelm Heinrich Riehl articulated with clarity and humour this state of affairs in the early 1850s:

> Among rural day laborers and poor cow-farmers, the woman does the same work as the man . . . Both work in the field, guide the plow and wagon together, sow, harvest and sell their crop together or changing at random from one to the other . . . Among factory workers, men and women, children and the elderly are often engaged in the same activity . . . For the shoemaker, the tailor, the innkeeper, small business and crafts in general, the woman is fully involved in the business. In bigger business and especially in the intellectual occupations, this status of women as co-workers comes to an end. The government minister's wife cannot help out in the cabinet as the shop-keeper's wife in the store. The higher the sphere of occupation, the more separate is the activity of man and woman.[9]

Even conceding that men and women did have such separate spheres of activity, there are questions about how separate these spheres were. Bourgeois men were involved with their families, and in bringing up their children; their female counterparts had their own forms of association and played a role – albeit, a distinctly female one – in public life. We could regard these instances as mitigating a bit the strictness of the separation of male and female roles without negating the basic fact that they were separated.

There is also the question of whether these different activities were oriented towards different or similar ends. When businessmen's wives, for instance, visited and took tea with each other – an elaborate social ritual that could go on at some length – or tried to arrange or facilitate their children's marriages, were they involved in an exclusively female domestic sphere of emotion and family life? Or were they making contacts and soliciting clients for their husbands' business, seeking partnerships through marriage and fresh capital via dowries, given that businesses, even very large ones, were still mostly family owned? Historians have written interesting works, arguing both sides of this issue, and it is difficult to make a definitive statement on this point. It might be fair to suggest that, among the mid-nineteenth-century European bourgeoisie, men and women did engage in more distinctly different kinds of activities than was the case with the less well off, but also that household and family, on the one hand, and business and public life, on the other, had more points of intersection than might be apparent at first glance.

What all these observations also suggest is that the ramifications of the big economic changes of the mid-century decades produced important structural changes in life and labour primarily among some elements of the upper and lower classes. The lives of agricultural labourers improved after the 1850s, owing to higher wages and steadier food prices, but their basic patterns of labour and family were not fundamentally altered as were those of industrial workers. Similarly, while members of the landed aristocracy rode the escalator of farm and property prices upwards, it was in the bourgeoisie that wealth accumulated particularly rapidly, new social contacts developed and different forms of relationships between men and women were consolidated. By contrast, among what was, overall, the single largest social group of the mid-century decades – smallholding farmers, craftsmen and retail merchants – previously existing forms of social relationships continued, with only gradual changes and the general softening of harder lines in life brought about by prosperity.

A WORLD OF ASSOCIATIONS

The one hundred years between 1750 and 1850 had seen the triumphant rise of a new form of sociability in Europe, the voluntary association. These were clubs or societies whose organization, membership and institutional goals were not legally fixed, as would have been the case, for instance, with the old regime guilds, but were freely devised by the members themselves. The development and growth of such associations was a central element of the emergent civil society of property owners. Although these groups came in many different forms and were designed for many different purposes, two kinds were the most common.

One was the social club, in which the notables, the locally most influential and affluent men, came together to socialize, conversing, eating and drinking, playing cards or billiards, reading newspapers and other literature. There were a number of variations on these groups, including some with an elaborate ritual, particularly the Masonic lodges, while others were devoted to cultivating cultural interests with lectures, musical concerts, art exhibitions and the like, and still others included an interest in charitable contributions and other forms of public welfare. This last group encompassed organizations with a strong religious orientation, such as Bible and missionary societies among Protestants, and St Vincent de Paul charitable associations among Catholics.

The second typical group was the mutual benefit or friendly society, whose members came from the urban lower classes, including labourers, factory workers, journeymen and master craftsmen, as well as clerks and shopkeepers. These groups existed to help out their members when they became ill, or, at least, to provide a decent funeral for them on their decease. Members paid modest dues to finance this assistance. The practical and material aims of these lower-class groups might seem somewhat different from the sociability cultivated by the societies of the notables, but the contrast should not be carried too far. Members of mutual benefit societies met regularly in a tavern, ostensibly to discuss the business and finances of their association, but also to consume some of the groups' benefits in liquid form.

While none of these associations were explicitly political, they proved to be extremely important for the development of politics. During the French Revolution of 1789 and the broad wave of revolutions encompassing continental Europe in 1848, these societies and associations became the model for, or were quickly transformed into, political clubs, whose activities were central to the revolutionary process. In post-1820 Britain, clubs and societies became important political players in the search for reforms, whether the abolition of slavery, equality of rights for Catholics, reapportionment of seats in parliament and changes in the parliamentary franchise, autonomy for Ireland, or the abolition of tariffs on imported grain. This use of social organizations for political ends would certainly continue after 1850, particularly in the 1860s and 1870s, but these decades would also see important changes in the voluntary associations themselves, two of which stand out: (1) the considerable expansion in the number of associations and their spread to areas or social groups where they had not before existed; and (2) the formation of new kinds of associations with occupational and professional goals, in conjunction with the creation and growth of a consciousness of belonging to a nation.

As early as 1818 there were already over 900,000 members of friendly societies in Great Britain. By the early 1870s, membership had grown to over 4 million, concentrated in large cities and industrial areas. In 1874, to take one example, the town of Preston, a centre of textile manufacturing in the Lancashire industrial region, counted 108,000 members of burial societies, but only 86,000 inhabitants. Many of the mutual benefit societies had joined together into national federations, such as the Independent Order of Oddfellows and Ancient Order of Foresters, each of which counted hundreds of thousands of members. In France, there were almost 2,500 mutual benefit societies, with some 240,000 members in 1852; by 1867, these numbers had more than doubled to 5,829 societies with 750,000 members.[10] Great Britain and France are the only two countries for which such global figures are available, but there is no doubt that mutual benefit groups increased on a similar scale across Europe in the decades after 1850.

Part of this increase involved reaching a somewhat different membership. In the post-1850 era, mutual benefit societies began to extend beyond industrial regions and large cities. The number of such groups in, for instance, the very rural French department of Loire-et-Cher, situated along the River Loire to the south-west of Paris, went from just 7 in 1851 to 44 in 1868, as small-town craftsmen and village farmers and winegrowers began to form and join these societies.

An even bigger change was the expansion of sociable and cultural voluntary organizations down the social scale, from the notables to the lower-middle class of small businessmen and master craftsmen, and still further, to journeymen artisans and factory workers. In the German states, there were no less than 225 workers' educational associations founded between 1860 and 1864. At that time, the UK counted some 425 of these groups, 250 of which were members of a national federation, the Working Men's Club and Institute Union, founded in 1862. Similar organizations existed in Italy, the Società Operaie, in France and in the more urban and industrial areas of the Habsburg Monarchy.

These groups met in the evenings after their members' long working day to hear lectures on practical topics, such as bookkeeping and mechanical draftsmanship, but also on the latest scientific advances (Darwin's theory of evolution was a favourite), current events, or new trends in the arts. There was plenty of drinking and socializing to go with these, as was the case with mutual benefit societies, but also an assertion of the lower classes that knowledge of science, high culture and the important events of the day was something they could claim for themselves. This attitude made workers' educational societies schools of potential political and economic action, mobilizing their members for support of liberal or left-wing politics, and training potential or prospective trade union leaders. They did so far more than mutual benefit societies, in spite of the authorities' fears that the latter groups would be hotbeds of subversion, and their consequent close regulation – even in liberal Great Britain, where the government usually took a more laissez-faire attitude towards the regulation of public life than was the case in continental Europe.

Another form of expansion of voluntary associations was geographical. Voluntary associations began to increase in numbers across the eastern and southern parts of the continent after 1850. Government officials counted 2,200 associations of all types in what would later be the Austrian half of the Austro-Hungarian Empire in 1856; their number reached 5,200 associations in 1868, rising to 8,000 just two years later. Voluntary associations remained sparse in the Tsar's empire, where the society of orders had proved long lasting, and a civil society of property owners was only beginning in the third quarter of the nineteenth century, but even there the number of private charitable societies grew from 49 in 1855 to 348 in 1880.

In some ways, the most interesting example of the extension of groups to new membership involved the place of women in voluntary associations. Women were rarely members of mutual benefit societies and most social clubs were male-only institutions. Yet there was an area of voluntary associations in which women – particularly more affluent women – were very much involved, and that was societies for charitable and pious purposes.

Even there, men had at first attempted to exclude or marginalize women, asserting that to be properly feminine they should be at home, and not taking part in public activities of societies, whether it was raising funds for charitable and religious purposes, disbursing them among the needy, or attending meetings where organization and policy were debated. In the 1820s, for instance, women were allowed to attend the meetings of the British Society for the Propagation of the Gospel, but only if they were hidden from sight of the male participants.

Women, however, were generally not willing to put up with such limitations. In Britain especially, they aggressively asserted their right to participate in charitable and religious associations, collecting funds for them, taking part in meetings or organizing such groups from scratch. In doing so, they generally did not challenge the idea that women's activities should be centred around home and family, they just interpreted their public activities as being directed precisely to such ends. They would help raise poor children by giving them Bibles, support poor families with food, cash contributions and home visits, sell the products of their sewing and knitting – eminently female, domestic activities – in bazaars and sales, raising thousands of pounds in doing so, very impressive sums of money for the time. By the third quarter of the nineteenth century, this female world of associations had been accepted as a matter of fact. The English philanthropist Barbara Bodichon (née Leigh Smith) wrote in around 1863: 'All over the Country, there are Ladies' Associations, Ladies' Committees, Schools managed by ladies, Magazines conducted by ladies, etc. etc. . . .'[11]

Contemporaries from the European continent were always impressed with the scope and aggressive character of the organizational activities of middle- and upper-class ladies in Great Britain, part of a broader British early start and greater extent of voluntary associations in general. Yet, particularly in the decades after 1850, women in continental countries developed their own network of charitable and pious associations. The Catholic Church sponsored St Elizabeth societies or 'Ladies of Charity' groups to help the poor, female pendants to the male St Vincent de Paul associations. Even as far off as the Bulgarian provinces of the Ottoman Empire, women in the 1870s founded associations to support education for girls, particularly poorer ones, whose families might be reluctant to let them go to school.

Just as workers' educational societies served as training grounds for political and trade union activists, so these female charitable societies became the training grounds for women's rights activists. The connection was clearest in Britain, where women's charitable and religious activities shaded over very quickly into the political – in anti-slavery societies, for instance, or in groups opposing prostitution. The most prominent example of this sort of activity, which impressed contemporaries very powerfully, was the campaign waged by the Ladies' National Association in the 1870s against the Contagious Disease Acts, which had required police registration and compulsory medical examinations for prostitutes working in garrison and port cities.

If this campaign shows the way that previously existing voluntary associations could be used to new ends with new groups of members, it was also the case that the post-1850 decades saw the development of new kinds of voluntary associations. One such was professional and occupational associations. The most obvious of these were trade unions, but their importance in the post-1850 decades should not be overrated. Unions had a substantial presence in Great Britain, where they were grouped into a national federation, the Trades Union Congress, founded in 1868, whose affiliated unions counted almost 1.2 million members in the early 1870s. By contrast, in continental Europe, unions were openly illegal or on the margins of legality throughout the entire period; workers were often more interested in creating production cooperatives than in forming unions. Union membership in continental countries was much smaller. A maximum figure might be the 60,000 or so members the three rival trade union federations in the German states counted at the end of the 1860s. Nationwide trade unions in continental European countries, to say nothing of federations of these unions, besides having considerably fewer members than their English counterparts, were far less permanent, unlikely to survive economic downturns, employers' hostility and government repression.

More significant in this period was the creation of professional associations among middle-class occupations that combined the self-interest of the groups in question with aspirations to influence public policy. French pharmacists, for instance, had been holding regular national congresses since the end of the 1850s, and began organizing societies and associations at the local level soon thereafter, their ranks quickly joined by those of veterinarians. The League of Education (Ligue de l'Enseignement), founded in 1867, was a sort of national education lobby in which teachers and the interested middle-class public worked to promote secular public schooling. (There was a Belgian predecessor to this group, and a British counterpart pursuing similar aims, the National Education League, was formed in 1869.) There was a whole series of professional national congresses and associations founded in the German states in this period: economists (1858), engineers (1859), lawyers (1860), chemists (1868), primary school teachers, architects (both 1871) and physicians (1873). As usual, these sorts of organizations were fewer in the economically less well-developed regions of eastern and southern Europe, although examples could be found there, such as the Russian Technical Society, founded in 1866, which was both an organization of engineers and a lobbying group for the improvement of industrial and technological education.

It was no accident that all these groups were national in character. Even, as was the case in France, where many occupational groups rejected nationwide organizations, they nonetheless held national congresses at which, for instance, pharmacists, from the entire country, could meet and debate professional and occupational questions. In Germany, professional organizations were founded on a 'nationwide' scale, even before the creation of a German nation-state in 1871. This fact demonstrates an important feature of the growth of voluntary associations in the post-1850 decades: their close connection to the development of nationality and nationalism.

Although nationwide societies and meetings of all types were connected to the growth of nationalism, there were three groups in particular that exemplified the links between voluntary associations and nationalism: choral, gymnastics and sharpshooting societies. In one sense, the groups' activities articulated and spread nationalist sentiments. Members of choral societies sang national folksongs and national patriotic tunes; gymnasts and sharpshooters paraded behind national flags. These societies, though, did not just articulate pre-existing nationalist ideas; rather, their activities were nationalism. The massive group singing of the choral societies, the unison movements of the gymnasts (whose gymnastics were more akin to contemporary marching societies than to the individual athletic performances we associate with the term today), the parades and marksmanship contests of the sharpshooters all provided, for participants and spectators, a sense of togetherness, of belonging to a widespread yet close-knit community, the nation as nationalists understood it. These associations were like the social clubs, of which they were a variant, all-male organizations, and the sense of nationhood they embodied was linked with a distinctly paramilitary ideal of uniformed, disciplined men, acting in concert. Even before the wars of national unity occurring between 1859 and 1871 actually took place, the nationalist associations created the link between the nation, militarism and orderly, organized, disciplined masculinity.

These associations first took their nationalist form in the German states during the thirty-five years between the uprisings against Napoleonic rule and the revolution of 1848. Originally small groups of young men from the upper classes, especially secondary school and university students, they became larger, mass movements, with tens of thousands of participants during the 1840s, acquiring members and supporters from lower down the social scale. Suppressed or severely restricted following the defeat of the mid-century revolution, the associations rebounded in the 1860s, the gymnastics societies counting some 170,000 members in over 1,900 separate clubs by 1864. The national congress of German sharpshooting societies, held in Frankfurt in July 1862, turned into an enormous nationalist demonstration, a public expression of the will to national unity.

At the same time as the German sharpshooters were holding their nationalist demonstration, nationalist associations were spreading to other nationalities. The year 1862 saw the creation in Prague of the first Czech gymnastics society, the Sokol or falcons. Founded by two German intellectuals, Heinrich Fügner and Emanuel Tirsch (both of whom changed their names to more Czech-sounding ones: Jindřich Fügner and Miroslav Tyrš), the existence of this society showed the growing influence of Czech nationalism, or, more precisely, the willingness of German-speaking burghers and Czech-speaking craftsmen and peasants in the Austrian province of Bohemia to think of themselves as members of a Czech nation. Throughout Bohemia, Czech gymnastics and choral societies were founded in the 1860s, either independently created or splitting off from German-speaking ones, once again demonstrating the progress of the idea of a Czech nation. By the 1870s, there were 72 such Sokol societies with some 7,200 members in the Austro-Hungarian Empire.

Their numbers and membership would grow rapidly over the following decades, but what is of interest is the way that these groups reached other Slavic nationalities in the empire and in neighbouring countries as well. By the 1870s, there were Slovene, Croat and Polish Sokol, followed in subsequent decades by Ukrainian, Serb and Slovak societies. The creation of these gymnastics societies shows the progress of nationalism across the multinational Austro-Hungarian Empire.

In western Europe, where nationalist ideas were longer-standing and nation-states often in existence before 1850, these kinds of societies were less common, although there as well they would come into existence in places where nation-states were challenged and nationalist movements developed. In Ireland, for instance, the Irish Republican Brotherhoods of the 1860s, in part conspiratorial nationalist groups, also had a public face as gymnastics societies. Following the French defeat in the Franco-Prussian War of 1870/71, gymnastics groups began to spread in France, and to incorporate sentiments of French nationalism seeking revenge for wartime defeat and loss of territory to the Germans.

From all these examples, we can bring together some features of the development of voluntary associations in the third quarter of the nineteenth century. Growth and expansion were perhaps the most important aspects of their development. Numbers of groups and group membership grew strongly; new social groups were reached and associations developed in rural areas or in southern and eastern Europe and associations developed some new functions as well. As was the case with other aspects of post-1850 social and economic developments, none of this was unique to the mid-century period, and there were many precursors in the first half of the century. Directions and activities of voluntary associations remained primarily at the local level, although national congresses and federations gradually developed which did try to provide local groups with leadership and guidance. Finally, the growth of voluntary associations was understood by contemporaries as part of the spirit of progress so characteristic of the age. One observer in the Lake Constance region of south-west Germany, commenting in the 1860s on the growth of voluntary associations, connected them with progress in politics, economics and culture, noting the

> breath of a fresh development, which has promoted a powerful upswing in associational life, increasing the public interest in religion, politics and local government, reinforcing the entrepreneurial spirit among craftsmen and businessmen, creating with bubbling humor, a wonderful Mardi Gras festival, filling the halls with spectators for scientific lectures, bringing to the theater an increased interest and greater expectations . . .[12]

CHAPTER 4

THE ARTS AND SCIENCES

Looking at the development of cultural and intellectual life in post-1850 Europe, we can point to three major trends. One was the expansion of opportunities for participation: increased and improved education, especially primary schooling, resulting in an expansion of literacy. Closely linked to this expansion was a growth in reading matter, particularly the periodical press. A second major feature was the development of a new attitude towards scientific research, characterized by a rejection of speculative and philosophical assumptions about the nature of knowledge and their replacement by an emphasis on rigorous empirical investigation, whether in the laboratory, as would be the case for physics, chemistry and medical research, or in the field, as would be true for geology and biology. This viewpoint would also influence, to a somewhat lesser extent, the humanities and social sciences – at least in part as an imitation of the physical and natural sciences. Parallel to these developments in the sciences and not directly tied to them, were similar trends in the arts, in particular the growing influence of artistic realism that sought to portray the world as it was empirically observed, rather than as religious or philosophical doctrines and public morality asserted that it ought to be. Taken together, these three trends posed a direct challenge to the intellectual, cultural and social position of revealed religion, and its adherents were faced with the choice of modifying their piety in line with the new intellectual trends or rigidly rejecting the new ideas. Intellectual confrontations between the devout and the adherents of new developments – whether over important specific issues, such as Darwin's theory of evolution, or, more broadly, over the validity of the idea of progress – were a typical feature of the post-mid-century decades.

EXPANDING THE CULTURAL UNIVERSE

The post-1850 decades saw a widespread if very uneven expansion of the number of people in Europe who knew how to read and write. In some parts of Europe, particularly the Scandinavian and German-speaking countries, literacy was already widespread at the middle of the nineteenth century, with upwards of 70 per cent of adults being able to read and write. By the end of the 1870s, literacy rates in these lands were close to 100 per cent. In Great Britain, France and the Low Countries, techniques of reading and writing were not quite so widespread at mid-century, with between 40 and 67 per cent of adults being literate. By the 1870s, upwards of 70 per cent of the adult population could read and write, with even higher figures among the younger generation.

The situation was quite different in southern and eastern Europe. In the 1870s, perhaps three-quarters of the inhabitants of Spain and two-thirds of those living in Italy could not read and write. In mid-century Russia, around 85 per cent of the Tsar's subjects were illiterate. Yet even in those countries, some modest progress occurred after mid-century. The 1881 census, for instance, recorded that some 70 per cent of Italians born between 1817 and 1826 could not read or write, with this figure falling to 55 per cent for those born between 1857 and 1866. Just over half the men in that latter group could read and write, while the situation was somewhat worse for women. In general, the more literate a country was, the smaller the gap in literacy between men and women.[13]

A central reason for the growth in literacy in this period was the expansion and reorganization of elementary education. In France, for instance, the number of children enrolled in school grew from some 2.8 million in 1840 to 4.8 million in 1875, an increase of 71 per cent, while the total population only grew by 8 per cent at the same time. In England and Wales, there were 2.1 million children attending primary school at mid-century, and 3.1 million twenty-five years later. These sorts of increases in school attendance were characteristic throughout Europe, found even in countries with low levels of literacy. The number of Spanish children attending primary school grew from 0.8 million at mid-century to 1.4 million in the early 1870s; the number in Russia increased at a similar pace, from 450,000 in 1856 to 1.1 million in 1878. Admittedly, these made up a very small proportion of children of school age, but the growth in their numbers is still noticeable.

Beyond the rapidly growing sphere of primary education lay a much smaller and less dynamic world of secondary schooling and universities. The vast majority of children finished their education between the ages of 12 and 14; secondary schools attracted well under 5 per cent of the 14–20 age group and their numbers and enrolment showed little expansion. With curricula focused primarily on the Latin and Greek classics, secondary schools offered a very different kind of education from that offered by primary schools. Such schools were exclusively for boys and young men; even fewer girls enjoyed any post-primary education, and that mostly from nuns or in finishing schools, where they learned French, music, sewing and other activities appropriate for cultured young ladies.

Rather as was the case with secondary schools, university education remained a minority phenomenon, attracting at most 0.5 per cent of the early twenties age group in the post-mid-century decades. University enrolments showed, at best, modest increase in the period. The number of students entering Oxford and Cambridge each year, for instance, had reached some 1,000 by the 1860s, about 20 per cent above 1830 levels. In the German states, there were actually about one thousand fewer students attending university at the beginning of the 1870s than there had been forty years previously. In contrast to the relatively static enrolment figures, universities developed new and growing institutions for scientific and scholarly research. Prominent scientists of the age, such as the German physiologist Rudolf Virchow (1821–1902), famed for his studies of the cellular basis of the human organism, the British physicist James Clerk Maxwell (1831–79), who formulated the basic equations of electrodynamics, or the German physicist Hermann von Helmholtz (1821–94), the leading German expert on electromagnetism, were all professors. Yet the greatest scientific figure of the period, Charles Darwin (1809–82), had no university affiliation at all. A gradual trend towards university affiliation of scholars in the humanities and the still nascent social sciences can also be observed, although in these fields the proportion of prominent figures not associated with universities was much more considerable than was the case in the physical and natural sciences. In sum, while universities were not directly educating many more people in this period, they were producing a good deal more knowledge that would, in indirect fashion, reach a much broader public. One important way in which this could happen was via the periodical press, for which the quarter-century after 1850 was an era of expansion.

A better-educated and more affluent population increased the market for the periodical press, while improved technology, from telegraphs to steam-powered printing presses, made it easier and cheaper to publish. Both the number of newspapers and their press runs increased. The number of English newspapers published outside London almost quadrupled, from 234 in 1851 to 916 in 1874. A mid-century maximum press run might have been 50,000 copies daily, but by the late 1860s the Parisian *Le Petit Journal*, was printing almost 600,000 copies every day. Admittedly, this newspaper was in a class by itself. The top English newspaper, the *Daily Telegraph*, managed about one-fifth as many copies ten years later, and the largest press runs of major newspapers in most continental European countries were in the 20,000–60,000 range. Most newspapers, of course, were not major national ones but more modest local and provincial news-sheets, printing between 1,000 and 2,000 copies once or twice a week.

Newspapers themselves generally remained small, some 8–12 pages an issue, as typesetting was not mechanized, thus putting strict limits on what could be done each day. By today's standards, newspapers were unbelievably tedious, with front pages full of unedited transcripts of parliamentary debates and the back pages containing dry reports of current events. Europe's most successful newspaper, *Le Petit Journal*, broke this mode, with lots of sensationalist crime reporting and no politics at all. Equally successful were popular weekly and monthly magazines that featured illustrations and simplified coverage of current events, especially via human interest stories and short pieces of fiction and poetry. Drawing, particularly, a female readership, the leading example of this sort of publication, the German magazine *Die Gartenlaube* (*The Arbour*) achieved a circulation of some 400,000 by the mid-1870s. Its British counterparts, the *London Journal* and the *Family Herald*, had similar circulation figures.

With increasing literacy and prosperity, the readerships of periodicals were expanding, including growing numbers of women and of skilled, urban workers. As a result, an increasing proportion of the population could learn about the major events of the day and the latest trends in the arts and sciences – if not, necessarily, at a terribly sophisticated level. Most inhabitants of rural areas still tended to be outside this communication network, and, as usual, the lower literacy rates and slower economic growth in southern and eastern Europe meant that such trends were weaker there. Still, the closely linked expansions of primary education and the periodical press were a characteristic of the mid-nineteenth century age of progress. While there had previously been brief moments of large public attention to politics via a widespread periodical press during the high point of the French Revolution or in the revolutions of 1848, by the 1860s this considerable public attention had become, in many parts of Europe, an established and permanent state of affairs.

SCIENCE ON THE ADVANCE

The post-1850 decades were a period of the steady progress and intellectual consolidation of the natural and physical sciences, the culmination of decades of scientific enquiry, ranging from laboratory experiments to mathematical derivations to the collection of natural specimens and geological excavations, leading to the formulation of general scientific principles. While this broader pattern of development could be found in chemistry, physics and biology, it occurred in each of these specific scientific disciplines – whose distinct and independent nature was emerging in this period, although by no means definitely established – in somewhat different ways, including relations to past and future trends in scientific research, the institutionalization of science, and the public impact and significance of newly proposed doctrines.

Since the last decades of the eighteenth century, chemists had developed a steadily increasing body of knowledge, based on several overarching theoretical principles and confirmed by ever more elaborate laboratory experiments. They saw substances as divided into basic units, elements, often assumed to be made of atoms, fundamental chemical particles. These elements combined to form molecules; chemistry was about the investigation of the formation and re-formation of such molecules. Chemists distinguished different elements by measuring their atomic weights, using ever more accurate instruments; they ascertained their valences, their electrical charges, which determined how they combined to form molecules, and investigated the different forms of chemical reaction, the interaction of chemicals under the influence of heat, catalysts, pressure and electrical charges, leading to the creation in the laboratory of chemicals found in nature and also to the synthesis of previously unknown substances.

A classic example of this growing knowledge of molecular structure was the discovery, in 1865, by the German professor of chemistry Friedrich August Kekulé

(1829–96) that the atoms in the benzene molecule are arranged in a hexagonal shape, the celebrated 'benzene ring'. Another example of the classification of chemical knowledge was the 1860 Karlsruhe international chemical congress, called to develop a standardized system of chemical notation, so that the chemical composition of molecules could be presented in clear and unified fashion. One of the congress attendees, Dmitri Mendeleev (1834–1907), a professor of chemistry at the University of St Petersburg, returned home thinking about the nature of the chemical elements. He arranged them in systematic form, based on their atomic weights and their valences, producing his celebrated periodic table, showing the relationship of the chemical elements to each other, and enabling Mendeleev to predict the existence of hitherto undiscovered elements and to list their chemical properties – elements duly discovered by researchers. This remarkable success suggests the extent to which chemistry had become an organized science in the post-1850 decades.

The reader may have noticed that all the individual chemists mentioned above were university professors, and this period saw the development of university-sponsored chemical research. It was the German chemist Justus Liebig (1803–73), who developed the idea of the university chemical laboratory, well equipped with the necessary chemicals and increasingly sophisticated equipment, in which a professor carried out his research, assisted by his students, who were, in that way, educated as chemists. Liebig's model, begun in the 1830s at the University of Giessen, quickly spread after mid-century, throughout central Europe, but was only very partially and incompletely imitated in other European countries. As a result, Germany became the world's chemical laboratory, a status it would retain into the 1930s.

Developments in physics show some striking parallels with those in chemistry, but also a number of sharp distinctions. Rather as had been the case in chemistry, the post-1850 period saw in physics the consolidation of a decades-long history of scientific theorizing – in the case of physics, carried out with the use of advanced mathematics – and experimentation. Central to this body of knowledge were investigations into the nature of electricity, magnetism, heat and energy, all of which were increasingly understood as interrelated. There were a number of examples of such theoretical synthesis, the most important of which were the celebrated Maxwell equations. Building on past investigations and theoretical insights into electricity and magnetism, James Clerk Maxwell, professor of physics at Cambridge, devised four differential equations that described the relationships between electric currents and magnetic fields, showing that the two were aspects of one electromagnetic force. Maxwell's work also demonstrated that light was a form of electromagnetic radiation, thus integrating the study of optics, electricity and magnetism.

This synthesis of knowledge seems very similar to what was occurring in chemistry at the time, but there was one significant difference. The synthesis of chemists' knowledge was part of a rejection of older, pre-1780 theories of alchemy or ideas about phlogiston. By contrast, there was an existing body of physicists' knowledge, dating back to Isaac Newton, which was not undermined by the new lines of research. The work of Newton and his many followers dealt, instead, with a different topic, namely mechanics, the motion of particles under the influence of forces, particularly gravity. The basic structures of Newton's physics were particles, while in the more recent developments, they were waves and fields. (In view of this trend, physicists of the time were rather more sceptical about the existence of atoms than were chemists.)

This newer physics did not directly contradict Newtonian mechanics and it continued to be developed in different ways – studying the motion of particles in fluids, for instance, or the orbits of bodies in the solar system – in the nineteenth century as it had been since Newton's day. However, physicists found it intellectually disquieting that these two branches of physics were unconnected. Maxwell had tried to bring them together, theorizing that electromagnetic phenomena were the result of movement of particles in vortices, but the more he developed his electromagnetic theories, the less valid his mechanical premises came to seem to him. The further development of chemistry in the last quarter of the nineteenth century would reinforce the syntheses developed after 1850, but the continuing development of the physics of electromagnetism would not just remain separate from Newtonian mechanics, but would undermine it, ultimately leading to the great pre-1914 revolutions in physics, quantum mechanics and the theory of relativity.

As a result of these great innovations, twentieth-century physics would become the classic example of 'big science', of research carried out at considerable expense with elaborate apparatus and large teams of researchers, generally funded by governments or big business. In the post-1850 period, if there was any scientific discipline even faintly approaching twentieth-century big science, it was chemistry. Physics, by contrast, was a much more modest affair, with just a few dozen researchers in all of Europe. Most of them had no laboratory, and the apparatus used in existing labs was not much different in 1870 from what it had been fifty years previously. One chemist, Liebig, had, all by himself, more students than there were physicists in mid-nineteenth-century Europe. Like the post-1850 advances in chemistry, the physics of electromagnetism had considerable economic potential but, as was the case with chemistry, the industrial application of the post-1850 progress of physics would have to wait for the final decade of the nineteenth century.

Biology might at first glance seem to have followed a somewhat different path from that of chemistry and physics. Charles Darwin's 1859 work *On the Origin of Species*, with its introduction of the 'theory of evolution' – not an expression Darwin used, incidentally – would seem a drastic break with past views of the development of life on earth. The 'Darwinian revolution', which is how both biologists and historians describe the impact of Darwin's ideas, endorses this understanding of them.

Darwin's ideas were certainly much more controversial among fellow scientists than, say, Kekulé's deciphering of the structure of the benzene ring or Maxwell's equations. They also attracted much greater public interest, sparking vigorous debate and controversy, and had a far more important and much broader impact on intellectual life in general than mid-century developments in other branches of science. Yet Darwin's great work was also a synthesis of biological and geological research over a series of decades, much like parallel syntheses in chemistry or physics. There was an important element of novelty in Darwin's theories, his concept of natural selection, but, ironically, a good part of the public impact of Darwin's work emerged from a neglect or misunderstanding of this concept.

The idea of a progression of life forms emerging in the course of a long natural history of the earth, of one species developing from another, rather than an initial creation of all the species, stems from eighteenth and early nineteenth century thinkers, the best-known of whom was the French natural history museum curator Jean Baptiste Lamarck (1744–1829). Among Lamarck's English followers was Darwin's own grandfather, Erasmus Darwin. In 1844, the anonymously published *Vestiges of the Natural History of Creation*, proposing such a 'transmutationist' or 'evolutionary' account of life on earth had been a great success, running through fourteen editions and selling some 40,000 copies. The book sparked enormous controversy and debate in Great Britain, and was widely read throughout the population, from members of workers' educational societies to members of the royal family, with Prince Albert reading excerpts from the book to Queen Victoria.

Other scientific developments supported these evolutionary views. The systematic study of animal embryos revealed that embryonic stages of one species closely resembled the adult forms of other species. Ironically, the development of 'uniformitarian' views in geology – the idea that the earth's physical features formed gradually over eons rather than being the result of sudden catastrophes such as the biblical flood – supported the idea of changing forms of life by suggesting an earth tens of millions of years old, with the time needed for the development of different life forms.

What was unique about Darwin's work, therefore, was not the idea that different species, including the human race, developed from each other over long periods of time, but the mechanism by which these changes occurred. Previous ideas about evolution had postulated the existence of some innate biological or spiritual force propelling the development of species, from more primitive forms to more advanced or progressive ones. The ultimate end of evolutionary developments – humanity – was, in this view, contained in life from its very beginning. Darwin's concept of natural selection broke with such teleological notions, suggesting, instead, that among a range of natural variations those animals best adapted to their environment would survive to reproduce, and the repeated use of this mechanism of natural selection, over long periods of time in different natural environments, would lead to biologically distinct species. This process had no inherent goal or tendency but reflected instead the long-term interaction of species with their environment.

This idea posed a sharp challenge to existing forms of religion. Of course, the idea of development of species over very long periods of time contradicted the literal account of the creation of the world in the Book of Genesis – which enraged biblical literalists, as it still does today. More importantly, though, the idea of natural selection strongly undermined basic ideas about the presence and power of God in the world, ideas that had brought together scientific knowledge and Christian faith. Both scientists and theologians had pointed to the diversity of species and their inter-action as examples of Divine Providence. The simultaneous existence of a species of bird and of bushes containing berries they ate was proof of the intentions of a Creator – for how else could the two exist simultaneously? Natural selection provided an entirely non-religious explanation. Birds who could eat the berries survived and passed this characteristic on to their offspring, while those who could not tolerate this form of food found less to eat and were less likely to survive and reproduce. Conversely, plants producing fruit that birds could eat, would find their seeds broadcast over a large area, ensuring their survival, while competing species unpalatable to birds would not do so well.

Darwin's world was one without any apparent divine presence; it was an invita-tion to atheism, or, at the very least, to a deism that postulated a very distant God, who did not repeatedly intervene in His creation, and had not created humanity in His own image, as was the case with the Judaeo-Christian deity. Darwin himself under-stood very well that his theories would provide a profound challenge to religion – one reason he had sat on them for almost two decades before finally bringing them out in published form. Prominent supporters and popularizers of Darwin, such as his leading English advocate Thomas Henry Huxley (1825–95), or the German zoology professors Carl Vogt (1817–95) and Ernst Haeckel (1834–1919), assertively linked Darwin's ideas to materialism and religious scepticism. Darwin's French translator Clémence Royer turned her introduction to the French edition of *The Origin of Species* into a passionate assertion of anti-clerical rationalism and advocacy of progress:

> The doctrine of M. Darwin is the rational revelation of progress, pitting itself in its logical antagonism with the irrational [Christian] revelation of the fall. These are two principles, two religions in struggle . . . It is a quite categorical yes and no between which it is necessary to choose . . . For myself, the choice is made: I believe in progress.[14]

As Royer's rationalist profession of faith suggests, much of the support and popu-larity which Darwin's ideas enjoyed among scientists, especially in continental Europe and among the general public, emerged from the belief that these ideas offered a biological proof for the existence of progress. Nature went over time from lower to higher forms; society and its forms of knowledge progressed in a similar way, if perhaps at a more rapid pace. Ironically, this popularity rested, to a great extent, on a misunderstanding. Darwin's concept of natural selection involved the explicit rejection of a progressivist and upward-striving understanding of the development of species. As he asserted dryly in his unpublished notes: 'It is absurd to talk of one animal being higher than another', adding that humans would regard the development of cerebral structures as evidence of higher rank, while bees would doubtless see the developments of instinct as decisive.[15] As would later be the case with the other tower-ing scientific figure of the years 1850 to 1914, Albert Einstein, Darwin's ideas achieved their greatest public impact at least in part because they were misunderstood. The theory of natural selection, with its rejection of any teleology of evolution or progress in nature, became the intellectual apotheosis of the age of progress.

PROGRESS AND POSITIVISM IN THE HUMAN SCIENCES

The post-mid-century decades saw the gradual emergence of specific disciplines in the humanities and social sciences, or, as the French like to say, and perhaps more accurately for this period, the human sciences. Even as the human science disciplines were becoming specialized and separated from one another, they were increasingly based on common core ideas of progress and empirical investigation. The clearest source of this common core were the two most influential – although certainly not the most subtle or deep – social scientists of the era, the Frenchman Auguste Comte (1797–1857) and the Englishman Herbert Spencer (1820–1903).

Comte, who invented the term 'sociology' in 1839, described human history as progressing upwards through three stages, each of which had its characteristic form of cognition: the religious, the metaphysical and the positive. In the last stage, whose era he saw as dawning in the mid-nineteenth century, cognition would be based on the practice of science, involving the systematic formulation of hypotheses, and their testing by experiment or careful empirical investigation. In this way, Comte thought, the intellectual rigour of physics, mathematics or chemistry could be brought to the study and guidance of society, creating a 'social science'. Comte named this form of investigation positivism, and his coinage has been used ever since to designate a philosophical approach that sees the methods of scientific enquiry as the basis for all forms of knowledge.

Herbert Spencer, the first person to use the term 'sociology' in English, was also an adherent of the idea of progress, and progress was a leitmotif of all his work, best seen in his 1857 essay 'Progress: Its Law and Cause'. Like Comte, Spencer saw human society as progressing through phases, but in his case only two: militant and industrial. Also like Comte, Spencer linked his understanding of human society to science, but he preferred biology to physics. Spencer understood the 'evolution' – one of his favourite words – of human society as paralleling biological processes, and the appearance of Darwin's *Origin of Species* simply reinforced his arguments about evolutionary progress in nature and human society. Indeed, the phrase 'survival of the fittest', often understood as expressing the quintessence of Darwin's theories, was actually coined by Herbert Spencer.

Spencer's views were an early example of 'social Darwinism', the idea that the mechanisms for the development of different species over time that Darwin understood as underpinning nature were also the basis for human society. Social Darwinism has acquired a bad reputation in the twentieth century following its adoption by the Nazi regime, which saw the human equivalent of the struggle for survival between species in warfare between different races and took the notion of survival of the fittest with a chilling literalness. Precursors of such thinking – by no means limited to Germany – can be traced to the pre-1914 era, particularly to the last quarter of the nineteenth century, when notions of race and racial superiority became more common in European thought.

As historians look more closely at the application of Darwin's ideas to the study of human history and society, particularly in the earlier phases, shortly after the appearance of *The Origin of Species*, they discover a somewhat different state of affairs. Evolution and progress were the watchwords of the early application of Darwin's ideas to human society, as they were (incorrectly) for the general understanding of Darwin's theories; racial metaphors and invocations of warfare were less common. Followers of Darwin were spread across the political spectrum, but disproportionately on the left – although pro free market liberals, such as Spencer, and anti free market socialists both found ways to apply Darwin's theories. As was the case with the application of Darwin's theories to biology, the use of his ideas to study human history and society generally told against revealed religion and orthodox forms of Christianity.

Such social Darwinist ideas were part of the development of anthropology, whose emergence as a separate discipline crystallized in the formation of anthropological societies in major European countries during the post-1850 decades. Anthropologists studied 'primitive' peoples, that is, tribal societies outside Europe, and understood them as remnants of an earlier stage in the progress of culture and science. Studying would reveal how humanity had progressed from lower, past stages. There was some dispute among anthropologists and other social scientists about the possibilities for progress among non-European peoples, more generally. Some thought that they were racially incapable of reaching European levels whereas others believed that with the right (i.e., those of post-1850 Europe) political, social and economic institutions, non-Europeans could progress quite nicely.

Economics, or political economy as most contemporaries would still have said, was already an established intellectual discipline by the middle of the nineteenth century. Its basic propositions, such as the efficiency of free markets, the labour theory of value, or the doctrine of comparative advantage in international trade, had been developed by Adam Smith in the eighteenth century and his early nineteenth-century successors David Ricardo, Thomas Malthus and Jean-Baptiste Say. Important criticisms of these propositions, particularly the argument for protectionism developed by Friedrich List that was widely popular in continental Europe, were also pre-1850 products. Post-mid-century economics, unlike other social sciences, owed less to Darwin's theories than Darwin owed to it, since Darwin himself admitted that his ideas of natural selection and the struggle for existence had been developed after reading Thomas Malthus's economic theories of population.

What distinguished post- from pre-mid-century political economy was more a change in tone, from pessimistic to optimistic. Adam Smith had been quite guarded about the long-term prospects for economic growth, while Ricardo and Malthus had been downright pessimistic, seeing a future of economic decline or at best stagnation, leading to Thomas Carlyle's celebrated characterization of political economy as a 'dismal science'. By contrast, their successors, such as John Stuart Mill (1806–73), whose *Principles of Political Economy* was published in 1848 and was very influential in the post-mid-century decades, employed the same economic theory to outline a more cheerful future of broader prosperity. (Mill is generally remembered today as a political philosopher, for his 1859 essay 'On Liberty' or his 1869 book *On the Subjugation of Women*, but his contemporary reputation was based above all on his economic works.) Rather than a dismal science, political economy would be a science of progress.

Even the communist economist Karl Marx (1818–83), whose 1867 book *Capital* was very much in the tradition of Ricardo and Malthus in predicting a dismal economic future for the working class (and, given Marx's doctrine of a falling rate of profit, things were not looking so good in his theory for the capitalists), praised the progress of the capitalist economy in creating ever more commodities ever more productively. Marx saw this development of capitalism as preparing for a new, communist stage in human history – Marx agreeing with contemporaries on the idea of progressive stages in human history, although having his own take on what these stages were – that would be an arena of progress.

Both the positivist notions of progress over time and knowledge based on close empirical investigation would seem to be relevant to historical studies, and for many historians of the era progress was a main theme of their work. The 'Whig historians' of Britain undertook to explain their country's history as a story of progress in liberty leading up to its post-1850 political, social and economic institutions. Nationalist historians, such as the Germans Heinrich von Treitschke (1834–96) and Heinrich von Sybel (1817–95), wrote lengthy works describing the progress of the ideas and institutions of the nation in central Europe. Some historians, such as the British scholars Henry Thomas Buckle (1821–62) and John Morley (1838–1923), specifically related their historical practice to the ideas of Auguste Comte whereas others took a more generic view of human history as a story of progress.

However, it is among historians that we can begin to see some of the limits to the ideas of progress in the human sciences. One way this occurred was the contrast between this idea and the ideal of close empirical investigation. Buckle's broad panorama of progress, in particular, came under heavy criticism for not conforming to the facts of the past as empirically determined. There was a substantial group of historians, all dedicated to the close empirical examination of the past, who rejected the idea of progress. The great German scholar Leopold von Ranke (1795–1886) and his student Johann Droysen (1808–84), for instance, or the 'liberal Anglican' historians in Britain, all followed Ranke's celebrated dictum that every epoch of human history is equally close to God.

Yet even these historians, if sceptical of broader visions of the progress of human history, were not disinclined to see their own era as one of progress, or to pose an outright opposition to the idea of progress and develop a theory of human society in decline. This was a relatively infrequent idea in the human sciences of the period. Two pessimists one could mention are the German Wilhelm Heinrich Riehl (1823–97) and the Frenchman Frédéric Le Play (1806–82), both of whom are generally described as folklorists, although their studies had elements of what would today be regarded as anthropology and sociology. Riehl and Le Play did not so much disagree with descriptions of social evolution provided by Comte or Spencer as value them negatively, seeing them as examples of a decline in morality and social cohesion.

There was one discipline, of all the human sciences the one most closely affiliated with universities, that was distinctly opposed to the ideas of progress, namely philology, the study of the evolution of languages. Very obscure today, but one of the great triumphs of nineteenth-century empirical scholarship, philology traced relationships among human languages and explained the development of human language groups, such as the Indo-European group, which includes most European languages, as the result of changes in speech from an original ancestor language existing in the past. As a scholarly discipline it was closely linked both to classics and to theology. Philologists such as Max Müller (1823–1900), a German academic who became an Oxford professor and a very prominent intellectual in post-1850 Great Britain, asserted that the development of languages showed, if anything, degeneration and decline over time. Müller saw the earliest human beings as living in the highly developed cultures of ancient India and Egypt, and was unable to perceive early human history as an example of continuous progress. Müller would stubbornly defend his ideas, even as the development of archaeology uncovered the existence of less advanced, prehistoric stages of human history. His attitude, and that of philologists more generally, was a definite exception to the vision of progress characteristic of the post-1850 human sciences.

REVEALED RELIGION FACING AN AGE OF PROGRESS

Part of Max Müller's rejection of the idea of progress stemmed from his Protestant piety and his unwillingness to consider the protagonists of the Old and New Testaments as lower down on a scale of progress than his mid-nineteenth-century contemporaries. His discomfort with the ideas of progress was part of a broader problem that adherents of revealed religion faced in the quarter-century following 1850. Scientific discoveries directly contradicted biblical accounts of human creation, providing a naturalistic account of the physical and natural world with no room left for divine intervention, thus encouraging the development of materialist and atheist, or at least deist, ideas. Empirically detailed historical scholarship applied to the world of the Old and New Testaments also undermined the certainty of revelation. The idea of progress as an advance from a religious to a scientific view of the world provided a specific alternative to a guide to life based on revealed truths of Christianity or Judaism, downgrading and marginalizing revealed religions.

One possible response was to seek an accommodation with the new trends in science and scholarship, and with the ideals of progress. The Protestant Association, formed in Germany in 1865, strove for a 'renewal of the Protestant church in the spirit of evangelical freedom and in harmony with the overall cultural development of our time'. For members of the Protestant Association, religion would not conflict with the age of progress, but would itself progress, developing away from old dogmatic certainties and restating itself in a form appropriate to an age of science and empirical scholarship. There were examples of this attitude in all Christian denominations and in Judaism as well in post-1850 Europe, but it was most common among Protestants of both central and northern Europe as well as the British Isles.

The question arising with this attitude was just what would be left of revealed religion after it had reconciled itself to a culture of progress. One example, which both impressed and infuriated contemporaries (and received a papal denunciation), was Ernest Renan's *Life of Jesus*, published in 1862. The French author described Jesus very positively, as a heroic individual who had devised an ethically superior religion, a major advance on Judaistic monotheism, which Renan (1823–92) regarded as the product of a people incapable of progressing. For all its positive portrayal, there was nothing of the divine in Renan's Jesus. No longer the Son of God, he was now an adherent of ethical and moral progress, and this attitude was widely perceived as the end result of attempting to reconcile Christianity and the culture of progress.

The alternative response was to reaffirm a connection to revealed religion and reject the idea of progress and its underpinnings in scientific discovery and empirical scholarship. In part, it was possible to attempt this by beating the positivists at their own game, by reading the fossil record as proving biblical accounts of Genesis, or at least as suggesting that each species was created separately rather than evolving one into another, by criticizing as empirically inaccurate broad vistas of progress across human history. Such a stance, however, meant meeting the sceptics on their own terrain, engaging in scientific and scholarly debate, and so undermining the very ideals of revelation. Indeed, attempted refutations quickly turned into angry sarcastic attacks, as was the case with the conservative Russian journalist Mikhail Pogodin, whose anti-Darwin pamphlet *Simple Words about Wise Things* denounced Darwin's ideas as atheistic, materialistic and alien to the devout Russian soul. At the other end of Europe, Bishop Wilberforce of Oxford asked the audience in a famous debate with Thomas Henry Huxley in 1862 about Darwin's theories, whether they were descended from apes or angels.

These two examples involve Orthodox and Protestant (in this case Anglican) rejection of ideas of the age of progress, but the strongest opponent and main dissenter to the dominant post-1850 intellectual trend was the Catholic Church. Praising the culture of the Middle Ages, reviving the scholastic philosophy of Thomas Aquinas, or building churches in the Gothic style, Catholics aggressively opposed ideas of progress and asserted the superiority of the medieval world over that of the nineteenth century. Far from accepting positivist and scientific ideas, the church strongly promoted religious devotion to the Virgin Mary and the Sacred Heart of Jesus, widely proclaiming the miracles occurring in their name, such as those occurring at Lourdes, in south-west France, site of a celebrated apparition of the Virgin Mary in 1858. For most Catholics, all the accoutrements of progress, from liberal political or social and economic institutions, to the development of a materialist science and a secular scholarship, were just evidence of moral decline and decay. Both leading and symbolizing this forthright rejection of the age of progress was Pope Pius IX, who ruled from 1846 to 1878. The famous 1864 Syllabus of Errors denounced the idea that the Pope should reconcile himself to 'progress, liberalism and modern civilization'. The harsh statements of the syllabus are evidence of the place of the Catholic Church as the single most important opponent of the culture of progress in post-1850 Europe.

THE ARTS UNDER THE BANNER OF REALISM

Like many other features of the period, realism as an artistic movement had begun in the first half of the nineteenth century but reached its peak of influence in the post-mid-century decades. Preceding artistic forms, particularly the duo of classicism and romanticism that had been predominant in the century before 1850, had looked both to past human eras – antiquity for classicism, the Middle Ages for the romantics – for artistic models and had developed ideal criteria for artistic forms – restraint, proportion and unity in classicist art, wild nature and unrestrained individual emotional expression for the romantics. Realism, by contrast, involved a different approach to artistic creation, one that fitted better with the positivist ideals of the age of progress.

Realists wanted an art that carefully and exactly portrayed the social, psychological and physical circumstances of the current day, an art that rejected ideal and idealized criteria of artistic representation in favour of close empirical analysis and observation. The English novelist G. H. Lewes, better known by her pen name George Eliot (1819–80), offered an account of the claims of realism in an essay of 1858, brief, trenchant and unusually effective, but just one of many similar manifestos issued at this time by writers, critics and painters:

Realism is . . . the basis of all Art, and its antithesis is not Idealism, but *Falsism*. When our painters represent peasants with regular features and irreproachable linen; when their milkmaids have the air of Keepsake beauties, whose costume is picturesque and never old or dirty; when Hodge is made to speak refined sentiments in unexceptionable

English, and children utter long speeches of religious and poetic enthusiasm . . . an attempt is made to idealize, but the result is simply falsification and bad art . . . Either give us true peasants, or leave them untouched; either paint no drapery at all, or paint it with the utmost fidelity; either keep your people silent, or make them speak the idiom of their class.[16]

Today's literary critics, who make fun of the idea that works of fiction could express the truth and who doubt that language refers to anything outside itself, have been generally hostile to realism. They certainly have their point, although many nineteenth-century realist writers and artists were well aware of the philosophical and aesthetic problems involved in creating a work of art that would actually reflect, in some way, reality, at least as the artists and writers perceived it. Yet all these criticisms rather miss two of the central and impressive features of realist art. One is the desire to expand the range of artistic subjects, to portray all segments of society, peasants, workers and craftsmen as well as the propertied elites, to deal with issues such as indebtedness, commercial transactions and factory labour as well as the psychological dynamics of courtship and marriage. The other is the vigorous effort to create a new form of artistic representation, one based on contemporary society, rather than looking to past ages for models and ideals. Both of these features gave realist art its force, which can be felt even today.

If artistic realism proceeded from some of the same intellectual bases as did the nascent social sciences in the age of progress, the attitude of the two closely parallel movements towards this age was quite different. Social scientists were adherents of progress and most had a positive attitude towards the developments of the post-1850 decades. There were artistic realists with similar attitudes, but a critical stance was more typical. Perhaps the greatest realist novelist of the age, Gustave Flaubert (1821–80), painted a far more negative picture of his contemporaries in his 1857 novel *Madame Bovary*. The title character, Emma Bovary, living in a French provincial town whose inhabitants, including her dreary husband, are all philistine adherents of the ideals of progress, finds this cultural world stifling and oppressive. Her efforts to escape this environment, to live her aspirations for emotional and aesthetic fulfilment, via two adulterous love affairs, only result in her self-destruction.

The realist novel found many accomplished practitioners in Russia and England, Europe's two peripheral nations. Most prominent among a galaxy of Russian realists, ranging from Leo Tolstoy to Ivan Turgenev to Nikolay Gogol, was Fyodor Dostoevsky (1821–81). Himself a long-term member of St Petersburg intellectual circles endorsing the ideas of progress, Dostoevsky, when he became a novelist, broke sharply with his former associates. In *Crime and Punishment* (1866) and *The Possessed* (1871), he denounced the contemporary culture of progress, insisting that its adherents' rejection of eternal verities of revealed religion invariably led to madness and murder. No less critical was the great English literary realist Charles Dickens (1812–70). In *Hard Times* (1854), Dickens savagely depicts and fiercely denounces the culture of progress in industrial England, mocking tenets of political economy, dramatizing the way industrialization and economic growth cripple human feelings and portraying primary education as turning children into fact-filled idiots. Like Flaubert, Dickens's portrayal of middle-class marriage in a culture of progress describes the crushing of a young wife's spirit, although given the greater rectitude of Victorian England, Louisa Gradgrind, the disillusioned wife of *Hard Times*, can just contemplate, with mingled fascination and disgust, an adulterous affair rather than actually engaging in one, as Emma Bovary does. Rather like Dostoevsky, Dickens also denounces political radicalism and calls for a revival of Christian verities as the only appropriate response to the social questions of the industrial era.

Dickens was a fabulously successful best-selling author, whose works were first printed in serial form in magazines, before appearing in hard covers, selling hundreds of thousands of copies. Other realists enjoyed much less success with a public that appreciated the close descriptions of contemporary life, including social problems, but disliked the realists' often harsh portrayals of personal life and psychological reality. The most popular novel of the realist era in France was Eugène Sue's *Mysteries of Paris* (1842–43) which described, with great acuity, the difficulties of working-class life in the capital. Its sentimental solution to the social question, though, in which hard-hearted capitalists suddenly and improbably metamorphose into generous philanthropists, made the book an object of scorn for realist authors and sophisticated literati, but a big success with the reading public. Realist literature was continuously stalked by the constant temptation to sentimentalism. Dickens, the most successful realist author, was particularly plagued by this temptation and many passages of his works – to say nothing of whole books, such as *A Tale of Two Cities* – are suffused with it.

Today's ideas about realism in the visual arts are shaped by the experience of the twentieth century, in which abstract art and distorted representations of human figures or landscapes stood against 'realistic', that is, more exact or 'photographic' representations of the world. However, this was not the meaning of mid-nineteenth-century realist art. Since the Renaissance, artists had been making paintings or drawings containing two-dimensional projections of three-dimensional human figures or landscapes. Realist artists continued this tradition of exact representation but wanted to portray subjects from everyday life in their everyday activities rather than painting or drawing them as if they were posing for portraits or as if their bodies looked like ancient sculptures of Greek gods.

Good examples of this viewpoint come from the two leading realist artists in mid-nineteenth-century Europe, 'two ringleaders of *Realism*', as contemporaries mockingly named them, the French artists Gustave Courbet (1819–77) and Edouard Manet (1832–83).[17] In Courbet's 1849 painting, 'The Stonebreakers', a carefully constructed and detailed scene of two stonebreakers at work, the viewer sees the labourers from behind as they go about their work, not posed and facing an audience. Manet's

---

BOX 4.1

Photography and artistic realism

Realist art and fiction is often described as 'photographic', as an imitation of the process of mechanical image reproduction. This viewpoint, a result of twentieth-century developments, does not conform well to the nature either of art or of photography in the nineteenth century. The high point of artistic realism, the quarter-century after 1850, was also a boom time for photography, as a technological innovation – the collodion process – made photography cheaper and faster than the previously used method of daguerrotypes. Photographs of nature, public events (the Crimean War of 1853 was the first to be photographed), individual or family portraits and pornographic scenes were soon omnipresent. Although photographs were wildly popular, the basic products of photography were generally not understood as art. At the 1855 Paris Exhibition, photographers were not allowed to display their work with the artists but were put in the pavilion with industrial products. Photographs might be perceived as artworks only after the negatives had been altered in the printing process (so that the print was not an exact photographic reproduction) or if elaborately staged and posed scenes, quite unlike those of realist artists, were photographed.

Because of the long exposure times required in early photography – an hour for daguerrotypes, some five minutes for collodion process – the large and clumsy cameras used, and the need to shield them from outside light, a 'candid' photograph, the shot of an unaware subject, was technologically impossible before the 1880s. Rather than realist artists imitating photography, it might be fairer to say that photographers, when they had better equipment towards the end of the nineteenth century, would begin to imitate realist art, with its detailed and unposed views of ordinary subjects going about the business of everyday life.

1863 portrait 'Olympia', of an up-market Parisian prostitute, is a formally posed nude, but the woman herself is not depicted with the lush curves characteristic of female nudes in the classical tradition, but with sharp angular lines. Contemporaries were horrified at the painting, not for its nudity, which was perfectly common in art, but for its portrayal of a de-idealized female body, and vigorously denounced Manet's work as pornographic.

As the response to Manet's work suggests, realist painters, not unlike their literary counterparts, had trouble with the public. Contemporary artists who painted lush, classical nudes, heroic battle scenes, or cute genre pictures in which innocent children were posed staring at the viewer, are today deservedly forgotten. At the time, however, they were far more popular, sold many more works and took the best places at large public exhibitions, while the realists were stuck in odd corners or sometimes not allowed in at all.

Realism did not pervade all the arts after mid-century. Architects, for instance, continued their practice of imitating past styles, whether Greek temples, Gothic churches or Renaissance palazzos. If there was a debate among architects about the construction of buildings appropriate to the age of progress, it usually concerned which past style to imitate. As for music, it is difficult even to imagine what a realist music could be.

Admittedly, the two dominant figures of European artistic music in the post-1850 era, the composer and pianist Franz Liszt (1811–86) and his son-in-law, the operatic composer Richard Wagner (1813–83), both saw their creations as part of the age of progress. Liszt explicitly called for 'progress' in music, and the creation of new musical forms appropriate to the age, while Wagner described his operatic multi-media spectacles as part of a 'music of the future'. However, both men also saw their work as a continuation of the great romantic composers, especially Beethoven, and stressed the extent to which their works would involve the expression of strong emotions in the romantic tradition. Wagner's operas, set like *Die Meistersinger* or *Tristan* in the Middle Ages, or in a Germanic never-never land of Nordic gods, as was the case with his enormous *Ring of the Nibelungen* tetralogy, were certainly not much like the realist insistence on the careful portrayal of contemporary society.

Music was thus the one major art in which the romantic forms of the first half of the nineteenth century continued unbroken following 1850. The critic and musicologist Carl Dahlhaus has suggested that such a development made music the great cultural exception in the age of progress, positivism and realism.[18] There is definitely some truth to that statement, but in another sense realist art in general was something of a cultural exception. Certainly sharing the ideals of positivism and close empirical investigation characteristic of the natural, physical and human sciences, artistic realists were rather more sceptical about the ideals of progress than were scientists and other scholars, or, at the very least, offered a more critical portrait of the age than its more enthusiastic supporters.

CHAPTER 5

THE POLITICS OF THE PEOPLE

Political life in Europe during the third quarter of the nineteenth century was characterized by four major trends: the triumph of reform, the domination of the notables, the hegemony of liberalism and the appeal of nationalism. In this chapter we will look at each of these trends in turn and then consider their influence on the organizational and intellectual development of the major political tendencies of the period, conservatism, liberalism and radicalism.

AN ERA OF REFORM

Reform was a signature of the age. The two most impressive reform works, to contemporaries and later historians, occurred in the peripheral Great Powers. To the east were the Great Reforms in the Russian Empire, beginning with the abolition of serfdom in 1861 and continuing in a series of decrees on local government, censorship and the judiciary. In the west, there was the Second Reform Act of 1867 in Great Britain, which drastically lowered the property qualification for voting, increasing the size of the electorate by about two and a half times. Yet these large and dramatic examples were only the tip of an iceberg of legal changes and improvements encompassing the entire continent.

When we look at the content of reforms, we can see two main areas of governmental action and improvement. One was removing impediments to a free market in land, labour and commodities. The abolition of serfdom in Russia and in the Danubian Principalities was a large example, but the guilds were abolished in the Low Countries in the 1850s, and in Scandinavia, the German states and the Austro-Hungarian Empire during the following decade. The creation of a united German nation-state between 1867 and 1871 cemented these reforms and added to them freedom of occupation, movement and marriage, thus liberating labour from any existing restraints. The promotion of free markets also occurred across national borders, the celebrated Chevalier–Cobden Treaty of 1860 between France and Great Britain sharply lowering tariffs and launching a round of bilateral commercial agreements across Europe.

The second area of reform was the expansion of political participation, which took a number of different forms. The abolition of the old-regime-style estates in Sweden in 1865–66, and their replacement with a bicameral legislature elected by a property franchise, was in effect a rearguard struggle and had been completed in most places before 1850. More typical of the era was the growth of the franchise, the Second Reform Act of 1867, or the introduction of universal manhood suffrage in a unifying Germany between 1867 and 1871. 'Manhood' is an important phrase here, and the idea that franchise expansion should reach women as well remained, in continental Europe, a rare and eccentric view. By contrast, the idea found numerous supporters in Great Britain, with petitions carrying thousands of signatures, and 81 votes in its favour in parliament during the consideration of the Second Reform Act – just over one-quarter of the MPs, to be sure, but the question of women's suffrage was never even posed in the parliaments of other European countries at the time. Between 1869 and 1872, women in Britain meeting the property qualification received the right to vote in elections to municipal government and for school and poor law boards.

Besides these reforms to local elections, there was another non-parliamentary aspect of the expansion of political participation. The Great Reforms in Russia are the prime example, since they included the introduction of jury trials for felonies, the institution of municipal self-government and, most importantly, in a very heavily rural empire, the creation of provincial rural self-government, the zemstvo. Similar reforms were introduced in the United Principalities of Moldavia and Wallachia in 1863–64. While these reforms fitted well with the promulgation of a constitution in the United Principalities, also in 1864, they were more sensitive matters in an autocratic tsarist regime, by the 1860s the only non-constitutional government in Europe, and Russian authorities tried hard to keep this political participation strictly limited. Juries were not allowed to sit in judgment over defendants accused of political crimes. Any zemstvo that dared to call for a constitution was dissolved, zemstvo publications were subject to government censorship and the authorities banned any kind of joint action by the zemstvos of different provinces.

One final aspect of the expansion of political participation was the development of a more inclusive concept of citizenship and civic rights. The prime example of this development was the emancipation of the Jews, the granting of equal rights to them, or, putting it somewhat differently, the implementation of the principle that political participation and civic rights should not be limited because of religious affiliations. We can see this process in Great Britain, with the seating of the first Jewish MP in 1857 and the abolition of religious oaths for MPs nine years later. Removal of restrictions on freedom of occupation and movement, and full suffrage rights, in both parliamentary and local elections, were granted to Jews in the south German states of Baden and Bavaria in the early 1860s – characteristically, as part of a broader reform package involving abolition of the guilds and their restrictions on freedom of occupation and movement – and became part of the constitution of the united German nation-state between 1867 and 1871, at exactly the same time as the Jews were emancipated in the Austro-Hungarian Empire. The decade of the 1860s saw the emancipation of the Jews in the Low Countries and in Scandinavia, as well as in Italy where national unification under the Kingdom of Piedmont-Savoy brought its emancipation of the Jews, first established during the revolution of 1848, to the entire Italian peninsula – a particular blessing to the Jews of the former Papal States who had suffered an unusual degree of legal discrimination on the part of Pius IX's government.

None of these legal changes meant that informal discrimination against the Jews, whether exercised in private life or by government agencies, came to an end. Nor was Jewish emancipation universal. The government of the newly united principalities of Moldavia and Wallachia (the future Romania) rejected it, and emancipation was not even seriously considered in the country with the world's largest Jewish population, the Russian Empire. For all these limitations and restrictions, the very fact of the granting of formal legal equality to the Jews across much of Europe during the 1850s and especially the 1860s, was evidence of a new, reformed position on the nature of citizenship and political participation.

These reforms were certainly sweeping, covering a wide swathe of society and politics; their significance and consequences were already recognized by contemporaries and have been emphasized by historians. Yet the reader may have noticed some absences in the reform efforts. Education, while it expanded considerably in this period, generally did so along pre-existing lines rather than involve substantial changes in curriculum or governance. More importantly, all of what was called before 1850 and after the mid-1870s 'social' reform – measures for the provision of occupational health and safety and affordable housing, or to ameliorate the problems caused by unemployment, illness and old age – was basically lacking. The reforms of the 1860s stemmed from a different principle. They would fit out individuals with the political rights and economic freedoms to make their own way in the world without requiring regulations or assistance. This principle was both the reforms' strength and their weakness.

Turning from the content of the reforms to their form, we can see two different versions of the reform process in the peripheral powers. In Russia, the reforms were devised and implemented by an enlightened government bureaucracy, acting largely in secret with the authorization and direction of a benignly minded autocratic ruler. What little public comment there was, largely from the nobility, frequently occurred as the result of official encouragement. By contrast, in Britain the expansion of the franchise was the work of parliament and political parties, responding to vigorous public debate, articulated in the press, in mass petitions and in public meetings with tens or hundreds of thousands of participants. The reforms of the European countries lying between Russia and Great Britain contained elements of both bureaucratic and public initiative.

Whatever the driving forces behind them, the reforms were precisely reforms, that is, changes brought about in legal fashion, preserving political and constitutional continuity, in sharp contrast to the previous thirty years, which had seen major revolutions in 1820, 1830 and 1848 throughout continental Europe, as well as many failed attempts at revolution. To be sure, in Britain the reform process had taken hold before 1850, as important examples of increasing political participation and creating freer markets – Catholic Emancipation in 1829, the Great Reform Act of 1832 or the repeal of the Corn Laws in 1846 – had occurred within the existing legal and political system. However, such early reform had come about only after large-scale political agitation so massive and so threatening to the existing legal and constitutional order that it seems to be of a different dimension from the still considerable, but smaller and much less violent or threatening, British extra-parliamentary politics of the 1850s and 1860s.

Fears about the possible outbreak of revolution and hopes and expectations of its imminent outbreak remained present for much of the 1850s and 1860s, but actual revolutionary violence was sparse, generally limited to individual countries, not spreading across the continent as it had in the first half of the nineteenth century. The Spanish Revolution of 1854–56 might be seen as something of a belated version of the revolutionary wave that encompassed much of Europe in 1848–49, but the revolutionary interval of 1868–75, which included the rule of three different dynasties and a briefly existing Spanish Republic, involved a politics quite different from that of legal reform. Similarly, the 1860 campaign of Garibaldi in southern Italy that destroyed the Kingdom of the Two Sicilies and, with it, much of the opposition to the national unification of the Italian peninsula, above all via widespread peasant uprisings, also involved drastic, extra-legal change. Of course, the proclamation of the republic in France in 1870, and the uprising of the Paris Commune the following year, one of the concluding events of the post-1850 period, were distinctly revolutionary. However, the events in Spain and southern Italy were very much on the periphery of Europe and failed to spark similar uprisings elsewhere, as had been the case in 1820 and 1848. The 1870–71 revolution in France was largely a Parisian affair, not spreading, as had Parisian revolutions in 1830 and 1848, to the rest of the continent. All three of these post-1850 uprisings were the result of military action – a military coup, or *pronunciamiento* in Spain, and in the wake of warfare in Italy and France – quite in contrast to the string of European revolutions from 1789 to 1848, occurring in peacetime against governments in full possession of means of repression. These post-1850 revolutionary movements were the proverbial exceptions that prove the rule of a period of – often vigorous – change occurring in non-revolutionary fashion.

THE REIGN OF THE NOTABLES

The prevalence of reform both reinforced and interacted with another characteristic feature of the period, the domination of the notables, that is, the locally most influential men. Local and influential are the key words here, and they express the two basic features of notables' politics. One is that political life was dominated by those with influence, stemming from their wealth and property and/or from their connections to the government. Such domination could be seen most clearly at election time, in voting systems still generally involving a property franchise or public balloting. (Even in the few examples of secret, universal manhood suffrage, the ostensible secrecy of the ballot generally was not guaranteed.)

Perhaps the very model of the politics of the notables during these mid-century decades was to be found in Ireland. Elections there were run by great Liberal and Tory landlords (or, in the few urban and industrial areas, merchants and manufacturers), each of whom mobilized their supporters, typically dependent tenant farmers and tradesmen. The latter were marched to the polling places, supplied richly with whiskey and beer, offered substantial cash payments, and sent off to vote. Many constituencies were not contested, but in those that were, the mobilized and generally very inebriated voters could engage in violent donnybrooks that would require army detachments to break up, but it was all done at the behest of the English elites in Irish society. Ireland was, admittedly, something of an extreme case, in combining the small size and great wealth of the elites running politics, with rowdy public demonstrations at the polls, but it shows in exaggerated form a characteristic of the period: the direction of public life by a small group of influential men, sometimes organized into formal political parties, sometimes just meeting informally at a social club; sometimes working things out amicably among themselves; sometimes clashing with each other or with the state authorities, but, with very few exceptions, having a dominant role.

The other crucial element in this picture of notables' politics is the word 'local'. Politics was often very local in scope, with elections turning on such questions as which candidate could do the most to bring government money, in the form of roads, bridges, railways and harbours, or subsidies and tax breaks for local economic activities, to the locality. Particularly in the 1860s, there was a greater tendency towards the creation of national or state-wide political platforms, but the strong local element in elections remained. Politics was also local in direction, as 'national' political parties tended to consist of a caucus of parliamentary deputies, without much of a political apparatus, depending on the voluntary adherence of local notables for their support. There were efforts to create nationwide political organizations, such as the German Nationalverein and the Italian Società Nazionale – both names mean National Association – centralized steering committees, working for the national unification of the German and Italian states respectively, with a modest subscription-paying membership (the Nationalverein counted about 25,000 members at its peak in the mid-1860s), and a political influence that was largely exerted by the efforts of the notables who were their members.

As was the case with the politics of gradual reform, there were exceptions to the rule of notables' politics, largely concentrated in the late 1860s. The growing republican opposition in France to the rule of Emperor Napoleon III, the agitation for a democratic franchise in Britain, the re-emergence of a nationalist political movement in Ireland, the massive nationalist agitation in the Austrian provinces of Bohemia and Moravia, or the first steps towards a socialist labour movement in Germany, all involved political campaigns that were either more nationally oriented or of a more popular character than the politics of the notables. But all of these were partial, exceptional and limited; overall, there is a striking contrast between, on the one hand, the notables' politics of 1850–70 and the turbulent mass politics of the revolution of 1848–49, and, on the other hand, the mass campaigns of increasingly centrally organized political parties and special-interest or single-issues groups that would become ever more crucial for political life in the last quarter of the nineteenth century.

LIBERALISM AND NATIONALISM

Both the triumph of reform and the domination of the notables are examples of the fundamental hegemony of liberal ideas in this period. As William Gladstone said of Great Britain, liberalism was 'the solid permanent conviction of the nation'.[19] The liberalism he described was the nineteenth-century variety, centred on the belief in a government with constitutionally guaranteed separation of powers – ideally, a constitutional monarchy – a social order based on the free disposition of property, and a preponderant political influence for the owners of this property. In this sense, the reforms of the period, with their gradual expansion of political participation and liberation of markets, exemplified liberal principles. The measured pace of reform, as opposed to the drastic changes of revolution, also fitted liberal ideas. In a similar way, the politics of the notables corresponded to liberal ideals of a society of property owners, even if the practice of politics by the notables might not always have been as high-minded as liberal thinkers would have liked.

In Britain, this domination of liberal principles was the result of Liberal governments, which were in office throughout the entire third quarter of the nineteenth century except for a few brief periods of minority Tory rule occurring when quarrels among Liberal parliamentarians prevented a Liberal government from being formed. In much of continental Europe, by contrast, liberal governments were few and far between in the 1850s, limited to the Swiss Republic, the northern Italian kingdom of Piedmont-Savoy and, on occasion, Spain. Additional liberal governments came into office during the 1860s – the 'Liberal Empire' in France, liberal governments in the smaller states of southern Germany, in the Low Countries and Scandinavia – but even in these liberal governments, conservative influences remained strong, both among the government ministers and outside the ministry. In Russia certainly, and to a considerable extent in the Kingdom of Prussia and in the united German nation-state that Prussia created by military conquest between 1864 and 1871, it was conservative and authoritarian regimes that implemented liberal policies. In an odd way, it is a signature of the liberal nature of the age that the many conservative-dominated or conservative-influenced governments in continental Europe could not turn back the triumph of liberal principles and even helped to bring them about.

In many respects, nationalism was the joker in the European political deck of cards during the post-mid-century decades, the issue that threatened to break apart the measured pace of reform and the elite domination of notables' politics. The basic doctrine of nationalism, that the nation should have the highest place in an individual's political loyalty and that each nation should have its own nation-state, was responsible for this disruptive political potential. Nationalists wanted to take all thirty-seven states of the German Confederation or all seven of the Italian peninsula and merge them into one; they aspired to break up the multinational Austrian Empire into different nation-states, to have Ireland terminate its connection with Great Britain, or to reconstruct an independent Polish nation-state, which would have involved carving chunks out of Russia, Austria and Prussia. Now, there was nothing new in the post-1850 period about this nationalist doctrine or the potential effects of nationalism; in the revolutions of 1848–49, Europe had had the first look at the possible effects of nationalism.

Before 1850, there had been plenty of other disruptive elements, particularly the effects of declining standards of living and chronic economic crises of the preceding decades. In the more prosperous post-1850 era, economic reasons for political disruption rather faded, leaving nationalist ideas as more prominent. There were two other reasons for the potentially disruptive effect of nationalism in this period. One was the result of social and economic changes – the growth of education, the increase in urbanization and the founding of voluntary associations. All of these contributed to a growing sense of nationality, of being part of a nation – feelings that were noticeably less common in an uneducated rural population – and so gave nationalism an increasing impetus, made nationalist political movements more important and encouraged political groupings to promote nationalist demands.

Closely related to this increasing salience of nationalism was the way that nationalist goals became part of government policy. This had not been the case in the first half of the nineteenth century, when nationalism had usually been associated with oppositional movements, mostly on the left of the political spectrum, and established governments had been at best sceptical about, but more generally openly hostile to, nationalist aspirations. In the 1848–49 revolutions, nationalist demands and nationalist aspirations had powered a large part of the insurrectionary activities, but few governments, and none of the Great Powers, had been willing to use their diplomacy and armed forces for the benefit of nationalist policies. This relationship between nationalism and government policy changed fundamentally after mid-century. Beginning with the emperor Napoleon III in France, and continuing with the Piedmontese prime minister Camillo di Cavour, and culminating with the Prussian prime minister Otto von Bismarck, ambitious statesmen, out to legitimize their rule, often against vehement opposition, to increase their country's power and to expand its territory, began to take up nationalist demands in order to do so. The use of nationalist demands would provide a boost of power, and above all of legitimacy, to the European governments that adopted them. Conversely, the adoption of nationalist demands by governments, particularly the Great Powers among them, meant that these demands not only had a far greater prospect of realization but also that their realization would be coupled with warfare between the Great Powers, possibly eventuating in a Europe-wide war. Although this great war never did break out between 1850 and 1870 – it would have to wait until 1914 – its prospect hung over the mid-century decades and the wars between the powers that did take place in those years all involved, in one way or another, governments utilizing nationalist demands. Nationalism carried by the armies of a Great Power would be *the* violent and disruptive aspect of the otherwise peaceful and reforming mid-century decades.

OLD POLITICAL TENDENCIES IN A NEW ENVIRONMENT

The major political tendencies of post-1850 Europe, moving from the left to the right, radicalism, liberalism and conservatism, had received their names, been shaped in their basic doctrines and, to a surprising extent, in the pattern of their supporters, during the years 1800 to 1840. The great explosion of political participation in the revolutions of 1848–49 had seen all these tendencies become, however briefly, political mass movements that attempted, sometimes with unexpected results, to realize their doctrines. In the two subsequent decades, the doctrines and supporters changed relatively little, but the result of their existing in a new political and socio-economic environment, characterized by prosperity and economic growth, the spread of education and the periodical press, the growth of voluntary associations, the triumph of the cultural imperatives of realism and positivism, and the growing salience of nationalism, meant that the same doctrines and the same tendencies began to take on a different meaning in different surroundings.

As explained in the previous section, nineteenth-century liberals were supporters of a constitutional government with limited powers and civic rights. They saw the free disposition of property in the marketplace as a crucial goal of public policy and a central feature of society. Theirs was a politics of property owners, and their supporters and activists were generally situated among the notables. After developing in the first half of the nineteenth century, these liberal principles and liberal supporters had met the turbulent realities of mass politics in continental Europe, during the revolution of 1848, and had found the reconciliation of principles and supporters on the one hand and mass politics on the other a difficult, often insurmountable, task.

In the two decades after 1850, liberalism generally continued along the same lines as in the first half of the century, and liberals generally found the era of notables' politics and gradual reform easier to contend with than the mass politics in the 1840s. There were some subtle changes that can be noted in the development of liberalism. One concerned changing composition of the notables. Increasing industrialization and expansion of markets brought an ever greater number of businessmen into the ranks of the locally most influential men, and, under their influence, liberals became steadily more attuned to economic issues. In a similar way to the progress of industry and economic growth, the progress of nationalism and national identity helped shape the nature of post-1850 liberalism. Endorsement of nationalist ideas had always played a role in liberal thinking, but it became increasingly salient in the post-mid-century decades. In the disunited states of the German Confederation and the Italian peninsula, and in the multinational Habsburg Monarchy, liberalism was ever more closely identified with nationalist ideas. Liberals increasingly believed that their causes – a free market in commodities, labour and capital, for instance, or a constitutional monarchy with parliamentary government and basic civic rights – would triumph via the creation of a nation-state. *'Durch Einheit zur Freiheit'* (through [national] unity to freedom), was how German liberals put it.

One final and paradoxical feature of liberalism in this period was the way it developed tendencies towards becoming a mass movement in spite of itself. Liberals were organized very largely in parliamentary caucuses, communicating with their supporters in the country via their speeches reprinted in the periodical press, and read by elite members of social clubs. As the circulation and readership of the periodical press increased, as members of the middle and lower classes began joining voluntary associations in greater numbers, liberal politics developed more of a mass following. This development was particularly noticeable in Great Britain, where the Liberal MPs increasingly split into two groups: the Whigs, using the older name for the party, who pursued a politics of the notables, and the Radicals, mostly MPs from northern industrial cities, who were willing to consider a political style and a political platform aimed at a broader audience. Similar disjunctions existed among the leaders of the Unión Liberal party which governed Spain between the end of one revolution in 1856 and the outbreak of another in 1868, among liberal politicians of the Progressive Party confronting the authoritarian government of Otto von Bismarck in Prussia, or in the ranks of the liberal opponents of the rule of Napoleon III in France, some of whom were willing to work with adherents of a republic whereas others were not. Overall, it would be fair to say that while notables' politics continued to be the dominant liberal political style, tendencies towards a more popular liberal mass politics were on the rise.

Turning to the left end of the political spectrum, we find radicalism in post-1850 Europe largely continuing in the vein in which it had developed during the 1840s and, particularly, in the revolutions of 1848. Radicals before and after mid-century continued to be adherents of a democratic and republican form of government; they expected such a government to institute reforms that would assist the lower and middle classes in their economic difficulties. Radicals continued to be supporters of nationalism, and generally to envisage a Europe made up of nation-states, whose different constituent nationalities would cooperate closely with each other. The revolutionary nationalist exploits of the Italian radical Giuseppe Garibaldi (1807–82) made him a continent-wide hero. Radicals across Europe continued to be strong supporters of

Polish nationalism and the very last nineteenth-century attempt of Polish national-ists to re-create a Polish nation-state, the failed Polish uprising against Russian rule in 1862–63, attracted continent-wide radical sympathies.

Such an emphasis on the continuity of radical ideas and political aspirations might seem surprising in view of the common understanding of the post-1850 decades as a seedtime of working-class politics and the development of an independent socialist movement. The key piece of evidence in favour of such an assertion would be the founding of the International Workingmen's Association in 1864. Later to be known as the 'First International', a precursor to the socialist 'Second International' of 1889 and the communist 'Third International' of 1919, the creation of this organ-ization might seem to suggest the progress of socialist ideas and a commitment to working-class politics in post-mid-century European radicalism. Historians have usually connected this movement towards a socialist and proletarian politics to the growth of industrialization, the development of a factory working class, and growth of trade unionism.

On closer examination, though, this whole picture begins to dissolve. There certainly were outspoken socialists among the founders of the International Workingmen's Association, such as the German revolutionary exiles Karl Marx and Friedrich Engels (1820–95), to say nothing of the wild Russian anarchist Mikhail Bakunin (1814–76), but other prominent members included the anti-socialist Italian democrat Giuseppe Mazzini, and English trade union leaders who were supporters of the Liberal Party. The International itself was not a novel institution: having emerged out of past efforts to create a Europe-wide federation of radical democrats involving the cooperation of radical émigrés from the continent living in London with English leftists, it was formed at a meeting held to support the Polish revolution against Russian rule. As for industrial workers, most of them were not involved with either radical politics or trade unionism; most 'working-class' radicals and unionists of the post-1850 era were journeymen artisans and outworking mas-ter craftsmen. Where industrial workers were organized in trade unions, as was the case with textile and engineering operatives in Great Britain, they were not advocates of socialism or of an independent working-class politics. Indeed, advocacy of an inde-pendent working-class politics in Britain was stronger among the radical Chartists of the 1830s and 1840s than it was in the post-1850 decades.

Rather than a break with existing radicalism, we can trace some modest, gradual and hesitant moves in the direction of independent working-class or socialist pol-itics. Fed up with the relatively moderate opposition of the Progressive Party to the conservative regime of Otto von Bismarck, and the notables' politics of the National Association, the veteran German radical Ferdinand Lassalle (1825–64) founded, in 1863, the General German Workingmen's Association – a group advocating typically radical ideas, such as national unification and democratic suffrage, but also gradu-ally developing into a labour party that proclaimed its exclusive attachment to the working class. Other radical groups in Germany, however, opposed this orientation;

they included, interestingly enough, the ones Marx and Engels themselves favoured. Perhaps a more typical example from the period would be the 1871 national congress of the Società Operaie, the federation of Italian workers' educational societies, held in Rome, the new capital of the united Italian nation-state whose creation had been a nationalist goal that the societies' working-class members had strongly endorsed. At the meeting, a resolution was proposed that the working-class members of the societies should not cooperate with people from other social groups. The motion was debated and was neither accepted nor rejected, but both its very proposal and uncertain reception suggest something of the development of radicalism by the end of the period.

More important for post-1850 radicals than the very modest onset of socialist ideas was the persistent experience of frustration and defeat. The widespread revolutions of 1848, culmination of almost two decades of increasing mass politics, had created an expectation of a future of ever broader mass politics and more dramatic change. Quite the opposite occurred. Repression in the early 1850s, ranging from mild in Great Britain to severe in much of continental Europe, destroyed left-wing political organizations and suppressed public political manifestations. Even with the onset of a more favourable political atmosphere at the end of the 1850s, political organizations remained small – often one or two orders of magnitude less than they had been in the 1840s – and echoes of efforts at mass politics were, at best, limited. Attempts at revolution, whether in Spain between 1854 and 1856 and again in 1868–75, in Poland in 1863 or in France in 1871, turned out to be failures. Even successful left-wing political campaigns, such as Garibaldi's invasion of Sicily in 1861, or, in a more peaceful vein, the 1866–67 suffrage agitation in Great Britain, involved compromises, as radicals were forced to settle for a good deal less than they had hoped for.

To be sure, this need to compromise, to come to grips with a reality that was not always in accord with their wishes, was something adherents of all political groups had to face. The German author Ludwig August von Rochau coined a phrase in 1853 to describe this attitude, one that has become a standard concept and remains in use today: *Realpolitik*, a politics that deals with conditions as they factually exist, not as they should ideally be. The post-1850 era was an age of *Realpolitik*, a state of affairs that was particularly painful for radicals, since they, of all political groups, had the most ambitious plans to change the status quo, and the need to come to terms with its persistence was especially difficult for them.

In many ways, though, of the three major political groups it was the conservatives who embraced *Realpolitik* to the greatest extent, maintaining some of their core values while adapting others to a new socio-economic and political environment. One crucial value that conservatives maintained, very resolutely, was the belief in the link between throne and altar, the insistence that an effective and legitimate government needed to be based on an established church. The leader of the British Tories, Benjamin Disraeli (1804–81), in opposing the disestablishment of the Church of Ireland, stated quite flatly, 'If a government is not divine it is nothing. It is a mere affair of the police office, of the tax-gatherer, of the guardroom.' The Count de Chambord (1820–83), the heir to the French royal dynasty of the old regime, and Legitimist claimant to the French throne, made the point in even sharper, almost apocalyptic terms:

> A Christian nation cannot tear out pages from its long history with impunity, break the chain of its traditions, inscribe the negation of the rights of God in the preamble of its constitution, banish all religious ideas from its laws and public education . . . Under these conditions, it can never put a halt to disorder; it will oscillate indefinitely between Caesarism and anarchy, the two equally shameful forms of pagan decadence . . .[20]

As both these statements suggest, conservatives of the period continued to be adherents of law and order and of political stability, of security for property owners and possessors of established privileges, and, consequently, opponents of disorder and revolution. Their support for an established church was directly related to this stance, since conservatives felt that a population devout according to the rules of the established church would be a peaceful, orderly and loyal population as well.

None of these attitudes would have surprised conservatives of the first half of the nineteenth century. But post-1850 conservatives took this defence of order, stability and existing privileges in a different direction from their predecessors. Defending an aristocrat's privilege to serf labour was a lost cause. No one tried to reverse the abolition of serfdom that had occurred as a result of the revolution of 1848; even in Russia, when the government abolished serfdom, conservatives mostly limited their opposition to getting the most favourable terms for the nobility. Pre-1850 conservatives had strongly opposed constitutional government and advocated either an absolutist monarch or a government based on the old-regime society of orders. There were certainly many conservatives in the 1850s who continued to oppose constitutional government: the conservative rulers of the states of southern Italy, the Kingdom of the Two Sicilies and the Papal States would have nothing to do with constitutions; the rulers of the Austrian Empire governed without one; some extremists in Prussia wanted to abolish that kingdom's constitution. Most Prussian conservatives, though, opposed the idea of abolishing the constitution and, by the 1860s, conservatives in all of Europe – except in the Tsar's empire – had come to terms with constitutional governments, guarantees of civic rights and legislatures elected on the basis of a property franchise, following the pioneering role of British conservatives, who had taken this position in the 1830s. Conservatives would increasingly engage in politics on liberals' terms.

Such a statement implies that conservatives were on the defensive, playing, as it were, on the liberals' home turf – and often they were. But there were also new departures in conservatism during this period, in which conservatives set out to make aggressive use of the new political environment not to defend themselves against the dominance of liberalism and the age of progress, but to master and dominate them.

The two major versions of these new conservative departures went by the names of Bonapartism and ultramontanism.

The first of these is associated with Louis Napoleon Bonaparte (1808–73), or, as he called himself, Emperor Napoleon III, whose rule over the Second Empire, lasted from his coup d'état in 1851 until his defeat in the Franco-Prussian War, nineteen years later. The Second Empire, beginning with the defeat of a revolutionary movement and including the strict preservation of public order and striving for close connections with the Catholic Church, had many conservative elements in it. But Louis Napoleon introduced three distinct innovations into conservative politics, which both fascinated and horrified contemporaries. One was that encouraging free markets and economic growth would preserve political stability and public order. Pre-1850 conservatives had been extremely suspicious of capitalism and free markets, seeing them as upsetting hierarchy and social stability, and some conservatives were still fighting to retain the guilds in the 1860s, so Louis Napoleon's views marked a distinct innovation on this point – and, all things, considered, a very successful one.

The second innovation of Louis Napoleon was reconciling conservatism with universal manhood suffrage, or, more precisely, with a guided form of democracy. All adult men in France during the Second Empire had the vote, although the legislature they elected did not have much power. Louis Napoleon also devised a clever instrument of democratic political manipulation, the plebiscite, in which voters were presented with a fundamental decision of his – such as proclaiming himself emperor – and asked to vote yes or no, while being told, implicitly and explicitly, that the choice was between Louis Napoleon and chaos. The proportion voting yes in such plebiscites, down to the very end of the regime, was regularly over 90 per cent. Another ingenious way to manipulate democracy was via the agency of the 'official candidate', a government-backed candidate for parliament, who ran for office with the full support of the state bureaucracy. To take one example, in an 1863 election in Alsace, the official candidate on his campaign tour was accompanied by the sub-prefect in uniform and twelve gendarmes: 'From morning to night they criss-crossed all the communes in the arrondissement and everywhere held out seductive promises concerning . . . nominations to the offices of mayor, cantonal medical officer, justice of the peace, together with subsidies for churches, synagogues, etc.'[21]

While many conservatives were horrified by this acceptance and exploitation of democracy, others found it an interesting idea. Independently of Louis Napoleon's example, Benjamin Disraeli continually toyed with the idea of making the Tories, at least rhetorically, the party of the people in British politics, and ultimately carried through a substantial expansion of the franchise in 1867. The Prussian prime minister Otto von Bismarck (1815–98) was very clearly influenced by Louis Napoleon's example when he introduced universal manhood suffrage in a united German Empire between 1867 and 1871. Neither Disraeli's nor Bismarck's hopes that an

BOX 5.1

Louis Napoleon Bonaparte

Son of the great Napoleon's brother Louis (King of Holland, 1807–14), and of Hortense, the daughter of Napoleon's first wife Josephine de Beauharnais, Louis Napoleon's early political career was marked by almost farcical failure, particularly his two attempts, in 1836 and 1840, to seize power in France by means of a military coup. When, as a result of the upheaval of the revolution of 1848, he was elected president of France, and then, following his successful coup of 1851, proclaimed himself emperor, the image of his past failures continued to haunt him. In the immediate aftermath of the coup, the author Victor Hugo referred to him as 'Napoleon the Petty', in contrast to his great uncle; Karl Marx's celebrated pamphlet *The Eighteenth Brumaire of Louis Bonaparte*, also written at the time, was a philosophical and historical meditation on how such a mediocrity could rise to the rank of emperor. Louis Napoleon's rule added fuel to that condescending fire. Between his succession of mistresses, his corrupt and meddling entourage, and the series of foreign policy and military disasters that plagued the final decade of his rule, the picture – sometimes sinister, mostly comic – of the incompetent on the throne became his historical characterization.

Over the past fifty years, another, noticeably more favourable, picture has emerged, one of Louis Napoleon as technocratic modernizer. Under his direction, capable subordinates rebuilt urban infrastructure and took measures to encourage economic growth. The modernization of his realm is perceived in political terms as well, ending the cycle of revolution and reaction that had played out repeatedly in France since 1789, preparing for a government representing informed citizens who shared agreement on the fundamental principles of the regime. This more favourable viewpoint was perhaps inspired by the career of Charles de Gaulle, an authoritarian modernizer of twentieth-century France, but it stems primarily from English-speaking historians; French ones seem rather more sceptical.

There is no question that Louis Napoleon Bonaparte was a highly successful political innovator, although his strengths lay less in the development of constitutional government than in the exploitation of war and nationalism for political purposes and the use of the distinctly anti-constitutional plebiscites. When it came to foreign and military affairs, the older picture of an incompetent, out of his depth, susceptible to the importuning of his mistresses and his entourage, still has its validity, although one has to wonder about the extent to which his foreign policy adventurism was a product of inability and intrigue and the extent to which it was a response to the domestic and international political situation in which Napoleon III found himself.

expanded electorate would prove reliably conservative actually came to pass, but the very fact they tried such measures – anathema to conservatives of the first half of the century – is suggestive of a realistic turn in conservative thought.

Louis Napoleon's third, most impressive, and most controversial innovation was to harness the power of nationalism for the conservative cause, particularly by the use of the armed forces. His realm was characterized by a series of wars – in the Crimea,

1853–56, in northern Italy, 1859, in Mexico 1861–67, and, finally, and disastrously, against Prussia in 1870 – all of which, besides their real and imagined foreign policy causes, were designed to improve the prestige of the regime by achieving glorious victories in the national cause. It is important to understand just what a novelty this path was. Conservatives of the first half of the nineteenth century had rejected nationalism as a subversive, indeed heathen, principle – setting up the nation as an individual's highest loyalty instead of divinely sanctioned monarchical rule – and they had generally rejected aggressive warfare as leading to the outbreak of revolution. There were plenty of conservatives in the post-1850 world who agreed thoroughly with these estimates, and they were horrified by Louis Napoleon's actions. But the initial success of his actions brought with them imitators: Camillo di Cavour (1810–61), prime minister of the Kingdom of Piedmont-Savoy, who brought the very conservative Piedmontese royal family to endorse Italian nationalism and to go to war for it; and, especially, Otto von Bismarck, who hitched the conservative Prussian government he headed to the cart of German nationalism with far-reaching results, particularly negative for Louis Napoleon, from whom Bismarck had learned these ideas.

The second new version of conservatism went by the name of ultramontanism. Literally, this referred to the idea that the Pope (who lived in Rome, *ultra montanes* or beyond the Alpine mountains) should be the central director and ruler of the Catholic Church, cutting back on the authority over the church exercised by secular rulers or by the bishops gathered in national church councils. Developing as a doctrine and aspiration in the first half of the nineteenth century, ultramontanism was generally supported by those Catholics who opposed rationalist and positivist ideas and advocated anti-rationalist religious practices, such as the veneration of the Virgin Mary and the Sacred Heart or the frequent use of the rosary. As rationalism and positivism increasingly became keywords of the age of progress after 1850, ultramontanism and its supporters became ever more powerful in the Catholic Church, strongly encouraged by the Pope, Pius IX (1792–1878), who opposed the whole culture of progress and the modern world it represented.

Ultramontanism broke with pre-1850 conservatisms in two distinct ways. First, it rejected the idea of an alliance of throne and altar, which conservatives had upheld, placing the altar well above the throne. Ultramontanists were certainly happy with pro-papal conservative regimes, such as Louis Napoleon's government in France, that had intervened militarily in favour of the Pope in 1849, or the government of the Austrian Empire which signed a concordat with the Vatican in 1855, but would not hesitate to turn against a conservative government if it threatened the papacy, as happened in France after Louis Napoleon changed course and allied himself with Italian nationalists in 1859. Indeed, a general characteristic of this period in France is the gradual movement of conservatives away from placing their primary loyalty in a dynastic claimant to the throne, whether from the Bonaparte or the Bourbon family, towards the Catholic Church and the Pope who both ruled and symbolized it.

Ultramontanists also had a more instrumental attitude towards constitutional government and the citizens' rights embodied in them than did pre-1850 conservatives. They made vigorous use of such rights where they might be helpful to the church, as happened in Prussia during the 1850s when Catholic-clerical politicians vigorously

---

BOX 5.2

Pope Pius IX

Born in 1792 into a noble family of the Papal States, Giovanni Maria Mastai-Ferretti, following his decision to take up a religious vocation, advanced quickly in the Catholic hierarchy, being named Bishop of Imola in 1832, elevated to the College of Cardinals in 1839, and then elected Pope in 1846, taking the name of Pius IX. He was something of a compromise candidate between liberals and conservatives in the Catholic Church, and in the early years of his pontificate, the new Pope seemed to favour liberal causes. Pius IX's liberal sympathies were more the projections of overly enthusiastic Italians than they were his own ideas, as quickly became apparent during the revolution of 1848. The Pope's opposition to revolutionary principles such as nationalism and popular sovereignty led the radicals in Rome to overthrow the papal government and proclaim a republic. The Pope was forced to flee and could return only after French troops had defeated the revolutionary regime.

This deeply traumatic experience shaped the rest of his long papacy, lasting until 1878, and moved him firmly in the direction of politically conservative and doctrinally ultramontanist ideas. His theological initiatives included the 1854 declaration on the Immaculate Conception, stating that the Virgin Mary was without sin from the moment of her conception, a particularly strong endorsement of the ultramontanist sponsoring of devotions to the Virgin. The 1870 declaration of the First Vatican Council, voted by the assembled bishops but largely arranged in advance by Pius IX and his supporters, that the Pope was infallible when he spoke in his official capacity (*ex cathedra*) on matters of faith and morals, was a high point for the ultramontanist programme of the supremacy of the Pope in the Catholic Church.

Pius IX's political actions were also part of ultramontanism. His denunciation, in the 1864 Syllabus of Errors, of liberal ideas such as constitutional government or freedom of religion – indeed of liberalism altogether – showed the conservative face of ultramontanist politics. Pius was a bitter and determined enemy of Italian nationalism; in 1871 he described his struggle with it as being between 'Christ and Belial, between light and darkness, between truth and lies, between justice and usurpation'. In spite of some initial sympathies in the 1850s, the Pope found that Europe's Catholic Powers – particularly the Kingdom of Piedmont-Savoy, which would later become the Kingdom of Italy, Louis Napoleon's French Empire, and even the Austrian Empire and Spain – ultimately disappointing, unwilling to enforce his political ideas or even to defend his political rule against the nationalist demands for the unification of the entire Italian peninsula. He found himself turning ever more for political, military and financial support, to say nothing of approval and encouragement, to the Catholic faithful across the entire world. In all these respects, Pius IX became the living symbol and adherent of ultramontanism.

wielded the guarantees of religious freedom in the Prussian constitution, to oppose government efforts to prohibit the activities of the Jesuits. By contrast, ultramontanists did not hesitate to reject appeals to human rights if they stood against the rules of the Church. The case of Edgardo Mortara, a 6-year-old Jewish boy living in Bologna (then under papal rule), became a Europe-wide *cause célèbre*. Edgardo was seized from his family in 1858 by papal authorities because the family's servant claimed she had secretly baptized him. He was imprisoned in a convent in Rome, but the Vatican simply refused all appeals for his release.

Ultramontanism was a spur to action. Catholic noblemen from all across Europe journeyed to Rome to join the Papal Guard to protect the Pope from the threat of Italian nationalism. The faithful organized societies to collect 'Peter's Pence' and send financial support to Rome. New religious associations, such as Marianic sodalities, were formed, gaining large membership; by the 1860s, Catholics in different European countries expanded these organizational initiatives in the direction of forming associations for social groups, such as workers, journeymen artisans, farmers, master craftsmen and household servants. Pius IX in his Syllabus of Errors had condemned liberalism, progress and modern civilization, but the ultramontanist movement was more than willing to use the tools of voluntary association and civic action, so characteristic of the liberalism, progress and modern civilization of the third quarter of the nineteenth century, for its own ends.

These new tendencies in conservatism were an example of the practice of *Realpolitik*. Conservatives would adapt their practices – and, ultimately, their principles – to a world of constitutional government, nationalism, industrialization and economic growth, and a vigorous and varied landscape of voluntary associations. It was via this process of adaptation to a new political and socio-economic environment, most apparent in conservatives but running through all the political tendencies of the post-1850 decades, that political groupings gradually evolved even while maintaining a rhetorical continuity with previous periods.

CHAPTER 6

THE POLITICS OF THE POWERS

Relations among the powers, and especially the Great Powers, of Europe in the two decades after 1850 were characterized by four features, one of which was a continuation of a previous state of affairs, while three were distinctly new and marked a break with the world of diplomacy that had existed in Europe since the Congress of Vienna in 1815. The one continuing feature was the preoccupation of the Great Powers with events in Europe itself and the relatively modest attention they paid to the extra-European world. If this extra-European world remained less important for diplomacy, the extra-diplomatic world, those situated outside the narrow circle of diplomats and high government officials – whether in the form of parliamentary deputies, nationalist associations, readers of the periodical press, or, most generally, as the vague formulation has it, 'public opinion' – had become far more relevant than previously to the formulation and implementation of foreign policy. The second new feature was the collapse of the system of international relations between the Great Powers that had guaranteed stability and peace since the end of the Napoleonic Wars in 1815. Instead, there would be efforts on the parts of several of the Great Powers to establish a dominant or hegemonic position in Europe, and to do so not just by diplomacy but also by force of arms. The period 1853–71 would see the one round of Great Power warfare in the otherwise largely peaceful century between 1815 and 1914. It was not just that the Great Powers went to war with each other in this period, but that warfare itself changed too, under the impact of industrialization, technological progress and strategic innovations.

EUROCENTRIC DIPLOMACY

The years between 1815 and 1850 had marked a sharp break with the previous three centuries of Great Power interaction, in which the search for overseas colonial possessions and various forms of maritime and colonial warfare had been a central element. After 1815, Britain was the only Great Power with a substantial overseas empire (the only other European country with major overseas holdings, the Netherlands, was a negligible quantity in European diplomacy); interest in and struggle over colonial acquisitions during the subsequent thirty-five years was, at the very most, brief and episodic. This state of affairs did not change much in the quarter-century after 1850; the Great Powers showed little interest in overseas possessions and questions concerning such possessions did not play a substantial role in the relations between the Great Powers.

There were modest signs of growing interest in extra-European affairs, whether from Great Britain, focused not so much on expanding its empire as in consolidating its hold on it after disturbances in New Zealand, the West Indies and a massive uprising against British rule in India in 1857. France's Napoleon III launched imperial ventures in South-East Asia and in Mexico; the latter ended badly, with his puppet Mexican emperor Maximilian executed by the Mexicans in 1867. (The French were supported in both these imperialist ventures by Spain, which also engaged in a brief war with Morocco in 1859–60.) Louis Napoleon's imperialist efforts, however, were not just – and not even primarily – directed at overseas goals. He was much more interested in seizing territory in northern Italy, western Germany and the Low Countries than in lands beyond the oceans, and his overseas ventures ended up fatally diverting forces from his primary, continental goals.

The major extra-European involvement of the Great Powers in this period occurred as a result of the Civil War in the United States. Both Britain and France, with an eye to securing sources of cotton, a crucial industrial raw material, toyed with the idea of intervention, of offering diplomatic recognition and perhaps even military assistance to the secessionist, slaveholding Confederacy. By contrast, the Russian Empire, continuing the strange eighteenth and nineteenth century diplomatic friendship between the Eurasian autocracy and the North American democratic republic, threw its weight on the side of the North, the legitimate American government. (The other two Great Powers, Prussia and Austria, were pro northern but, lacking navies, had no way to make their influence felt.) In the end, both Britain and France, fearing a military confrontation with the United States, decided to postpone intervention until the Confederacy scored a decisive military victory – which would have made their intervention unnecessary – and let the Civil War run its course to the Confederacy's final and complete defeat. The very fact that the single most important extra-European concern of the Great Powers ended with them not actually doing anything is compelling evidence that continental matters retained priority in the third quarter of the nineteenth century.

FOREIGN POLICY AND PUBLIC OPINION

While eighteenth and early nineteenth century European governments had sought to rally public opinion, and foreign affairs had played an important role in the revolutions of 1848, the post-1850 period was distinct from previous decades in three different respects. First, as a result of the growth of the periodical press there were a lot more people paying attention to international affairs, and newspaper coverage of them was far more elaborate. The Crimean War of 1853–56 was the first newspaper war, with extensive reporting from journalists on the spot, and even pictures from press photographers. Garibaldi's invasion of Sicily in 1860 and the resultant national unification of the Italian peninsula was front-page news across the continent.

Second, the spread of constitutional government and elected legislatures created a new forum for debate on foreign policy. Great Britain, as was typical for constitutional developments, set the pace here, with the course of the Crimean War leading to a parliamentary committee of enquiry and a change in government. The pace of legislative involvement in foreign policy picked up in the 1860s. The diplomatic confrontations of the 1860s and the wars of German unification in 1864 and 1866 were matters of parliamentary debate and public discussion in the Kingdom of Prussia and in the smaller German states. Following Prussia's victory over Austria in 1866, the run-up to war between France and the German states between 1867 and 1870 was accompanied by a drumbeat of parliamentary debate and criticism of government policy on both sides.

Finally, governments themselves began increasingly to take public opinion into account in planning their foreign policy. Dramatic diplomatic successes, particularly victorious wars, became a way to defeat domestic political opposition, ensure the election of parliamentary candidates favourable to the government, and mobilize support for the regime. It was the French emperor Napoleon III who raised this kind of public opinion warfare to an art form, and its use was a characteristic feature of Bonapartism, but Liberal governments in Great Britain and conservative ones in Prussia were by no means averse to gaining domestic support via peaceful or violent foreign policy successes.

However, the search for domestic support via victories abroad was a risky business. Once a government had let the genie of public opinion out of the bottle, it was impossible to put it back in. In an age of a mass circulation press, a growing parliamentary self-assertion and a network of voluntary associations, foreign policy failures could not remain hidden or relegated to the diplomatic corps, but would reverberate negatively against the regime, leading to domestic political defeats and possibly undermining its legitimacy. Newspaper editorials, parliamentary speeches, sometimes even public meetings and street demonstrations, would put forward foreign policy demands to a government which might find it difficult to evade them. Napoleon III, the crafty practitioner of a foreign policy designed for domestic political success, would find both of these developments occurring in the second half of the 1860s, setting in motion a train of events leading to his disastrous war with Prussia in 1870 and the end of his rule.

THE CHANGING NATURE AND IMPORTANCE OF WARFARE

This Franco-Prussian War of 1870–71 was the culmination of a series of Great Power wars occurring in this period, beginning with the Crimean War of 1853–56, and continuing with the northern Italian war of 1859, the Prussian and Austrian war against Denmark in 1864 and the Austro-Prussian War of 1866. This repeated warfare was a reflection of the collapse of the Vienna settlement of 1815, the formal and informal rules that had preserved the peace following a quarter-century of French Revolutionary and Napoleonic warfare. This settlement was aimed at avoiding any recurrence of that revolutionary warfare and its upsetting of existing ruling dynasties and international boundaries. Such wars were to be deterred by the cooperation of the European powers, especially the two strongest of the Great Powers in 1815, Britain and Russia.

The Vienna settlement had lasted from 1815 to 1853, surviving even the 1848 revolutions, which had been widely expected to bring large-scale warfare and associated upheavals to Europe. Instead, the revolutions had ended by reinforcing Russia's powerful position. As Queen Victoria's husband, Prince Albert, put it in 1852, 'The [Russian] Emperor Nicholas is master of Europe.'[22]

Russia's defeat in the Crimean War at the hands of an Anglo-French coalition completely exploded both major features of the Vienna settlement, eliminating the anti-French coalition and the joint action of the peripheral Powers. The way was free for wars of aggression on the part of the Great Powers, for major changes of boundaries, and for the rise of a new hegemonic power. France, under its Napoleonic ruler, was the logical choice for a new dominant power in Europe, and Napoleon III certainly aimed for such an outcome. In the end, rather to everyone's surprise, it was the Kingdom of Prussia, the least populous and ostensibly the militarily least threatening of all the Great Powers, in the 1850s often regarded as little more than a Russian puppet state, that defeated first Austria and then France, united the states of Germany under its rule, and emerged as the new continental European hegemon.

This unexpected outcome was a direct result of the changes in the nature of warfare occurring in this period. Through the 1850s, strategic doctrines and battlefield practice followed the initiatives first tried out successfully in the wars of the French Revolution and developed to a very high degree by Napoleon Bonaparte. Battles were decided by raising a large army – superiority in numbers was crucial to battlefield success – and then taking the offensive. Troops charged enemy lines in columns, bayonets fixed, while skirmishing sharpshooters laid down covering fire. Such massed charging columns prevailed over fixed line formations, characteristic of eighteenth-century warfare, and it was only when Napoleon's enemies adopted his tactics that he was defeated.

Two new features of the rapid industrialization in the post-mid-century decades changed this strategic equation. The first was the building of a rail network. Railways made possible the rapid mobilization and concentration of forces at a given point, so that with skilful use of the railways a country with fewer men under arms than its opponent could nonetheless enjoy a numerical superiority on the battlefield. The second feature was the increase in firepower, a result of progress in metallurgy and steel manufacture. Breech-loading rifles, steel artillery, and, at the very end of the period, the *mitrailleuse*, a hand-cranked machine gun, all had greater range, accuracy and firepower than older weapons. Against a defensive position, well provided with such new weapons, Napoleonic-style bayonet charges were suicidal; a successful offensive would no longer involve a frontal attack, but a more complex pattern of manoeuvre outside the range of enemy weapons, aimed at outflanking and encircling the opposing forces.

The unexpected military success of Prussia was a direct result of the kingdom's military planners recognizing these new realities and understanding that they provided a way out of a very threatening situation. With some 17 million inhabitants in this period, Prussia's population was about one-half that of Austria or France, and one-third that of Russia and so could not support armies of comparable size to those of the other Great Powers, and the kingdom's strategic thinkers were plagued by the

---

BOX 6.1

Helmuth von Moltke and nineteenth-century warfare

Although his social background – the landed aristocracy of north-eastern Germany – was typical for a high-ranking Prussian officer, Helmuth von Moltke's early military experiences, which included a spell as a military adviser to the Ottoman Empire, were not. It was perhaps this unconventional history which encouraged him to think more deeply about military affairs than did most of his contemporaries. As early as the 1840s, even before there was much in the way of railways in continental Europe, he recognized the importance of rail transportation for mobilization and deployment in future warfare.

After his appointment as chief of the General Staff in 1857, Moltke developed his military planning. The Prussian army would be equipped with breech-loading rifles and steel artillery, allowing a high rate of fire to repel enemy offensives. To take the offensive in a battlefield dominated by firepower, Moltke rejected frontal attacks and proposed, instead, to have his forces outflank and encircle the opposing forces. Troops would be concentrated on the battlefield by rail transport, and the General Staff developed elaborate plans for the use of the rail network in case of war. Moltke saw the battle plans he developed as primarily defensive in nature, given the precarious position of Prussia in Great Power politics; the outflanking and encircling battle he planned was to take place in the vicinity of the Prussian capital, Berlin, against invading French or Austrian forces.

Under Bismarck's political leadership, Moltke proceeded to use his planning for the new warfare in distinctly aggressive fashion – against the Danes in 1864, the Austrians in 1866 and the French in 1870 – with considerable success, making him first into a Prussian and then a German national hero. In the concluding years of his life and military career, he developed more defensive battle plans, designed to retain the position of the German Empire as the dominant power of Europe. The steady increases in the firepower of both infantry and artillery weapons, though, caused him to be extremely pessimistic about the consequences of future warfare between the Great Powers – a pessimism that would be only too well confirmed by the First World War.

nightmare of a conflict between an outmatched Prussia and another of the Great Powers, or worse, against an alliance of two of them.

It was the Prussian officer and strategist Helmuth von Moltke (1800–91) who recognized most clearly this situation and took the obscure planning division of the Prussian army, the General Staff, which he had been assigned to lead, and used it to implement the new strategic doctrines. The other Great Powers did not. Russia lacked the industrial development for a war of rail mobility and firepower. The Austrian army's officer corps was hopelessly backward in its strategic thinking. French planners did have an inkling of these new strategic realities, and made use of them to some extent, but in the crucial situation of 1870, the French government and army officer corps, from the emperor himself on down, proved unable to adapt either their broader plans of campaign or their battlefield tactics to them.

Historians sometimes describe the post-1850 strategic realities as an example of the development of 'industrialized warfare'. It is certainly true that industrialization was a presupposition for the construction of a rail network and for the manufacture of infantry weapons and artillery pieces possessing much greater firepower. Yet what counted even more than these economic and technological advances was the ability to make use of them. This required systematic military advance planning, or 'staff work', on an unprecedented scale to prepare the use of railways in case of a conflict and to arrange for the manufacture of high-firepower weapons, their distribution to the armed forces and the training of soldiers in their proper use. The diplomatic competition among the Great Powers following the collapse of the Vienna settlement in the 1850s, a competition stirred up and increased by the attempts of governments to use foreign policy successes for domestic consumption, and the growing influence of nationalist sentiments, would ultimately only be decided by armed force. The outcome of the clashes at arms would itself be decided by careful military preparation and planning that took into account new economic and technological realities.

CHAPTER 7

THE DYNAMICS OF POWER

Looking at the broad sweep of political developments occurring in individual countries and in international relations, in relatively peaceful fashion and in violent conflicts, the period between 1850 and 1871 can be divided into two broad parts. The first, during most of the 1850s was dubbed by contemporaries the 'age of reaction', with reaction used both in its literal sense of a reaction to events – in this case the revolutionary uprisings of 1848–49 – and in the political meaning of the domination of militantly conservative regimes. In some ways undermined by the Crimean War, the domination of reaction, in both senses, was visibly weakening in the last years of the decade and was brought to a final end by the northern Italian war of 1859 and its unexpected ramifications. What followed was a quite different decade of political and socio-economic reforms, liberal and nationalist initiatives, and, towards the end of the 1860s, a renewal of mass politics, which, if still beneath the level of the 1840s, was greater than anything seen since 1850. Accompanying this more labile political situation and interacting with it was a competition for hegemony among the Great Powers, with all these trends coming together and reaching at least a provisional conclusion in 1870–71.

THE AGE OF REACTION, 1850–59

The 1850s began with the repression of the revolutionary movements of 1848–49. The failure of the very last flare-up of the mid-century revolutions, the unsuccessful uprising in rural areas of central and southern France against the December 1851 coup d'état of Louis Napoleon Bonaparte, the decisive step on his path to crowning himself Emperor Napoleon III, made it very clear that hopes of a renewal of the revolutionary movement would not be fulfilled, either in France or anywhere else in Europe. As the radical challenges to the existing order were suppressed, the position of liberals became ever more precarious. Their hold on power, usually a consequence of the 1848 revolution itself, proved tenuous, so that by 1853 outside republican Switzerland the only liberal government left on the European continent was in the small north-west Italian kingdom of Piedmont-Savoy. Britain became an island stronghold of liberal ideas and liberal government in this period, although there was a brief period of Tory rule in 1852.

Conservative government in the reaction era took on a particularly repressive form, so that contemporaries spoke of a 'police state'. The police presence, particularly in capital cities, was strongly reinforced, so that by the mid-1850s the number of policemen in Berlin and Paris had quadrupled over that ten years previously. Police stepped up political surveillance, spying on and harassing potential opposition political leaders, at home and in exile, closing down clubs and associations that might be connected to oppositional political activity. In large cities of France, Prussia and Austria, police commissioners were required to produce daily reports of suspicious occurrences – and one might think about the mindset that expects suspicious occurrences every day. In the German states there was even a special newspaper published for the political police, containing handy tips on how to suppress dissent and opposition. It was this extension of political policing, often carried out without bothering too much with proper legal forms, that, more than anything else, made the reaction era one of a police state.

It is not that proper legal measures were excluded, since the early 1850s saw a series of enormous political trials against the insurgents of the later phases of the 1848 revolutions, counting tens of thousands of defendants or potential defendants in France, south-western Germany and Hungary. Although the death penalty was only occasionally imposed and many of the defendants enjoyed, either immediately or some years later, an amnesty – both measures that, by the standards of twentieth-century regimes, appear downright gentlemanly – to contemporaries of the 1850s, the repression appeared quite substantial. This impression was compounded by cruel and brutal punishments, such as the practice of Austrian army officers who took Hungarian noblewomen related to the insurgents, stripped off the upper half of their clothing and whipped them in the public square.

Reaction era governments extended their authoritarian and repressive practices with a view to the long term. Public education, in rapid expansion, was one arena of action to influence the minds of future generations. Thousands of primary school teachers lost their jobs as a result of the left-wing sympathies they had demonstrated in 1848. In France, secondary school and university teachers were ordered to shave off their beards – a symbol of radicalism in the mid-century revolution – or face dismissal. Churches were accorded more influence in public education, and religion was made central to the curriculum in the evident belief that a devout population would be a politically docile one. Thus, in Prussia, the government decreed that in the primary schools for the Protestant population, twenty-six of twenty-nine weekly hours of instruction should deal with religion. This encouragement of religion as a means to political ends was another characteristic of the era, whether in the form of the Austrian Concordat or the Prussian government's practice of prohibiting public dances and demanding that shops and taverns be closed during hours of both morning and afternoon Sunday church services.

Looked at more closely, the politics of the reaction era differed regionally across Europe. Repression was most severe in Russia, which had escaped any revolutionary uprisings in 1848, but where Tsar Nicholas I and his extremely conservative advisers wanted to ensure they would never occur. Censorship, already strict, was tightened to an astonishing degree, with the censors prohibiting the appearance of the published letters of the eighteenth-century tsarina Catherine the Great because of her enlightened scepticism towards religion, and banning the performance of Shakespeare's *Richard III* for the play's ostensible dangers to morality. The government minister of public instruction proclaimed: 'theology is the strong foundation on which all useful education is based', or as the censor Alexander Nikitenko put it, his superiors were engaged in a 'Holy War against scholarship and knowledge'.[23]

Not far behind Russia in a mixture of oppression and piety was the Austrian Empire, where the authorities not only abolished the constitution worked out in the revolution of 1848, but also refused to restore the Diets, the pre-1848 provincial old-regime-style legislatures. Instead, they instituted a centralized, bureaucratic and absolutist rule across the entire territory of the empire. This authoritarian rule was tempered by the regime's advocacy of an alliance of throne and altar. Breaking with the older practice of close regulation of the Catholic Church in the empire, the reaction era regime allowed the church substantial liberty regarding self-administration, in the – generally justified – expectation that it would uphold the system of authoritarian rule. Much the same system of authoritarian government combined with a more independent Catholic Church existed in the states of the Italian peninsula, with the characteristic exception of Piedmont-Savoy, which retained its 1848 constitution and whose liberal government ministers attempted to increase state control over the church.

By contrast, in the Low Countries (and likewise in Scandinavia), the era of reaction was much weaker and briefer. Constitutional government, in the reformed version introduced during 1848–49 remained in place, and the conservative governments in power during the early 1850s were replaced with liberal ones by the middle years of the decade. Between these eastern realms of severe repression and western ones of brief conservative ascendancy lay the German states and the French Second Empire. There, authoritarian regimes, with an active and expanding political police, coexisted with constitutions, elected legislatures and a press nominally free of censorship. Reaction era rule in theses states involved subverting rather than overthrowing constitutional government – elections, but with 'official candidates' nominated and elected to largely docile legislatures, uncensored newspapers, but ones subsidized if they printed pro-governmental news and threatened with legal action if they did not. These policies of repression were eminently effective, but, unlike the absolutist practices in southern and eastern Europe, they retained the institutions of constitutional government and opened the possibility of a legal transition to a more liberal form of rule.

Whether openly absolutist or nominally constitutional, the governments of reaction era Europe successfully repressed political opposition. Radicals, adherents of democratic and republican ideas, could not operate openly; their efforts at underground organization were quickly broken up by the political police. Left-wing leaders of the 1848 revolution, if they were to escape jail, or even a firing squad, had to flee, and found their best refuge in Britain, where both the government and public opinion supported liberal principles of political asylum. As a Great Power, the British government could, and did, reject demands for extradition of radicals, which intimidated smaller countries, such as Switzerland or Belgium, and even refused to prevent leftists from conspiring against continental governments. London became the radical exile headquarters, where activists from a number of European countries founded a European Democratic Central Committee that issued manifestos and attempted to guide political opposition on the continent. These efforts proved unavailing and the exiles quickly fell to fruitless quarrelling among themselves.

In contrast to radicals, advocates of liberal ideas could work openly, at least in the states that continued to have constitutional regimes. Liberals attempted to engage in opposition, trying interesting political alternatives, such as supporting Catholic and ultramontanist opposition to authoritarian Protestant governments in Prussia and the south-west German Grand Duchy of Baden (a rare example of liberal–Catholic cooperation in nineteenth-century continental Europe), but most of these efforts had little success. Discouraged by the failure of their aspirations in 1848–49, many followers and leaders intimidated by the repressive policies of the reaction era, liberals in continental Europe found themselves mostly waiting, biding their time in the hope that the situation would take a turn for the better and they could resume political activities.

Up to about 1857, the reaction era appeared quite stable; the one major threat to its continued existence was the Crimean War of 1853–56. The war was the first example of the adventurous foreign policy of the French emperor Napoleon III. He was driven to such policies by a combination of domestic and international imperatives, for Louis Napoleon Bonaparte never felt entirely secure on his imperial throne. Radicals hated him for his overthrow of the republic; liberals distrusted his authoritarian rule; conservatives tolerated him as a lesser evil but their hearts belonged to other causes such as the Legitimist pretender, heir to the Bourbon dynasty that had ruled France before 1789, or the Pope and the Catholic Church. Inhabitants of large cities and industrial areas had never trusted Louis Napoleon, and the naïve peasant support he had enjoyed, as nephew of his great uncle, began to drain away as expanding public education, growing prosperity and agricultural specialization and market orientation made rural inhabitants more aware of the world.

So Louis Napoleon was constantly seeking great military victories in the footsteps of his uncle to legitimate his rule and shore up his support. But the diplomatic situation when he came to power was as unfavourable to France as it had been since 1815, with the Great Powers, led by Britain and Russia, arrayed against him. His first foreign policy initiative, which would enable all others, was to break up this anti-French coalition. The vehicle he would use to that effect was the 'Eastern Question', the chronic problem of nineteenth-century European diplomacy.

The Eastern Question referred to the potential future of the Ottoman Empire, once a Great Power extending from south-eastern Europe across North Africa into the Middle

East, but since the eighteenth century in steady decline. Would this empire continue to exist, and if so in what form, or would its rule, particularly over south-eastern Europe, cease, and if so, what would replace it? By 1850, the Russian Empire in particular had been expanding to the south for a good century, seizing territory of Islamic rulers in the Caucasus and the Crimea, and fighting several wars with the Turks. The tsars and their ministers were casting an acquisitive eye on the Balkans and on Istanbul (or, as Europeans still called it, Constantinople), the Ottoman capital located on the Straits of the Dardenelles at the border between Europe and Asia. The city controlled the outlet from the Black Sea, and from Russia's great Crimean harbour Odessa, into the Mediterranean. The other Great Powers had always looked with suspicion on these Russian aspirations.

BOX 7.1

The Ottoman Empire in nineteenth-century Europe

The relationships between the Ottoman Empire and the Great and not-so-great Powers of nineteenth-century Europe were complex, probably the most complex of any relations between the European and extra-European world. One way to look at this relationship is to consider the three great extra-European realms: the Ottoman, Persian and Chinese Empires. Until the eighteenth century, at least the Europeans' equal in economic output and military power, by the nineteenth these three empires had clearly fallen behind. They had not only missed out on the industrial revolution and the broader improvements in economic productivity in nineteenth-century Europe, but also failed to achieve an efficient bureaucratic state administration. As a consequence of these two shortfalls, the three empires were noticeably inferior in military capacity. As a result of these disparities, the European Powers were able to push the three empires around, split off pieces of them, or treat them as subordinates, but they were too large to be completely subdued, conquered and colonized.

In contrast to Persia and China, though, the Ottoman Empire was noticeably closer to Europe – it was, in fact, not an entirely extra-European power, but a Euro-Asiatic one, like the Russian Empire. Indeed, in the mid-nineteenth century over half of the Ottomans' subjects lived in the Balkans, in south-eastern Europe, and this area was the economically most advanced and dynamic portion of the Empire. This close proximity to the rest of Europe meant that there was a considerably greater involvement of the European Powers in Ottoman affairs than there was in the other two empires, and at an earlier date.

Intellectual and political currents prevalent in nineteenth-century Europe also had a greater effect, and at an earlier time, on the Ottoman Empire than on the other two empires. Ottoman reformers, inspired by doctrines of European liberalism, made repeated, although generally unsuccessful, attempts to reshape the empire. Nationalist ideas increasingly penetrated the Ottomans' realm, gradually transforming the older antagonism between the ruling Muslims on the one hand, and their subordinate Christian subjects on the other, into a more intransigent and potentially more violent and destructive clash between different nationalities.

Louis Napoleon's strategy was to provoke Russia into aggressive action in this sensitive area and to align the other Powers against it. His 1853 demand that the Ottoman government replace Russia with France as the official protector of the Christian holy places in Jerusalem (Palestine being part of the Ottomans' realm) enraged the Russians, who responded to the Ottoman granting of the French request by sending their armies into the Balkans and occupying the principalities of Moldavia and Wallachia, semi-autonomous parts of the Ottoman Empire. Tsar Nicholas and his foreign policy advisers expected few problems with this step, since their country was, by treaty, the protector of these Christian principalities under Islamic rule, and Russian forces had been in them before, most recently in 1848 to suppress revolutionary movements there. Not just relying on treaty rights, the Russians counted on their seemingly dominant military position in Europe.

Their calculation failed. The Ottoman Empire declared war and was quickly supported not only by France but also by the Liberal government of Great Britain, suspicious of growing Russian power in general in the eastern Mediterranean and in central Asia, bordering on India, and hostile to the arch-reactionary tsarist regime. To the considerable disappointment of the Tsar, the other Great Powers failed to rally to the Russian cause. Quite the opposite. The Austrians, whose empire bordered the Ottomans' Balkan provinces and who looked on Russian activity there with suspicion, demanded Russia withdraw its forces from the Balkan principalities. Prussia, the weakest of the Powers, the one with the least reason to go to war and the least ability to fight one, cleverly used its situation to remain neutral, letting Austria absorb all the Tsar's hostility at the lack of support he was receiving from a regime that his forces had saved from revolutionary upheavals in 1849.

The Tsar did give in to the Austrian ultimatum, so that Austria remained out of the war, which was fought between Great Britain and France on the one hand, and Russia on the other. An Anglo-French expeditionary force crossed the Straits, entered the Black Sea, landed in the Crimea and, following several months of militarily inconclusive encounters, laid siege to the great fortress of Sebastopol. The fighting was characterized by extreme military incompetence on both sides; most casualties in the war were actually the result of disease rather than of armed action, so that the deciding factor in the war was the economic and technological position of the opposing parties. British and French troops could reach the Crimea via steamship in three weeks, whereas it took Russian soldiers three months of marching from Moscow to reach the theatre of operations in their own country. Both the infantry rifles and the artillery pieces of the Western Powers were more modern and had a longer range and greater accuracy than those possessed by the Russian forces. The hostility of Tsar Nicholas I and his advisers to economic development, industrialization and the construction of railways, a relic of pre-1850 conservative attitudes, now made itself felt.

Following the fall of Sebastopol, the Russian government decided to accept the Western Powers' peace terms rather than continue the war with a very uncertain

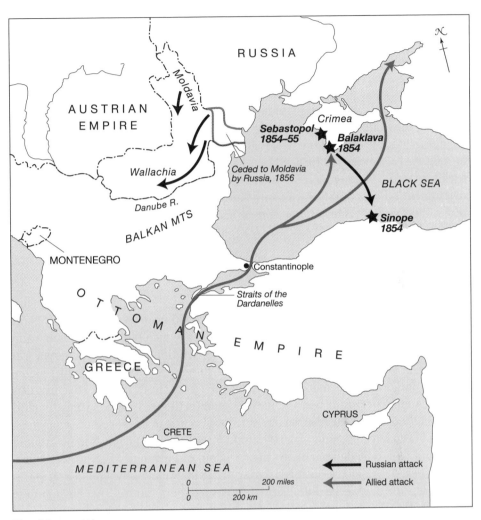

The Crimean War
Source: From *THE MAKING OF THE WEST 3E* by Lynn Hunt et al., Copyright © 2009 by Bedford/
St. Martin's. Reproduced by permission of Bedford/St. Martin's.

outcome. Russia agreed not to put any warships in the Black Sea, thus not threatening the Straits with a naval force, ceded a small strip of territory – southern Bessarabia
– to Moldavia and agreed that Moldavia and Wallachia would be put under the protection of all the Great Powers rather than of just the Russian government. (The two
principalities chose a common prince in 1859, who introduced a unified government
over the next five years, steps in the direction of a future Romanian nation-state.) It
was less the actual terms of the peace treaty than the results of the fighting which
made it clear that the post-1815 Russian military predominance in Europe was at
an end, along with Anglo-Russian cooperation to preserve territorial boundaries in
Europe, and thereby the entire settlement arranged at the Congress of Vienna.

The Crimean War was the first in a series of changes that heralded an end to this period of post-1850 conservative domination in continental Europe. Between 1856 and 1858, liberal governments came back to power in Denmark, Belgium and the Netherlands. Another signpost was the 1857 recession, a blow to reaction era governments and their plans for political quiescence through economic development. Finally, these years saw the replacement of two reactionary Great Power monarchs following the death of Russia's Nicholas I (1796–1855), and the physical and mental incapacity of Prussia's Friedrich Wilhelm IV in 1858. The two rulers' respective successors, Alexander II (1818–81) and Prince Wilhelm (1797–1888), the latter regent in 1858 and king in 1861, both began to pay attention to liberally minded government officials and to break with the policies of the reaction era. By the late 1850s, this era was visibly evaporating in Europe; its final demise was the result of another military action of Louis Napoleon in 1859.

POLITICS IN MOVEMENT, 1859–71

Scarcely was the victory parade in Paris for the Crimean War over when Louis Napoleon moved on to the next phase in his efforts to gain popularity at home and increase French power in Europe by means of a victorious war. His new target was the Austrian possessions in northern Italy, the provinces of Lombardy and Venetia, site of his uncle's first great military victories in the 1790s. The expulsion of the Austrians from the Italian peninsula was a long-time Italian nationalist cause, which touched a personal chord with the French emperor since his first political venture as a young man had been in connection with revolution of 1830 in Italy. Louis Napoleon could also count on a reliable Italian ally, the Kingdom of Piedmont-Savoy, whose rulers had twice tried to expel the Austrians during the 1848 revolutions without Great Power assistance, and had been humiliatingly defeated both times. The Piedmontese monarch Vittorio Emanuele (1820–78) and his formidable prime minister, Count Camillo di Cavour, were looking for a way to confront Austria again, this time with bigger battalions on their side. They had even joined the Western Powers in the Crimean War, not out of any foreign policy grievance against Russia, but in order to put themselves in a more favourable position for future activities against Austria.

Making this all a propitious venture was the precarious diplomatic position of the Habsburg Monarchy. By taking an anti-Russian stand in the Crimean War, the Austrians had lost the support of the Tsar, so helpful to them in suppressing the revolutionary government of Hungary in 1849. Prussia's new rulers, aiming to resume ambitions, most recently thwarted by the Russians in 1850, to replace Austria as the dominant power in central Europe, would be unlikely to stand with the Habsburgs. The liberal government of Great Britain, concerned with its overseas possessions, and vaguely sympathetic to ideals of Italian nationalism, would not help the Austrians either, leaving them diplomatically isolated.

In a famous secret meeting in the resort town of Plombières, in July 1858, Louis Napoleon and Cavour signed a treaty of alliance, aiming at a war with Austria. There was nothing secret about the military preparations the two governments began making. In a repetition of Russian behaviour in the Eastern Crisis of 1853, the Austrian government let itself be provoked into issuing an ultimatum against Piedmont in April 1859 and then declaring war. Lacking the – mistaken – Russian belief in their military superiority, the Austrian decision was even more dubious. As Austria's emperor, Franz Joseph, would admit some years later when describing his policy, 'We were very honourable, but very stupid.'[24] French troops crossed into Italy – not on foot, over the Alps, as Napoleon had led them heroically in the 1790s, but more comfortably, on the railway. Joining with the Piedmontese army, they defeated the Austrians in the bloody battle of Solferino at the end of June 1859.

Having liberated Lombardy from Austrian rule, Louis Napoleon suddenly changed course. Instead of continuing to Venetia, as previously agreed with his Piedmontese allies, he negotiated an armistice, leaving this Italian province under Habsburg rule. The war had been victorious and relatively easy up until Solferino; a further campaign, involving attacking Austrian positions in their Alpine fortresses, the 'Quadrilateral', threatened to become more difficult and costly, both in economic and human terms, raising the possibility of war on other fronts as well, and creating a situation that would decrease rather than elevate the emperor's popularity.

The armistice guaranteed Louis Napoleon's goals with less effort. His Piedmontese ally, in return for acquiring the very rich province of Lombardy, centre of industrialization and economic development in post-1850 Italy, would cede to France the border district of Savoy and a strip of Mediterranean coastline around the city of Nice, in the next century to be famous for the introduction of the bikini. These were two regions that had been part of France during the Revolutionary and Napoleonic era and lost in the Treaty of Vienna in 1815; their acquisition was the first territorial revision of the treaty provisions in France's favour. Finally, all the kingdoms and duchies of the Italian peninsula would be gathered into a confederation, under the presidency of the Pope, a step towards the nationalist demand for an Italian nation-state, but just a very moderate one.

This was *Realpolitik* in action, and it was a settlement that would pass muster with the Great Powers. It lasted barely a few months, overturned by a combination of mass politics, nationalism and clever Piedmontese diplomacy. Nationalist insurgents in the small central Italian duchies of Parma and Modena, ruled by relatives of the Austrian Habsburgs, overthrew the governments and demanded their annexation by Piedmont. Then, in May 1860, the radical revolutionary of 1848, Giuseppe Garibaldi, along with his one thousand red-shirted followers, took ship from the port city of Genoa, under Piedmontese rule and thus with tacit cooperation of the Piedmontese authorities, heading for the island of Sicily.

The arrival of the insurgents led to an enormous uprising in Sicily and in the mainland regions of southern Italy, all part of the Kingdom of the Two Sicilies, one of the most reactionary countries in Europe, whose arch-conservative king Fernando II was a sworn enemy of Italian nationalism. Most of the insurgents were impoverished peasants, day labourers and sharecroppers, who were primarily interested in seizing disputed forest lands for themselves, but their actions completely destroyed the rule of the kingdom's authorities, and Garibaldi entered Naples in triumph. Count Cavour saw this wild revolutionary action as a danger – namely, that Garibaldi might continue his victorious march on to Rome, overthrow papal rule (radicals, including Garibaldi, had already done this in 1848) and embroil Piedmont with its French ally, whose troops were protecting the Pope. But Cavour understood that Garibaldi's southern Italian revolution was not just a danger but also an opportunity. He sent the Piedmontese army marching south, annexing the Grand Duchy of Tuscany and a large chunk of papal territory in central and southern Italy as it went, reaching Garibaldi in October 1860, when a celebrated meeting took place between Garibaldi and the Piedmontese monarch in which Garibaldi greeted the latter with the words, 'Hail Vittorio Emanuele, king of Italy.'

The greeting was a gesture of *Realpolitik* on the part of the revolutionary. As a republican and a democrat, Garibaldi was an opponent of the monarchical form of government; as the leader of a successful revolution, he was surrendering sovereign authority to what was, at most, a moderately liberal regime. But the encounter involved an even greater degree of *Realpolitik* for the Piedmontese monarch. By accepting Garibaldi's greeting, he was rejecting the principle of the legitimacy of existing boundaries and ruling dynasties that was an integral part of the Vienna settlement of 1815, and receiving his new territories from the hands of a radical revolutionary who had just finished destroying a legitimate ruling dynasty in the Kingdom of the Two Sicilies and whose peasant followers were wreaking havoc on noble landlords. What these two very disparate figures had in common was nationalism, the belief that all individuals of the same nationality should be citizens of a common nation-state. Vittorio Emanuele became not, as originally envisaged, the ruler of an expanded but still distinctly limited Kingdom of Piedmont-Savoy, but instead the monarch of an Italian nation-state whose territory extended across the entire peninsula except for the north-eastern province of Venetia, still in Austrian hands, and a small region around Rome, the 'Papal patrimony', under French military protection. The House of Savoy would rule Italy 'by the grace of God and the will of the people', thus uniting two seemingly contradictory principles: the conservative one of divinely sanctioned dynastic rule and the radical one of the sovereign authority of the nation.

It is difficult to overestimate the impact of the events of 1859–60 on the entire European continent. Garibaldi was a dynamic, charismatic figure, and with the growth of the periodical press, we could say that he became Europe's first mass media celebrity. Even in phlegmatic England, tens of thousands of people gathered in London's Hyde Park for meetings supporting him, the participants brawling with angry Irish Catholic defenders of the Pope. When Garibaldi toured England in 1864, he

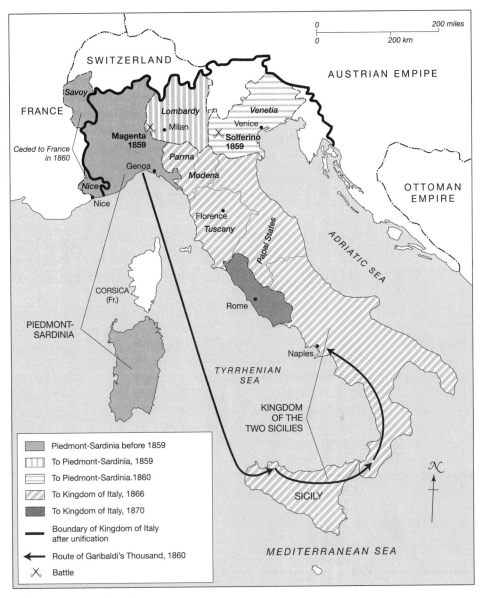

Italian national unification
Source: From *THE MAKING OF THE WEST 3E* by Lynn Hunt et al., Copyright © 2009 by Bedford/
St. Martin's. Reproduced by permission of Bedford/ St. Martin's.

received a hero's welcome everywhere he went, culminating in a London parade attracting some 400,000 spectators.

Beyond his individual characteristics, Garibaldi personalized a broader political moment, the end of the era of reaction. Political initiative shifted leftwards, as liberals increasingly pressed their claims, while conservatives found themselves more and more on the defensive. Garibaldi's campaign revealed in drastic fashion another feature of the era: that political initiative was no longer restricted to the government, as had largely been the case in the 1850s, but could be taken by members of the public, working through nationalist associations or via nascent political parties.

In many ways, the chief distinction between the different European countries in this period was the point at which the political situation changed, and the degree of upheaval this change generated. Liberal reforms proceeded without difficulty in Scandinavia and the Low Countries. Among the Great Powers, the smoothest line of political development was in Britain. Lord Palmerston (1784–1865), the veteran Whig politician, who had already been prime minister from 1855 to 1858, returned to office in 1859 after a brief interlude of minority Tory government, and continued his policies aimed at increasing administrative efficiency, expanding and improving education, and cutting taxes. Counter-balancing Palmerston's more moderate image was his chancellor of the exchequer, William Gladstone (1809–98), who enjoyed support on the left wing of the Liberal Party and among British radicals. This duo kept politics on course until the question of expanding the suffrage split British Liberals in the mid-1860s.

Russia's Tsar Alexander II and his advisers faced a much more difficult situation than did British politicians, with their stable and well-functioning political system. The early 1860s was the period in which Alexander was introducing major reforms into Russia, moving society and even the state in a more liberal direction – above all, liberating the serfs, but also introducing jury trials and rural provincial self-government, and loosening strict press censorship – yet trying to ensure, in spite of these changes, the continuation of an autocratic regime. It was a delicate balancing act, at which the Tsar and his authorities largely succeeded. Liberally minded state officials and aristocrats, the major figures in public life, in a still very undeveloped civil society, cooperated in the reforming measures; their efforts to go beyond them, to use the zemstvos to petition for the introduction of a constitution, for instance, were suppressed. To be sure, Russian radicals became more active, with the creation of an illegal underground organization, Land and Liberty, dedicated to overthrowing tsarist rule. Their membership was confined to a small group of intellectuals, above all students at the university in St Petersburg, and their efforts did not get very far throughout the 1860s.

The one spot in the Tsar's empire where this delicate balancing act collapsed was in the empire's Polish territories. Peasants there, as elsewhere in the empire, were excited at the prospect of the end of serfdom, if also suspicious of the terms on which it would be carried out. Much of the politically active population – the Polish version of the notables, which meant primarily the nobility but also some of the more affluent inhabitants of urban areas – understood the reforms as an expression of weakness, a sign that the Tsar's rule over Poland was collapsing, and an independent Polish nation-state might soon emerge. Underground Polish radicals, organized illegally like their Russian counterparts (and, like them, with a lot of university students among

BOX 7.2

William Ewart Gladstone

Arguably the leading liberal politician and statesman in Europe during the second half of the nineteenth century, and a continent-wide inspiration for and symbol of liberalism, William Ewart Gladstone's life and career demonstrated both the typical features of liberalism as well as his own personal, idiosyncratic ones, both the strengths of this political movement and its weaknesses.

Gladstone's background was quite atypical for liberals. A devout adherent of the Church of England, his faith made him an exception in a political tendency whose supporters were disproportionately anti-clerical or adherents of free (that is, non-established) churches. As might be expected from his religious beliefs, he began his political career as a Conservative, and it took about two decades, from the late 1830s to the late 1850s, for him to move from the Tories to the Liberals.

In contrast to his personal piety and political antecedents, the policies Gladstone followed when in office as chancellor of the exchequer and prime minister during the 1850s, 1860s and 1870s, were classic exemplars of nineteenth-century liberalism. He advocated lower taxes, lower government expenditures, a balanced budget and free trade; he tried to create a more efficient civil service and government administration, and provided aid to education. Gladstone was sympathetic to nationalist aspirations, particularly supporting the movement towards Italian national unity and the struggle of the Bulgarians for independence from the Ottoman Empire. His attempt to implement these principles in Britain itself, by introducing autonomy or home rule for Ireland, would prove, in the 1880s, to be his political downfall.

Gladstone was also a prime example of liberalism as political mass movement in spite of itself. Already a popular figure, dubbed 'the people's William' in the 1860s, for his abolishing taxes on articles of mass consumption and the periodical press, in his 'Midlothian campaigns' of 1879 and 1880 Gladstone became a mass orator, attracting audiences of ten to fifteen thousand, with his passionate speeches widely publicized in the periodical press. His public appearances were enormous spectacles, turning a politician who was a firm believer in a society of property owners and a free market economy, and who was no supporter of universal manhood suffrage, into a passionately adored working-class hero.

their members), but in larger numbers, with ties to the Polish exile communities in western Europe, launched an uprising in January 1863. The insurgents were unable to gain control of any urban centres and retreated to the countryside, where they attempted to engage in guerrilla warfare. With relatively few exceptions, though, the peasants were sceptical of the insurgents, remembering the close connections between Polish nationalism and the serf-owning nobility. Insurgents responded by threatening the peasants and even publicly hanging recalcitrant villagers. This did not increase popular support, and after six months of fighting the insurrection collapsed. Like the Polish nationalist uprisings of the first half of the nineteenth century, this one showed that the rural Polish lower classes had little sympathy for nationalist ideas, or even identified greatly with the Polish nation. Polish nationalists of the last third of the nineteenth century would generally give up efforts at armed insurrection in favour of actions designed to convince the peasants that they truly were Poles and that their political loyalties should lie with the idea of a Polish nation-state.

In France, the situation for most of the 1860s, while still under governmental control, was becoming shakier for the emperor. His military victories of 1859 had boosted his popularity, but they had also alienated an important group of conservative supporters, pious Catholics, who were outraged by the way that France's ally, Piedmont-Savoy, had seized large chunks of papal territory, threatening the independence and autonomy of the head of the Catholic Church. Although liberals and radicals largely approved of the 1859 war, for the same reason as conservatives had opposed it, they remained opposed to Louis Napoleon's authoritarian rule and, indeed, increased their political activities against it. In the 1863 elections, votes for all the oppositional candidates, both on the left and the right, increased by about 50 per cent over the previous ballot in 1857. Particularly embarrassing for the government was that all ten of the deputies representing Paris were oppositional, nine republicans who wanted an end to the empire altogether, and one more left-wing liberal.

In contrast to the short, victorious war of 1859, the emperor's military initiatives in the 1860s, the attempted colonial acquisitions in South-East Asia and in Mexico, were lengthy, expensive and much less popular. There were practical reasons for these efforts, namely attempts to gain control of economically useful raw materials – silk in Indochina and silver in Mexico – but the costs, particularly of the Mexican expedition, began to outweigh the benefits. By contrast, the conditions for further and more popular European military victories in the Napoleonic tradition seemed much less favourable. If not yet facing a crisis, the imperial regime was seeing its support steadily leak away. On a smaller scale, the political situation in Spain showed distinct similarities to those in France. The Spanish prime minister between 1856 and 1863 was a military strongman, the general Leopoldo O'Donnell, whose moderately liberal but distinctly authoritarian government faced growing radical opposition in spite of several modest overseas military ventures, largely in the wake of France.

In face of mounting opposition, the government in France nonetheless remained in charge throughout the 1860s, as did that in Spain, albeit somewhat more precariously, until the outbreak of revolution in 1868. By contrast, the new authorities of the united kingdom of Italy had very great difficulties in establishing their rule in the Italian peninsula south of Rome. Part of the problem stemmed from the continued resistance of the conservative forces defeated in 1860. Pius IX refused to accept the Italian nation-state, excommunicating Vittorio Emanuele and all his government ministers, denouncing them as 'subalpine usurpers'. The deposed Bourbon dynasty of the

Kingdom of the Two Sicilies was no less resistant to the new state of affairs. Their sympathizers demonstrated against the new regime, engaged in plots and conspiracies against it, and worked to gain the support of gangs of armed bandits, who were a common feature of life in nineteenth-century southern Italy. The result was a state of endemic lawlessness and lack of government authority, climaxing in a massive counter-revolutionary uprising in the Sicilian capital of Palermo in 1866, which enjoyed widespread sympathy in the countryside, controlled the city for a week and required the massive deployment of the army to suppress.

Part of the reason that conservative resistance to the Italian kingdom was so successful was, paradoxically, because the radical hopes raised during Garibaldi's campaign in 1860 were not fulfilled. Unlike the rural Polish population, which saw no benefits to them from the nationalist uprising in 1863, the impoverished peasants of the Italian south responded to the call of the one thousand red-shirted insurgents, and made it possible for them to conquer the largest state in the Italian peninsula. But the aftermath disappointed the Italian peasants' aspirations to gain control of the land. To be sure, the new authorities auctioned off the property of the Catholic Church, and some badly intimidated noble landlords sold part of their own holdings, but the new proprietors were generally members of the urban middle class, or former substantial peasant farmers. Perhaps the chief characteristic of these new landowners in Sicily was their formation of a secret society to protect their property from armed bandits, and to collect protection money from other landlords for doing so. They called their organization the Mafia and it was the forerunner of the organized crime families of the twentieth century.

The new liberal regime thus gave the rural lower classes of southern Italy no benefits, but placed additional burdens on them in the form of higher taxes, new bureaucratic regulations and conscription of young men into the army, deploying large numbers of soldiers and paramilitary police, the *carabinieri*, to compel the population to bear the burdens. It is not surprising that many small farmers and landless labourers became supporters of the conservative and clerical counter-revolution or, sometimes, of an odd mixture of radical and conservative ideas. It was during this period that Davide Lazzari, a self-proclaimed prophet and messiah, was active. Lazzari held enormous mass meetings calling on the peasants to boycott paying taxes in the name of Jesus Christ.

Considered more broadly, the fate of the Italian south in the new Italian kingdom raised questions about the success of the liberal and nationalist initiative that would be characteristic of the 1860s. Once in power, nineteenth-century liberalism, a movement of property owners devoted to a free market economy, did not necessarily have a lot to offer the propertyless classes, especially in an environment, as was typical of much of southern Europe in this period, where economic growth was lagging and where railway construction, industrialization and agricultural specialization were not making much progress. The experiences of the united Italian kingdom in the southern part of the peninsula raised even more questions about nationalism.

Contrary to the nationalists' assumption that everyone in the peninsula thought of him- or herself as an Italian and wanted to belong to an Italian nation-state, the inhabitants of southern Italy and the island of Sicily showed very little identification with the nation-state in which they lived, ignoring its laws, despising (or, on occasion, trying to kill) its officials and police. Most southern Italians did not speak standard Italian – itself a northern dialect – and so lacked the common language needed for a sense of national belonging. Indeed, so alien were northern Italians in the south that Sicilians thought schoolteachers from Piedmont were Englishmen.

This situation was summed up in a famous phrase, usually, although incorrectly, attributed to Cavour's successor, Massimo d'Azeglio: 'We have made Italy; now we must make Italians.' This was the nationalist cause, as seen in the disillusioned gaze of *Realpolitik*. If the inhabitants of the Italian peninsula did not have the loyalties and sentiments that nationalist idealism insisted they should, then the new 'national' government would have to instil these loyalties and sentiments in them, via coercive measures – compulsory public education, military conscription, and the actions of a government bureaucracy. It was a long-term project that, arguably, took a century and more to complete.

A different, although equally difficult, result of the combination of liberalism and nationalism occurred in the Austrian Empire, where the absolutist reaction era government was badly shaken by military defeat in 1859. Dismissing the discredited conservative government ministers and making one concession after another, Emperor Franz Joseph in the 'February patent' of 1861 granted a constitution and called for elections to a legislature based on a property franchise, in effect giving the notables their political voice. This opening to a more liberal political system did not produce the expected result, in view of the close affiliation of liberalism and nationalism. German-speaking, Czech-speaking, Magyar-speaking, Polish-speaking and Croatian-speaking liberals in the Austrian Empire may have agreed on political and economic principles, but they wanted these principles implemented in separate nation-states, or at least autonomous provinces of the empire, rather than in a multinational regime. Consequently, almost all the liberal deputies elected to the imperial parliament refused to take their seats since the elections were not for their own national legislatures. The only group willing to go along was the German-speaking liberals, but this was because they understood the entire empire, in spite of its many different ethnic, linguistic and national groups, as being part of a potential German nation-state. Most liberals in the rest of the German-speaking world rejected this understanding and aspired to a united German nation-state that would not include the Germans of the Austrian Empire.

The decade of the 1860s would see an increasing realignment of politics in the Austrian Empire in terms of competing nationalism. A good example would be the developments in the Bohemian city of Budweis/Budejovice, best known for its Budweiser beer. The population of this city included both German- and Czech-speakers, with most inhabitants bilingual to a greater or lesser degree. In the early

1860s, lines of division among the town's politically active inhabitants (mostly its more affluent ones) ran between conservative-clericals on the one hand, and anti-clerical liberals on the other. By the end of the decade this clash had transmuted into one between opposing German and Czech nationalists. Differences in the political spectrum would only be possible among members of the same nationality, a trend which would become ever more influential in the politics of the Habsburg Monarchy in the years down to 1914.

In the other states of the German Confederation – the Great Power Kingdom of Prussia and the many smaller and medium-sized states such as Baden, Bavaria and Saxony – there was no disagreement among the inhabitants that they were all Germans, so the liberal and nationalist initiatives of the post-1859 period at first went from strength to strength. The 1859 Schiller Festivals, celebrating the one hundredth anniversary of the birth of the famous poet, became widespread demonstrations in favour of liberal reforms and national unity. The early years of the 1860s saw the rapid growth of nationalist gymnastics, choral and sharpshooting societies, as well as of workers' educational associations, all endorsing liberal political principles. The National Association of 1860, with its 20,000, largely notable, members, across all of central Europe, coordinated effectively the actions and activities of these associations, liberal parliamentarians and liberal journalists, pressing for the creation of a united, liberal German nation-state. Liberal government ministers were appointed in a number of the German states; liberal politicians were victorious in parliamentary elections almost everywhere in central Europe.

Yet this liberal initiative would ultimately prove incapable of realizing its nationalist goals unaided. Part of the problem was the limitations of liberal political conceptions. Liberal leaders refused to lower dues to allow workers to join the National Association, so Germany's working-class activists formed their own national group, which gradually developed in the direction of an anti-liberal labour party. Catholics, especially in southern and western Germany, were suspicious of and frequently hostile to liberal plans for free market reforms, anti-clerical ideas among liberals and liberal plans to unite the German states without Austria, central Europe's Catholic Great Power. For all these difficulties, it was in the domain of national unification itself that the liberal initiative would face its greatest difficulties.

The question for central Europe's nationalists was which state would be Germany's Piedmont, would take the diplomatic – and, if necessary, military – initiative to unify the German states. Most of Germany's liberals put their hopes in the Kingdom of Prussia, and the initial policies of the prince regent and then king, Wilhelm I, and his moderately liberal ministers – contemporaries called it the 'New Era' government – suggested that their hopes were well placed. To encourage this trend, leaders of the National Association formed a new political party in Prussia in 1860, the German Party of Progress, whose very name was a political programme. It was the party of progress, thus embodying the spirit of the age; it was a German party, not a Prussian one, so that the progress it envisaged was in the direction of a united German nation-state.

A coalition of liberals and radicals – in the spirit of *Realpolitik* the latter largely deferring to the former and their programme of seeking cooperation with the Prussian government – the party did well in the 1861 elections and emerged as the major political grouping in the Prussian parliament. However, the intended cooperation quickly gave way to a bitter conflict which was, ironically, over an issue closely related to the liberal programme for national reunification, namely the reshaping of the Prussian army. The plans of Prussian generals to fight future wars, which seemed a likely prospect after 1859, involved attempts to outflank and encircle enemy armies, a task requiring more soldiers. The generals proposed to obtain these troops by incorporating the militia (*Landwehr*) into the regular army during wartime.

This was not an unreasonable notion, or one that the liberal politicians, who saw Prussia and its army as crucial to their hopes for a united German nation-state, would have been inclined to oppose had the government been willing to reach out to them. But the government was not – to be more precise, many of the government ministers were not opposed to doing so, but the minister of war, Albrecht von Roon (1803–79) and the leading general, Edwin von Manteuffel (1809–85), flatly refused. They were supported in this respect by their monarch, who had no interest in conceding any authority over the army to the liberal politicians. For the Prussian king, his generals and much of the realm's landed nobility, control over the armed forces – armed forces crucial to liberal plans of national unification – marked the limit of their cooperation with liberalism.

It took just a few months for the Party of Progress, formed to cooperate with the government, to become its bitter enemy. The parliamentarians, using the power of the purse they had under the Prussian constitution, refused to pass the government's budget or consent to the levying of taxes until the army reorganization was arranged with their cooperation. The government responded by dissolving the parliament and calling new elections, in which the authorities employed all the techniques of the official candidacy from the era of reaction: state-supported candidates, pressure on government employees and contractors to vote for them, threats against those who opposed the authorities. What was successful in the 1850s failed badly in 1862. Liberal notables, in an election system involving public voting and a franchise that weighted votes by the amount of direct taxes the voter paid, dominated the polling, so that the opposition swept the elections by a wide margin. After the elections, the moderately liberal and moderately conservative government ministers of the 'New Era' resigned, leaving the monarch with a difficult decision.

King Wilhelm was unwilling to appoint ministers who would cooperate with the liberal parliamentarians, but it was also unclear how his kingdom could be run without a budget and legal authority to collect taxes. The monarch seriously considered abdicating in favour of his son Friedrich, a son-in-law of Queen Victoria and heavily influenced by his liberal, English wife. As a last, desperate step before abdication, the king decided to appoint a new prime minister, the Prussian ambassador in Paris,

Otto von Bismarck. The new prime minister, in view of his past political history, had the reputation of being an extreme conservative, an enemy of parliaments and constitutions, and an opponent of liberalism and nationalism.

His actions, once in office, seemed to uphold that reputation. Bismarck simply ignored the legislature and its constitutional prerogatives, and went on collecting taxes and expending funds without its approval. He found ways to harass opposition newspapers, make punitive transfers of judges who supported the liberals – another act in violation of the constitution – and generally to behave in an aggressively authoritarian and reactionary fashion. Contemporaries, both Bismarck's friends and his

---

BOX 7.3

Otto von Bismarck

After what could fairly be called a wasted youth, Bismarck became involved in politics via his wife, Johanna von Puttkamer, who came from a prominent family of aristocratic, Prussian, born-again Christians, or Pietists as they were called in Germany. Such devout Protestants were on the right of the political spectrum, and Bismarck first made a name for himself during the 1848 revolution as a prominent, if eccentric, figure on the extreme right. Following the suppression of the revolutionary movement, the reaction era Prussian government rewarded him by appointing him to a major diplomatic post, as Prussia's representative to the German Confederation in Frankfurt.

In Frankfurt, and in a later diplomatic posting in Paris, Bismarck's circle of acquaintances and his intellectual and political horizons widened. He met members of Germany's capitalist class in Frankfurt, an important commercial and financial centre, and observed closely the innovative right-wing political style of Napoleon III in Paris. Still viewed as the hard-line reactionary of 1848 when he was appointed Prussian prime minister in 1862, Bismarck astounded contemporaries by co-opting his liberal opponents' ideas, creating a united German nation-state under Prussian leadership. The diplomatic skill and daring he showed in doing so, and the equally skilled and daring successes of the Prussian army in carrying out his plans, made him into a national hero – an unexpected role for a one-time religious conservative who had viewed nationalism as idolatry. The final two decades of his career, 1871–90, when he was simultaneously prime minister of Prussia and chancellor of the German Empire, were primarily devoted to preserving the domestic and foreign policy accomplishments of 1862–71.

Bismarck has been as controversial a figure to historians as he was to contemporaries, with a major question being the relationship between his actions and those of later German leaders, such as the Emperor Wilhelm II and Adolf Hitler. Condemned as an unscrupulous manipulator, using wartime victories, nationalism and personal charisma to subvert constitutional government and the rule of law, Bismarck has also been defended as a devout statesman who subordinated both power politics and nationalism to his religious and ethical ideals. Without choosing between these two interpretations, it would be fair to say that Bismarck's use of nationalism and armed conflict for his political purposes set a bad precedent for his successors, who lacked both his diplomatic skill and his sense of limitations.

enemies, generally assumed that Bismarck's foreign policy would correspond to his reactionary domestic policies, that he would be an opponent of liberal plans for national unification.

In this assumption contemporaries were simply wrong. Taking a leaf from the book of Louis Napoleon Bonaparte, whom he had observed closely when he was in Paris, Bismarck set out to implement the liberals' programme of German national unification under his conservative leadership. The first step was the 1864 war with Denmark, after the Danish government announced its intention, in liberal and nationalist fashion, to incorporate the separately administered border province of Schleswig, inhabited by both Danish- and German-speakers, directly into the Danish kingdom. The cause of the German-speaking inhabitants of Schleswig, and its neighbour province Holstein, was a popular one with German nationalists, strongly supported by the National Association and the gymnastic societies. Bismarck manoeuvred to have the German Confederation, the league of all the states of central Europe, declare war on Denmark. The ensuing conflict, pitting the Confederation in general, and the two Great Powers, Prussia and Austria in particular, against Denmark, was a rather one-sided affair, but Bismarck made sure that the heroic deeds of Prussian soldiers, such as their storming the Danish fortress of Düppel, were widely reported in the press as nationalist victories.

In spite of the successful outcome of the war, which involved the Danish cession of the provinces of Schleswig and Holstein to Prussian and Austrian administration, Bismarck had not yet succeeded in breaking the liberal opposition to his government. He turned in 1865 to planning the next and decisive step in his campaign, a war with Austria to make Prussia the dominant state in central Europe. Once again borrowing from Louis Napoleon's ideas, he systematically provoked Austria into war, his key provocation a call in April 1866 to transform the German Confederation from a league of states into a united nation-state, with a parliament elected by universal manhood suffrage.

Bismarck's attempt to provoke Austria certainly worked, only not quite as he had planned. Almost all the other German states, and their league, the German Confederation, joined Austria in declaring war on Prussia in June 1866, supported in this decision by most liberals and nationalists in central Europe. Germans looked apprehensively at France, expecting Napoleon III to send French troops into western Germany to seize territory along the River Rhine – repeating another conquest from the French Revolutionary and Napoleonic era – once Prussian troops were withdrawn from the region to fight the Austrians. Bismarck himself, expecting just such a French move, was more than a little apprehensive about the situation he was in.

His fate, that of the Prussian government, of central Europe, and of the European powers more generally, would depend on the campaign of the Prussian army. It proved to be a successful application of the new military doctrines developed by that army's General Staff. Although outnumbered overall, Prussian troops were concentrated very quickly by rail in Bohemia, achieving a local superiority over the Austrians. At the decisive battle of Königgrätz (Sadowa) on 3 July 1866, Prussian forces exploited their superiority in firepower, firing seven times as many shots as the Austrians, while the latter took seven times as many casualties. So complete was the Austrian defeat that the government was forced to sue for peace, and the entire Austro-Prussian war was over in six weeks – too quickly for Louis Napoleon, many of whose best troops were mired in Mexico, to intervene.

The victory of the Prussian army marked a dramatic change in the territorial organization of central Europe and, as a result of this reorganization, an equally drastic change in its political orientation. The defeated German Confederation was dissolved. Prussia annexed several of the states, such as Hanover, Hessen-Kassel and the city of Frankfurt, which had opposed it, and gathered the remaining German states north of the River Main – the traditional dividing line between north and south Germany – into a new governmental body, the North German Confederation. This was not like its predecessor, the German Confederation, a league of sovereign states, but a federal state with not only a central government but also state governments – Prussia, Saxony, Braunschweig, and so on – with constitutionally delegated powers. The president of the Confederation was the king of Prussia, who was also commander-in-chief of the Confederation's armed forces. There was a lower house of parliament, the Reichstag, elected by universal manhood suffrage – and here we see Bismarck joining other unconventional conservatives of the era, such as Louis Napoleon Bonaparte or Benjamin Disraeli, in endorsing a democratic franchise. However, this parliament had strictly circumscribed powers. The Confederation's prime minister, its chancellor (Bismarck, of course), was appointed by its president, the king of Prussia, so the democratically elected parliament had no power over the Confederation's executive. Laws the parliament passed required the consent of the Federal Council, a body made up of representatives of the different state governments in the Confederation, and dominated by the representatives of the Prussian government – once again, led by Bismarck. These complicated constitutional arrangements guaranteed that the king of Prussia and his prime minister would dominate the government of the Confederation.

The German states south of the River Main – Baden, Bavaria, Hessen-Darmstadt and Württemberg – would have an independent sovereign existence, not part of any larger league or confederation (Napoleon III had insisted on this) so that all that was needed to complete the unification of Germany, which the nationalists envisaged, was the adherence of these states to the Confederation. By contrast, the Austrian Empire was expelled from German affairs and came close to collapse. Although Austrian forces defeated the Italians, who were Prussia's ally, the Austrian defeat by Prussia meant that Austria had to cede its remaining Italian province, Venetia, to the Kingdom of Italy. The only thing that saved the empire from dissolving into different nation-states was the gentle treatment by its victor. Bismarck renounced any war indemnity, territorial annexation, or even, much to the annoyance of Prussia's generals, a victory parade in Vienna.

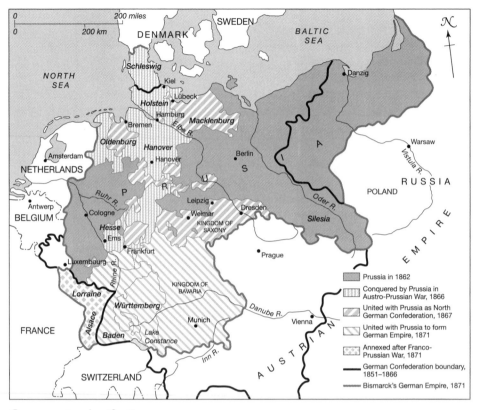

German national unification
Source: From *THE MAKING OF THE WEST 3E* by Lynn Hunt et al., Copyright © 2009 by Bedford/
St. Martin's. Reproduced by permission of Bedford/St. Martin's.

To avoid the triumph of all the nationalist movements in his realm, Emperor Franz Joseph had to make concessions to the most powerful of them, the Hungarians. In 1867, he and his ministers reached an agreement with the Hungarians, known as the *Ausgleich* (Compromise), which divided the empire into two autonomous states, Austria and Hungary, each with its own constitution, parliament, prime minister and council of ministers. The two halves of this Dual Monarchy, or Austro-Hungarian Empire, as the realm would be known from 1867 until its demise in 1918, would have a common armed forces and foreign policy, jointly arranged government finances, and a joint sovereign, Franz Joseph, who was emperor of Austria but king of Hungary.

These central European constitutional arrangements may all seem like tedious legal details to the reader, but it is important to understand that they amounted to a revolutionary change. Prussia's annexation of sovereign states – which included a few interesting acts, such as confiscating the private fortune of the Hanoverian royal family, or threatening to pillage the city of Frankfurt unless its inhabitants handed over 20 million gulden for Prussian troops – was the final nail in the coffin of the

1815 Vienna settlement and its principle of respecting the territorial integrity and ruling dynasties of the existing states of Europe. Since the late Middle Ages, the Austrian ruling dynasty, the house of Habsburg, had been the dominant power in German affairs, until 1806 as Holy Roman Emperor, following 1815 as president of the German Confederation – and was now completely driven out of these affairs by a government purporting to represent the ideas of the nationalist movement in Germany. This territorial revolution produced a political revolution as well.

For many of central Europe's conservatives, Bismarck's actions were those of a dangerous, radical revolutionary. Catholics in particular were outraged by defeat of their champion, the Habsburg emperor, by a Protestant Prussia in close alliance with the Kingdom of Italy that had seized the lands of the Pope. Many Protestant conservatives, certainly in annexed territories such as Hanover, but even in Prussia, were outraged by Bismarck's flouting their political principles. It was particularly galling to them that it was one of their own who had acted that way.

By contrast, a substantial number of liberals and even some radicals re-evaluated their position on Bismarck. He had successfully united most of the German states, as they had never been able to. The Party of Progress split, with many of its adherents forming a new National Liberal Party which endorsed Bismarck's actions as the path to a united and liberal German nation-state. Ironically, Bismarck, having offended many of his former conservative supporters, found himself cooperating with his new liberal allies. Liberal reforms, such as freedom of movement and occupation, complete emancipation of the Jews, even the legalization of trade unions, were implemented in the North German Confederation in the late 1860s. A similar trend emerged in Austria-Hungary. The more conservative government ministers, who had led Austria to disaster between 1859 and 1867, were discredited. Parliamentary elections in both halves of the empire, still under a property franchise, led to liberal victories and cooperation between governments and parliamentarians in implementing a similar set of liberal reforms. Thus the war planned by a steadfast, if daring and eccentric, conservative led to the climax of the era of liberal reforms in central Europe.

The results of the Austro-Prussian War also transformed the contest among the Great Powers for hegemony in Europe. The blows to Russia in the Crimean War and to Austria in the northern Italian war had seemed to enhance the power of the Louis Napoleon's Second Empire, and its ruler had initially welcomed the prospect of a further Austrian defeat in 1866 as a reinforcement of France's situation, rather as a repetition of the events of 1859–60. Yet the military superiority Prussia demonstrated in the war, and the subsequent creation of a North German Confederation uniting most of the German states, had resulted in a much more powerful neighbour than the Kingdom of Italy. The speed of Prussia's victory made it impossible for Napoleon III to obtain pieces of German territory as he had pieces of Italy in 1859. His attempt to gain compensation by annexing Belgium in 1867 was blocked by Prussia, as was the further effort, the following year, to annex Luxembourg. When you cannot annex Luxembourg, you know there is a problem. Consequently, the North German Confederation and the French Empire, Otto von Bismarck and Louis Napoleon Bonaparte, faced each other anxiously and warily between 1866 and 1870, circling like two wrestlers, waiting for an opportunity to clinch.

Exacerbating this diplomatic impasse was the upsurge of mass politics during the final years of the 1860s. This period saw public political participation in Europe at its greatest extent since the 1848 revolution. In Great Britain, differences among Liberal Party politicians about whether to expand the franchise spilled over into broader public life as the Reform League, founded in 1865 and with 65,000 members in 600 local groups, agitated ever more vigorously for a democratic suffrage. Hundreds of thousands of supporters participated in its greatest demonstrations in London in July 1866. The concessions to Hungarian nationalists in the Austro-Hungarian Empire only encouraged other nationalist groups to press their demands: there are said to have been over 1 million participants in a series of demonstrations in Bohemia and Moravia demanding an autonomous government for the Czech Lands, in effect calling for the transformation of the Dual Monarchy into a triple monarchy. Generally, the existing political systems proved able to accommodate this mass politics. In Great Britain, for example, when the Liberal Party split over the suffrage, a minority Tory government under Benjamin Disraeli introduced the Second Reform Bill, which expanded the franchise considerably without granting it to all adult men (to say nothing of women). The one outright exception to this trend was in Spain, where the political system collapsed in 1868 into seven years of revolution and civil war. In France and the German states, the incipient mass politics of the 1860s would be far from overthrowing governments but could not be entirely absorbed by the existing system either. They would affect state policy and encourage riskier diplomatic strategies, leading to war in 1870.

In France, the growing political participation increasingly took the form of open opposition to imperial rule. The republicans were especially active, defying the regime by publishing radical newspapers, forming election committees and holding public mass meetings – particularly aggressively in the capital city and its suburbs, but also in urban and rural areas all across the country. In the 1869 elections, 30 per cent of the votes were cast for republican candidates, a threefold increase over the previous elections of 1863. On the announcement of the election results, crowds in Paris surged into the streets, denouncing the emperor and clashing with the police. Striking workers in the commercial city of Toulouse and in the coal-mining town of Anzin, marched through the streets chanting 'Down with the emperor!' and 'Long live the republic!'

The regime's military and foreign policy defeats only encouraged this opposition. The withdrawal of French troops from Mexico and the execution of France's puppet emperor Maximilian by Mexican insurgents in 1867 ended an unpopular and fruitless military adventure in a débâcle. Back in Europe, a site of much greater concern for the press and public opinion than overseas, the victory of Prussia and the failure of the emperor to extract compensation could only be seen as a national humiliation. If Napoleon III had previously used military and diplomatic victories to reinforce his support and the legitimacy of his rule, his post-1866 defeats and failures in these spheres had precisely the opposite effect.

Forced to make concessions, the emperor appointed as his new prime minister a one-time republican leader, Émile Ollivier (1825–1913), and made a series of concessions in 1869–70, enhancing the power of the elected legislature, proclaiming that his realm would henceforth be a 'liberal empire'. A plebiscite in early 1870, a tool still used effectively by the emperor, endorsed these reforms by a wide margin. Having temporarily mollified the opposition by renouncing some of his powers, the question emerged of whether Napoleon III might seek a new military victory to gain them back. At the same time as opposition was growing to Louis Napoleon's rule, Otto von Bismarck was facing similar, if not so extreme, difficulties in the new state of affairs in Germany. The inhabitants of the south German states, in a series of elections between 1868 and 1870, some under a property franchise, some with universal manhood suffrage, but all with a good deal of public campaigning and high turnouts, rejected candidates who proposed that these states adhere to the North German Confederation and complete the unification of Germany. Catholic conservatives in the south and radical democrats there were united in their opposition to Bismarck's ideas, and the National Liberals who supported him could make no headway. In fact, Bismarck began to wonder whether these same oppositional groups might not score successes in the elections scheduled for the North German Confederation in 1870. Rather like Napoleon III, he too began to look for a foreign policy success to reinforce the popularity and legitimacy of his regime.

The opportunity for such a confrontation came with events in Spain. Following the 1868 revolution, the Spanish legislature, the Cortes, was looking for a new monarch, and in February 1870 they offered the crown to Prince Leopold of Hohenzollern, a distant relative of the Prussian royal family. It was not a totally implausible choice, since four years previously Leopold's younger brother Prince Carol had received, following an insurrection and palace coup, the rule of the Danubian Principalities. Bismarck systematically promoted the negotiations between the Spanish parliament and the potential monarch – a *démarche* celebrated in diplomatic history as the Hohenzollern candidacy. News of this proposal leaked to the press, and the French government was furious at this effort to put a German monarch on France's south-western border. It immediately issued an ultimatum in July 1870 demanding the candidacy be revoked, to which the Prussian government agreed. Having achieved a foreign policy success, Napoleon III and his less than competent foreign minister, the Duke of Gramont, decided to push for more, sending the French ambassador to Berlin to issue a further demand to the king of Prussia that the candidacy never be repeated. The demand was actually made at the spa town of Ems where King Wilhelm was taking the waters, just a few days after the original ultimatum. The monarch refused to make the desired concession and wired a statement, known in diplomatic history as the 'Ems dispatch', to Bismarck in Berlin.

Bismarck altered the statement to make it sound hostile and personally insulting to the French emperor, and released it to the press. Louis Napoleon's whole use of foreign policy for domestic political purposes now rebounded on him, and to avoid being publicly humiliated and so weakened and delegitimized still further, he and his close advisers saw little else to do than to declare war. In doing so, he appeared as the aggressor, letting Bismarck pose as the defender of all German territory, including that of the reluctant south German states, against a new French invasion. In effect, Bismarck had used the very tactic Napoleon III had employed so effectively against Russia in 1853 and Austria in 1859, provoking a country until it declared war, but with the additional point of making use of a growing periodical press and its readership for his purposes. Historians disagree about whether Bismarck had this outcome in mind when he first supported the Hohenzollern candidacy or if he just took advantage of the second ultimatum, but in either case his plan worked very effectively.

The ensuing Franco-Prussian War of 1870–71 was the single most consequential confrontation of the European Powers in the largely peaceful century between the end of the Napoleonic Wars in 1815 and the outbreak of the First World War in 1914. French hopes for a Great Power ally were in vain, since Louis Napoleon's own previous wars against Russia and Austria had alienated them, and Great Britain, guardedly sympathetic to the Prussians in any event, was not about to intervene in a continental conflict. Still, the outcome of a war between France and the German states – basically Prussia, since the south German contingents were of relatively little military value – was not a foregone conclusion. Both sides were about equally matched in population and industrial output. Armaments were roughly equivalent as well. Most contemporary observers, including a number of the victorious generals in the recently concluded American Civil War, expected a French victory.

The initial battles of the war, in August 1870, fully confirmed Moltke's doctrine of firepower dominating the battlefield, as frontal attacks by infantry columns, attempted by both armies, were thrown back with heavy losses. What made the difference in the conflict was the superior Prussian military organization and staff work. While the troops of Prussia and its allies, along with their weapons, munitions and supplies, were placed on the railways and sent systematically into eastern France, the opposing French mobilization was a picture of chaos. At the end of July, Napoleon III found only 40,000 troops under his command at the frontiers, instead of the 100,000 who were supposed to be there. The soldiers had excellent new breech-loading rifles, but the cartridges for them had not arrived. Supplies were left at the railhead and did not make it to the troops, leading to shortages of bread, coffee, sugar, rice and even drinking water. The French army, it turned out, had only military maps of German territory, so when the fighting was in France, the French officers had literally no idea where they were. This strategic incompetence was accompanied by tactical ineptitude, as French commanding officers at the opening battles of Spicheren and Froeschwiller (both on 6 August 1870) failed to order a counter-attack after their massed firepower had repelled Prussian infantry offensives. The French suffered one defeat after another, until, on 2 September, just a month after the war began, the main French army, commanded by the emperor personally (who, very much unlike his great uncle, had no military abilities whatsoever), was forced to surrender at Sedan.

With the emperor himself a captive, it seemed that the Franco-Prussian War would end just as quickly as the wars of 1859 and 1866, but, unlike the defeated Austrian monarch, the French emperor was no longer in charge of events. When the news of the defeat at Sedan reached Paris, crowds gathered in the streets, marched to the legislature and demanded that the republic be proclaimed. The resulting 'Government of National Defence', following in the footsteps of its predecessor in 1793 when France had been invaded by Prussian troops, proclaimed an all-out war. German forces pushed on, encircling, besieging and bombarding Paris. The minister of war in the new government, Léon Gambetta, escaped besieged Paris in a balloon and went to unoccupied southern France to raise new armies. In occupied territories in eastern and northern France, civilians – contemporaries called them *franc-tireurs*, we might say today guerrillas or partisans – began ambushing and shooting German soldiers at night. The Germans responded by taking civilians hostage and announcing that the hostages would be shot if further German soldiers were ambushed. This duly happened and the execution of the hostages simply encouraged more civilians to start sniping at the occupying army. These developments all suggested a new kind of warfare, which would become very familiar in the twentieth century; one in which nationalist passions are loosed, the civilian population of the combatant nations becomes involved, and the fighting takes on a new quality of ferocity. However, the full potential – or horror – of such warfare had to wait for 1914 and 1939; after four months of trying, the republican government admitted that it would not be able to expel the invaders, arranged an armistice and entered into negotiations with the Prussians. This victory over the national enemy, widely celebrated throughout the German states, was what Bismarck needed to complete the work of national unification, bringing the south German states into the North German Confederation, on a wave of nationalist sentiment, keeping all its constitutional arrangements but changing its name to the German Empire, while the title of the king of Prussia went from confederal president to German emperor.

The new empire's creation was integrally related to the peace negotiations. Defeated France would not be treated as nicely as Austria had been in 1866. It would pay the German Empire a very large war indemnity, with occupation troops stationed until the indemnity was paid off, and, most gallingly, would have to cede the border regions of Alsace and Lorraine to the newly united Germany. These areas had been annexed by France from the Holy Roman Empire in the seventeenth century, and many of their inhabitants spoke a German dialect as their native language, but they had little interest in becoming part of a German nation-state, as they would demonstrate quite resoundingly. For German nationalists, the opinions of the Alsatians and Lorrainers were irrelevant; they were part of the German nation whether they liked it or not, and they belonged in the German nation-state. Bismarck consciously encouraged this attitude, subsidizing expressions of it in the press, as its spread would help obscure political differences that had previously kept the south German states out of the North German Confederation.

The outcome of the war had a few additional implications beyond the direct combatant powers. French defeat meant the withdrawal of the French garrison in Rome protecting the Pope. Consequently, Italian troops were able to seize the last remnants of papal territory and make Rome the capital of a united Kingdom of Italy. Pius IX proclaimed himself a prisoner in the Vatican and continued his policy of non-recognition of the Italian nation-state. The Russian government took the occasion of the war between France and the German states to send its warships into the Black Sea, thus revoking one of the humiliations of the Crimean War when the architect of that war, Napoleon III, met his nemesis.

One last issue remained, namely how to end the war, since it was unclear who was entitled to sign a peace treaty on behalf of defeated France. There was the former emperor, now a prisoner in Germany, and the unelected provisional government of the republic. Any regime could take credit for a victory, but one accepting a defeat would require definitive legitimacy. For that reason, Bismarck, the conservative statesman, adopted a radical and democratic viewpoint: legitimacy could only arise from the people, so he insisted on democratic elections for a French constituent national assembly to form a government with the popular sanction to admit that France had lost the war. These elections, held throughout France, including the areas occupied by German troops, in February 1871, demonstrated the state of public opinion. In Alsace and Lorraine, candidates demanding the regions stay with France won overwhelming victories – which did the Alsatians and Lorrainers no good: their fate was sealed. In most of the rest of the country, conservative monarchists, adherents of the old-regime Bourbon dynasty that had been deposed for the last time in the revolution of 1830, standing for election as the peace party and, willing to bring the war to an end, obtained the best results. It was only in besieged Paris that the pro-republican radicals, with the heroic but thoroughly unrealistic demand that the armistice be revoked and the war continued, were victorious.

The meeting of the constituent national assembly, with its conservative, anti-war and monarchist majority in the Paris suburb of Versailles, was a direct rebuke to the political activists and most of the inhabitants of Paris. They responded by proclaiming on 18 March 1871, an autonomous Parisian municipality, a commune, as they said. The Paris Commune's ensuing three-month-long existence has become a touchstone in the history of socialism and communism. Karl Marx, in his famous pamphlet *The Civil War in France*, described the Commune as a living example of a communist dictatorship of the proletariat. Vladimir Ilyich Lenin, on the date in 1918 when the Bolshevik government had lasted seventy-three days, one day longer than the Paris Commune, went outside and danced in the snow, since the Bolsheviks had become the holder of the world record for the longest existing communist regime.

Among the many organizations that supported the Commune's government and brought it into existence, including trade unions, political clubs, and detachments of the National Guard, there certainly were some self-proclaimed communists and socialists, including individuals affiliated to the International Workingmen's Association. Much more numerous, though, were old-fashioned Jacobin radicals, who saw 1871 as a second edition of 1793, supporters of workers' cooperatives, and 'social' democrats in the tradition of the revolution of 1848, as well as a great mass of French patriots and supporters of the republic, activists of the vigorous left-wing election campaign of 1869. The government of the Commune took no measures to seize private property or otherwise act in socialist fashion. Its enemies were not capitalists but landlords charging high rents and the former authoritarian and unelected government of the Paris municipality, led by the slum-clearing prefect, Baron Haussmann. The Commune was very much the expression of political radicalism in the middle decades of the nineteenth century; its appropriation by communists and socialists is indicative of the way they would become the typical radicals of the late nineteenth and early twentieth centuries, not of the political situation in 1871.

Communist or not, the Commune was a challenge to the authority of the newly elected French government, which would not tolerate its existence. After procuring the necessary troops, mostly ex-prisoners of war conveniently released by Bismarck for this counter-revolutionary enterprise, the French government invaded its capital city at the end of May 1871. The forces of the Commune defended themselves fiercely, setting fire to public buildings, taking, and later shooting, hostages, including the Archbishop of Paris. There were a number of women among the insurgents, whose presence (often greatly exaggerated) wielding weapons and fighting on barricades attracted an enormous – and generally unfavourable – public echo across Europe and North America.

The larger and much better armed forces of the republic – who did not hesitate to use artillery against the defenders of the Commune, destroying whole blocks of the recently rebuilt capital city – were victorious and took a savage revenge. Some 10,000–20,000 captured insurgents were shot in the space of a week, a conservative political massacre that might be compared with the 30,000 killed by the radicals during the year-long Reign of Terror in 1793–94. There were few people, inside and outside of France, who had much sympathy for the vanquished. Only a relatively small number of radicals dared to defend them – most typically, avowed socialists, such as Karl Marx or the German socialist leaders Wilhelm Liebknecht and August Bebel, their advocacy helping to create the image of the Commune as communist government. Most public opinion, from the bourgeois ladies of Versailles, who gathered to see the Communard prisoners carried off and poked them with their umbrellas as they went by, to Pope Pius IX, who described the insurgents as 'devils risen up from hell, bringing the inferno to the streets of Paris', was unreservedly hostile.[25]

Taken together, the Franco-Prussian War and the Paris Commune brought to an end the period of movement in European politics that began with the war of 1859.

Three results of this 1859–71 period stand out. One was the question of the resolution of the post-Congress of Vienna international order. After Russia's defeat in the Crimean War and the increasing orientation of British foreign policy towards the overseas world, the remaining Great Powers engaged in a contest for hegemony. By 1871, the result was clear: the Kingdom of Prussia, leading a federation of the German states under the title of the German Empire, had become the dominant power in continental Europe. In 1859, when this period of political movement and uncertainty began, gamblers would have been unanimous in describing this result as the long-odds choice. It came about because Prussian statesmen and generals had recognized crucial features of the age of progress, from the influence of the periodical press to the growth of nationalism, from the development of steel production to the growth of a rail network, and made use of them in their plans and actions.

The second result was another form of hegemony, namely the hegemony of political liberalism in the politics of the various European countries. This political movement, representing better than any other the ideals of the age of progress, had become the dominant form of political organization. Radicals could influence the way liberal and nationalist ideas reached fruition, as Garibaldi's remarkable campaign in southern Italy demonstrated, but they could not bring their own ideas to bear, as the suppression of the Paris Commune or, a few years later, the short-lived Spanish Republic of 1873, made all too clear. Conservatives were, in this period, stronger opponents of liberalism than radicals were, but conservatism as well had not prevailed. Some conservatives had been swept aside: the Italian ruler Fernando II of the Kingdom of the Two Sicilies had been dethroned, and Pope Pius IX reduced to a prisoner in the Vatican. Even autocratic monarchs, such as Austrian Emperor Franz Joseph and Tsar Alexander II, had been forced by military defeat to introduce reforms implementing at least some – more in Austria-Hungary, less in Russia – of the liberal socio-economic and political programme. Other conservative rulers – Disraeli, Bismarck, in some respects Napoleon III – voluntarily implemented substantial parts of the liberal programme as a way to strengthen their political position.

This paradoxical situation of conservatives implementing liberal reforms shows the third feature of the period. In some parts of Europe, Great Britain above all, but also the Low Countries and Scandinavia, where liberalism achieved its dominant position through the processes of notables' politics without a violation of the constitutional order, liberal ends and liberal means coincided. Elsewhere they did not, and it took the distinctly un-liberal means of revolutionary victories, Great Power warfare, or the decreed reforms of absolutist monarchs and authoritarian government ministers to achieve liberal ends. Achieving progress, the great liberal ideal, required, at times, a somewhat cynical recognition of existing power structures that went under the name of *Realpolitik*. Progress and realism were the two watchwords of the age, and they sometimes complemented each other, but also sometimes worked at cross-purposes.

NOTES TO PART I

1   Cited in Bernard Porter, *The Absent-Minded Imperialists: Empire, Society and Culture in Britain* (Oxford, 2004), 95.
2   Figures from Jordan Goodman and Katrina Honeyman, *Gainful Pursuits: The Making of Industrial Europe 1600–1914* (London, 1988), 195.
3   Cited in Roger Price, *People and Politics in France, 1848–1870* (Cambridge, 2004), 187–8.
4   Ibid., 58.
5   R. J. Morris, 'Urbanization', in R. J. Morris and Richard Rodger (eds), *The Victorian City: A Reader in British Urban History 1820–1914* (London, 1993), 49–50.
6   Figures from Friedrich Lenger, *Zwischen Kleinbürgertum und Proletariat* (Göttingen, 1986), 235, 251–5.
7   Cited in Françoise Choay, 'Pensées sur la ville, arts de la ville', in Georges Duby (ed.), *Histoire de la France urbaine*, 4 vols (Paris, 1980–83) 4: 182–3.
8   Quoted in Trevor Lummis, *The Labour Aristocracy 1851–1914* (Aldershot, 1994), 37.
9   Wilhelm Heinrich Riehl, *Die Familie*, 2nd edn (Stuttgart, 1852), 29–31. A larger English-language excerpt of Riehl's observations can be found at http://germanhistorydocs.ghi-dc.org/document.cfm?document_id=445.
10 Figures from P. H. J. H. Gosden, *The Friendly Societies in England 1815–75* (Manchester, 1961), 16; Eric Hopkins, *Working-Class Self-Help in Nineteenth Century England* (London, 1995), 22; and Allan Mitchell, 'The Function and Malfunction of Mutual Aid Societies in Nineteenth-Century France', in Jonathan Barry and Colin Jones (eds), *Medicine and Charity before the Welfare State* (London, 1991), 184.
11 Cited in F. Prochaska, *Women and Philanthropy in Nineteenth Century England* (Oxford, 1980), 32.
12 Cited in Klaus Tenfelde, 'Die Enfaltung des Vereinswesens während der Industriellen Revolution in Deutschland (1850–1873)', in Otto Dann (ed.), *Vereinswesen und bürgerliche Gesellschaft in Deutschland* (Munich, 1984), 55.
13 Carlo Cipolla, *Literacy and Development in the West* (London, 1969), 94.
14 Quoted in Robert E. Stebbins, 'France', in Thomas F. Glick (ed.), *The Comparative Reception of Darwinism* (Austin, TX, 1974), 126.
15 Quoted in Michael Ruse, *The Darwininan Revolution: Science Red in Tooth and Claw*, 2nd edn (Chicago, 1999), 168.
16 Cited in Linda Nochlin, *Realism* (Harmondsworth, 1971), 35.
17 Quote from Patricia Mainardi, *Art and Politics of the Second Empire: The Universal Expositions of 1855 and 1867* (New Haven, CT, 1987), 141.
18 Carl Dahlhaus, *Nineteenth Century Music*, trans. J. Bradford Robinson (Berkeley, CA, 1989), 192–3.
19 Quoted in Jonathan Parry, *The Rise and Fall of Liberal Government in Victorian Britain* (New Haven, CT, 1993), 1.

20 Two quotes from Paul Smith, *Disraeli: A Brief Life* (Cambridge, 1996), 150, and Steven Kale, *Legitimism and the Reconstruction of French Society 1852–1883* (Baton Rouge, FL, 1992), 270, respectively.

21 Cited in Roger Price, *The French Second Empire: An Anatomy of Political Power* (Cambridge, 2001), 110.

22 Cited in Bruce Lincoln, *The Great Reforms: Autocracy, Bureaucracy and the Politics of Change in Imperial Russia* (DeKalb, IL, 1990), 36.

23 Ibid., 34.

24 Cited in F. R. Bridge and Roger Bullen, *The Great Powers and the European States System 1814–1914*, 2nd edn (Harlow, 2005), 132.

25 Cited in Matthew Beaumont, 'Cacatopianism, the Paris Commune and England's Anti-Communist Imaginary, 1870–1900', *English Literary History*, 73 (2006): 465–87.

PART 2

THE AGE OF UNCERTAINTY, 1871–1895

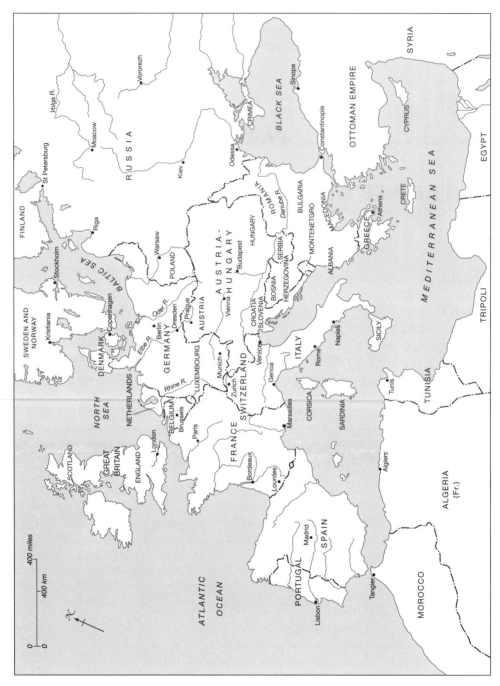

Europe in 1871

Source: From *THE MAKING OF THE WEST 3E* by Lynn Hunt et al., Copyright © 2009 by Bedford/
St. Martin's. Reproduced by permission of Bedford/St. Martin's.

CHAPTER 8

OVERVIEW OF THE AGE OF UNCERTAINTY

THE SHAPE OF AN ERA

The 1870s and 1880s, and at least the early part of the 1890s, appeared to contemporaries as a sharp and unexpected break with the age of progress in the third quarter of the nineteenth century. Processes that had been running reasonably smoothly since 1850 ground to a halt or went off in entirely different, and generally unwelcome, directions. Policies that had been successful no longer produced good results; ideas that had previously seemed self-evident came into question. Most broadly, the sense of being borne along by a gradual but firm and inevitable wave of progress, so much a feature of the post-1850 decades, was increasingly replaced with suspicions that progress was an illusion, with fears of regression and decline, and with a feeling of uncertainty about the nature of the present and the prospects for the future.

This break and resulting uncertainty was apparent in many different aspects of late-nineteenth century European life. It was strongly perceptible in the economy, where the long post-1850 economic upswing gave way, at different points during the 1870s in different European countries, to a less favourable economic situation characterized by much slower rates of economic growth, sharper and deeper recessions and falling prices. In these circumstances, the major economic policy assumption of the two post-1850 decades, that opening up and freeing markets – abolishing serfdom and seigneurialism, abolishing the guilds, tearing down tariff barriers – led to affluence for all, came strongly into question. The uncertainty could also be found in political life. By the early 1870s, liberal policies and liberal ideals, although not necessarily always liberal politicians, seemed to have triumphed over conservative and radical options. In the two subsequent decades, triumphant liberalism, rather than going from strength to strength, stumbled over obstacles, found its policies perceived as unsuccessful, generated increased opposition, and experienced a number of different forms of challenges to the notables' politics with which liberals had previously been so comfortable. In particular, the growth of socialist political parties, the transformation of ultramontane Catholicism into a political movement, the reinvigoration of conservatism, and the rise of a new, more radical and populist form of right-wing politics, all represented challenges to the hegemony of liberalism, even if none of them by themselves – or even all together – could, yet, completely undermine the position of liberal politicians and liberal ideals.

The triumph of the idea of the nation-state had been another feature of the turbulent politics of the 1859–71 period. This triumph brought with it, though, new problems, particularly in central and eastern Europe. The Germans were united into a nation-state, but this meant that members of other nationalities living in the German Empire, particularly the large Polish population to the east, and the formerly French inhabitants of newly annexed Alsace-Lorraine, now had a new and different status, one at odds with the existence of the nation-state itself. The compromise of 1867 had granted the demands of Hungarian nationalists for autonomy in the Austro-Hungarian Empire, but this success of the Hungarians only encouraged other national groups to make the same demands for themselves. Christian subjects of the Ottoman Empire in the Balkans redoubled their efforts at obtaining independence from Turkish rule, with their aspirations increasingly articulated in national rather than religious terms.

In comparison to the twenty years preceding the First World War, clashes of nationalities with each other and with the states of central and eastern Europe remained muted and subdued in the final decades of the nineteenth century, and could still be resolved within the existing structures of domestic politics and international relations. However, the quarter-century after 1870 saw the development of new ideas about the nature of the nation and the meaning of belonging to a nationality, ideas drawing on, among other sources, biological conceptions deriving from Darwin's theories (often from rather misunderstood versions of them). These new conceptions of the nation would prove to have politically upsetting and, ultimately, deeply pernicious consequences.

This upsetting of the previously accepted was also a feature of the intellectual and cultural life of the age. As scientists explored more deeply some of the great scientific triumphs of the previous decades, such as Darwin's theory of natural selection, or the formulation of the physics of electromagnetism, it became increasingly clear that these advances raised at least as many questions as they resolved. In a parallel fashion, the techniques of realism in literature and the visual arts, or of changing chromatic scales in musical compositions, were utilized so vigorously, and pushed to their very extremes, that they too began to seem less like successful answers to aesthetic questions than presuppositions of an aesthetic dilemma. The basic philosophical principles that had underscored the human sciences in the third quarter of the nineteenth century, the positivist view of the world and the application of the idea of evolutionary progress to the history of human society, came into question and the problematic features of these principles became steadily more evident. This emergence of questions and doubts across a broad range of artistic, scientific and scholarly preoccupations was not accompanied by the development of satisfactory answers to the questions, or the resolution of the doubts, so that the closing decades of the nineteenth century were characterized by a climate of intellectual uncertainty.

THE MAIN EVENTS

In contrast to the 1850–71 period, with its interrelated linear narratives of Great Power conflicts for hegemony in Europe and aspirations towards national unification, the major events of the years 1871 to 1895 do not fit into quite so neat a pattern, and lack any exact concluding event, like the Franco-Prussian War and the Paris Commune in 1870–71. Probably the easiest way to characterize the trend of events would be to say that, in the 1870s, liberalism was the dominant force in domestic politics of most European countries, and political occurrences arose from the liberals' agenda, whereas the following decade saw a swing to the right, and the events of domestic politics followed from conservatives' ideas. The major diplomatic focus of the 1870s was the Eastern Question, while the 1880s and early 1890s saw something of a shift towards overseas expansion as a focus of European diplomacy, although the Eastern Question, and the related issue of tensions between Germany and Austria-Hungary on the one hand, and Russia on the other, by no means disappeared from view.

Liberal governments in different European countries during the 1870s tried to introduce a wide variety of reforms; the most controversial of them concerned the place of religion in state and society. Among the features of these reforms were a secularization of public elementary education, both in terms of its administration and its curriculum, the introduction of civil marriage, and the establishment of equality before the law of citizens of all religious confessions. Particularly in central Europe – Austria-Hungary, Switzerland, and Germany – a part of this package was a broad attempt to control the Catholic Church and to curtail its public influence. This campaign reached its most extreme level in Germany. The *Kulturkampf* (struggle for civilization), as it came to be called, quickly degenerated into a bitter struggle between church and state, in the course of which first the Jesuits and then the other religious orders were expelled, hundreds of priests were arrested and almost all the bishops forced to flee the country. Catholics organized their own, very successful, political party – a decision quickly emulated throughout central Europe – and firmly resisted the government's initiatives.

Domestic politics followed somewhat different lines outside central Europe. In the Russian Empire, liberalism, rather than becoming more aggressive in the 1870s, faltered, as Tsar Alexander II was unwilling to cap his Great Reforms of the 1860s with the introduction of a constitution and an elected legislature, so that an underground revolutionary movement developed. France was ruled for most of the 1870s by Catholic conservatives, who saw a government using the police to enforce religion and persecute anti-clericalism, rather than the other way around. These conservative plans, which included restoring the monarchy, were vigorously opposed and the liberal adherents of a republican form of government came to power following a political crisis, the 'sixteenth of May', named after the date in 1877 when the crisis came about. Because the Tories controlled the government in the UK in the second half of the 1870s, the crucial moment for liberal reforms came in the years 1882 to 1885, when the Liberal hero William Gladstone was prime minister. In a predominantly Protestant country, the controversial point of liberal reform was not opposition to the Catholic Church, but the Liberals' attempt to introduce autonomy, or home rule, in Ireland.

The major diplomatic event of the decade of the 1870s was the Eastern Crisis of 1877–78. It began with uprisings against Ottoman rule in Bosnia and Bulgaria (then provinces of the Ottoman Empire), which were very brutally suppressed by the Sultan's soldiers. This provided an excellent pretext for Russian intervention, and the Tsar's armies marched into the Balkans, and, after a not very well run campaign, succeeded in almost reaching Istanbul and imposing peace terms which provided for the creation of independent, pro-Russian states in the former Ottoman provinces. The British government vigorously opposed this policy, openly threatened war, and sent the fleet through the Straits into the Black Sea. This was the one time between the end of the Franco-Prussia War in 1871 and the beginning of the pre-First World War diplomatic crises in 1905 that a war between the Great Powers seemed a serious prospect. Bismarck's skilfully planned mediation culminated in the Berlin Conference of 1878, which restored some of the Balkan provinces to the Ottomans and limited Russian influence in the region. The Balkan principalities of Serbia, Montenegro and Moldavia-Wallachia, previously still subject to the Sultan, became independent sovereign kingdoms, the last under the name of Romania. Austria-Hungary occupied the still nominally Ottoman province of Bosnia-Herzegovina.

In terms of domestic politics, the 1880s were rather the mirror image of the previous decade, with a resurgent conservatism dominating most European countries. The failure of the free market policies of liberal governments to deal with the prolonged economic crisis of the 1870s and 1880s played an important role in this transition, as did the increasingly hostile reception of liberals' anti-clerical policies. Finally, some spectacular events – the two attempted assassinations of the German emperor Wilhelm I in 1878 and the successful assassination of Tsar Alexander II by a terrorist suicide bomber in 1881 – helped to discredit liberal governments and liberal ideas. Conservative policies included a turn away from the free market via the introduction of protective tariffs, a persecution of the nascent socialist labour movement, and, particularly in central Europe, greater measures of government intervention in the economy, including the creation of social insurance programmes, first proposed by Bismarck in 1881, and the reinstatement of the guilds. In Russia, Alexander II's son and successor Alexander III, repudiated even the modest and reluctant reform policies of his father and followed a policy of autocracy – absolutist rule of the tsar – and support for and promotion of the Eastern Orthodox state religion.

Particularly in Mediterranean Europe, liberal governments clung to power, but only with increasing difficulty, and were forced to engage in questionable electoral and parliamentary manipulation to do so. The disastrous defeat of the Liberals in the 1885

British parliamentary elections hit liberalism in its nineteenth-century European stronghold. The main reason was that many Liberals deserted the party over the idea of home rule for Ireland, and formed a secessionist Liberal Unionist party, which supported the Tories. Scandinavia was the only part of Europe where liberals enjoyed success and expansion during the 1880s.

Another main aspect of that decade was the rise of a new form of right-wing politics. One important feature of it was the growth of political anti-Semitism. The widespread anti-Semitic riots in Russia in 1881, pogroms – a term that was quickly adopted by most European languages to describe anti-Semitic mob actions – were a sign of increasing hostility towards Jews. More organized and usually less violent anti-Semitism – petition campaigns, political parties, congresses – appeared in central Europe. Another feature of this new right-wing politics was its nationalist and populist character, two characteristics previously associated with the left. The famous campaign of General Boulanger in France in 1888–89, who called for a more authoritarian government and a war of revenge with Germany, his efforts ending in an abortive coup d'état – all financed by royalists and extreme conservatives – was a good example. This basic political situation of beleaguered liberals, influential conservatives, and a still small but growing radical right and a resurgent socialist movement (in spite of government persecution) continued in most European countries through the mid-1890s. Dramatic changes in the head of government, such as the dismissal of Bismarck by the young German emperor Wilhelm II in 1890, or the retirement of the British Liberal leader William Gladstone in 1894, after a five-decades-long political career, did not fundamentally change the basic situation.

There were two major developments of international relations during the 1880s. One was the rapid growth of overseas expansion, a distinctly new departure after seventy years of relatively little interest in it on the part of almost all the European Powers, except for Great Britain. The 'scramble for Africa', in which almost the entire continent was partitioned out in the course of the 1880s, according to the diplomatic rules set down in the Berlin Africa Congress of 1884, was the most prominent example of imperialism, but all the available territory in Asia and the Pacific was also snatched up. A whole new group of countries, including Belgium, Germany and Italy, joined an overseas imperial enterprise, until then limited to the Atlantic maritime nations. This sudden wave of imperial expansion proceeded relatively smoothly, with disputes over territory claimed by more than one European Power settled without too much difficulty, certainly compared with the much tenser relations among the Great Powers in Europe itself.

It was the tensions between Germany and Austria-Hungary on the one hand, and Russia on the other, which were the other major diplomatic development in the decade. Following the victory of the German armies over France in 1870–71, Bismarck, chancellor of the newly created German Empire, decided that the only threat to this nation-state would be France gaining an ally and undertaking a war of revenge. He resolved to deal with this problem by joining diplomatically with the two Great Powers,

Austria-Hungary and Russia, who would have been France's potential ally. (Britain, absorbed by its empire and unwilling to intervene in continental affairs, was not much of a possibility.) In an elaborate series of treaty arrangements and non-aggression pacts – the League of the Three Emperors (of Germany, Austria-Hungary and Russia) in 1873, the Three Emperors' Alliance in 1881, the 1882 Triple Alliance linking Germany, Austria-Hungary and Italy, and the 1887 Reinsurance Treaty, or non-aggression pact between Germany and Russia – Bismarck attempted to keep any possible French allies tied to Germany.

This elaborate structure fell apart for two main reasons. One was tension between Russia and Austria-Hungary over the Balkans; the Russian government was not happy about the way its victory over the Turks in 1877 rebounded in favour of Austria-Hungary in the Berlin Conference the following year. In addition, Russian–German relations became increasingly strained. Economics played an important role; high German tariffs on imported grain cut off Russia, a major grain exporter, from a profitable market. Russia retaliated with tariffs on German industrial exports. Bismarck, in the later 1880s, struggled to maintain a friendly diplomatic posture with Russia while taking a harsher economic line, banning Russian government loans from the Berlin capital market. After Bismarck was dismissed from office in 1890 by the young German emperor Wilhelm II, German policy became increasingly anti-Russian, and the Russian government responded by opening negotiations with France. In 1894, the two countries signed a mutual defence pact, the Franco-Russian Alliance. Although it was not entirely clear if this pact was aimed at Britain, a perennial maritime and colonial rival of the two countries, or at Germany, the diplomatic realignment of the Great Powers seen in this pact was probably the single clearest sign of the end of an era in international relations.

CHAPTER 9

POPULATION AND THE ECONOMY

The initial economic experience of the age was the crash. Vigorous economic expansion in the late 1860s and part of the 1870s was accompanied by the formation of new financial, industrial and railway corporations whose shares were eagerly purchased by an investing public. Purchasers of these shares and of government bonds were not content to leave them in their portfolios, but traded them in increasingly speculative fashion. The number of transactions on the major European stock exchanges rose steadily, and share prices moved strongly upwards. As the financial markets boomed, they attracted new investors, from different and often more modest backgrounds than had previously been the case, whose personal finances had improved as a result of the post-1850 economic upswing. Even factory workers in Lancashire purchased shares in textile manufacturing firms, the so-called Oldham Limiteds. About 30 per cent of the investors in the textile corporations of this town during the 1870s were millworkers, and about one inhabitant in five of Oldham put money into textile manufacturing shares. At the other end of the social scale, landed aristocrats, who had previously shunned such dishonourable means of making money, became large investors. This growing public interest, the additional funds – and, even more, the buzz they created – drove share prices up still further.

What happened next will come as no surprise to readers who have experienced similar stock market booms. Some contemporaries were also aware of what was about to occur. The brother-in-law of the German steel manufacturer Alfred Krupp wrote to him in 1872 'that the gigantic founding [of new corporations] swindle . . . must lead us to an enormous general business crisis'.[1] With great suddenness, the boom ceased. Share prices fell, and banks and industrial enterprises were unable to make their payments. Indeed, many of the newly founded companies turned out to have been rather shady affairs, better at running share prices up than actually producing anything. Spectacular large-scale bankruptcies, generally accompanied by evidence of questionable business practices, such as those of the railway magnate Henry Strousberg in Germany, the City of Glasgow Bank in Scotland, or of the Union Générale bank in France, replaced reports of stock market advances in the financial press. Investors were wiped out. In Vienna, the site of the first crash, one hundred and fifty of them committed suicide. The shockwaves from the crash moved out of the financial sector into the producing economy, and it was plunged into recession. This sort of crash was a pan-European event, occurring in Austria-Hungary and Germany in 1873, in the UK in 1878, in France in 1882, and in Italy in 1893.

Such financial crashes were not new, having occurred before on a Europe-wide scale in 1847 and 1857–58. What was different about the circumstances was the recession resulting from these financial crashes: unlike the short 1857–58 recession, the major crisis of the post-1850 decades, the recession following the post-1870 financial crashes was deep and prolonged; the recovery from it was weaker and short-lasting. The post-crash recession in central Europe lasted six years, from 1873 to 1879, and the resulting recovery gave way to new recessions in 1882–86 and, again, in 1890–95. Such a development was typical of the economy of most European countries in this period. In Germany and Austria-Hungary, the downswing was sharpest in the 1870s, in France and the UK during the following decade, in Italy at the end of the 1880s and in the first half of the 1890s.

What was true everywhere was that these crashes introduced a long-term phase of slower economic growth, as Figure 9.1 demonstrates. The actual quantities being considered differ for the different countries, including national income, gross national product and gross domestic product, but in each case they tell a common story. Yearly economic growth rates in the twenty years after mid-century, in some cases averaging almost 3 per cent, eminently respectable even by today's standards,

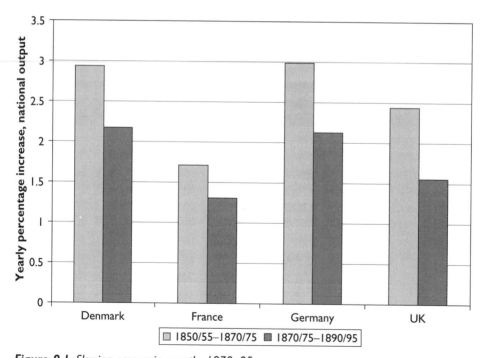

Figure 9.1 *Slowing economic growth, 1870–95*
Source: Derived from B. R. Mitchell, *International Historical Statistics: Europe, 1750–1993*, 4th edn (London, 1998).

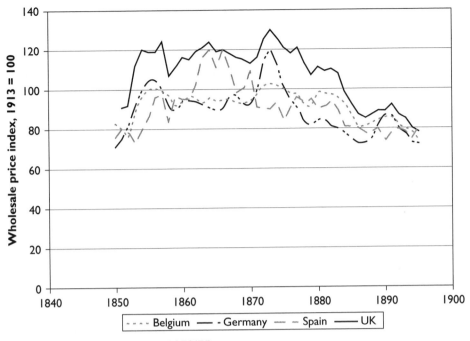

Figure 9.2 *Falling prices after 1870/75*
Source: B. R. Mitchell, *International Historical Statistics: Europe, 1750–1993*, 4th edn, 1998, Palgrave Macmillan, reproduced with permission of Palgrave Macmillan.

fell off sharply after 1875. The solid and persistent economic progress of the quarter-century after 1850 had come to an end.

Accompanying this deceleration of economic growth was a broad decline in prices. Figure 9.2 shows wholesale price indices for four countries. Unlike the chart of real wages (Figure 2.2), the indices for this chart are specific to each country. (The fact that the curve for the UK is persistently higher than the one for Belgium does not mean that prices were higher in the UK than in Belgium, but that prices in the UK during this period were higher in comparison to UK prices in 1913 than were Belgian prices in comparison to Belgian prices in 1913.) The curves all move more or less in the same direction, showing a period of rising prices, usually peaking at some point in the 1870s, and then falling off sharply, by as much as 50 per cent by the mid-1890s.

It is these three features – frequent and long-lasting recessions, slower rates of economic growth and declining prices – that characterized economic developments in Europe during the concluding decades of the nineteenth century. Their combination meant that wealth grew much less than in the age of progress; standards of living even declined for a time and recovered only slowly. Just as prosperity in the previous period had been broad based, so in these years economic difficulties reached throughout the social scale as businessmen and master craftsmen battled weak demand and growing inventories, and farmers faced persistently falling prices. Real wages did actually increase in these years, not because money wages went up – they declined, too – but they declined less than prices did, so that blue-collar workers received less pay than before but found they could purchase more with it. However, workers could only purchase more with their wages if they were earning them. As a result of the recessions and slowing economic activity, unemployment moved noticeably upwards. In Great Britain, the sole country for which we have even remotely reliable figures, the unemployment rate was over 7.5 per cent for four straight years, from 1884 to 1887, the only time this happened until after the First World War. When

BOX 9.1

Was there a 'Great Depression of the nineteenth century?'

One of the ways historians have often understood the economic situation in the 1870s and 1880s is through use of the phrase the 'Great Depression of the nineteenth century'. This was, obviously, not a term contemporaries used, but a linguistic retrofitting, developed by analogy with a twentieth-century event, the Great Depression of 1929–39, a decade-long period of worldwide economic crisis. The 'Great Depression of the nineteenth century' was used to refer to the period 1873–96, which were seen as a parallel to 1929–39. This coinage was generally part of a broader understanding of the nineteenth century as consisting of long periods of economic upswing, such as the years 1850 to 1873, or 1896 to 1914, and other periods of economic decline.

In recent years, this concept has come in for a lot of criticism. Unlike in 1929–39, which was, at least in some countries, a period of absolute economic decline, where national output was lower at the end of the decade than at the beginning, economic growth continued over the whole period 1873–96, albeit at a slower pace than in previous or subsequent years. Also, the idea that the years 1873 to 1896 are a consistent period of any kind has come into question. Summing up economic growth over somewhat different periods of time, with different beginning and end points, can lead to the conclusion that the 1870s, 1880s and early 1890s saw mixed periods of more rapid and slower economic growth, as did other years in the century.

These are certainly valid criticisms, but they can also be taken too far. Economists sometimes denigrate the whole notion of a longer period of slower economic growth by stating that 'it's just a change in the second derivative', which may be mathematically correct but ignores the very material effects that slower economic growth had on contemporaries, both on their standards of living and on their perception of their situation. Although the specific years of slower growth may not be the same for different European countries, all of them nonetheless experienced a prolonged phase of sharp recessions and weak recoveries at some point in the decades of the 1870s, 1880s and early 1890s; all of them experienced a long-term price decline as well. These may not have been a 'Great Depression of the nineteenth century', but they add up to a distinct phase in the economic development of nineteenth-century Europe.

real wage series are adjusted for unemployment and short hours, they show a decline or, at best, stagnation, from the mid-1870s to the mid-1890s. Such calculations are only possible for some occupations in Great Britain, but the workers of the Esslingen machine shop, to take a German example, whose post-1850 rising standards of living were noted in Part 1, were frequently forced, in the 1870s and 1880s, to pawn those material possessions that had been a symbol of prosperity – Sunday suits, sofas, grandfather clocks – as prolonged unemployment ate up their assets.

The macroeconomic picture of the late nineteenth century was thus generally not too cheerful. Most individual economic sectors had their problems and a focus on them illuminates three further characteristics of the period: (1) the way that economic processes previously leading to prosperity now had different outcomes; (2) changing policy preferences as a result of the new situation; (3) a glimmer of hope, in that some of the difficulties of the period laid the foundations for more favourable future developments.

INDUSTRY IN 'PROFITLESS PROSPERITY'

The phrase 'profitless prosperity' was coined to refer to developments in the steel industry during this period. Major innovations in steel manufacturing led to a very substantial increase in the output of steel, but the combination of high investment costs and declining steel prices meant that steel firms were not making any more money on their increased production.

Through the 1870s, highly mechanized forms of steel manufacture, the Bessemer process or the Siemens-Martin (open hearth) process, required high-quality, low-phosphorus-content iron ore, so that most steel was produced by the craft-like process of puddling, which could employ cheaper, acidic iron ore, but which was only one-twentieth as productive. In 1879, two British inventors, Sidney Thomas and Percy Gilchrist, showed that the addition of lime neutralized the acid in the phosphorus and made it possible to use lower-quality ores in a Bessemer Converter.

This innovation revolutionized steel manufacture. Within four years of the invention of the process, there were eighty-four Thomas–Gilchrist furnaces in operation in Europe and total steel produced in the eight most important European steel manufacturing countries more than tripled from 3.04 million metric tons in 1880 to 10.42 million in 1895. The investment required to build the large, complex facilities to manufacture all that steel was considerable, and the price of steel produced in them was sinking rapidly, declining by some 80–90 per cent between the mid-1860s and the mid-1890s. With these declining prices, steel firms had a hard time making much of a return on their investments. The Gutehoffnungshütte in Oberhausen, one of Germany's most technologically advanced steelworks, averaged a yearly return of just 2.7 per cent on its invested capital between 1878 and 1895, including two years of zero returns, and eleven more when returns were 3.0 per cent or less.[2] This firm, like most of its counterparts, was producing ever more steel, but earning little money while doing so: a profitless prosperity.

The investments in technological innovations and increased capacity were thus not paying off as they had in the two post-1850 decades. They certainly had the potential to, and, after the mid-1890s, investments in steel manufacturing would yield excellent returns. In this intervening period, though, the whole complex of iron–coal–railways, the post-1850 leading economic sector, no longer played such a role. Contemporaries, as they thought about this problem, generally attributed it to the falling price of steel. They began to consider ways that the price of steel might be increased.

Textile manufacturing, the other major branch of industrial production, also suffered price declines, although for somewhat different reasons. The late nineteenth century did see the completion of the mechanization of textile manufacture, even for difficult fibres such as silk, and the elimination of handloom weaving. Yet the increase in textile output from the mid-1870s through to the mid-1890s occurred at a slower pace than had been the case in the mid-century decades. As Table 9.1 shows, post-1870s output growth followed a different path. Although Great Britain remained by far the dominant cotton manufacturing country in Europe, and in the world, the expansion of its cotton manufacturing came almost to a halt during the fifteen years between 1877 and 1892. In central and western continental Europe, where industrialization had been well under way since the 1840s, there were increases in the number of cotton spindles after 1877, but relatively modest ones. By contrast, in the more peripheral countries, Russia and Italy, the last quarter of the nineteenth century saw a rapid increase in cotton manufacturing capacity.

In other words, cotton production (and this development was true of the manufacture of other fabrics as well) was beginning to shift to peripheral countries where the cost of labour was lower, resulting in downward pressure on the price of textiles. Just getting under way in this period, the production shift would accelerate after the

Table 9.1 *Development of cotton manufacturing, 1867–92*

	Cotton spindles (Thousands)				
	UK	**Belgium**	**Germany and France***	**Russia**	**Italy**
1867	34,215	625	8,800	2,500	450
1877	44,207	800	9,700	?	880
1891/92	44,509	930	11,131	7,146	1,680

*Germany and France are taken together because the annexation of Alsace-Lorraine in 1871 brought a considerable part of the French cotton industry into German possession.
Source: B. R. Mitchell, *International Historical Statistics: Europe, 1750–1993*, 4th edn, 1998, Palgrave Macmillan, reproduced with permission of Palgrave Macmillan.

beginning of the twentieth century as textile manufacturing began in Asia – in this case, in India and Japan. Ever since then, production has moved within and between countries and continents in search of a low-wage workforce. Manufacturers in higher-wage countries needed to find a way either to lower wages or to increase the prices charged by their low-wage competitors.

Thus, business interests in both textile and steel manufacture, still the most important branches of industry in the last quarter of the nineteenth century, came increasingly to understand their difficulties in terms of declining prices. This understanding led them to reconsider one of the most important economic dogmas of the previous twenty-five years: the freeing and expansion of markets. Instead of being part of an irresistible march of progress, steadily improving prosperity, as they had from 1850 through to the mid-1870s, these open markets seemed instead to be leading to falling prices, declining profits and decreasing market shares. Rather than continuing to allow markets to have their way with prices and profits, businessmen began to consider forms of intervention in the market to reverse the negative trends.

Over the forty years between the mid-1870s and the First World War, manufacturers in Europe would develop a wide array of different strategies and institutions to accomplish these ends, whose effects would remain, to a greater or lesser extent, until the last two decades of the twentieth century. The first measure to which they turned was a rejection of international free trade. Hesitantly at first, but with growing impetus, textile and steel manufacturers began to demand protection, that is, a tariff or tax on imported manufactured goods, which would raise the price of imports and so help domestic manufacturers both retain market share and enjoy higher prices. By the mid-1890s, this system of protectionism had encompassed most European countries, excluding just a few smaller nations with small domestic markets compared with their export possibilities – Belgium, the Netherlands, Switzerland and Denmark – and, among the major powers, only Great Britain, the model pro-free trade country. Even in Britain, ever stronger pressures began to develop for the institution of protective tariffs, although free-traders were still able to fight them off.

This turn to protectionism is suggestive of a gloomier and more pessimistic mood in the textile and metallurgical industries, which had been the mainstays of industrialization in Europe. By the late nineteenth century, though, there was more to industry than spinning-mills and steel mills. One area of innovation was in the two new industries of chemicals and electrical equipment, beginning to emerge at this time from scientific laboratories into mass production. These were potential bright spots in an economically gloomy environment, offering the possibility of more rapid economic development, not just for themselves but, as leading sectors for the entire economy, replacing textiles and the steel–coal–railways–metalworking complex, which no longer seemed to be the engines of broader economic growth.

By the 1880s, the electrical industry had begun manufacturing a wide variety of products, ranging from the turbines and generators which produced electricity, to the power lines and transformers through which electricity was moved from generating station to customers and consumers, to devices using electrical power, ranging from aluminium refineries to electric motors, to light bulbs to telephones. However, this entire effort faced a considerable bottleneck, namely the need to construct and install an electric grid, a network of power lines distributing generated electricity. Throughout this period, major technical controversies – between the use of alternating and direct current, or between the two-phase and three-phase electric motor – impeded agreement on a single standard for power generation. Without such a standard, every piece of electrical equipment would have to come in multiple forms, to work with the different ways that generated current was distributed, and each form would work only with one version of current generation. It would not be until the 1890s that such disputes over standardization were settled (in fact, in Great Britain, they were still not settled as late as the outbreak of the First World War) and it would be possible for the electrical industry to begin developing its full economic potential. In the 1871–95 period, this potential remained just out of reach.

Chemical manufacturing, the other scientifically advanced industrial branch, by contrast, was already revealing its potential in this period. A series of scientific advances, mostly dating from the 1850s and 1860s – the production of synthetic dyestuffs, the invention of dynamite by the Swedish inventor Alfred Nobel, and, most important, the Solvay process, by which the Belgian inventor Ernest Solvay made possible the cheap and efficient production of sodium carbonate, the initial substance for a wide variety of alkaline products – were brought to production in the 1870s and, especially, the 1880s. Some of the firms manufacturing these products, including Bayer and BASF in Germany and Sandoz and Geigy in Switzerland, would become, by the early twentieth century, the giant industrial enterprises they remain today. They had not quite reached that point *c.*1890, and major advances in chemical manufacturing, particularly those relating to pharmaceuticals and petrochemicals, remained for the future. Chemicals were an economic growth sector in an otherwise slow growth period, but they had not yet quite acquired the production and sales volume to stimulate the entire economy.

If we turn our attention away from these spectacular, high-tech industrial developments, we can note another feature of this period: the beginning mechanization of consumer goods production. The production of items such as shoes and leather goods, furniture, paper products, or kitchenware, before the 1870s exclusively the domain of artisanal workshops, began to make use of steam power. One sign of this was the very considerable increase in total horsepower in steam engines between 1875 and 1895, slightly more than threefold in Germany and slightly less than threefold in France. The mechanization of consumer goods production, given an additional impetus with the introduction of electric motors, would continue gradually down to the First World War and beyond.

The two decades from the mid-1870s to the mid-1890s were certainly a period of technological innovation, increasing output, broadening mechanization and shifting locations of production. Yet they were also a period of falling prices, lower profits and frequent brushes with bankruptcy. In some cases, these relatively difficult years were a period in which fundamental investments were made that would lay the foundations of future prosperity; in other instances, they were the beginning of a long-term economic decline. They certainly marked a fundamental shift in economic policy, away from the universal endorsement of ever freer markets. In retrospect, these two decades might seem more promising, as historians and economists can emphasize the brighter prospects of the decades immediately preceding the First World War. Contemporaries, lacking knowledge of what the future would bring, would have emphasized the negative, more impressed with crisis and the upsetting of previous certainties.

AGRICULTURE IN CRISIS

If there is some debate about whether European industry was in a crisis during the closing decades of the nineteenth century, there can be no doubt about the very difficult position of agriculture, characterized by falling prices, rising debts and one enormous natural disaster. This crisis was universal, affecting every European country, all social groups involved in agriculture, from noble landlords to farm labourers, and all forms of farming, whether cultivation of grains, the raising of livestock or the growing of speciality, non-subsistence crops. The crisis of the post-1870 period was a direct result of improvements in transportation, the subsequent opening up of markets, and the possibilities for specialization introduced by this state of affairs, that had led to the agricultural prosperity of the post-1850 decades.

By the mid-1870s, improvements in transportation and the growth of a world market made it possible to transport grain grown in the immensely fertile virgin soil of the midwestern United States, ship it across the Atlantic and sell it at prices lower than those for grain grown just a short distance away from European port cities. The upshot was a very sharp decline in the price of grain in the second half of the 1870s; grain prices remained depressed for the following twenty years, declining irregularly, with the ups and downs of each year's harvest, to about 50 per cent of the levels of the early 1870s. As the final decades of the nineteenth century wore on, and global transportation networks improved still further, Canada, Argentina, Australia and New Zealand joined the United States as important exporters of agricultural products to Europe. The development of refrigeration technology – an advance involving both high-tech industries of the day – made it possible to export meat products on a large scale, as well as grains, thus putting price pressure on yet another sector of farm products – although never quite to the extent of grain prices.

Complementing this very difficult economic environment was the great natural disaster that befell European viticulture, namely the phylloxera epidemic. A parasitic insect native to the Americas, phylloxera lived off of the roots of the grapevines, only its feeding on those vines also killed the vines. Accidentally brought into Europe in the mid-1860s, the insect's progress became noticeable by the end of the 1870s, and swept through winegrowing regions of Europe over the following fifteen or so years. The efforts involved in re-establishing viticulture were sweeping in scope, tedious in implementation and expensive in execution. The diseased vines had to be uprooted and the vineyard soil rid of the parasite by use of sulphur. Fresh soil then had to be added, and disease-resistant American rootstocks imported, on to which the vines could be grafted.

European producers might try to meet overseas production head on, by increasing crop yields so as to sell more at lower prices. One part of the new product palette from the growing chemical industry was artificial fertilizer, which would be a mainstay of – ultimately successful – attempts to increase grain yields. Not unlike circumstances in the steel industry, making use of artificial fertilizer on a large scale was an expensive investment that would have to be paid for by the sales of a commodity whose prices were declining steeply. Another possibility, practised in various parts of northern Europe, and with the greatest success in Denmark, was not to fight the influx of cheap grain from overseas but to make use of it by shifting the emphasis in agriculture from crop-growing to dairy cattle, and using the foreign grain as a cheap source of feed.

The single most common reaction, though, was to demand government intervention to raise prices – above all, by establishing protective tariffs on imported farm products. Indeed, the introduction of protectionism in continental Europe was a joint effort of manufacturers and agriculturalists. The first protective tariff in Germany, implemented in 1879, was known to contemporaries as the 'marriage of iron and rye'. This pattern of protection for agriculture and industry simultaneously was repeated throughout Europe: Austria-Hungary in 1882, Romania in 1886, Italy in 1887, Sweden in 1888, France, Spain and Portugal in 1892, to mention just a few examples. Tariffs on farm products were not limited to grains; duties were also levied on meat and dairy products, fruits and vegetables, and wine. Once tariffs were implemented, their rates were steadily increased. They were quickly joined by a galaxy of other forms of government assistance, including tax breaks, export premiums and outright subsidies. Indeed, the last quarter of the nineteenth century marked a fundamental turning point for European agriculture. From that point onwards, and down to today's EU agricultural policy, farmers would no longer operate in a free market but would be dependent on different forms of government assistance designed to raise prices and to suppress foreign and overseas competition.

CRAFTS, COMMERCE AND FINANCE IN DEPRESSED CIRCUMSTANCES

The slowing of economic activity in the last quarter of the nineteenth century also had a commercial impact While both international and domestic wholesale commerce continued to increase in these decades, they did so at a slower pace than in the quarter-century after 1850, a result of both slower economic growth and the introduction of protective tariffs. This period was not one of substantial innovation in financial institutions, as had been the case after 1850. If anything, the many financial crashes and crises had cast suspicion on banking corporations, suggesting that the line between them and outright fraudulent enterprises was difficult to draw. International capital flows collapsed in the aftermath of the financial crashes occurring in the different European countries. These capital flows did recover as the effects of financial crashes diminished, and again reached levels comparable to those of the 1850s and 1860s, or, in some cases even exceeded them. Overall, however, they showed sharper swings than had been the case in the economically less troubled post-mid-century decades.

If international trade and finance largely continued along previous lines, although perhaps more slowly and uncertainly, the last decades of the nineteenth century saw a number of changes and innovations in the circumstances of crafts and retail commerce. Taken together, and occurring in a more depressed economic environment, they added up to a difficult situation in this economic sector.

Times were hardest for the crafts. Even in the more prosperous 1850s and 1860s, master craftsmen were not entirely happy with economic trends, and looked with concern as outworking made advances in the organization of their crafts, reducing many masters to a condition of dependency on merchant capitalists. The masters became considerably more unhappy in the 1870s and 1880s, as larger firms and industrialization became more prevalent in consumer goods production. One large, local example of this form of capitalism was the mechanized shoe factory of Adolf Fränkel, founded in 1881 and the first of its kind in Vienna. Six years later, Fränkel opened a chain of ten shoe shops in the city, selling his wares at 20 per cent below the prices that master shoemakers charged. Not only did Fränkel charge lower prices for his shoes, he also paid his workers higher wages, so that many journeymen shoemakers abandoned their masters' craft shops to work in Fränkel's factory. The master shoemakers, and Vienna's master craftsmen more generally, made Fränkel's name into a swear word for decades after.[3]

What made this mechanized competition particularly difficult for master craftsmen was the depressed economic environment of weak consumer demand and falling prices. Instead of sharing a buoyant market and rising prices with mechanized competition, perhaps taking over different market segments or niches, the masters had to compete directly for a stagnant or only slowly increasing consumer market while prices fell. Masters had to exploit themselves, to work harder for longer hours, in order just to maintain a declining standard of living.

While some crafts – the construction and food trades in particular – enjoyed more favourable market conditions and less large-scale competition, most artisans struggled with the combination of a continuation of the growth of outworking, the expansion of mechanized consumer goods production and the decline in the price level. In Germany, where government statistics were more detailed and reliable than in many other countries, the total number of small production enterprises (primarily craftsmen's shops) declined from 2.17 million in the 1882 census to 1.99 million in 1895; the number of people working in these enterprises, both employers and workers, dropped in the same period from 3.26 million to 1.88 million.[4] For the first time in the nineteenth century, craftsmen, both as a percentage of the workforce and in absolute numbers, began to decline – a telling measure of artisans' economic difficulties.

Just as was the case with industry and agriculture, craftsmen, as a group less enthusiastic about the free market than were other occupations, even during the prosperous post-1850 decades, began demanding government intervention in the market. Since their competitors were merchants and manufacturers in their own countries, protection was of little use. Artisans called instead for higher taxes on their large-scale competitors, or for set-aside government contracts, such as reserving for master craftsmen a proportion of the boots made for the army. In Germany and Austria-Hungary, master craftsmen pushed for a restoration of the guilds, succeeding with these demands by the 1880s. The restored guilds were weaker organizations than their predecessors: although allowed some price-fixing powers for craft products, they were unable to set wages for journeymen or to take measures against the merchant capitalists and industrial manufacturers who were making craftsmen's lives miserable.

Throughout the nineteenth century, craft production and retail sales had gradually been separating – a process largely completed in economically advanced Britain by 1850, but still ongoing in the early twentieth century in the Russian Empire. In much of continental Europe, the last quarter of the nineteenth century saw an acceleration of this trend, as the number of craft workshops declined or stagnated, while retail establishments became more common. The number of grocers in Paris, for instance, grew by one-third between 1860 and 1891. In the northern Italian industrial centre of Milan, the number of restaurants, inns and taverns doubled between 1881 and 1896, grocery stores grew by 83 per cent and the number of clothing shops by 45 per cent, while the number of craft workshops increased by only about 13 per cent.[5]

It is not always clear how many of these shopkeepers were prospering. Their ranks may have been swelled by the unemployed trying to earn a living or by recent immigrants from the countryside fleeing from the poor prospects of declining farm prices. Still, the general expansion of retailing is suggestive of a somewhat different situation from that which existed for the hard-pressed master craftsmen.

Shopkeepers faced potential competition as well, from the multi-headed hydra of larger retail establishments: department stores, chain stores and consumers' cooperatives. The initial examples of such enterprises were certainly present in late nineteenth-century Europe. The continent's and the world's first department store, Paris's Bon Marché, had been founded in 1869 and, by the 1880s, had become a giant palace of consumer pleasures and the newest of the capital's many tourist attractions.

It quickly found its imitators, such as Selfridge's in London or Bocconi in Milan. In Britain, the Army and Navy Stores, consumers' cooperatives open to civilian employees of the armed forces, were doing a brisk business by the 1880s. Smaller retail businessmen were already uneasy about the development of such competition and beginning to demand government action to protect them from it.

Yet large-scale retail enterprises were at this time mostly limited to western Europe, especially to England and France. Their continent-wide expansion and surge of big retailing would take place primarily in the quarter-century before the First World War. It was then that shopkeepers would begin to organize themselves and to demand that the government take measures to protect them from their larger and better-capitalized competitors. The earliest examples of these organizations did begin towards the very end of the period under consideration. The ponderously named Syndicalist League of Labour, Industry and Commerce, an organization of French shop-keepers, primarily Parisian ones angered by the competition of large department stores, was founded in 1888, and claimed close to 150,000 members by the mid-1890s. It called for government assistance in the form of legislation setting restrictions and imposing higher taxes on its members' large competitors. In this respect part of the broader trend of the period, the demand for government intervention to cor-rect the result of market trends, this association, founded in the European continent's avant garde of retailing, was also a preliminary sign of broader controversies that would continue and even escalate through the end of the nineteenth century and the initial decade of the twentieth.

POPULATION MOVEMENTS: OLD TRENDS AND NEW

Looking back at economic developments between the beginning of the 1870s and the middle of the 1890s, we can note repeated breaks with the post-1850 trends. Some of these breaks, such as a slower rate of economic growth, would themselves be reversed after the mid-1890s; others, for example the end of a free market in European agriculture, would be permanent. Population movements showed a similar trend of breaks with previous development, some of which would later be reversed whereas others would mark off a new demographic direction with consequences reaching to the present day. In contrast to economic developments, the breaks in the demographic trends would not be so sharp, nor were they immediately noticeable to contem-poraries. Their long-term effects, though, would be much greater.

Probably the single most important demographic trend was the decline in the birth rate, starting in a number of European countries around 1880. The crude annual birth rate in England and Wales, which had averaged about 35 births per thousand inhab-itants for most of the nineteenth century, and had, if anything, increased up to the 1870s, declined by about 14 per cent over the two following decades, to 30.02 per thousand in the 1890s, a new low point. Starting at a somewhat higher level, an annual average of about 39 births per thousand inhabitants in the 1870s, the birth rate in Germany fell some 7 per cent to 36 per thousand by the 1890s. There were similar declines in the birth rate over these years in France, the Low Countries, Scandinavia, Russia and Hungary. Between 1890 and the First World War these declines intensified and reached other countries, such as Spain, Italy and Austria, which had not experienced them before 1890.

This broad downward pattern of fertility, following decades of steady and, indeed, often rising, birth rates, was almost unprecedented; of all European countries, only France had previously experienced such a decline at the beginning of the nineteenth century. This decline in the birth rate also occurred in a distinct fashion, demonstrably different from past demographic behaviour. It was not due to a decline in the proportion of the population marrying, or a rise in the age of marriage; with some exceptions, age at marriage declined and the marriage rate rose in the late nineteenth century. Nor was it what demographers call 'non-parity specific' fertility limitation, decreasing the number of children by increasing the amount of time between births, say by abstention or prolonged breast-feeding of infants and small children. Both of these methods of decreasing birth rates had occurred in earlier periods of European history. Rather, the post-1870 decline in birth rates was 'parity specific'; it occurred because women had their last child on average at a younger age. The decline in the birth rate corresponded roughly to a decline in the average age of women at last birth from 40 to 35.

There is no particular evidence for a growing knowledge of forms of birth control or the introduction of new forms of contraceptive technology which could be associated with the sharp decline in fertility. Some demographers have suggested that knowledge of birth control was available, but in the prosperous decades after 1850, couples saw little need to practise it. By contrast, in the economically more difficult 1870s and 1880s, they began to make use of their knowledge. This is, however, just speculation; no one is entirely sure what caused people to change their intimate behaviour on such a wide scale, across much of the European continent, and, with many differences in extent and timing, in different social, cultural and religious groups.

The other main demographic feature of the period was a renewed growth of emigration. The 1880s saw emigration at levels unseen since the 1850s. Overseas emigration from Germany, at about 1.34 million in the 1880s, was an all-time high, about 25 per cent higher than its previous peak some three decades earlier. Emigration from Sweden and Norway surged in the 1880s. Just over half a million people left those two countries for North America in the course of that decade, around one-twelfth of their entire population. This growing exodus from the Nordic countries added to the existing streams from the British Isles and central Europe but did not change the mid-century character of emigration as a predominantly northern and central European affair. Emigration from Italy was already picking up in the 1880s, but it would only be after 1900 that departures from southern and eastern Europe would reach very high levels and come to dominate trans-Atlantic departures from the European continent.

In contrast to the mysteries of declining fertility, the rise in emigration seems easier to explain: it was directly linked to the crisis in agriculture. Emigrants were very disproportionately agricultural labourers, crofters and sharecroppers, people at the low end of the rural social scale, who ended up shouldering much of the burden of the decline in farm prices and agricultural profitability. Lacking political power, social organization and economic clout, their response was simply to leave, in large numbers.

The differing developments in fertility and emigration might serve to sum up the economic character of the era more broadly. Increasing emigration was a reflection of the quarter-century after 1870 as a period of long-term economic difficulties, some of which took the form of a drastic crisis, while others were more in the form of a less severe but chronic problem. By contrast, the decline in birth rates suggests that the nature of the post-1870 period was one of new departures, with considerable ramifications for the future – ramifications, however, that would only become apparent and reach their full force and effect after the 1890s. This combination of a crisis-filled continuation of existing trends and a still nascent and potential development of new ones typified economic developments in the closing decades of the nineteenth century.

CHAPTER 10

SOCIAL STRUCTURES AND SOCIAL INSTITUTIONS

In terms of both social structures and social institutions, the post-1870 decades saw largely a continuation of post-1850 trends, sometimes at an accelerated and sometimes at a decelerated pace.

URBANIZATION AS ROUTINE

Growth of cities and of the proportion of the population living in urban areas continued after 1870 as it had after 1850, but the dramatic acceleration of the post-mid-century decades was gone. The decline in growth rates was sharpest in France. There the urban population increased by about 2 per cent each year between 1851 and 1881 (except for the years of the Franco-Prussian War and Paris Commune); after 1881, urban growth rates were just half that level. There was a similar deceleration of the urban growth rate in Switzerland, Spain and Norway, and a more modest one in England and Wales, where the urban population grew at an annual rate of 2.1 per cent between 1851 and 1871, and 1.9 per cent over the following years. In the German Empire, by contrast, the urban population increased about as rapidly after 1871 as before. There were exceptions to this rule of decelerating urban growth, most noticeably in European Russia, although Sweden, Denmark, Belgium and the Netherlands also had post-1871 increases in urban growth rates.[6]

In the last quarter of the nineteenth century, cities continued to grow, and to grow at a faster rate than the population as a whole, meaning that the proportion of the population living in urban areas continued to rise. But the rate of urbanization had in most – although by no means all – European countries slackened off or just held its own. This modest pace of urbanization was a result of the slowing of economic growth in the post-1870 years, the rise of unemployment and the declining, or at least not radically increasing, prospects for jobs in urban areas.

Moving beyond statistics on the growth of the urban population, it would be fair to say that the exciting forms of urban development, so evident after 1850 in Haussmann's Paris or in Vienna's new boulevard, the Ringstrasse, was lacking in the 1870s and 1880s. Perhaps one could mention the construction of the Eiffel Tower in 1889, although that was more of a tourist attraction than a significant shaping of urban space. More commonly, the 1880s and 1890s saw the construction in smaller cities and more peripheral areas of some of the great building projects – boulevards, water and sewer systems, or railway stations – of the post-1850 period.

None of this was a permanent state of affairs; new urban projects, connected with the creation of an electric power grid, particularly the building of electric tram-lines and underground railway systems, would dramatically alter Europe's great metropolises in the quarter-century before the First World War. Rates of urbaniza-tion, or sometimes suburbanization, would rebound and contemporaries would be powerfully impressed – or sometimes deeply depressed – by the dynamics of early twentieth-century metropolitan life. The 1870s and 1880s, by contrast, were some-thing of a pause, or at least a time of less dramatic urban growth, packed between two phases of rapid expansion.

EXTENSION AND EXPANSION OF VOLUNTARY ASSOCIATIONS

The vigorous world of voluntary associations that had developed in Europe in the two decades after 1850 only expanded further in the 1870s and 1880s. In the Austrian half of the Austro-Hungarian Empire, the 8,000 or so voluntary associations existing in 1870 had almost doubled to 15,000 in 1880 and doubled again to 30,000 ten years after that.[7] Similar trends could be found all across Europe.

This growth of voluntary associations reflected not only the penetration of asso-ciations into areas and among social groups where they had previously not existed, but also the broader expansion of groups where they were already well represented. A good example of this development comes from the gymnastics societies, discussed in Part 1 as sites of national identity and nationalist emotions. The already large German gymnastics movement, with 168,00 adherents in the mid-1860s, counted 530,000 members thirty years later. Czech Sokol gymnasts, the east European pion-eers of this form of nationalism, went from some 9,000 members in 1871 to 37,000 by the end of the 1890s. Gymnastics reached other east European nationalities in the 1870s and 1880s, with thousands of Croatian and Polish gymnasts around 1890. Gymnastics had been less common in France before 1870 but paramilitary gym-nastics and sharpshooting societies multiplied rapidly there in the two decades following the French defeat in the Franco-Prussian War.

This pattern of both extension and expansion could also be found in other forms of voluntary associations that had been prevalent since mid-century and before: mutual benefit societies, social clubs, educational and charitable societies, and professional associations. A characteristic feature of the late nineteenth century was the new develop-ment or considerable expansion of previously existing forms of associations devoted to economic questions: cooperatives, trade unions and economic special-interest groups. The growth of these organizations was integrally linked to the economic crises of the period, although they would not vanish with the return of prosperity in the 1890s but would continue to expand until the outbreak of the First World War.

Cooperatives had been developing in the quarter-century after 1850. The most promin-ent examples were the Rochdale cooperative stores in Great Britain – 350 of them, with 100,000 members in 1863 – and the Schultze-Delitzsch cooperatives (primarily credit unions and savings banks) in Germany, with 700 branches and half a million members by the 1870s. Cooperatives' growth accelerated in the last decades of the nineteenth century, with over 1 million members of British cooperatives by 1897.[8]

In a fashion similar to the gymnastics societies, cooperatives underwent not just expansion but also extension. The big innovation of the 1870s and 1880s was the creation of farmers' cooperatives for agricultural purchasing, marketing and credit: there were 1,600 of them in Germany by the mid-1890s. Legalized in France only in 1884, there were 648 of them just six years later, with 234,000 members united in the ponderously named Central Union of the Syndicates of the Farmers of France. The cooperative movement was very vigorous in Scandinavia. There were 600 Danish farmers' cooperatives founded between 1882 and 1888, and in Norway the National Dairy Association, a league of dairy farmers' cooperatives, was formed in 1881. The consumers' cooperative movement was also well represented in the (admittedly few) urban areas of Norway. Moving south from the Baltic to the Mediterranean, the first agricultural cooperative savings bank in Italy, the Banco Populare (People's Bank) was started in 1864. The total number of cooperative banks and credit unions increased from 171 in 1881 to 738 in 1890. In 1886, Italian cooperatives joined together into a national federation, the National League of Italian Cooperatives.

There was a strong element of idealism in the cooperative movement; leaders and activists saw it as the beginning of a new and better way of life. J. T. W. Mitchell, president of the wholesale business of the British Rochdale cooperatives expressed this opinion when he stated that cooperatives would 'solve all social problems, destroy poverty, eradicate crime, and secure the greatest happiness to the greatest number'.[9] For all this idealism, it would be difficult to deny that the growth of cooperatives was closely tied to more practical motives, above all the need to respond to the economic difficulties of the 1870s and 1880s, falling prices, especially for farm products and frequent unemployment. As the spread and success of both consumers' and farmers' cooperatives became evident, other economic groups, such as master craftsmen and small shopkeepers, began to think about setting up their own cooperatives.

In this period, there was one social group with a long history of interest in cooperative enterprises that was steadily moving away from them and towards other forms of organization. This group was the working class: journeymen artisans, factory workers and urban day labourers. Strong working-class support for producers' cooperatives in the first two-thirds of the nineteenth century had been combined with aspirations towards economic independence, towards having one's own workshop. Joining together with other workers in a cooperative workshop would be one way to do it. This attitude continued as late as the Paris Commune, many of whose supporters were enthusiasts for producers' cooperatives.

By the 1870s and 1880s, though, blue-collar workers in Europe could look back on one, sometimes even two, generations of working-class life and see that aspirations towards achieving economic independence were becoming increasingly unrealistic. They were facing a lifetime as wage-earners, and began to consider more seriously the formation of voluntary associations to deal with this state of affairs, namely trade unions. Just a change in workers' attitudes would not have entirely sufficed to found unions, since both unions and strikes had been either illegal or of dubious legal status in the first two-thirds of the nineteenth century. This state of affairs came to an end in the following decades. Unions were legalized in Germany and Austria in 1869, in France in 1884, Spain in 1887. Italy lagged a bit, with unions being fully legalized only in 1900. While unions had been legal in Great Britain since the 1820s, legislation passed in 1875 substantially improved their legal status.

These legal changes were generally the work of liberal governments (or, in the case of Britain, of a conservative government seeking to steal the liberals' issue), whose members, like most nineteenth-century liberals, were generally supporters of a free market economy, opposed to unions' non- or anti-market forms of action. Yet, as liberals, they were as strongly supportive of freedom of association as they were of the free market, and decided they could not deny workers the right to organize themselves. They would have preferred that workers' organizations be educational or mutual benefit societies or consumers' cooperatives, but were willing to accept the consequences of freedom of association, even if it led in unwelcome directions. In countries where liberal principles had little influence – the Russian Empire, especially – unions were not legalized in any way, shape or form. It would take a revolution in 1905 for unions to gain any freedom of action in Russia.

The combination of changes in workers' attitudes and in legal possibilities for expressing these attitudes led to an extension and expansion of trade unions in the last quarter of the nineteenth century. These developments were expressed in four different ways: the formation of unions on a national or countrywide scale, the establishment of national trade union confederations, the growth of union membership and the dramatic articulation of workers' attitudes in the form of large-scale strikes, attracting wide public attention. Except in Great Britain, where nationwide union organizations had developed starting in the 1850s, these developments took place in two stages, a smaller one in the 1870s and a larger and more significant one at the end of the following decade.

Through the 1870s, most labour organizations and their actions tended to be very localized. There had been some brief exceptions, during the revolutions of 1848, and, more persistently in Great Britain, where a few 'amalgamated' unions, nationwide mergers of more municipally based groups, came into existence, the largest and best known of which was the Amalgamated Society of Engineers, founded in 1850 and counting almost 40,000 members by the mid-1870s. In Germany, there were no less than thirty-six nationwide unions in 1877, although their total membership was about that of the Amalgamated Society of Engineers.

Indeed, outside Great Britain, union membership in this period was very small, and organized workers represented just a tiny proportion of their trades. Trade union membership in Britain peaked at around 1 million to 1.3 million in the mid-1870s, only to fall back to half that number by the end of the decade. It was also only in Great Britain that these scattered national unions and the much more numerous regional groups came together, to form municipal trades councils, in at least twenty-four different cities, and, in 1868, a national joint group, the Trades Union Congress.

Much of this changed, and changed quite drastically, at the end of the 1880s and the beginning of the 1890s. Union membership soared: less than 100,000 following legalization in France in 1884, but increasing fourfold in the following decade; going from about 80,000 to 250,000 in Germany during the same period; hitting about 1.5 million, at or going a bit beyond the mid-1870s peak, in Great Britain by the early 1890s. In economically less developed southern and eastern Europe, union membership lagged behind – just some 8,000 union members in Spain in the mid-1890s, although having grown from only 3,000 at the middle of the previous decades. As the unions grew, they began to form national confederations, the Spanish General Union of Workers in 1888, the General Commission of Germany's trade unions in 1890, the Austrian Trade Union Commission in 1893, the French General Confederation of Labour in 1895. In other European countries, such national union federations would follow in the subsequent decade.

The strongest unions were in craft occupations, particularly the construction trades, or among highly skilled workers such as printers and typesetters. Since the early nineteenth century, these were the working-class groups that had been most likely to form organizations or associations and to engage in strikes. The period also saw the extension of union activities to working-class groups not previously involved: textile workers, coal miners, railway workers, dockers and waterfront labourers, or farm workers. In Britain, there had been examples of organization of these groups at an earlier time, but their massive organization made a very large impression on contemporaries, who spoke of a 'new unionism', involving unskilled workers, organized by industry, rather than skilled workers organized by their craft.

The most remarkable example of this extension of union activity to social groups where it had previously been uncommon or even unknown was the great strikes of the second half of the 1880s. In terms of sheer size and public impact, they represented something new and unprecedented. It was particularly coal miners' strikes that impressed contemporaries. The 1885 strike in the French mining town of Decazeville, in the course of which the striking miners invaded and ransacked the coal company headquarters, and threw a particularly hated engineer-supervisor out of a window to his death, would be immortalized by the naturalist writer Émile Zola in his lurid novel about coal mining, *Germinal*. The following year, striking coal miners in the Belgian town of Charleroi marched through the streets, calling out steel- and glass-factory workers, destroying industrial establishments and the homes of their employers. The Belgian government had to deploy 20,000 soldiers to bring this small-scale insurrection to an end. Coal miners of the Ruhr Basin, Germany's major centre of heavy industry, were more orderly when they went on strike in 1889, but their astonishing numbers – 150,000 miners were on strike – overwhelmed the public. The young German emperor Wilhelm II received a delegation of the striking miners, an unprecedented step for a ruling monarch to take.

It was not just coal miners who went on strike in such impressive numbers. Far to the north, the 2,000 construction workers who went on strike in Helsinki in 1896, demanding a ten-hour day, represented a labour struggle at a level never before seen in Finland. London was quite shaken in 1888–89 by three very large strikes, carried out by workers previously not involved in trade union activities: in 1888, the 'match girls' (young women, unskilled factory workers, who manufactured matches), the following year the gas workers and then the dockers. Massive picketing and marches of tens of thousands of strikers through the streets made a powerful impression. In contrast to the violence of continental coal miners, the London strikers were peaceful and orderly; their struggles gained a good deal of middle-class public support, including feminists who helped the match girls, and the Catholic Cardinal Manning who endorsed the demands of the dockers, there being many pious Irishmen in their ranks.

These massive strikes were generally not called by unions; rather, they were largely spontaneous outbursts that led to the creation of unions. A number of these new creations, particularly the ones organizing unskilled workers, proved ephemeral and quickly collapsed under employer pressure. But the upsurge in labour action and trade union organization of the late 1880s and early 1890s set in motion an irreversible trend. As was the case with cooperatives, trade unions could no longer be excluded from the economic, social and political scene anywhere in Europe. The number of organized workers, their degree of organization, the strikes they undertook and the influence they exerted would increase steadily down until the First World War and beyond.

Cooperatives were a way of allowing individuals with little or no capital to band together and take part in a market economy, although at least some of the cooperative activists understood their organizations as a way to go beyond the capitalist market. Trade unions certainly represented a further step in this direction, since collective demands for higher wages, whether implemented via strikes or through collective bargaining (this latter still a great rarity before 1900) definitely did not conform to market forms of action. This drive to form economic interest groups to circumvent or counteract market forces and market actions was by no means limited to the working class. Another feature of the late nineteenth century was the development of economic interest groups representing business and agriculture.

These associations were formed primarily in order to press demands for protective tariffs. The classic example of such a group was the ponderously named Central Association of German Industrialists, a group representing, in spite of its name, primarily steel and textile manufacturers with a pronounced interest in protectionism.

Formed at the height of the economic crisis in the mid-1870s, the organization showed considerable skill in arranging public hearings, whose carefully chosen witnesses blamed free trade for Germany's recession, supporting financially protectionist parliamentary candidates and drafting protectionist legislation with government officials. Paralleling the efforts of the industrialists' association was the Society of Tax and Tariff Reformers, a group of large-scale agriculturalists, mostly noble landlords from eastern Germany, who pushed, in similar ways, for protective tariffs on farm products.

The introduction of protective tariffs in France occurred in basically the same fashion. It was powerfully supported by the Committee of the Forges, a steel manufacturers' special-interest group, which endorsed protectionism and, along with similar interest groups, such as the Committee of Coal Mines, or the Syndicalist Chamber of Beet Sugar Manufacturers, sponsored the founding of the Association of French Industry, which pressed politicians to endorse protectionism. It was joined in its efforts by the Society of French Agriculturalists, representing France's large landowners.

Examples from other European countries could be cited, such as the Italian Wool Association, formed by woollens manufacturers in 1877 to press for protective tariffs. In the early 1880s, a similar protectionist lobbying group, the National Fair Trade League, was founded in Great Britain. Unlike similar organizations on the continent, it made little headway; free trade remained the ruling dogma. Most business special-interest groups in Britain had a different orientation, directed against growing union organization. The National Federation of Associated Employers, formed in 1873, fought, unsuccessfully, efforts to improve the legal status of trade unions, and following its failure, soon dissolved. With the new and much larger wave of labour unrest would come new employers' groups, such as the Shipping Federation, organized in 1890, to break the dockers' unions.

Taken together, all the developments of economically oriented voluntary associations in the years between *c.*1875 and *c.*1895 suggest a growing reluctance to accept, unquestioningly, the dictates of the market. By banding together voluntarily, individuals and businesses, from unskilled labourers and small farmers to industrialists and noble landlords, were attempting to gain a better position in the market, to counteract its effects or to pressure the government to intervene in it. This tendency in the formation of voluntary associations, which would only increase between 1895 and 1914, marked a fundamental change from the post-mid-century high point of endorsement and acceptance of market forces.

EXPANSION, EXTENSION AND TENTATIVE TRANSFORMATION OF PUBLIC EDUCATION

The 1870s and 1880s saw a continuation of previous trends, dating back to the middle of the nineteenth century, or even earlier, towards the expansion of elementary (primary) education. As we saw above, voluntary associations experienced a similar trend, and, as was the case with them, the expansion of public education was also an extension of it, bringing it to countries and regions where it had not previously been prevalent: the usual southern and eastern European suspects, such as Sicily or the Russian Empire, but also some unexpected areas, such as parts of Great Britain. This extension was not just geographical; in the late nineteenth century, primary schooling increasingly encompassed girls equally with boys.

Primary schooling did not just expand in this period, it also began to change. Compulsory education laws were enacted, where they had not existed; fees for primary schools were abolished and national governments began to pay more attention to, and provide more money for, schooling. A new curriculum developed, displacing previous emphases and introducing new elements into elementary instruction, which would persist through and beyond the First World War.

By contrast, changes in secondary and university education were more modest in the later decades of the nineteenth century. Enrolments did increase, but at a much slower pace than was the case with primary schooling. Although there was a growing feeling that secondary education, in particular, needed revamping, this sentiment did not yet lead to decisive action. Curricular and structural innovations were frequently considered, but only occasionally implemented, and did not yet have the scope and impact of parallel developments in primary schools. Mostly, the post-1870 decades saw a slow accumulation of discontent with the structure of secondary education, which would lead to new initiatives after the first half of the 1890s. Yet even then, existing institutions proved resistant to change.

In much of western and central Europe, primary schooling was very widespread by the 1870s. A rough guess would put the percentage of school-age children attending school at between 70 and 90 per cent. By the 1890s, that figure was approaching 95 per cent and above, as young people from poorer rural areas and working-class districts – especially girls – were cajoled or coerced into the classroom. Literacy among young people was very close to universal, even if the quality of reading and writing skills was not always very high.

Things moved more slowly in Italy, where the proportion of 5–15-year-olds in school rose from 35 per cent in 1881 (that figure itself a significant increase over the 1860s) to 38 per cent in 1896. Looking at the Italian figures more regionally, we can see a considerable distinction between industrialized, urbanized and more affluent northern regions, such as Piedmont and Lombardy, where about 75 per cent of boys and 67 per cent of girls attended school, to the much poorer and less education-friendly south. Yet even there, education was on the rise: the number of girls aged 6–14 attending school in Sicily grew from 23 per cent in 1881 to 34 per cent twenty years later. In a similar way, the number of elementary school pupils in the Russian Empire increased dramatically from 1.1 million in 1878 to 3.8 million in 1896. Just under 18 per cent of schoolchildren in Russia were girls in 1878, the number growing modestly to 21 per cent eighteen years later.[10]

These increases were to a great extent the result of changes in public policy towards elementary education: it was to be free, compulsory and guaranteed by the national government. The classic example here is that of France. Although there were tendencies in this direction during the 1860s, they were finalized and made permanent by a barrage of legislation enacted two decades later: the law of 1881 instituting free elementary education, one of 1882 making it compulsory for all children between the ages of 7 and 13 and one of 1889 transferring schoolteachers' salaries from village and municipal budgets to that of the national government, a decisive recognition of education as a national responsibility. There were a number of variations on this theme in different European countries. In Great Britain and in Prussia (in the federal governmental system of the German Empire, education was a responsibility of the individual states), teachers' salaries were paid out of municipal budgets, but these payments were organized, supplemented and regulated by central authorities. Compulsory schooling began earlier in Italy, with the Casati law of 1859, but this law remained a dead letter for decades, largely because the central government at first did not help finance elementary education. As expenditures grew from half a million lire in 1859 to ten times that thirty years later, the idea and practice – regionally very different – of compulsory education became more plausible. Compulsory education laws had been on the statute books in the German states for a long time, in some cases since the eighteenth century, but reached the British Isles in 1880, about the same time as in France.

These sorts of changes – and similar ones occurred in Belgium, the Netherlands and Switzerland during the 1870s – were eminently political. They all reflected the political impetus of liberalism, at the height of its influence, and the considerable priorities that nineteenth-century liberals had always placed on schooling. They also demonstrated the secularist bent of liberalism, its desire to restrict the place of religion, especially established religion, in public life. Liberal school reforms coincided with, and were an integral part of, political clashes between liberals and clerical-conservatives in Germany, Austria, France, Switzerland, Belgium and the Netherlands. In Catholic countries, these school reforms involved ousting the clergy from their place as inspectors of public schools or teachers in them. This was a long, slow process in Italy, since in 1859 half of the schoolteachers in the country were priests or religious. In France, the confrontation was shorter and sharper, involving, especially, a government effort to expel nuns from teaching girls; the expansion of primary education to girls in France went along with a sharp reduction in the number of female religious who were teachers in public girls' schools. These sorts of measures involved an improvement of the position of schoolteachers vis-à-vis the clergy. This, combined with generally rising salaries for teachers, made them strong protagonists of this programme.

There were two exceptions to this secularizing trend, in the peripheral powers, Russia and Great Britain. In Russia, far from elementary education being secularized, much of the expansion of schooling in the 1870s and 1880s involved the creation of schools under the auspices and direction of the Holy Synod, the supreme authority of the Orthodox Church. The established Russian religion thus increased its position in elementary education, in open competition with schools under the authority of the state ministry of education. The autocratic Russian Empire was, in this respect as in so many others, a stronghold of opposition to liberal ideas.

The situation was a bit more complex in Great Britain since the underlying conflict was not so much between liberal secularists and supporters of an established religion as between two groups of adherents to religion: supporters of the established Anglican state church and proponents of different forms of independent Protestant churches. Before 1870, primary schools had been run either by the Anglican church, using public funds, or by private groups, including the 'independent' dissenting churches. New legislation in that year established elementary schools run by local school boards and financed by local property taxes ('rates') as the alternative to schools sponsored by the established church, which continued to receive government funds. The dissenting churches promptly terminated their own schools in favour of the newly created ones. These two different, and both tax-supported, educational systems – one aligned with the established church, and one notionally secular but supported by dissenting Protestants – continued to exist, although the growth in public education was largely in the rate-supported schools that over the decades encompassed an increasingly large portion of schoolchildren.

This large-scale realignment of public elementary education involved curricular changes. Religious instruction – hymns, prayers, Bible study – the centrepiece of public elementary education in the first two-thirds of the nineteenth century, lost its central intellectual place. It was only in France that religion was banished altogether from the public schools and replaced with instruction in a secular, or as the French said, 'laic', morality. Elsewhere, religious instruction continued, but in a greatly reduced portion of class time. More attention was paid to basic skills: reading, writing and simple arithmetic. The period saw the increasing introduction of new topics, particularly history, civics and nature study. Increases in funding made it possible for classrooms to have maps and collections of natural objects, reinforcing these curricular innovations.

These new curricular items all had a central focus, the nation. In history, students were taught about the long past of their nation, even if some of that nationhood – the ancient Germanic tribesman Arminius who fought with the Romans as part of a millennia-old German nation, for instance – was largely fictional, or, in attributing the ancestry of the inhabitants of Great Britain to the Teutonic Angles, Saxons and Jutes, rather eliminated any Celtic peoples. Aspiring French schoolteachers, asked in exams what the purpose of history instruction was, almost unanimously said that it was to create feelings of national identity and nationalism. Geography and maps showed the very shape of the nation to the schoolchildren, pointing out to them the place of their community in the larger nation. Nature study focused on flora and fauna that were part of the nation. Guidelines for teacher training in

Italy summed this whole theme up by stating that 'the educator of the people should not be unfamiliar with anything that might induce knowledge and love of the fatherland'.[11]

Even (or perhaps especially) elementary school readers promoted nationalist ideas. A particularly popular one in French schools, *Julien and André Go on a Tour of France*, described two boys from Alsace whose dying father's last wish was that his offspring leave their annexed province to reside in their nation. Arriving in France, the two boys tour the country, discovering its geographic features, its cities and its people; the last words of the book are 'duty and fatherland'. Or take this text of a reader used in the public schools of Bavaria:

> Why do you love your fatherland? You love it, because your mother is a German, because the blood that flows through your veins is German, because the earth is German in which the dead are buried – dead your mother mourns and your father honors; because the place you were born, the language you speak, because your brother, your sister, the great nation in whose midst you live, the beautiful nature which surrounds you and everything you see, you love, you learn, you admire is *German*.[12]

As these examples suggest, the new moral centre of public education, replacing religion, was the nation and nationalism. It is, admittedly, hard to know just how widespread this sort of instruction was. Its intent is well documented for France and Germany – two nations whose former school pupils would fight each other with great vehemence in the First World War – although it is hard to know just how effective it was in not atypical large classrooms of 50–70 pupils. It is less clear how common, and how effective, such nationalist instruction was in other European countries. In Great Britain, for instance, as late as 1889, history was taught only in 20 per cent of all primary schools. It does seem that in Russia, where religion retained an important role in public education, the curriculum was less imbued with nationalism.

In contrast to these quite dramatic changes in primary education, secondary schooling was less visibly affected in this period. While primary education became an ever more common, often universal, experience, only a very small proportion of the population attended secondary schools – under 3 per cent of the 10–19 age group everywhere in Europe in 1890, with the exception of Switzerland. University education was even less common, with at most 1 per cent of 20–24-year-olds attending university that same year.[13] Secondary schooling was, unlike primary education, not free. Furthermore, it began before primary school ended, so that there was no direct track from primary to secondary education. Finally, secondary school was for boys. An advanced education, contemporaries asserted, would make girls unmarriageable, ruin their morality, or in a Darwinian mode, overtax their smaller brains.

There were some secondary schools for girls, known in Germany by the particularly charming name of 'higher daughter schools'. As this name indicates, their purpose was to prepare cultivated young ladies for life as bourgeois wives, teaching them French, the piano, needlework and other skills appropriate to an elegant mistress of the house. Proponents of an intellectually more rigorous curriculum for young women certainly existed, especially in Great Britain where feminist ideas were stronger than in continental Europe, but remained, before 1890, a distinct minority.

Of course, the intellectually rigorous curriculum provided to boys in secondary schools might not have been an ideal model for emulation. It was centred on ancient languages, with the study of Latin and Greek far and away the most important and most time-consuming items in the curriculum. No less than 43 per cent of classroom time in French secondary schools in 1890 was devoted to Latin and Greek, more than three times as much as the next most important item, the French language.[14] This emphasis on the classics to the detriment of modern languages, science, mathematics, technology, modern history and the contemporary world more generally, was increasingly apparent, and different versions of secondary school that made up for these gaps began to be proposed: *Realgymnasium* and *Oberrealschule* in Germany, *enseignement spécial* and *enseignement modern* in France, *scuole tecniche* in Italy. As all these names suggest, these institutions offered more instruction in modern, scientific and technological subjects, and less in the classics. Enrolment in them gradually increased, although the dominant and most prestigious standing of classical secondary education was unchallenged before 1890 and would remain so, if perhaps to a lesser extent, down until the First World War.

Education in the late nineteenth century, as was the case with other social developments, shows both a continuation and culmination of previous trends and an uncertain search for new directions. Elementary education offers a good example of continuation and culmination. Not only was the scope of elementary education expanded, but the virtues of such education as an end in itself – not just as an adjunct to religion – was increasingly recognized in public policy and public expenditures. Secondary and university education largely showed a continuation of previous trends, but these were being brought into question, although as yet no convincing new alternatives had emerged.

THE ARTS AND SCIENCES

Perhaps more than any other area it was in intellectual and cultural life that the uncertain nature of the era came to the fore. Certainly, in many ways the developments of the age of progress continued into the late nineteenth century. Whether in the writing of realist novels, the synthesis of organic compounds, the exploration of the electromagnetic spectrum, or the classification and organization of past and present human societies, scientific and artistic endeavours of the post-1870 decades built on the foundations of their post-1850 predecessors. Sometimes, though, the very extension of this progress began to undermine its intellectual assumptions. The more physicists learnt about the electromagnetic spectrum, the less their new knowledge fitted with their basic physical theories; as literary naturalists and artistic impressionists pushed the boundaries of artistic realism, their work began to point beyond realism. In other cases, newly uncovered evidence seemed to contradict previous assumptions. This was above all the case with the linked (or mis-linked) ideas of evolution and progress, so important in the quarter-century after 1850. A host of questions were raised about Charles Darwin's theories, arising both as a result of their direct evaluation and also from the progress of other areas of biology.

Even more than Darwin's theories, the notion of progress itself came into dispute. Observers were more apt to see evidence of degeneration and decay than of progress in contemporary history and society. The positivist, scientific-empirical approach to the production of knowledge, another pillar of the post-mid-century worldview, was brought into question as well. The post-1850 embrace of progress and positivism had gone along with a vigorous criticism of religious orthodoxy. Growing doubts about these post-1850 affirmations generally did not lead to a resurgence of religious orthodoxy; rather, the upshot was a more persistent malaise and lack of certainty. The German philosopher Friedrich Wilhelm Nietzsche took this intellectual malaise and uncertainty and turned it into a new and disquieting form of affirmation. Doing so made him the thinker whose ideas were as emblematic of the intellectual world of the late nineteenth century as Auguste Comte and Herbert Spencer were of the mid-century decades.

A MORE AMBIVALENT FORWARD MARCH OF SCIENCE

Of all the natural sciences, chemistry was the public face of continued, uninterrupted progress in the latter decades of the nineteenth century. The synthesis of indigo dye in 1880 by the German chemist Adolf Baeyer was a continuation of previous successes in synthesizing organic chemicals. The discovery of elements such as gallium, scandium and germanium between 1875 and 1886 confirmed, very effectively, Dmitri Mendeleev's predictions in his periodic table of the elements. At the very end of the period, in 1894–95, the English chemists John Stutt, Lord Rayleigh and William Ramsay discovered the inert gases, introducing a whole new column into the periodic table.

There was a similar form of scientific progress in physics, building on previous accomplishments and seen in the laboratory work exploring the electromagnetic and optical phenomena described in theoretical form in Maxwell's equations. In 1888, the physicist Heinrich Hertz sent electromagnetic radiation across his laboratory; in other words, he was the first to broadcast radio waves. Seven years later, another German physicist, Wilhelm Röntgen, demonstrated the existence of high-energy electromagnetic radiation, or as contemporaries quickly dubbed them, X-rays. Both these experimental advances were only possible with new technological devices, oscillators and vacuum tubes, and reflected the progress of the manufacturing of electrical equipment.

Although these findings certainly exemplified Maxwell's theories, other developments were raising questions about them. One was in the rather arcane area of 'blackbody radiation', the electromagnetic radiation emitted when a physical substance is heated under specific conditions. Experiments kept turning up distributions of the radiation frequencies that differed noticeably from the ones that theory predicted.

The reconciliation of Maxwell's theories of electromagnetic radiation with the older physics of Newton's mechanics required expanding Maxwell's equations to include electromagnetic radiation in bodies in motion, or, as physicists said, in moving coordinate systems. The theoretical and mathematical challenges involved were considerable. Making this work more difficult were the results of the attempts by the American physicist Albert Michelson to measure precisely the speed of light. Michelson's 1881 experiments showed that the earth's motion had no effect on light's speed, a result difficult to reconcile with either Maxwell's or Newton's theories.

Both the theoretical resolution of these questions and the further development of the study of electromagnetic radiation would, in the twenty years before 1914, reach the attention of the public in spectacular ways – from wireless communication, to X-ray photography, to Marie Curie's investigations into radioactive substances, to Albert Einstein's theory of relativity – helping to set physics on its path to being the foremost science of the twentieth century. In the two decades before 1895, physics was on the verge of this new departure but had not yet reached it.

The same combination of impressive new laboratory results and further theoretical investigations with questions about previous theoretical advances characterized biological science in the late decades of the nineteenth century. In contrast to physics, though, the disparity between previous theories and new results was much sharper in biology, and the results of new investigations reported to a wide circle of the public in dramatic fashion, not just circulated in obscure scientific journals in the form of differential equations.

If the 1860s saw a great scientific and public debate about Darwin's theory of natural selection and the supporters of Darwin's ideas in the ascendant, starting in the 1870s and continuing over the following decades, doubts about the centrepiece of Darwin's theory, the idea of natural selection, came to the fore. Most of these doubts centred on the way that natural selection would operate from one generation to the next. Individual members of species might have specific characteristics that would enable them to survive, but when they mated with other members of the species would these characteristics be passed on in full to their offspring or would they be watered down? The British biologist Francis Galton (1822–1911), Darwin's cousin, subjected the process of natural selection to mathematical analysis and concluded that, over time, rather than the extremes in a range of variations coming to dominate a species, there would be a 'regression towards the mean' (the statistical technique of regression, which Galton invented, gets its name from his analysis of natural selection), so that natural selection could not work as Darwin proposed.

The physical mechanisms of heredity also remained little understood, and the process by which variations, particularly extreme ones, could arise, was unclear. The German biologist August Weismann (1834–1914) proposed that hereditary material in living beings, which he called 'germ plasm', was completely separate from and unaffected by changes in the rest of the body. In support of this point of view, he performed a celebrated experiment in which he cut off the tails of white mice, but found that their offspring all had their full tails. Weismann saw himself as a supporter of Darwin's ideas, and his theories would ultimately form the basis of modern genetics, but to contemporaries it seemed that he had made the link between adaptation to the environment and inheritance of traits, both needed for natural selection, even harder to understand.

The upshot was a growing scepticism by the 1880s and 1890s of Darwin's theory of natural selection. This scepticism did not lead to a revival of theistic versions of the understanding of biological diversity, explained by divine creation, a notion that had disappeared among scientists by the late nineteenth century. Rather, there was a growing acceptance of notions of biological or spiritual progress ingrained in nature. Both older ideas of Lamarck and the newer theory of 'orthogenesis' asserted that life on earth evolved over time because it had an inherent tendency to become more complex. Of course, much of the popular acceptance of Darwin's ideas in the first place had been because of their confusion with broader theories of progress. Now it seemed that scientific biology itself was moving in such a basically pre-Darwinian direction.

In many ways, the cutting edge of biological research in the post-1870 decades moved away from discussions of the evolution of life forms and the origins of biological diversity towards the investigation of microscopic organisms. The major figure here was the French biologist Louis Pasteur (1822–95). Already a celebrated figure for his pre-1870 work on the actions of microbes, Pasteur's investigations of the 1870s and 1880s made him into a French national, and even Europe-wide, folk hero, when he discovered the microbes that caused anthrax and rabies and used them to devise a vaccine preventing these diseases. This investigation into pathogenic microbes was taken up by other biologists, particularly Pasteur's German rival, Robert Koch (1843–1910), who discovered the microbes responsible for tuberculosis and cholera.

The research of these biologists and their students and emulators firmly established the still controversial germ theory of disease, demonstrating that major nineteenth-century illnesses, besides cholera and tuberculosis, typhus and typhoid fever, and many of the childhood diseases, were the result of the actions of micro-organisms. While this research had no direct bearing on Darwin's theories, and both Pasteur and Koch retained a discreet silence about the relevance to their work to evolution, such research did disprove the theory of 'spontaneous generation', the idea that life could originate from dead organic matter, by showing that such life was actually the product of living micro-organisms. Theories of the development of life on earth over very long periods of time, whether Darwinian or non-Darwinian in nature, tended to assume that life had begun originally from non-living matter and supposed contemporary examples of spontaneous generation would support such an assertion. Evidence that spontaneous generation was the result of eminently living, if very small, micro-organisms, posed yet another problem for Darwin's theories.

There were two broader ramifications of the trend towards microbiology. One was the move in biology away from naturalism, the collection of specimens of living organisms, and the fossils of dead ones, towards laboratory investigations and systematic experiments. Darwin himself was a naturalist, and his theory of natural selection the result of lengthy naturalistic observation; the new forms of experimental biology, while not disproving any of Darwin's ideas or even eliminating naturalism from biology, did tend to take the main currents of biological research in a new direction.

The other point about this new direction in biology was its political implications. Darwin's theories, with their undermining of theistic understandings of the world, possessed a noticeably left-wing implication, and these ideas – albeit often misunderstood as a biological proof of the existence of progress – had been taken up by liberals, radicals and socialists of various sorts. Both Pasteur and Koch, by contrast, were personally devout and politically conservative; their ideas did not give aid and comfort to opponents of an established order. Indeed, the establishment of the germ theory of disease tended, if anything, to undermine the connection between improving health and raising standards of living, since it was not poverty or poor-quality housing in general that caused disease, but micro-organisms, which could be combated by vaccinations, pasteurization (heating milk to kill micro-organisms), and the building of water and sewage systems, rather than by making poor people better off.

The fate of Darwin's ideas in the late nineteenth century is suggestive of the development of scientific thinking. The intellectual advances of the 1850s and 1860s, which had undermined previous, often theistic, certainties were not refuted, nor were these previous certainties reinstated. But the closer examination of the major intellectual concepts of the post-mid-century era, an examination frequently carried out in precisely the spirit of these concepts, showed gaps, weaknesses and insufficiencies in them for which no entirely satisfactory resolution could be found. Tentative new suggestions and the revival of older ones created an atmosphere of intellectual uncertainty. This sort of uncertainty was every bit as pronounced in the social sciences as in the natural and physical ones.

THE SOCIAL SCIENCES REORIENTED AND REALIGNED

In the post-mid-century decades, the emergent social sciences had been characterized by two main themes. One of these was conceptual, an understanding of human society and human history as a story of progress, generally understood as running through distinct stages, and frequently given a biological, evolutionary interpretation. The other was methodological, a positivist commitment to the empirical examination of evidence, modelled on or considered in parallel with the natural and physical sciences. In the later nineteenth century, the ever more firmly articulated and separated social science disciplines generally continued to work within these broad parameters. Examined more closely, though, we can see how the previous affirmation of these two major principles was amended, questioned and placed in doubt.

If this was the case with historical studies, sociology and anthropology, the situation in another social science discipline was quite different, although in its way equally characteristic of the uncertainty of the era. Economics was placed on a quite new intellectual foundation during the two post-1870 decades, and in many ways became a fundamentally different discipline – a change symbolized in western Europe, at least, by a new name, 'economics', in place of the previously preferred 'political economy'. Yet, while absorbing this conceptual revolution, economists insisted on the continuity of their discipline with the ideas of increasingly iconic past figures such as Adam Smith. If most of the social sciences seemed to continue in their previous intellectual path while subtly taking side routes and detours, economics went off at a sharp angle all the while insisting it was going in a straight line.

One of the points of intellectual discomfort was the idea of progress. By the 1870s, some historians were beginning to have their doubts about understanding their subject as a chronicle of progress. The British historian Leslie Stephens offered a mild version of this discontent when he asserted that progress did not move 'in a straight line . . . but in a spiral curve'.[15] If Stephens implied an alternation of periods of progress and regressions, his French contemporary, the critic and historian Hippolyte Taine (1828–94) was more open and explicit in his pessimism. In the 1850s and 1860s author of a number of acclaimed works in which he applied Comte's positivist ideas to the study of literary criticism, Taine's optimistic view of human progress soured after the experience of the Paris Commune. In his *Origins of Contemporary France*, which appeared in five volumes between 1875 and 1894, Taine perceived the history of his country over the previous century as one of decay and degeneration, in which biologically degenerate revolutionaries obtained an ever more influential position.

Questions about progress began to appear in the works of anthropologists as well. Sometimes these doubts reflected the influence of ideas about biological evolution, whether evolution was understood – or misunderstood – in Darwinian or non-Darwinian terms. One famous example of this attitude was in the work of the Italian anthropologist and criminologist Cesare Lombroso (1835–1909). By measuring skulls and analysing other physiological features, Lombroso attempted to show that criminals' bodies were closer to those of apes than were those of honest citizens. Poverty and criminality thus became evidence of individuals' biological backwardness, a state that Lombroso found existing in women, children and Africans as well.

Lombroso's work was by no means universally accepted, and was the subject of vigorous criticism by fellow criminologists. Still, what is striking about his efforts is the attention to and focus on – sometimes the obsession with – failure to progress, on degeneration, on individuals of a 'lower' evolutionary state. Francis Galton, whom we met above raising statistical questions about Darwin's theories, generalized this attitude by observing that his contemporary society was characterized not by natural selection, in which the fittest were reproducing, but by an 'unnatural selection', in which the poor and ignorant, assisted by charity and social welfare, had many children, while the affluent and intelligent had steadily fewer. As a response to these ostensible circumstances, Galton advocated and coined the term 'eugenics', policies to encourage evolutionarily 'superior' people to reproduce and to discourage or to prevent their supposed biological inferiors from doing the same. Eugenics would take off in the twentieth century, especially after the First World War. In its initial phase, it reflected a rejection of the optimistic post-1850 affirmation of progress and a fear that the biological and social opposite of progress was occurring.

Questions about progress were important to late nineteenth century debates in anthropology. Some anthropologists argued that contemporary tribal peoples of Asia and Africa represented an earlier stage in human evolution, hunter–gatherer societies of several thousand years ago, and still had the potential to progress towards civilization. As English anthropologist Edward B. Tylor (1832–1917) put it in 1871: 'the savage state in some measure represents an early condition of mankind, out of which the higher culture has gradually been developed or evolved, by processes still in regular operation as of old'.[16] By contrast, the German anthropologist Adolf Bastian (1829–1905) asserted that the tribal peoples of Africa and the South Seas were *Naturvölker*, peoples or races of nature, to be contrasted with European *Kulturvölker*, peoples or races of culture and civilization. The latter had evolved from more primitive states in the past to higher forms of civilization in the present, while the former were permanently stuck in a timeless, lower stage of development. Unlike Lombroso or the eugenicists, who perceived lack of progress and even regression as existing within European society itself, this anthropological trend tended to locate lack of progress among non-Europeans, but the attention paid to such conditions was part of a broader developing doubt about progress and its inevitability.

In one social science discipline, namely economics, fundamental philosophical and epistemological questions came to the fore in the last quarter of the nineteenth century, resulting in an intellectual reorientation. The starting point of this new turn was an increasing dissatisfaction with the 'classical' doctrines of economics, as they had developed from Adam Smith, Jean-Baptiste Say and David Ricardo. From this common beginning, two different and ultimately hostile schools of thought emerged.

One version of this dissatisfaction involved a growing scepticism about the way the classical economists had described social reality and proposed economic policies on the basis of their theories. Critics of the classical economists' procedure, most prominently a group of economists in Germany who became known as the 'historical school', called for empirical analysis of the economy, for developing statistics on wages, prices, working and living conditions, in good positivist fashion, before deriving theories about the way the economy worked. This critique of the historical school, already developing in the 1860s, received added emphasis in the harsher economic climate of the 1870s and 1880s. Both the sharp economic crises and the longer periods of slow economic growth seemed to suggest that key doctrines of classical economics, such as the primacy of free markets to promote economic growth, and the theory of comparative advantage in international trade, did not correspond to the empirically observed facts as the economists of the historical school saw it.

As a result, a number of these economists, most prominently their leading figure, Gustav Schmoller (1838–1917), professor of economics at the University of Berlin, came increasingly to advocate different forms of government intervention in the economy, including wages and hours legislation, social welfare initiatives, measures to support craftsmen and small shopkeepers, and, most controversially, the institution of protective tariffs. Although by no means all members of the historical school were protectionists, this advocacy of protectionism came to be associated with them and met with strong opposition on the part of adherents of classical economic doctrines. When a number of Italian economists began to propose similar doctrines to their German counterparts, supporters of classical ideas responded by forming the charmingly named Società Adamo Smith to promote the pure doctrines of free trade and free markets.

The major riposte to the historical school, though, did not come from the upholders of Smithian – more exactly, Ricardian – orthodoxy, but from the proponents of a new version of economic theory. Like the historical school, these economists also had their doubts about classical economics, but they did not criticize it for being too abstract and theoretical. Instead, they found it not theoretical enough, or, perhaps more precisely, lacking in the right kind of theory.

What irked these economists was the classical idea of the labour theory of value, in which commodities' values were determined by the amount of labour put into them.

Instead, they proposed that objects' values were determined by the usefulness to individuals consuming them, their utility. They measured utility by considering the usefulness of the last object acquired, or, as they said, its 'marginal utility'. This approach could then be used to analyse prices, costs (the 'marginal cost', for instance, being the cost of the last item produced) and productivity. It was susceptible to advanced mathematical analysis, since understanding this last item as not one item, but an infinitely small increment over the previous one, made it possible to use calculus in economic reasoning.

This whole approach has come to be known as the 'marginal revolution' in economic theory. Its basic ideas were first clearly formulated in the 1870s by a trio of economists, the Englishman William Stanley Jevons (1835–82), the Austrian Carl Menger (1840–1921) and the Frenchman Léon Walras (1834–1910). As this polyglot mixture makes clear, unlike the historical school, an intellectual movement that clearly began in central Europe and was strongest in Germany, the marginalists came from all over the continent. The ranks of the initial adherents were reinforced by a slightly younger group, including the English scholar Alfred Marshall (1842–1924), the Swedish economist Knut Wicksell (1851–1926) and the Italian Maffeo Pantaleoni (1857–1924).

In contrast to the historical school, the marginalists generally emphasized their similarities to their predecessors, Smith, Ricardo et al., so that their doctrines are also known as 'neo-classical' economics. There certainly were similarities between classical and neo-classical economists, particularly in the advocacy of a free market, about which the marginalists were particularly vehement, but the differences between the groups are at least as striking. The respective theories of value – the philosophical basis of economics – were very much opposed. Neo-classical economic theory was strongly mathematicized, expressed in equations, or graphically, as supply and demand curves, while the classical economists used little or no mathematics. The classical economists studied, above all, the preconditions of economic growth and the way the economy's output was distributed to members of different social classes. Their neo-classical successors generally rejected this object of study (they only returned to the study of economic growth at about the same time as biologists returned to Darwin's doctrines of natural selection, in the 1940s) and concentrated on the analysis of the interaction of individual consumers and firms in a market, emphasizing the formation of prices and the creation of an economic equilibrium.

Both the marginalists and the proponents of the historical school began their versions of economics with a criticism of the lack of intellectual rigour in classical economics. But the respective intellectual tools they used – mathematical formulations of the marginalists and statistical investigations of the historical school – and the policy proposals they endorsed – pro-free market for the marginalists, pro-governmental action for the historical school – set them strongly against each other. Particularly in central Europe, partisans of the two schools of economics engaged in a series of savage polemics. In Germany, the historical school was the winner, but in the wider European context and from a longer-term perspective, the marginalists obtained the victory. Contemporary economics is the intellectual descendant of the neo-classical theories first developed in the 1870s and 1880s.

Like the other social sciences, economists had come to have increasing doubts by the late nineteenth century about existing modes of investigation and analysis. While most of the social sciences were unable to develop new conceptions in this period and continued to work with ones dating from the 1850s and 1860s, only to question them subtly, economists succeeded in moving from doubts about previous forms of investigation to a new disciplinary focus. Ironically, economists were reluctant to admit this, and presented their new focus as a continuation of the previous one they had criticized. Both the inability to break with previous ideas, in spite of doubts about them, and the ability to do so but a reluctance to admit it, were characteristics of the social sciences in an age of uncertainty.

PROGRESS AND ITS DISCONTENTS

In 1886, the British poet laureate Alfred Lord Tennyson wrote, read publicly and published his poem 'Locksley Hall Sixty Years After'. Much of the lengthy poem is a pessimistic reflection on the failures of the ideal of progress:

> Gone the cry of 'Forward, Forward', lost within a growing gloom;
> Lost or only heard in silence from the silence of a tomb.
> Half the marvels of my morning, triumphs over time and space,
> Staled by frequence, shrunk by usage into commonest commonplace!
> 'Forward' rang the voices then, and of the many mine was one.
> Let us hush this cry of 'Forward' till ten thousand years have gone.
>
> . . .
>
> Evolution ever climbing after some ideal good,
> And Reversion ever dragging Evolution in the mud.
>
> . . .
>
> Is it well that while we range with Science, glorying in the Time,
> City children soak and blacken soul and sense in city slime?
> There among the glooming alleys Progress halts on palsied feet,
> Crime and hunger cast our maidens by the thousand on the street.[17]

We could just dismiss these lines as the sour mood of an 80-year-old author, and elsewhere in the poem Tennyson admits that his scepticism about progress is in part a product of his advanced age. Yet his sentiments were not unique to the elderly. Lots of younger intellectuals of the late nineteenth century also devalued the importance of material and economic advances, questioned the significance of science for life and a tide of regression swamping the pretensions of progress.

In view of this rejection of the ideals of progress and positivism, so powerful in the third quarter of the nineteenth century, the question might be, what would replace them? One possibility might have been a return to the certainties of revealed religion. There were certainly some efforts in that direction. The 1880s, for instance, was probably the only decade over about the past two hundred years in which church attendance by Protestants in Germany actually increased. Most intellectuals of the late nineteenth century, though, tended to accept the criticisms of revealed religion developed by adherents of progress and positivism, even if they could no longer share the latter's affirmations.

An illuminating example of a search for new forms of affirmation appears in the work of the German philosopher Friedrich Wilhelm Nietzsche (1844–1900). An obscure figure during his lifetime (or at least his rational lifetime, since he became incurably insane in 1889), Nietzsche's fame would increase steadily in the pre-1914 years. His intellectual development, notwithstanding his many personal idiosyncrasies, offers a revealing guide to the possibilities and problematic features of the late nineteenth century acceptance of the criticisms made by the mid-century adherents of progress and positivism, but rejection of these adherents' ideals.

Nietzsche certainly endorsed the positivist criticism of metaphysics, insisting that any other forms of knowledge about the world than empirical observation, based on perception, were simply delusions. And like the positivists, Nietzsche, at least at times, saw the natural and physical sciences – as he understood them (Nietzsche's own intellectual training was in the classics) – as the appropriate models for the acquisition of knowledge. But Nietzsche continued beyond the positivists, asking, if one rejects metaphysics, something beyond and underscoring perceptions, how can we know if our perceptions are valid? In his 1888 book *The Twilight of the Idols*, he asserted: 'We have suppressed the true world [i.e. a world lying beyond our perceptions]: what world survives? The apparent world perhaps? Certainly not! In abolishing the true world we have also abolished the world of appearance!'[18]

Nietzsche was even more vehement and scornful in his rejection of the other dominant post-mid-century ideal, that of progress. Everywhere around him he saw decay and degeneration, and he found past eras – the Roman Empire, for instance, or the rule of the Borgias in Renaissance Rome – vastly superior to his own. As was the case with many of his contemporaries, Nietzsche perceived this degeneration in biological terms, resulting from the breeding and social tolerance of racially and biologically inferior individuals. There was a Darwinian element to this, but Nietzsche, as was also typical of his time, felt that Darwin's theory of natural selection lacked a spiritual element of life striving for perfection.

What affirmations would Nietzsche put in place of positivism and progress? His solution to the problems of epistemology came in two slogan-like phrases, the 'will to power' and 'eternal recurrence'. An exposition of these phrases would be as long and complex as they are short and pithy. To be ruthlessly and misleadingly brief, they involved connecting perceived reality with the strength of individuals' wills and envisaging the world as fixed and finite, repeating itself exactly over and over again, across enormously long periods of time.

More interesting, and certainly more influential, was Nietzsche's search for affirmation, following his rejection of the idea of progress. A return to revealed religion and its eternal verities was unacceptable to him. If there is one phrase associated with Nietzsche, which most people know, it is his blunt exclamation that 'God is dead'. The philosopher made no secret of his hostility to Christianity, denouncing it in unusually colourful language as life-denying, fraudulent and deeply pernicious in its intellectual and social consequences. Thinkers of the eighteenth-century Enlightenment and the post-1850 positivists had criticized Christianity in similar ways (maybe not with Nietzsche's unique brand of invective), and the clash between socially and politically conservative adherents of revealed religion on the one hand, and, on the other hand, more secular or free-thinking, progress-minded supporters of liberal, democratic and, by the 1880s, socialist ideas, was a typical feature of the intellectual and political scene in Europe. Nietzsche, though, rejected this affirmation of secular ideals, and, in an intellectual move he called the 'revaluation of all values', turned it on its head.

We can see this best in Nietzsche's celebrated attack on the anti-Semites of his day. Nietzsche knew them well (his sister was married to a leading German anti-Semite) and condemned them not so much for denouncing Jews as for denouncing Jews while professing to be Christians. For Nietzsche, the worst thing that could be said about Jews was that they had invented Christianity, a religion devoted to helping the weak and inferior, and entrapping biologically superior, strong-willed individuals in a net of guilt-ridden prohibitions. Then, Nietzsche went on, liberalism, democracy and socialism were secularized versions of Christianity, all containing its endorsement of the weak and inferior, and its hostility to the powerful and superior.

Thus having dissolved the dichotomy between conservative revealed religion and progressive free-thinking, by describing the latter as an equally pernicious version of the former, Nietzsche unveiled his own form of social affirmation: an end to the coddling of the inferior and the unleashing of the biologically superior to impose their will without feelings of guilt. The exact details of this programme, as was often the case with Nietzsche's writings, were left vague. Still, a passage of *The Twilight of the Idols* in which he praises the ancient Hindu law of Manu and its measures to ensure the extirpation of the racially inferior Chandalas, comparing it favourably with Christian or socialist calls to exalt the poor, reads very unpleasantly when we think of the mass murders of the twentieth century, some carried out by self-professed supporters of Nietzsche. Seeking alternatives to the mid-nineteenth-century belief in progress and positivism did not always lead in the most wholesome of directions.

BOX 11.1

Nietzsche and his followers

Had Nietzsche's sanity lasted long enough to see the growing popularity of his ideas, he would have been amazed at the diversity of followers he attracted in the quarter-century before the First World War. Found in every European country, and not just in German-speaking ones, post-1890 Nietzscheans included right-wing extremists as well as socialists and anarchists, militarists and pacifists, misogynists and feminists, anti-Semites and Jews, racist proponents of eugenics and strong enemies of racial thinking, rigorously rationalist philosophers and mystical, avant-garde artists, even devout Christians and atheists. One might want to throw up one's hands at the contradictory ideas propounded by Nietzsche enthusiasts, or perhaps attribute them to Nietzsche's notoriously aphoristic style and his refusal to put forth a systematic argument. On closer examination, though, there are three general observations that can be made about Nietzsche's followers.

One is that whatever their viewpoint, they tended to be dissenters from dominant, conventional views, and adherents of unusual opinions. Nietzscheans remained a minority, suggestive of the limitations on the resonance of their guru's criticisms of positivism and progress. A second point concerns a broader division in the ranks of Nietzsche's followers. Decades ago, the American historian Crane Brinton suggested that one could divide them into two groups, the 'hard' and the 'soft' Nietzscheans. Both were excited about the idea of a transvaluation of all values, but the former took the master's praise for warfare, cruelty, the right of the stronger, overcoming outdated Christian feelings of guilt, and the subordination or elimination of the inferior rather literally, while the latter understood them as spiritual or aesthetic in nature. Although there have been many criticisms and modifications of Brinton's basic argument – he tended to place the hard Nietzscheans all on the political right, for instance, while there were, in Russia especially, hard Nietzscheans on the left – the basic observation still seems, at the very least, a helpful way to understand Nietzsche's followers.

Finally, and in this respect Nietzscheans seem a lot like social Darwinists, we can observe a gradual political progression in Nietzscheanism from left to right. The big change for Nietzsche's ideas was the First World War, which brought the literal meanings of warfare and extermination to the fore and paved the way for the appearance of fascist political movements whose leaders claimed to be disciples of Nietzsche and of a particularly hard form of his ideas. Since the Second World War, it would be fair to say, the pendulum of Nietzscheanism has swung in the opposite direction and softer interpretations of Nietzsche, focusing on the way he saw ethics and epistemology as artistic and creative concerns, sometimes with vaguely left-wing political implications, have become more the rule – although it could be argued that such interpretations leave out a lot of the more unpleasant side of Nietzsche's ideas.

THE ARTS IN TRANSITION

In surprisingly close conjunction with the trends in the sciences, in scholarship and philosophy, artists of the late nineteenth century continued in the practices of the post-1850 decades and, by extending them to extremes, began to call them into question. This development was most pronounced in the visual arts, somewhat less so in literature and music, but apparent in all areas of artistic endeavour.

The practice of realism, so vigorous in the literature of the post-1850 decades, continued strongly in the last years of the nineteenth century. The great Russian realist Fyodor Dostoevsky, for instance, published his late masterpiece *The Brothers Karamazov* in 1880. In the Iberian peninsula, realist novels began to be written only in the 1870s and 1880s. The Spanish author Benito Pérez Galdós (1843–1920) and his Portuguese counterpart José Maria de Eça de Queirós (1845–1900) wrote a series of realist novels in the 1870s and 1880s in an anti-clerical vein, commenting critically on what they saw as the problematic influence of the Catholic Church in Iberian society. Their contemporary José María de Pereda (1833–1906) retorted with his own realist novels of Spanish provincial society, which praised the influence of the church and criticized secularizing trends.

Realism had been an influential literary movement in the German-speaking world since the 1840s at least, but it was only in the last decades of the nineteenth century that the individual generally regarded as the greatest German-language realist novelist, Theodor Fontane (1819–1898), produced his fictional works. The books often considered his masterpieces only appeared in the 1890s: *Frau Jenny Treibel*, an ironic comedy of manners that was also a penetrating dissection of the social values, political allegiances and personal and marital relations of the Berlin bourgeoisie, in 1892, and *Effi Briest*, a study of a woman's adultery and the resulting dissolution of her marriage and her life, the 'German *Madame Bovary*', in 1894.

In all these respects, the late nineteenth century literary scene in most European countries might appear as a continuation of the post-1850 realist trend. Yet there was also an alternative or, perhaps more precisely, a supplement to realism that made artistic waves in the 1870s, 1880s and early 1890s: the literary movement known as naturalism. If realism was characterized by an attempt to develop an empirically accurate portrait of society and social institutions, naturalism went one step further by attempting to derive this empirically accurate portrait from scientific doctrines and procedures. As Émile Zola (1840–1902), the leading naturalist author not just in France but across all of Europe, put it: 'The experimental novel [Zola's name for his naturalist fiction] arises out of the scientific advances of the century; it is a continuation and a completion of physiology ... the study of abstract, metaphysical man is replaced by the study of natural man, subject to physio-chemical laws and determined by the effects of his milieu ...'[19] Fiction, one might say, would become a lab report.

In contrast to literary realism, which was a Europe-wide artistic movement, naturalism was regionally more limited. Zola was *the* naturalist author and found a number of followers in France, most today forgotten except perhaps for the short-story writer Guy de Maupassant (1850–93). There were naturalists in Belgium, in Italy, where they were known as the 'verists', and to some extent in Spain, where the realist Pérez Galdós flirted with Zola-style naturalist novels. Although Zola's work was known and admired by literary circles in Russia, fiction writers did not attempt to imitate them. More generally, there was little in the way of naturalist novels in northern Europe or in Great Britain, where Zola's works came under heavy literary fire, were condemned by the House of Commons, and where the publisher of an English edition of Zola's novels was sent to jail.

Northern Europe did see another version of naturalism, namely in theatre, particularly in the writings of the playwrights Henryk Ibsen (1828–1906) of Norway, August Strindberg (1849–1912) of Sweden and Gerhart Hauptmann (1862–1946) of Germany. In their case the vagueness of the borders of literary movements is particularly apparent because all three of these authors can be categorized not only as proponents of an older, pre-naturalist version of realism, but also as exemplars of literary modernism, a distinctly post-naturalist movement. Nonetheless, at least some of their works fitted into the naturalist approach and were seen by contemporaries as examples of this literary movement.

What was most apparent to contemporaries about naturalist fiction was its dwelling on the dark side of life. The Anglo-Irish author George Moore, one of the few self-professed naturalists in Great Britain, took a trip to investigate the town of Hanley as the background for a novel, because the latter had the reputation of being the ugliest town in England. Naturalist works were often epics of disease and decay. Zola's *Nana*, his 1880 novel about a Parisian prostitute whose body, after its extensive sexual exploitation, is wracked by syphilis, but dies of smallpox, just to add an additional disease, was a characteristic and notorious example. Hauptmann's 1892 play *Before Sunrise* describes the protagonist's romance with a young woman, which he breaks off on discovering that his beloved comes from a family of alcoholics, ends with the jilted girl committing suicide, while her drunken sister gives birth, offstage, to a stillborn child.

This fascination with individuals' ruin through alcohol, sexually transmitted disease and other forms of decay produced a very hostile reaction in prudish late-Victorian England, which is how Zola's English-language publisher ended up in jail. Yet it also raises the question about the connection between a literature claiming to articulate a scientific view of the world and the morbid, depressing writing it produced. This connection was not a coincidence, nor was it the result of a discrepancy between the ostensible aims of the naturalists and their actual literary works. Instead, it was directly linked to the late nineteenth-century post-Darwinian understanding of heredity and degeneration.

The widespread fear that something had gone wrong with evolution, that the contemporary world was heading for degeneration and decay rather than towards progress (all this involving the common misunderstanding of Darwin's ideas of evolution as a form of progress in the first place), was widespread in naturalist literature. Zola's *Nana* was part of a multi-volume series on the Rougon-Macquart family during Louis Napoleon's reign, which described in lengthy and lurid detail the downfall of the family over several generations, as hereditary weaknesses, especially a tendency towards alcoholism, led to inevitable degeneration and decay. Similarly, the protagonist of Hauptmann's *Before Sunrise* breaks up with his fiancée because he fears that the hereditary alcoholism of her family would destroy their offspring. Two of the Scandinavian naturalists' most celebrated plays deal with the topic of inherited decay: Ibsen's *Ghosts*, about hereditary syphilis, and Strindberg's *Miss Julie*, a tragedy of a young woman whom the author described as 'a retrogressive step in evolution, an inferior species who cannot endure', driven to suicide by the hereditary characteristics transmitted from her mentally ill mother.[20]

Thus, in a number of different respects, naturalist literature was a characteristic artistic product of the late nineteenth-century age of uncertainty. Its method and style continued the ideals of realism but carried them to extremes: the critical, empirical examination of social reality dissolved into a 'scientific' evocation of human biology in action. The naturalists' conception of hereditary decay and their fears of degeneration were an integral part of the pessimistic re-evaluation of the social consequences of Darwin's theories. Finally, the pessimistic, rather morbid tone of naturalist writing – which today seems almost hysterical in its exaggeration – carried the critical examination of society by literary realists virtually to the point of absurdity.

This role of problematic successor to realism was also apparent in impressionism, the major thematic trend in the visual arts during the 1870s and 1880s. Contemporaries certainly saw the impressionists as a dramatic new artistic movement. The name itself comes from a critical attack on their painting, accusing them of not actually portraying scenes or individuals but just leaving a vague impression of them. Taking this critical denunciation as a badge of pride, the impressionists enjoyed their position as artistic rebels; they were the first group of artists to be known as the 'avant-garde', a designation they cherished.

The impressionists certainly were opponents of the academic school of painting, based on classical models, and the critics who endorsed this view. In doing so, though, they were continuing in the tradition of the mid-century realist painters, and it is no coincidence that Edouard Manet, one of the best-known French realist painters, was seen as the patron and leader of the impressionist artists. Impressionists continued the realist practice of painting unposed scenes from life. Claude Monet (1840–1926), probably the leading impressionist painter, focused on landscapes, which he liked to paint out of doors, avoiding studio retouchings of his art. By contrast, the work of Edgar Degas (1834–1917) focused, as the French realist painters often had, on portrayals of people at work. Admittedly, Degas's drawings and paintings had as their subjects women of the lower classes or in sexually charged occupations – dancers, washerwomen, prostitutes – although his portrayals of them were far from risqué or titillating.

In the end, the impressionists proved to be quite successful painters. With the end of Louis Napoleon's Second Empire and the creation of a republic in France, the French art world became more democratic, or at least less subject to the authoritarian control of classically minded professors of the art academies. Impressionists were able to show their paintings in major exhibitions and to gain a substantial public following. Originating as a distinctly French artistic movement of the 1870s and 1880s, impressionism spread throughout Europe and the entire world – there were significant groups of impressionist painters in Australia, Japan and the United States – in the quarter-century before the First World War, ironically only as impressionism was falling out of style in its home country and could certainly no longer lay claim to be an artistic avant-garde.

To see how this was the case we might take a look at the technique of the impressionists. Both Degas and Monet, as was the case with many although not all of the impressionists, were known for their distinctive brush strokes, which looked blurred when seen up close (hence the hostile critical designation 'impressionism'), but resolved into a realistic image when observed at a distance. In doing so they were continuing the realists' programme of portraying the world as they perceived it rather than based on idealized models and images. But what were the impressionists perceiving? Monet explained his ideal of painting around 1890 as follows:

> When you go out to paint, try to forget what object you have before you . . . Merely think here is a little square of blue; here an oblong of pink, here a streak of yellow, and paint it just as it looks to you, the exact color and shape, until it gives your own naïve impression of the scene before you.[21]

This statement, which is reminiscent of Nietzsche's remark that his philosophy, by destroying the world lying beyond human perceptions, had also abolished the world of appearances, suggests that in carrying to an extreme the realist programme of painting an empirically perceptible world, the impressionists were transferring artists' attention from the exterior world they were portraying to the shapes and colours used for representation. In doing so they were straining at the bounds of empirical representation, characteristic of realism, laying the groundwork for a very different, modernist art that would flourish in the quarter-century before the First World War.

Thus, both literature and the plastic arts in the last decades of the nineteenth century were characterized by a situation in which stylistic and aesthetic continuity led to stylistic and aesthetic innovation, with the innovation probably more pronounced in painting and sculpture and the continuity more in literature. Looking at music, we see a situation in which the balance between continuity and innovation was tipped much more strongly in favour of a continued domination of the romantic musical tradition, a state of affairs that was itself to a great extent a continuation of mid-century developments.

The 1870s, for instance, saw the apotheosis of Richard Wagner and his claim that his operatic works represented the continuation and culmination of Beethoven's symphonic works. After decades of searching, Wagner acquired in the 1870s a permanent home base in the Bavarian provincial town of Bayreuth. There, he was able to build not an opera house or concert hall but, as he described it, a 'festival perform-ance house', in which his operas could make their maximum impact on the spectators as giant multimedia performances. In 1874, he was able to stage there the premiere of *The Twilight of the Gods*, the concluding and climactic opera of his *Ring* tetralogy. Not only were the acoustic and line-of-sight conditions in the new location ideal, as anyone who has ever toured the facility can testify, the music festivals provided Wagner with a venue in which he could employ his compositions to exalt his mystical cul-tural and political ideas, particularly his vicious nationalist and anti-Semitic notions – a testimony, if not a particularly pleasant one, to the power of romantic music.

Wagner's contemporaries, such as Johannes Brahms (1833–97), Peter Ilyich Tchaikovsky (1840–93) and Antonín Dvořák (1841–1904), all composed symphonic works, consciously following in the romantic tradition developed by Beethoven in the initial decades of the nineteenth century. Indeed, Brahms's first symphony of 1876 was hailed by contemporaries as a revival of the music and spirit of Beethoven. If late nineteenth-century music thus appears as a continuation of early nineteenth-century musical romanticism and its mid-nineteenth-century successors, there was one area in which it took existing forms and pushed them to their limits.

This was in regard to chromatic transitions, of composing a symphonic movement or smaller musical phrase in one key, and then the next in another, and returning at the end to the original key. The tension evoked by this movement of keys and its resolution by the return to the original key of the composition provided an import-ant part of the excitement and dynamism of romantic music. Late nineteenth-century composers, particularly Wagner but even Brahms, began using this technique in modified form, introducing dissonant tones to heighten the musical tensions, and not always returning to the original key at the expected time. A younger generation of musicians, first appearing on the scene around 1890, such as Richard Strauss (1864–1949), Gustav Mahler (1860–1911) and Jean Sibelius (1865–1957), pushed this technique to its limits, changing keys in their works in ever shorter intervals, using more dissonant elements, or never reverting to the original key. In continuing the romantic practice of sharp tonal contrasts and raising it to new heights, their musical works raised the question of whether music needed to be chromatic, whether it would be possible to devise musical works in which the preferred rela-tionship of certain notes to each other, which made up a musical key, would not exist.

Admittedly, such a question can be raised mostly in hindsight. The concert-going public would have heard more continuity than change in works by Brahms or Mahler – perhaps less so with Strauss, whose premieres often became critical and public scan-dals, although mostly after the turn of the century. Still, if less pronounced than in literature and, especially, painting, the tendency to push the existing aesthetic envel-ope to the point where it began to burst and the hint of new artistic forms tumbled out was also present in music and characteristic of the arts in an age of uncertainty.

CHAPTER 12

THE POLITICS OF THE PEOPLE

To contemporaries, the second half of the 1860s might have seemed like a challenge to the politics of progress and gradual reform which had been a broader characteristic of the post-1850 decades. Yet in spite of a surge of mass politics, Great Power conflicts, including two large-scale, if ultimately limited, wars and the revolutionary episode of the Paris Commune, in the end the liberal ideas of progress and reform and the political style of the notables seemed, by the early 1870s, to have emerged triumphant. In much of Europe at different times during the 1870s and 1880s the liberal reform programme continued, often in more vigorous and demanding ways than before. Paradoxically, the result of this activity was not a strengthened liberalism but a weakened one, not a continuation of the politics of the notables, but a challenge to it. One reason for this result was that liberals overreached, believing a bit too much that their policies were at the vanguard of unstoppable political and social progress, leading to a vigorous reaction against them. The resulting political movements, in part a continuation of pre-1870s trends, in part novel developments of the last quarter of the nineteenth century, challenged liberalism. But this decline of liberalism also stemmed from social and economic changes, particularly the prolonged economic slowdown and declining prices of the late nineteenth century. It was also related to intellectual changes: the questioning of the idea of progress, the growth of notions of degeneration and of a Darwinism applied to human history and society. The upshot was not just a decline of liberalism and a rise of its opponents, but a broader political realignment.

HIGH POINT AND CRISIS OF LIBERALISM

Generally in the 1870s, although in some countries in the subsequent decade, liberal politics reached its nineteenth-century high point. Liberalism itself, as a result of post-1850 developments, had become increasingly broad and diverse. We can point to three separate patterns – not absolute distinctions, of course, but general tendencies – each of which held sway in different parts of Europe. In France, Switzerland, Great Britain and Scandinavia, liberalism was shot through with radical and democratic elements, more popular in character than elsewhere, more willing to consider the techniques of mass politics and to endorse an expanded franchise. By contrast, in the Low Countries, Italy, Spain and Romania, liberalism of the 1870s and 1880s preserved to a greater extent the heritage of notables' politics and a distance towards and scepticism about mass political participation. In the empires of central and eastern Europe, Germany, Austria-Hungary and Russia, there was a third pattern, in which possibilities for liberal politics were tied more closely to the government bureaucracy and liberalism was less of an independent political movement.

Common to all these different forms of liberalism was something of a shift of emphasis from the post-1850 decades. Liberals had been predominantly concerned then with creating a free market, establishing constitutional and parliamentary government, and supporting movements of national unification. It was not that these concerns vanished after 1870. Particularly in multinational empires, such as Austria-Hungary or Great Britain (one might not think of the nineteenth-century British Isles as a multinational empire, but there were plenty of people in Ireland who did), issues of national self-determination remained politically salient. But having achieved a considerable amount of success with these earlier priorities, liberals moved on to other matters which had previously not been at the top of the to-do list or at the centre of political confrontations. There were three major new issues: education, anti-clericalism and administration.

As noted in the discussion of education in Chapter 10, the 1870s and 1880s saw the vigorous expansion of public education across Europe, as new schools were built, compulsory education laws introduced or vigorously enforced and the number and salaries of schoolteachers increased. Expansion, though, was just one prong of the liberal educational programme; secularization was the other. Education was placed directly under government control – generally a combination of central and local government – and the influence and control of the churches decreased or eliminated altogether. Curricula were secularized and religious education reduced in importance.

This secularization of public education was part of a broader programme of anti-clericalism designed to reduce the influence of organized religion, particularly of the Catholic Church, in public life. Measures against the church were most extreme in Germany, where political life in the 1870s centred on the confrontation between the government and the Catholic Church, a politics dubbed by Germany's liberals a *Kulturkampf*, a struggle for civilization. The close relationship between state bureaucracy and central European liberalism was particularly apparent in this political struggle as the government resorted to distinctly authoritarian means, including the arrest of many of Germany's Catholic bishops and hundreds of priests, the expulsion of the Jesuits and the abolition of many of the religious orders and congregations. There were similar clashes between a government pursuing liberal and anti-clerical policies and a Catholic Church opposing these in Switzerland and Austria-Hungary, albeit in less dramatic fashion than in Germany. French liberals' return to political power at the end of the 1870s also marked the beginning of an anti-clerical policy that would include legalizing divorce, repealing restrictions on Sunday work, and secularizing public education, without – at least not yet – employing the more extreme, authoritarian measures used in central Europe.

By contrast, this strongly anti-clerical tinge of liberal policy was largely missing in the predominantly Protestant countries of northern Europe. Protestant churches had, as a group, not taken the intransigent stand against liberal ideas of progress that the Catholic Church under Pius IX had in its 1864 Syllabus of Errors or the 1870 declaration of Papal Infallibility. Also, contrasts between established Protestant churches and non-established 'free' or 'dissenting' churches, a characteristic feature of religious life in both Great Britain and the Scandinavian countries, diluted the potential confrontation between an anti-clerical liberalism and an established state church.

The third feature of liberal policy in this period was the realignment and reform of administration, characterized by a paradoxical mixture of decentralization and centralization. Liberal governments worked to turn city and village governments into arenas of local self-government and municipal autonomy. In countries where a centralized state had run local affairs, municipalities received greater autonomy. Cities, towns and villages received the right to elect their own mayors in France in 1884 and in Italy in 1888 (admittedly with the exception of Paris in France, and towns and villages with a population under 10,000 in Italy, where municipal government continued to be in the hands of the central state). Where local administrative autonomy existed, it was expanded and reformed. In Prussia, rural county administration was reformed in the 1870s, taking power away from the landed nobility – the first time this had happened in some sixty years. The Local Government and Public Health Acts of 1871 and 1872 in Great Britain expanded the powers of municipalities over poor relief and public health, and simplified the procedures needed to borrow money for public improvements and the provision of public services. In Russia of the 1870s, liberals pressed for increased power and radius of activities of the zemstvo, the organ of provincial self-government created during the Great Reforms of the previous decade. By far the largest and most controversial example of decentralization was the celebrated 1885 proposal of William Gladstone, the Liberal prime minister of Great Britain, for home rule, or as one might say today, regional autonomy, for Ireland. Such a proposal marked both the very acme of liberal efforts at decentralization and also the beginning of a reaction against them, an important part of the late nineteenth-century crisis of liberalism.

Liberal decentralization proposals went, perhaps oddly, hand in hand with parallel attempts at centralization. The liberal governments of newly united Italy and Germany, having got their inhabitants behind a common set of borders, also tried to bring them closer together within these borders. Measures to do so included the creation of a central bank and a common currency, a national post office, and the institution of a common criminal and civil code (not an easy undertaking; the creation of an all-German code of civil law took twenty years). Governments promoted the construction of branch railway lines, to bring more isolated rural areas into the net of national life. Such measures were not restricted to newly unified countries; the building of branch railways was also strongly supported by liberal governments in France during the 1880s.

Internal unification came with coercive features. The liberal government of the newly created German nation-state began demanding that its Polish-speaking citizens in the east and its French-speaking citizens of newly annexed Alsace-Lorraine use the national – German – language in public education and public meetings, a policy meeting strong resistance on the part of the indigenous populations. In France, the government's promotion of universal and secular education went along with a war on local dialects and non-French regional languages, such as Breton or Basque. Schoolchildren were required to learn and speak the official language of the nation.

Liberal provincial and clerical enemies coincided. The French and Polish national minorities in Germany were mostly Catholic and the church, itself under attack by the liberal government, supported the efforts of the minorities to use their own languages. In France, the church generally supported the dialects and non-French languages, with priests preaching and catechizing in them, and even seeing them as a bulwark against the liberal policy of secularization. As one priest in Brittany said, praising the use of Breton, 'It is in French that all the bad [secular, anti-clerical] books are published.'

Looking at this programme, both its relatively non-controversial aspects, such as codifying civil law and building railways, and its more discordant ones, such as taking on the Catholic Church or promising the Irish self-government, what we see is a broader effort to build on the successes of the previous quarter-century and to find ways to make them permanent. Codes of law and networks of rails would set future standards in ways that would solidify the changes of the 1850s and 1860s. A secular and nationalist public education would shape the minds of the coming adult generation in support of liberal social, economic and political principles. Potential opponents of this liberal future, the Catholic Church especially, but national minorities and regionalist provincials as well, would find their access to the public and their influence permanently circumscribed. An increase in local administrative autonomy, implemented under the watchful eyes of a liberal central government, would introduce a new venue for liberal politics and even expand – cautiously – the political universe, in ways that would be favourable to liberals.

This ambitious effort, although achieving certain successes, primarily in the less controversial aspects of the liberal programme, ultimately did not reach its goals for two main reasons. One was that liberals overreached themselves. In central Europe, the attack on the Catholic Church backfired. Rather than cutting off the faithful from the cultural or political influence of the clergy, it had the opposite effect, bringing the two closer together and increasing the influence of the church. Gladstone's bold effort to solve the 'Irish question' by keeping Ireland in the United Kingdom but granting it a very large measure of autonomy barely satisfied Irish nationalists while alienating a large portion of Gladstone's and the Liberal Party's own supporters.

In the Russian Empire, this liberal overreach occurred through the actions of the opposition, not the government. Increasingly frustrated with Tsar Alexander II's refusal to follow up his reforms of the 1860s with the introduction of a constitution and an elected legislature, young intellectuals turned to projects of political opposition, con-spiring at forms of radical revolution, ultimately leading to the practice of 'terror-ism' (probably the first usage of the word in the way it is employed today), planning the assassinations of government leaders, culminating with the shooting of the Tsar himself in 1881. Far from bringing on political reform, these terrorist acts promoted the victory of conservatives and downright reactionaries, under Alexander III, son and successor of the assassinated tsar.

The second reason for the failure of the liberal project was the change in the eco-nomic and cultural environment. The strong nineteenth-century liberal belief in the virtues of a free market was at odds with the economic crises of the 1870s and 1880s. Responses of liberal governments to these crises – basically, do nothing, since gov-ernment interference in the economy would only make things worse – did not prove to be very effective. Businessmen and farmers who had previously supported liberal politics became increasingly disillusioned with it. The growing disenchantment with the idea of progress, so closely identified with liberal politics, also undermined the political position of liberals and produced a growing cadre of thinkers and jour-nalists with different and opposing opinions. While liberals were striving to insti-tutionalize and make permanent the changes of the two post-1850 decades, many aspects of these changes were themselves becoming undone.

Such increasing difficulties of the liberal project in the 1870s and 1880s manifested themselves in two different ways. One was the revival of right-wing opposition to lib-eralism, in the form of a politicized ultramontanist Catholicism and of a revived and transformed conservatism. The other involved the transformation of political radi-calism, a process beginning in the 1880s and continuing down to the First World War. Pre-1870 radicalism, while not disappearing, tended to decline. In its place and emerging from it, there appeared two diametrically opposed groups: an organized socialist labour movement that would increasingly become the face of the political left in Europe, and a radical nationalism, often turning into a force on the extreme right, articulating racist and anti-Semitic ideas.

FORMS OF OPPOSITION TO LIBERALISM

Probably the single biggest political story of the 1870s and 1880s in central Europe – Germany, Austria-Hungary, Switzerland, Belgium and the Netherlands – was the creation and success of a Catholic political party. An important background to this development was the rise of ultramontane Catholicism during the middle decades of the nineteenth century. Reshaping popular piety by promoting pilgrimages and processions and devotions to the Sacred Heart and the Virgin Mary, increasing the effectiveness and cohesion of the ecclesiastical hierarchy, and the influence of the clergy on the faithful, promoting the formation of voluntary associations under clerical leadership, ultramontane Catholicism was also a sharp critic of the liberal ideas of progress and positivism. Yet, before 1870, this religious, cultural and social movement had not been politically very well organized or influential. Two important developments of the years 1865 to 1880 changed this state of affairs and led directly to the politicization of the ultramontane movement.

One was the outcome of the wars of 1866 and 1870, in which the Catholic Great Powers, Austria and France, were defeated by an eminently Protestant Prussia. These wars also led to the incorporation of all the territory under the rule of the Pope into the Italian nation-state. Following the 1870 entry of Italian troops into Rome, Pius IX, both the symbol and the promoter of ultramontane Catholicism, proclaimed himself a 'prisoner of the Vatican', a prisoner whose position as head of the worldwide Catholic Church was now compromised by Italian national unity.

The second development was the actions of liberal governments from the late 1860s onward. Whether requiring civil marriage, introducing free, compulsory and secular public education, or expelling the Jesuits, these governments seemed bent on taking actions that drastically offended Catholic sensibilities, opposed Catholics' moral values, and threatened the freedom and independence of the church. In the eyes of both liberals and Catholics, outcomes of the wars and the actions of the liberal governments blended together. As one Catholic newspaper in Germany announced in 1874: 'The liberal leaders declare that the war is now just really starting; we have made peace with France; with Rome (that is, the Catholic Church), we will never make peace.'[22]

This feeling of being under siege, of 'religion in danger', propelled the rapid organization and equally rapid success of Catholic political parties. First formed in 1871, the Centre Party, what Germany's Catholics called their group, was already the second-strongest political party at the elections in 1874 and had gained the support of about 80 per cent of Catholic voters. After liberals in Belgium introduced a system of free, compulsory and secular public education in 1879, Catholic politicians reorganized, gained the support of a majority of the electorate and ended a twenty-five-year period of liberal rule. The Catholic party would dominate Belgian politics until the First World War.

Although the political background of most of the leaders of these parties was generally on the conservative side of the political spectrum, the parties themselves were characterized by vigorous mass political agitation, complete with public meetings, and large membership political organizations. The Association of German Catholics, which agitated in favour of the Centre Party until it was prohibited by the government, counted some 60,000 members and was the largest explicitly political group in central Europe between the revolutions of 1848 and the rise of large-scale political organization in the 1890s.

The Catholic parties of course opposed the liberal governments' anti-clerical and secularizing measures. They tended to be sceptical of liberal ideas about economics too, showing a preference for protectionism and the guild system, and endorsing government economic intervention. In areas where most of the employers were Protestant, as was the case in the industrial regions of western Germany, these parties were willing to support trade unions as well. Catholic politicians were generally opposed to liberal plans for centralization; they supported and encouraged the demands of the (strongly Catholic) French and Polish national minorities in Germany for use of their native language in public life; in Belgium they were closely associated with the Flemish-speaking population, then generally poorer and less influential than the French-speaking Walloons.

This Catholic politics played less well in much of western Europe. In Italy, Pius IX condemned the Kingdom of Italy and demanded that devout Catholics have no part in its government. Pius's successor as Pope on his death in 1878, Leo XIII, was in many respects more moderate, but he continued his predecessor's hard line on Italy so that a Catholic political party could not come into existence there. There were somewhat belated efforts to construct a similar Catholic political party in France, but they met with little success, in part because France's Catholics were, as a group, less devout and more given over to anti-clericalism (something that could be said of many Catholics in Italy and Spain, too), in part because devout Catholics in France were oriented politically in other ways, supporting adherents of a restoration of the monarchy or the imperial rule of the Bonaparte dynasty, or, somewhat later, of a conservative republic.

In Ireland, the generally quite conservative and ultramontane Catholic hierarchy lined up behind the adherents of Irish nationalism and their demand for autonomy or home rule. These Irish nationalists were generally allied with the Liberal Party, making the United Kingdom one of the very few places in Europe where the Catholic Church and the liberal movement came to some sort of agreement. This agreement, though, was only in the House of Commons – and even that would prove controversial. At the local level, English Liberals and Irish Nationalists had their own separate political worlds: Catholic Ireland, where the Irish nationalists had largely driven the Liberals out of politics, and Protestant England, where the Liberals and the Tories battled it out as to which could be the most Protestant political party.

If Catholic political parties played an important role in bringing the liberal era to an end, with a few exceptions, such as Belgium, they were not the main beneficiaries of the end of liberal dominance. Rather, it was conservative parties and conservative politicians who came to power in the 1880s and 1890s and much of the conservative politics of this era is linked to the conservatives' leaders, such as Robert Cecil, Marquis of Salisbury (1830–1902), the Tory prime minster of Great Britain, Constantine Pobedonostsev (1827–1907), head of the Holy Synod (the Russian government administration of the Orthodox Church) and close adviser of Alexander III of Russia, Eduard von Taaffe (1833–95), Austrian prime minister from 1879 to 1893, and Germany's chancellor, Otto von Bismarck, who, after an initial period in the 1860s as an innovative conservative politician, and another in the 1870s leading a largely liberal government, reinvented himself as a different kind of conservative during the last twelve or so years of his career, from 1878 to 1890. Looking at them together, we can see distinct features of conservative politics in the late nineteenth century, building on some of the initiatives of innovative conservatives of the 1860s, such as Disraeli, Napoleon III and the younger Bismarck, but also differing from them and taking political conservatism in a new direction.

One place where we can see clear lines of continuity with pre-1870 conservatism is in favourable attitudes towards nationalism and warfare, although due to clever diplomacy, changing arenas of military expansion and the altered balance of power, they had the advantage of a warlike foreign policy without ever actually having to go to war with another Great Power. Conservatives of the late nineteenth century increasingly embraced an aggressive and chauvinistic nationalism, characterized by the desire to aggrandize their own nationality and promote its superiority over others. Under Bismarck's conservative policies of the 1880s, the German government took an even harsher line towards the Polish and French national minorities than it had when Bismarck was endorsing the liberals in the 1870s. The one issue which led to a two-decades-long period of Tory domination in Great Britain was the opposition to home rule, or self-government, for Ireland, in effect a demand for the subordination of the Irish to English domination. Tsar Alexander III and his adviser Pobedonostsev vigorously worked to Russify the many nationalities in the empire, prohibiting, for instance the use of non-Russian languages, particularly Polish, in primary education. Conservatives all across Europe supported imperialist ventures in this period, leaving no doubt about their nationality's superiority to colonized peoples in Africa, Asia or the South Seas. The Marquis of Salisbury combined different forms of aggrandizing nationalism by asserting, in a notorious election speech in 1886, that the Irish were no more capable of self-government than the Hottentots in Africa. The one major exception to this attitude occurred in the multinational Austro-Hungarian Empire, where conservative leaders continued the older tradition of opposing nationalism, since granting demands of the different nationalist movements would have brought the empire to an end.

If conservatives of Louis Napoleon's day had endorsed economic growth via free trade, their counterparts of the last quarter of the nineteenth century were, in a noticeably less prosperous economic environment, much more sceptical of the free market. Strong endorsement of protective tariffs was one way that conservatives were able to undermine liberal positions. Conservative hostility to free markets showed a strong west–east gradient. Even supporting protective tariffs was a minority position among the British Tories, testimony to the power of free market ideas in Britain. Conservatives in France, Italy and Spain generally endorsed protectionism; their counterparts in central Europe went further, by restoring the guilds. In Russia, Alexander III could not quite consider restoring serfdom, although he did make a vague gesture in that direction by instituting the office of the 'land captain', a nobleman in each canton who had the power to order peasants around and override the decisions of their village government. Yet even Alexander III's very conservative government did not oppose the growth of industry in his realm, as early nineteenth-century conservatives had, and, in fact, took measures to encourage it.

The innovative conservatives of the 1850s and 1860s took great pains to present themselves as friends of the working class. Some of that attitude did continue into the later part of the century. In a sensational move, Bismarck introduced public health insurance for blue-collar workers in Germany in 1881, quickly following up this initiative with programmes of disability insurance and old-age pensions. Count Taaffe, Bismarck's Austrian counterpart, followed his example, but conservatives elsewhere in Europe showed no such enthusiasm for social insurance programmes. Tories in Great Britain did try to gain workers' support, not on economic issues but on cultural ones – aggressively promoting Anglican Protestantism and vigorously defending the right of the workers to spend as much of their free time in pubs as possible, against the many Liberals who were dissenting Protestants, enemies of the state church and friends of teetotalism. More characteristic of late nineteenth-century conservatives, though, was an orientation towards the lower middle class, restoring the guilds in central Europe, and supporting the interests and concerns of clerks and salesmen in Great Britain, establishing a close connection between the Tories and white-collar occupations which would continue for the following century.

Late nineteenth-century conservatism also demonstrated three political features typical of the social and cultural climate of the age of uncertainty. One was a scepticism about the idea of progress, an idea conservatives linked with their political opponents. As the Marquis of Salisbury, a Tory noted for both his intellectual reflection and his quirky sense of humour, remarked, 'When the Liberals tell you they are the party of progress, is it impertinent to ask them where they are progressing to?'[23] If conservatives tried to tie an increasingly discredited idea of progress to their liberal opponents, they tried to claim for themselves the mantle of the defence of property – not just the property of the landed nobility as had been the case in the past, but of commercial, industrial and financial property as well. Promoting protectionism, denouncing trade unions and a still nascent socialist labour movement, conservatives attempted, with some success, to represent themselves as the political tendency that would defend business against the economic and social dangers threatening it.

This effort at becoming the party of all property was enhanced by another unique feature of the era, the extent to which conservatives were able to gain the political alliance of groups of liberals. The 1886 and 1887 elections in Great Britain and Germany, respectively, saw a group of liberals, the Liberal Unionists in Britain and the National Liberals in Germany, form an electoral alliance and a post-election parliamentary coalition with conservative political groupings. Economic considerations, including support for lower taxes, protectionism and opposition to unions, played a role in these alliances, but the most important role was undoubtedly played by nationalism. The pro-Tory liberals in Great Britain called themselves Liberal Unionists, endorsing the Conservatives' opposition to home rule for Ireland and their fervent wish to keep the United Kingdom united. Their German counterparts strongly supported Chancellor Bismarck's call for substantial increases in the strength of the armed forces to deal with the ostensible danger of a revenge-seeking attack by Germany's defeated rival France.

Another example of such a liberal–conservative coalition at about the same time, although with nationalist liberals as the senior partner, occurred in Italy under the prime minister Francesco Crispi (1819–1901). A one-time radical and close associate of Garibaldi, Crispi's policies, although including some liberal ideas such as local government reform, were increasingly focused on the implementation of protective tariffs, the promotion of nationalism, the repression of the labour movement and the cultivation of an Italian overseas empire in Africa, all policy points which won his government support from a growing number of conservatives.

Liberal–conservative coalitions, which governed Great Britain, Germany and Italy in the years around 1890, did have some historical precedent, particularly during the very unusual circumstances of the revolutions of 1848, but for most of the nineteenth century, liberals and conservatives were strongly at odds. Even a partial agreement between them was a novelty and reflected the unsettling circumstances of the 1870s and 1880s.

RADICALISM DIVIDED AND TRANSFORMED

Looking at the left end of the political spectrum, one might expect the economic and social difficulties and the broader feeling of uncertainty prevalent in the late nineteenth century to have been favourable for political radicalism, allowing leftists to recover from the defeat they had suffered at the time of the Paris Commune. In some ways, this was the case, as the 1880s and early 1890s saw a number of new, radical political initiatives. Although often emerging from a common origin, these initiatives proved to be quite different, leading in diametrically opposed political directions – and generally not coordinated with existing forms of radical politics. The upshot was a divided radical politics that was more disturbing or even threatening than effective.

One clear example of new forms of radical politics was the rise of socialist political parties. While there had been socialist ideas and socialist political tendencies present in Europe since the 1820s, socialists had generally worked within a broader left-wing political climate, as had been the case in the International Workingmen's Association of the 1860s and the Paris Commune in 1871. This situation changed very quickly in the last quarter of the century, as working-class-based and working-class-oriented political parties were created by radical activists. Between 1875 and 1896, no less than twenty-three different socialist or social-democratic parties were founded in Europe, including, to mention just a few, in Germany (1875), Spain (1879), France and Hungary (1880), the Netherlands (1881), Belgium (1885), Switzerland (1888), Austria and Sweden (1889), Serbia and Italy (1892).[24]

For most of the 1870s and 1880s, these parties were still new and not very impressive, enjoying little support in Great Britain, divided into squabbling sectarian groups in France, or illegal, as were socialist parties in Germany and Austria-Hungary during the 1880s and in Russia until 1905. (Ironically, leftists in the Tsar's empire who focused on organizing workers were the moderates compared with their counterparts who promoted the terrorist assassination of high government officials.) The one real breakthrough in popular support came towards the end of the period, in 1890, when the social democrats in Germany received about 20 per cent of the votes cast in the general elections of that year, about as many as all the liberal parties or all the conservative parties together. Similar political victories for socialists elsewhere in Europe would have to wait until the first decade of the twentieth century.

Yet the nascent socialist labour movement had an impact that went well beyond the modest ranks of its adherents. Behind them loomed the many massive strikes that broke out across Europe in the 1880s and early 1890s. The socialists had not organized these largely spontaneous strikes, and the strikers themselves generally had no socialist or any other political affiliation. Rather than socialists inspiring the strikers, the latter inspired the socialists. Representatives of socialist parties from a number of European countries met in Paris in 1889 to found a league of socialist parties, quickly dubbed the 'Second International' in reference to the International Workingmen's Asssociation which had dissolved in the 1870s. The new group's chief activity was to issue an appeal for public demonstrations on 1 May, May Day, in favour of a workplace-oriented goal, an eight-hour working day. Sure enough, 1 May 1890 did see such demonstrations in urban areas of many parts of Europe.

With this measure, the socialists made the many large-scale strikes of the late 1880s their own. Combined with the uncertainty generated by the difficult economic conditions prevailing in the period, this advocacy made the still quite modest socialist movement appear impressive and threatening. Francesco Crispi, the moderate liberal Italian prime minister, articulated this fear when he announced in 1888: 'Modern socialists are enemies of the family, of property and of the fatherland. They give new opportunities to would-be thieves to loot and steal. Today people are trying to deceive and seduce and to disguise what is really an attack on property and the family with misleading phrases.'[25]

As socialists were very slowly organizing themselves and gradually making headway, a different form of radicalism was having a larger and more dramatic impact on politics in Europe during the later 1880s and 1890s. Like the socialists, these new forms of radicalism originated in the broader radical political milieu; also like the socialists, in the tradition of political radicalism they were committed to mass political mobilization. In contrast to the socialists, with their orientation towards the labour movement and their international political connections, these radicals tended to stress older political themes of the left: nationalism, hostility to banks and big business, and support for small business, master craftsmen and small farmers – a political stance generally accompanied by a generous dose of hostility to the Jews. One more feature of this radicalism deserves particular attention because it set the stage for political events for the next five or six decades: these radicals obtained substantial support, both open and covert, from the political right and pioneered a new form of right-wing mass politics.

One such radical was the French general Georges Boulanger (1837–91), one of the few pro-republican generals in the French army, with close ties to radical politicians, whose furious 1888 political campaign against political corruption and the influence on politics of banks and big business and for a nationalist war of revenge on Germany, brought him to the brink of political power – which he might have achieved had he heeded his followers' demands to march on the Elysée Palace (seat of the French parliament) rather than hiding in his mistress's apartment. It later turned out that Boulanger's campaign had been financed by royalists and extreme conservatives, and many, perhaps even most, of the voters who supported him came from the right.

Other such radicals were the two ethnically German Austrian leftists, Karl Lueger (1844–1910) and Georg Ritter von Schönerer (1842–1921), both supporters of the radical Linz programme of 1882; a fellow radical and adherent of the programme was Viktor Adler (1852–1918), who would go on to found the social democratic party in Austria. Schönerer and Lueger, though, went in other political directions. The former became a militant German nationalist, calling for the secession of the ethnic Germans from the Austrian Empire and their adherence to the German nation-state. He also developed into a vehement, obsessed anti-Semite, denouncing Jews as 'sucking vampires', exploiting Germanic farmers and craftsmen, sending his followers to beat up Jewish journalists. Similarly radical and anti-Semitic politicians, with similar sorts of campaigns, appeared in Germany itself in the late 1880s and early 1890s.

Lueger, by contrast, began associating with Catholic conservatives and never played the nationalist card quite so blatantly as did Schönerer. Instead, he launched an appeal to the small businessmen, master craftsmen and small property owners of Vienna, condemning both the socialist labour movement and the large capitalists as their enemies, and asserting that behind both groups of enemies of the lower middle class were the Jews. Eventually elected mayor of Vienna in 1897, Lueger enormously impressed a young Austrian provincial who had moved to the capital city. In his memoirs, Adolf Hitler would describe Lueger as the 'greatest man of his day'.

The mention of Hitler is not coincidental. The sort of radical but anti-socialist, often nationalistic and generally anti-Semitic mass politics represented by these figures (while Boulanger himself was not an anti-Semite, his former followers were deeply involved in anti-Semitic movements in France during the 1890s), first developed in the 1880s, was clearly at the origins of fascist movements in Europe after the First World War. Both these mass right-wing movements and the socialists developed out of broader radicalism in this period. Between the two offshoots, the radicals who continued to appeal to an older political tradition of support for democracy and republicanism, and some non-class-specific governmental support for the common people, had a harder time, losing voters, supporters and influence. In western Europe, especially in Great Britain, France or Switzerland, radical political parties or political tendencies maintained themselves fairly well, although generally as part of a broader coalition with more moderate liberals; in Denmark and Norway, the 1880s even saw the triumph of *Venstre* (left) parties, with a radical agenda. By contrast, in central and eastern Europe, one of the important political realignments of the age of uncertainty was the declining fortunes of an older political radicalism.

NATIONALISM, RACISM AND ANTI-SEMITISM

The development of anti-Semitism in radical movements of the 1880s moving from the left to the right was part of a broader feature of politics in this period: the rise of more intransigent and frequently racist forms of nationalism and the reorientation of hostility towards the Jews into a new form, dubbed with a name coined during this time, anti-Semitism.

The years around 1880 in particular saw a wave of vehement hostility towards Jews in central and eastern Europe. In 1881, there were some 250 anti-Semitic riots in the Russian Empire, where enraged mobs attacked Jewish districts, destroying homes and businesses, assaulting, raping, looting and killing their inhabitants. The Russian word used for these riots, *pogrom*, was quickly applied to anti-Jewish mob violence more broadly. Although contemporaries suspected the Tsar's authorities of having secretly fomented the riots, evidence since uncovered by historians suggests this suspicion is incorrect. However, it also shows that the authorities demonstrated remarkably little enthusiasm about taking action to bring this extreme public disorder to an end, and that they decided in some cases the best way to pacify the situation was to expel as many Jews as possible from the affected locality.

In central Europe, action against the Jews was usually more disciplined and orderly. A massive petition drive, counting half a million signatures, to the German legislature was launched, demanding that Jews be stripped of their citizenship. At the same time, in the Hungarian town of Tisza, Jews were arrested and accused of killing Christian children and using their blood in religious rituals. These charges of ritual murder would arise in eastern and central Europe repeatedly over the next twenty years.

These actions marked a dramatic reversal of a decades-long history of progress, of the gradual granting of legal equality to Jews across Europe. To contemporaries, these actions against the Jews, both violent and orderly, were a very visible sign of the end of the age of progress. They seemed like a reversion to backward, medieval bigotry, undermining the triumph of scientific principles and of liberal political ideas so characteristic of the post-1850 decades.

The so-called blood libel, the accusation that Jews used the blood of Christians in religious rituals, was, in fact, a product of the Middle Ages, but the growth of hostility towards the Jews in the 1880s was at least as much a result of modern, scientific, intellectual developments as it was a religious atavism. A typical feature of hostility to Jews in the period was a reorientation from a perception of Jews as practitioners of a non-Christian religion, to Jews as members of a distinct racial group, the Semites. The German author Wilhelm Marr (1819–1904), in his 1879 book *The Victory of Jewry over the Teutons*, coined a new phrase to describe hostility to Jews as members of a racial group: 'anti-Semitism'. The new name caught on quickly, and within three years the first international Anti-Semitic Congress was meeting in Dresden.

This new understanding of what it meant to be a Jew, derived from applications – or misapplications – of Darwin's theories, prevalent at the time, implied a fundamentally different basis for hostility towards Jews. If hostility towards Jews was the result of their accepting a different religion, one that many Christians saw as cursed by God, then changing their religion, converting to Christianity, would, at least in theory, remove the basis of hostility. By contrast, if being Jewish was a matter of heredity, of belonging to a 'Semitic' as opposed to an 'Aryan' race, then Jews' nature, and the grounds for hostility towards them, were biologically fixed and could never be changed. Jews who became Christians would still be, racially, Jews. Followers of the Austrian anti-Semite Georg Ritter von Schönerer used to sing a little ditty about this, which would later become a favourite of the Nazi SS: 'Jew or Christian, it's the same to me / Race is the problem, don't you see?' Looking back in 1899, the French conservative Count Edouard de Lur-Saluces described very precisely this shift in opinion in the recent past:

> . . . a few years ago . . . many people found anti-Semitism to be frightening . . . they evoked the specter of religious wars. Today . . . there is a sense that individual beliefs are not at issue. Everyone has understood that we are struggling *against a race* and defending ourselves against its cosmopolitan power.[26]

This racial attitude, as we have noted above, typical of intellectual and cultural life at the time, also came increasingly to be applied to the understanding of differences as nationalities. Different national groups were perceived as belonging to different races; conflicts of nationalities appeared as biologically inevitable struggles for existence. Schönerer, whose extreme attitudes make his assertions particularly useful for historians, since he came right out and said what others thought more discreetly, once asserted that equality between Germanic and Slavic races was impossible, as impossible as equality between a lion and a louse. In other words, his nationality was a race at a biologically more advanced level than the race of opposing nationalities.

Just as a biological understanding of what it meant to be Jewish created a new and much more intransigent form of hostility to Jews, such a biological understanding of national differences also had consequences for conflicts between nationalities in the multinational Austrian and Ottoman Empires, or for relations to national minorities in nation-states, such as the German Empire. If nationality was primarily cultural in nature, then one national group could attempt to assimilate another by encouraging it, or forcing it, to adopt the first group's language and national culture. The policies of the liberal German government during the 1870s towards Germany's Polish and French national minorities were governed by such an assumption; the efforts of the French government to eliminate the use of regional dialects and non-French language in education followed along similar lines.

If nations were biologically created entities, then simply changing a people's culture and language would not change their national identity, and, if culture and language were linked to biology, the whole effort would be doomed to failure. Conflicts between nationalities could only end with the expulsion or even extermination of the defeated nationality. The full effect of such biological conceptions of nationhood would only be seen in the twentieth-century age of total war. In the 1880s these were still ideas, and by no means universally accepted ones. Politically, the nationalities' conflict in the Austro-Hungarian Empire was quite subdued; the conservative 'Iron Ring' government of Count Taaffe strictly opposed the ideas of German nationalists and accepted the support of Polish, Czech or Slovene nationalists only if they muted very substantially their political demands.

New, biological understandings of differences between religions or nationalities were by no means universally accepted, nor were they necessary for the expression of violent hostility. Participants in the Russian pogroms of 1881 had never heard of Charles Darwin or his theories of natural selection; accusations that Jews used the blood of Christian children in their religious rituals did not necessarily have any racial overtones. In Romania, of all European countries the one whose official policies were most hostile to the Jews, intellectuals rejected racial theories and proclaimed their vehement hostility to the country's Jewish population as a result of its not sharing the dominant religion or cultural tradition. Still, it is hard to avoid the impression that a new, harder, more intransigent attitude towards national and religious differences was making its way around Europe as an integral part of the political developments of the age of uncertainty, and that biological understandings of these differences were an important justification for such attitudes.

CHAPTER 13

THE POLITICS OF THE POWERS

If the keynote of European diplomacy in the years 1850 to 1871 had been the confrontation of the Great Powers, leading to wars between them in 1853–56, 1859, 1866 and 1870–71, circumstances would be quite different in the following two decades. Then, the diplomatic scene would be characterized by a freezing of Great Power confrontations in the European heartland, and a turning outwards of policy, ambitions and potential conflicts. This outward turn was focused on two quite different regions: one was in the Balkans, in south-eastern Europe, the latest version of the perennial Eastern Question, while the other was overseas, in Africa, Asia and the Pacific, in what has come to be known as the 'new imperialism'. These three developments – the end to direct Great Power confrontations, the renewed saliency of the Eastern Question and the striking rise of overseas expansion – were the main features of international relations in Europe between the early 1870s and the mid-1890s.

BISMARCK'S ALLIANCE SYSTEM

To understand the reasons for the end of almost two decades of warfare between the Great Powers, we need to consider the position of the newly formed German Empire as it emerged from war between Prussia and the other German states on the one hand, and France on the other, in 1870–71. Otto von Bismarck, who was the chancellor, the head of government, and very much in charge of foreign policy, from the empire's creation in 1871 until his forced retirement in 1890, saw the post-1890 united German nation-state not only as the most powerful on the continent but also, as he said, a 'saturated power', content with the post-1871 status quo and determined to preserve it. The chief danger to this status quo, Bismarck thought, would be a French war of revenge, but to engage successfully in such a war France would need a Great Power ally.

The Kingdom of Italy, united into a nation-state at the same time as Germany, was a Great Power by courtesy only; its economic, diplomatic and, especially, military capabilities were no serious danger to the Germans. Great Britain was a more serious prospect, but its government, under both Liberal and Conservative leadership, had been, since the 1850s, moving away from playing a military role in continental Europe to concentrate its efforts and expenditures on its overseas empire. The statement of the Tory prime minister Lord Salisbury that Great Britain would pursue a policy of 'splendid isolation', comes from the 1890s, but its spirit was already apparent two decades earlier. This left as potential French allies just Austria-Hungary and Russia. The key to Bismarck's policy was to be on good terms with both of these Great Powers, thus fully isolating France.

Bismarck accommodated these two Powers by enmeshing them in a series of treaty obligations, the League of the Three Emperors (that is, the emperors of Germany, Austria-Hungary and Russia) of 1873, and the Alliance of the Three Emperors of 1881. Complementing the tripartite structures, and, by the end of the 1880s, replacing them, were separate treaty structures involving Germany and one of the two Powers: the Triple Alliance of 1882, linking Germany, Austria-Hungary and Italy, and the German–Russian Reinsurance Treaty, or, as we would say today, non-aggression pact, of 1887. This elaborate network of treaty obligations has come to be known as the 'alliance system', and has often been regarded as one of the causes of the First World War. This observation is inaccurate. Bismarck's original alliance system was for the purpose of preserving Germany's strong but not totally dominant position that it had won in the war with France in 1870–71, to be achieved by preventing another war instead of preparing for one. The First World War emerged not from the alliance system but from its collapse.

The potential problems in Bismarck's system were twofold: Germany maintaining good relations with both Austria-Hungary and Russia, and Austria-Hungary and Russia maintaining good relations with each other. Both these problems would prove increasingly difficult to resolve, although, Bismarck, utilizing to the maximum his very considerable diplomatic skills, was able to keep them at bay for twenty years. His successors were not so fortunate, and even in the last years of Bismarck's term of office the difficulties were becoming increasingly apparent.

Although Prussia's dominance in central Europe emerged from its 1866 defeat of Austria, and the Prussian kingdom and the Tsar's empire had been on good terms since the late eighteenth century, it was German–Russian relations which created post-1871 problems, not German–Austrian ones. The Habsburg monarch, Franz Joseph, and his officials contented themselves with the role of Germany's junior partner. They looked to the German Empire as a power that could guarantee the existence of Austria-Hungary against the intertwined danger of foreign war and unrest among the monarchy's many nationalities.

By contrast, German–Russian relations became steadily tenser in the post-1870 decades. Economic issues played a major role, the introduction of protective tariffs on agriculture in Germany cutting off the Russian Empire, a major grain-exporting country, from a lucrative foreign market. Another reason for growing tensions was racialized thinking about international relations. From the late 1880s onwards, statesmen, army officers and journalists in both countries began to perceive their relations as part of a potential conflict between Teutonic and Slavic racial groups – a conflict which, in the social Darwinist interpretation of the world was inevitable and unavoidable. Bismarck himself never thought in such racialized terms, but as Bismarck aged and a younger generation, more open to racial thinking, came to occupy high government posts by the late 1880s, a group that would have the ear of the new German emperor, Wilhelm II, the potential for conflict increased considerably.

THE RETURN OF THE EASTERN QUESTION

If German–Russian relations were becoming increasingly strained in the 1880s, relations between Russia and the Austro-Hungarian Empire, the other major element of Bismarck's alliance system, had a built-in source of tension, the Eastern Question, the problems raised by the declining power of the Ottoman Empire. The Eastern Question had already estranged the Tsarist and Habsburg Monarchies, at the time of the Crimean War, and it heated up again in the 1870s. The decade between 1875 and 1885 saw the question of the future shape of the Balkans reach a new intensity, with war between Russia and the Ottoman Empire in 1877–78 opening the possibility of a broader war between the Great Powers. While the difficult issues developing were ultimately resolved in peaceful fashion, another triumph of Bismarck's diplomatic skill, the resulting settlement contributed to a further estrangement between Russia and Austria-Hungary, further undermining Bismarck's larger effort to maintain peacefully Germany's leading position among the Great Powers.

There were a number of reasons for the return of the Eastern Question to the diplomatic centre stage in this period, all linked with the broader trends in the post-1871 age of uncertainty. Economic difficulties further weakened the already precarious hold of the Ottoman Empire on the region. The triumphant conclusion of German and Italian national unification encouraged both indigenous nationalist movements and the policies of the semi-sovereign states of the region – the principalities of Serbia and Montenegro and the United Principalities of Moldavia and Wallachia. These new developments tended to force the hands of Great Powers, who were drawn into a potential confrontation with each other. While they succeeded in avoiding this confrontation, many of the issues generating it increased over time, so that the Eastern Question would ultimately lead Europe into the First World War.

The banking and financial crisis developing in the 1870s, and the ensuing period of slow economic growth, placed the Ottoman Empire in a difficult position. Already heavily indebted to European creditors – by 1875, about half the government budget was going to pay interest on the debt – the Sultan's officials were forced to renounce payments in 1876 and officially declare a state bankruptcy three years later. Attempts to increase taxes to avert this disastrous outcome led to the 1875 uprising in Bosnia-Herzegovina, rapidly spreading to Bulgaria, which initiated the crisis decade in south-eastern Europe.

Ottoman rule in the Balkans had been regularly punctuated by uprisings in the nineteenth century, and generally the Sultan's armed forces, badly organized and undersupplied and underpaid as they usually were, had proved capable of dealing with them, provided there was no outside interference. The 1875 insurgents were supported by the semi-sovereign European principalities of the region, still nominally subject to Ottoman rule but enjoying considerable autonomy – Serbia, Montenegro, and the largest and most powerful of these realms, the United Principalities of Moldavia and Wallachia. They had been ruled by one prince since 1859, with a joint constitution since 1864, and since 1866 under the rule of Prince Karl (in Romanian, Carol; 1839–1914) from the Hohenzollerns of south-western Germany. Political precedents from western Europe, particularly the national unification of Italy in the 1860s, encouraged these principalities; Serbia, in particular, hoped to become 'the Slavic Piedmont of the Balkan Peninsula'.[27] The government of Greece, which had won its independence from Turkish rule in 1830 but still had territorial claims on the Ottoman Empire, also joined in supporting anti-Ottoman insurgencies.

In these events of 1875–76, and again in a further uprising in Bulgaria in 1884, it was indigenous forces in the Balkans which initiated the crisis and forced the hand of the Great Powers, quite in contrast to the previous flare-up of the Eastern Question during the Crimean War, when the Great Powers – in that case, Russia, France and Great Britain – had taken the initiative and the indigenous political forces had followed. The intervention of the Great Powers, above all the Russians, remained the decisive element, though. Russian policy ranged from encouraging individual volunteers to join the wars and uprisings, to what we might today call covert action (secretly providing weapons and military leadership), to open and massive military intervention, with aims ranging from the modest – full independence for the semi-sovereign Balkan principalities – to the more aggressive – a reorganization of the entire region into Russian satellite states – to the extreme – the conquest of Istanbul and the partition of the Ottoman Empire.

Unlike the previous Balkan crisis during the Crimean War, when Napoleon III's Second Empire had opposed the Russians, the weakened and defeated French Republic of the 1870s carefully avoided involvement in the Eastern Crisis. By contrast, the Conservative British government under Disraeli was quite as active in the 1870s as its Liberal predecessor had been in the 1850s in determinedly resisting Russian actions – although in the 1870s this proved to be possible without needing to go to war – and propping up the Ottoman Empire. There were ideological distinctions – the 1850s liberals proclaimed their political opposition to the reactionary Russian Empire whereas Disraeli presented opposition to Russia in terms of Great Power self-interest and nationalist self-assertion – but the basic diplomatic reasons for British involvement remained the same: to secure the eastern Mediterranean and links to India against Russian power.

The Austrian Empire had played an ambiguous role in the Crimean War, largely alienating both sides. The renamed Austro-Hungarian Empire, by contrast, achieved much greater diplomatic success in the Balkan crises of 1875–85, limiting the expansion of Russian power and increasing the influence of the Habsburg Monarchy in the Balkans – and accomplishing all this without fundamentally alienating the Russians, since it was Britain which did the heavy diplomatic work in opposing Russia's plans for the expansion of its territory and influence. If the Habsburgs' diplomatic success was greater in this second round of Balkan confrontations, the dangers it posed to the monarchy were more grave, a reflection of the development of nationalism over the two decades since the previous crisis of the Eastern Question.

The crisis of the 1870s was all about the creation of nation-states from the body of the multinational Ottoman Empire, raising the unpleasant prospect that the multinational Austro-Hungarian Empire might be carved up in similar fashion. The way different nationalist groups in the Austro-Hungarian Empire lined up on different sides of the crisis made that threat painfully clear. Czech and Romanian nationalists raised money for the anti-Ottoman insurgents, celebrated their victories and even volunteered to join the fighting. The liberal Hungarian government encouraged Hungarian nationalists to support the Turks, and Hungarian and Polish nationalist volunteers formed armed detachments that fought on the side of the Ottomans. In effect, the nationalist movements in the Austro-Hungarian Empire were divided into pro- and anti-Russian forces: their proposed policies, besides threatening the empire's actual policy in the crisis, showed the potential for the disintegration of the multinational realm of the Habsburgs into different, hostile nation-states. While the empire survived the 1875–85 crisis of the Eastern Question, and even, under the conservative Austrian Iron Ring government of the 1880s, was able to tame, temporarily, competing nationalist movements, their potential dangers, exposed in the middle decades of the 1870s, remained. The next crisis of the Eastern Question in the years 1908 to 1913 would renew this danger to the empire, and in a period of greatly expanded nationalist movements. The ultimate response of the government of Austria-Hungary to this renewed manifestation of the Eastern Question would bring on the First World War.

The position of the Kingdom of Prussia during the Crimean War was very similar to that of its successor state, the German Empire, during the Eastern Crisis of the 1870s and 1880s. Both the Prussian kingdom and the German Empire claimed no strategic or diplomatic interest in south-eastern Europe. Bismarck explained his policy in a celebrated phrase when he asserted that the Balkans were 'not worth the bones of a single Pomeranian grenadier'. If equally disinterested, Bismarck's Germany was much more powerful and influential than 1850s Prussia, so it was more actively involved in diplomacy, mediating between Austrian-Hungary and Russia and between Russia and Great Britain, successfully sponsoring diplomatic initiatives and international conferences, which ultimately defused the tensions between the Powers.

The decade-long period of political upheaval, military action and diplomatic uncertainty concerning the Balkans was, in part, a repeat of previous confrontations over the region, ranging from the Greek and Serbian uprisings of the early decades of the nineteenth century to the Crimean War of the 1850s. Some features of the situation, such as the decline of Ottoman power, Russian expansion, British concern about the eastern Mediterranean, were characteristic of past crises, and could even be dated back to the eighteenth century. By contrast, nationalist themes, while not entirely lacking in past crises of the Eastern Question, played a larger role in the actions of the inhabitants and governments of both the Balkans and Austria-Hungary in the later nineteenth century. While the conflicting positions of the Great Powers, and the clashing demands of nationalist movements could ultimately be resolved, the underlying tensions would return in force after 1900 and be an important factor in leading up to the First World War.

RISE OF THE 'NEW IMPERIALISM'

Although the crisis concerning the Eastern Question was not fully resolved until the mid-1880s, its high point had come at the end of the previous decade. There was another new feature of foreign relations in this period, rather more prominent in the 1880s and early 1890s: the remarkable overseas expansion of European countries. Historians call this phenomenon the 'new imperialism'. It marked a break with the years 1815 to 1880, a period of relatively modest European diplomatic interest in overseas territory and even with the three-century-long (1500–1800) competition for overseas empire. This round of colonial expansion went beyond the usual suspects, the Atlantic maritime powers, to include such unlikely imperialists as Germany, Belgium and Italy, and, spreading beyond Europe, found emulation in Japan and even the ostensibly anti-imperialist United States. Overseas acquisitions occurred on a very large scale, the clearest example of which was the division of an entire continent: the 'scramble for Africa'. In 1880, European political control in Africa was confined to a few coastal enclaves; the entire vast interior of the continent was ruled by indigenous kingdoms or inhabited by tribal societies. By 1914, the entire continent had been partitioned into European colonies, with just two (barely) independent African nations, Liberia and Ethiopia, remaining. In addition to this scramble for Africa, all the available territory in East Asia and the Pacific Ocean was seized by different European powers. All in all, between 1880 and 1914 European colonial possessions more than doubled in area and the size of the colonized population increased by 78 per cent.[28]

The term 'imperialism' itself, while not a new one, came into common use in this period to refer to overseas empires. (Previously, it had designated the rule of Louis Napoleon in France.) This linguistic re-coining characterizes the post-1880 period of expansion as a distinct break with at least the recent past and has led historians and other interested parties since then to enquire about its causes and consequences. Explanations of this wave of imperial expansion have a continuing contemporary relevance, since they cast light on the nature of relations between economically advanced countries and the less developed portions of the world, today, and, in particular, on whether these relations can be seen as a continuation of the period of colonial rule.

One school of explanation tends to focus on economics, on the idea that 'trade follows the flag', or, even more commonly, that the rapid growth of colonial empires was related to the increase in overseas investments by colonizing countries – a theory first developed at the beginning of the twentieth century by the British radical J. A. Hobson, taken up by V. I. Lenin, the founder of twentieth-century communism, and still widely asserted in the underdeveloped world today. There certainly was plenty of overseas investment in late nineteenth and early twentieth centuries, and plenty of seizure of overseas territory, only the two did not have very much to do with one another.

BOX 13.1

The Hobson–Lenin thesis

J. A. Hobson, in his 1902 book *Imperialism: A Study*, developed a theory linking imperialism not just to economic motivations but to broader economic conditions as well. Hobson argued that, as a result of low wages, there was not enough purchasing power in economically advanced countries, such as England, so that businessmen were reluctant to make investments at home because of the difficulties they would have in selling the products of their investments. Instead, they looked to overseas territories as sources of investments and pressed governments to annex territories in which they had invested or planned to invest.

Writing during the First World War, the communist V. I. Lenin, in his 1916 *Imperialism: The Highest Stage of Capitalism*, took Hobson's thesis and expanded it into a theory of the structural development of capitalism. Unlike older, pre-1870 free-trade capitalism, in which international trade took the form of the export of goods, according to Lenin, late nineteenth and early twentieth century 'monopoly capitalism', characterized by large monopolistic corporations and a commanding role for banks, engaged in the export of capital. Lenin used as an example of capital export the building of railways in Asia, Africa and the Americas, so he probably meant by it something like infrastructure investment that would enable European capitalists to engage in profitable mining and plantation agriculture enterprises.

This was a powerful theory, which became an integral part of the world communist movement and post-1945 decolonization movements, and still finds a lot of approval in the southern hemisphere today. However, it is simply not correct. Not only did European powers not invest all that much in their newly acquired colonies, the connections Lenin made between changes in economic structure and export of capital are dubious. Both Great Britain and France were major capital exporters in late nineteenth- and early twentieth-century Europe, but neither had large monopolistic corporations or a business sector dominated by powerful financial institutions. Germany, by contrast, which did have these characteristics, and seems to have been Lenin's model for monopoly capitalism, did not export that much capital but instead made most of its investments in its domestic market.

Great Britain was the nineteenth-century world's leading colonial power and also the leading overseas investor. A very large chunk of its investments, though, went outside the empire to independent countries, such as the United States and Argentina, as well as to various nations in continental Europe – about 46 per cent of the approximately £3.8 billion invested overseas in 1914. Much of the rest, another 25 per cent, was in Canada, Australia and New Zealand – long-term settler colonies well on their way to autonomy and independence and not exactly the result of post-1880 imperial expansion. About 10 per cent of overseas investments were in India, a better example of imperialism, although also not exactly a new acquisition. Recently acquired territories in Africa and South Asia made up a grand total of 2.6 per cent of overseas investment.[29] Britain was by far the champion of colonial investment. French investors put a good deal of money into foreign countries, although mostly European ones, especially the Russian Empire, but very little into their colonies. This same lack of investment was typical of the other colonial powers. There may well have been more British investment in the German Empire, for instance, than German investment. Figures on trade with colonial possessions show the same results: European countries' best markets were each other and the independent nations of the Americas, followed, at some distance, by long-term colonial possessions, and, far at the end, by the acquisitions of the new imperialism.

The case for investment or, more broadly, overseas economic matters, as a driving force for the new imperialism is thus a hard one to make. Historians often make recourse to two other versions of explanation, one centring on diplomatic and strategic issues, the other on ideological ones. Both strands of explanation are helpful in understanding the development of empires in this period, but both are ultimately as unsatisfactory as the Hobson–Lenin thesis.

The strategic explanation sees the acquisition of overseas territory as primarily part of the military and diplomatic chess game the Great Powers played with each other in Europe. However, attempting to make the case leads to difficulties. Exactly what was the strategic and diplomatic value of New Guinea, Senegal or Togo? Sometimes, the argument is made that colonial acquisitions were really part of a more Eurocentric strategic thinking. Otto von Bismarck was a notorious sceptic about colonies, who once said to a German Africa explorer: 'Would you like to see my map of Africa? There is France on the west and Russia in the east, and we are in the middle.' Yet, in the mid-1880s he moved to acquire colonial possessions for Germany in southern and central Africa and in the South Pacific. This move has been explained as an effort to create animosity with Great Britain and so convince France, another colonial rival of Britain, that Germany was really on its side. Such an explanation is, at best, far-fetched, and was contradicted by Bismarck's actual policy, which was quite solicitous of British interests.

A comparison with the Eastern Question helps put the rush for colonies into a better strategic perspective. The Great Powers followed closely the upheavals in south-eastern Europe and were prepared to go to war over them – and, in 1914, ultimately did. No such hostility appears in colonial acquisitions, where territorial disputes of the 1880s were settled amicably and with little conflict. There would, later on, be more contentious colonial disputes, the Fashoda Affair of 1898 or the Moroccan crises of 1905 and 1911, but these, too, were settled peacefully and it was probably the case that the colonial focus of the disputes was a pretext for strategic issues in Europe. The one long-standing strategic issue of colonial acquisitions, control of the buffer zone (today's Afghanistan) between British India and the central Asian possessions of the Russian Empire, known in the nineteenth century and to readers of contemporary historical thrillers as the 'Great Game', pre-dated the rush for colonies by decades.

If strategic explanations of colonialism seem insufficient, perhaps ideological ones might be more helpful. The traditional ones advanced are religion and nationalism; in more recent years racism and attitudes about masculinity have been added to the explanatory mix. The contribution of these factors to the development of imperialism is undeniable, although large claims for them seem less clear and self-evident. Religion clearly did play a role in imperial expansion, as can be seen from this African saying: 'When the whites first came, they had the Bible and we had the land . . . Now they have the land and we have the Bible.'[30] Missionaries did ask for political support of the European powers to spread the Gospel, and, to be fair, often criticized the excessive brutality and oppression of the indigenous population by settlers and imperial administrations, if rarely questioning the legitimacy of colonization itself. While religious motives were very strong in the initial wave of European overseas expansion during the age of the Reformation, the centrality of religious motivations in the much more secular nineteenth century, though, seems harder to assert. Also, missionary efforts in Africa and Asia had been ongoing for much of the nineteenth century; it is difficult to see them as behind the sudden outburst of colonial acquisitions.

If older intellectual influences stemming from religion seem less likely to be a cause of imperial expansion in the 1880s, newer intellectual trends, such as nationalism and racism, might seem more apt. It is certainly the case that the possibilities for national aggrandizement inside Europe, as had existed in the 1850–70 era, were no longer so prevalent in the last decades of the nineteenth century, making overseas territories a logical outlet for nationalist ideas. As colonial empires expanded, nationalists got on the colonial bandwagon and began praising overseas possessions as part of the nation. In Great Britain, where for most of the nineteenth century the empire had existed with a surprising lack of official glorification and public attention, government officials, Tory politicians and journalists began promoting imperial causes and imperial identities from the 1870s, starting with Benjamin Disraeli's declaring Queen Victoria Empress of India in 1876. Yet imperial expansion and nationalism did not always go together. Jules Ferry, the leading advocate of the creation of a French empire in Africa and South-East Asia during the 1880s, was always attacked by nationalists for concentrating France's energies overseas and ignoring the vital national cause of revenge on Germany. As Camille Pelletan, just such a critic, said, 'Alsace Lorraine is under the Prussian jackboot and our army is leaving for Tonkin [in South-East Asia].'[31]

Racist and social Darwinist ideas were being formulated and gaining increasing currency at the time of colonial expansion. The Darwinist (or pseudo-Darwinist) notion that Europeans were biologically more advanced than Asians or Africans became an excuse for and justification of imposing European colonial rule on those self-same Asians and Africans. The Paris International Exhibition of 1900 exemplified in a nutshell this point of view. Not only did the colonial pavilions include caged displays of flora and fauna of the colonies, but caged displays of the indigenous human inhabitants as well. The International Congress of Colonial Sociology, held at the exposition, provided scholarly investigations along these lines, with the academics present calling on colonial bureaucrats to treat the natives as their biological nature called for. One participant explained, emphasizing hereditary biological differences between Europeans and non-Europeans, 'A race can no more be assimilated [i.e., treated by the colonial authorities as Europeans] than metals can be transmuted.'[32]

As with nationalism, a note of caution might be struck here as well. Racism certainly justified and helped legitimize imperial rule; it is rather less clear that it caused it. Europeans' attitudes about race and racial superiority were probably centred more on other Europeans than on colonial peoples. The Austro-Hungarian Empire was a hotbed of racist thinking and racial anti-Semitism, although it was the one Great Power with no overseas colonial possessions.

Colonial officials and European settlers did find all sorts of possibilities for sexual escapades with indigenous women (or men, for that matter), escapades they were unlikely to have enjoyed in Europe. It would be stretching plausibility, though, to suggest that a search for sexual indulgence was a motive for imperial ventures. In the late nineteenth-century scramble for colonies, growing numbers of women became involved in the imperial enterprise – either joining colonial societies or as resident wives and female dependants of administrators and settlers. They seemed to be every bit as enthusiastic about empire as their male counterparts. Colonialists often described the indigenous population as weak and passive – stereotypically feminine characteristics – and used this as a justification for their rule. Of course, they were also likely to describe indigenous peoples as wild, violent and savage – or more favourably, as was case with the British and the Sikhs and Gurkhas, as virile warriors – typically masculine characteristics. Of all the intellectual justifications for colonial expansion, ideas of masculinity seem to be the least plausible.

Perhaps the largest problem with all these explanations of colonial expansion is that they do not relate very well to the specific late nineteenth-century era in which European powers carved up the entire world. A consideration of the economic conditions of the period provides the most plausible moving factor for the growing imperial enterprise. It should be located, primarily, in the period of slow economic growth and frequent and severe recessions which were typical of the 1870s and 1880s.

Businesses were having a hard time selling their goods; inventories were building up – characteristic of recessions – and businessmen saw the situation as one in which they had lost their markets. If markets were lost, then new ones would have to be found to replace them.

The period was characterized by a search for these new markets. As protectionism became more common in the 1880s, possibilities for expanded markets in economically more developed countries of Europe or North America became less likely. Colonies were a potential source of such markets. Of course, no one knew if they would actually be there, but if they were and another country took possession of them, then they would be permanently lost. Hence the pre-emptive character of the scramble for Africa. Lord Salisbury put it just that way in a parliamentary debate of 1891:

> I do not, of course, say that the trade of Africa will be an immediate compensation for what we may lose in consequence of the existence of Protectionist beliefs in America, but it is a motive for preventing territory from falling into the hands of other Powers, that those Powers will probably use the dominion which we should concede to them for the purpose of crippling the trade that we otherwise should possess; and that seems to be a legitimate motive for the accession of territory which might otherwise be wanting.[33]

Francesco Crispi and Jules Ferry, the leading Italian and French advocates of colonial expansion, made precisely the same argument, linking the need for colonies as a potential source of markets for goods and investment with the growth of protectionism.

This version of explanation may sound like the Hobson–Lenin thesis, but it differs in not taking expectations for reality. Those markets and sources of investment that Europeans hoped to find in Africa, East Asia or the South Pacific were a chimera. The pre-emptive action was all in vain; when prosperity returned, as it did from 1890/95 onwards, European countries' international trade and opportunities for investment were mostly with each other or with independent nations in the Americas. Once the colonies had been set up, though, once they had been justified as national possessions, as places to spread the Gospel or to rule biologically inferior races, once a colonial civil service was in place, subsidized steamship lines in motion, perhaps even some settlers on location, they were there to stay. It would take the violent disruptions of two world wars – and several decades after that – to bring them to an end.

With some individual exceptions, of which India is probably the most prominent, European colonial ventures were, overall, enterprises that ran at a loss. The expense of creating and supporting a colonial government complete with officials, police and an army and of offering subsidies to various economic interests connected with the colonies, was greater than the benefits gained by trade and investment. Particular special interests certainly benefited, but the economies of the colonizing powers did not. Indeed, it would have been cheaper and more beneficial to humanity if the tax-payers of the colonizing countries had simply given the money directly to the colonial administration and army, settlers, steamship lines and colonial investors, and not bothered with building any empires.

Instead, European governments launched colonial ventures, which did not yield the expected profits but which did very considerably disrupt and transform indigenous societies in the colonized areas. Some forms of colonial rule were cruel, brutal and horrifying: the German government's suppression of the uprising of the Herero

BOX 13.2

Leopold II's Congo kingdom

Leopold II of Belgium, even before he came to the throne in 1865, envisaged expanding the power and prestige of his modestly sized country by means of an overseas empire. As a constitutional monarch facing a liberal government lacking interest in such activities, he had no opportunity to fulfil his vision until the changed climate of the 1880s. Working through the celebrated Africa explorer Henry Stanley, of 'Dr Livingstone, I presume' fame, and two anti-slave-trade front groups he created, the International Africa Association and the International Association of the Congo, he began laying claim to large swathes of territory in central Africa along the River Congo. At the beginning of the scramble for Africa he got his associations' claims recognized by the Berlin Africa Congress of 1884 and renamed the territory the Congo Free State.

Governing this territory required a substantial army of mercenaries and officials, which Leopold tried to fund by requiring the indigenous inhabitants to gather ivory for him. In the 1890s, when the development of the chemical industry led to a growing demand for rubber, this new product was added to the roster of compulsory labour. Leopold's officials summarily conscripted Congolese to perform this work from their villages, or rounded them up and marched them off to veritable slave labour camps. Not surprisingly, this treatment met with resistance, which led to drastic punishments, including beatings with the *chicotte*, a whip made of dried rhinoceros hide, cutting off the hands of the recalcitrant or of their children and relatives, or simply shooting them.

Even by the not very demanding human rights standards of the European colonial enterprise, the treatment of the indigenous population of the Congo Free State was abusive and extreme. At the beginning of the twentieth century, opposition to Leopold's private state increased, spearheaded by the Congo Reform Association, one of the first non-governmental organizations, founded by the British radical journalist E. D. Morel and the British colonial administrator turned Irish nationalist Roger Casement. Growing international public pressure forced Leopold to turn the Congo over to the Belgian government in 1908, a belated version of the trend in the new imperialism away from private companies running overseas territory towards governmental colonial rule.

The new Belgian state administrators abolished the system of coerced labour and virtually unlimited brutality and slaughter that had characterized Leopold's Congo Free State. By levying taxes on its African subjects, though, they found a gentler way to require them to continue to gather raw materials for their European rulers.

tribesmen in south-west Africa (today's Namibia) in 1905–06, for instance, which involved the systematic slaughter of about 80 per cent of the Hereros. Perhaps the worst was Belgian colonial rule in the Congo, or, more precisely, the private rule of Belgian king Leopold II (1835–1909), whose Congo Free State was, in effect, his personal possession. The inhabitants were conscripted into slave labour to harvest wild rubber in the rainforests by Leopold's administrators and his private army. The labour itself and the ever harsher forms of coercion used to get unwilling inhabitants to perform the work cost hundreds of thousands, perhaps even millions, of lives.

Now, colonial rule was not just murder and slave labour. As a large, apologetic historiography – begun in the 1950s and 1960s by colonial administrators who were unemployed as a result of decolonization – has pointed out, the European colonial powers introduced schools and promoted literacy, improved public health and increased life expectancy. The growth of the indigenous population in the colonized countries shows that such assertions are not totally without foundation. Colonial rule may not have promoted economic development or may have pushed economic development in potentially less promising directions, such as plantation agriculture, but the economic fate of African or Asian countries that were never colonized – Afghanistan, for instance, or Ethiopia – does not suggest that the poverty of large portions of today's underdeveloped countries is the result of imperialism.

Even taking these points into account, the most appropriate way to judge the new imperialism of the late nineteenth century might be in terms of the ideas of nationalism that were so prevalent at the time. Nationalists believed strongly in the idea of national self-determination, that each people should have the right to govern itself. From that perspective, the colonial enterprise, one people ruling over another, was a dubious one, a form of oppression not to be excused by the building of schools or clinics, or by the fact that the enterprise was run at a financial loss. This viewpoint is one that has prevailed on a global scale, although it took until the last decades of the twentieth century for its triumph to be complete. Based on a vision of trade and investment thoroughly unconnected to reality, justified by pernicious and scientifically dubious racist ideas, violating what have come to be seen as basic principles of international justice and equity, the new imperialism was one of the least attractive products of European society in the age of uncertainty.

CHAPTER 14

THE DYNAMICS OF POWER

The twenty-five years after 1871 fall into two distinct periods so far as both domestic politics and foreign policy are concerned. The 1870s was the liberal decade in domestic politics. In most European countries, liberal governments were in power and attempting an aggressive programme of reforms. There were conservatives in power in some countries for some or all of the decade, including in Russia, the Scandinavian countries and, more surprisingly, in France and Great Britain, countries which contemporaries saw as the liberal western powers. Yet these conservative governments were under fire from a strong liberal opposition and very constrained in their actions and accomplishments. While the autocratic rule of the tsars would maintain itself in Russia, conservative rule would come to an end in Britain and France by the end of the decade, and in Norway by the mid-1880s.

In international relations, the first half of the 1870s was concerned with sorting out the results of the Franco-Prussian War and establishing Germany as the strongest of the Powers, but not a dominant or hegemonic one. Diplomacy in the second half of the decade was centred on the Eastern Question, as insurrections against Turkish rule in the Balkans led to war against the Ottoman Empire, first by the smaller, semi-independent states of the region and then by the forces of the Tsar. This Russo-Turkish War of 1877–78 produced the greatest diplomatic crisis Europe experienced between the end of the Franco-Prussian War and the Moroccan Crisis of 1905, the one time in those thirty-four years when a war between the Great Powers was even remotely a possibility. The peaceful resolution of this crisis at the Congress of Berlin in 1878 produced a framework for dealing with the Eastern Question that would suffice to render harmless a further flare-up in the mid-1880s.

In terms of domestic politics, the 1880s were a mirror image of the previous decade, with conservative governments ruling most European countries. The movement to conservative rule was often a drastic one, seen, for instance, in Bismarck's celebrated political about-face of 1878–79, in the deeply reactionary policies of Russia's Tsar Alexander III, come to the throne following the assassination of his father in 1881, or the virtual self-destruction of the Liberal Party in Great Britain in 1885. There were liberal exceptions to the conservative tide, in France, Switzerland, Spain, Italy and Scandinavia, but these were frequently beleaguered governments facing considerable opposition and unable to achieve much politically.

Diplomatic relations in this decade centred on overseas expansion, with another Congress of Berlin, this one on the partition of Africa in 1884–85, providing a resolution of international disputes. Quite in contrast to the previous Congress of Berlin on the Eastern Question, though, this congress did not avert a war or resolve a crisis, but set down rules for the division of the African continent among the European Powers.

In contrast to the earlier period, which had a fairly clear ending in the years around 1880 – in domestic politics, the movement from a preponderance of liberal policies and governments to a preponderance of conservative ones, in international relations, the outbreak and resolution of a crisis stemming from the Eastern Question – the later period had no clear end point. At the beginning of the 1890s there was certainly a developing discontent with primarily conservative policies (although liberal governments, in countries such as France or Italy, were having their problems as well) but there was no return to liberal governments and policies of the sort that had been so prominent in the 1860s and 1870s. Rather, newer forces began to influence political life ever more strongly, among them, socialist parties, forms of political Catholicism and versions of radical nationalism and radical right-wing politics. However, neither by themselves nor in conjunction with each other were they able to come to power and direct government policy. Instead, politics generally became more unstable and changeable in the decade of the 1890s, a fitting conclusion to an age of uncertainty.

In some ways, international relations followed a similar pattern. The late 1880s saw the gradual unravelling of Bismarck's alliance system, as relations between Germany and Russia became distinctly less friendly. The ultimate outcome of this development would be the Franco-Russian Alliance of 1894, breaking France's long diplomatic isolation and creating, at least potentially, a new strategic situation in Europe. One possibility for this situation was a confrontation between newly allied France and Russia on the one hand, and Germany and Austria-Hungary on the other. This would be the actual state of affairs two decades after the signing of the Franco-Russian Alliance at the time of the outbreak of the First World War. Such a situation was by no means predetermined in 1894, though. The relation of Great Britain and Italy to the new alignment of the other Powers was unclear, as was the assumption of a continuing conflict between Russia and Germany. As in domestic affairs, the age of uncertainty ended with international relations in an uncertain state.

POLITICAL STRIFE AND INTERNATIONAL TENSIONS IN THE 1870S

The 1870s saw vigorous liberal initiatives in a number of European countries that built on accomplishments of the previous decades, but went well beyond them. Great Britain had been the standard-bearer of mid-nineteenth-century liberalism, and the liberal governments in power from 1868 to 1874, and again from 1880 to 1885, introduced a series of reforms, continuing the implementation of liberal principles while bringing them to bear on broader segments of the population than property-owning adult men. Local governments were reorganized more efficiently and their powers expanded to include public health and sanitation and public libraries. The expanded franchise of 1867 was reinforced with the introduction of a secret ballot in 1873 and the prohibition ten years later on bribing voters and other corrupt electoral practices. The liberal combination of promotion of public education and opposition to established religion appeared in the establishment of state schools not controlled by the Church of England (the Education Act 1870), the admission of non-Anglicans to university study at Oxford and Cambridge and the disestablishment of the Church of Ireland, a state-supported Anglican church in a predominantly Roman Catholic island, whose Protestant minority was mostly Presbyterian.

These measures went along the lines of past liberal practice, but others showed the expansion of liberal ideas. Liberals believed in a society of property owners, but generally male ones; married women were to be represented by their husbands. Now, the liberal government in Great Britain began extending the rights of property owners to women. While proposals to grant women the vote in parliamentary elections failed (albeit narrowly, by just sixteen votes in 1883), property-owning women received the vote in municipal elections in 1869 and in school board elections the following year. The Married Women's Property Act of 1882 guaranteed married women control over property they brought into their marriage or acquired within it.

The working class also received the favour of the liberals, with legislation passed securing the legal position of trade unions and preventing them from being sued for damages in case of strikes. There was some modest health and safety legislation implemented – initiatives that would be continued, on an equally modest scale, by the Conservative government of 1875–79. Legislation in 1880 protected tenant farmers, especially in Ireland, from their landlords, preventing arbitrary rent increases or evictions, giving them a property-like right to their tenancies. Capping all these measures in favour of male non-property owners was the expansion of the franchise. The Third Reform Act of 1884 equalized suffrage requirements in rural areas with those implemented for urban ones in the Second Reform Act of 1867, so that about 60 per cent of adult men had the right to vote – not quite democratic circumstances, but the franchise was no longer restricted to substantial property owners either.

This was a distinctly British pattern of advanced liberal politics, with relatively little on the continent to conform to it, except perhaps in Scandinavia, particularly in Norway, where the liberal leader Johan Sverdrup (1816–92), 'Norway's Gladstone', became prime minister in 1884. His government was the first in any Nordic country to be based on a parliamentary majority. Among its legislative accomplishments it was able to lower the property requirement for the franchise and, in 1889, to strip the state church of control over state schools.

The population of Norway, as elsewhere in Scandinavia, was almost entirely Protestant, and this marked a contrast with liberal rule in other European countries with a substantial Catholic population where 1870s liberalism involved a sharp clash with the Catholic Church, most extreme in the newly united German Empire. For most of the 1870s, the national government and the governments of the individual federal states, such as Prussia, Bavaria or Baden (the reader needs to remember that the German Empire was a federal polity where powers were divided, in complex fashion, between the imperial government and the governments of the thirty-seven individual German states), followed liberal policies, and had the support of liberal parliamentary majorities – although the governments themselves, unlike circumstances in western Europe, were never actually parliamentary governments.

Some of the governmental policies pursued in the German Empire during the 1870s followed along the lines of previous liberal ideas – introducing or reinforcing freedom of trade and freedom of occupation, expanding self-government of urban municipalities and rural counties, or completing national unification by introducing a national postal system and central bank. The most aggressive and contentious policies added up to an assault on the Catholic Church. Clergy were forbidden to preach sermons on political topics; education, appointment and discipline of the Catholic clergy were placed under state control. First the Jesuits and then the other religious orders were expelled from the country. The church's influence on public education was sharply restricted; civil marriage and registration of vital events were made compulsory. The ecclesiastical hierarchy and ordinary priests refused to obey these laws so the authorities ended state subsidies to the Catholic Church, seized church property and arrested hundreds of priests, from parish assistants to the Archbishop of Cologne. Most of Germany's bishops ultimately fled the country.

These extremely interfering and coercive policies failed completely in their intent. Catholic laypeople stood powerfully behind their clergy, holding large-scale mass meetings in support of them and against government policy, turning up in their thousands when priests were arrested – and sometimes brawling with the police when that happened – appearing in impressive numbers to vote for the Catholic political party, the Centre Party, which scored major victories in the Prussian elections of 1873 and the German national elections of 1874. The response of the Catholic population to the government's authoritarian, hostile and persecutory policies was a major example of mass political mobilization, at a level fully equal and probably beyond that of the national campaigns of the 1860s, the most impressive political mass movement in the German states during the half-century between the revolution of 1848 and the 1890s.

What was at stake in these confrontations between a liberal government and the Catholic Church can be seen from the phrase coined about them by Rudolf Virchow, a Berlin professor of pathology, one of Germany's leading scientists and also a radical parliamentary deputy. He called the clash with the Catholic Church a *Kulturkampf*, literally a struggle for culture or civilization. His coinage hit the spot and was quickly adopted by partisans of all religious and political points of view in Germany, and even outside the German-speaking world, and is occasionally still used today to describe political campaigns centring on religious, moral or ideological issues.

Virchow's phrase gets to the heart of the matter. Germany's liberals, continuing, in the 1870s, in the political and intellectual traditions of the post-1850 decades, saw the Catholic Church as the leading enemy of a future united, liberal Germany. (Germany's Protestants, by contrast, were generally understood by liberals, whether themselves Protestant, Catholic or Jewish, as more open to liberal political and theological ideas.) By secularizing public education and controlling the appointment and education of the Catholic clergy, liberals and Otto von Bismarck – both chancellor of the German Empire and prime minister of the Kingdom of Prussia, the empire's largest federal state, then cooperating politically with the liberals – would shape Germany's future in the direction of progress, positivism, free markets, and a society in which property owners' points of view were dominant. The Catholic Church had been the leading opponent in the post-1850 decades of the culture of progress and science, an opposition only cemented by the victory of ultramontane clergy at the First Vatican Council of 1870, and the council's promulgation of the doctrine of Papal Infallibility. The ultimate failure of the campaign against the church, the inability of the forces of science and progress either to convince Germany's Catholics to reject their allegiance to an ultramontane Catholicism, or to force them to do so, already apparent by the mid-1870s, became yet another reason for people to doubt the validity of the ideals of the post-1850 culture of progress.

Liberal opposition to the Catholic Church was strongest in Germany, where it was mixed in with conflicts dating from the era of national unification, emerging from two wars between predominantly Protestant Prussia and the Catholic Great Powers Austria and France, but flourished in many other European countries of the time. Similar policies of civil marriage, secular public education and control of the Catholic Church were implemented by the liberal government of 1870s Switzerland, the most democratic country in Europe. Some of the measures of the *Kulturkampf* had been carried out by the liberal governments of post-1867 Austria and Hungary, and were planned by liberal governments in the Netherlands and in Belgium in the later 1870s. Liberal political oppositional groups in Italy, France and Spain proposed similar anti-clerical policies. It would be fair to say that the policies of the *Kulturkampf* were as characteristic of the militant phase of European liberalism in the 1870s as were the plans of British liberals to take liberal ideas beyond the circle of property-owning adult men.

In many ways, the issues involved in the *Kulturkampf*, just with the political signs reversed, were central to the policies of western Europe's leading conservative government of the 1870s, that in France. This government, chosen in good parliamentary fashion by the monarchist majority elected in 1871, tried to implement a conservative programme called the 'regime of moral order'. This was an effort to destroy the post-1850 culture of progress, which French conservatives saw as a reign of godlessness and immorality leading their nation into divinely inspired chastisement by the Prussians in 1870–71.

The conservatives set out to close taverns, promote church attendance, increase clerical control of public education, prohibit non-religious funeral ceremonies and fire large numbers of godless schoolteachers. They sponsored the building of the Basilica of the Sacred Heart in Montmartre, on the highest point in the city of Paris. Today a major tourist attraction, the church was designed to be a measure of expiation and repentance. France would renounce the godless evils of the reign of Napoleon III and the Paris Commune by dedicating itself to Jesus. Not content with appealing to divine support, the conservatives used some distinctly human means as well, enforcing tight restrictions on the press and public meetings, stripping municipalities of the power to elect their mayors and having them appointed by the central government. The whole project was to be capped by the National Assembly voting to restore the monarchy.

Efforts of French conservatives to use the police in order to destroy the culture of progress were no more successful than the attempts of German liberals to use the police to enforce that culture. The pretender, the Count de Chambord, refused to govern with a constitution or accept a tricolour flag, proclaiming that he would rule in divinely inspired fashion. This was too much for the more moderate conservatives, former supporters of the Orléans dynasty which had ruled France from 1830 to 1848, or adherents of Napoleon III and the Bonapartist dynasty. France remained a republic, admittedly with a conservative general as president, but also a republic in which the conservatives' political stock was steadily declining. By-elections brought more and more republican candidates to office, their campaigns often led by innkeepers and schoolteachers, open opponents of the regime of moral order. In 1876, republicans gained a majority of deputies, and the attempt the following year of President MacMahon to dismiss a republican prime minister who had majority parliamentary support, the so-called crisis of 16 May, ended with the conservatives' complete defeat.

France would be a republic, albeit not a Jacobin republic as it had been during the Reign of Terror in the 1790s or a social democratic republic, as was attempted during the revolution of 1848, but a liberal republic, one in which property was protected and civil liberties were assured. The liberal government of this Third French Republic (the First lasted from 1792 to 1804, the Second from 1848 to 1852), like those of contemporary Switzerland or, to a lesser extent, Great Britain and Norway, was one in which liberal political principles were married to a broader franchise, including all or a majority of adult men, not just substantial property owners. The French liberal governments of the late 1870s and 1880s promptly secularized public education, increased financial support for it, and combated the influence of the Catholic Church. The fate of conservatism in France can be seen as the exception that proves the rule of the liberal decade of the 1870s, and towards the end of that decade and at the beginning of the next conservative governments gave way to more liberal ones in Spain, Italy, Romania and Norway, leaving the Tsar's empire as the one major European country never to experience a period of liberal rule.

At first, international relations were relatively little affected by the period of liberal hegemony in domestic politics. Bismarck's 1873 League of the Three Emperors, uniting Germany, Austria-Hungary and Russia, one of whose ostensible points was to fight the radicalism of the Paris Commune – itself, already fully repressed – seems more like a conservative counterpart to the German chancellor's more liberal domestic stance. The 'war in sight' crisis of 1875, when Bismarck purported to be fearing an imminent French attack and took preparatory measures for war, such as prohibiting the export of horses, was also political shadow-boxing, and not very successful shadow-boxing at that. The other Great Powers, including Germany's allies, saw no evidence of French action and rather sympathized with France against what they saw as Bismarck's bullying.

Far more significant and a much greater threat to the peace were the events in the Balkans, which brought up, once again, the Eastern Question. They began in 1875 with an uprising of the inhabitants of Bosnia-Herzegovina against Ottoman rule. The principalities of Serbia and Montenegro, both officially still subject to the rule of the Sultan, but largely autonomous in their own affairs, promptly joined the insurgents and went to war against their own ruler. By contrast, the United Principalities of Moldavia and Wallachia, like Serbia and Montenegro, an autonomous dependency of the Ottoman Empire but, unlike them, having a substantial and effective army, stayed out of the conflict. The government of the United Principalities did tolerate Bulgarian nationalist revolutionaries gathering on its territory and crossing the River Danube to spark an uprising in the Ottoman Empire's Bulgarian provinces, in effect attempting to repeat Garibaldi's performance of 1860.

All this military action against Ottoman and Islamic rule generated a considerable stir in public opinion across Europe. Anti-Ottoman forces in Bosnia and Bulgaria were joined by political radicals from many parts of Europe – veterans of Garibaldi's campaigns in Italy, a number of former activists of the revolution of 1848, for whom this was their revolutionary last hurrah, as well as younger radicals from France, Belgium, Germany, Austria's Czech provinces, and even Norway. The struggle in Bosnia was probably the major European event for radicals in the 1870s, a decade in which they were mostly on the defensive following the suppression of the Paris Commune. Even some Russian revolutionaries took a break from opposing the rule of the Tsar to join in the insurrections, ironically, since in doing so they were supporting the Tsar's foreign policy. Militarily, though, the anti-Ottoman forces were no match for the Sultan's armies, which defeated, without too much difficulty, both the irregular insurgents and the ragged regular armies sent against them. This might have been an end to the matter had it not been for the behaviour of Turkish troops in Bulgaria: not content with suppressing the uprising, some of them, quite out of control, went on to murder anywhere from 5,000 to 20,000 civilians.

This massacre provided a very handy pretext for Russian intervention. After reaching agreement with Austria-Hungary, the other Great Power bordering on the Balkans, Russian forces entered the war in April 1877, bringing along with them the reluctant government of the United Principalities as an ally. The major battles of the war, including the six-month siege of the fortress of Plevna in the latter half of 1877, revealed Russian strategic and tactical failures. The outnumbered Turkish defenders of Plevna dominated the battlefield with their firepower, American long-range rifles and

German steel cannon, considerably superior to the Russians' weapons. Russian frontal assaults were thrown back with large casualties and only the full use of the allied contingents from the United Principalities – whose military exploits made them celebrated national heroes of Romanians in the Principalities and in the Austro-Hungarian Empire – enabled the Russians to take the fortress and then, with an eight-month delay, march south, accepting an armistice on the outskirts of Istanbul.

The peace terms kept the city in the Ottomans' hands, but they lost everything else in the Balkans. The nominally subordinate principalities became sovereign states; a newly 'independent' Bulgaria was created in the rest of the region, but it was occupied by the Tsar's troops. Ironically, the Russians' chief ally, the United Principalities, was also a loser, as its government was forced to return Bessarabia, which Russia had been compelled to cede at the end of the Crimean War in 1856. This quite foreseeable outcome was why the government of the United Principalities, in spite of widespread sympathies for the anti-Ottoman insurgents, had been reluctant to get involved in the war.

The long delay involved in the siege of Plevna, though, made possible outside intervention. The British Conservative prime minister Benjamin Disraeli opposed the expansion of Russian power resulting from the war as a threat to British imperial interests. Disraeli's nationalist and jingoist stance (the word jingoism was coined then) trumped the implicitly pro-Russian efforts of William Gladstone, leader of the Liberal opposition, to emphasize moral questions, the 'Bulgarian horrors' as he called the slaughter of the Balkan Christians by the Islamic soldiers of the Sultan. Secure at home, Disraeli gained support abroad from Austria-Hungary, whose rulers were uncomfortable with the extent of the Russian victory. British actions introduced, at least briefly, the possibility of a war between the Great Powers, in the spring of 1878.

Bismarck's diplomatic mediation produced, instead, the Congress of Berlin, which met in June and July 1878 and drew up new peace terms. The former Ottoman subject states did acquire their independence, and the United Principalities got to rename themselves the Kingdom of Romania, receiving, in addition, some modest compensation bordering the Black Sea for the loss of Bessarabia. In what was definitely a diplomatic novelty, the Great Powers tried to impose liberal political principles on a smaller state by insisting that the independent Romania grant the Jews residing in its territory equal citizenship, a move that the Romanian government and the entire politically active Romanian population fiercely resented. Ultimately, Romania was forced to agree to the Great Powers' conditions, but in practice Romanian authorities found various bureaucratic subterfuges to ensure that almost no Jews became citizens. Bulgaria was no longer to be a sovereign nation but an autonomous principality still under Ottoman sovereignty, and greatly reduced in size, with the remaining territory reverting to direct Ottoman rule. Austria-Hungary received compensation in the acquisition of Bosnia-Herzegovina as a protectorate although still nominally under Ottoman sovereignty, and Great Britain walked away with Cyprus as a new territory of the empire.

The Balkans in 1878

Source: From *THE MAKING OF THE WEST 3E* by Lynn Hunt et al., Copyright © 2009 by Bedford/
St. Martin's. Reproduced by permission of Bedford/St. Martin's.

The work of the Congress preserved the peace of the European continent and shored
up the tottering existence of the Ottoman Empire. The new settlement pacified,
temporarily, the Balkans (actually, it took several years of fighting insurgents in the
mountains before Austrian rule over Bosnia was secured) and remained in place for
the next two decades, the one change being territorial expansion of Bulgaria in
1885–86. On the other hand, the Congress also involved a degree of frustration among
the victorious powers. The United Principalities had helped the Russians win the war,
and received honorary distinctions – a new name, *de jure* as well as *de facto*
sovereignty – and material disadvantages, in the loss of Bessarabia and the very

considerable interference of the Great Powers in its internal affairs. As a small country, this outcome had only domestic ramifications – the coming to power of the liberals on a wave of nationalist resentment. By contrast, the victorious Great Power, the Russian Empire, had seen its victory largely annulled by the other powers. Long-term feelings of ill will against Great Britain increased; Russian resentment against Germany and especially Austria-Hungary grew. If these developments would lead to conflicts in the long run, in the short-term a reconciliation with Germany and even Austria-Hungary, in the form of the Three Emperors' Alliance of 1881, proved possible. France continued to be diplomatically isolated – Bismarck's main concern in the whole affair.

A CONSERVATIVE TURN IN THE 1880S

The transition from predominantly liberal to predominantly conservative governments took place in different European countries from the late 1870s through to the mid-1880s. A constant background to this power shift was the economic crisis of the period, the sharp recessions and prolonged periods of slow economic growth, and the principled refusal of liberal governments, believers in free market economics, to do anything about them. Another part of the background was a growing disillusionment with the aspirations of the culture of progress, particularly in its 1870s militant, anti-Catholic form. Yet by themselves these background doubts were generally not enough; it typically took a precipitating event, often of a violent or dramatic nature, to bring about a change of government. In the Austrian half of the Austro-Hungarian Empire, it was the refusal of the liberal government ministers to go along with the Austrian occupation of Bosnia-Herzegovina – as mostly German liberal nationalists, they felt the empire had all the Slavs it needed – that led Emperor Franz Joseph to dismiss the liberal ministers and appoint the conservative, 'Iron Ring' cabinet led by Count Taaffe in 1879. Changes in government in Russia, Germany and Great Britain were considerably more dramatic.

In the German and Russian empires, the political transition at the end of the 1870s was precipitated by assassinations or attempted assassinations of the respective emperors. The assassination of Russia's Tsar Alexander II emerged from a double frustration. First, there was frustration over the emperor's unwillingness to cap his Great Reforms of the 1860s with a constitutional government and an elected legislature. Students and educated young people responded to this frustration by forming secret societies aiming at a radical revolution and the overthrow of tsarist rule. Their different groups were generally known as Populists, from their effort to engage in political agitation among the people, especially the peasants, the vast majority of the population. The illiterate and unsophisticated peasantry, for all its grievances loyal to the Tsar, was indifferent to the agitation or downright hostile, turning agitators over to the police. Frustrated again by lack of popular support, one wing of the Populists, members of the secret society 'The People's Will', began a campaign of assassinating high-ranking government officials, hoping that the dramatic impact of these assassinations would shock an indifferent population into taking action against their oppressors. After practising on police commissioners and provincial governors, the group turned to the emperor himself: several attempts failed, but at the end of February 1880 a suicide bomber from the group blew himself up and the emperor with him.

BOX 14.1

Radicalism in Russia

The Russian Empire never had a constitution in all the years of its existence; it was only following the 1905 revolution that an elected legislature existed, checking the tsar's powers in any way, or that there were any, even partial, guarantees of civil liberties. By the last quarter of the nineteenth century, this legal and constitutional state of affairs was unique to Russia among all the powers of Europe. Combining this state of affairs with the Russian social structure, not unique to it, but part of an economically less advanced zone of eastern and southern Europe – largely rural population, agriculture still dominant over industry – produced some very distinct forms of politics. Russian radicals, in particular, barred from any legal forms of political action, practised two rather different forms of political action, forms which continued in one way or another until the end of tsarist rule in the revolution of 1917.

One such distinct form was the practice of terrorism, of the systematic assassination of high government officials, both to intimidate them into changing their policies and to spark a revolutionary uprising. This practice involved a fundamental redefinition in the meaning of terrorism in European politics. Beginning during the radical phase of the French Revolution, the Reign of Terror in 1793–94, terrorism referred to a revolutionary government that suppressed, intimidated and, when necessary, executed its enemies; to be a terrorist was to be a proponent of such a government. This understanding of terrorism continued as late as the Paris Commune of 1871, whose supporters were widely accused of being terrorists. The new meaning and practice of terrorism, invented by Russian radicals in the 1870s, would be taken up by European and North American anarchists of the late nineteenth and early twentieth centuries; after 1945, anti-imperialist movements and, more recently, Islamicist ones, have made it into a key political strategy.

A second point about late nineteenth-century Russian radicalism was its efforts to gain support among the peasantry. While there were agrarian radicals in late nineteenth-century Scandinavia, and the nascent socialist movement in the rest of Europe did not totally neglect the peasantry, leftists in Europe increasingly turned their attention to the urban population, especially the industrial working class. By contrast, the largest radical party in Russia, down through the revolution of 1917, the Socialist Revolutionaries, besides being prominent practitioners of terrorism, saw its supporters and its goals primarily in terms of the peasants and rural society. A socialist labour movement did gradually arise in the 1880s and 1890s – ironically, often being a more moderate part of the left in Russia – but its practices and aspirations continued to be shaped by the unique features of the political situation.

There was popular violence in the aftermath of the assassination. Rather than an uprising against the government as the Populists hoped, pogrom rioters attacked the Jews and blamed them for killing the Tsar. The assassinated Alexander II, the ruler who had liberated the serfs and instituted the other Great Reforms of the 1860s, might have been unwilling to go any further in a liberal or emancipatory direction, but his son and successor Alexander III (1845–95) put politics into reverse gear, restricting further the competence of the zemstvos, limiting the free actions of the peasantry, removing from office senior government officials who sympathized with liberal ideas, prosecuting even more vigorously any attempt at an open discussion of public affairs, and even prohibiting schoolteachers (an occupation under suspicion as a group of subversives) from holding professional association meetings. The result of the assassination carried out by The People's Will – most of whose members were duly rounded up by the police and either executed or sentenced to long terms in prison or Siberian exile – was exactly the opposite of what the Russian radicals wanted, and instituted a twenty-five-year phase of repressive and oppressive rule, only partially ended by the 1905 revolution.

By contrast, the two attempts on the life of the elderly German emperor Wilhelm I were perpetrated by mentally ill individuals who acted alone. German chancellor Bismarck claimed that the potential assassins had ties to the socialist labour movement, and called on the parliament to pass legislation outlawing the social democratic party. Certainly more influential than the handful of Russian conspirators, the German socialists of the 1870s were still a small political movement, with only very modest levels of political support. Bismarck's actions were aimed not at the socialists but at the liberals, whose free trade policies had not helped resolve the severe post-1873 recession and whose anti-clerical *Kulturkampf* had alienated Catholics from Germany's government.

When the parliamentary liberals, though, showing strong support for civil liberties not apparent in their previous support for measures persecuting the Catholic Church, refused to pass these 'anti-socialist' laws, Bismarck dissolved parliament and held new elections on the question of whether the voters should tolerate deputies who coddled terrorists and subversives. Held in an atmosphere of widespread suspicion and political hysteria, the elections resulted in the liberals' loss of a substantial number of seats and corresponding gains by the conservatives. The newly elected legislature outlawed the socialists and went on to pass legislation implementing protective tariffs. Bismarck dismissed his liberal advisers, replacing them with more conservative figures, and continued in office now as a conservative head of government rather than a liberal one.

Political turnabouts in both these empires reflected a belief that liberalism had gone too far, producing a radicalism with fatal consequences. Conservative officials surrounding Alexander III lost no time in asserting that the terrorist revolutionaries were the result of liberal demands for constitutional government, a point the new tsar was only too willing to believe. Both conservatives and Catholics in Germany used the attempted assassinations of the emperor to denounce the liberals' *Kulturkampf* for having destroyed respect for religion and encouraged the growth of a godless socialism, whose adherents, besides wanting to abolish the family and private property, would dare to attack the emperor, the symbol of the nation. In retrospect, these accusations seem distorted and almost perversely incorrect – violent radicalism was much more a result of authoritarian rule than of liberal political principles – but they found a sympathetic audience in an age when the former certainties of progress and positivism were increasingly in doubt.

In the three empires of central and eastern Europe, traditions and practices of authoritarian rule were more pronounced even during the decades of liberal reform and liberal government. By contrast, in western Europe, liberal policies and constitutional rule were more firmly established, yet the years between 1878 and 1885 saw the decline of liberal rule there as well. In both Belgium and the Netherlands, it was legislation passed in 1878–79 establishing a secularized state school system, that led to the creation of a Catholic political party (a Protestant conservative party also developed in the Netherlands, with its large Calvinist population), securing substantial success in the subsequent elections, bringing down liberal governments. These developments show that it did not require the massive persecution of the *Kulturkampf* to incite a strong political response from the Catholic Church in an age of ultramontanism and strong doubts about the culture of progress.

The end of liberal government in Great Britain, for decades the European stronghold of liberal politics, was a more complex affair. The economic crisis of the 1870s, elsewhere devastating to liberal governments, worked to the disadvantage of the Tories, who had come to office in the 1875 general elections under their long-term leader Benjamin Disraeli. The next general elections in 1880 were a sweeping victory for the Liberals, led by Disraeli's long-term nemesis William Gladstone who conducted a massive speaking tour in Scotland – the celebrated 'Midlothian campaign' – to enormous media attention. The vigorous and successful reform programme that Gladstone's government implemented was to culminate with his proposal in 1885 to introduce home rule, or as we would say today, autonomy, for Ireland, thus resolving, or so Gladstone hoped, a problem that had plagued the United Kingdom for the previous nine decades. The proposal was a disaster; a large portion of the Liberal MPs refused to support it, seceding to form a Unionist party that would uphold the unity of the United Kingdom. After receiving a majority of votes cast at every single general election between 1852 and 1880, the Liberals would lag behind the Tories at every general election from 1886 to 1900. From being the party of government for four straight decades, the Liberals would be in power for only three of the next twenty years.

Although a serious political miscalculation, the proposal also reflected an important change in the political situation in Ireland, part of the development of radical nationalism in this period. The sharp decline in farm prices resulting from the agrarian crisis of the 1870s meant that Irish tenants of English landlords were often unable to meet their rents and were faced with the threat of eviction. There were clashes with the police when evictions occurred, and new tenants taking over from evicted farmers were murdered by anonymous night-time attackers. The situation was so out of control between 1879 and 1882 that contemporaries began talking about it as a 'land war'. Under the energetic leadership of Charles Stewart Parnell (1846–91), ironically, himself a Protestant landowner, Irish nationalists were able to connect their cause with the grievances of tenant farmers. Working closely with Parnell's group, the Land League, which had as many as 1,800 branches across Ireland, the nationalists reversed three decades of political marginalization and captured all the predominantly Catholic parliamentary constituencies in Ireland, largely to the detriment of the Liberals. Increasingly, the Liberal position in parliament came to depend on the votes of Irish nationalists, making Gladstone's disastrous effort to placate them an understandable choice. In a broadly European context, we could see this situation as a distinctly British version of a characteristic trend of the age of uncertainty: the decline of notables' politics and the rise of more aggressive forms of nationalism – in this case, two clashing nationalisms, the Irish nationalism of Parnell's supporters, calling for at least a partial separation of Ireland from Great Britain, and the nationalists of the Unionists and the Tories, who were determined to maintain Ireland as British territory.

Conservative governments coming to power in the 1880s followed a negative policy of rejecting the liberal project of continuing upon and expanding the reforms of the post-1850 decades. Neither home rule nor a further extension of the franchise were on the agenda during the three post-1885 Tory cabinets of Lord Salisbury; after his turn to the right, Bismarck began slowly and carefully, one by one, to repeal all the anti-Catholic measures of the *Kulturkampf*. More generally in this respect, conservative governments throughout central Europe – in Austria, Germany, Belgium and the Netherlands – rejected the idea of any further secularization of public life. Under Alexander III, there was no thought of any further continuation of the Great Reforms of the 1860s his father had introduced.

Political repression was also part of conservative rule: outlawing the socialists in Germany and Austria-Hungary, and a crackdown on all independent political initiatives in Russia. The Tory governments in Great Britain responded to Irish nationalism by arresting Irish nationalists and Land League agitators. In contrast to the reaction era of the 1850s, these repressive measures – outside of Russia at least – were generally taken within a framework of legality and constitutional rule. Opposition continued to exist and to battle the governments at election times and in parliaments. In Germany, due to a peculiar quirk in the law – the social democratic party was outlawed, but social democratic candidates could stand for office and even run pro-socialist election campaigns – the prohibition of the socialists hampered but did not eliminate their political activity.

Conservative regimes also took their own initiatives, most noticeable in two areas. One was vigorous state intervention in the economy. Bismarck's post-1878 policies are exemplary: protective tariffs; the introduction of a social insurance system, beginning with state-sponsored health insurance and moving on to disability and old-age insurance; restoring the guilds; public works in the form of railway and telegraph construction, to combat unemployment; and seeking a colonial empire to provide a captive market for goods. While many of these measures were copied in Austria-Hungary, in strongly pro-free market Great Britain, even Conservative governments, in spite of some sympathy for protectionism on the part of Tories and their Liberal Unionist allies, could not go that far. The most they could dare was the introduction of state-funded workmen's compensation for industrial accidents in 1897.

The second initiative of conservative governments was a more aggressive, more militaristic foreign policy. The new imperialism of the 1880s and 1890s cannot be ascribed to conservative governments, since liberal ones, in France and Italy for instance, were also involved, but it is probably true that conservatives were more likely to press more strongly and on a larger scale towards the building of empires. Closely connected to this imperialist endeavour was a tendency towards expanded armaments expenditure. Bismarck's last major political victory came in the German elections of 1887, in which the coalition of conservative and liberal parties supporting his government campaigned on a programme of a substantial increase in arms expenditures. The introduction of the 'two power standard' in the 1889 Naval Defence Act, committing Britain to maintaining a navy equal to that of its two largest competitors combined, was another example of a conservative government sponsoring a major increase in its arms budget.

Just as the previous decade had proved a difficult environment for conservative governments, so the 1880s would pose a challenge to liberals in power. A few years after the republicans – whose views roughly corresponded to those of liberals and radicals in other European countries – had come to power in France, they found themselves buffeted by the sharp winds of the economic crisis of the period, most severe in France during the 1880s. The 1884 elections showed ominous gains for the monarchists and the Bonapartists. The campaigns of General Boulanger in 1888–89 and the 'Panama scandals' of 1892, in which it was revealed that a number of parliamentary deputies had accepted pay-offs from a French company formed to build a canal across the isthmus of Panama, rocked the government and raised the question of whether the republic could survive.

Yet liberal government survived in France, as it did in Italy. Dubious political manipulations played a role – the French Chamber of Deputies declaring the elections of conservative candidates invalid, the Italian liberals making deals with the Mafia to deliver constituencies in Sicily. Religious questions also helped liberals in Italy, since even Pius IX's much less intransigent successor, Leo XIII (r. 1878–1903), refused to allow devout Catholics, and thus potential supporters of conservatism, to participate in politics. In a different way, religion was helpful to liberals in the Netherlands, where the Catholic and the Calvinist conservative parties distrusted each other even more than they opposed the liberals. Liberals also adopted some of the policies of conservative governments, in particular introducing protective tariffs and seeking colonies overseas as a way of combating the economic crisis, abandoning the long nineteenth-century liberal support of free trade. Finally, we can observe a gradual shift of liberal governments to the right, as fairly radical governments in France and Italy of the late 1870s and early 1880s gave way to much more moderate ones by the beginning of the 1890s, including some conservative government ministers, although the opening to the right went rather further in Italy than in France.

Looked at across the European continent, the ultimate upshot of the economic, cultural and political crisis of the 1870s and 1880s was that liberal governments and parliamentary regimes were more likely to be present in western Europe, and more conservative and anti-parliamentary regimes in the east. There were exceptions of course – persistent post-1880 Catholic-conservative governments in Belgium, and liberal ones in Romania – but, more generally, liberal political principles and parliamentary government were firmly implanted in the western half of Europe, even when, as was the case in Great Britain, Conservatives dominated the government, while the three central and eastern European empires, Germany, Austria-Hungary and Russia, remained centres of non-parliamentary rule and weakness of liberal political parties.

AN UNCERTAIN BEGINNING OF THE 1890S

Within this broader picture of a more conservative and authoritarian eastern and central Europe, and a more liberal and parliamentary western half of the continent, which would persist until the outbreak of the First World War, cracks and fissures began to appear at the beginning of the 1890s. New political forces made an appearance – radical nationalists, such as General Boulanger in France, or the German nationalist Georg Ritter von Schönerer in Austria, and his equally vociferously Czech nationalist opponents, the Young Czechs. In Germany, the 1890 elections resulted in an unparalleled victory for the still illegal social democrats; the 20 per cent of the vote they received was more than that of any other political party. If the 1890 elections marked a victory for left-wing opposition to the government (the non-socialist radicals also did well that year), the next elections in 1893 saw a victory for the radical right, with both moderate liberals and non-socialist radicals losing votes and seats, while the anti-Semitic political parties reached the high point of their pre-1914 success – admittedly, just a modest 5 per cent of the votes cast.

A number of long-term government leaders left the stage. In 1893, Count Taaffe's attempts to reconcile competing demands of German and Czech nationalists was rejected by all the parties and all the nationalities. Emperor Franz Joseph reluctantly decided that his prime minister, after fourteen years of service, had reached the end of his effectiveness. Otto von Bismarck, who had effortlessly dominated the elderly German emperor Wilhelm I, having guided him through the political controversies of the 1860s when Wilhelm was king of Prussia, and the wars of German unification, faced an uncertain fate when the elderly emperor died at the age of 91 in 1888. His son and successor, Friedrich III, came to the throne dying of cancer and lived just ninety-nine days, but Friedrich's son, the youthful Wilhelm II (1859–1941), was in no mood to be dominated by the elderly chancellor. Following the victory of the opposition parties in the 1890 elections, the young emperor

BOX 14.2

Wilhelm II

It was not long into his reign before the moustachioed German emperor Wilhelm II gained a reputation for tactless and impetuous behaviour, uncontrollable and excessive verbosity and intellectual eccentricity. This was the man who, on watching the King of Italy board a ship, loudly proclaimed, 'Watch that dwarf climbing the gangplank!' The hostile designation of the Germans as Huns during the First World War was not an invention of Germany's enemies, but came from a speech Wilhelm himself gave, calling on German troops helping to suppress the Boxer Uprising in China to act like the ancient barbarian tribe. Wilhelm's own ideas were at least as problematic as his behaviour: he believed in the divine right of kings – a noticeably archaic view by 1900, except perhaps in the Russian Empire – but also in social welfare programmes. He envisaged his generals and government ministers as his medieval vassals, but was fascinated by industrialization and by Germany's growing navy and commercial fleet. Wilhelm was given to making all manner of racist, anti-Semitic remarks, but he invited Jewish businessmen to his court and some became surprisingly close companions.

Historians, investigating the Hohenzollern family documents, have argued that there were organic causes for Wilhelm's odd behaviour: manic depression (bipolar disorder) and possibly brain damage caused by the same difficult birth that left one side of his body partially paralysed. A broader question that divides their interpretation of his rule concerns his influence over events. Some regard him as a central figure, as the powerful ruler making policy, appointing subordinates who would follow his plans, and generally being in charge. This was certainly the attitude of the victorious allies in the First World War, and they brought war crimes charges against the emperor, which he evaded by fleeing in 1918 to the Netherlands, whose government refused to extradite him to face trial.

Another interpretation sees Wilhelm II as largely a figurehead, someone enjoying pomp, ceremony and display, spending his working hours signing thousands of papers granting government bureaucrats various honours and titles, and thinking he was in charge, but being, both for personal reasons and in view of the increasingly complex structure of German government and society, incapable of actually ruling. It would be fair to say that Wilhelm started out by trying to be a strong ruler – his dismissal of the domineering chancellor Bismarck in 1890 a clear sign of this intent – but as his reign progressed, his inability to be in charge became increasingly evident, and he became steadily more of a figurehead. From time to time he did summon up the energy and concentration to intervene in government affairs, particularly with regard to personnel choices for top government and military offices; these interventions generally had negative consequences.

dismissed the elderly chancellor. What this dismissal would mean for German politics was quite unclear, especially as different ideas of the mercurial and eccentric emperor ranged across the political landscape, from the extreme right to the liberal left. Most of the 1890s would see both domestic and foreign policy, in Europe's most powerful nation, now lacking Bismarck's strong guiding hand, contested among government insiders and in a state of uncertainty and indecision.

Italians may have thought they had a strong man when the veteran nationalist – former radical turned liberal seeking compromise with conservatives – Francesco Crispi became prime minister in 1887, serving in that office from 1887 to 1891 and again in 1894–96. Crispi's second term proved to be a disaster. Domestic chaos, reflecting the way that the economic crisis of the late nineteenth century hit Italy hardest towards the end of the period of low growth and steep recessions, included an enormous scandal concerning government bailouts of some of Italy's major banks following their very dubious investments, massive demonstrations and land occupations of the rural lower classes in Sicily and of students and blue-collar workers in Italy's industrial north. Crispi's vigorous advocacy of imperialist foreign policies, for economic and nationalist reasons, met with disaster at the battle of Adua in early 1896 when Italian troops in north Africa were decisively defeated by the Ethiopians – more Italian soldiers died in one day of that battle than in all the wars of Italian unification in 1859–61 – the only such crushing and definitive defeat suffered by a European imperial power before 1914.

Even in conservative and absolutist Russia, the final years of the rule of Alexander III were marked by the famine of 1891–92, when the government's inability to get relief supplies to areas of widespread hunger caused a loss of public confidence in the regime. Alexander's son and successor, Nicholas II (1868–1918), coming to the throne in 1894, was determined to continue the conservative and authoritarian policies of his father, but it was unclear if he would be able to do so. Rounding out this picture of political indecision and uncertainty was a twelve-year-long conflict in Denmark between conservative governments and liberal parliamentary majorities. Beginning in 1889 as a clash over military expenditures and the taxes needed to pay for them, the disagreement escalated into a conflict over whether the country would have a parliamentary government, that is, whether government ministers would be accountable to parliament or to the king.

This general impression of domestic affairs politically adrift in most of Europe by the early to mid-1890s also applies to the condition of international relations. For much of the 1880s, the attention of the European Powers was turned to overseas expansion, which proceeded relatively smoothly with little impact on the intra-European situation. The existing pattern of diplomacy was shaken by two factors that drove a wedge between Russia on the one hand and the two central European powers on the other. The first of these was a recurrence of the Eastern Question, which occurred in the context of intensive Great Power diplomatic manoeuvring. The issue concerned the accession to Bulgaria in 1884 of Eastern Rumelia, part of the territory withheld from Bulgaria by the Berlin Congress of 1878. Austria-Hungary ultimately imposed a pro-Habsburg government in Sofia (Bulgaria's capital) over Russian opposition.

Russia broke with Austria-Hungary, refusing to renew the Three Emperors' Alliance of 1881. Bismarck, continuing his policy of good relations with both Austria-Hungary and Russia, so as to maintain the diplomatic isolation of France, now retreated to a set of two treaties. One was already in existence, the Triple Alliance of 1882, a mutual defence pact between Germany, Austria-Hungary and Italy. The second he devised was the Reinsurance Treaty of 1887, a German–Russian mutual non-aggression pact. As can be seen from the nature of these two agreements, German–Russian relations had become noticeably more distant than German–Austrian ones.

Even this German–Russian détente was not of long duration. Bismarck's conservative turn at the end of the 1870s had meant a commitment to agricultural protective tariffs, which had a sharp and negative effect on Russian grain exports to Germany. Russian retaliation in the form of a tariff on imported industrial goods led Bismarck to his 1887 decision to ban Russian government bonds from the Berlin capital market. Bismarck's policy of diplomatic conciliation of Russia was paired with one of economic hostility.

This would have been a difficult balance even for a diplomatic genius like Bismarck to maintain, but in the late 1880s, as his power waned in Berlin with the accession of the new emperor Wilhelm II, different voices were beginning to be heard in German policy-making circles. A growing number of individuals, including such prominent figures as the chief of the General Staff, Count Waldersee, and one of the senior diplomats, Friedrich von Holstein, began suggesting that German policy should take on a more strongly anti-Russian, pro-Austrian orientation. Both strategic calculations and racialized visions of national conflict – thoughts of a coming war between Teutonic and Slavic races – motivated their policy decisions. The new emperor, who was simultaneously inexperienced, headstrong and opinionated, found their views increasingly congenial, and their influence on Wilhelm II was another one of the reasons that Bismarck was dismissed in 1890. Germany's new foreign policy team promptly refused to renew the Reinsurance Treaty that very year.

Russia's realignment towards a pro-French policy followed in steps corresponding to Germany's steps in rejecting Russia. Following Bismarck's prohibition on the sale of Russian bonds in Berlin, the Tsar's officials turned to the Paris capital market, and Russian bonds quickly became a big favourite of French investors. French and Russian financial ties steadily increased from the late 1880s through to 1914. The non-renewal of the Reinsurance Treaty and, with it, the end of a German guarantee not to attack Russia, brought the next step, expanding the Franco-Russian entente from the financial to the diplomatic and military arenas. Staff talks between Russia and France began in 1891, leading the following year to an agreement on mutual defence in case of attack. The agreement was finally ratified by the two governments at the beginning of 1894, and has come to be known as the Franco-Russian Alliance.

This agreement was a step into the unknown, one that required a good deal of negotiation and the overcoming of a considerable amount of reluctance, particularly on the part of the Russians. It marked a decisive break in European diplomacy, bringing to an end the era of French isolation and unchallenged German primacy, but in doing so it also raised the possibility of a major war between the Great Powers. The peripheral engagements the Powers had cultivated in the two decades following the Franco-Prussian War – colonial expansion and the Eastern Question – remained very much live issues, but following the Franco-Russian Alliance these peripheral engagements were no longer an alternative to direct clashes between the Great Powers, but a possible lead-in to them. When combined with the political uncertainty and the rise of new political forces developing in most European countries by the 1890s, it is easy to see how this new diplomatic situation would be potentially unstable and dangerous. Further developments in the two decades before 1914 would only intensify this state of affairs.

NOTES TO PART 2

1 Cited in Hans-Ulrich Wehler, *Bismarck und der Imperialismus*, 4th edn (Munich, 1976), 58.
2 Figures from B. R. Mitchell, *International Historical Statistics: Europe, 1750–1993*, 4th edn (London, 1998), 466, and Wilfried Feldenkirchen, *Die Eisen- und Stahlindustrie des Ruhrgebiets 1879–1914* (Wiesbaden, 1982), table 126a.
3 John W. Boyer, *Political Radicalism in Late Imperial Vienna* (Chicago, 1981), 44.
4 Figures from Friedrich Lenger, *Sozialgeschichte der deutschen Handwerker seit 1800* (Frankfurt, 1988), 115.
5 Figures from Robert Gellately, *The Politics of Economic Despair: Shopkeepers and German Politics, 1890–1914* (London, 1974), 31; Alain Faure, 'The Grocery Trade in Nineteenth Century Paris: A Fragmented Corporation', in Geoffrey Crossick and Heinz-Gerhard Haupt (eds), *Shopkeepers and Master Artisans in Nineteenth-Cenetury Europe* (London, 1984), 161, and Jonathan Morris, *The Political Economy of Shopkeeping in Milan 1886–1922* (Cambridge, 1993), 33–4.
6 Figures from Peter Marschalk, *Bevölkerungsgeschichte Deutschlands im 19. und 20. Jahrhundert* (Frankfurt, 1984), 181; Boris N. Mironov, *Social History of Imperial Russia, 1700–1917*, 2 vols (Boulder, CO, 2000) 1: 465; Adna Weber, *The Growth of Cities in the Nineteenth Century* (Ithaca, NY, 1963), 99, 103, first published 1899.
7 Figures from Stefan-Ludwig Hoffmann, *Geselligkeit und Demokratie* (Göttingen, 2003), 63.
8 Figures from W. Hamish Fraser, *The Coming of the Mass Market* (London, 1981), 123–4; Brett Fairbairn, 'History from the Ecological Perspective: Gaia Theory and the Problem of Cooperatives in Turn-of-the-Century Germany', *American Historical Review* 99 (1994): 1204–39; Gellately, *Politics of Economic Despair*, 39.
9 Cited in Fraser, *Coming of the Mass Market*, 125.
10 Italian figures from Marzio Barbagli, *Education for Unemployment: Politics, Labor Markets, and the School System – Italy, 1859–1973*, trans. Robert Ross (New York, 1982), 75, 79; Russian figures from Ben Eklof, *Russian Peasant Schools* (Berkeley, CA, 1986), 287.
11 Cited in Christopher Duggan, *Francesco Crispi 1818–1901* (Oxford, 2001), 446.
12 Cited in Werner Blessing, *Staat und Kirche in der Gesellschaft* (Göttingen, 1982), 214.
13 Figures in Hartmut Kaelble, *Social Mobility in the 19th and 20th Centuries: Europe and America in Comparative Perspective* (New York, 1986), 40, 42.
14 Antoine Prost, *Histoire de l'enseignement en France 1800–1967* (Paris, 1967), 251.
15 Cited in Jeffrey Paul von Arx, *Progress and Pessimism: Religion, Politics, and History in Late Nineteenth Century Britain* (Cambridge, MA, 1985), 35.
16 Cited in George W. Stocking, Jr, *Victorian Anthropology* (New York, 1987), 163.
17 'Locksley Hall Sixty Years After', in *The Poems of Tennyson*, ed. Christopher Ricks (London, 1969), 1359–69.
18 Friedrich Wilhelm Nietzsche, *The Twilight of the Idols*, in *The Portable Nietzsche*, ed. Walter Kaufman (New York, 1968), 486.

19 Quoted in Lilian Furst and Peter Skrine, *Naturalism* (London, 1971), 30.
20 Quote from David Baguley, *Naturalist Fiction: The Entropic Vision* (Cambridge, 1990), 101.
21 Cited in John House, *Impressionism: Paint and Politics* (New Haven, CT, 2004), 148.
22 Cited in Fred Sepainter, *Die Reichstagswahlen im Großherzogtum Baden* (Frankfurt, 1983), 94.
23 Cited in Richard Shannon, *The Age of Salisbury, 1881–1902: Unionism and Empire* (London, 1996), 50.
24 Taken from the very handy list in Geoff Eley, *Forging Democracy: The History of the Left in Europe, 1850–2000* (Oxford, 2002), 63.
25 Cited in Duggan, *Francesco Crispi*, 539.
26 Cited in William D. Irvine, *The Boulanger Affair Reconsidered* (New York, 1989), 173. Emphasis in original.
27 Cited in Veselin Traikov, 'Bulgarian Volunteers in the Serbo-Turkish War of 1876', in Bela K. Kiraly and Gale Stokes (eds), *Insurrections, Wars and the Eastern Crisis in the 1870s* (Boulder, CO, 1985), 166.
28 Figures from H. L. Wesseling, *The European Colonial Empires, 1815–1919* trans. H. L. Wesseling (London, 2004), 144.
29 Figures from Robert Johnson, *British Imperialism* (Basingstoke, 2003), 54. Different total figures are cited in other sources, but the distribution of investments remains the same.
30 Cited in ibid., 99.
31 Cited in M. E. Chamberlain, *The Scramble for Africa*, 2nd edn (London, 1999), 85.
32 Quoted in Raymond Betts, *Tricoleur: The French Overseas Empire* (London, 1978), 48.
33 Cited in Michael Bentley, *Lord Salisbury's World: Conservative Environments in Late-Victorian Britain* (Cambridge, 2001), 226.

PART 3

THE AGE OF CLASSICAL MODERNISM, 1890–1914

Legend:
- Triple Alliance, 1882–1915
- Triple Entente, 1907–1917

NORWAY

FINLAND

St Petersburg

SCOTLAND
Glasgow

NORTH
SEA

SWEDEN

Moscow

IRELAND
Dublin

GREAT
BRITAIN

DENMARK

BALTIC SEA

RUSSIA

ENGLAND

NETHERLANDS

Hamburg

London Amsterdam

Brussels

GERMANY

Berlin

POLAND

BELGIUM

Frankfurt

ATLANTIC

Paris

Prague

OCEAN

Orleans

Vienna

Budapest

FRANCE

Bern

AUSTRIA–HUNGARY

SWITZERLAND

Bordeaux

Lyons

Turin Milan

Venice

MONTE-
NEGRO

ROMANIA

Marseilles

Genoa

Sarajevo

Belgrade

Bucharest

BLACK
SEA

PORTUGAL

Barcelona

CORSICA

ITALY

ADRIATIC SEA

SERBIA

Sofia

Lisbon

Madrid

SPAIN

Rome

BULGARIA

Constantinople

SARDINIA

ALBANIA

BALEARIC IS

GREECE

AEGEAN
SEA

OTTOMAN
EMPIRE

Athens

SICILY

CRETE

MOROCCO
(Fr.)

ALGERIA
(Fr.)

TUNISIA
(Fr.)

MEDITERRANEAN SEA

LIBYA
(It.)

0   400 miles
0   400 km

Europe on the eve of the First World War
Source: From *THE MAKING OF THE WEST 3E* by Lynn Hunt et al., Copyright © 2009 by Bedford/St. Martin's.
Reproduced by permission of Bedford/St. Martin's.

CHAPTER 15

OVERVIEW OF THE AGE OF CLASSICAL MODERNISM

THE SHAPE OF AN ERA

The quarter-century preceding the First World War has very recently passed entirely out of living memory. What remains are images, now typically seen in television mini-series: women in long skirts and men in coats with stiff collars, spending long sunlit afternoons on large, green lawns in amiable conversation and stately pastimes. It all leaves the impression of an age of peace and prosperity, of a time of order and stability. These images and the impressions they evoke are the electronic version of a long-held designation of the age, known in most European languages by its French name, the 'belle époque' – literally, the beautiful era, or, translated more freely, the 'good times'.

This designation was not coined during the years to which it refers, but only retrospectively, a reflection of the way that the First World War brought this period of European history to a sudden and catastrophic end. The war itself involved an unprecedented slaughter of combatants, as well as enormous economic, social and political upheaval. But the end of the war did not bring any relief: it was followed by revolution, counter-revolution and civil war in much of Europe, and by social and economic chaos. After a few years of relative stability in the mid-1920s, there came the Great Depression, the rise of Nazism and a second world war, far more murderous, far more disruptive than the first, and another post-war sequel of revolution and socio-economic disruption. It was only at some point between 1950 and 1960 that standards of living in most European countries finally reached and permanently surpassed their 1913 levels. In the interval, an entire adult lifetime had passed and the years before 1914 appeared in a rosy light, whose projection continues into the present.

Since the past fifty years have been, all things considered, a period of unprecedented peace and prosperity in Europe, the contrast between a dark and cloudy present and a pre-1914 era of sunlit afternoons has begun to fade. As a result, historians have been posing inconvenient questions about the belle époque: above all, if the pre-1914 era was an idyllic time of peace and prosperity, how did it lead to such a devastating war? Focusing more closely on the years 1890 to 1914 reveals an era with a more divided character. It was certainly a period of (relative) peace, but also one of arms races, diplomatic brinksmanship, and the exploitation of nationalism and militarism for political purposes. The late nineteenth and early twentieth centuries were a time of prosperity, especially in comparison to the troubled decades after 1870, but this prosperity was the result of rapid and unsettling economic changes. Compared with the Russian Revolution and Civil War, with Stalin's purges, or with the Nazi seizure of power and Hitler's bellicose and murderous totalitarian regime, the quarter-century before 1914 was a period of order and political stability, but it was also a time of dynamic mass politics, involving unprecedented political mobilization and political confrontations on a very large scale. By today's standards staid and old-fashioned, easily lending itself to portrayal in stuffy television dramas, the pre-1914 era was also a period of dynamic intellectual, artistic and scientific innovation.

With these developments in mind, we can see that the designation of the years 1890 to 1914 as a belle époque is more nostalgic than exact. What is needed is something that more accurately captures the characteristic of the era at the interface of the nineteenth and twentieth centuries, a conclusion to a long period of relatively peaceful historical development, also the lead-in to a very different era of total war, and, beyond that, at the origin of ideas, structures and institutions that would shape – for good or ill – much of the next seven or eight decades. A useful alternative is to crib a term from art historians and talk about the pre-1914 years as an age of 'classical modernism'. Art historians use the phrase to refer to artists whose career began at that time, such as Picasso or Matisse. They were pioneers of new artistic endeavours, creating a 'modern art' which, continuing nineteenth-century trends but doing so in radical fashion, broke with classical traditions in search of forms appropriate to portray what they and their contemporaries understood as the modern world. At the beginning of the twenty-first century, that 'modern' world is one hundred years old, and no longer quite so modern; the forms of modern art first developed then are no longer contemporary and 'modern' in the sense of being about the present, but have become, in their turn, classic, belonging to the past.

Expanding on this understanding of art and applying it more broadly to the pre-1914 era, we could say it was then that 'modern' forms of political, economic, social and cultural life developed that would continue on through much of the twentieth century. Today, though, many of these modern forms, whether large-scale steel manufacturing, labour parties, Freudian psychology, or European domination of world politics, seem more than a bit old-fashioned; they, too, have become classic and are no longer contemporary. This triple designation behind the term 'classical modernism' – the culmination of the nineteenth century, the run-up to a very different era of total war, and the setting of trends that have continued through the first three-quarters of the twentieth century but which increasingly seem old-fashioned today – lays out the main themes for this third part of the book. Leaving behind the nostalgic view of a belle époque, we will explore a period of dynamic and unsettling change, with powerful short-, medium- and long-term consequences, yet also an era departing from living memory and fast receding into the past.

THE MAIN EVENTS

The dynamic and unsettling character of the era is certainly apparent in the main political events. The quarter-century before 1914 was crowded with vehement controversies, mass actions, including a revolution in Europe's largest country, and a whole series of smaller wars and diplomatic confrontations leading up to the First World War. The best way to structure these many and dramatic occurrences, in both domestic and international politics, is to think of the period as divided into three parts: the years 1890–98, which saw mostly a continuation of trends from the 1880s; a transitional period, 1898–1906, marked by warfare, major diplomatic realignments, political disputes leading to the very edge of legality and beyond, and elections bringing about important political changes; finally, the years 1906–14, characterized by clashes over political reform in many European countries, and an international scene of diplomatic confrontations and crises perpetually on the brink of war.

The first two-thirds of the 1890s was a period of conservative, or, in the Mediterranean countries, of moderate liberal governments, which sought a reconciliation with more conservative forces, much like the situation in the previous decade. Probably the most important domestic events in this period were the rise of political extremes. On the left, the victory of the social democrats in the 1890 German elections, in which they received more votes than any other political party, was followed by socialist election victories, albeit on a much more modest scale, in most of Europe during that decade. On the right, the 1893 elections saw the pre-1914 high point of anti-Semitic political parties in Germany; the Austrian anti-Semitic leader Karl Lueger was elected mayor of Vienna in 1897 taking control of a long-time liberal stronghold. Nationalist political parties in the multinational Austro-Hungarian Empire grew steadily stronger and more intransigent, making life increasingly difficult for the government.

International relations in this period also ran along lines of the 1880s, as European countries continued their imperial expansion. In 1898, French and British expeditions aimed at expanding their African empires met at the village of Fashoda, in today's Sudan. For a few months there was the threat of war over colonial acquisitions, until the French backed down and the matter was solved peacefully.

If the major political events between 1890 and 1897/98 largely involved a continuation of the trends of the 1880s, the years 1898 to 1905 were ones in which a series of wars and crises led to a complete diplomatic realignment. One reason for this realignment was the end to the period of effortless imperial expansion. The Boxer Rebellion of 1899–1900, a massive uprising against European imperial pretensions in China, and the Boer War of 1899–1902, in which the descendants of eighteenth-century Dutch settlers in southern Africa opposed the incorporation of their small republics into the British Empire, both involved powerful opposition to European imperialism, and both were followed with close attention worldwide. Although the

Boxers and the Boers would eventually be defeated, it was only after considerable effort and difficult and expensive fighting. A different kind of check on European expansion became evident in the Spanish–American War of 1898 and the Russo-Japanese War of 1904–05. Both of those wars, ultimately originating in struggles for power and influence in East Asia, saw the defeat of a European colonial power by a rising non-European state. The Japanese victory over Russia was particularly striking and unexpected to contemporaries.

Great Britain's military and political leaders, following the enormous expense and difficulty of the Boer War, felt that the nation's economic and human resources could no longer support an open-ended, worldwide imperial commitment. Formal and informal agreements with Japan and the United States limited British engagement in Asia and South America; the Franco-British Entente of 1904 resolved disputed colonial questions and set the two countries, which had been maritime and colonial rivals for the previous two centuries, on a course of gradual military and diplomatic cooperation. A similar entente would be reached with the Russian Empire, another long-term colonial rival, by 1910, allowing Britain to concentrate its military resources, particularly its fleet, on defending the empire and the British Isles.

While the British were scaling back their potential military commitments, the Germans were increasing theirs. Following the Franco-Russian Alliance of 1894, German military planners prepared for a war on two fronts, best known in its 1905 version, the Schlieffen Plan, which called for a German invasion of France followed by an offensive against Russia. In 1897, the German government began the development of a battleship fleet, a high seas navy that would threaten British naval supremacy, as part of a plan to develop a large German colonial empire. By the middle of the first decade of the twentieth century, the British military and strategic recommitment was increasingly directed against the growing German naval threat, producing a new diplomatic and military realignment, pitting Germany and its Austro-Hungarian ally against a loose coalition of France, Russia and Great Britain.

At the same time as these military conflicts and diplomatic realignments were proceeding, domestic politics in the major European countries was being transformed. Sometimes these transformations occurred in peaceful and constitutional form: the victories of the social democrats in the German elections of 1903 and of a Liberal–Labour–Irish Nationalist political alliance in the British elections of 1906 indicated the widespread desire in the two countries for a new period of social and political reform, following decades of conservative rule. In France, the political system remained within the bounds of legal constitutional change, although things did get closer to the edge.

The reason was the Dreyfus Affair, which developed out of the trial and conviction in 1895 of the Jewish army officer Captain Alfred Dreyfus on charges of passing military secrets to the German. As time went on, evidence mounted that Dreyfus had been framed by a right-wing clique of anti-Semitic officers on the General Staff, and a growing campaign to have his conviction overturned, increasingly supported by left-of-centre political parties, was met by a vociferous insistence on his guilt from both older conservatives and newer, right-wing radicals. The 1898 elections were punctuated by anti-Semitic riots. In 1902, a pro-Dreyfus coalition of liberals and socialists won a major election victory and took steps against conservative forces in France, dismissing anti-republican army officers, and, in 1905, separating the state and the Catholic Church – a step that caused riots throughout the country. The governing coalition won an impressive election victory in 1906, setting the path, contemporaries thought, for further reforms.

The most drastic form of change came in absolutist Russia, where the Tsar's autocratic rule was shaken by his country's defeat in the war with Japan. Most of 1905 was taken up with social and political unrest: mass meetings demanding a constitution and elected legislature, land riots of the peasants, enormous strikes of industrial and craft workers, demands for independence on the part of the Russian Empire's national minorities, particularly the Poles. Eventually, Tsar Nicholas II was forced to agree to limits on his power and an elected parliament, or Duma. But no sooner were the concessions made than the counter-revolutionary forces took the initiative, beginning with an unprecedented wave of pogroms and followed by the gradual suppression, over the course of 1906, of the revolutionary movement. Shock waves from this revolution, particularly the politicized labour unrest and the nationalist demand for secession from a multinational empire, reverberated across Europe.

Following this tumultuous interlude, politics in most European countries centred around a confrontation between proponents of reform, sometimes in danger of being outflanked to their left, and enemies of reform. Among the reforms of the Liberal government in Great Britain were the introduction of a social insurance system, financing both that system and an arms build-up with higher taxes on landed property, instituting home rule in Ireland and breaking the power of the Tory-dominated House of Lords to prevent these proposals from becoming law. Just initiating these measures required two dramatic confrontations with the Lords and two general elections in 1910. Home rule for Ireland was still not implemented before 1914, and the Tories were leading a ferocious opposition to it, even flirting with opposing the government by armed force. At the same time, the Liberal government was faced with oppositional mass movements, in the form of enormous strikes and labour unrest, and an increasingly militant women's suffrage movement.

In Germany, a conservative government, funding its social insurance and military expenditures by taxing business interests and consumers instead of large landowners, faced a liberal and socialist opposition that triumphed in the 1912 general elections. At the same time, there were a growing number of conservatives and extreme rightists who felt that the government was not conservative enough – not doing enough to suppress the socialists, or pursuing an aggressive enough foreign policy. They formed what they called a 'national opposition'.

Prospects for social and economic reform in France, which had seemed so bright in the 1906 elections, quickly faded, and French politics fell into two separate camps. On the one hand, there was a group of left-wing liberals and socialists who wanted to see the introduction of social insurance programmes financed by a progressive income tax; they had a relatively peaceful foreign policy. On the other hand were more moderate liberals and conservatives who vigorously opposed social reform and progressive taxation but who strongly supported increased defence spending and an aggressive foreign policy – the so-called national reawakening. The second group succeeded in 1912–13 in increasing arms expenditures and terms of military service, but the 1914 elections brought a victory for the first group, who seemed about ready to take over the government.

For all the increasingly vehement political disputes in France, Germany and Great Britain, their governments were still functional; the governments of Austria-Hungary were having difficulty functioning in this period, as increasing popular support for nationalist groups, who wanted to secede from the empire to create their own nation-states, brought the political process to a halt. To be sure, there were both Catholic and socialist political parties who opposed this trend towards nationalism, and in the first election in Austria held under universal manhood suffrage in 1907 they scored a substantial victory. But the 1911 elections brought gains to the nationalists, so that the future of the multinational empire seemed in doubt.

Tsarist Russia was on an authoritarian course following the victory of counter-revolution in 1906. Prime minister Peter Stolypin hoped this strong position of the Tsar's government would enable him to implement a series of reforms that would solidify support for the regime. Stolypin's attempts to introduce a free market in rural landownership were partially successful, but his efforts to modernize the empire's administration and introduce equality before the law for all nationalities and religions were blocked by the very conservative forces his counter-revolutionary policies had brought to power. Growing opposition, in the form of labour strikes and a terrorist campaign of assassinating high-ranking government officials – including Stolypin himself in 1911 – made the political situation very problematic.

As these domestic political confrontations over reform were occurring (and similar ones were under way in the smaller European countries at this time as well), the Great Powers were launched on a path of diplomatic crises and military confrontations leading to the First World War. The series of crises began with the first Moroccan crisis of 1905, in which the German government exploited ostensible colonial disputes with France over Morocco to intimidate the latter power, while its Russian ally was suffering military defeat and revolution. Although occurring at a favourable moment, the German initiative failed because the country's rulers backed down from a preventative war against France, and at the 1906 Algeçiras conference to settle the dispute, all the countries in attendance, including the United States, either lined up behind France or showed little enthusiasm for the German position. Germany's emperor Wilhelm II asserted that his country was 'surrounded by a ring of enemies', which his policies had helped to create.

The second major crisis followed the Young Turk revolution of 1908 in the Ottoman Empire. Responding to the unclear legal and diplomatic situation created by this uprising, and the possibility of the dissolution of the entire empire, the government of Austria-Hungary formally annexed the province of Bosnia-Herzegovina, which it had ruled as a protectorate since 1878. This brought about the prospect of a war between Austria-Hungary and the neighbouring kingdom of Serbia, in view of the large ethnic Serbian population in Bosnia. Serbia received strong diplomatic support and potential military assistance from Russia, and the threat of a war between Austria-Hungary and Serbia backed by Russia, leading to a general European conflict was present. This was how war would begin in 1914, but in 1909 Russia's French ally was not enthusiastic about such a war, and Russia itself was militarily too weak to fight on its own, so it was forced to give way.

In the Second Moroccan Crisis of 1911, basically a renewal of the one six years earlier, the prospect of such a general European war was very apparent, and at the height of the crisis in the summer of 1911 the outbreak of a war was widely expected – as it would not be three years later when the war began. The crisis was settled with minor French concessions, a German diplomatic defeat. Following the resolution of the crisis, the French, German and Russian governments all began taking major measures to increase the size of their armies, the firepower of their weapons and the speed with which the troops could be mobilized in case of war. This land arms race, in conjunction with the Anglo-German naval arms race, ongoing since c.1900, destabilized the diplomatic situation and made a war as the result of a diplomatic crisis much more likely.

The Balkan Wars of 1912–13, in which a coalition of smaller Balkan powers attacked and defeated the Ottoman Empire, and then fought each other over the spoils, was the immediate precursor to the Great War. The conflict was a French proxy victory, since the victorious Greek, Serb and Romanian forces used French weapons and had been trained by French military instructors, while the German-sponsored Ottoman and Bulgarian armies were defeated. The Russian government, while pleased by the victories of anti-Turkish Slavic nations, was upset at the prospect raised by the war of the dissolution of the Ottoman Empire and control of the Straits at Istanbul, a crucial choke point of Russian maritime commerce, coming under the control of a potentially hostile power. The government of Austria-Hungary was particularly dismayed by the war, fearing that the nationalist victories over the multinational Ottoman Empire would only encourage the already vociferous and militant nationalist movements still further. The Habsburg government was particularly concerned with the kingdom of Serbia, both a major victor of the Balkan Wars and a supporter of Serb nationalist movements within Austria-Hungary itself. Since Austria-Hungary was the only remaining ally of a German government increasingly worried about an Anglo-French-Russian coalition against it, the Austrians' concerns touched a nerve in Europe's militarily strongest Great Power.

These fears were realized in particularly striking fashion, just three and a half months after the signing of the final treaty ending the Balkan Wars. On 28 June 1914, the Archduke Franz Ferdinand, heir to the Habsburg throne, while making an official visit to Sarajevo, capital of Bosnia-Herzegovina, was assassinated by Bosnian Serb terrorists enjoying the support and patronage of the Serbian army. The government of Austria-Hungary resolved to respond by crushing Serbia once and for all. As the Bosnian crisis of 1908 had shown, this might lead to Russian intervention, so the Habsburg government, before taking any action, conferred with its German ally, receiving from it permission to go to war. In agreeing to support an Austrian attack on Serbia, the German government, well aware that such an attack might lead to a Russian intervention, and that its own war plans called for beginning a war with Russia by an attack on France, was accepting the possibility of starting a great European war.

This is precisely what happened following the Austrian assault on Serbia at the end of July 1914. The Russian government began to mobilize its armies; the Germans responded by declaring war on Russia, and, as their military planning required, hurling the bulk of their armed forces against France. Thus, by 1 August 1914, the day that Germany declared war against Russia and invaded France via Belgium, a great continental European war was in progress. Turning it into a world war required the intervention of the worldwide British Empire. Officially, Great Britain entered the war because the German invasion of France proceeded via Belgium, whose neutrality and inviolability had been agreed to by all the European Powers in 1839. In reality, the British government feared the possibility that its major maritime rival would be victorious in a continental European war and emerge stronger than ever. The outbreak and progress of the global conflict begun in the summer of 1914 would destroy once and for all most of the political, social and economic structures that had developed in Europe since 1850, and institute a three-decades-long period of total war, social and economic upheaval and totalitarian rule in much of the European continent.

CHAPTER 16

POPULATION AND THE ECONOMY

The overriding economic feature of the period was an increase in growth rates following the depressed years of the 1870s and 1880s. At different point in the 1890s in different countries, economic growth began to accelerate and continued at a more rapid pace down until the First World War. Figure 16.1 offers examples of this increase in growth rates in five countries, from which it can be seen that the acceleration in growth rates ranged from extremely sharp – almost doubling in Italy over the previous twenty years – to more modest, as was the case with France and the UK. Overall, economic growth in the quarter-century prior to the First World War came close to, but fell just short of, the prosperous post-1850 decades. Also like those decades and very much unlike the period 1870–95, the period from 1896 to 1914 had just two recessions – in 1901 and 1907. Both were short and followed by vigorous recoveries.

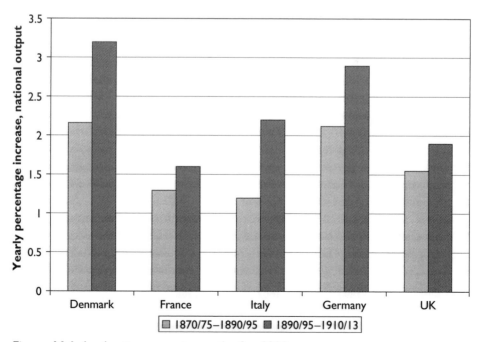

Figure 16.1 *Accelerating economic growth after 1895*
Source: Derived from B. R. Mitchell, *International Historical Statistics: Europe, 1750–1993*, 4th edn (London, 1998).

Accelerating economic growth and few and short recessions suggest a period of prosperity, and the pre-1914 decades were exactly that. In contrast to the difficult years of the late nineteenth century, businesses found the pre-war period a consistently profitable one. For example, the German steel manufacturer, the Gutehoffnungshütte, which had averaged a meagre yearly return of just 2.7 per cent on its invested capital between 1878 and 1895, saw that figure rise to an impressive 12.5 per cent between 1896 and 1914. Yearly returns over this entire period never dropped below 7 per cent, and were in double digits for fourteen of nineteen years, peaking at 20.2 per cent in 1896/97.[1] It was not just large, modern enterprises, such as the Gutehoffnungshütte, which experienced the prosperity of the period. Unemployment rates were noticeably lower than in the depressed 1870s and 1880s; some particularly economically vigorous regions even experienced labour shortages at times. Real wages rose through most of the pre-1914 years, and increasing consumption of both basic necessities – per capita wheat consumption in Italy, for instance, rose 50 per cent between 1900 and 1915 – and consumer goods was a feature of the period. Farmers, small businessmen, master craftsmen and the growing social group of salaried employees also participated in the general prosperity.

Small producers, farmers in particular, were pleased by another feature of the era, a rise in prices. As in Figure 9.2, each line in Figure 16.2 refers to a price level in a specific country; the lines cannot be used to compare price levels in different countries.

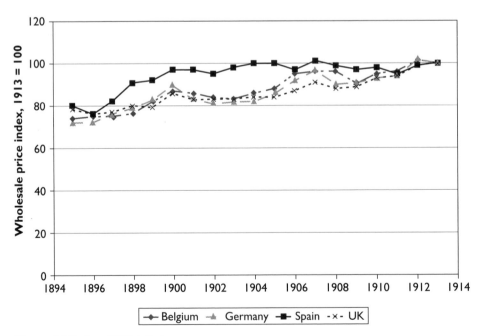

Figure 16.2 *Post-1895 inflation*
Source: B. R. Mitchell, *International Historical Statistics: Europe, 1750–1993*, 4th edn, 1998, Palgrave Macmillan, reproduced with permission of Palgrave Macmillan.

They do show that, in all the countries, prices rose by between 25 and 35 per cent over the two decades from their low point in the mid-1890s until the First World War. The increase in prices was especially noticeable after about 1905 and there were increasing complaints to be heard in the pre-1914 decade about the cost of living. In several countries, most prominently France and Great Britain, price increases limited or even brought to an end gains in real wages. Individuals with fixed incomes or in occupations with gradually increasing salaries – civil servants and many white-collar workers, for instance – found themselves falling behind the rise in prices.

By today's standards, the price increases were quite moderate, generally not exceeding some 3 per cent per year. For contemporaries, accustomed to a nineteenth-century of steady or falling prices, especially the sharp price declines of the century's final years, this rise in prices was both unwelcome and unsettling. It was nothing compared to the wild inflation seen during and after both world wars, or even to the oil price shock years of the 1970s and 1980s, but the modest rises in prices after the mid-1890s marked a transition from a mostly deflationary nineteenth to a mostly inflationary twentieth century.

A SECOND INDUSTRIAL REVOLUTION

Central to this favourable economic environment was the blossoming of two new branches of industry, the manufacture of chemicals and electrical equipment. Their rapid growth, technological innovations and many spin-offs made them the leading sectors of the economy, a role they would continue to play through the first two-thirds of the twentieth century. So great was the impact of these industries in the period, that historians have taken to referring to their introduction as a 'second industrial revolution'. To show just how apt this phrase was, we will mention just a few of the products of these industries that were either first developed or first came into widespread use in the quarter-century before the First World War.

This period saw the beginning of large-scale pharmaceutical manufacturing. Several prominent products of the period include acetylsalicylic acid, which we know by the trade name given to it by the Bayer Chemical Company when it brought the chemical to market in 1898 – aspirin. About that time, Bayer Chemicals also introduced a new product for treating sore throats, which it named heroin – a drug that turned out to have some other uses. In 1909, the chemist Paul Ehrlich synthesized Salvarsan, the first effective treatment for syphilis and the first manufactured drug that actually cured a disease – and a disease that was a major killer and a social scourge – as opposed to treating its symptoms.

There were new household products, including the development around 1900 of hydrogenated vegetable oils, better known by the trade name introduced then of margarine. Persil, the first laundry detergent, was invented by the German chemist Fritz Henkel (1848–1930) and marketed by his firm in 1907. Chemical bleaches were not

BOX 16.1

Paul Ehrlich and the invention of Salvarsan

Today, in an age of AIDS, we can better appreciate the enormous apprehension in early twentieth-century Europe caused by syphilis, a potentially fatal, incurable sexually transmitted disease. The exact prevalence of the disease is unknown, although contemporaries certainly thought it was very widespread. The militant feminist Christabel Pankhurst even asserted in 1913 that between 75 and 80 per cent of all adult men in England suffered from venereal disease.

Since the sixteenth century, physicians in Europe had known of a treatment for syphilis, giving those infected doses of mercury. Mercury does, in fact, kill the spirochete that causes syphilis, but the dosage needed to do so kills the spirochete's human host as well. The medical treatment for syphilis thus consisted of giving patients almost enough mercury to kill them, which caused all sorts of unpleasant side effects, and weakened the syphilis spirochete without eliminating it.

The biologist Paul Ehrlich, a pupil of the great nineteenth-century bacteriologist and Pasteur's rival, Robert Koch, an expert in the staining of micro-organisms with chemical dyes, resolved to use the possibilities inherent in the progress of organic chemistry to develop treatments for infectious diseases. Ehrlich's idea was to start with an organic chemical compound and systematically alter it, by attaching different substances to its benzene ring, until he found one that would kill bacteria without harming the life form in which the bacteria lived. He was searching for a cure for sleeping sickness when he discovered, by accident, that the 606th substance he tried killed the syphilis spirochete but left its human host unharmed. Given the trade name Salvarsan, Ehrlich's chemical compound was hailed as a 'magic bullet' for the dread disease. In practice, the use of the drug proved to have considerable toxicity risks, although far less than mercury treatment, and with far more effect on the micro-organism causing the disease. Salvarsan's production was a triumph of the science of organic chemistry and the possibilities for manufacturing products based on scientific chemistry. It began a new era of scientifically designed pharmaceuticals for the treatment of infectious disease, an era that continues to the present day.

new to this period, but new methods of producing chlorine and hydrogen peroxide made their manufacture much cheaper and their use far more widespread.

New industrial applications of chemistry included the acetylene torch, chemical refrigerants, and the electrolysis of aluminum, invented in 1886 and brought into industrial production in the 1890s, making possible the cheap mass production of aluminium from the readily available deposits of bauxite, aluminium ore. Dynamite, a stable, easy-to-use explosive, invented by the famous Swedish engineer Alfred Nobel, had been in production since the 1870s, but smokeless powder, introduced in 1887, revolutionized military explosives. Synthetic dyestuffs had also been manufactured since the 1870s, but their output and consumption increased enormously in the quarter-century before the First World War; the same can be said of chemical fertilizers. Petroleum products in and of themselves were not new to this period, but the refining of crude oil to produce petrol and diesel fuel to power internal combustion engines was. The decade before the First World War saw the manufacture of the first plastics and the first synthetic fabrics. Their widespread use would have to wait until later in the century.

In regard to electrical equipment, the period 1890–1914 did not so much see the invention of new products as their introduction on a large scale. The first electric-powered subway systems were built in the 1890s, in Budapest, London and Paris, with Berlin soon to follow. Tramcars, horse-drawn until then, were electrified, and steam-powered suburban railways converted to electric power. In major cities, these years saw the transition from gaslights to electric street lighting. The production of aluminium from bauxite was as much a triumph of electrical as of chemical manufacturing, because the electrolysis process required massive amounts of electrical power. Electric motors came into widespread industrial use; on the eve of the First World War there were almost 37,000 such motors in Berlin, most commonly in metal- and woodworking, but in a variety of other uses too, employed to drive elevators or sewing machines, in paper mills, hat pressing or bakeries. All these uses of electricity were possible only as a result of the building of power grids, networks of electrical generation and transmission, with their power stations and substations, high-voltage lines and transformers. The construction of such power generation and transmission networks was a great triumph of engineering.

Before 1914, this triumph was still very partial and incomplete; most private households were not yet hooked up to the grid, less than 6 per cent in Berlin, for instance, Europe's electrically most advanced metropolis. As a result, and in strong contrast to chemical manufacturing, with its wide array of pre-1914 consumer products, most consumer products running on electric power, from light bulbs to toasters to vacuum cleaners, to sewing and washing machines to radios (pre-1914 wireless had exclusively military or navigational applications), would have to wait for a later period, either the years between the world wars or the third quarter of the twentieth century.

In spite of these differences, both industries had one crucial feature in common. They were the first 'high-tech' industries, whose products and processes were the result of scientific theory and experiment – in organic chemistry and the physics of electrodynamics – and whose competitiveness and success in the marketplace depended on continuing scientific research. Of the 4,000 university-trained chemists in Germany at the end of the 1890s, some 3,000 of them worked in the chemical industry. The large chemical firms BASF and Bayer each employed 150 chemists on their staff. This close relationship to scientific theory and experiment and dependence on university-trained scientific personnel, first apparent in chemical and electrical manufacturing, would become a feature of leading economic sectors and a determinant of the broader fate of national economies in the course of the twentieth century and down to the present day.

Besides these two high-tech industries, a third industry was crucial to the general economic upswing of the period, and that was steel manufacturing. Output of steel grew enormously in this period, tripling or quadrupling between the mid-1890s and 1913 in Austria, Belgium, France, Germany, Russia and Sweden. In contrast to chemical and electrical manufacturing, this growth of output was not the result of scientific or technological innovations; rather it represented a pay-off for the previous investments of the 1870s and 1880s in mechanized steel manufacturing through the Siemens–Martin and Thomas–Gilchrist processes.

Older branches of industry, although certainly doing better in the pre-war era than in the difficult 1870s and 1880s, lost a good deal of their dynamics. By c.1900, the rail network in Great Britain and most western and central European countries was complete, and there was little additional rail construction, an important economic stimulant through the 1880s. Even in parts of Europe very under-served by railways – the Balkans in particular – there was little rail construction in this period. The Russian Empire, with its large non-European territories, was the one country to experience a substantial increase in its rail network, which roughly doubled from 31,000 kilometres in 1890 to 67,000 in 1910. The story was much the same with textile manufacturing, where the trend, begun in the 1870s and 1880s, for manufacturing to shift to peripheral countries with lower wages continued. As Table 16.1 shows, the number of cotton spindles in Italy, for instance, increased by about two and a half times between the early 1890s and the First World War. By contrast, the pace of increase in Russia slowed considerably after the early 1890s, and in Spain there was even a decline in the number of cotton spindles. In western and central European countries with a long-established industry, there were examples of substantial growth in output, a recovery from the slower pace of the 1870s and 1880s, as in Germany, but also a clear slackening of the pace, as can be seen in Great Britain and France.

One industry developing in this period deserves mention not so much for what it was then, as for what it would become. This was the manufacture of motor vehicles, which have often been seen as the quintessential product of the second industrial revolution, combining, as they do, chemical and electrical technology in the internal combustion engine. Such engines were first developed by the German engineers Nikolaus Otto (1832–91) and Rudolf Diesel (1858–1913) in the 1880s and used to

Table 16.1 Development of cotton manufacturing, 1877–1913

	Cotton spindles (thousands)					
	UK	**France**	**Germany**	**Italy**	**Russia**	**Spain**
1877	44,207	5,000	4,700	880	4,400*	1,865*
1891/92	44,509	5,040	6,071	1,686	7,146	2,050
1913	55,653	7,400	11,186	4,600	9,212	2,000

*1882–83.

Source: B. R. Mitchell, *International Historical Statistics: Europe, 1750–1993* 4th edn, 1998, Palgrave Macmillan, reproduced with permission of Palgrave Macmillan.

power wheeled vehicles by two other engineers, Gottlieb Daimler (1834–1900) and Carl Benz (1844–1929). (The Daimler firm named one of its early models after its financial backer's niece, Mercedes.) Surprisingly, though, it was not Germany, Europe's emerging industrial powerhouse and leader in high-tech industry, that developed into the leading motor vehicle manufacturer but France, where entrepreneurs such as André Citroën (1878–1935) and Louis Renault (1877–1944) made that country into the world leader of motor vehicle production until overtaken by the United States in 1904. Before 1914, France exported more motor vehicles than any other country and would continue to be Europe's top motor vehicle producer through the 1920s. Quite in contrast to the United States, where forms of mass production, including Henry Ford's celebrated assembly line, set in very quickly before 1914, motor cars in Europe were produced one at a time, in very small production runs, with considerable craft work and skilled labour put into each car. Renault, Europe's largest motor vehicles manufacturer, was averaging all of 5,000 vehicles yearly in the five years before the First World War. Production runs in the three or even two figures per year were typical of all but the very largest firms.

Most motor vehicles produced went into commercial use, as lorries or taxicabs, and private ownership was limited to an affluent minority. Admittedly, motor cars powerfully captured public attention at a very early date, with the 1898 Paris Motor Show attracting 140,000 visitors, and motor races becoming major public spectacles. Yet the true pre-1914 personal transportation product of the second industrial revolution was not the automobile at all, but the bicycle – with its aluminium frame and pneumatic rubber tyres a product of electrical and chemical manufacturing advances. On the eve of the First World War, there were about 125,000 motor vehicles in France, as against 3.5 million bicycles. In Europe, the role of the automotive industry as paragon of the second industrial revolution, leading economic sector and source of mass consumption, would have to wait for the inter-war era and, really, for the 1960s.

SHIFTING CENTRES OF INDUSTRY

It was clear to contemporaries that the new industries of the second industrial revolution opened up previously unknown possibilities for economic development. The Italian engineer Giuseppe Colombo, who directed the building of Europe's first electric power station in Milan in 1883, stated:

> The utilization of electricity in the transmission of power over long distances is of such enormous importance for Italian industry that not even the most fertile of imaginations could begin to perceive the consequences it will have. It is something that could completely change the face of this country, bringing it up one day to the level of the strongest of nations.[2]

The basic point of Colombo's observation was completely correct. The growth of the two components of the second industrial revolution and the enormous expansion of steel manufacturing in the years 1890 to 1914, along with the increasing importance of scientific knowledge and the exchange of information for economic growth, led to a reshaping of the industrial map of Europe and of the world. There were three major components to this change. One was that Great Britain, the once-dominant industrial nation of the entire world, and still, by far, the leading manufacturing power in Europe as late as 1890, lost its position and was replaced by Germany, which became Europe's pre-eminent industrial nation. The second component was the economic and industrial rise as a result of the new industries of one-time marginal and peripheral countries that had had little part in the initial industrial revolution or had lagged badly behind. While Portugal and Greece remained quite poor, and economic progress in the Balkans and in Spain was modest, Italy, Russia, Sweden and Norway made good use of the opportunities provided by the industrial innovations of the period. The third change was the economic rise of the United States, whose manufacturing output was about equal to that of the entire European continent, a fact of which some people were uneasily aware before 1914, but which would reveal its major effects during and after the two world wars.

Figure 16.3, showing the growth of steel output between 1890 and 1913, illustrates these first two points. Still far in the lead in 1890, producing almost twice as much steel as second-place Germany, Great Britain's output – which had by no means stood still but had doubled over the following twenty-three years – was far outclassed by Germany's, which now produced as much as the other four leading European producers put together. (The United States was then producing as much steel as these four producers and Germany.) France and Belgium, among the early industrializers

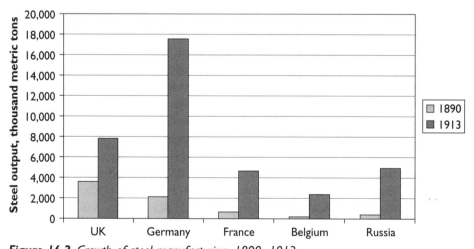

Figure 16.3 *Growth of steel manufacturing, 1890–1913*
Source: B. R. Mitchell, *International Historical Statistics: Europe, 1750–1993*, 4th edn, 1998, Palgrave Macmillan, reproduced with permission of Palgrave Macmillan.

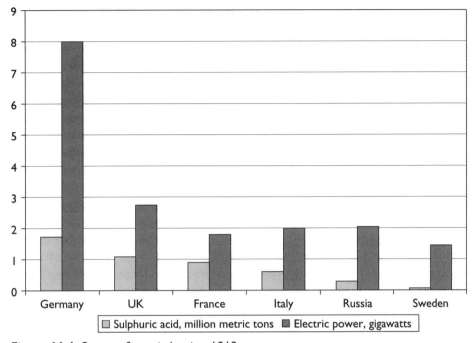

Figure 16.4 *Output of new industries, 1913*
Source: Derived from B. R. Mitchell, *International Historical Statistics: Europe, 1750–1993*, 4th edn (London, 1998), 541, 562–3.

of western Europe, saw substantial increases in steel output, but so did Russia, for most of the nineteenth century an economically backward nation, whose total steel production was greater than that of France on the eve of the First World War. Admittedly, with over four times as many Russians as Frenchmen, France still had a much larger per capita steel output.

Turning to the industries of the second industrial revolution, Figure 16.4 shows a similar picture. On the eve of the First World War, German production of sulphuric acid – which, because it is employed in so many different chemical processes, makes a good proxy for total output of chemicals – was twice that of Great Britain, precisely reversing the state of affairs of 1890. French chemical production had grown in the interval, almost catching up to the UK. Germany was producing about as much electrical power in 1913 as the next four countries put together; and previously not very industrialized nations, such as Italy, Russia and Sweden, had taken advantage of this new source of power and were producing substantial amounts of it. Norway, also a substantial producer of electrical energy, was using it to become a major centre of aluminium manufacturing.

As was explained above, both of these newer branches of industry presupposed scientific and engineering knowledge; we could see them as early examples of a knowledge or information economy. We could also try to measure the exchange

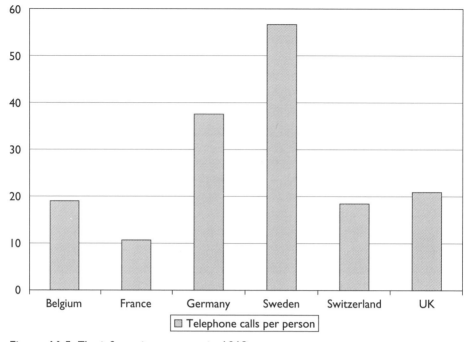

Figure 16.5 *The information economy in 1913*
Source: Derived from B. R. Mitchell, *International Historical Statistics: Europe, 1750–1993*, 4th edn (London, 1998), 85, 87, 766–8.

of information more directly. Figure 16.5 gives one version of the volume of information, namely per capita telephone calls. Since installed telephones in pre-1914 Europe were very largely for business purposes, we can assume that the information exchanged over them – rather unlike today – was economically useful. The chart shows, once again, Germany in a leading position, with about two to three times the number of telephone calls per capita as other major economic powers in western Europe. The champion in per capita telephone calls, though, was Sweden, suggesting a country with extensive stores of information being vigorously exchanged. Sweden and, like it, Norway, among the poorer nations – at least in western and central Europe – during the nineteenth century, were able to use the new industries of the second industrial revolution and a generally well-educated population to elevate themselves over the first half of the twentieth century into the ranks of Europe's and the world's most affluent countries.

Thus an integral part of the second industrial revolution was the shift in centres of industrial activity. One aspect of this shift, which has been long debated both by contemporaries as well as by later economists and historians, is Britain's decline: why Great Britain, Europe's and the world's leading industrial nation for more than a century, fell off the pace and was so quickly overtaken by its continental competitors. As economists like to point out, this decline was not all-encompassing. Until 1914, output per capita was still greater in the UK than in any continental European nation, the UK remained the world's leading exporter and still led Europe overall in manufacturing output, or, somewhat contradictorily, capital was being shifted in the UK from manufacturing to the more profitable service sector, in areas such as international commerce and finance. None of the economists' assertions is empirically incorrect, but they all ignore the direction of the trends. British per capita GDP or industrial output was still higher in 1913 than its European competitors, for instance, but the gap had closed considerably and at a rapid rate since 1890, as had not been the case at earlier points in the nineteenth century. There were real changes in the pace of economic development that need to be explained.

Historians have proposed many explanations for this trend; three seem most significant. One concerns the role of science and technology, and the exchange of information. Great Britain was well behind its competitors, particularly Germany, in this area, with noticeably fewer secondary school students and fewer university students studying key scientific subjects, especially chemistry. A second strand of explanation concerns what economists call 'path dependence'. Great Britain was the world's first industrial nation; it had the oldest industrial facilities, and all the money sunk into them made entrepreneurs reluctant to invest in newer forms of production which would make their old facilities obsolete. This was an important factor in both chemical and steel manufacture; the large investments in gas lamps for street lighting and the infrastructure of the gas industry that powered them slowed the pace of the adaptation of electric lights.

Finally, there is the question of what we might call economic organization. All three of the leading economic sectors required very substantial amounts of capital investment; and before capitalists would put up the money required, they needed some guarantee of return. Britain's banking system, with many competitive small banks offering only short-term loans, could not provide the long-term capital needs of such investments, as the larger banks of its competitors, especially the Germans, could. There was a very vigorous stock market in London, but it raised capital primarily for investments overseas and in some of the colonies, not for domestic manufacturers. Pro-free market government policies also seem to have played a role in discouraging large industrial investments. Instead of having municipal and national governments working closely with industry to create one electric power generation and transmission system, as was the case in Berlin (or Chicago, for that matter), the London power grid was the subject of vigorous competition from sixty-five different utility companies that produced power at twenty-four different voltage levels. The result was smaller, less efficient electricity networks, producing more expensive power and, since there were so many different voltages, creating a major burden for manufacturers of electrical equipment. This was a very significant factor in the problems of British electrical manufacturing, an area of industry where, unlike in chemistry, scientific and engineering personnel were as good and as numerous in the UK as in Germany.

Related to economic organization were tariff policies. With a home market protected by high tariffs, continental European and American businessmen could make the large investments needed in the three leading sectors of the period, with the knowledge that foreign competitors could not lower prices and disrupt their returns. Their British counterparts, whose government followed free trade policies, and so had an unprotected domestic market, could not do the same, and were increasingly inclined to leave their older, technologically obsolescent plant in place, and to divert investments towards trade, finance and services. In the changes of manufacturing over the years 1890 to 1914, we can see very clearly the character of the period as an age of classical modernism. The new industries of the second industrial revolution, along with steel production, and their offshoots such as motor vehicle manufacturing, would be the economic leading sectors for much of the twentieth century, far overshadowing previously important branches such as textiles or railway building. The new industrial powerhouses of the period, Germany and the United States, would play an ever more important role in the world economy, as would the rising Russian Empire and its successor state, the USSR, while the place of the formerly dominant Great Britain would gradually shrink. Yet today, with the development of new leading sectors in microelectronics, telecommunications and biotechnology, and the rise of Asian economies on the world stage, the modern economic developments of the pre-1914 decades seem to be receding rapidly into the past.

AGRICULTURE, CRAFTS, FINANCE AND COMMERCE

Industrial leading sectors were not the entire story of the pre-1914 economy. After suffering through the gloomy years of declining agricultural prices between the mid-1870s and mid-1890s, farmers were able to enjoy a reversal of the trend in the two decades before 1914. Accompanying rising prices was growing agricultural productivity, the result of two important developments: the increasingly widespread use of artificial fertilizers and the beginning of the mechanization of farm work. The rapid growth of the chemical industry made a broader variety of fertilizers available on a larger scale. To take just one example, the use of phosphate fertilizers increased tenfold in Italy between 1893 and 1913, rising from 112,000 to 1.14 million tons.[3]

While this use was widespread across western and central Europe (much less in the Russian Empire, the Balkans or the easternmost reaches of Austria-Hungary), mechanization of agriculture was still distinctly a minority phenomenon, confined to large landowners and more substantial farmers. Typical of agricultural mechanization were the steam-powered threshing machine and the mechanical separator, the latter for turning milk into butter. Tractors, the quintessential product of agricultural mechanization, would have to wait for the inter-war period and, like other products using internal combustion engines, the 1950s and 1960s.

The upshot of all these innovations was an expanded agricultural productivity, as crop yields grew by 25–35 per cent in different European countries over the pre-1914 decades. These productivity increases generally required considerable capital investments, in fertilizers and sometimes farm machinery – naturally, not the vast amounts needed for a steel mill or chemical plant, but still considerable in relation to the generally smaller economic units involved in farming. Protective tariffs in agriculture, as in industry, offered at least the possibility that these investments would yield returns.

Such tariffs were all the more important for European agriculture in view of the ever growing overseas competition. Agricultural tariff rates were raised steadily over this period, and their range expanded from the imports on which they had been levied in the 1880s, primarily grains, to include beef and pork products. What economists call non-tariff barriers, prohibitions, for instance, on the import of supposedly unhealthy American pork, were also introduced. Tariff rates for grains were generally higher and the best protected agriculturalists were large landowners who grew grain or sugar beet on their estates; farmers on medium- or smaller-sized holdings, with a more diverse production, including dairy products and farm animals, received less protection from foreign competition.

Free trade in agricultural products had become almost a curiosity in this period, limited to just two European countries, Denmark and Great Britain; even otherwise free-trading nations, such as Switzerland, introduced protective tariffs for their farmers. Danish farmers, using imported grains to feed their farm animals, developed a vigorous trade in dairy, pork, beef and poultry products. Exports of these products more than doubled in the two decades before the First World War. While agriculture in Great Britain made a similar shift from grain-growing to specializing in animal products, the net results were less favourable. British agriculture recovered poorly from the long downturn of the late nineteenth century; yields on grain remained stagnant for decades; farm revenues did not do much better. British consumers did enjoy the benefits of American grain, Australian mutton and Danish bacon, but the agricultural sector of the economy, free-trading in a protectionist world, did not share in the better times seen in continental Europe.

Turning from agriculture to the crafts and retail commerce, we see very largely a continuation of the trends of the 1870s and 1880s. The number of artisans and artisanal production more generally continued to shrink, relatively and absolutely. In Germany, small production enterprises, employing five people or less, declined in number from 1.99 million to 1.87 million between the censuses of 1895 and 1907; the people employed in such workshops went from 43 per cent of workers production enterprises to 32 per cent in the same time.[4] The more favourable economic situation of the pre-First World War decades, as compared to the depressed years of the late nineteenth century, eased circumstances for craftsmen, especially for the more prosperous construction and food trades. The growing use of electric motors, which, unlike steam engines, would fit into small workshops, made it more possible for craftsmen to use their own power tools. New industries created new craft trades, such as bicycle and motor vehicle repair. Still, overall the picture for artisans was not encouraging. Karl Kautsky, the German social democratic leader who, as a Marxist, was no fan of small business, nonetheless hit the nail on the head when he compared master craftsmen's condition with a 'lottery: a few get a winning ticket, but the majority draw a blank, and pay, not just for the winners, but for the whole enterprise'.[5]

In retail sales, the post-1890 years also saw a continuation of the trends already apparent in the 1870s and 1880s, towards an increase in the number of shops. The number of licensed traders in France grew from 1.3 million in 1881 to 1.5 million in 1905; in Germany, the number of people owning a retail sales business went from one for every 38.8 inhabitants in 1895 to one for every 30 in 1907.[6] While small retail shops proliferated, their large-scale competition became more pervasive, as department stores and consumers' cooperatives increased in extent and total sales. Although today we think of department stores as the characteristic example of large-scale retail establishments, at the beginning of the twentieth century actively growing consumer cooperatives were also very important. The pre-1914 era was the golden age of the cooperative movement. By the first decade of the twentieth century, cooperatives in Great Britain accounted for 7–8 per cent of all retail sales. In 1913, German consumers' cooperatives counted 1.96 million members; cooperatives' gross receipts had reached three-quarters of a billion Marks. Italian consumers cooperatives counted 1 million members on the eve of the First World War.

Department stores also proliferated in this period. The largest stores were giant enterprises; Harrods in London, then, as today a model of up-market retailing, had 6,000 employees in 1914. Such enterprises were not typical of the retail business, nor did they dominate it in the way that giant firms dominated chemical, electrical or steel manufacturing. Department stores were found primarily in larger cities; their price-cutting competition threatened smaller retailers but did not stop the expansion of their stores. In contrast to the shrinking crafts, retail sales continued to be a place where it was still possible to earn a living – admittedly a precarious one.

Part of the secret of the survival and, indeed, expansion of small retail establishments in spite of the competition of cooperatives and department stores was the sheer growing volume of retail sales, which could be spread out over all kinds of establishments. This commercial expansion of the period was also seen at the wholesale and international levels. The pre-1914 era was a long-term high point of global commerce. In 1913, exports made up 8.2 per cent of the gross domestic product of the world's seventeen economic leading nations – primarily in Europe but including a few in the Americas and Japan. In 1950, the figure was just 5.2 per cent, and only surpassed its 1913 levels in the 1970s. The global dynamics of economic expansion powered an increase in trade, in spite of the ever higher tariff barriers designed to halt imports.[7]

Capital flows reached a similar peak in this era. Encouraging international capital movements was the universal adoption of the gold standard for currencies, as countries such as Austria-Hungary and Russia, which had previously a bimetallic standard or floating currency, went over to gold (in 1892 and 1897, respectively, in these two cases). The security of prices and exchange rates, and the ability to convert currencies freely as a result of this development encouraged international capital flows. London was the centre of the world capital market. In the pre-war decade, almost half of total capital formation in the UK went into overseas investment. The pound sterling, in spite of its silver name, was as good as gold. French banks and the Paris bourse were also involved in capital export, albeit on a smaller scale, while German financial institutions catered primarily to a vigorous domestic market.

In this environment, the possibilities for wholesale commerce and navigation were considerable. The key innovations in these areas had occurred in the middle decades of the nineteenth century, and the pre-war era primarily saw the expansion of already existing institutions. This was a golden age of trans-Atlantic commerce and navigation, symbolized by the building of luxury ocean liners – the celebrated *Titanic*, that met its unfortunate fate in 1912, was a rather less successful version of a very vigorous business. Shipping became an important economic factor in previously largely landlocked countries such as Austria-Hungary and Germany. The Hamburg–America line, Germany's leading shipper, had 21 ships in operation in 1884 and 442 in 1914. Another example of the expansion of shipping was the growth of the merchant marines of Greece and Norway. Consisting of a few sailing vessels at mid-century, by 1914 they had reached 1.8 million and 1 million tons, respectively, in modern steam-powered vessels. All this varied and multiple commercial and financial activity marked a sharp rebound from the more depressed circumstances of the last quarter of the nineteenth century – and this rebound was the dominant economic feature of the era.

RAPID POPULATION MOVEMENTS

The quarter-century before the First World War was a period of very rapid demographic change in Europe. Both vital events and migration showed sharp changes from preceding years. The reshaping of population structures and population movements was one of the most important and long-lasting changes occurring in the belle époque.

Perhaps the single most important demographic feature of the period was the decline in birth rates. As Figure 16.6 shows, this decline was universal in Europe, occurring in high-birth-rate countries, such as Russia, and in low-birth-rate ones, such as Sweden or France, as well as in those between. Beginning the 1880s, and in some cases as early as the 1870s, the decline in birth rates accelerated after *c*.1900, so that

Figure 16.6 *Declining birth rates, 1880–1913*
Source: B. R. Mitchell, *International Historical Statistics: Europe, 1750–1993*, 4th edn, 1998, Palgrave Macmillan, reproduced with permission of Palgrave Macmillan.

by the eve of the First World War birth rates were between 12 per cent and 25 per cent lower than they had been at the beginning of the 1880s. This unprecedented decline in fertility was quite perceptible to contemporaries and the reasons for it were hotly debated, including such odd suggestions as damage to female reproductive organs due to excessive bicycle riding. As more astute observers realized, what was actually occurring was the increasingly widespread practice of birth control.

The declines in the birth rate represented the phasing in of the practice over the course of several decades. Initial practitioners included couples from the upper and professional and white-collar middle classes, gradually joined by blue-collar workers and farmers. The progression is usually described as being from skilled and well-paid workers, to unskilled and less poorly paid ones, and then to the rural population, but closer analysis shows a more erratic course among blue-collar workers and craftsmen, with some groups lagging behind, particularly coal miners, whose marriages were astonishingly prolific. Generally, birth rates were lowest in large metropolitan areas and highest in the countryside, although there were rural areas, particularly in France, with very low birth rates. Cultural and religious factors were important in the progress of birth control, with Jews and Protestants adopting the practice before Catholics and Orthodox, and with the more secularized from all religious confessions being more likely to practise birth control than the devout – no

BOX 16.2

Practising contraception at the beginning of the twentieth century

Birth control was – and is – an intimate area of people's private lives, so that its practice has not left behind a lot of detailed evidence for historians to study, besides the statistics of birth rates. There were certainly a lot of advertisements at the beginning of the twentieth century, whether in the periodical press or via posters and flyers, promoting various devices, creams and jellies. Just how well these worked is open to question. Condoms, the premier mechanical birth control device, certainly existed but were quite expensive – a six-pack costing a worker's weekly wages – and were thick and very stiff, often requiring a half-hour's soaking in hot water before they were ready for use. Modern latex condoms were first manufactured in the 1930s.

Abortion – everywhere illegal – was practised, but probably the most common method used was withdrawal, which, in Sicily, received the charming sobriquet – and a nice reference to the cultural impact of motor vehicles – as 'going forward in reverse gear'. Another commonly practised method, apparently especially prevalent in England, was simply cutting down on the frequency of sexual relations within marriage. Especially when compared with the birth control pill and its offshoots, introduced since the 1960s, none of these methods was a guarantee against pregnancy. Margot Tennant, wife of British prime minister Herbert Asquith, is reputed to have quipped that she and her husband had four children, each the product of a different form of birth control. When practised on a broad scale, though, the still very primitive methods of contraception, if not preventing any individual pregnancy, overall sufficed to bring about the reduction in birth rates.

surprise, given that representatives of all organized religions before 1914 were unanimous in condemning contraceptive practices as severely sinful.

If fertility was declining in the pre-1914 decades, population growth was continuing at a vigorous pace, because death rates were declining even faster. As Figure 16.7 shows, this decline in mortality was every bit as widespread across Europe as the decline in fertility; death rates were 20–40 per cent lower on the eve of the First World War than at the beginning of the 1880s. The reasons for this very substantial decline in mortality – not quite so unprecedented as the fall in fertility, since there had been more modest declines earlier in the nineteenth century – were not mysterious at all. They included a rising standard of living, and the concomitant increase in protein intake powering the immune defence system, improving public health, both in the wider provision of vaccination against infectious diseases and the building of sewer and water systems, as well as other advances in sanitation, such as the pasteurization of milk. All these improvements had their greatest effect on infants and small children, whose mortality rates declined particularly rapidly.

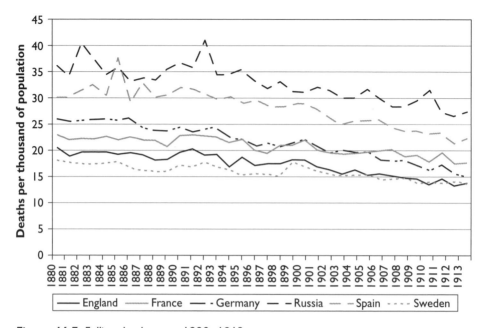

Figure 16.7 *Falling death rates, 1880–1913*
Source: B. R. Mitchell, *International Historical Statistics: Europe, 1750–1993*, 4th edn, 1998, Palgrave Macmillan, reproduced with permission of Palgrave Macmillan.

By today's standards, infant mortality rates remained very high. Even in Sweden, which had among the lowest rates in Europe, close to one in every ten children died in their first year of life, an infant mortality rate about eighteen to twenty times as high as is seen in many European countries today. Still, in comparison to nineteenth-century infant mortality rates of 200–300 deaths in the first year of life for every thousand children born, or even higher, it was a real decline. The fall in both birth and death rates in the belle époque began a long-term trend. In spite of occasional interruptions – the rise in mortality during the world wars, or the increase in fertility during the 'baby boom' of the 1950s – their decline has continued in Europe through to the present day.

If birth and death rates were going down before 1914, the other major demographic feature of the period, geographical population movements, were going in the opposite direction. The pre-1914 decades were a high point of population movements, within localities, within state borders, across these borders and across oceans. The most evident feature of such population movements was overseas emigration. While this emigration reached new peaks in the years before the First World War, its sources changed noticeably. In previous centres of emigration in northern and western Europe, Germany and Ireland, for example, the extent of emigration declined, while in southern and eastern Europe it expanded greatly, as Figure 16.8 shows. Emigration became a big business, as steamship companies sent their representatives

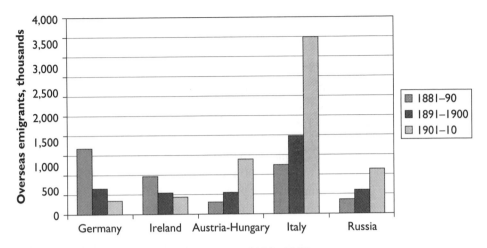

Figure 16.8 *Changing centres of emigration, 1880–1910*
Sources: Derived from B. R. Mitchell, *International Historical Statistics: Europe, 1750–1993*, 4th edn
(London, 1998); Kerby Miller, *Emigrants and Exiles* (New York, 1985).

to the province of Galicia at the far eastern end of the Austro-Hungarian Empire,
or to mountain villages of southern Italy, with brochures, price lists and discount
ticket offers. Sometimes they were arrested as spies or under the – generally justified
– suspicion of trying to hustle conscription-age young men out of the country before
they had done their military service.

Overseas emigration was part of a broader pattern of long-distance population
movements. While in some parts of Europe the pattern of rural–urban migration over
relatively short distances continued to prevail – about 80 per cent of immigrants to
Moscow, for instance, came from the eight surrounding provinces – rapidly growing heavy industrial centres on the European continent developed such an enormous
need for labour that surrounding rural areas no longer sufficed. Germany's steel manufacturing and coal mining centre, the Ruhr Basin, located at the far western end of
central Europe, recruited hundreds of thousands of Polish-speaking labourers from
a thousand miles away, at the far eastern end of the German Empire, near today's
Lithuania, and from the Russian and Austro-Hungarian Empires. Italian workers
manned the steel mills of Lorraine, in eastern France. There were similar developments in agriculture, as half a million Polish workers came from the Russian Empire
to harvest grain and potatoes on the Pomeranian estates of Germany's noble large
landowners; Italians picked the fruit and vegetable crop in southern France.

It is important to understand that these migrations, as was the case earlier in
the century, were not just in one direction, but involved large-scale back-and-forth
movement. With the development of fast and relatively cheap trans-Atlantic transport, even emigrants to the Americas could come and go on a regular basis. Between
1908 and 1914, the number of people leaving the United States was 52.5 per cent of

those entering it. The *golandrinas* (Spanish for 'swallows') were Italian labourers who went to Argentina every year from December to April to harvest the southern hemisphere wheat crop.

What was true in a trans-Atlantic dimension was even more the case within Europe. People moved from country to city, between cities and within them at an unprecedented rate – a rate that declined drastically after the First World War and has never again achieved its pre-1914 levels. At the beginning of the twentieth century, about 17 per cent of Moscow's inhabitants moved to or from the city in any one year. To take a broader example, in the period 1908–13 in German cities with a population of over 100,000, for every 100 inhabitants, 38 moved either into or out of the cities every year. Comparable population movement rates today are about one-third that level. This rapid, dynamic population turnover might stand as a more general sign of economic and demographic conditions in Europe during the quarter-century before the First World War: a period of rapid change and dynamic movement.

CHAPTER 17

SOCIAL STRUCTURES AND SOCIAL INSTITUTIONS

The rapid and dynamic economic and demographic changes in Europe during the quarter-century before the First World War led to equally dynamic transformations of social structures and social institutions. Class structures evolved, following the developments in industry and agriculture. A second, closely related, change was the rapid increase in urbanization: the growth of very large metropolitan centres and urban networks, and the transformation of cityscapes. A third was the continued expansion of voluntary associations and their centralization and reorganization. Finally, the period saw the increasing development of mass consumption and the tentative beginnings of a consumer society in Europe, at the intersection of new media, new forms of retailing and new versions of leisure and recreation. Every one of these developments, but the first and the third particularly, had a profound effect on structures of gender and gender relations.

SOCIETY IN THE AGE OF THE SECOND INDUSTRIAL REVOLUTION

Looking most broadly at social structure in pre-1914 Europe, we can observe two tripartite divisions. One concerned the economic sector in which people worked. Except in Great Britain, where agriculture employed under 10 per cent of the workforce, shortly before the First World War farming remained an important employer of labour, ranging from about 25 per cent of the workforce in urbanized and industrialized Belgium to 55–60 per cent in Italy and Russia. The proportion of the population in agricultural pursuits was steady or declining, though; by contrast, the numbers employed in industry, construction, transportation and services were increasing, making up a majority of the workforce in most European countries.

The other major division concerned social class. People who earned their living by working for a wage, doing physical labour – blue-collar workers, as we would say today – were the single largest portion of the workforce – almost three-quarters of employed men in Great Britain before 1914, and about the same figure of all gainfully employed in Germany, according to the 1907 census. In countries with a larger rural population, consisting mostly of peasants owning at least some property, the proportion of participants in the workforce was smaller, but blue-collar workers were, overall, the single largest social group in belle époque Europe. Besides blue-collar workers, there was a middle class – probably, a lower-middle class would be a more accurate description – consisting in part of small proprietors, especially in agriculture, but also in crafts and commerce, whose numbers were substantial but declining or, at best, increasing modestly. A new feature of the period was a different aspect of the middle class, the still relatively small but rapidly growing number of salaried employees, particularly in commerce, but also in larger industrial establishments. The most affluent 10–15 per cent of the social structure was composed of the same large landowners, professionals, merchants and industrialists who had been typical members of elite groups since the mid-nineteenth century. Their ranks were being supplemented by a still small group of corporate managers.

One might say that the pre-1914 decades were the years in which the working class came of age. The large-scale institutions of the labour movement – labour and socialist parties, trade unions, consumers' cooperatives, and a wealth of associations affiliated with them – demonstrated a rising group self-consciousness and a claim to a major role in society and politics. On a more personal level, the increasingly widespread practice of birth control suggested a desire to plan and control individual futures and improve children's circumstances. The working week was shortening, towards 55–60 hours, particularly with the introduction of the 'English Saturday', when work ceased around noon. Blue-collar standards of living were, generally, increasing – if, at certain times and places, inflation was beginning to counteract the trend. This overall picture of an increasingly affluent, self-confident and cohesive working class, if generally the case, does have three important exceptions.

One was the state of housing, particularly in Europe's major urban centres and in rapidly growing areas of heavy industry. Population increases in these areas outstripped housing supply, with resulting shortages and persistent poor quality. Perhaps conditions were generally not as bad as in the Donets Basin, the heavy industrial centre of the Russian Empire, where peasants rented out their chicken coops to coal miners and steelworkers, but overcrowded accommodations, lacking privacy, space and indoor lavatories, were the rule rather than the exception. There was no affordable public housing built in pre-1914 Europe; large employers sometimes provided cheap – and generally somewhat better quality – housing for their workers, but living in such housing meant accepting employers' rules and being evicted on taking another job or going on strike. Although conditions did gradually improve in the inter-war and post-1945 periods, particularly with the widespread construction of public housing, inadequate housing remained an issue in working-class life through to the third quarter of the twentieth century.

The second exception was workers' continuing economic insecurity. While long-term unemployment was less common before 1914, periodic short-time in seasonal trades caused regularly recurring income shortages. Serious illness of a parent threatened to plunge a working-class family into poverty. Above all, old age remained a looming disaster in working-class life. Later in the century, government-financed social insurance programmes would help workers cope with these difficulties stemming from both the business cycle and the life cycle, but such programmes were in their earliest stages before 1914 and even rudimentary versions were available in only a few, wealthier European countries. Workers had to rely on their own resources – small life insurance policies for burial expenses (very popular for children as well as adults) or the ubiquitous pawnshop. Londoners held 42 million pawn tickets before 1914, or about six items per person.

The third exception was in the position of married women. While younger, single women were gradually carving out a better position for themselves in working-class family life (although often not in industrial occupations, but as domestic servants or employees in white-collar jobs), being more likely to have gainful employment and keep part of their pay rather than turn it all over to their parents, once married their lives became an accumulation of time-consuming burdens. Little had changed in household technology before 1914, and scrubbing clothing, furnishings, housing – and even the street in front of the house – by hand, as well as lugging tubs of water up flights of stairs, continued to characterize married women's lives. Cooking and food preparation was no less demanding. Birth rates, and infant and child mortality rates, if declining, were still high so that childbirth and child-rearing continued to take a heavy toll on women's energies. Managing the family budget – assuming they could wrest the money for it away from their husbands – in straitened circumstances remained a source of working-class wives' anxiety and stress. Any energy left over after childcare, cooking and cleaning, had to be spent on sewing and mending clothing, or earning a little extra money by taking in boarders or doing industrial homework, such as making paper flowers or matchboxes. Interviews that historians carried out in the 1970s and 1980s with people growing up in the pre-1914 era usually included a comment by the latter about how their mothers never had a moment's free time.

At the beginning of the twentieth century, in many parts of Europe, the industrial revolution had been under way for three and even four generations. Long-term industrial cities, such as Manchester, Aachen or Liège, and even London, the great metropolitan centre, had a relatively settled working-class population, living in well-established neighbourhoods (admittedly, often moving around in these neighbourhoods in search of cheaper accommodations), working at the same jobs across generations, belonging to clubs and societies, taking out insurance, practising well-established leisure pastimes, including those two English favourites, pigeon-breeding and betting off-track (and illegally) on the horses.

By contrast, the centres of heavy industry – Germany's Ruhr Basin, the Russian Empire's Donets Basin, or the Lorraine steel district in France, for instance – were areas of rapid social movement and instability. The workers were not locals, but, literally, foreigners coming from far away: half the coal miners of the Ruhr Basin spoke Polish as their native language; 70 per cent of the iron miners in Lorraine were Italian; and although the Donets Basin was in Ukraine, virtually none of the workers there were Ukrainian. Population and job turnover was astonishing. Managers of the Decazeville coal mines in central France noted that, by 1910, they had to hire five workers to find one who would stay long term. In some Donets Basin coal mines,

80 per cent of the workforce worked for three months or less before moving on. Annual population turnover in the fast-growing coal mining village of Hamborn (which went from 6,000 inhabitants in 1900 to more than 100,000 in 1912) on the western edge of Germany's Ruhr Basin was greater than 100 per cent.

The workers in these regions, generally young, male and single, were not much given to family life, joining clubs or raising pigeons. Their entertainment included heavy drinking – 150,000 of the 350,000 rubles weekly wages bill in a Donets Basin steel mill was spent on vodka (an enormous amount, even by hard-drinking Russian standards) – and brawling with each other and the police. The village of Hamborn was part of an area known in the broader Ruhr Basin as 'der wilde Westen' – the 'wild west', a sort of a central European Dodge City, a wild and chaotic mining boom town.

Yet these divisions within the working class pale before those of the lower-middle class in pre-1914 Europe. It was the German economist Gustav Schmoller who first pointed out these divisions in an 1897 lecture entitled 'What do We Understand as the Middle Class?' Schmoller suggested that the middle class was divided into two groups, an 'old middle class', a social formation that had been around for quite some time, consisting of small businessmen, smallholding farmers and master craftsmen, and a 'new middle class', a newer group of salaried employees working in supervisory, administrative, technical and sales positions. Schmoller's lecture was intellectually influential because he had hit on a key social trend. While the new middle class was definitely less numerous than the old (particularly if smallholding farmers are included in the latter's ranks), it was growing rapidly as the old middle class was declining. In Germany, the number of proprietors – most of whom could be placed in the old middle class – went from 32 per cent of the workforce in 1882 to 22 per cent in 1907, while in the same period salaried employees' share in the workforce grew from 2 per cent to over 5 per cent.[8] This growth in the number of salaried employees and decline in the ranks of small proprietors was a trend that has continued to the present day.

One source of employment for the new middle class were the large firms of the second industrial revolution, which required foremen and supervisors to run their production processes, office workers to coordinate their far-flung activities, salesmen to move their product, and engineers and technicians for research and development. A good example of the growth of white-collar employment comes from the German electrical manufacturer Siemens. In 1865, when the firm was a small manufacturer of telegraphs and telegraph wire, there was one salaried employee for every 11.3 blue-collar production workers; by 1912, when it was a giant high-tech producer of every kind of electrical product, employing some 56,000 people, the ratio of blue-collar production workers to salaried employees had shrunk to 3.5 to 1.[9]

Growing urbanization, particularly the increase in the population of large cities, was another crucial factor in the growth of the new middle class. Business offices and large industrial establishments were likely to be found in big cities, but, above all, the concentration of population meant an increase in retail sales establishments, the branch of the economy where the salaried employees were most numerous and most common. In Paris, for instance, there were 126,000 white-collar workers in 1866, 245,000 twenty years later, and 353,000 in 1911.[10] The new middle class was thus going with the flow of economic development while the old middle class was bucking the trend, as the decline in the farm population, the increasing difficulties master craftsmen had in competing with industrial enterprises, and the tendency towards larger units of production and distribution took their toll on small, independent proprietors.

The growth of the new middle class demonstrated another important social trend of the period, this one in gender terms: the expanded job market for women. The increase in white-collar jobs was disproportionately large among women. The growth in the number of white-collar workers in Paris mentioned in the previous paragraph, breaks down to a 123 per cent increase among men, from 108,000 salaried employees in 1866 to 241,000 in 1911, and a 522 per cent increase for women, from 18,000 in 1866 to 112,000 forty-five years later. Women were generally confined to the lower end of the pay and prestige scale, as office clerical help or, especially, as shop workers – in the decade before the First World War 35 per cent of English shop workers and almost 80 per cent of their German counterparts were female – likely to keep their positions only until they were married, and rarely employed in a senior or supervisory capacity. In spite of these considerable limitations, the growth of white-collar occupations opened new possibilities of employment and new fields of social action for women.

For all these differences in their relationship to major economic trends, members of both the new and the old middle class had a common complaint in this period: the relative decline in their incomes and social prestige, the perception that they were being squeezed between the giant social formations of an organized working class on the one side, and capitalist large enterprise on the other. Shopkeepers and master craftsmen fumed about the competition from department stores and large factories; they denounced trade unions and workers' consumer cooperatives. Salaried employees often noted that their chances of going into business for themselves (a typical career pattern for shop workers and office clerks earlier in the nineteenth century) were steadily declining, leading to a lifetime of earning a salary. Yet, they asserted, their salaries could be even lower than the wages of blue-collar workers and they were subject to such proletarian indignities as being required to punch a time card – a requirement particularly galling to engineers, who generally did not have to worry about their pay.

At least to some extent, these complaints were not entirely unjustified. Small proprietors were having a hard time as a result of capitalist competition – master craftsmen perhaps more than retailers. While their standards of living were increasing, it is not impossible that they were growing more slowly than those of blue-collar workers, and certainly those of the upper classes. The large influx of women into white-collar occupations, coupled with technological innovations in office work, such as the introduction of the typewriter (reaching a large scale in the years around the turn of the century), had led to a lowering of salary levels for male shop workers and office clerks, producing a hostility towards female competition which they were quick to articulate. Generally, white-collar workers continued to earn more than their blue-collar counterparts, and certainly had greater security of employment, but salaries did tend to move up at a slow pace, which became particularly noticeable in the decade of rising inflation before the First World War.

Turning now to the upper-middle and upper classes of the belle époque, it would be fair to say that continuity of condition and position rather outweighed change. The comfortable and downright well-to-do of 1870s Europe were the comfortable and well-to-do of Europe in 1910. Large, often noble, landowners, especially in Great Britain and in eastern and southern Europe (less in the west and north of the continent), bankers, wholesale merchants and manufacturers were the very wealthiest members of society; smaller businessmen and the members of the learned professions, both those practising these professions independently and those working as senior civil servants, were members of an upper-middle class. Within these broad lines of continuity, though, we can note three embryonic elements of change.

One was in the position of noble large landowners. They were very wealthy, true, and the increase in farm prices over the twenty years before 1914 only enhanced their economic position. But this wealth, as contemporaries vaguely perceived, was fragile, centred in a declining economic sector, propped up by protective tariffs and government subsidies. In Great Britain, home of the world's wealthiest noble landlords, but also a country politically committed to free trade and willing to let its agricultural population take the consequences, its aristocratic great landowners were becoming aware of a gradual decline in their fortunes – at least if their landholdings did not include lucrative urban or coalfield real estate.

A second point concerns the position of Europe's leading entrepreneurs. As a growing number of large firms began to be reorganized in the form of corporations, the pre-1914 decade saw the gradual development of a group of corporate managers – entrepreneurs who were not owners of the firm they ran. They were noticeably more likely than firm owners to have attended a university and pursued studies in science or engineering. While the development of such a managerial class would proceed apace over the entire twentieth century, one should not exaggerate the importance or influence of managers before 1914. Most firms, even most large firms, continued to be individually or family owned. When businesses went public, it was often the case that the original family owners continued to possess large shares of stock and a considerable influence on corporate policy, as we can see from firms as different as Siemens, the German manufacturer of electrical equipment, and Cadbury, the British manufacturer of confectionery.

The third point about this social group is the new arena of occupation opened up for women among it, through the development of a growing group of distinctly female professional occupations such as nurses and social workers. Steadily more women found work in primary, and even some more affluent and prestigious positions in secondary, education. In some countries, where primary education was expanding from the 1880s onward – the UK and Russia in particular – primary education became predominantly female. Elsewhere, most teachers continued to be men, but the number of women taking up teaching as a career was everywhere growing steadily.

It could be argued that such occupations, considering the generally modest incomes attached to them, belonged more to the lower-middle class. But a considerable number of the women initially holding such positions were from affluent backgrounds, and these sorts of posts were attractive to the small but rising number of women attending universities. In all these respects, they suggested new possibilities and life choices for women from bourgeois and even, on occasion, aristocratic families. Women in these occupations would play an important part in the development of feminist and women's movements before 1914.

Some aspects of the social structure of different European countries during the belle époque represent a continuation of longer-running past developments: the decline in the agricultural population and in smaller units of production are probably the two best examples. Others, such as the rise of the new middle class and the expansion of employment options for women, were new developments, just getting started in the twenty-five or thirty years before the First World War and would continue on – if not always smoothly or continuously – throughout the twentieth century and into the twenty-first. In western and central Europe, the years between 1890 and 1914 saw a high point in the extent of the blue-collar working class; the strong and visible presence of an industrial working class was an important feature of the age of classical modernism.

THE PRESENCE OF THE CITY

The quarter-century before the First World War was a period of an increased presence of the city in European life. This was partly a matter of actual social developments: urban areas growing in size and population, an ever larger proportion of the population living in these urban areas in general, particularly in large cities, and a new wave of construction within these cities. It was also a matter of perception, of understanding urban life, especially as it was lived in major metropolitan centres, as striking and dramatic, as new and different, as threatening and intimidating, or as full of possibility and offering new chances for change and reform. Larger, dynamically growing cities were the laboratories of social change in the age of classical modernism.

The British Isles had been a predominantly urban country since the mid-nineteenth century, but by the eve of the First World War, almost 80 per cent of the population of England and Wales lived in urban areas, 44 per cent in large cities of over 100,000 population. Between 1880 and 1910, city dwellers went from 40 per cent to 60 per cent of Germany's inhabitants; there were similar, if more modest, advances in the urban populations of France, Italy and Spain. Urban life was not dominant everywhere on the European continent: only 13 per cent of the inhabitants of Serbia and Finland lived in urban areas in the early years of the twentieth century; just 18 per cent in Russia – although that figure was double the 9 per cent urban population of the first half of the nineteenth century.

It was the great cities of the era that caught the eye of contemporaries – the London metropolitan area reaching 7 million, Berlin, Paris and Vienna with 2 million apiece, Moscow and St Petersburg each with 1.5 million. These metropolises were the epitome of modern urban life, offering both awe inspiring and frightening spectacles of traffic jams, brightly illuminated shopping districts, throngs of people in the streets, and crowded slums. Yet the rapid growth of smaller industrial cities and regional centres was, if anything, more typical of the era. There were just four cities with over 100,000 population in the newly united German Empire of 1871, but forty-eight of them in 1910.

In some ways, though, neither the impact of the great cities nor the rise of smaller industrial towns captures the nature of urban developments in this period, which were characterized by two major trends: decentralization and conglomeration. Decentralization was a hallmark of the development of large urban centres. One good example would be a smaller metropolis, the Belgian capital of Brussels. Between 1890 and 1910, the population of the city of Brussels itself just went from 176,000 to 177,000, while the population of the Brussels region grew over that twenty years from about half a million to three-quarters of a million. All the population growth occurred in the city's suburbs. If redevelopment and expansion of city centre locations was a characteristic of 'Haussmanization', in the previous period of dynamic urban growth, the 1850s and 1860s, the quarter-century before 1914 saw a different trend: the rapid outward expansion of major urban centres, sometimes into independent suburban municipalities, sometimes into the outer districts of the major cities themselves, while the population of their oldest, inner districts held steady or even declined.

This decentralization was the result of two major developments. One was the shaping force of industrialization. In the 1880s, the town of Praga on the east bank of the River Vistula across from Warsaw was a hamlet, best known for its livestock market, but on the eve of the First World War it had become a working-class suburb of 90,000 inhabitants, many of whom earned their living working in the newly built railyards and textile mills. If industrial development attracted populations to the outskirts, the transformation of public transportation made it possible to live there yet work or shop closer to the centre of town. This change was a direct result of the second industrial revolution, in particular the electrification of public transport, underground railway systems in the largest cities and, far more widespread, light rail transport in the form of trams or trolleybuses. Horse-drawn buses had been around since the middle of the nineteenth century, but they were expensive – feeding and caring for all those horses – slow, worked poorly in bad weather and could not cope with steep hills. The 1890s were the breakthrough decade for electrification, with just 96 kilometres of electrified trolley lines in 1890, and almost 2,900 just eight years later. Unlike underground railways, trams were not confined to giant urban centres like London and Paris, but were found in smaller cities such as Kiev, Remscheid or Limoges. By the eve of the First World War, municipalities, whether industrial cities and regional centres such as Leeds, Nottingham, Breslau and Hanover, or capital cities like London and Berlin, were averaging from 150 to 300 tramway trips per person per year.

The decentralization of major cities was a part of the second broader trend, the way that cities were beginning to grow into each other. The English phrase to describe this development, 'conurbation', was coined in 1915, right at the end of the period under consideration. Certainly, such conurbations would include the capital cities and their surroundings, but they were characteristic of major industrial regions as well: the Ruhr Basin in Germany, the Turin–Milan–Genoa triangle in northern Italy, the Lyons–Saint-Étienne and Roubaix–Turcoing industrial regions in France, the south-east Lancashire conurbation, including Manchester, Salford, Bolton, Rochdale and Stockport. Although less exciting than the great capital cities, and generally rather drearier places to live, these massive urban industrial areas shaped the face of large portions of Europe, and continue to do so today, often in even drearier form as the industry is gone, and the jobs with it, but the depressing urban industrial landscape remains.

The urban presence in pre-1914 decades was not just a question of physical change, of growing populations, electrification of transport or expansion of suburban municipalities. Rather, this presence was also manifest in ideas about large cities and perceptions of them. Such perceptions ran the gamut of judgements, from hostile to apprehensive to favourable. It was a characteristic of the period that the more negative opinions were the best articulated.

This negative opinion was, to a great extent, a moralizing one. Cities, especially large ones, it was asserted, were centres of criminality, immorality, godlessness and degeneration. Cheap and entrancing pleasures led innocents astray, so that prostitution, illegitimacy and venereal disease flourished. Deaths outnumbered births and the surviving inhabitants were stunted and degenerate, poor fare for staffing an army or maintaining an empire. The famous crimes of Jack the Ripper, a serial killer stalking prostitutes in London's impoverished East End at the very beginning of the pre-1914 era, in 1888, and the terror and horrified fascination they generated, seemed a living example of this moral decay. Or to take just one of an enormous number of condemnations of urban life, consider this denunciation by the French economist Louis Wuarin in 1900:

> There are, moreover, all sorts of spectacles . . . the thousand traps set for vanity and sensuality, the evil relationships having to do with business and pleasure that quietly

lead the victim into the abyss. There are the vagabonds and the criminals who form a sort of secret society in order to thwart the power of the law. Just as one no longer finds the healthy air of the countryside in the populated centers, the moral atmosphere here is also polluted.[11]

Against this sort of rhetoric, affirmations of urban life tended to sound defensive. Statisticians could observe that urban death rates were declining, or that high illegitimacy rates were in part a result of single pregnant women from rural areas going to the cities to give birth. Partisans of urban life could describe cities as centres of progress and economic development. Leaders of municipal government and practitioners of the developing field of urban planning could point to the successes of public health measures, the construction of mass transit systems, electric street lighting, parks and monumental public buildings. These accomplishments were enshrined in the 1903 German City Exhibition held in Dresden, where 400,000 paying visitors saw examples of such successful public policy from 128 different municipalities. Yet these rational responses lacked the power and impact of the negative, moralistic messages.

Another response was the advocacy of urban reform. Particularly strong in Great Britain, and only gradually reaching the continent, this reform movement included the foundation of settlement houses, in which charitable young men – and, especially a novelty, young women – from the upper classes lived in urban slum areas and attempted to ameliorate what they saw as the social evils of these areas. Housing reformers, such as the Frenchman Tony Garnier (1869–1948), the German Adolf Damaschke (1865–1935), and, most influential, the Englishman Ebenezer Howard (1850–1928), proposed to create new, planned neighbourhoods, with sanitary and spacious housing, in peripheral areas with lots of green space. Very influential in shaping urban policy later in the twentieth century, the ideas of these housing reformers were widely discussed but little implemented before 1914.

The actions of Europe's rural lower classes were a distinct rebuke to those enemies of urban life who contrasted it unfavourably with rural society. The population movements of the belle époque, which were, overall, from rural areas to urban ones, especially to the largest cities, suggest that, for all their problems, the cities appeared to offer better prospects than were available in the countryside. A popular song circulating at the beginning of the twentieth century in the Baltic provinces of the Russian Empire concerning the booming seaport and industrial city of Riga, the empire's seventh largest city, articulates very nicely this preference for urban over rural life:

> Brothers, we will go to Riga
> In Riga life is good;
> In Riga gold dogs bark
> And silver cocks crow.[12]

HIGH POINT AND TRANSFORMATION OF VOLUNTARY ASSOCIATIONS

The twenty-five years before the First World War was both a high point of voluntary associations and a conclusion to their process of growth and expansion which had been going on across the entire nineteenth century. Never before had such groups been so numerous, so widespread or with so large a membership. Yet at the same time, economic, social and cultural changes were under way that would both transform the nature of voluntary associations and limit their appeal. The pre-1914 acme of voluntary associations was also the prelude to a twentieth-century transformation and decline.

The sheer numbers of these groups and their steady pre-1914 increase is overwhelming. Figure 17.1, documenting the growth of voluntary associations in the Austrian half of the Austro-Hungarian Empire, shows how they doubled every decade, reaching over 100,000 voluntary associations on the eve of the First World War. Even in the Russian Empire, where the lack of clubs and societies had been quite conspicuous to observers across the first three-quarters of the nineteenth century, these groups increased in extent dramatically, some 4,800 founded between 1906 and 1909 alone, in part a result of the liberalization of association laws following the revolution of 1905. The Russian provincial town of Saratov, which had had just 2 voluntary associations in 1850, counted 37 in 1899 and 111 by 1914.

This spread and expansion of voluntary associations was generally not the result of the formation of new kinds of groups. Rather, expansion occurred within the basic contours set earlier in the nineteenth century. Women's associations for charitable

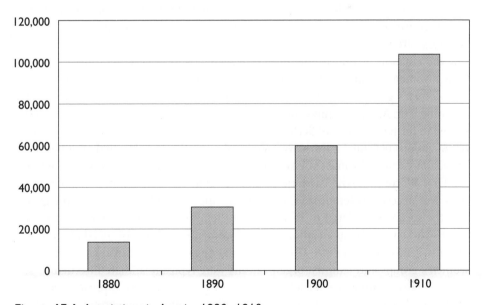

Figure 17.1 *Associations in Austria, 1880–1910*
Source: S. L. Hoffman, *Civil Society*, 2006, Palgrave Macmillan, reproduced with permission of Palgrave Macmillan.

purposes or moral improvement had a long nineteenth-century history. In Great Britain, the largest of such groups, the Women's Temperance Association, founded in 1876, was organized on a national scale and counted 50,000 members by the early 1890s. That decade, though, saw a continent-wide expansion of women's groups founded to deal with social problems, often associated with moral issues: alcoholism, child abuse, venereal disease, prostitution and the 'white slave trade', the purported seduction of unknowing young women into prostitution in large cities and overseas. Others, such as the Russian Elisabeth Society, provided day-care for working women. Generally closely connected with these organizations were women's professional and occupational associations, founded as women moved in increasing numbers into new lines of work, in white-collar and professional jobs. For example, in the German provincial capital of Hanover, women formed nineteen different associations between 1890 and 1906, including groups for women primary and secondary school teachers, a society of female salaried employees, a society to guard lower-class young women against the dangers of prostitution, an association that sponsored childcare and nursery schools, and, especially, the Protestant Women's League, a church-sponsored group that engaged in a wide variety of moral and social welfare campaigns. Perhaps two thousand women, from the city's middle and upper classes, were involved in these organizations.

If such groups were at first local in orientation, they quickly became affiliated in national federations. One of the first was the Danish Women's Progress Association of 1886. The League of German Women's Associations was founded in 1894, a Russian Women's Mutual Benefit Society the following year (the misleading name was chosen because of the government's repression of most forms of organizations). The Patriotic League of Frenchwomen was formed 1900, following a national congress of Catholic women's charitable and social welfare groups. The next year saw the creation of the competing, more secular and liberal, National Council of Frenchwomen. A National Council of Women was formed in Italy in 1903 and fifty-two women's groups united to form a National Council of Women in Hungary the following year. About this time, the twenty-seven women's charitable societies in Serbia united to form the 'Circle of Serbian Sisters'. Some of these federations and national organizations obtained impressive membership totals. The affiliated societies of the League of German Women's Associations counted 500,000 members on the eve of the First World War; the Patriotic League of Frenchwomen claimed 585,000 members. Not necessarily feminist in orientation – indeed, quite a number of the groups and the societies affiliated to them opposed feminist demands such as female suffrage – these women's associations offered women new forms of social and political activity. Feminists of the pre-1914 era usually began their political careers in these women's groups and feminist organizations were typically affiliated to them.

Nationalist gymnastics societies, already vigorous and widespread before the 1890s, reached new heights in the pre-1914 decades. The German groups, largest and longest established, almost tripled in size during this period, going from half a million to 1.4 million members. Czech Sokol grew sixfold from 1888 to 1912, reaching 120,000 members in 1,100 societies in that year. There were thousands or tens of thousands of Croatian, Ukrainian, Serb, Bulgarian and Slovene gymnasts, as well as Polish and Russian groups, united in 1908 into an international federation of Slavic Sokol.[13]

To take an example of another kind of voluntary association, the mutual benefit or friendly society, a kind of organization first begun in Great Britain and always most prevalent there. Membership in friendly societies, not including burial societies, grew from 2.75 million in 1877 to 5.6 million in 1904.[14] Now, a substantial portion of these groups were the 'collecting societies', not local clubs whose members looked after each other – as mutual benefit societies had originally been – but large, centralized organizations run by salaried employees. Membership in such an association required little activity besides paying dues and receiving benefits; there was essentially no membership participation. There was little to distinguish such associations from commercial insurance companies, or the nascent state-sponsored social insurance programmes. Indeed, both of these would tend to replace friendly societies, whose membership in Great Britain between the world wars was somewhat below their pre-1914 level.

This trend towards organization and centralized control was a major feature of associational life during the belle époque, most apparent in voluntary associations organized to deal with the economic difficulties of the later decades of the nineteenth century. These groups increased in membership and developed an ever more tightly organized and centralized administration in the more prosperous post-1890 decades. One prime example of this kind of organizational development was in trade unionism. Already on the upswing at the beginning of the 1890s, union membership rose greatly over the following twenty years, reaching very large numbers on the eve of the First World War: 4.14 million in the UK, 2.5 million in Germany, just under 1.1 million in France, some 840,000 in Italy. This growth also occurred in smaller European countries: 148,000 union members in Spain, about 85,000 in Sweden and 36,000 in Norway. These numbers all marked very considerable increases from the early to mid-1890s, of the order of 2.5 times as many, to as high as ten times. Accompanying these massive jumps in membership was the development of a considerable organizational apparatus. Individual craft or industrial unions were organized on a national scale, and joined together into giant national trade union federations. All levels of the unions' administrative apparatus, from the policy-making central offices to the local ones providing services, were run by paid, full-time union officials.

Contemporary observers, most famously the German-Italian sociologist Robert Michels, analysed this tendency towards bureaucratization. Michels, who was an anarchist before he became a supporter of Mussolini's fascists, decried the creation of a bureaucratic elite of the labour movement, which, he thought, destroyed the workers' revolutionary energies. But if unions with tens or hundreds of thousands of members were to accomplish anything, especially in view of the enormous geographic mobility of substantial segments of the working class, they needed just such a bureaucratic organization and a paid staff to administer it.

This development of centralized and bureaucratic administration was characteristic of all economic special-interest groups in the pre-1914 era. Although occurring everywhere on the European continent, the process was probably most advanced in Germany. Whether it was one of the three national trade union federations, one of the three national farmers' associations, one of the four competing national groups of salaried employees (male salaried employees, since female ones had their own associations), one of the two competing federations of small businessmen and master craftsmen, one of the two competing business federations – the more protectionist Central Association of Industrialists, the more free-trade League of Industrialists – or one of the galaxy of regional special-interest groups, ranging from the League of Saxon Industrialists to the Association of Berlin Industry, to the League of Bavarian Industrialists to the Association for the Preservation of the Common Economic Interests of the Rhineland and Westphalia (this latter known as the 'Association with the Long Name'), they all had a dues-paying membership that supported a substantial full-time paid staff and a bureaucratic organization. Just as, before 1914, locally oriented, individually or family-owned small businesses were gradually losing ground to bureaucratically organized corporations with a much larger scope of affairs, so too were voluntary associations with a local scope, an active membership and unpaid officers being slowly superseded by large, nationally organized associations with a relatively passive dues-paying membership and a well-organized full-time staff.

INTIMATIONS OF A CONSUMER SOCIETY

One of the major features of twentieth-century European history was the development of a consumer society, where consumption choices and leisure activities became steadily more important in individuals' lives and a focus of personal and group identification. Rising pre-1914 standards of living, and a gradually shortening working week, made it possible for consumption and leisure to assume a greater salience in the lives of a significant portion of the population. Still very far from what it would be in the second half of the twentieth century, or even in the years between the world wars, a universe of consumption was beginning to take shape in the quarter-century before 1914. Both building on older trends and encompassing new developments, the nascent consumer society was characterized by standardization, commodification and spectatorship. It was most apparent in three forms of leisure: commercial entertainment, sports and fashion.

Of the many kinds of commercial entertainment prevalent in the belle époque, print media were the most important. The pre-1914 years saw the triumph of the mass or boulevard press, newspapers designed to be successful business enterprises through entertaining a mass readership, rather than, as newspapers had tended to be for much of the nineteenth century, advocates of a political viewpoint that might or might not make money. The boulevard press was hawked on the streets and in kiosks and railway stations, rather than available just by subscription. Issue prices were low as plenty of advertising met publishers' costs, and advertisers were willing to pay, as the daily print run of such newspapers in capital cities, the London *Daily Mail*, the *Petit Parisien* or the *Berliner Morgenpost*, had crossed the 1 million mark by the beginning of the twentieth century. Yet the impact of the mass press was not just in its print run but also through its content and layout, which featured urban spectacles, lots of sports reporting, sensationalist crime features and plenty of illustrations – still mostly line drawings before 1914, rather than photographs.

Another form of print entertainment developing in the period was pulp fiction, stories of adventure or romance. Often in the form of serials, with individual episodes appearing on a weekly basis, or in daily instalments in the boulevard press, sold, like that press, from door to door, on the street, or in kiosks and railway stations, this pulp fiction increasingly featured three genres: science fiction, Westerns and detective stories. Tales of invasions from Mars, of future wars with super-scientific weaponry, of cowboys and Indians in a poorly understood American West – say New Mexico portrayed as a tropical rainforest – or of crime and its investigation in a pronouncedly urban setting became dominant themes of popular reading matter.

This popular reading matter, and popular entertainment more generally, was often viewed with alarm. Conservative and religious pressure groups, such as the German League against Filthy and Trashy Literature, or the French National Alliance against Depopulation, denounced it as vile, godless, pornographic and unpatriotic. Such groups tried to offer alternative, devout and nationalist cheap fiction, although generally without much success – perhaps most in Great Britain, where magazines aimed at teenagers, such as the *Boy's Own Paper*, combined imperialism, piety and adventures. Interestingly, socialists tended to share their conservative enemies' opinion about the entertainment media, holding that it diverted the workers' attention from the class struggle to Martians or Indians in the New Mexico rainforests, complaining that workers would rather read about sensational murder cases in the boulevard press than the tariff question, in – notoriously dull – socialist newspapers.

Historians and literary scholars who have studied popular reading matter of this period have found examples of both right-wing and left-wing political opinions. Perhaps more to the point is the subject matter of this pulp fiction: scientific advances, emigration to the United States, the criminal terrors and investigative fascinations of life in great metropolitan centres. Unlike older forms of popular reading matter, tales of knights, dragons, adventurous peasants, and other distinctly old-regime topics, still quite popular in economically less advanced countries such as the Russian Empire, the subjects of pulp fiction were taken from the age of classical modernism. Their widespread consumption is evidence that Europeans understood themselves to be

BOX 17.1

Pulp fiction and literature

The enormous expanse of late nineteenth- and early twentieth-century pulp fiction is best known today for the few authors who escaped from the pulp universe into a broader popularity. Champion of this process was the French science fiction writer Jules Verne (1828–1905), whose books became Europe-wide bestsellers, translated into dozens of languages; UNESCO has ranked him as one of the three most translated authors of all time. His counterpart in Westerns was the German author Karl May (1842–1912), whose imaginary visions of cowboys and Indians – May never actually visited the United States – were enormously popular in the German-speaking cultural world, and still are today. Unlike the frequently translated Verne, May's popularity has remained limited to central Europe. The classic author of crime fiction was Arthur Conan Doyle (1859–1930), whose character Sherlock Holmes was the first fictional figure to become far more popular and far more real to the reading public than his creator.

Yet for all the very considerable financial and popular success of these writers, their reputation never quite made it out of the pulp realm into the world of fiction with serious literary aspirations. There were a few serious authors – mostly English-speaking ones – of the early twentieth century who played with pulp genres. Two good examples are the English writer, cultural commentator and historian H. G. Wells (1866–1946), whose science fiction novels *The War of the Worlds* and *The Time Machine* dealt with questions of eugenics and social Darwinism, or the author, literary critic and political commentator, G. K. Chesterton (1874–1936), whose crime thriller *The Man Who Was Thursday* articulated his conservative political views. Although their pulp fiction-like writings are what these authors are known for today, to contemporaries their more conventional literary fiction and non-fiction works were at least as important, rather separating them from popular pulp authors.

living in a new and modern era; reading them today is evidence of just how distant that modern era has become.

Joining printed entertainment was a new mass medium, first emerging in this period, motion pictures. Like so many other features of the time a product of the second industrial revolution – created by the invention of celluloid film and of electrically powered film projectors which could show a rapid sequence of images – the motion picture process was successfully developed by the Lumière brothers in France, whose first film was ready in 1895. Rather as was the case with another product of the second industrial revolution, the automotive industry, France would be the centre of film making in Europe and, in fact, of the entire world, until about 1910. At first a novelty item, shown at fairs or between acts at music halls, in the five to seven years before the First World War films quickly became a major feature of leisure-time activity. The first cinema – a building devoted to nothing but showing films – was built in the UK in 1908; by 1914 there were 4,500 of them. In that same year there were about 1,500 cinemas in Germany, and 160 in Paris alone. Giant pleasure-palace movie houses had already opened – the Gaumont in Paris, with 5,000 seats and the Alhambra in Berlin with 2,000, both in 1911, the Palads Teatret in Copenhagen with 3,000 the following year.[15]

Along with cinemas went the development of a motion picture industry led by the Pathé Brothers who, by 1908, were Europe's and the world's leading film makers. Films themselves developed to fit their new venues, going from brief demonstrations of motion – the Lumières' first film, which fascinated and terrified audiences of the 1890s, showed a train coming into a station – to feature-length stories, containing characters, a plot and dynamic camera work. Feature films' plots tended to come from the genres of pulp fiction and movies began to generate some of the fears and disdain of pulp fiction as well, with denunciations of cinematic immorality and calls for government censorship. By the outbreak of the First World War, cinema was well prepared to take on the role it would have in the forty years following 1920 as the leading element of popular entertainment.

Possibly the single greatest novelty in leisure-time activity of the belle époque was the rapid rise of sports, as both spectator and participant activity. While bicycling was a popular pastime and the period saw the institution, in 1903, of the Tour de France bicycle race, the prime example was association football, the sport Americans stubbornly insist on calling soccer. The modern form of the sport and its offshoot, rugby, developed in Britain during the 1860s. By 1888, there were 1,000 clubs affiliated to the Football Association; their ranks rocketed to 10,000 by 1905. The Association's national championship, the 'Challenge Cup', attracted an astonishing 111,000 spectators in 1901. This remarkable interest reflected the increasingly detailed and spectacular coverage of sports in the boulevard press. So many spectators meant huge gate receipts, more affluent clubs and the development of a class of professional athletes emerging from the top ranks of the many amateur club athletes.

British students and industrial workers brought the game to continental Europe, The first soccer clubs there began appearing towards the beginning of the belle époque: Ogeryte IS in Gothenburg, Sweden, in 1887, MTK Budapest in 1888, or FC Dresden in 1892. FIFA, the international soccer association, was founded in 1904. MTK's new stadium, built in 1912, had room for 20,000 spectators, which was at the very peak of what pre-1914 soccer would achieve on the continent. Professional players, the World Cup, and six-figure audiences would have to wait for the 1920s and 1930s. Fan riots, on the other hand, were already a feature of athletic life. At the 1913 Scotland *v* France rugby match (this sport was surprisingly popular in southern France), held in Paris, fans, dismayed at what they saw as the referee's unfair pro-Scots calls, invaded the field and assaulted the referee, who had to be rescued by the police.

Characteristic of all forms of mass athletics was the need for some sort of organizing and structuring institution to standardize the conditions for competition. Before the formation of national and international soccer associations, for instance, each soccer club had its own version of the rules, and games began with negotiations about how they were to be played – and could be broken off if the two teams were unable to reach agreement. The ultimate sports standardizing body was the International Olympic Committee, formed in 1894 to promote quadrennial athletic competitions presented to the world as a revival of the ancient Greek Olympic Games. The Frenchman Baron Pierre de Coubertin (1863–1937), who, in league with Greek tourist promoters, was the moving force behind the modern Olympics, began his career in athletics as one of the founders and the first permanent president of the Union of French Gymnastics Societies, a national federation of sports clubs that attempted to set regular organized rules, first for gymnastics and then, more broadly, for track and field sports. With varying degrees of success, the earliest modern Olympic Games, especially the last pre-war games, held in Stockholm in 1912, set the stage for one of the major organized sports spectacles of the twentieth century.

Unlike pulp fiction or the cinema, sports enjoyed favourable public opinion. Conservative contemporaries endorsed mass athletics as hardening young men's bodies for war and reinforcing nationalist sentiments. Indeed, from their very beginning the modern Olympic Games involved competitions between national teams. Clergy saw sports as a way to take young men's minds off sex. Even socialists appreciated athletics and sought to sponsor their own workers' sports clubs.

As these perceptions of athletics suggest, the pre-1914 world of sports was a largely masculine one. While there was some limited female competition at the early Olympic Games, and even a few women's bicycle races, virtually all professional athletes and the overwhelming majority of amateur club players were men. Physicians often regarded athletic activity as dangerous for women's health, and religious groups tended to be strongly opposed to the immoral public sight of female bodies. It would only be in the inter-war years that less restrictive women's clothing, and the sponsorship of totalitarian regimes – lacking moral qualms about women showing their legs in public and feeling that sports, far from endangering women's health, would make them stronger mothers – began to bring women into the sports world.

If women before 1914 did not have sports as a realm of leisure and consumption activities, they did have another one that came into its own in this period, namely fashion. Developing its own versions of rules and standardization during the belle époque, fashion was heavily promoted by the boulevard press and was part of a new form of public spectacle and commercialized leisure activity, department store shopping. The fan base for fashion, as it were, could certainly hold its own in size with the fan base for sports.

The nineteenth century had seen the growth of Paris as Europe's and the world's fashion centre, the number of specialized *couturier* shops growing from 158 in 1850 to over 1,600 in 1895. By the 1890s, the yearly change of fashions had become well established. Parisian shops showed their new original creations, which were bought by wealthy purchasers at high prices, and sold rights to the designs to department store buyers who commissioned cheaper versions for sale in department stores and other mass retail outlets. Through this process, fashions were standardized across

Europe. The fashion scene of the time was especially focused on ladies' hats, which were very elaborate creations, topped with artificial flowers and other decorations.

A crucial element in this development of fashion was the department store. The pioneering stores of the 1860s, 1870s and 1880s, brought forth very large numbers of imitations in the post-1890 period – four hundred department stores in Germany, for instance, on the eve of the First World War. Department stores made their impact through a number of important innovations in retailing, in particular accepting a very low profit margin on each individual good sold, but running up substantial profits by selling in volume. To do this, department stores turned the activity of purchasing into a spectacle and leisure pastime with brilliantly lit and elaborately decorated stores, extensive advertising in the boulevard press, and encouragement of browsing with no commitment to purchase, which led customers to buy still more. Although stores offered a very wide variety of household goods, it was clothing, particularly women's fashions, that was at the heart of their product line.

Contemporaries had no doubt that fashion shopping in department stores had become a major leisure-time activity for women, and a wide variety of opinions developed about this activity. There was a lot of viewing with alarm, with fears widely expressed that women would waste family resources on fashion, be tempted into shoplifting or even lured into extramarital affairs. Suspicions were expressed that the desire for modern fashions was leading country girls to move to the city – and this was a period when standardized fashions increasingly replaced folk costumes in many rural areas. In England, department store shopping became, by contrast, a source of female respectability, a way for women from London's middle and upper-middle classes to appear in public without the need for a male escort.

In all these respects, fashion shared three of the central characteristics of a still tentatively emerging consumer society. One was standardization, so that people across Europe could compete in the same sport with the same rules, see the same film, wear the same fashions, and read the same novel by Jules Verne. Another was the increasing organization of leisure activities, whether by commercial interests in department stores, the boulevard press or sports magazines. The third was commodification, the way that leisure activities had become something individual consumers purchased, rather than something they did for themselves.

The extent of these three developments should not be exaggerated. There was still plenty of self-generated leisure activity in pre-1914 Europe, in clubs, societies and associations, or in rural areas, particularly on the poorer, economically and commercially less developed southern and eastern fringes of the continent. Most households lacked the income to make shopping a regular leisure activity, and the long hours of work and running a household limited the amount of leisure time available. Conversely, commodification of leisure activities was not a unique development of the quarter-century before 1914; earlier examples existed in the eighteenth and even the sixteenth centuries. Nonetheless, it is hard to avoid the impression that the years before the First World War marked a turning point, when standardized, organized and commodified versions of leisure, often involving intellectual and technological innovations, became the way that ever greater numbers of people aspired to spend their free time.

These forms taken of the nascent consumer society in pre-1914 Europe might well stand in for the broader trends in social development. Whether considering class structure, urbanization, the formation of voluntary associations or the development of consumerism, the 1890–1914 period saw the culmination of trends running since at least the mid-nineteenth century. Yet the result of this culmination was the creation, as yet in an initial and tentative form, of something distinctly new and modern which would develop further, in spite of the upheavals of two world wars and their aftermaths, throughout the twentieth century.

CHAPTER 18

THE ARTS AND SCIENCES

The twenty-five years before the First World War were an era of triumphant intellectual innovation whose consequences would echo across the twentieth century. This
was the period of the rise of artistic and literary modernism, of the formulation of
the classic sociological theories of Émile Durkheim and Max Weber, of Sigmund Freud's
psychoanalysis and of what contemporaries were calling revolutionary new theories
in physics – in retrospect, a fully justified designation.

As is usually the case with such sweeping comparisons and generalizations, there
are a number of caveats and exceptions. In some intellectual disciplines – biology,
chemistry and economics come to mind – the crucial innovations came earlier in the
nineteenth century, and the pre-1914 years were more about the continuation and
refinement of previous innovations. Many of the bold new ideas of the belle époque
built on or were anticipated by intellectual and artistic trends of the late nineteenth-
century age of uncertainty, and the new ideas developed before 1914 by no means
resolved all the problems and uncertainties of the earlier era. Most of all, though,
one should be sceptical of efforts to tie all of these new developments together. James
Joyce's literary modernism, Pablo Picasso's cubist artworks and Albert Einstein's theory of relativity were all products of the first decade of the twentieth century, but it
is questionable to see them, as historians often do, as part of some broad recon-
ceptualization of perception, space and time. Rather as was the case in an earlier period
with the idea of progress and Charles Darwin's theory of natural selection, the relationship between new intellectual and artistic notions on the one hand, and new
scientific ones on the other, was marked more by common misunderstandings than
by common elements.

A NEW WORLD OF SCIENCE

The pre-1914 era was one of rapid and intense progress in the natural and physical
sciences, whether in the formulation of new scientific theories or in the perfection
and demonstration of older ones, in the attainment of striking research results or
in the technological and engineering application of this research. This scientific
progress did not remain hidden in laboratories and scholarly journals but reached
a large public audience, making knowledge about the advances of science a significant part of the perception of living in a modern era.

Public knowledge of scientific advances in chemistry was hard to avoid in view of the central role of chemical manufacturing in the second industrial revolution. Synthetic dyestuffs, new drugs, or new industrial products, from cellulose to plastics, to acetylene to petrol, all delineated the public contours of the science of chemistry. Yet these applications were primarily a reflection of the advances in basic chemical research over the last third of the nineteenth century. Perhaps the most significant development in chemical research during this period, the fixation of atmospheric nitrogen by the German chemist and future Nobel Prize winner Fritz Haber (1868–1934), in 1908, which would make possible the synthesis of nitrogen-containing fertilizers and explosives, was, like other important chemical discoveries, the culmination of a longer period of experimentation and research.

In some respects, developments in biology were similar to those in chemistry. Research into microbes and causes of infectious disease followed along the lines set down in the 1870s and 1880s by Louis Pasteur and Robert Koch. An important expansion of their research programme was the discovery during the 1890s, primarily by the Russian biologist Dmitri Ivanovski (1864–1920) and the Dutch botanist Martinus Beijerinck (1851–1931), of a new kind of disease-causing micro-organism, much smaller than bacteria, quickly dubbed a virus. As with chemistry, aspects of previous biological research found industrial and commercial applications in this period. The spread of pasteurized milk – milk which has been sterilized to destroy potentially harmful micro-organisms – seems to have played an important role in the decline in infant mortality that occurred throughout much of Europe, especially in the large cities, during the quarter-century before 1914.

Circumstances in regard to the other great development of nineteenth-century biology, Darwin's theory of natural selection, were somewhat different. The major questions raised in the concluding decades of the nineteenth century about this theory concerned the mechanisms of heredity, the process by which biological characteristics are passed from one generation to the next. The post-1890 period saw the discovery, or, actually, the rediscovery, of the basic rules of genetics, the division of inherited characteristics into dominant and recessive strains, and the results of their crossing. First proposed by the Austrian monk Gregor Mendel (1822–84) during the 1860s, but published in a very obscure and little regarded journal, the ideas were rediscovered by the Dutch plant physiologist Hugo de Vries (1848–1935) in 1900. Another piece of the biological puzzle of heredity was the discovery, by the American biologist Thomas Hunt Morgan, of the existence of mutations, intergenerational changes in genetic structure.

The discovery of these mechanisms of heredity had the potential to deal with one of the key questions raised about natural selection, but at first scientists perceived these new developments more as confirming than as resolving existing doubts. Mutations were seen as enormous macro changes in an organism, in effect the creation of a new species from one generation to the next, and so seemed to provide an alternative to natural selection in explaining changes in species over time. It would take until the 1940s to incorporate genetics into evolutionary theory, by understanding mutations as involving smaller changes, increasing the range of variability within a species, thus enhancing the possibilities for natural selection, rather than as creating a new species altogether. Combining this with the mathematical analysis of Mendel's laws of descent, as applied to an entire species – population genetics – provided an understanding of the mechanisms of heredity through which natural selection operates. Biologists refer to this merger of natural selection and genetics as the 'modern synthesis', and it remains the focal point of today's scientific biology.

Thus, the pre-1914 era produced the basic discoveries in biology that would come to drive that science over the course of the twentieth century, although contemporary scientists at first did not perceive them as such. By contrast, the quarter-century before the First World War saw an avalanche of new experimental findings in physics, and remarkable new theories to explain them. These new theories would not just set the course of physics from the first decade of the twentieth century down to the present day, but also turn physics into the pre-eminent science of the twentieth century, the one that had the greatest and most pronounced impact, to the point of creating the capability to destroy most life on earth.

By the 1890s physicists were having problems reconciling the classical physics of Isaac Newton, centred on the study of the motion of particles under the impact of forces, with the newer, nineteenth-century study of electromagnetic radiation. In the physics section of the 1895 meeting of the German Association of Natural Researchers, the most important annual conference of Germany's scientists, the advocates of a Newtonian 'mechanics' and an electromagnetic 'energetics' descended into a shouting match over which form of physics should have priority. Compounding these unresolved theoretical problems was the appearance of a series of striking experimental results, coming closely together in less than a decade, for which existing theories had no explanation.

First was Wilhelm Röntgen's 1895 discovery of a mysterious form of energy discharge from a vacuum tube, receiving the name of X-rays. The following year, the French physicist Henri Becquerel (1852–1908) discovered that certain chemical substances – in his case, uranium salts – spontaneously emitted energy. Following up on Becquerel's findings, the physicist duo Pierre Curie (1859–1906) and Marie Curie *née* Sklodowska (1867–1934) found that other radioactive substances contained hitherto unknown chemical elements – which they named polonium and radium – and that these elements emitted considerable and visible energy, enough heat to bring water from near freezing to a boil, or radiant energy enabling them to glow in the dark. Marie Curie dubbed this energy 'radioactivity', a name that has resonated through the following hundred years. More detailed investigation by the physicist Ernest Rutherford (1871–1937), originally from New Zealand but working in the physics laboratory at Cambridge, the centre of physics research in the UK, showed that radioactivity took different forms – soon to be dubbed alpha, beta and gamma rays – with different amounts of energy and different electrical charges.

In an age of rapidly expanding mass media, the new experimental results quickly became public spectacles. The eerie ability of X-rays to penetrate physical barriers, in particular to reveal human skeletal structure under the skin, was made for a show. Germany's emperor Wilhelm II summoned Wilhelm Röntgen to give a command performance of X-ray photography at the imperial palace. Within a year of his discovery, the *Illustrated London News*, one of the new mass newspapers, had published X-ray pictures of the hands of the Duke and Duchess of York. Europe, as one American observer noted, was afflicted with 'Roentgen mania'. Little tubes containing a small quantity of radium were sold to the public so they could see it glowing in the dark. Spurred on by the speculations of physicists such as Becquerel or Pierre Curie on the possibilities inherent in 'atomic energy' – a phrase coined at this time – science fiction writers began penning works about radium-propelled aeroplanes and radium bombs.

This public fascination with radioactivity was focused, perhaps more than anywhere else, on the person of Marie Curie, who became Europe's first celebrity physicist. Her unique status as a leading scientist, the 1903 Nobel Prize winner, and a woman – in fact, a wife and mother – in an extremely male-dominated field of intellectual endeavour only heightened public interest. Her life was detailed in the boulevard press, in the serious, political press, and even in the magazine *Paris Sport*. Pierre Curie explained in a letter to an acquaintance that he and his wife '. . . have been pursued by journalists and photographers from all the countries of the world, they have gone so far as to reproduce the conversation of my daughter with her maid and to describe the black and white cat who lives with us'.[16]

All this attention for a very obscure science was flattering, if also annoying, since, as Pierre Curie complained, the incessant attention was making it impossible for his wife and himself to get any physics done. The major theoretical challenge that physicists faced was resolving the contrasts between Newtonian mechanics and nineteenth-century electrodynamics, while also explaining the striking new experimental results. Two new physical theories, both of which were proposed in the first decade of the twentieth century, would begin to accomplish this task: quantum theory and the theory of relativity.

The first of these two theories dealt with the nature of energy, asserting that energy is emitted in discrete units or quanta. First proposed in 1900 by the German physicist Max Planck (1858–1947) to explain the nature of black-body radiation, the idea was taken up in 1905 by Albert Einstein (1879–1955), whose theoretical explanation of the photoelectric effect – the way that light rays impinging on a substance can cause it to give off electrical energy – demonstrated that light energy was also quantized, existing as spatially localized particles rather than in the form of waves spreading out through space, with infinitely variable amounts of energy. On the eve of the First World War, the Danish physicist Niels Bohr (1885–1962) used these quantum ideas to explain atomic structure as a miniature solar system, with electrons orbiting around a central nucleus and the quantized emission of electromagnetic radiation tied to the movement of electrons from one orbit to another.

The other major theoretical advance, the theory of relativity, has attained a celebrity status in the public mind, comparable among scientific theories only to Darwin's evolutionary ideas. Relativity theory dealt with the problem of reconciling Newton's mechanics and nineteenth-century theories of electromagnetic radiation. The very title of Albert Einstein's celebrated 1905 paper, in which the theory was formulated, 'On the Electrodynamics of Moving Bodies', indicates the point, taking James Clerk Maxwell's electromagnetic field equations and showing how they needed to be transformed to deal with moving sources of electromagnetic radiation.

Just as was the case with quantum theory, which was the product of the work of a number of different physicists, including Einstein himself, the development of a mathematical model that would explain the electrodynamics of moving bodies was something of a joint creation, based in part on the work of the Dutch physicist Hendrik Antoon Lorentz (1853–1928), regarded as the leading theoretical physicist of his day, (among his accomplishments was developing the idea of a particle carrying an electric charge, the electron) and the French mathematician Henri Poincaré (1854–1912). Einstein's theories, although mathematically similar to those of Lorentz and Poincaré, differed in decisively rejecting previous ideas of a universal rate of the passage of time and of the existence of an ether, a universal medium of electromagnetic radiation.

Although at the time he published his basic papers on physics in 1905, Einstein was an obscure figure, a technical expert in the Swiss patent office, his theories quickly impressed physicists, particularly German-speaking ones, who regarded his work as revolutionary in its implications for the study of the physical world. The reformulation of Einstein's theories by the Göttingen mathematician Hermann Minkowski in 1909, involving the non-Euclidean geometry of a four-dimensional space–time, introduced the seductive idea, which would come to be associated with Einstein, that time was the 'fourth dimension'.

Although provoking considerable debate and fruitful experiments, neither quantum theory nor relativity were completely formulated before 1914. Both theories would be completed over the following fifteen years. Since then, a central topic of physics has been reconciling relativity and quantum mechanics, a theoretical, mathematical and experimental task that has proved more difficult than reconciling Newtonian mechanics and electromagnetic radiation, and continues down to the present day.

It was also in the 1920s that both new theories of physics went beyond their narrow scientific audience and reached a broad public, in doing so turning Albert Einstein into the ultimate celebrity physicist, whose worldwide appeal put his predecessor Marie Curie in the shade. In the wake of this popular interest in revolutionary physical theories, questions have been raised about the relationship of the post-1900 new physics to broader cultural and intellectual developments. Historians, philosophers and various assorted thinkers have sometimes linked the new physics to new portrayals of space in cubism, new understandings of time, consciousness and selfhood in literary modernism, or new conceptions of ethics and morality. Most of the people who draw these connections do not understand physics very well. The connection between artistic modernism, new philosophical ideas and the new physics of the early twentieth century is based on an even greater misunderstanding of science than the connection between Darwin's theory of natural selection and the idea of progress in the 1860s and 1870s.

If there was a link to external factors in the development of new physical theories in the post-1890 period it was probably in a much more closely related area, namely the second industrial revolution. The development of electrical manufacturing made possible the sort of apparatus needed to carry out the study of radiation. Einstein, whose father and uncle had run a business manufacturing devices used in electric power stations, who evaluated electrical and electromagnetic inventions for the patent office, and who was himself an inventor, patenting a number of electrical devices, was personally well tuned in to matters electromagnetic. The crucial intellectual

---

BOX 18.1

Why the theory of relativity does *not* say that everything is relative

One of the most commonly proposed links of the post-1900 new physics to broader cultural change is the idea that the theory of relativity asserts that everything is relative. This assertion, the argument goes on, connects Einstein's theories to modernist art, with its replacement of previous universal aesthetic standards by the artist's own subjective conceptions, to literary expressions of the perception of different rates of the passage of time or of a rejection of universally valid moral values, and an advocacy of a relativity of ethics and morals. Unfortunately for such assertions, even a brief and thoroughly non-technical consideration of the theory of relativity shows their very dubious nature.

Einstein did propose a principle of relativity, namely that physical laws are the same in all inertial frames of reference, that is, in all bodies travelling at constant rates of speed. His rigorous mathematical development of this principle led to seemingly bizarre results, such as the fact that time passes more slowly in objects going at higher rates of speed. This passage of time, however, is not a subjective perception, as might be seen in a literary portrayal of boredom. Time actually passes more slowly in one frame of reference than another; unstable elementary particles, for instance, exist longer before they decay into other particles when they are travelling close to the speed of light, than when they are at rest or going at slower velocities.

Even more to the point, Einstein's theory of relativity consists of two basic principles, one the assertion about inertial frames of reference, the other the assertion that the physical constant c, the speed of light in a vacuum, is the same in all frames of reference. In Einstein's system, the speed of light or of other forms of electromagnetic radiation in a vacuum is absolute and unchanging, no matter what the velocity of the emitter of that radiation or the observer of it. All of Einstein's conclusions, from the relativity of the passage of time to the famous equation $E = mc^2$, depend on this absolute, thoroughly unrelative velocity.

concept in Einstein's theories of synchronizing clocks via an exchange of light signals may have been related to the development of a network of synchronized electrical clocks in Europe's railway systems occurring at the beginning of the twentieth century. These sorts of connections between the new physics and broader changes may seem more prosaic and less cosmic than a convergence of artistic, scientific and ethical perceptions of time and space, but are probably a better reflection of actual intellectual influences.

SOCIAL SCIENCE BETWEEN REASON AND THE IRRATIONAL

The quarter-century before the First World War saw a remarkable flowering of the social sciences, which would set the stage for much of their intellectual development over the course of the twentieth century. To mention the names of just three of the figures putting forth their ideas in the pre-1914 era suffices to make the point: Émile Durkheim (1858–1917), Max Weber (1864–1920), Sigmund Freud (1856–1939). On closer examination, these innovators, and many of their contemporaries rather less well known today – Werner Sombart, Wilfredo Pareto, Georges Sorel, Robert Michel and Gaetano Mosca, to mention a few – built their insights on the foundations of the previous half-century. They took up not only the ideas of Comte and Spencer about human history as involving progress through different forms of society, and the relationship of these ideas to Darwin's theories, so popular in the mid-century decades, but also the doubts expressed about the ideal of progress in the later nineteenth century.

The thinkers of the belle époque gave these ideas their own distinct twists. One was to accept the distinctions between earlier, more primitive and later, more advanced forms of society, but to drop either the positive or the pejorative connotations that adherents of progress or proponents of degeneracy had tied to this social and historical development. A second was to accept the enormous importance of the irrational in human life, in human psychology and in human society, while insisting on the importance of rational and positivist forms of investigation and study. The link between rationality in human action and rationality in studying human action – a link strongly endorsed by the positivists of the third quarter of the nineteenth century, and equally strongly rejected by the late nineteenth-century critics of positivism, such as Nietzsche – was broken.

Setting the stage for the new developments in sociology was the 1887 work of Ferdinand Tönnies (1855–1936), *Community and Society*. According to Tönnies, these were two different forms of social organization, the former based on shared beliefs and values, expressed by individuals' desires and actions, the latter based on individual self-interest and reasoned calculation. Tönnies identified community with past societies, the Middle Ages, for instance, with its guilds, lords and serfs and universal church, but he also saw communal forms of social organization in the present: in families, villages or small towns. By contrast, he identified society with market economics, large cities, industrial production, bureaucracy and constitutional government. This distinction was not unlike the stages in human social development defined by Comte or Spencer, but for Tönnies the movement from community to society was not praiseworthy progress but instead involved alienation and loss. At the same time, Tönnies, unlike many of the mid- and late nineteenth-century critics of progress, did not call for a return to a communitarian form of social organization. This was impossible in an increasingly urban and industrial age; in melancholy fashion, Tönnies could only regret the change.

Both the distinction between two forms of social organization and the ambivalent attitude towards them were characteristic of leading social scientists of the period. In his study of the division of labour, Durkheim distinguished between the 'mechanical solidarity' of artisan guilds and peasant villages (like community) and the 'organic solidarity' of the industrial division of labour (like society); in his book on suicide, he endeavoured to show that suicide rates were lowest among social groups with strong community-like ties and highest where 'anomie', the lack of such bonds, existed. Max Weber's contrast between 'traditional' and 'bureaucratic' forms of authority moves in a similar direction. The distinction in contemporary sociology and mass media commentary between 'tradition' and 'modernity', although not coined in exactly this way during the 1890–1914 era, goes back to it.

Community and tradition were precisely not characterized by critical and rational thinking, so this mode of social analysis led to a new appraisal of non-rational elements in human society, such as belief, or feelings of solidarity. Durkheim, in his *Elementary Forms of Religious Life*, asserted that 'In reality, then there are no religions which are false. All are true in their own fashion . . . The reasons with which the faithful justify them may be, and generally are, erroneous; but the true reasons do not cease to exist and it is the duty of science to discover them.'[17] Like his positivist precursors, Durkheim was rejecting religion's claim to transcendental validity, and asserting the priority of empirical evidence and reasoning in understanding the world, but, very much unlike Comte and Spencer, he was praising religion for the non-rational feelings of solidarity it generated. Max Weber's famous attempt to demonstrate the crucial importance of Calvinist religious obsessions in the development of economic rationality, in his book *The Protestant Ethic and the Spirit of Capitalism*, shows a similar kind of positive appraisal of the social role of religion, without accepting its literal truth.

If appreciating non-rational forms of community, early twentieth-century social science inversely cultivated a discontent with modern, bureaucratic rational society. A number of sociologists developed strong sympathies with the labour movement, hoping to find in it a new form of community. They were generally disappointed, as was the case with Robert Michels, whose contact with socialists in Germany and Italy led him to the discouraging conclusion that even these movements of social emancipation ended up creating bureaucratic organizations dominated by a small group of leaders – a result he called the 'iron law of oligarchy'. Max Weber, who was oppressed by the 'iron cage' of bureaucratic organization he saw increasingly encompassing modern society, looked for ways to break through it. Like Tönnies, he saw no chance of return to past forms of community. Instead, he looked to the potential of 'charisma' (Weber invented the modern, non-religious use of this phrase), those magnetic personality traits allowing an individual to elicit followers' overwhelming and distinctly non-rational loyalties, as a way to break out of the politically confining structures of bureaucracy. Weber was also a passionate German nationalist, actively supporting efforts to turn his native country into a world power. Such a combination of a charismatic leader with passionate nationalism – admittedly not in a way Weber had envisaged – would have unfortunate consequences for Germany later in the twentieth century. Its pre-1914 advocacy is evidence of the pronounced position of the irrational in the positivist social science of the period.

Rational analysis of the irrational was a central feature of the life and work of Sigmund Freud. The basic doctrines of psychoanalysis, the intellectual discipline he founded, were worked out in the quarter-century before the First World War. Freud and his followers came to understand psychoanalysis as a very expansive discipline: a form of medical therapy of psychiatric disorders, a theory of human mental functioning, a form of sociological and anthropological investigation and a version of cultural criticism. As a result, the intellectual and social influences of Freud's ideas have been multifarious and considerable, generating passionate adherence and violent opposition, so that the origins of his doctrines in the pre-1914 era are often obscured. Three aspects of Freud's ideas are characteristic of the social and biological science of the period.

One is the empirical and scientific investigation of human sexuality, a form of human behaviour in which the instincts and non-rational emotions play a pronounced role. Freud was one of a larger group of investigators which included such figures as Richard von Krafft-Ebing (1840–1902), a professor of psychiatry at the University of Vienna whose 1886 book *Psychopathia Sexualis* dealt with deviant forms of sexuality not as examples of sin and moral decay but as medical conditions, and his British counterpart Havelock Ellis (1859–1939). While today the best known of the late nineteenth-century sexologists, Krafft-Ebing and Ellis were just two of a galaxy of investigators of human sexual behaviour whom Freud cited and in whose ranks he was generally placed by contemporaries.

A second aspect of Freud's work was its close relationship to late nineteenth-century Darwinist conceptions, a version of Darwin which owed much to the assertions of Lamarck, namely that acquired characteristics could be inherited. When questioned about the universal empirical reality of central features of his theory of sexual development and the origins of neuroses, such as the 'primal scene', the young child witnessing his or her parents having sexual relations, Freud would say that these had actually occurred in early stages of human evolution and been transmitted by inheritance ever since.

Finally, Freud's thought was part of the same trend of thinking about the rational and the irrational that was such a prominent feature of early twentieth-century sociology and anthropology. Freud emphasized the power of the irrational in human life, the role of the instincts in shaping human behaviour, the centrality of the unconscious to human mental functioning, the way that neurotic behaviour overwhelms individuals' reason. The psychoanalytic method of free association, in which patients said whatever came into their mind, was designed to make unconscious traumas conscious and to bring the irrational under rational control. Freud – and in this respect, his attitudes are similar to those of Weber or Tönnies – saw human civilization as depending on the suppression of irrational instincts, particularly those of a sexual nature, so that individuals could engage in rational, economic behaviour, yet he also saw this triumph of rationality and repression of the instincts as leading to neurosis and personal unhappiness.

Just as Einstein took insights widely spread through the study of theoretical physics and brought them together into a powerful theory, so his contemporary, Freud, brought together a number of contemporary intellectual trends to form his unique theory of psychoanalysis. Both of these new theories would come to attract broader intellectual and popular interest, in small ways before 1914, and, much more substantially, after the First World War. However, there is one very distinct difference between the work of the two men. Einstein's theory of relativity has been persistently and consistently verified over the past century; it stands as a landmark of successful science. Freud's theories have not fared so well. Any similarity between them and actual human cognitive activity or sexual behaviour seems coincidental; psychoanalysis, whether performed by the master himself or by his disciples, has had a singularly poor therapeutic track record. If connections between cultural change and the early twentieth-century revolution in physics seem largely to derive from intellectual misunderstandings, it is the 'scientific' nature of psychoanalysis that is the misunderstanding; its significance emerged from its relationship to the intellectual and cultural changes of the pre-1914 period.

Freud himself was a physician in private practice and the International Psychoanalytic Association he created was a society quite separate from universities and academic life. Yet Freud was also an adjunct lecturer in the faculty of medicine at the University of Vienna, and he always hoped that academics would come to appreciate and support his theories. In this respect, psychoanalysis, like other forms of social science developing in the quarter-century before the First World War, reflected the transformation of secondary and higher education in the period. This transformation was not primarily a result of a substantial growth in advanced educational institutions. Enrolments remained small; less than 3 per cent of the relevant age group. Rather, there were structural changes. Women were admitted to university study – amounting to about one-fifth of British university students in 1910 – and secondary education for them was reshaped to prepare them for attending a university. The scientific and modern language tracks of secondary education, still not quite respectable before 1890, and clearly behind the classical language tracks, gained substantial numbers of students and recognition as appropriate forms of preparation for university studies.

Universities themselves, retaining their earlier focus on subjects such as law, theology and medicine, gained new branches of study and research, in technology and engineering. Investigation in the natural sciences took place almost exclusively in universities. Einstein, the leading scientist of the period, who formulated his theories while working as a patent examiner, might seem like an exception, but he had enjoyed a thorough technological and scientific education at the Federal Institute of Technology in Zurich and quickly moved into university employment once his scientific theories became known and appreciated. Sociology, an intellectually very vigorous discipline in the 1890–1914 period, became one practised almost exclusively in universities. This movement of intellectual life into formal academic institutions was another feature of the belle époque that would continue and expand across the twentieth century.

THE RISE OF ARTISTIC MODERNISM

The innovative, often unsettling, always challenging initiatives in the arts during the belle époque have come to be known as modern art or artistic modernism. Although these phrases were occasionally used before 1914, they were primarily, like the belle époque itself, a retrospective designation, seen, for instance, in the 1929 founding of a museum of modern art in New York City – a celebrated institution, still very much present today. Before 1914, there was a wide variety of artistic trends – post-impressionism, expressionism, fauvism, symbolism, atonalism, cubism, futurism, constructivism, to mention just a few. Although art historians, musicologists and literary critics have separated these into nicely discrete aesthetic movements, contemporaries applied the terms freely and inconsistently.

We might give up looking for any common elements in these artistic movements, but to do so would probably be a mistake. As was vaguely apparent to contemporaries, and is quite clear today, characteristic of all these trends was a feeling that long-existing artistic forms were no longer adequate to represent the reality of the modern world – both its exterior reality in the development of science and technology or the growth of giant urban centres, and its interior reality of individuals' conscious and unconscious mental states. As the Russian artist Kasimir Malevich (1878–1935) said: 'It is absurd to force our age into the old forms of time past.'[18] Consequently, artists sought new forms that would serve their purposes. Sometimes they based this search on previous artistic innovations, such as impressionism, realism in literature and painting, or the rapid changes of key typical of late romantic music. Another focus of the search was forms of art outside the canon of high culture – European folk art, 'primitive' art (that is, art of tribal peoples, especially in

Africa), even creations of children or the mentally ill. Sometimes this search for innovation created artistic forms that seemed like drastic breaks from anything previously done. Before 1914, these innovations occurred to a very different degree in the visual arts, music and literature, and they received different versions of public notice, approval or hostility. But everywhere they proliferated and set the stage for artistic developments, certainly through to the 1960s, and, in some ways, until the present.

Artistic innovations were most vigorous and most apparent in painting, drawing and sculpture. At the risk of distorting a complex aesthetic feature, we might divide these artistic innovations into two separate trends – in which there were many personal and artistic overlaps. One trend involved finding new ways to represent external reality. The Italian futurists and Russian constructivists were two groups of artists whose work moved in this direction, but the most dramatic and famous example – at the time and ever since – of the new representation of external reality was the artistic movement of cubism, whose leading figure, the Franco-Spanish artist Pablo Picasso (1881–1973), launched himself on a career that would make him the leading artist of the twentieth century.

Along with his friend and collaborator Georges Braque (1882–1963), Picasso rejected the artistic technique of perspective, in use since the fifteenth century, to represent three-dimensional space on a two-dimensional canvas. Instead, Picasso and Braque showed three-dimensionality by representing the same object with different perspectives, by mixing up the interior and exterior of an object to be represented, and by placing in the same artwork representations of different spatial planes at right angles to each other. In doing this, once familiar objects would look odd and barely recognizable – in a word, strange. Picasso would note of his use of collage, in which the cubist perspective was enhanced by placing actual objects, such as newspaper fragments, into the work of art: '. . . this strangeness was what we wanted to make people think about because we were quite aware that our world was becoming very strange and not exactly reassuring'.[19]

Such an effort to convey emotions was central to the other main trend of artistic modernism. It appears in a group of mostly French artists, the 'post-impressionists', including Vincent Van Gogh (1850–93), Paul Gauguin (1848–1903), Paul Cézanne (1830–1906) and, especially, Henri Matisse (1869–1954). As Matisse put it in 1908: 'Composition is the art of arranging in a decorative manner the diverse elements at the painter's command to express his feelings.'[20] Post-impressionist painters did so by using strong dashes of colour, often in ways that would not have been seen in nature, or by rearranging the portrayal of human figures to articulate emotions rather than to represent exactly physical appearance. Strongly influenced by these painters was another group of artists, primarily in Germany and the Scandinavian countries, the expressionists, whose work, as their name indicates, was all about the expression of emotions. All too often these emotions were negative ones – fear, pain and terror, all seen in one of the founding paintings of expressionism, the Norwegian artist Edvard Munch's (1869–1944) 1893 work 'The Scream', in which a crudely portrayed man radiates inner angst. The expressionists often painted scenes of apocalyptic destruction, which have been interpreted as foreshadowings of the First World War, although if those paintings were portraying any external reality, as opposed to the artists' own internal ones, it was a vision of all-encompassing workers' revolution, not of a total war.

The expressionists' search for new forms to represent the modern world often led them away from literal portrayals of their surroundings. One of the expressionists, the Russian-born Wassily Kandinsky (1866–1944), who worked before 1914 in Munich, an important centre of modernist art in the German-speaking countries, began to turn out canvases with no relation to external objects, and which he called 'abstract' paintings. This kind of artwork has led to the opinion, on the part both of art critics and of the general public, that modern art involves a rejection of realism and its desire to portray accurately the physical and social world. Yet Kandinsky described his abstract art as a way to represent the 'non-material strivings of the soul', which he contrasted with the increasingly modern scientific world in which he lived.[21] Such remarks suggest a different relationship between realist and modernist art. Even the non-representational works of early twentieth-century modern artists shared with their realist predecessors the wish to break with long-existing forms of artistic creation and to find new forms needed to represent reality. Certainly, though, both the break with previous forms and the use of new ones were much more drastic in artistic modernism. Of course, artists working in the modernist styles, as a result of the social, economic, political and intellectual changes of the pre-1914 era, understood reality differently from the realists, and, as a result of the artistic innovations of the impressionists of the 1870s and 1880s, also had a different understanding of what it meant to represent reality. Yet this search for new artistic forms adequate to reality was common to both realist and modernist artists, and might lead us to surmise that artistic modernism was not so much a rejection of artistic realism as its continuation by other means.

As was the case with the plastic arts, the quarter-century before the First World War saw the development of a distinctly modernist music. Just as modernist art showed both a continuity and break with its realist predecessor, so modern music also involved a continuity and break with romanticism, the dominant musical tradition of the nineteenth century. Composers of the 1880s and 1890s used the romantic technique of sharp tonal contrasts, rapid changes from one key to the next and insertion of ever more dissonant elements into their composition. The next step, seen in the work of Claude Debussy (1862–1918), including his 1892–94 composition *Prelude to the Afternoon of a Faun* and his 1905 tone poem *The Sea*, were sections which seemed not to be in any key at all, although the pieces ultimately reverted to being in major and minor keys, expressions of musical harmony as had been practised in European musical composition for centuries. Other composers active in Paris, particularly the Russian Igor Stravinsky (1882–1971), continued Debussy's experiments in tonality, and added to them unconventional expressions of rhythm and metre, most dramatically in the music Stravinsky composed for the ballet *Rite of Spring*, which had its Paris premiere in 1913.

The Austrian composer Arnold Schoenberg (1874–1951) worked in a similar vein as can be seen in his 1899 sextet for strings *Verklärte Nacht* (*Transfigured Night*) that carried the late romantic changes of tonality to extremes. After 1900, Schoenberg, along with his two pupils, Alban Berg (1885–1935) and Anton Webern (1883–1945), began composing completely atonal pieces, music not in any key at all, where the long-existing musical harmonies were simply rejected in favour of other forms of melodic arrangement. Personally close to a group of German expressionist painters, the 'Blue Rider' school of Munich, Schoenberg understood their artistic endeavours as fundamentally similar to his, both involving the dramatic rejection of past artistic forms and the search for – often difficult – new ones, in order to express the artist's emotions in the context of an increasingly unfamiliar modern world.

The development of literature in the pre-1914 era parallels that of painting or music, albeit with a somewhat different chronology and somewhat different relation to previous versions of artistic expression. Like other forms of artistic modernism, literary modernism involved a rejection of previous artistic forms and a search for new ones, in order to represent the new and unfamiliar aspects of the modern world. A central element of literary modernism was the development of new methods to represent human consciousness, above all the technique known as 'stream of consciousness' or 'interior monologue', in which authors attempted to show the unmediated experience of perceiving the world and the self. Classic works of literary modernism, such as the multi-volume novel *Remembrance of Things Past* by the French author Marcel Proust (1871–1922), or the novels of the Irish author James Joyce (1882–1941), *Portrait of the Artist as a Young Man* or *Ulysses*, demonstrated different versions of this technique, more refined and stylized in Proust's work, more vigorous and wildly expressed in Joyce's – but all breaking with the conventions of the realist novel in its representation of thought and perception. A variation on this technique was practised by the German modernist author Thomas Mann, best seen in his 1912 novella *Death in Venice*, in which an individual's conscious perception, in this case a writer's inarticulate longing for a beautiful boy (representations of homosexual desire were very common in modernist writing), was observed and analysed from different angles, producing an effect perhaps not unlike that of stream of consciousness writing.

In all these respects, literary modernism seems, like artistic modernism, a continuation of the realist project by describing new versions of reality with non-realist forms of artistic representation. However, in contrast to the situation in the visual arts, it is striking how little progress literary modernism had made before the outbreak of the First World War. James Joyce's first major work, the beautiful but eminently realist short-story collection *Dubliners*, was published in 1914. His *Portrait of the Artist as a Young Man*, with its many stream of consciousness sections, followed in 1916, and *Ulysses*, in which the stream of consciousness quite overwhelms everything else, only in 1922. The very first volume of *Remembrance of Things Past* was published at the end of 1913. Other prominent literary modernists, such as the German-Czech-Jewish author Franz Kafka (1883–1924) or the British author Virginia Woolf (1882–1941), had published little or nothing before 1914; their chief literary works would have to wait for the 1920s.

Among the important European modernist authors, it was only Thomas Mann, who had published a substantial amount and developed a significant literary reputation in the belle époque, and much of Mann's reputation rested on his 1901 novel *Buddenbrooks*, whose story of three generations of a German merchant family was very much in the tradition of nineteenth-century realism. In contrast to the visual arts, and to music, older nineteenth-century realist forms remained quite vigorous in pre-1914 literature. More typical of the high literature of the pre-1914 era were realist authors, such as the Anglo-Irish playwright George Bernard Shaw (1856–1950), whose works appear rather tedious today, or the now largely forgotten French novelist Roger Martin du Gard (1881–1958), whose 1913 novel *Jean Barois* is a neglected masterpiece. Literary modernists were still just formulating their ideas and their literary works.

If literary modernism was largely under the educated public's radar screen before 1914, in the art world modernism was eminently visible. The great 1912 international art exhibition in Cologne, at which expressionist, post-impressionist and cubist artworks from all across Europe were on display, testified to the arrival of artistic modernism. Well beyond the circle of connoisseurs, Parisian cabarets and theatrical farces were featuring cubist artists and showing parodies of their art in the five or so years before 1914. In spite of these jokes, and the frequent complaints about the nonsensical character of modernist art by individuals famous – such as the German emperor Wilhelm II – and obscure, the truth is that critics and the public were surprisingly accepting of early twentieth-century modern art. Certainly compared with the enormous hostility shown previously in the nineteenth century to the realist and impressionist artists, the reception of modernist works was quite favourable. The French art critic Théodore Duret noted, disillusioned in 1912, that he had lost his allies in upholding traditional artistic values: 'Those unhappy "bourgeois" who, in the last century, exposed their dullness before artists and were self-satisfied in their incomprehension, have been definitively shamed . . . They too have aspired to comprehension . . . Now nothing scandalizes them. They are prepared to swoon before any eccentricity.'[22] In music, by contrast, critics and the educated public were well aware of the progress of modernism but had a much less favourable attitude. The premiere of Stravinsky's *Rite of Spring* was marked by the riot of a hostile audience. At the initial public performance of Schoenberg's String Quartet No. 2, his first venture in fully atonal music, a prominent critic was so horrified that he jumped out of his seat after only the fifth measure and screamed at the musicians to stop playing.

These very different receptions of artistic, musical and literary modernism in the quarter-century before 1914 reflect their broader fate over the next hundred years.

BOX 18.2

Modernism and postmodernism

Scholars and critics have argued endlessly about how to define artistic modernism and postmodernism, what (if anything) separates and distinguishes the two, and in what era these two artistic movements flourished. What follows is one idiosyncratic take on this definition.

Artistic modernism, as is suggested in the text, arose from the search for new artistic forms and styles adequate to represent the reality of the modern world. This search led to an often drastic break with long-existing, conventional and familiar forms of artistic representation. Modernist artists also inherited an idea from earlier nineteenth-century artistic innovators, expressed in the famous slogan 'art for art's sake'. Art was not to serve a higher, transcendental purpose, such as religion or the nation, but was its own purpose – and one partaking of the solemn and transcendental character of religion or of nationalism, as it was increasingly understood in the nineteenth century.

For postmodernists, by contrast, art does not represent anything but itself. The question of which artistic forms and styles best represent the modern – or any other world – is irrelevant to them, since they do not see art as representing any kind of reality exterior to it. Postmodernist artists do make use of the stylistic innovations of modern art, but they also use older artistic forms as well, often mixing different forms and styles in arbitrary fashion, a practice known by its French name of *bricolage*. Besides dropping any sense of art as representation, postmodernists have also rejected the idea that art has transcendental significance. Their motto might be, in place of 'art for art's sake', 'art for nothing'.

Although postmodernist elements can be found in even the earlier phases of modern art, it would be fair to say that artistic modernism was the predominant aesthetic movement from around 1890 to 1960, and postmodernism has come increasingly to the fore since then.

Modernism has completely dominated painting and the visual arts, at least until the rise of its successor and competitor postmodernism. Millions of visitors attend special museum exhibitions of modernist art and purchase reproductions of modernist works to hang in their homes; modernist designs appear everywhere on tablecloths, couch fabric and curtains. Modernist, atonal music, by contrast, has never attained even an approximately similar degree of public acceptance. The lucid, crystalline works of modernist composers (at least this is how this author feels about them) have been widely rejected, and the performance of 'classical' music remains stuck in its nineteenth-century repertoire, largely ignoring twentieth-century composition. In literature, the contrast between realism and modernism was less stark than in music or the visual arts; realist and modernist forms and themes have developed together over the course of the twentieth century. In this respect, as in so many others, the years 1890 to 1914 were the seedbed of future artistic, cultural and intellectual developments.

CHAPTER 19

THE POLITICS OF THE PEOPLE

There were three main characteristics of political life in pre-1914 Europe, all multi-faceted and with far-reaching and long-lasting effects. The most important of these characteristics, containing within it all the others, was the emergence of mass politics: large-scale political organization, mobilization and participation, activities reaching hundreds of thousands and even millions of people. The institutions of such politics included the mass-membership political party, the special-interest group and the single-issue group that contemporaries often referred to as a league. This mass politics certainly operated in the familiar venues of parliamentary elections, but it found new forms of expression as well, in mass street demonstrations and political action across the borders of sovereign states. Such a mass politics would naturally have a substantial ideological component, one that could reach a wide audience. While there were many different ideological trends in the period, it would be fair to say that the second characteristic of pre-1914 political life was the primacy of socialism and nationalism as the most important ideologies of mass politics.

The third characteristic of the period was the central and underlying issue of mass politics, the struggle for democracy, both the institution of parliamentary government and universal manhood suffrage in those countries – particularly in central and eastern Europe in the German, Russian and Austro-Hungarian Empires and the smaller kingdoms of Romania, Bulgaria and Serbia – where they did not exist, and the extension and improvement of them where they did. It was typical of this period that, for the first time, the demand for universal suffrage went beyond the male half of the population, with the growth – to a very different extent in different European countries – of movements in favour of women's suffrage.

Demands for votes for women had been voiced on a number of occasions, starting in the 1840s. The same point could be made about all the features of the mass politics of the belle époque, and in this respect political life in the period was like social and economic or cultural and scientific trends, all of which can be seen as the culmination of earlier developments. But, just like these other features of the age, the political trends can also be understood as a break with the past, as basically new, and as setting the stage for the twentieth century. This latter view of pre-1914 politics as primarily a new development seems ultimately more convincing. Previous instances of mass politics, in Great Britain during the 1820s and 1830s, in continental Europe during the revolutions of 1848, in both Britain and the continent during the 1860s and again in the 1880s, if prefiguring later developments, nonetheless had all tended to be ephemeral, giving way to the more limited politics of the notables. By contrast, the mass politics of the 1890–1914 period largely swept away notables' politics and initiated a twentieth century of large-scale political mobilization. Let us keep in mind the fundamentally novel character of these three features of political life as we consider the structures of mass politics, the issues of mass politics and the effects of mass politics on political parties and on forms of political confrontation.

STRUCTURES OF MASS POLITICS

A crucial innovation, coming to fruition in the 1890–1914 period, was the mass political party, one with a large membership, in five, six or even seven figures. This membership was not just impressive in size but also dues-paying, so that even modest dues would generate a substantial income, enabling a mass party to support a permanent paid staff at the national, regional and local levels. Between the permanent staff and the large membership, mass political parties were very active – certainly in carrying out election campaigns, by sponsoring public meetings, handing out leaflets and putting up posters, going door-to-door to canvass votes and, on election day, engaging in get-out-the-vote drives. But the combination of professional politicians and a mass membership meant that these parties could be active, engaging in public campaigns, all the time, and not just in the run-up to elections. Mass membership parties generally had more structured connections to their membership, via close cooperation or outright incorporation of special-interest groups and other kinds of voluntary associations. These connections only augmented the strength and influence of this new kind of political party.

Both the novelty and the strength of the mass political party are most apparent when we compare them with the practices of notables' politics, the previously dominant form of political life. In notables' politics, the informally organized, self-co-opting group of the locally most influential men was the political actor, not a dues-paying mass membership organization. The notables took public political action – and even that generally on a modest scale – only at election time; their party had no standing presence between elections. Notables were the *locally* most influential men; their political action lacked the nation- or state-wide coordination of a party organized on a broader scale with close ties to interest groups and voluntary associations, themselves broadly organized. Just listing the differences between mass politics and notables' politics suffices to show why a direct competition between the two would leave the latter at a distinct disadvantage.

Mass politics first reached belle époque Europe primarily via the parties of the labour movement. Their rapid rise, in most continental countries, from marginal status or downright illegality at the end of the 1880s to the party receiving the most or the second most votes by the eve of the First World War, was a striking indication of what organized mass political parties could achieve. The strength of these parties was not just in their card-carrying and dues-paying membership, but also in the socialist parties' role as the central nexus of a broad variety of affiliated organizations. There were working-class economic interest groups, such as consumers' cooperatives and, especially, the trade unions, whose members outnumbered those enrolled in the party by two to one and three to one, respectively. In Great Britain, where, quite in contrast to continental Europe, trade unionists were still mostly committed to the Liberal Party before 1914, the Labour Party had a hard time making headway, and the Liberals had more of the attributes of a mass membership political party than their European counterparts. Beyond economic interest groups was a galaxy of other affiliated societies: socialist sports clubs (like the German Solidarity Workers' Bicycling Association, with 100,000 members by 1914), youth groups, women's groups, lending libraries. A supporter of the labour movement could drink in a socialist tavern, or, if he preferred, not drink in a socialist abstinence society. Upon decease, the party faithful who were members of socialist cremation societies could receive a suitably non-religious funeral. One could be a socialist from the cradle to the grave. This support for the mass political party in the form of a network of organizations was at its most elaborate in Germany, Belgium and Scandinavia, but it existed to a greater or lesser extent everywhere in Europe, and in fact throughout the world, as the socialist parties were organized into a worldwide federation, the Second International, that tried to coordinate the ideology and actions of these parties across national boundaries. This network of organizations, within and beyond borders, points to a basic strength of the pre-1914 socialist parties: they were not just political parties, not just even mass political parties, but a whole way of life.

And as such, they appeared dangerous and subversive to adherents of other political tendencies, who often responded with calls to prohibit socialist parties or to renew the previously existing prohibitions on them. Gradually, politicians of other parties began to realize that they would need to beat the socialists at their own game. They began to institute dues-paying memberships, hire a permanent paid staff, hold more aggressive election campaigns, and work more closely with single-issue and special-interest groups, accosting the latter, particularly those associated with business and agricultural interests, for additional funds. In 1907, the liberal and conservative parties in Germany coordinated their election campaigns with an anti-socialist single-issue group, the Imperial League against Social Democracy, whose efforts culminated on election day when it offered voters free rides to the polls in motor cars. (The use of motor vehicles in electioneering, common in a number of European countries, was a sign of liberal and conservative commitment to mass politics.) It was the one election setback the socialists suffered in Germany over the almost thirty years from the general elections of 1884 to those of 1912.

A major issue in these 1907 elections was the contention that the German socialists were enemies of nationalism, and another major source of mass politics in pre-1914 Europe was nationalism and nationalist political parties. Particularly in the eastern portions of the continent, in much of the Austro-Hungarian Empire, and in those parts of the Russian Empire inhabited by non-Russian nationalities, nationalist mass political parties, such as the Polish National Democrats, or the Czech National Socials, themselves allied with recreational groups like the Sokol gymnastics societies, pre-dated and often overshadowed socialist ones. Just as socialist parties, via their Second International, crossed national borders, so too nationalist movements in different countries – Polish nationalists in Germany, Austria-Hungary and Russia or Serb nationalists in the Kingdom of Serbia, and the Austrian province of Bosnia-Herzegovina – worked together across the boundaries of sovereign states.

It would not be unfair to say that nationalism was at the heart of the other major formation of mass politics in the pre-1914 era, the leagues. These were the primary agency of right-of-centre mass politics, as the mass-membership political parties were for groups to the left of centre. A good example of such a league was the League of French Action, generally known, even in English, by its French name, Action Française. Emerging from a pre-history dating back to the 1880s, which included groups such as the League of Patriots and the League of Anti-Semites, the Action Française was devoted to promoting nationalist ideals, supporting the armed forces and denouncing groups and individuals it regarded as the enemies of the nation. The group sponsored public demonstrations, distributed its literature and sold its newspaper in the streets, and its supporters – particularly numerous among students at the Sorbonne, in Paris – had the nasty habit of assaulting their political opponents.

The violence of Action Française, an ugly foreshadowing of what fascists would do in Europe after the First World War, was still rather the exception in pre-1914 Europe. Other leagues garnered mass memberships, in the tens and hundreds of thousands, employed a full-time paid staff, which sponsored public campaigns, including mass meetings, the distribution of literature and the holding of multimedia spectaculars, such as 'magic lantern' (an early version of photographic slides) shows. In Germany, where associations in general were very numerous, the leagues, most of which had an aggressively nationalist orientation, included the Navy League, the Army League, the Agrarian League, the Pan-German League (probably the closest to the later Nazis), the Eastern Marches Society (anti-Polish) and the Protestant League (anti-Catholic).

The oldest example of a league was certainly conservative but not so militantly right wing. Founded in 1884 by Tory politicians, the English Primrose League would come to count some 2 million members by 1910, making it by far the largest of the leagues. Rather than assaulting its opponents, it was known for sponsoring teas and flower shows, attracting a substantial female membership. These women members, who did not have the vote, nonetheless showed their political mettle by going door to door to canvass voters and bring them to the polls for the Conservatives. There were plenty of male members of the Primrose League who had their own forms of activities, such as bicycling clubs. Common to the activities of both male and female members was a noisy nationalism, flying the Union Jack, emphasizing loyalty to the queen or king, and stressing the glories of the worldwide British Empire.

Although the leaders of the Primrose League were prominent Tory politicians, the group itself was formally independent from the Conservative Party, and its members had no voice in setting party policy, quite unlike the situation with other mass political parties, where mass membership went along with at least a pretence at members' democratic influence on party policy. This was a very convenient state of affairs, because it enabled the Tories to have all the benefits of a mass political party while preserving the structures of notables' politics. As Lady Salisbury, wife of the wily Conservative prime minister, said about relationship of the mass politics of the Primrose League to a party still dominated by local elites: 'Vulgar? Of course it is vulgar, but that is why we have done so well.'[23] The (Catholic) Centre Party in Germany, with its affiliated People's Association for Catholic Germany, developed a similar, and similarly successful, relationship between a moderately conservative political party, still run along the lines of notables' politics, and a political league with a million-strong mass membership.

These new organizations of mass politics also developed new forms of political activity in the period, two of which deserve special emphasis. One was the street demonstration, the organized, hopefully orderly (although not always so in practice), large-scale, public march of supporters of a cause or issue – a major political form of the twentieth century. While both previous street demonstrations, in the revolutions of 1848, for instance, and subsequent ones, such as those in eastern Europe in 1989 leading to the overthrow of communist rule, had insurrectionary connotations, those of the belle époque were generally designed to press drastic demands within the existing legal and constitutional system.

Here as well, it was the socialists who were the political pioneers of demonstrations, beginning with the annual May Day parades, held on 1 May, or sometimes the following Sunday, every year from 1890 onwards. Socialists used demonstrations at other times and for other issues as well, such as the mass demonstrations held in Austria in 1905 and Prussia in 1909 in favour of the introduction of a democratic franchise. A mass demonstration, with at least 150,000 participants in the Russian capital of St Petersburg, arranged, ironically, by a secretly government-sponsored anti-socialist labour organization, led to the outbreak of the 1905 revolution, when troops fired on the demonstrators.

If in terms of mass political organization the counterpart to socialist parties was the right-wing nationalist leagues, this was less true in regard to street demonstrations. There were nationalist street demonstrations in western Europe, whose participants were known to mix in anti-Semitic slogans, but these were on a noticeably smaller scale than the socialists' efforts and were sometimes hard to distinguish from brawling and riots. Massive right-wing street demonstrations, on a scale comparable to those propounded by the left, would have to wait for the post-1918 era. In the Austro-Hungarian Empire, nationalist demonstrations were larger – 10,000 demonstrators turned out to support Croatian nationalist demands in Zagreb in November 1912 – although such demonstrations often turned into violent clashes between nationalist demonstrators and the police, or between opposing groups of nationalists, Czechs and Germans for instance, or Slovenes and Italians.

For the English-speaking world, probably the best-known sponsors of mass demonstrations in the pre-1914 world were the advocates of women's rights and women's suffrage. The suffragette campaign in Great Britain included mass demonstrations, such as the 30,000 women who marched through London in favour women's suffrage in July 1908; there are said to have been half a million people at the rally concluding their march. This sort of massive women's rights demonstration, by contrast, was quite unknown in continental Europe, where socialists and nationalists made the running in street politics.

ISSUES OF MASS POLITICS

What was true of arenas of politics in the years 1890 to 1914 was true of political issues as well. None of the issues that came to the fore in this period were entirely new, and some, such as confrontations over religion, were distinctly old. Nonetheless, their discussion in front of an ever greater audience, an audience that was receiving the message about these issues in ever more penetrating ways, gave them a new salience that they had not enjoyed in the age of notables' politics. If we categorize the major political issues of the period that were prevalent throughout Europe, understanding that individual countries had their own particular issues or combinations of them, we can list no less than six different areas of politics: (1) budget and taxation; (2) economic and social questions, especially free trade versus protectionism, and social welfare and labour protection legislation; (3) the armed forces and the threat of war; (4) the nation and nationalism; (5) religious controversies; (6) the demand for democracy. Looking at the long run, we might say that while the years 1850 to 1875 were a period of liberal domination and liberal reforms, and the subsequent two decades one of conservative resurgence, the 20–25 years before the First World War saw a renewed surge of proposals for reform and political change, although often along quite different lines from the previous liberal reform period.

Especially among the Great Powers, and particularly in the decade before 1914, government budgets came under a lot of strain, primarily the result of steadily increasing military expenditures, but also, to a lesser extent, due to the growth of social welfare spending. The idea, so prevalent later in the century and today, that chronic government budget deficits are acceptable, and may even be desirable, was unthinkable in the belle époque. Deficits were shameful; temporary shortfalls could be met by borrowing, but longer-term borrowing was unacceptable, and printing more money to meet the government's needs was impossible under the international currency regime of the gold standard.

There was no way around it: with budget cuts politically impossible and chronic deficits conceptually unimaginable, taxes had to be raised, and the period saw battles between the left and the right over whether to raise direct taxes, as the former preferred, or indirect ones as the latter wanted. What created the passion in the situation was not support of one kind of taxation, but the rejection of the other. The famous 'People's Budget' of 1909, by which the radical chancellor of the exchequer, Lloyd George, in the Liberal government of British prime minister Asquith, sought – quite successfully as it turned out – to provoke the opposition Conservatives, relied, for doing so, on increases in direct taxes, particularly those on land. The Social Democrats and the liberals in Germany proposed to finance the government's massive naval and land arms build-up by land, inheritance and wealth taxes; the conservatives and the Catholic Centre strongly preferred indirect taxes on consumer goods, such as matches or beer, and a tax on stock transfers. In a debate on the introduction of an income tax in Italy, one parliamentary deputy, a duke, became so outraged at the prospect, that he threw his chair at the parliament speaker. The proposal of the French government to institute an income tax in 1914 was greeted by conservatives as the end of western civilization.

Another issue generating a fair amount of venom was the contrast between protectionists and free traders. This was sometimes a right versus left clash, with the former protectionist and the latter against tariffs, although there were a number of exceptions, in the form of left-of-centre parties in Scandinavia, France and Germany, for instance, whose supporters were hard-pressed small farmers fearful of foreign competition. The protectionists, who had the most effective special-interest groups behind them, generally had the most success in policy terms, as tariffs kept getting steadily higher throughout the pre-1914 period. The one major exception to this record was in Great Britain, where free trade remained popular, the Liberal Party aggressively campaigned for its preservation, vigorously raising the spectre of expensive food as a result of agricultural protective tariffs (aggressive support of free trade as a popular measure was one way that the Liberals in the UK maintained themselves as a popular party in the age of mass politics) and even the Conservatives, quite unlike most continental countries, were divided about advocating protectionism. The chief proponent of protectionism, the one-time radical turned Tory politician, Joseph Chamberlain (1836–1914), had to disguise his position by calling for 'tariff reform' and 'imperial preference', that is, tariffs on imports from outside the British Empire, and free trade for imports from the colonies. He was never able to obtain any policy successes or even a party endorsement for his demands.

In contrast to the sharp controversies over taxes and tariffs, questions of social welfare or labour protection legislation proved easier to resolve. Health and safety regulations, factory inspection, and even legislation limiting work on Sundays proved relatively uncontroversial, perhaps because big businesses, with the resources to deal with such laws, had more influential special-interest groups at their disposal, while small businesses, which were more affected, lacked political clout. Unions and strike activity were generally legal; even in the authoritarian phase of the Russian Empire before the 1905 revolution, the secret police had decided that unions were useful and had started to found its own. Italy's calculating liberal prime minister Giovanni Giolitti caused quite a stir at the beginning of the twentieth century when he ordered the police not to intervene in strikes in favour of employers, but his actions reflected the generally more secure place of unions in the law. Social insurance programmes, including health insurance, unemployment insurance and old-age insurance, with their substantial expenditures, have been a major source of political strife in the twentieth century and continue to be so, but were not in the pre-1914 period, largely because there were few such programmes existing – in Germany and Austria, primarily – and new ones were only occasionally proposed.

In the pre-1914 period, military expenditure, the shape and structure of the armed forces, and the threat of war became an item of hot public debate in which the government and all the political parties joined in. Positions taken in these debates generally broke down along left–right lines. Politicians and governments on the political right glorified the armed forces, demanded their expansion and the larger military budgets needed to do so, and were not shy about supporting, endorsing and even advocating their use in warfare. Beyond policy questions, lionizing the armed forces and condemning any criticism of them as virtually treasonous was a central element of right-wing politics. Conservative election victories often turned on military questions, the 'Khaki Elections' of 1900 in Great Britain for instance, where the ruling Tories made support for the British troops fighting the Boer War into their main platform, denouncing the Liberal opposition as anti-war, and even 'pro-Boer', sympathetic to the enemy. Later in the decade, themselves in opposition, the Tories would taunt the Liberal government as weak on national defence, demanding a vigorous expansion of the Royal Navy's battleship force, using the slogan 'We want eight [battleships] and we won't wait.' The 'Hottentot Elections' of 1907 in Germany involved a similar kind of right-wing victory on supporting the troops, and one of the major right-wing single-issue groups, the Navy League, had been involved in a permanent campaign for more battleships ever since its founding. In French politics, the Dreyfus Affair became increasingly a clash between conservative political forces, who glorified the army, and left-wing ones, who attacked it. Right-wing forces hoped to recover from their ultimate political defeat in the Dreyfus Affair in the post-1910 'national reawakening', one of whose major points was the expansion of the French army by increasing conscripts' term of service from two years to three. It would be possible to go on in this vein at some length, pointing to examples of pro-military positions among the political right in Italy, Austria-Hungary, Russia, Spain (where it helped fuel a disastrous war with the United States in 1898) and a number of the smaller European powers, but the basic point of the close affinity of conservatives and the armed forces, the promotion of 'militarism', as contemporaries said, is clear.

Militarism was a major strength of the right, a central political resource, particularly in the post-1900 period, when the forces of the left seemed to be on the offensive. Left-of-centre parties found this use of militarism difficult to counter. They could continue to use older strategies to deal with the issue, emphasizing the considerable expense of the armed forces and the higher taxes they would require, call for free trade and international agreements as a means of preserving the peace, and advocate the introduction of a militia system based on the Swiss model – all adult men receiving six months of military training and then a long-term commitment to serving in a military reserve – as the best form of the armed forces. In an age of protectionism, arms races, and the increasing technological complexity of weapons systems, most of these proposals seemed old-fashioned and out of date. Calls for cutting military expenditure and lowering taxes were the most effective of the left's older attitudes towards the armed forces, but the whole approach lacked the emotional appeal of supporting the troops and defending the nation against foreign dangers, which conservatives could use.

Particularly among the socialists, a new attitude towards questions of war and peace began to emerge in this period, namely an aggressive rejection of the armed forces and the values they stood for, and a denunciation of the use of military force as a tool of ruling elites, linking capitalism, nationalism and warfare, and opposing them with a vision of peaceful international cooperation of the working class. Socialists exposed instances of abuse of conscripts by their officers and NCOs; some, on the extreme left of the socialist labour movement and among the anarchists, advocated draft resistance and desertion. Even when not taking such extreme steps, socialists campaigned, ever more stridently, against the danger of a great European war. The 1912 congress of the Socialist International in Basel was one enormous anti-war demonstration. Some leftists proposed a drastic response to such a war: a general strike across Europe through which working-class action would bring military mobilization to a halt. This proposal was rejected by the Socialist International and never endorsed by any member parties. In retrospect, we can understand its futility, especially as, in August 1914, all the socialist parties endorsed their respective countries' positions and went to war with each other. Still, no one could know that in advance, and all the major European countries had drawn up plans to arrest socialist and trade union leaders at the outbreak of a war, showing that government authorities took leftists' anti-militarism very seriously.

In a number of ways, the political implications of attitudes towards nationalism in pre-1914 Europe were similar to those regarding the armed forces. By this period, the long slide of nationalism in the political spectrum from left to right, begun in the 1850s, had largely reached its conclusion. Political conservatives proclaimed themselves the guardians and supporters of the nation and put its glorification and promotion centre stage. The leagues, in particular, articulated an aggressive nationalism, but right-wing political parties were generally close behind, with the occasional exception of some of the more moderate conservative groupings associated with the Catholic Church. Liberals were placed somewhat more awkwardly, as they had been on military questions, with most liberals endorsing a nationalist stance, and just a minority – politically more to the left, but also more old-fashioned in their orientation – showing somewhat more distance. By contrast, radical support for nationalism, still fully on display at the time of the Paris Commune in 1871, had dissipated. One-time radicals who endorsed nationalism had moved over to the political right and were often involved with the leagues, while those continuing to stay on the left, particularly in the labour movement, heralded an internationalism that challenged all the tenets of nationalist politics. A simple and eminently audible measure of this change was the replacement of the *Marseillaise* as the anthem of extreme left-wing politics with the *Internationale*, a song whose very name makes the point.

All of this suggests a radical reversal of political fronts by 1910 when compared with 1850, with nationalism going from being a radical, subversive notion, deeply upsetting to the status quo, to a powerful force in defending the existing state of affairs. In a good deal of Europe, particularly in the west and centre of the continent, this would have been the case. In the multinational empires to the east and the south – the Austro-Hungarian Empire, the Ottoman Empire, primarily, but also those portions of the German and Russian Empires not inhabited by the dominant nationality – there was a quite different story. In those regions, nationalism was a powerfully disruptive force, demanding the break-up of multinational regimes into individual nation-states, and the secession of national minorities from existing realms to found their own government. This had been the case for most of the nineteenth century, but the subversive force of nationalism was magnified in an era of mass politics.

By the beginning of the twentieth century, nationalism was everywhere: reaching peasants and workers as well as the educated middle class, and expanding to include any and all imaginable nationalities, as Ukrainians, Lithuanians, Latvians, Estonians, Slovaks, Macedonians and even Jews joined a movement once limited in central and eastern Europe to Poles or Germans. If we add to this mixture the increasingly intransigent and racist nature of nationalist thinking, as it had been developing since the 1870s and 1880s, we have a highly explosive cocktail, the very opposite of the preservation of the status quo.

The ways in which extreme nationalism disrupted the political life of the Austro-Hungarian Empire in the years after 1900 have become legendary. Czech-nationalist and German-nationalist deputies marched out of the Bohemian provincial parliament, each singing their respective national anthems. Clashes between German and Italian nationalist students at the University of Innsbruck in 1904 resulted in the death of one student and the need for troops to restore order. Ukrainian representatives in the Reichsrat, the parliament of the Austrian half of the Dual Monarchy, spoke in Russian, intimating they wanted to see their home province of Galicia annexed by the Tsar; one threw a desk at the parliament's presiding officer. A Ukrainian nationalist assassinated the Polish-nationalist provincial governor of the province of Galicia and escaped to the United States, where he was hailed as national hero by Ukrainian immigrants. The list of such national clashes could be extended at considerable length.

In the Hungarian half of the Dual Monarchy, the Magyars or Hungarian-speakers made up a bit less than half the population, but that did not stop the Hungarian nationalist politicians who ran the Hungarian government from attempting to impose the Magyar language on members of other nationalities, arresting and charging with treason Croatian and Serb nationalist politicians, or even kidnapping Slovak babies to bring them up as Hungarians. Not content with defining the Hungarian half of the Dual Monarchy as a Magyar nation-state, these same politicians pushed for dissolving the last links connecting the two halves of the monarchy. In 1906, the imperial authorities, frustrated beyond all measure by such policies, sent in the army to dissolve the Hungarian parliament.

Recently, historians have argued that these examples give a false impression of the state of the Habsburg realm, that such noisy nationalist demonstrations were not typical, or at least did not herald the imminent demise of the multinational empire and its dissolution into smaller nation-states. They mention the political successes of anti-nationalist socialist and Catholic political parties, and point to the many instances of bilingualism, of people in, for instance, Bohemia, speaking both Czech and German, and not necessarily identifying themselves as belonging to either nationality. Yet, in the end, these objections are not entirely convincing. Nationalism was popular and deeply rooted; it was by no means limited to the educated middle class. Extreme nationalists did well in elections, under both a property franchise and universal manhood suffrage. The empire's leaders themselves were painfully conscious of the existential threat that nationalism posed to the monarchy. Furthermore, this extreme nationalism was very much on display in other parts of central and eastern Europe, among the Polish and the Lithuanian populations of the German and Russian Empires, for instance, or the Slavic subjects of the Ottoman Empire in south-eastern Europe.

Some of the nationalists in multinational empires, such as the Polish National Democrats and their contentious leader Roman Dmowski (1864–1939), stood, in other respects, politically more on the right wing. Other nationalists in these circumstances, such as Dmowski's main opponent, Józef Pilsudski (1867–1935) were more on the left, Pilsudksi even describing himself as a socialist. In general, nationalists in the multinational empires in the east and south-east of Europe represented a broader spectrum of political opinions than their counterparts in the nation-states of the centre and west of the continent. Yet there can be no doubt that there was an increasingly intolerant edge to the nationalist movements of the multinational empire, whose proponents had, among other things, a strong tendency to be vehement anti-Semites. When two nationalist groups clashed over the same territory, such as Germans and Czechs in Bohemia, or Poles and Ukrainians in Galicia, both tended to attack the Jews and each asserted that the Jews supported the other side. This atmosphere of increasingly intolerant, racist and anti-Semitic nationalism in eastern Europe is part of the background for the growth of Jewish nationalism in this period. The best-known Jewish nationalists were the Zionists, who responded to the racist and anti-Semitic nationalism prevalent in early twentieth-century Europe by aspiring to found a Jewish nation-state in Palestine among their fellow Semites, the Arabs, with whom they expected to get along better than with the racially 'alien' Slavs or Aryans – rather a miscalculation, one would have to say. There were also Jewish nationalists who wanted an autonomous political unit for Jews in the territory of the Russian Empire.

Although we do not think of the British Isles as composing a multinational empire, Irish nationalists of the period certainly did. Their nationalism, which in the course of the twentieth century would acquire a reputation for extremism, was, before 1914, rather different from that of their east European counterparts. Irish nationalists were closely allied to the Liberal Party in British politics; the main nationalist demand was not for an independent Irish nation-state, but for autonomy within the British Empire, or 'home rule' as the nationalists said. If there were nationalist extremists, it was mostly the British Conservatives and their allies among the Protestants of Northern Ireland, who reacted with vehemence and hostility to the possibility of home rule, opposing it by all legal means and toying with violent and illegal ones.

This mention of the political situation in Ireland brings up one other important political issue of the period: controversies over religion. Past patterns of religious confrontations continued into the age of mass politics – and were probably amplified by them. In the religiously mixed zones of central Europe, Catholics and Protestants continued to eye each other with suspicion. The Protestant League had the largest membership of all of Germany's leagues, and devoted most of its resources to the odd task of trying to convert the German-speaking Catholics of the Austro-Hungarian Empire to Protestantism. In the Mediterranean countries, left-wing politics was still characterized by an intransigent anti-clericalism, while conservatives continued to promulgate an equally intransigent Catholicism. Certainly typical of these circumstances was that the ultimate political upshot of the Dreyfus Affair was the coming to power of a centre-left French government that proceeded in 1905–06 to separate church and state, over the vehement and frequently riotous objections of devout Catholics and political conservatives. In multinational eastern Europe, nationalism and religious loyalties continued to be mixed, as was the case in the Austrian province of Slovenia, where the Catholic clergy was so sympathetic to the Slovene nationalist cause that Germans in the province refused to be married by them, leading to colossal illegitimacy rates of 80 per cent and more in some German-speaking villages.

In a sense presupposing all these other issues was the struggle for democracy. One phase of it was the effort to rein in the powers of the emperors and monarchs of eastern Europe. The most dramatic instance of this struggle was the Russian Revolution of 1905 that brought Europe's last autocracy to an end, although the parliament emerging from the revolution, the Duma, was still distinctly inferior to the Tsar in its powers. On a smaller scale, but no less dramatic were the turbulent street demonstrations in Belgrade in 1901, brutally suppressed by the police, and a military coup, two years later, complete with a massacre of members of the royal family, leading to the creation of a constitutional and parliamentary government in Serbia. In both the Austrian half of the Austro-Hungarian Empire, and in the German Empire, the emperor retained the right to name the government ministers, so that a parliamentary government, as understood in western Europe, where the prime minister and other government ministers were elected by the parliamentary majority, did not exist. Post-1900 Austrian and German governments, if not dependent on parliament for their constitution, found that they could no longer dominate the parliamentarians as effortlessly as Bismarck or the Austrian 'Iron Ring' ministers had done in the 1880s, but had to find ways to cooperate with parliamentary majorities.

Parallel to but different from the demand for parliamentary government was the call for a democratic franchise. Universal manhood suffrage was introduced in Belgium in 1894, following a socialist-led general strike, although the addition of an extra vote for older and more affluent men made this franchise less than completely democratic. All adult men were given the vote in Norway in 1898, in Austria in 1907 and in Italy in 1912. There were still plenty of countries holding out against universal and equal manhood suffrage, including Russia, Hungary, Prussia (votes in elections to the parliament of the most powerful federal state in the German Empire were weighted by the taxes that voters paid, as opposed to the democratic franchise for the imperial parliament), the Netherlands, Sweden and Great Britain, where only about 60 per cent of adult men had the vote following the Third Reform Act of 1884.

For the first time, this democratic tide came to include women as well, who received the vote in Finland (then a semi-autonomous dependency of the Russian Empire) in 1906 and in Norway in 1913. Movements for women's suffrage existed in most European countries, by far strongest in Great Britain, where the 'suffragettes' made a major impact on public life. Generally, though, feminist activists were foiled in their attempts: liberal and radical parties, who favoured women's suffrage in theory, were reluctant to implement it in practice, suspecting that women, more likely to be churchgoers than men, would, if given the vote, choose church-related, right wing political parties. Giovanni Giolitti, Italy's leading liberal politician, once came out and said what most liberals only thought in private, condemning a radical politician for proposing women's suffrage, saying, 'The only [party] that will be grateful to him and ought to erect a monument to him will be the clerical party.'[24] Conservative parties, by contrast, tended to disapprove of women's suffrage on principle.

In the end, it would take the sweeping and revolutionary changes occurring in the aftermath of the two world wars for women in most European countries to be given the vote. Yet even given the pre-1914 frustrations of the adherents of women's

BOX 19.1

Suffragettes

Calls for women's suffrage had been heard in Great Britain as early as the 1830s. From the time of the Second Reform Bill in 1867, there was an organizational continuity of existing women's suffrage groups, most of which merged into the National Union of Women's Suffrage Societies (NUWSS) in 1897. Although leaders of the NUWSS came from different political parties, the local activists and most of the women's suffrage movement were close to the Liberal Party, especially to its radical wing, with its support for temperance and close ties to Non-Conformist Protestantism (i.e., independent of the Anglican state church). The coming to power of a Liberal government in 1906 thus raised considerable hopes in the NUWSS, which quickly gave way to disappointment, because the Liberal prime ministers and key party leaders refused to introduce a bill for women's suffrage. Sexist attitudes aside, Liberal politicians feared that granting women the vote on the same property and taxpaying basis as men, would have enfranchised predominantly pro-Tory well-to-do women, while moving to a democratic franchise, giving all adult men and women the vote, was too drastic a step for them to take.

The failure of the NUWSS strategy encouraged the growth of an alternative women's rights group, first created in 1902, the Women's Social and Political Union (WSPU). Its founders, especially the veteran feminist Emmeline Pankhurst (1858–1928) and her daughter Christabel (1880–1958), originally had close ties to the English labour movement, especially its radical wing, and opposed an alliance with the Liberals. In their women's rights activities, they sharpened this radical stance by rejecting ties between women's groups and male political parties, publicly opposing the Liberals, their Labour ally and even the more left-wing, pro-socialist labour groups. If anything, they tacitly supported the Conservatives, as punishment of the more left-wing groups for opposing women's suffrage or not supporting it more vigorously.

Reflecting its radical strategy was the WSPU's ideological stance, its denunciation of male domination and call for women's suffrage to overturn the existing gender order – a demand summarized in Christabel Pankhurst's pithy phrase, 'votes for women and chastity for men'. The WSPU's tactics were equally radical; they included public demonstrations, attempts to disrupt parliamentary proceedings, bomb and arson attacks, hunger strikes by imprisoned members, and even committing suicide, as one activist, Emily Davison, did when she ran on to the course during the 1913 Derby, England's premier horse race, and died after being hit by the king's horse. WSPU activists and their sympathizers proudly adopted the hostile designation they had received from the conservative press, and called themselves 'suffragettes'.

Neither the drastic tactics and strategies of the WSPU nor the more restrained efforts of the NUWSS, whose leaders began to pin their hopes on the Labour allies of the Liberals, rather than on the Liberals themselves, brought women's suffrage to Great Britain before 1914. It would only reach the UK, as was the case in much of Europe, as a result of the upheavals of the First World War. But the campaigns of the women's suffrage activists are remarkable evidence of the growing demands for democracy, the widening of the political universe, and the development of new and more vigorous forms of political life in the belle époque, and make it clear that the pre-1914 era, in spite of the nostalgic view of it as peaceful and conflict-free, was a period of considerable political strife.

suffrage, and the lack of a fully democratic franchise for men in a number of major European countries, contemporaries had no doubt that the tide of democracy was surging. Adherents of all political positions and supporters of all parties looked – with feelings of both pleasure and apprehension – towards a steadily more democratic future, expecting that sooner or later legal and constitutional forms would have to catch up with the realities of mass politics.

REALIGNMENTS AND CONFRONTATIONS OF MASS POLITICS

The impact of mass politics led all the major political groupings to develop new programmatic initiatives, often the result of contentious programme debates. Versions of these initiatives and debates existed among the liberals, conservatives and socialists in most of Europe. The resulting political realignments were not the only consequence of the rise of mass politics. Another, equally consequential one was the growth of large-scale political confrontations, sometimes still within the boundaries of the legal and constitutional order, but sometimes well beyond them. Both realignments and confrontations pointed towards a turbulent political future, although the full implications of these new developments would become apparent only after the giant upheaval of the First World War.

Leading the way in political realignment were the liberal parties. In the decade of the 1890s, these parties had taken a pounding. Following a four-decades-long run as the dominant political party in Great Britain, the Liberals had been repeatedly and disastrously defeated by the Tories in general elections, a result helped along by the secession of the 'Liberal Unionist' (i.e., anti-home rule for Ireland) wing of the party. German liberals also suffered political splits and their proportion of the vote declined by about 20 per cent in that same decade, losing voters to socialists on their left, conservatives and anti-Semites on their right, and to abstention, as some of their core supporters gave up on politics. Liberals in Austria faced similar débâcles to those faced by their German counterparts, and for similar reasons, although the rise of competing radical nationalisms in the Habsburg Monarchy only made the situation worse. In the Mediterranean countries, France, Italy (less so in Spain), liberals, if also losing votes to competitors on both the left and the right, did somewhat better in the 1890s, generally holding on to political power, although their governments were buffeted by scandals, such as the 'Panama affair', in France, and by foreign policy catastrophes, such as the defeat of the Italians in Ethiopia in 1896.

Responding to these defeats was a programmatic renewal dubbed, in Great Britain, the 'new liberalism', a handy phrase that can be applied more generally, admittedly with many different national variants. It involved keeping some of the previous features of liberalism, such as support for legal equality and constitutional government, for education and anti-clericalism, but dropping the previous insistence on government non-intervention in the economy and endorsing social welfare programmes and labour protection legislation. As J. A. Hobson, whom we have met previously as a critic of imperialism, noted in 1896, the British Liberals would have to move in that direction if they were to 'avoid the shipwreck which Continental Liberalism had suffered when it was driven onto the submerged reef of the economic problem'.[25] Continental liberals were busily trying to get off that reef themselves, although, in contrast to their English counterparts, they were generally willing to endorse additional and more aggressive government actions, in the form of protective tariffs and also of an imperialist foreign policy – the former anathema to Liberals in the UK, and the latter strongly debatable among them.

All things considered, the political reorientation of the new liberalism was a success – albeit to a different extent in different countries. It certainly helped return the Liberals to power in Great Britain in 1906 and keep them there through to the outbreak of the First World War. Historians have been debating for some time whether the Liberals were successful in keeping the working-class vote before 1914, or whether they were gradually losing ground to Labour. There are good arguments on both sides, but what is certainly true is that, compared with their continental European counterparts, the pre-1914 British Liberals were extraordinarily successful among the working class – at least among those workers who had the vote.

The picture in continental Europe was more mixed. The agile Giovanni Giolitti (1842–1928), the dominant political figure in Italy, prime minister four times between 1901 and 1914, was a very successful continental new liberal, tolerating, almost encouraging, trade unions, passing workplace health and safety legislation, offering subsidies to cooperatives, nationalizing the Italian railways and the telegraph system, balancing the budget by refinancing the state debt at lower interest rates. He systematically expanded the franchise, reaching universal manhood suffrage by 1912, but kept liberals in a dominant position by the policies of *trasformismo*, that is, making deals simultaneously with the clerical and conservative right, and with the radical and republican left – although he never could quite bring himself to cooperate with the socialists. Giolitti also followed an aggressive, imperialist foreign policy, culminating in a war against the Ottoman Empire in 1911, resulting in the seizure of Libya and its conversion into an Italian colony.

Giolitti's policies and their relative success were matched on a smaller scale by the Spanish liberal prime minister José Canalejas (1854–1912), who was in office from 1910 until his assassination by an anarchist in 1912. Liberal reorientation was less successful elsewhere in continental Europe. In Austria, liberals had steadily less influence, and while nationalist liberals ruled the Hungarian half of the Habsburgs' dual monarchy, their policies remained the older ones of a property franchise, hostility to the labour movement and vehement nationalism. In France, the major liberal party, the Radicals, achieved a good deal of success and excellent vote totals on older issues, particularly the defence of the republican form of government and anti-clericalism. Attempts to move in a new liberal direction by proposing social and economic reforms weakened the party rather than strengthened it, leading to splits and growing vote totals for the socialists to its left and the conservative nationalists to its right. There was a very vigorous liberal rethinking in Germany, among its protagonists the sociologist Max Weber, but above all a Protestant pastor and social reformer turned politician named Friedrich Naumann (1860–1919). The upshot was that Germany's liberals supported social reform more vigorously, diluted their already weak ties to free market policies, toyed with the idea of allying with the very strong labour movement and its social democratic party, but also endorsed imperialism, rearmament and an aggressive and risky foreign policy. After 1900, liberals did recover some of their electoral losses of the 1890s, but their hopes for domestic reform were generally frustrated, while their endorsement of foreign policy measures leading to the brink of war succeeded only too well.

Yet this was a relatively favourable record compared with what liberals could accomplish in Russia. There, political parties became legal only after the revolution of 1905, so that the main liberal party, the Constitutional Democrats, or Kadets, began its life as a new liberal grouping. But between the conservative defenders of tsarist autocracy and the increasingly active and aggressive revolutionary socialist parties, the Kadets had trouble establishing themselves.

Conservative political parties, who had generally carried out their own reorientation at an earlier point, during the era of liberal dominance in the 1870s, with a fair amount of success, had less need to engage in a major post-1900 realignment. Rather, what we can see in this period is the gradual bifurcation of right-wing political parties into two distinct groups, sometimes different tendencies within the same party, sometimes represented in different parties. One of these tendencies was in the direction of radical right-wing thought, including racist and anti-Semitic ideas, support for an aggressive and warlike foreign policy, rigid opposition to the labour movement, a hostility to liberal, democratic and parliamentary institutions, in place of which such conservatives did not aspire to restore older forms of authoritarian rule but looked forward to new kinds of charismatic leadership. These sorts of viewpoints were particularly at home among members of the leagues and were perhaps not yet entirely part of the mainstream of conservative political parties. Yet we can see them in party politics, in those German Conservatives who began, after 1910, to call themselves a 'national opposition' because they found the conservative government not conservative enough, in the Austrian followers of the militant German nationalist Georg Ritter von Schönerer, in the Italian Nationalists, in the Polish National Democrats, among the parliamentary representatives of the Union of the Russian People and the followers of the Spanish politician Antonio Maura, perhaps even among some of the Ulster Protestants and their Tory allies, who were willing to take very extreme measures to keep Ireland in the United Kingdom.

All these groups might seem to have a distinctly fascistic tinge to them, and post-1918 fascists would look back on some of them as their predecessors. Adolf Hitler, for instance, had admiring words for Schönerer. At most, though, we could call these politicians of the belle époque pre-fascists. It would take the experiences of the First

World War – the deeply traumatizing ones of total war, at the front and at home, as well as the exhilarating ones of combat – to create both the jackbooted, uniformed fascists of the inter-war era, and popular support for their parties.

The other, rather more benign, tendency in pre-1914 conservatism was in the direction of what would later come to be known as Christian Democracy – church-related political parties, sceptical of democracy but willing to accept its inevitability, with often retrograde opinions about cultural, religious and educational issues but open to social reform and also restrained on militarism, bellicose foreign policy and flag-waving nationalism. The classic example of this sort of party was the (Catholic) Centre Party in Germany, whose political stance was not so much, as its name suggests, in the centre of the political spectrum, but on both the left and right ends simultaneously. The Centre was to the right in opposing democratic and parliamentary government, in supporting indirect taxes and protectionist tariffs, and calling for limitations on freedom of expression in cultural and artistic matters, when it infringed on the church's moral teachings. But it also supported labour protection legislation and expanding Germany's social insurance system, favoured trade unions – as long as they were led by devout Christians rather than atheist socialists – was doubtful about the German government's exploding military budget and its aggressive foreign and colonial policy, and spoke up in favour of the rights of Germany's Polish and French (both predominantly Catholic) national minorities. There were similar parties in other central European countries, including Switzerland, Belgium and the Netherlands, and gestures in the direction of creating such parties in both France and Italy, neither of which quite reached fruition, because of papal scepticism about devout Catholics participating in two political systems dominated by anti-clerical elements. Catholic political parties also appeared in the Austro-Hungarian Empire, albeit separate ones for different nationalities, including the Italians, Slovenes, Croats and Slovaks, with larger ones among the Czechs, Germans and Hungarians. Although with a number of similarities to other central European Christian Democrats, these parties were also known for their vehement anti-Semitism (Catholic politicians in France and Italy engaged in anti-Semitism as well), and they were not immune to the extremes of nationalism affecting every other aspect of political life in the empire. In the predominantly Protestant countries of Europe, in Great Britain and Scandinavia, conservative political parties, although certainly affiliated to the established churches, and mostly relatively moderate in their general political stance, lacked the specifically Christian attributes of the Catholic parties.

Turning to the left of the political spectrum, the rapidly growing socialist and labour parties had the most intense policy debate, emerging from the very success these parties enjoyed over the quarter-century before the First World War. Starting the period as relatively small groups of activists, engaged in illegal or only semi-legal activities, who were hostile to the existing social, economic and political order and strongly committed to revolutionary ideas – often, although not always, expressed through the theories of Karl Marx – they increasingly found themselves professional politicians leading mass political parties, major trade union federations and flourishing consumers' cooperatives, with an increasing stake in the status quo. Just what kind of revolutionary could you be if you were a city mayor, as were a number of French socialists?

The result was a growing tendency in the labour movement to reject an intransigent revolutionary stance, to advocate gradual reforms, constitutional and parliamentary politics, and cooperation with other left-of-centre political parties. This was not an attitude most socialists were willing to admit openly. When the German socialist Eduard Bernstein (1850–1932), a man with impeccable Marxist credentials, in his 1899 book *Evolutionary Socialism* made the celebrated statement that 'the [labour] movement is everything, the goal [i.e., the revolution bringing in a socialist state and society] is nothing', he touched off a firestorm of criticism. Karl Kautsky (1854–1938), the leading socialist theorist in Germany and Europe, known as the 'Pope of Socialism', wrote lengthy works refuting Bernstein, who was widely denounced as a 'revisionist', someone wanting to revise the sacred texts of Marx and Engels. Bernstein's ideas were officially condemned by both the German Social Democratic Party and the Socialist International.

Yet if we ask what socialists were doing in pre-1914 Europe, whether they were meeting in secret conspiratorial cells, gathering weapons and preparing an insurrection while calling on the workers to take to the streets and build barricades, or whether they were campaigning for parliamentary offices, organizing trade unions and consumers' cooperatives, holding positions on city councils, social insurance administration boards and industrial conciliation courts, and publicly demanding such non-revolutionary goals as an eight-hour day, universal suffrage for men and women, lower tariffs on imported foodstuffs and direct taxation, then the answer is largely the latter. The great socialist leaders of the pre-1914 era, such as Jean Jaurès (1859–1914) in France, or August Bebel (1840–1913) in Germany, were celebrated orators and parliamentarians, not underground conspirators or streetfighters. While condemning revisionist ideas, most socialists were actually practising them.

Yet in the authoritarian empires and kingdoms of central and eastern Europe, lacking any form of parliamentary government, and with ruling elites vehemently hostile to even mild calls for political, social and economic reforms, socialist advocacy of violent revolution seemed rather more plausible. In retrospect, the chief proponent of such policies was the socialist leader Vladimir Ilyich Ulyanov (1870–1924), better known by his pen-name, Lenin, future leader of communist revolution in the Russian Empire, whose Bolshevik faction of the Russian Social Democratic Party was meeting in conspiratorial cells, calling on workers to rise up, gathering weapons, and robbing banks to pay for this activity. To the mainstream of the European labour movement, though, Lenin was a distant, obscure figure, and the differences between his Bolshevik faction and its Menshevik opponents were incomprehensible quarrels. Before the First World War, the best-known representative of revolutionary intransigence in eastern and central Europe was Rosa Luxemburg (1870–1919), pre-1914 Europe's most influential female politician, who was active on the left wing of the Russian, Polish and German socialist parties simultaneously, and who proposed the propagation of mass strikes as a revolutionary tactic, replacing earlier forms of revolutionary struggle such as barricade fighting.

There were certainly sympathizers with these sorts of revolutionary tactics and aspirations among the socialists of western Europe and even in the eminently law-abiding United Kingdom. In the western parts of the continent, especially its south-ern, Mediterranean areas, the main proponent of revolutionary radicalism were the anarchists, who shared the socialists' radical economic and social goals but also wanted to abolish all forms of government. Some anarchists were terrorists, who advocated the assassination of leading figures as the path to revolution. Such terrorists were generally lone assassins; organized anarchists found some support among landless labourers in rural areas of southern Spain and in trade union movements of France, Italy and Spain, where they mounted a challenge to socialist leadership. Anarchist trade unionism, generally known under the name of syndicalism, propagated a hostility to elections and parliamentary politics, a suspicion of intellectuals in lead-ership positions and a willingness to use direct action, in the form of large-scale strikes, including general strikes of all employed workers, or even industrial sabotage, to gain the workers' ends.

Both intransigent Marxist revolutionaries and anarchists were a distinct minor-ity in the pre-1914 labour movement, and, seen from the beginning of the twenty-first century, their advocacy of revolutionary insurgency and syndicalist direct action seems to have been going against a trend towards greater prosperity and more democratic forms of peaceful and constitutional political participation. Yet such a retrospective judgement is possible only if one neglects an important feature of polit-ical life in the belle époque: the growth of dramatic confrontations, within and beyond the borders of legality and constitutionality. The big one was, of course, the Russian Revolution of 1905, the first revolution in a major European country since 1871, and the first to shake the entire, enormous Euro-Asiatic realm of the tsars, from Russian Poland to the Crimea to Siberia. There were also major outbreaks of polit-icized violence involving the rural population: the riots and land occupations of the *Fasci* (no relation to Mussolini's later Fascists) in Sicily at the beginning of the 1890s; strikes and demonstrations of landless labourers in Hungary at the same time; many rural actions during the Russian Revolution of 1905; the mass demonstrations and riots of French winegrowers in 1907, the peasant uprising in Romania that same year. All of these required military action to suppress: 120,000 troops were in action against the Romanian peasants, killing perhaps 10,000 of them.

Better known today are the strike actions of urban workers. Starting with the large-scale strikes of the late 1880s and early 1890s, the belle époque saw fluctuating but, in the long-term, increasing rates of strike action. As both unions and employers became better organized, labour conflicts became larger, involving more workers and more

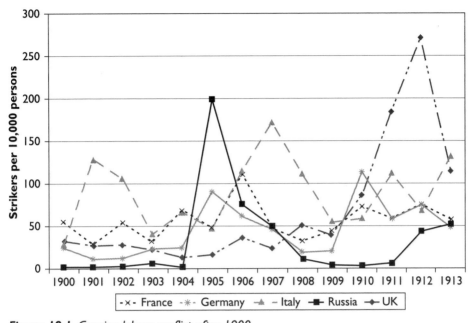

Figure 19.1 *Growing labour conflict after 1900*
Sources: Derived from figures in Leopold Hamson and Charles Tilly (eds), *Strikes, Wars and Revolutions in an International Perspective* (Cambridge, 1989); Edward Shorter and Charles Tilly, *Strikes in France 1830–1968* (Cambridge, 1974); Volker Berghahn, *Imperial Germany 1871–1914* (Providence, RI, 1994); B. R. Mitchell, *International Historical Statistics: Europe, 1750–1993*, 4th edn (London, 1998).

establishments per strike. Figure 19.1, giving strike rates per 10,000 population in five countries, shows both the overall increase in strike rates and the presence of two peaks, one in 1905–07 and another in 1910–14. Both were associated with major upheavals – the Russian Revolution of 1905 and major labour conflict on the eve of the First World War taking on near-insurrectionary character in Italy and Russia, and leading up to a general strike in Great Britain, planned for September 1914.

In the end, none of the many social and political conflicts of the pre-1914 era, whether violent or peaceful, whether stemming from tensions in rural society, from the rising labour movement, from increasing and more extreme nationalism, or from the onward march of democracy, permanently disrupted any country's government or brought about total revolutionary change. The introduction of an elected legislature in Russia after the 1905 revolution was the closest to this, but, even if no longer an autocrat, the Tsar remained an extremely powerful monarch. The dominant form of politics in pre-1914 Europe continued to be peaceful, legal and constitutional; it would take the upheaval of the First World War to bring about revolutionary change. Nevertheless, the sharp controversies of the mass politics of the belle époque were a clear sign of a more turbulent future ahead.

CHAPTER 20

THE POLITICS OF THE POWERS

If domestic politics was moving in steadily more confrontational directions after about 1900, a similar development was occurring in international affairs. In the late nineteenth century, the focus of the Great Powers' energies and aggression had been deflected away from each other and towards the acquisition of overseas empires or towards the south-east European periphery and the chronic Eastern Question; after 1895/1900 the diplomatic situation changed fundamentally. Imperialist ambitions did not decline, and the Eastern Question became more acute than ever before, but these peripheral preoccupations were no longer a diversion from potential clashes between the Great Powers in the heart of Europe. Instead, they fed directly into them. Following 1905, an almost uninterrupted series of crises, originating overseas or in the Balkans, became a cause of, or pretext for, Great Power confrontations, bringing them to the brink of war, until in the summer of 1914 one last crisis drove them over the edge.

There were five main reasons for this warlike turn in international relations. One was in the extra-European world, where, after 1900, the period of easy imperial acquisitions came to an end. The defeat of European powers in Spanish–American War of 1898 and the Russo-Japanese War of 1904–05, by rising non-European countries was a sign of the imminent end of European world domination. Just as easy overseas diversions were vanishing, the situation in the Balkans, even in the relatively peaceful 1870s and 1880s a source of potential Great Power confrontations, was both becoming more heated and showing greater possibilities for drawing in the Great Powers.

Third, and the main feature of the period, was the realignment of the Great Powers into two hostile blocs confronting each other: the combination of Germany and Austria-Hungary versus an allied France, Russia and Great Britain. This had certainly always been a possibility since the break-up of Bismarck's alliance system at the beginning of the 1890s and the creation of the Franco-Russian Alliance, but it was by no means a foregone conclusion. To get there, two major developments would be necessary. One was that Great Britain would have to be drawn away from its previous position of non-involvement in continental European matters, at the same time patting aside its maritime, colonial and Eastern Question rivalries with France and Russia, in the direction of an anti-German stance. The other was that German efforts to regain a Russian alliance, ongoing since the mid-1890s, would prove unsuccessful, leaving Austria-Hungary as Germany's only Great Power ally. By the second half of the 1900s, both of the developments had occurred and the possibility that a crisis would touch off a great European war was greater than at any time since the 1850s.

Only exacerbating this increasingly tense situation was the post-1906 arms race, a ratcheting up of the size and armaments of the armies and navies of the Great Powers, whose military expenditures grew by about 50 per cent in the seven or eight years before 1914. The arms race was a strategic seesaw – first one side introduced new weapons or increased the number of troops under arms, and then the other followed suit. In the interval, between the innovation on the one side and the response on the other, the side introducing the innovation had a temporary advantage and was subject to the temptation to launch a pre-emptive strike. This temptation was especially pronounced in view of the changes in military planning, emphasizing the importance of the offensive and of a first strike.

Finally, the role of the armed forces, defence spending, nationalism and foreign policy in an age of mass politics was yet another aggravation of a tense situation. The inclination to employ an aggressive and risky foreign policy both to defeat foreign rivals and to score domestic political points – generally something that conservative politicians and governments wanted to employ against their left-of-centre opponents – was apparent repeatedly from the 1890s onwards. Sometimes, the domestic uses of foreign policy would rather outstrip the foreign policy uses of foreign policy, and governments would engage in actions that were problematic in terms of a power-oriented strategy of international relations, but which made good sense in terms of the situation at home.

In retrospect, it is hardly surprising that such a diplomatic situation ended in the First World War. Indeed, the steadily increasing threat of such a war was the single largest piece of evidence against the portrayal of the belle époque as an idyllic era sharply separated from a later catastrophe. Instead, it points to the character of the period as a predecessor of the gloomier age of total war. Let us now look at each of the factors leading to such a fatal outcome.

GROWING OPPOSITION TO EUROPEAN OVERSEAS EXPANSION

After the partition of Africa, China was the next step for European imperial aspirations, and the very enfeebled Chinese governments of the late Qing Dynasty seemed more than willing to accommodate imperialist initiatives, including the establishment of protectorates and the granting of extra-territoriality, legal authority of European Powers over their own subjects residing in at least some regions of China. This process was broadly disrupted by the actions of the Society of Righteous Fists (hence the name 'Boxers'), a widespread, secret religious group, practising martial arts, whose members launched a series of attacks on European missionaries and Chinese converts to Christianity in 1899. As the movement spread, it broadened into attacks on all Europeans, and the Chinese imperial government began to see it as a vehicle to re-establish its full sovereignty, sending regular troops to support the insurgents. The insurrection was defeated by an international punitive force in 1900, including the European Great Powers, as well as troops from Japan and the United States, whose members killed thousands of insurgents as well as many Chinese civilians. The Chinese government was humiliated and forced to pay reparations, but the affair had made clear the scope of resistance in China to European initiatives.

While the Boxer Rebellion certainly created a stir in European public opinion and raised concerns about an entirely mythical 'Yellow Peril', its impact, either in Europe or the entire world, can scarcely be compared with that of the Boer War, occurring at the same time. The conflict itself was a product of the late nineteenth-century imperialist scramble for Africa, as the British expanded their rule from the Cape Colony at the southern tip of the continent northwards. This particular expansion was not directed towards the territory of indigenous kingdoms or tribal peoples, but to two small republics, the Transvaal and the Orange Free State, inhabited in part and ruled by the Boers, descendants of seventeenth- and eighteenth-century Dutch settlers. Unlike most territorial seizures in Africa, based on futile hopes of finding something to exploit economically, the discovery of gold in the Transvaal in 1886 demonstrated the existence of very tangible and very shiny economic resources. The famous 'Jameson Raid' of 1895–96, an attempt to seize the Transvaal mounted by Cecil Rhodes, who was both a gold-mining magnate and prime minister of the Cape Colony, mounted with the knowledge and tacit approval of the government in London, was a sign of the situation.

Although the Boers defeated the Jameson Raid, evidence of further British designs on their territory led them to declare a pre-emptive war in 1899, and to invade Britain's southern African colonies. The two tiny republics, with a total European population of around 250,000, went to war with the British Empire, and, at first, were actually winning, inflicting humiliating defeats on British forces present, and on reinforcements sent from England. Although substantially outnumbered, the Boers' modern German rifles were able to dominate the battlefield and foil British infantry assaults – a situation foreshadowing combat on the Western Front during the First World War.

A switch to more competent generals and massive reinforcements did enable the British to defeat the main Boer armies and to occupy Pretoria and Johannesburg, but from 1900 to 1902 the Boers resorted to guerilla warfare. The British forces responded by rounding up the civilian population and imprisoning them in 'concentration camps' – coining a phrase that would come to have a bad twentieth-century history – where thousands of internees died from hunger and disease. The last Boer forces surrendered in 1902, in a conflict that cost the British the astounding sum of £200 million, required the utilization of 400,000 troops, and left the world's greatest empire badly shaken.

Even clearer signs of the end of effortless European world domination than the Boxer Rebellion or the Boer War was the defeat of European Powers by non-European

BOX 20.1

The global impact of the Boer War

The Boers looked to other governments for support in their war with the British Empire, but found none willing to help them. (The German government did loudly express verbal sympathies but offered no actual assistance, thus offending the British without gaining anything by it.) The attitude of the public was different. British imperial aspirations to the Boers' territory and the counter-insurgency policies British forces adopted provoked anger and outrage worldwide. Mass meetings were held in support of the Boers, and volunteers from many European countries travelled all the way to South Africa to join the struggle, most prominently a contingent of Irish nationalists helping to fight a common enemy. J. A. Hobson's celebrated book-length theory and denunciation of imperialism, *Imperialism: A Study* (1902), was written as a result of the Boer War. His condemnation of the British foreign policy and the Jews – since, he claimed, Jewish capitalists in the gold- and diamond-mining industries were pulling the strings for the war from behind the scenes – found approbation, even in England itself, where a portion of the opposition Liberal Party, the 'pro-Boers' denounced the government's imperialist war.

This widespread support for the Boers and their anti-colonial war rather obscured their long history of brutal behaviour towards the indigenous inhabitants of southern Africa. Both Africans settled in urban areas and those living in tribal groups were virtually unanimous in supporting the British, and 30,000 of them ultimately served in the British forces. Indians living in the British colony supported the British as well – ironically, under the leadership of the future anti-imperialist hero Mohandas Gandhi. The Boers retaliated by shooting any African soldier they captured. The British, for their part, after defeating the Boers, promptly betrayed their African and Indian allies by joining their colonies to the conquered Boer states in a Union of South Africa and creating a system of self-government there that openly favoured the European population. In some ways, opposition to the Boer War, along with the agitation against Leopold II's rule in the Congo, occurring at the same time, marked the beginning of a global struggle against imperialism, but the anti-imperialist alignments of the Boer War seem less clear today in retrospect than they did at the time.

ones in two brief wars, fought around the turn of the century: the Spanish–American War of 1898 and the Russo-Japanese War of 1904–05. Both wars were, ultimately, about imperial ambitions in China, the latter directly resulting from competing Russian and Japanese ambitions in Manchuria and the Korean Peninsula; the former, although ostensibly about American assistance to Cuban insurgents against Spanish colonial rule, actually more about US desires to seize the Philippine Islands, to gain an East Asian naval strongpoint. Both wars featured humiliating maritime defeats of the European powers, the sinking by Admiral Dewey's flotilla of a Spanish squadron at anchor in Manila Bay, and Admiral Togo's destruction of the Russian Baltic fleet off Tsushima Island in the Sea of Japan, following that fleet's odyssey halfway around the world. The two wars' land battles, in Cuba and Manchuria, respectively, were somewhat more evenly matched, with both demonstrating, as had the Boer War, the way rapid-firing rifles dominated the battlefield, but they all ended with the victory of the non-European armies.

The defeat of a decrepit Spanish navy and army by the forces of the United States was not a great surprise, except perhaps in Spain itself which had begun the war full of illusions about its military power. The outcome of the Russo-Japanese War, however, had been a real shock. European military superiority could no longer be taken for granted and the powerful position of both Japan and the United States in Asia and of the US in Latin America would make further European colonial acquisitions impossible, and make it considerably more difficult even for European Powers to exert their influence.

THE EASTERN QUESTION YET AGAIN

Just as the overseas world was losing some of its attractiveness as a cockpit of power politics, the perennial sore spot of European diplomacy, the Eastern Question, was emerging from a two-decades-long hiatus into a permanent crisis condition. A major reason was the increasingly critical condition of the Ottoman Empire itself, especially after the Young Turk uprising of 1908, a military coup carried out by army officers determined to reinstate the liberal constitution of 1906, but which led more to chaotic and unsettled conditions than to the hoped-for reform or renewal. As the Young Turk policies moved steadily in the direction of Turkish nationalism, aiming to turn the multinational but predominantly Islamic Ottoman Empire into a Turkish nation-state, with subordinate national minorities, opposition to Ottoman rule mounted in the Balkans. This opposition, in part supported and even organized by the independent Balkan states of Serbia, Greece and Bulgaria, eventually encouraged them to try their hand at a military assault on the remaining European provinces of the Ottoman Empire in the Balkan Wars of 1912–13.

During the previous crisis over the Eastern Question, it had been Austria-Hungary and Russia among the Great Powers that had been the most involved. This involvement not only continued after 1900, but was ratcheted up considerably. The onset of the age of mass politics and the corresponding increase in the support for, and intensity of, nationalist movements within the Austro-Hungarian Empire made its ruling groups considerably more nervous about the possibility that a victorious anti-Ottoman nationalism would further encourage the already vociferous nationalist movements of their own subjects. They took stern measures: annexing Bosnia-Herzogovina in 1908 in response to the Young Turk revolution, seriously contemplating military intervention in the Balkan Wars, and then, in the crisis following the assassination of the heir apparent to the Habsburg throne by Serb nationalists in June 1914, going all out for war.

In all the crises surrounding the region from 1908 onwards, the Russian Empire regularly took the part of the smaller states, against both the Ottomans and the Austrians. Following the defeat of its expansionist plans in Asia by the Japanese in 1904–05, Russian diplomatic interests increasingly concentrated on south-eastern Europe. There were economic motives involved as well, since Russian exports from its booming port of Odessa had to pass from the Black Sea into the Mediterranean through the Straits at Istanbul, the Ottoman capital. The steady decline of the Ottoman Empire and its capital's increasing vulnerability – it was almost captured by Bulgarian forces in the Balkan Wars – made the Russian government hypersensitive about the situation in the region.

Another reason for Russian hypersensitivity was the increasing interest of the German government in the Balkans and the Ottoman Empire. By the early twentieth century, previous German declarations of lack of interest in the Ottoman Empire no longer rang true. German investments and trade had grown considerably. The celebrated Berlin-to-Baghdad railway – never actually built, still in the planning and financing stages as of 1914 – was a symbol of changing interests and attitudes. German efforts to regain a Russian alliance never quite worked out, so that as the Eastern Question grew more acute following 1908, there was no question about where Germany would stand in a confrontation between Austria-Hungary and Russia. Changing and expanding German interests in the region made the danger of the escalation of a regional crisis in the Balkans or the Middle East into a major European war much more likely.

A HOSTILE REALIGNMENT OF THE GREAT POWERS

A major European war as the result of a regional crisis was more likely because of a realignment of the position of two of the Great Powers, Great Britain and Germany. In both cases the reasons for the realignment centred on imperial realities and imperial aspirations, although for opposite reasons in each of the countries. British policy makers sought to diminish the burdens of running the world's largest empire whereas their German counterparts aspired to develop a large overseas empire while simultaneously retaining and even expanding their country's position as the dominant power in continental Europe. The intersection of these two developments would go a long way towards creating the preconditions for the First World War.

The Boer War brought about a moment of truth for British statesmen. The enormous expenditures required to fight that war – costing far more than the very expensive post-1906 arms race would – the manifest military unpreparedness and downright incompetence that the conflict revealed and the great effort required to defeat a minor opponent, whose war-making abilities lay far beneath those of the European Great Powers, all combined to demonstrate that the country's diplomatic and imperial commitments could not be continued indefinitely. Financially, the strain was too great, since both Conservative and Liberal politicians were committed to a fiscal policy of low taxes and balanced budgets. The ever more successful competition of German and American manufacturers raised questions about the future of Britain's industrial, commercial and financial hegemony, a major source of diplomatic and military power since the eighteenth century. Even if the money had been there, the manpower was not. Without compulsory military service – Great Britain was the only European country that did not practise conscription – there were not enough bodies for all the commitments of the armed forces.

After 1902, then, British policy was devoted to reducing its worldwide commitments in order to focus its available resources on crucial areas. The UK reached formal and informal agreements with the rising non-European powers, Japan and the United States, limiting its commitments in Asia and the Americas. An even more crucial step was reconciliation with long-term maritime and imperial rivals, France and Russia. By 1904, the so-called Entente Cordiale had resolved disputed colonial and maritime questions between Britain and France in Africa, Asia and the North Atlantic. The following year, British and French military experts even held staff talks concerning the coordination of the two country's naval forces in case of war.

These talks reached no formal conclusion and lapsed for five years, but were then resumed and continued through to 1913. Focused on naval issues, the talks involved the idea of France transferring its Atlantic squadron to the Mediterranean in case of a major war, while British forces would be concentrated in the Atlantic and the North Sea. In 1913, the French did move their Atlantic squadron to the Mediterranean but no accord was reached, no binding or treaty obligations were made, and most of the British cabinet did not even know that the discussions had been going on. Even if agreement had been reached, the exact military relevance of the discussions, at least as far as the French saw them, was not so clear. Maurice Rouvier, French prime minister at the time the staff talks began, made the cynical and later celebrated remark that the British navy 'did not run on rails', a reference to the fact that its assistance to France, should the latter's army engage the German army on land, would not be particularly great.

Yet the significance of these talks should not be underestimated, for the very fact of their being held. That the Committee of Imperial Defence, the top British military planning agency, whose creation was yet another result of the Boer War, should view France as a potential ally rather than a potential enemy represented a profound strategic realignment, even if no formal commitments to offer military assistance had been made. Part of the post-1902 British policy of limiting commitments involved crossing France off its list of potential enemies.

Russia was another, probably more salient British rival. The two countries had gone to war in the 1850s, and come close to war again over the Eastern Question at the end of the 1870s. The meeting grounds of the two empires' vast possessions and spheres of interest, in Afghanistan and in Persia (modern Iran), were constant sources of tension. The Russian and British Empires came close to war in 1904 following the Dogger

Bank incident in which the Russian Baltic fleet, steaming through the North Sea on its long voyage to confront the Japanese navy and be defeated off Tsushima Island, encountered some British fishing vessels, which the Russian sailors took to be Japanese cruisers. (Excessive consumption of vodka played a part here.) The Russians opened fire and sank them all.

Russia's defeat in its war with Japan encouraged a more conciliatory attitude on the part of the Tsar's diplomats, so that they, too, reached agreement with Great Britain, the Anglo-Russian Entente of 1907, which recognized Afghanistan as part of the Russian sphere of influence and divided up Persia into Russian and British spheres. Besides its strategic position, Persia was of interest to the Great Powers, because oil had been discovered there, so that this accord marked the beginning of the twentieth-century role of the Middle East as a crucial source of energy and so a focus of world politics. This very familiar aspect of today's world was weakly developed before 1914, as Middle Eastern oil was then just a small segment of world petroleum production (quite surpassed, for instance, by the Austrian province of Galicia) and the vast oilfields lying under the Arabian desert were completely unknown

By 1910 or so, the British reduction of commitments and diplomatic realignment was complete. Bringing together the Anglo-French and Anglo-Russian Ententes with the formal mutual defence accords of the Franco-Russian Alliance created what contemporaries referred to as the Triple Entente. By reaching agreement with the rising non-European powers and reconciling with previous European rivals, Great Britain was able to husband its financial and manpower resources so as to defend the empire and the mother country against what seemed like the major military threat emerging from Germany. Quite in contrast to France and Russia, Great Britain had been on good terms throughout the nineteenth century and as late as the 1890s with the Kingdom of Prussia and the German Empire emerging from that Prussian kingdom. To see how Germany had gone from a British friend to a potential enemy, we need to consider German policy of the post-1890 period.

A major goal of the foreign policy of the imperial German government in the two decades before the First World War was the expansion of Germany's economic, political and military influence on a worldwide scale. Contemporaries talked about *Weltpolitik*, which we could translate, a little loosely, as a 'worldwide foreign policy'. Behind this aspiration was an attitude about the condition of world affairs at the beginning of the twentieth century, an attitude that was shared widely among Germany's political, diplomatic, military, economic and intellectual elites: the nineteenth century had been the century of the European Great Powers, whose actions were mostly on a continental scale, but the twentieth century would be the age of the world empires, states with a global reach. As Germany's leaders looked around the world in 1900, they saw three such world empires: the British Empire, the Russian Empire and the United States. To play in the same league of twentieth-century politics, Germany would have to transcend the position it had held under Bismarck, as the most powerful of the continental European Great Powers, moving up to world-class status, while simultaneously defending and even expanding its position as the most powerful of the continental Powers.

To regain the continental position it held under Bismarck, the German government made strenuous efforts, from the mid-1890s onward, to win the Russian Empire back from its alliance with France. These efforts reached a climax at the time of the Russo-Japanese War. On the flip side of the Dogger Bank incident, the German government arranged for German commercial shipping to supply the Russian Baltic fleet with coal as it made its way around the world to the Sea of Japan. Following the Russian defeat against Japan, the 1905 Treaty of Björkö, a mutual defence pact between Germany and Russia, suggested Germany had attained its goal. Yet the treaty was never ratified, and Russia soon reverted to its ties with France, military cooperation between the two powers growing steadily closer in the years before 1914. There were a number of reasons for the failure of Russo-German reconciliation. One was a matter of German domestic politics, the high tariffs on imported grain, a permanent annoyance to Russian grain exporters. Aggressive subsidies for German grain exporters, which enabled them even to export to Russia, exacerbated this annoyance. Another key issue was Germany's desire to be a global power, leading to greater German economic, diplomatic and military interest in the Middle East and the Ottoman Empire, potentially threatening Russian interests in the continued opening of the Straits. The failure of Germany's diplomatic initiatives meant that attempts to preserve and enhance Germany's dominant position in continental Europe would have to be primarily military in nature.

If Germany was to pursue a worldwide foreign policy, beyond the borders of the European continent, it would need a worldwide navy to carry it out. Through the mid-1890s, the German navy had been a glorified coast guard, but Bismarck's policies, oriented primarily towards continental Europe, did not require much of a naval establishment. Wilhelm II, Germany's eccentric emperor who had dismissed Bismarck in 1890, was a big fan of navies and maritime affairs, celebrated in his saying that 'Germany's future lies on the water'. But attributing all responsibility to the emperor rather misses the broad consensus about the need for a world empire prevalent among Germany's elites. The actual naval policy developed by Wilhelm's secretary of state for the navy, Admiral Alfred von Tirpitz (1849–1930) (another great fan of the theory of world empires) called, in 1897, for the building of a large German battleship fleet, to be stationed in the North Sea, with the intent of threatening Britain's pre-eminent naval position. A thoroughly chastened and intimidated Great Britain could then fall in line behind German plans for colonial expansion.

What such planning, which was duly implemented in the decade following 1897, actually accomplished, was to make Germany seem like Britain's chief enemy, so that the post-Boer War British imperial retrenchment ended up concentrating the empire's maritime resources against the Germans. Having antagonized the British and not won over the Russians, to say nothing of France and its continuing anti-German policy, by 1905 or so Germany found itself, as the emperor said, 'surrounded by a ring of enemies' – which was true, although primarily because German policy had created them. There remained for Germany's security the Triple Alliance with Austria-Hungary and Italy, but Italian attachment to the alliance was increasingly dubious, and after 1905 the Austro-Hungarian and Italian General Staffs developed elaborate plans to go to war with each other. Thus, by the years between 1905 and 1910 the pattern of military and diplomatic affiliations among the European Great Powers increasingly pitted Germany and Austria-Hungary on the one hand, against France, Russia and Britain on the other.

ARMS RACES

As these Great Power alignments were being firmed up after 1905, two major arms races broke out which would help propel the European Powers in the direction of war. Armaments expenditures of the Great Powers had not changed much in the first five or six years of the twentieth century, except for Great Britain and Russia, both of whom were involved in wars – the Boer War and the Russo-Japanese War, respectively. When these wars ended, arms expenditures reverted to pre-war levels. Starting in 1906–07, though, this state of affairs changed drastically. Between those years and 1913, defence expenditures of the Great Powers increased in a range anywhere from 30 per cent to 100 per cent. This increasing preparation for war reflected the existence of not one, but two, arms races – one at sea and one on land – arms races that strained budgets, transformed military planning and, as moments of military superiority came and went, increased the likelihood of a Great Power seizing the opportunity to go to war.

The naval arms race followed directly from the implementation of German plans for the building of a battleship fleet. The British responded with a technological innovation, the 'dreadnought' class of battleships, whose guns were more powerful than any existing battleship, and whose turbine-driven engines could propel the ship faster than any existing battleship, thus making existing warships obsolete. Tirpitz had to start all over again, building the German version of dreadnought class ships. The British riposted by building still more dreadnoughts. The rapid pace of naval armaments became a growing fiscal burden. Naval disarmament talks were held between Germany and Great Britain in 1909 and again in 1912: they ended not with disarmament but with each side increasing the pace of battleship construction still further. The fashion for building dreadnoughts spread to the other European Powers, including such unlikely ones as Italy and Austria-Hungary, who were diligently building high-end battleships at the outbreak of the First World War.

Although naval spending was increasing much more rapidly than spending on land forces, all the Powers, with the exception of Great Britain, spent more on their armies than on their navies – about two to four times as much. Army expenditures and land-war planning were at least as big an element in the arms race that led up to the First World War. The story of the land arms race does go back to the strategic realignments of the 1890s, as does that of the naval arms race, but much of the actual expansion in arms spending and in the armed forces was compressed into the two or three years before 1914.

The origins of the situation lay in the Franco-Russian Alliance of 1894, which ended Bismarck's policy of leaving France isolated against Germany. The General Staff, Germany's military planning agency, considering the problem of a war against two Great Power opponents on two widely separated fronts, drew up two quite different battle plans, its 'eastern deployment' and 'western deployment', which called for concentrating the bulk of the troops at the outbreak of war against Russia or France, respectively, concentrating Germany's military effort on that power, and having the smaller number of troops facing the other in a strictly defensive stance. In 1905, with Russia taken out of the military equation by its war with Japan, Count Alfred von Schlieffen (1833–1913), the head of the General Staff, devised a radical war plan to defeat the French, involving using the entire German army to attack France, not along the heavily fortified and mountainous Franco-German border but in an enormous flanking movement to the north, through the flat lands of the Low Countries.

Schlieffen's successor as chief of the General Staff, Count Helmuth von Moltke the younger (1848–1916, the nephew of Helmuth von Moltke the elder, who had directed the German armies so successfully in their war against France in 1870–71), revised and expanded this enormous outflanking movement through Belgium. As Russia recovered from the débâcle of the war with Japan and the revolution of 1905, and the Russian army became a serious problem once again for the Germans, German military planning concentrated ever more on the idea of a western offensive at the beginning of the war, while leaving just a few troops in the east in order to defend against the Russians. Finally, in 1913, the General Staff scrapped its eastern deployment plan altogether: there was no option to beginning a war other than concentrating most troops against France.

As German war planning moved in the direction of the large-scale western offensive, its possibilities of success became hostage to three conditions, all related to the fact that at the outbreak of the war the large majority of German forces would be advancing through Belgium and northern France. One was the slowness of the Russian mobilization. It had to be assumed that the Russians would need most of the initial six weeks of the war to get their army mobilized and ready to fight, since German war plans called for the bulk of the army to be deployed during this six weeks in Belgium and northern France. The relatively poor state of rail networks and road conditions in the Russian Empire made that plausible, at least initially. Another condition was that the French stay on the defensive at the outbreak of the war, concentrating their forces in the vicinity of the Franco-German border fortifications that were to be outflanked. Should the French plan to launch an offensive into Germany, there would not be sufficient troops available to counter them. The third was that

Great Britain would remain neutral, or at least would not send ground troops to Belgium or northern France to combat the Germans.

In the years after 1910, every one of these conditions began to vanish. In 1912/13, the Russian government, with French financial assistance, began a programme of constructing strategic railways, to bring its troops to the front more quickly in case of war. Once this programme reached its planned completion at the end of the 1910s, German forces would no longer have six weeks to defeat the French without worrying about the Russians. French strategists planned an offensive into southern Germany, via Alsace and Lorraine, on the outbreak of war, a decision of which German intelligence was quite well aware. Forces needed to defend against the French offensive could not be used in the outflanking manoeuvre to the north. Finally, as the naval confrontation between Germany and Great Britain escalated, the possibility of British intervention in a war between Germany on the one hand, and France and Russia on the other, grew more likely.

By 1912, the German General Staff decided that the only way to deal with these threats to its war plans was to increase the size of the army, by some 300,000 troops. In the end, the actual troop increase was only half that, both for financial reasons and, more importantly, because the ministry of war did not think that there were enough reliable (i.e., politically conservative, socially aristocratic) individuals available to be officers of an expanded army. The French government increased the size of its army in turn, by raising the term of conscription from two years to three. As was the case with the naval arms race, both Austria-Hungary and Italy joined in the land arms race as well.

Thus, by 1913, there were two arms races going on full scale. Fiscal pressures were mounting up, creating political difficulties for the governments of the Great Powers. The land arms race, though, was particularly destabilizing, since the German plans for a quick defeat of France were threatened by the French military build-up, the Russian strategic railways plan, and the growing inclination of the British to join the Franco-Russian alliance in case of war. Thus the temptation grew in Germany to launch a pre-emptive strike while the circumstances for the planned western offensive were still favourable, to start a war with its newly expanded army before France's and Russia's plans reached fruition. In the crisis of 1914, this appraisal of the state of the land arms race would play a crucial role in turning the crisis into a fully fledged war.

FOREIGN POLICY AND DOMESTIC POLITICS

The reader will have noticed that many of Germany's foreign policy problems stemmed from the decision taken in the late 1890s to build a battle fleet to challenge British naval supremacy, when Germany and Great Britain were, diplomatically, on relatively good terms. It is difficult to make sense of this move if we think of foreign policy as being conducted by rational actors carefully calculating ways to expand their country's power. Admiral von Tirpitz himself noted another motivation for his fleet, namely that it would be a national task that would serve as a political weapon 'against educated and less educated social democrats'.[26] In other words, Tirpitz saw his plans for naval expansion, and the related idea of turning Germany from a continental power into a world empire, as helping to defeat the rapidly growing labour movement, the 'less educated social democrats', and the middle-class advocates of social reform, the 'educated . . . social democrats'.

This decision to build a navy against a country which was not, at least before the navy was built, an active national enemy, is a moment in which we can disentangle the interconnection between causes of foreign policy and military decisions in domestic politics, and in the relationship between the different powers. At other times, the two groups of motives were too closely entangled. Conservative advocates of the extension of the term of military service in France from two years to three in 1913 saw the proposal as a way to split apart the Radical Party and prevent it from forming a left-of-centre coalition government with the socialists. Yet they also thought that the expansion of the French army was needed to defend the country against the growing German army. In a similar way, the decision of the Tsar's ministers to take an aggressive line in the Balkans following 1908 not only reflected fears of other Great Powers gaining control of the Straits, but were also related to the need to pursue an aggressive foreign policy to counter liberal and socialist critics of the government following the revolution of 1905 – and the defeat of Russian forces by Japan had rendered Asia impossible as a site of Russian expansion. The taking of a hard line by the government of Austria-Hungary against the Serbs in 1914 was in part motivated by the outcome of the Balkan Wars, in which a coalition of smaller Balkan powers had defeated the Ottoman Empire. Yet it was driven at least as much by the nationalist agitation within the empire, especially by the Slavic nationalities. A military defeat of the Kingdom of Serbia would be a drastic political setback for anti-Habsburg nationalists. The Tory opposition politicians who kept pressing the Liberal government in Great Britain after 1906 to expand the plans for battleship building were seeking a convenient issue which would both be popular with the voters and divert the electorate's attention from other issues where the Tory positions were less attractive. But they also felt – and not without good reason – that the expansion of the German battle fleet was a national security danger to Great Britain, which needed to be met with energetic military counter-measures.

Although this interplay of domestic and diplomatic motives for foreign policy dated at least from the 1850s, there were three features of the post-1890 era that made it particularly explosive. One was the onset of the age of mass politics. Aggressive policies became the goal of political campaigns carried out by mass political parties or by nationalist leagues. As such, they could take on a life of their own and slip out of the hands of the politicians and statesmen who thought they were controlling them. The second was the development of the arms race after 1906. Expanding a country's army was generally a trump card of the political right, only in the crisis-ridden atmosphere of European diplomacy in the decade before the First World War, and in the context of the increasingly fixed alignment of the Great Powers, these increases in the size of the armed forces and upgrades to their logistics and weapons systems had immediate diplomatic and military ramifications.

The third was the development of the domestic political situation in the decade between the Russian Revolution of 1905 and the outbreak of the First World War. Erratically, at differing rates, and to differing extent from country to country, the forces of the political left, or at least those seeking dramatic change (nationalists in the Austro-Hungarian Empire, for instance, whose politics, although certainly subversive, were not always left wing), were generally on the advance, forcing proponents of the status quo to deal with them. In countries with democratic, or at least parliamentary, forms of government – France, Switzerland, Great Britain, Scandinavia, the Low Countries, to some extent Spain and Italy – the existing political system was flexible enough to deal with such a development, although it should be noted that by 1914 it seemed that the question of home rule for Ireland would prove too much for the arch-parliamentary political system of Great Britain. By contrast, in the authoritarian regimes in the centre and east of the continent – the German, Russian, Austro-Hungarian Empires and, in its own way, the Ottoman Empire – the institutions and expectations that might have made possible some sort of accommodation of these political forces were largely not present or were underdeveloped. There, the temptation to resort to aggressive foreign policy and military adventurism as a way to preserve the status quo was much greater. It is probably no coincidence that in the pre-war crisis of the summer of 1914 the parliamentary regimes of western Europe, Britain and France were cautious and reserved, while the central and eastern empires took more aggressive steps towards war – although, in the end all five of the Great Powers were willing to go over the brink into a world war.

CHAPTER 21

THE DYNAMICS OF POWER

Both the domestic politics of most European countries and their relations to each other during the quarter-century preceding the First World War can be grouped into two periods, with a dividing line running roughly from 1900 to 1906. The first period largely continued the trends of the 1880s. Domestic policy was generally in the hands of individuals or political parties to the right of centre, although the development of mass political parties, special-interest groups and the nationalist leagues made governing in conservative fashion more difficult than it had been in previous decades. In foreign policy as well, overseas expansion remained a primary concern of the Great Powers, with the 1890s seeing the culmination of the scramble for Africa. Admittedly, the estrangement between Germany and Russia, and the signing of the Franco-Russian Alliance in 1894, brought a new degree of movement to the relations of the Great Powers within Europe, but even there the ultimate consequences of this development remained unclear and the policy options emerging from these alliances were still flexible.

In the space of five or six turbulent years, around the immediate turn of the century, this whole situation changed, for three interlocking reasons. One reason for such a turnabout was foreign policy débâcles: the defeat of Italian troops by the Ethiopians in 1896, the Boer War of 1899–1902, or the Russo-Japanese War of 1904–05. Problems radiating out from these débâcles, including loss of trust in the government, both by the political class and the broader population, financial burdens, and the need for new directions in foreign policy, upset both the domestic politics and international relations. Another reason was drastic crises of regimes: the Dreyfus Affair in France and the resulting crisis (or at least perception of a crisis) of the republic in the years 1899 to 1900, the 1903 military coup in Serbia, the secession of Norway from Sweden in 1905 and, the overwhelming regime crisis of this period, the Russian Revolution of 1905. The series of regime crises was concluded on the margins of Europe with the Young Turk military coup in the Ottoman Empire in 1908. Finally, the period saw a number of dramatic election victories for the left: in France in 1902 and again in 1906, in Germany in 1903 and in Great Britain in 1906. The very first elections ever held in Russia, in the wake of the 1905 revolution, to the first two Dumas of 1905 and 1906, both resulted in victories for left-of-centre parties as well.

Following all these upheavals, domestic politics took on a quite different pattern, moving from an emphasis on the status quo to one on reform. Particularly in western Europe, left-of-centre governments, generally involving some kind of cooperation between liberals and labour parties, came to office with a programme of political, social and economic reform. By contrast, in the authoritarian regimes of the centre and the east of the continent, domestic policy continued to be run by conservative statesmen and politicians, although often with an admixture of reforming policies, apparent in the plans of the Russian prime minister Peter Stolypin or the German chancellor Theobald von Bethmann-Hollweg.

Such reform plans, whether drastic or much more modest, promptly touched off substantial political controversies. Forces on the left, particularly in the more militant wing of the labour movement, denounced them as insufficient. Increasing labour strife and strike activity provided a powerful social underpinning to such criticism. Other movements of political opposition, usually on the left but also containing different political elements with their own focus – women's rights movements in Great Britain, nationalist movements in multinational empires – were no less hesitant about denouncing the insufficient character of potential reforms. The very same reforms perceived as too modest on the left or among other oppositional groups, were rejected as far too drastic by many elements of the right. Plans for extra-legal and non-constitutional actions as a response to the domestic political situation began to circulate – perhaps not surprisingly in the authoritarian regimes of the centre and east of the continent, but even in arch-constitutional and legalistic Great Britain. Right-wing patronage of increasingly militant and vociferous nationalism, and support for an aggressive and warlike foreign policy as an alternative to reform, only sharpened the domestic political situation.

Just as domestic politics in many European countries were moving in the direction of sharpened conflict, relations between the Great Powers were becoming more strained. The realignment of Great Power relations into two conflicting blocs, and the growing arms races, developments first emerging around 1905 and being painfully clear some five years later, pointed in the direction of a major European war. A rapid succession of diplomatic crises – the First Moroccan Crisis of 1905–06, the Bosnian annexation crisis of 1908–09, the Second Moroccan Crisis of 1911, the Balkan Wars of 1912–13 – made the danger of such a war evident, and not just to the limited and specialized circles of diplomats, or even to the political class more generally, but, via the mass circulation press and the agitation of the political parties and nationalist leagues, to a large portion of the adult population. The combination of domestic political conflict and Great Power brinkmanship created the conditions in which the First World War began in the summer of 1914, bringing the entire period of post-1850 European history to its final, convulsive end.

HOLDING THE LINE IN THE 1890S

Governments of the right and the centre-right in 1890s Europe pursued a variety of political strategies. One could be called immobilism, a rejection of reforms or changes to the political system. Perhaps the prime example of this strategy was the actions of the British Conservatives. Coming to power with a major victory in the 1895 elections, after systematically thwarting all the initiatives of the Liberal government in office between 1892 and 1895, the Conservatives and their agile prime minister, Lord Salisbury, proceeded to do strikingly little in domestic affairs, except for providing more financial aid to the Church of England and cutting the taxes on large landowners. A similar attitude characterized the governments of the Spanish conservatives and their leader Antonio Cánovas del Castillo (1828–97), like Salisbury a veteran of the conservative resurgence of the 1880s.

Both Spain and Great Britain had seen influential periods of liberal reform in the nineteenth century, with the liberals understood as the natural governing party in the third quarter of the nineteenth century, so that conservative rule and political immobilism were something of novelties. At the other end of Europe, conservatism – indeed, extreme conservatism – had been the dominant political tendency in the Tsar's empire, except for the period of the Great Reforms in the 1860s. The ascension to the throne of Alexander III in 1881, following the assassination of his reforming father Alexander II, had initiated a period of conservative reaction, which historians call the Counter-Reforms. On Alexander III's (peaceful) death in 1894, his son Nicholas II announced his intention to continue autocratic, absolutist rule, heading the government himself without a prime minister. Many of the leading figures at the court and in the government during the previous reign, such as the procurator of the Holy Synod Constantine Pobedonostsev, remained in office. A new figure, though, was the minister of finance, Sergei Witte (1849–1915). Certainly a supporter of absolutism and an opponent of political change, Witte felt that economic development would be the best way to uphold the Tsar's rule. He took a number of measures to encourage industrialization, including instituting protective tariffs for industry and encouraging crucial foreign investments by putting the Russian currency on the gold standard. Rather than refusing to introduce any reforms, Witte's design was for economic change to bulwark political stasis.

Governments of the right in other European countries during the 1890s showed more interest in political realignment. Moderate liberals in both France and Italy attempted to create centre-right coalitions with conservative supporters of the Catholic Church, hoping to overcome the long-term hostility that devout Catholics felt both towards the Kingdom of Italy, which had seized Rome from the Pope, and towards the anti-monarchical French Third Republic. The resulting centre-right governments in both countries did indeed scale back anti-clerical measures, if generally not to the extent that devout Catholics had hoped, increased protective tariffs, conducted a strongly imperialist foreign policy, and were at best unsympathetic to the growing labour movement, and at worst, as was the case with Italian prime minister Francesco Crispi, sent in the army against striking workers.

Finally, in central Europe, the 1890s began with a break from previous conservative governments, symbolized by the dismissal of the two long-term conservative heads of government, Germany's Otto von Bismarck and Austria's Count Taaffe, at the beginning of the decade. Both Germany's youthful monarch Wilhelm II and Austria's elderly emperor Franz Joseph supported an opening to the left, and the new heads of government they appointed, General Leo von Caprivi (1831–99) and Count Kasimir Badeni (1846–1909), worked with the liberals, tried to defuse nationality conflicts, replaced a strategy of repression of the labour movement with one of making concessions to labour, in the hope of regaining workers' loyalties, and thought about modifying, if not abolishing, economic protectionism. This more moderate stance was also apparent in centre-right governments of Belgium and the Netherlands.

In an age of mass politics, it proved impossible to carry out this change of course. German and Czech nationalists both rejected Count Badeni's efforts to resolve the nationalities conflict in the province of Bohemia and nationalist agitation grew steadily throughout both the Austrian and Hungarian halves of the monarchy. Nationalist leagues and special-interest groups in Germany, including the powerful farmers' special-interest group, the Agrarian League, founded specifically to oppose Caprivi's efforts to liberalize trade, led increasingly successful campaigns against government policy. Far from gaining by the government's policy shift, liberal political parties lost votes, often to the radical movements of the extreme right. The 1890s marked the high point of anti-Semitic political parties in central Europe, with these parties' good results in the 1893 German national elections and the 1897 election of the anti-Semitic leader Karl Lueger as mayor of Vienna, a decisive change in a long-term liberal stronghold. On the left of the political spectrum, the social democratic parties in both Germany and the industrialized regions of Austria steadily gained strength, so that concessions to labour had the opposite effect from what central European governments had hoped.

The upshot was a swing to the right by the end of the decade. Badeni's successors gave up trying to conciliate the nationalists, and since nationalists made up a steadily larger element in the Austrian parliament, they also gave up trying to rule with parliamentary support rather than by emergency decrees. Caprivi's successors and Germany's mercurial emperor Wilhelm II toyed with even more extreme steps – abolishing the democratic franchise, reinstating the prohibition of the social democrats, significantly limiting freedom of speech and the press – but shrank from these confrontational and extra-legal policies. Ultimately, following the ideas of Admiral von Tirpitz and the veteran diplomat Bernhard von Bülow (1848–1929), appointed German chancellor in 1900, the German government tried to rally the conservative political parties, some of the liberals, the leagues and the special-interest groups behind a government policy of building a large navy to confront the British fleet and facilitate imperialist expansion and introducing new, even more extreme, protective tariffs.

This smorgasbord of conservative policies does suggest the extent to which the political solutions that had proved so successful at the end of the liberal era in the 1870s and 1880s were getting a little stale in the 1890s, and were not always well adapted to the newly developing political universe of mass parties, nationalist leagues and special-interest groups. A similar pattern of older foreign initiatives not adapted to new situations appeared in the diplomatic relations of the Great Powers.

The Eastern Question, that chronic problem of European diplomacy, was relatively quiet in this period, indeed in the two decades from 1885 to 1905. The Franco-Russian Alliance of 1894 demonstrated the end of Bismarck's alliance system and the isolation of France it had produced, yet the long-term effect of this new diplomatic combination remained unclear. We know now that it would be directed against Germany, indeed would ultimately involve the two powers, or, in the case of Russia, its successor state, the USSR, in not just one but two wars against Germany, but to contemporaries in the 1890s it was just as plausible that the Franco-Russian combination might be deployed against Great Britain, a perennial maritime and colonial rival of the two powers.

Such a conflict might have seemed especially plausible in view of the continuing focus of the European powers on imperial expansion in the 1890s. The partition of Africa culminated then and imperial enterprises continued in the South Seas and in Asia as well, such as the German creation of a protectorate in the Kiaochow peninsula of China in 1897 (best known today for the Tsingdao beer the imperialists began brewing in the town where their naval base was located), or the steady Russian penetration of Manchuria and Korea. This continuing imperial expansion led to the most considerable clash between European colonial powers since the wars of the eighteenth century, the Fashoda Affair of 1898, in which British and French troops met at the eponymous village, on the upper reaches of the Nile near Khartoum, capital of today's Sudan. Both countries were following a strategy of creating a trans-African colonial realm, but the British were there in considerably superior strength. The French troops, more of a survey expedition than an actual military force, were forced to yield control of the area to their colonial rivals.

This result was a blow to a centre-right French government already enmeshed in a bitter domestic quarrel over the Dreyfus Affair. For a few months, it looked as if there might be a war between France and Great Britain arising from this encounter. In the end, the French gave way and soon embarked on a series of negotiations with Great Britain over disputed colonial questions. Turning away from war over an economically worthless territory, frankly of not much strategic importance either, was an eminently sensible decision of French statesmen, but it also marked the end of a fifteen-year-long period in which overseas expansion had been a top foreign policy priority.

LARGE CHANGES AT THE TURN OF THE CENTURY

The conflict over Fashoda was one of a series of usually interrelated foreign policy and domestic political conflicts occurring around the turn of the century that helped bring the period of conservative government to an end, and introduced new governments, new political controversies and new diplomatic alignments. Both the timing and the extent of the changes varied from country to country, as did the relative importance of domestic and foreign policy causes.

The defeat of the Italian army by the Ethiopians in 1896 brought the resignation of the prime minister, Francesco Crispi. (By contrast, Spain's equally humiliating defeat by the United States in 1898 led to talk of a military coup and much soul-searching among Spanish intellectuals, but no immediate changes in government.) Yet Crispi's centre-right orientation persisted until a new government, with the innovative liberal leader Giovanni Giolitti as minister of the interior, came to power in 1901. Giolitti immediately made a name for himself by ordering the police not to intervene in strikes, commencing a reform-oriented domestic policy.

There was a similar interplay of foreign and domestic causes of change in government in turn-of-the-century Great Britain. As with Italy, the foreign policy impetus was a war arising from an aggressive colonial policy in Africa, in this case the Boer War of 1899–1902. Although starting badly, and revealing – at least to the upper ranks of armed forces, diplomatic service, civil servants and politicians – serious weaknesses in the armed forces, the war did end successfully for Great Britain. Encouraged by a wave of celebrations over military victories, such as 'night of Mafeking', the giant national festivities celebrating the relief of the besieged forces in this South African city, the ruling Conservatives launched an aggressive election campaign in 1900, the so-called Khaki Elections, identifying themselves with the troops and the Liberal opposition as treasonous 'pro-Boers'.

Yet the ensuing election victory was more pyrrhic than anything else. The very considerable costs of the war had to be met, leaving the government with the perennially unpopular choice of raising taxes or cutting spending. Domestic controversy weakened the Conservatives' position, a result of the split between the free traders, led by the new prime minister, Arthur Balfour (1848–1930), nephew of the deceased Lord Salisbury, and the protectionists, led by the ex-liberal Joseph Chamberlain, who had deserted the Liberal Party over opposition to its support for home rule in Ireland. Economic special-interest groups lined up behind each of the different leaders, although protectionists in Great Britain, quite unlike just about anywhere else in the pre-1914 world, were less influential than free traders, even in the ranks of political conservatives.

While the ruling Conservatives were facing the financial consequences of past policies and divided about how to meet future economic and fiscal challenges, the opposition Liberals were rearming themselves politically, fitting out older policies for a new environment of mass politics and developing new political issues. An emphasis on free trade, presented as a defence of cheap food against Tory desires to help noble landowners by raising food prices, was one long-successful Liberal talking point, regaining new relevance as a result of Chamberlain's protectionist campaign. The other was Liberal opposition to the Church of England and support for the Protestant Free Churches, some of whose ministers promptly drove motor cars around the countryside

campaigning for the Liberals. The Liberal reorganization also included an identification of liberalism with social reform, the 'new liberalism'. The Liberal Party
would sponsor parliamentary candidates chosen by the Labour Representation
Committee, an alliance of the trade unions and the smaller socialist groups in the
UK. The 1906 elections duly produced a very large victory for the Liberals and their
Labour supporters, and a Liberal government committed to a policy of reforms –
albeit reforms that would be an uneasy mixture of old and new liberal ideas.

Changes were fewer in central Europe, as conservative governments of the 1890s
tended to persist, sometimes under different leadership, into the beginning of the
new century. Yet in Austria the more the authoritarian government ignored the nationalists and their parliamentary representatives, the stronger and more drastic the
political campaigns of the different nationalist groups became. In Germany, the conservative realignments around a large navy, a continued bid for colonial empire, and
expanded protective tariffs were tested in public opinion by the general elections
of 1903, which centred on the large increases in agricultural protective tariffs
implemented the previous year. Turnout jumped to unprecedented levels, with over
three-quarters of eligible voters coming to the polls, and the Social Democrats, the
party of the socialist labour movement, campaigning on the eminently un-socialist
cause of free trade in foodstuffs – in this respect, quite similar to the Liberals in England
– won a major election victory.

The two largest political changes in the years around the turn of the century were
unquestionably in France and in Russia, the result of the Dreyfus Affair and of the
revolution of 1905. Each of these produced a political upheaval of remarkable
dimensions, if, admittedly, stopping short of creating a new political system, and each
had ramifications on a Europe-wide scale.

Of the two, the Dreyfus Affair seemed by far the more unlikely candidate for a
political upheaval. The trial and conviction in the winter of 1894–95 of Captain Alfred
Dreyfus (1859–1935), an officer of the French General Staff, on charges of passing
secret military information to the German embassy in Paris, was far from controversial, and the verdict of the court martial was widely greeted across the entire political spectrum. Over the next four years, though, the convicted officer's supporters,
at first primarily his family members, but, as time went on, an ever growing number of members of France's intellectual, literary and political elites, uncovered a mountain of material demonstrating not only that the intrepid officer had been convicted
unjustly, but also that the evidence against him had been forged by a cabal of anti-
Semitic officers in the General Staff, with the connivance of their superiors and
the military and civilian judges who had ruled on the case. The same individuals responsible for inventing a case against Dreyfus had suppressed evidence implicating the
actual traitor, a pious, aristocratic army officer badly in need of money, Count
Marie-Charles Esterhazy. As the ranks of Dreyfus's supporters swelled, and their attacks
on the army officers responsible for his treatment and the politicians who vouched
for them became more vehement, the proponents of his guilt came to be centred more

clearly on the political right – not only in the new nationalist right of the leagues, the League of Patriots, the League of the French Fatherland and the League of Anti-Semites, whose politics combined nationalism, militarism and anti-Semitism, but also in the older monarchist right and at least some of the France's leading Catholic clergymen. The 1898 elections were accompanied by anti-Semitic riots and street demonstrations, and, as the case in favour of Dreyfus made greater headway in the French parliament, activists of the League of Patriots attempted to mount a military coup against the republic in 1899 – an effort which, in practice, was less of a threat and more of a farce.

These turbulent events were followed closely across Europe and even in North America; the Dreyfus Affair became a broader *cause célèbre*. The political upshot in France was a realignment on the left and centre, not without some resemblance to events in Britain at about the same time, involving an alliance between left-leaning liberals and the labour movement. Centre-right governments that had dominated French politics in the 1890s gave way to a ministry of 'republican defence' more clearly to the left, which was supported by the socialists, dropping their previous practice of opposing all forms of capitalist politics, and even contained a socialist government minister. The left-wing forces did well in the 1902 general elections, and the newly elected government was launched on a programme of drastic political reform.

If the foreign policy implications of the Dreyfus Affair were primarily in the background – the prestige of the army and its role in defending France against potential threats from Germany – the Russian Revolution of 1905 was clearly the result of a foreign policy débâcle. The mounting defeats in the course of 1904 in Russia's war with Japan shook the foundations of the tsarist autocracy and encouraged the many elements of Russian society opposed to the emperor's absolutist rule to express their opinions. Beginning with a national conference of representatives of the zemstvos in November 1904, whose participants called for the institution of basic civil liberties and an elected legislature, the following months saw a wave of public meetings and demonstrations across the empire. Ironically, it was the policies of the Tsar's own secret police, which turned this oppositional activity, still largely centred in the educated and propertied classes of the empire, into a mass movement.

To weaken the strength of the illegal socialist labour movement, the Tsar's officials had been secretly sponsoring workers' associations. The leader of one of the largest of these groups, the Orthodox priest Georgii Gapon, went rather beyond what the police had in mind, when he proposed to mount a large public demonstration of the workers in St Petersburg, in front of the Tsar's palace. The demonstration was a strange mixture of the mass politics of the age of classical modernism, and the old-regime personal appeal to a patriarchal tsar. Held on 9 January 1905, its 100,000 participants, carrying icons and pictures of Nicholas II, marched to the Winter Palace in St Petersburg, where soldiers opened fire on the peaceful demonstrators, killing at least forty of them. As news of 'Bloody Sunday' spread it turned opposition to the Tsar's rule into a mass phenomenon.

BOX 21.1

The Dreyfus Affair

When the Dreyfus Affair reached its high point at the end of the 1890s, its divisive impact, at least at first glance, seemed overwhelming. Politicians, of course, were divided, but so were artists – Monet pro-Dreyfus, Degas anti – and writers – Zola, Proust and Anatole France in favour of the beleaguered captain, Maurras, Daudet and Barrès his determined enemies – and other French intellectuals. In fact, the very phrase 'intellectual' in its contemporary meaning comes from a 'Protest of the Intellectuals', a pro-Dreyfus public appeal which ultimately gained three thousand signatures. Long-term friendships were broken over the Affair, and even family members became estranged. Well covered by the contemporary press, the impact of the Dreyfus Affair was not just limited to France, but spread across Europe and North America. The Austrian journalist Theodor Herzl, covering the affair for the leading Viennese newspaper *Die Neue Freie Presse* and experiencing the violent hostility of Dreyfus's opponents, decided that their actions proved Jews could only be safe from anti-Semitism if they had their own country, leading him to launch an appeal in favour of a Jewish nation-state in Palestine, and to organize a Europe-wide Zionist movement in support of it.

More recently, historians have suggested that this whole picture of contention and hostility reaching almost obsessive levels was limited to the educated middle and upper classes of large cities. France's rural population, in particular, was relatively indifferent, and had paid a good deal more attention to the agitation of General Boulanger at the end of the 1880s than they would to the Dreyfus Affair a decade later.

This judgement certainly has something to it, but both the substantial anti-Semitic riots occurring in a number of French cities and towns during the 1898 elections and the 1902 election victories won by Dreyfus's supporters suggest that the affair was not just a matter for Parisian literati. The Dreyfus Affair became a touchstone for a whole variety of issues: anti-Semitism and the position of the Jews in a world of rising nationalism, certainly, but also the stability of the republican form of government in France, the relations between the Catholic Church and the French republic, the position of the army in French society, even anxieties about masculinity. All of these were read into the Affair, and the largely unknown figure of Captain Alfred Dreyfus himself – a conventional, unimaginative, if determined and courageous army officer – became the screen on to which individuals could project their hopes and aspirations, their passions and hatreds.

For much of 1905, the situation spiralled out of control. There was bad news from the front in Asia, still more and better attended public meetings issuing demands for constitutional governments, riots and disturbances in rural areas, emerging from peasants' discontent about the nobility's ownership of much of the land, demonstrations and strikes of secondary school and university students, calls for autonomy or even independence from the empire's national minorities, and, above all, a steadily growing number of labour strikes, culminating in a massive, empire-wide general strike in October. Repeated mutinies in the armed forces made it impossible for the government to restore order.

The authorities had no choice but to offer concessions to the revolutionary movement, culminating in the 'October Manifesto' in which the Tsar promised the introduction of basic civil liberties and the election of a parliament, the Duma, with law-making powers. At the same time, the Tsar named his technocratic finance minister, Sergei Witte, the chief proponent of this reforming course, as the prime minister, establishing, for the first time in Russian history, a head of government separate from the hereditary head of state. The October Manifesto was the high point of the revolutionary movement in Russia, but also the beginning of its decline.

The visible defeat of the Tsar's authority provided the incentive for his supporters to organize their own political movements, the most prominent of which was the extreme right-wing Union of the Russian People. Their most effective action was to encourage attacks on the Jews. There were over 600 pogroms within a few weeks of the signing of the manifesto, the largest of which, in the Crimean city of Odessa, left at least 800 Jews dead. Not unlike anti-Semites in Germany and the Austro-Hungarian Empire, or the enemies of Captain Dreyfus in France, these Russian rightists, known to contemporaries as the Black Hundreds, saw the Jews as pulling the strings behind the scenes of revolutionary movements and believed that attacking them would help to destroy the revolution. The government authorities, the police and the army, many of whose leading figures endorsed such anti-Semitic notions – as did Tsar Nicholas II himself – were conspicuous by their reluctance to take action against the rioters.

The mobilization of counter-revolution continued through 1906, which saw the steady return of order as the war with Japan was ended and the Tsar's officers regained control of their once mutinous soldiers. Members of the liberal Kadet party dominated the elections to the first Duma, or parliament, which was promptly dissolved by the government a few weeks after it met. A second Duma, in which the socialists were prominently represented, was dissolved as well, and the new prime minister, an unusually capable and ambitious state official, Peter Stolypin (1862–1911), replacing Sergei Witte, who had proved unable to deal with the revolutionary situation, embarked on a policy of rigorous political repression. While the Duma, with its law-making powers, continued to exist, the franchise for it was changed, so that the landowning nobility would elect a disproportionate number of the deputies; civil liberties were restricted; and no constitution was written, so that the Tsar's powers were not subject to any fundamental limitations.

In the end, the Tsar's rule had survived the revolutionary challenge, above all because the instruments of repression available to the regime had been weakened by the war with Japan, but not destroyed. As was the case with most revolutions in Europe between 1848 and 1989, it would take a far more fundamental military defeat and consequent dissolution of the armed forces for the regime to be overthrown – circumstances that would occur in Russia in 1917, as a result of the First World War.

Two characteristic features of the 1905 Russian Revolution were the enormous labour unrest and the widespread strikes and political campaigns emerging from them, and the nationalist demand – particularly prevalent in the Tsar's Polish provinces – for independence from a multinational empire. There were emulations of this politicized labour unrest elsewhere in Europe – calls for a general strike by socialists in Austria and Germany; the threat of such a strike helped to bring about the introduction of universal manhood suffrage in elections to the Austrian parliament, the Reichsrat in 1907. The nationalist effort to gain independence from a multinational empire, or at least autonomy, was part of a much more widespread trend of the period, ranging from the call for home rule in Ireland, to the demands for autonomy on the part of the Basques and Catalans in Spain, to the nationalist agitation among the Polish subjects of the German Empire (to a lesser extent its French, Danish and Lithuanian subjects as well), to the many nationalist movements in the Austro-Hungarian and Ottoman Empires.

Looking to the far north of Europe, this secessionist imperative was also apparent in one of the more overlooked events of the turbulent years at the beginning of the twentieth century, the creation of an independent Norway in 1905. Since 1814 an autonomous part of the Swedish kingdom, with its own parliament and constitution, the increasingly left-wing Norwegian body politic had, by the 1890s, come into continuous conflict with a conservative Swedish regime. The movement for full Norwegian independence, a coalition between a largely peasant-based radical party, a small but growing socialist labour movement, and a more urban and bourgeois group of political liberals, finally achieved its goal at the same time as the Russian Revolution, but through amiable agreement with a Swedish monarchy, whose leaders were not all that sad about seeing the kingdom's Norwegian subjects go. This drastic but peaceful resolution of major political issues would set a precedent for much of the politics of the Scandinavian countries in the twentieth century, but against the backdrop of continent-wide nationalist agitation, particularly in the Russian Revolution occurring in the same year, it can be seen as one more example of the rupture in political life and the turn to new directions characteristic of the initial years of the twentieth century. Certainly, contemporaries understood it that way. Nationalists in the Hungarian parliament, for instance, demanded the dissolution of the union of Austria and Hungary to cries of 'Norway for ever!'

A PLETHORA OF CONFLICTS: THE DECADE BEFORE THE OUTBREAK OF THE FIRST WORLD WAR

In some ways, both the European domestic political systems and the system of relationships between the Great Powers became overloaded with conflicts in the ten or so years before the First World War. Perhaps either of these sets of conflicts could have been managed – and some of Europe's smaller powers, including the

Scandinavian and Benelux countries, Switzerland and Spain seemed able to manage domestic political clashes – but their combination, in particular the intersection of nationalist hostility to multinational empires with the Eastern Question, and the promotion of militarism and a bellicose foreign policy by the forces of the political right, ended up in a great European and worldwide war.

Looking at the domestic political situation, we can point to three separate models among the Great Powers, with parallel trends in Europe's smaller states. One was the confrontation between a liberal–labour alliance, calling for social and economic reforms – and the political changes needed to implement them – and a hard-pressed but determined conservative grouping, with the reformers leading the government in Great Britain, and opposing the government in Germany. Domestic politics in pre-1914 Sweden might fit this model as well, as would developments in the Low Countries. A contrasting version might be called the Mediterranean option, seen in France, Italy and Spain, where such a liberal–labour alliance aiming at social and economic reform was never quite able to reach its potential. The final version of domestic politics, typical of the Austro-Hungarian and Russian Empires, involved governments and political movements each seeking their own version of changes and reforms, but with little cooperation and much hostility between the two.

The Liberal government in Great Britain, having won a landslide victory in the general election of 1906, found it difficult to get its reform proposals enacted into law, even though it enjoyed an overwhelming majority in the House of Commons, because the Tories used their powerful position in the House of Lords to block liberal legislative initiatives – a policy the Conservatives had already used very successfully against Gladstone's Liberal ministries in the 1880s and early 1890s. The response to this tactic, less from the colourless prime ministers Henry Campbell-Bannerman (1836–1908) and his successor Herbert Asquith (1852–1928), than from the clever and energetic chancellor of the exchequer David Lloyd George (1863–1945), was to link social reforms, rearmament and tax policy together, proposing to pay for the necessary expenditures in his 'People's Budget' of 1909, by sharply increasing the tax on landed property. Such a tax would fall primarily on pro-Tory large landowners not on the financial, commercial and industrial interests who continued to support the Liberals, or on the working-class adherents of the Liberals' Labour allies.

The Tory-dominated House of Lords rejected the finance bill, violating a long-standing tradition of never doing so, sparking, as Lloyd George had hoped, a constitutional confrontation. In new elections, called on this issue in 1910, Liberals and their Labour allies retained their majority and sent the new financial proposal back to the Lords. A substantial group of Tories wanted to reject the law again and create a constitutional crisis, but at the very last moment more moderate figures prevailed and the budget became law. The government then followed up on its victory by generalizing it with the Parliament Act, which eliminated the Lords' power to reject any bill passed by the Commons; at most, the Peers could delay its passage by three years. There followed the Lords' rejection and another dissolution and election campaign at the end of 1910, with about the same result. Once again, the disputed bill reached the Lords, but this time the matter was resolved when the new monarch, George V (1865–1936), made it known that if the Lords rejected the law, he would create as many new peers as necessary to pass it. The Liberals and their Labour allies seemed to have carried the day, albeit narrowly and with extraordinary effort, and they followed up their victory with the creation of a new, more elaborate social insurance system in 1911, the only new creation of its kind in pre-1914 Europe.

These reforming victories had a nationalist Achilles heel: the demand of the Liberals' Irish nationalist allies for home rule, a cause that had doomed Gladstone's Liberal governments two decades earlier. Following the 1910 elections, the Liberals were dependent for a parliamentary majority on the Irish Nationalists, so they put forth and passed a Home Rule Bill, that was promptly suspended by the Conservative-dominated Lords for three years. The Tories used the interval to campaign vigorously against the idea of autonomy for Ireland, certainly in England, but also among the large Protestant population in Ulster. The latter formed their own militia to oppose the government's plans, which was soon heavily armed and enjoyed the open sympathy of most Tory MPs and of leading army officers, who refused orders to disarm what was, in effect, a group of potential insurgents. The Conservative opposition was toying with the idea of armed resistance to the government.

If the Liberals were facing vehement opposition to their programme on the right, their left was also no longer entirely secure. The enormous strikes of 1911–13, involving millions of workers, clashes with strike-breakers, with the police and even the army, threatened to sever the political link between free-trading businessmen and organized labour, on which the Liberal government had been based. At the same time, the feminist campaign for women's suffrage was reaching a new height, whether in militant feminists' violent demonstrations or in more moderate ones' persistent lobbying of the Liberal government and parliamentarians. It is certainly true that advocates of these three different forms of opposition to the Liberal government were generally opposed to each other, so they could not combine their forces against it, but by 1912–14 the ability of the Liberal government to govern effectively, or to govern at all, was coming into question.

The situation in Germany during this time has a number of important similarities with that in Great Britain, in particular the creation of an alliance between elements of labour and business against politically conservative groupings, dominated by noble large landowners. The German chancellor Bernhard von Bülow had been determined to avoid such a development, but the coalition of liberal and conservative parties behind the government's imperialist policies and its naval arms race collapsed in 1908–09 when it became necessary to raise taxes to pay for them. Conservatives and the (Catholic) Centre Party supported taxes on basic consumer necessities, including beer, as well as taxes on financial activities, stock transfers and payments by cheque. Their financial solution was the exact opposite of Lloyd George's 'People's Budget', proposed at the same time. Bülow resigned at this rejection of his policy, and his successor as head of government, Theobald von Bethmann-Hollweg (1856–1921), tried to reconcile the different and opposing demands of political parties (at least the non-socialist ones), special-interest groups and branches of the armed forces.

Bethmann-Hollweg's task was not made any easier by the responses to the tax increases. Many businessmen were outraged and were even willing to consider supporting a British-style anti-landed property alliance between free-trading (or, in the German case, less protectionist) capitalists and a socialist labour movement. The liberal parties, largely financed by business interest groups, generally went along with this plan. In the general elections of 1912, this alliance scored a strong victory – its message for the voters helped along by a surge in sausage prices on the eve of the polling – although, unlike in Great Britain, it was the Social Democrats of the labour movement who were the big winners, with the liberals trailing behind. Since Germany did not have a parliamentary system of government, Chancellor Bethmann-Hollweg remained in office, but to get the budget through the German parliament, he had to make concessions to the opposition. Germany's enormous naval and land arms build-up was financed in 1913 by a capital levy, a one-time tax on all property.

As in Great Britain, there was increasing labour unrest in pre-1914 Germany, especially the great strike of the coal miners of the Ruhr Basin in 1912, with their clashes between strikers and strike-breakers and the use of troops to restore order. The relatively few German feminists were unable to match their British counterparts, but the political right in Germany was eminently capable of taking strong, potentially extra-legal action. Following the Social Democrats' election victory of 1912, proposals for a coup and the abolition of universal manhood suffrage made the rounds. Special-interest groups vehemently defended protectionism, support for agriculture and opposed any additional social welfare legislation. The unprecedented financial decisions of 1913 only increased the discontent of the special-interest groups, and the opinion spread among Germany's right-of-centre politicians, the activists in its nationalist leagues, among the aristocracy, the army officer corps and the upper ranks of state officials that Chancellor Bethmann-Hollweg and his government was not conservative enough – that the right needed to form a 'national opposition' to the government.

Both within this opposition and among the ranks of the government's supporters, the feeling grew that the best way out of domestic political difficulties would be a 'brisk, free war', as one Conservative journalist asserted, following the Social Democrats' election victory in 1912.[27] Just as Bismarck had defeated the liberal opposition in the 1860s by his successful wars with Denmark, Austria and France, so Germany's leaders at the beginning of the twentieth century – as a group, intensely conscious of Bismarckian precedents – would need a similar triumph. This domestic impetus towards war, combined with the strategic realignments produced by the arms race, would weigh heavily on decisions in the summer of 1914.

In some ways, the advocacy of a more bellicose and warlike foreign policy was also the result of domestic political controversies and frustrated reform hopes in France and Italy. The left-of-centre French government elected in 1902 took vigorous, if at times misdirected, action to safeguard the republic. Following the revelations in the Dreyfus Affair of widespread hostility to the republic among the officer corps, army officers were vetted for their political reliability – although there was considerable embarrassment when it was revealed that the government was depending on secret reports from members of Masonic lodges in order to do so. France's republicans had always been suspicious of the Catholic Church and the behaviour of some parts of the church, particularly the religious order of the Assumptionists, in the leading ranks of opponents of the government during the Dreyfus Affair, gave new life to their suspicions. Blaming the whole church for actions and ideas of just one part of it, the government resolved to undo Napoleon's post-revolutionary settlement of church–state relations by abolishing the Concordat, the treaty between France and the Vatican, and separating church and state.

This was not necessarily an exclusively anti-clerical measure. Following separation, the government would no longer offer financial support to the church, but it would also renounce its right to appoint the clergy. However, the Radical government, the Vatican and the French episcopal hierarchy – the latter caught between the Pope and the government – approached the proposal in a spirit of hostility. The government claimed that church buildings and all their furnishings were state property. It sent around commissioners to inventory the churches, which brought out large crowds of angry Catholics, particularly devout women, to mock, taunt and even assault the officials who seemed to be determined to confiscate the crucifixes and altar decorations as belonging to the government. However, the church also refused the government's proposals for a devolution of property on to an independent church, aggravating an already tense situation.

In the end, church and state were separated, and the general elections of 1906 resulted in a large victory for the anti-clerical Radicals and a smaller one for the socialists who had generally supported them. A logical next step for this centre-left government would have been the move from political to social reform. Events reinforced such a conclusion, the surge of strike activity in 1906 and the massive, riotous demonstrations of winegrowers in southern France the following year, suggesting the need for some tinkering with the existing economic and social order.

Changes in political personnel seemed to provide the ideal person for the role, with the election of Georges Clemenceau (1841–1929) as prime minister in late 1906. Although today mostly remembered as the politician who led France to victory in the First World War, Clemenceau was seen at the time as a figure of the radical left, the man whom the nineteenth-century communist revolutionary Auguste Blanqui had personally chosen as his successor. Yet Clemenceau, in the course of his long (by standards of the French Third Republic) premiership, from 1906 to 1909, sponsored no social reforms. His response to large-scale strikes was to arrest union leaders and to call out the army to shoot at strikers. For the CGT, the French trade union federation, Clemenceau's was the 'government of assassins'.

On closer examination, what was occurring under the prime minister, and continuing in the five years between the fall of his government and the outbreak of the First World War, was a growing difference of opinion within the Radical Party, the left–liberal grouping formed in the wake of the Dreyfus Affair and dominant in French politics from then until 1914. Some Radicals, like their liberal counterparts in Great Britain and Germany, were interested in social reforms, implemented in conjunction with the socialists – which, in the French context, meant the introduction of an income tax to provide a more equitable distribution of the burdens of government finance, and the beginning of a social insurance system. Others, like a minority of their British and German counterparts, opposed this idea, and, supported by business special-interest groups, such as the Committee for Fiscal Study and Defence, which united pro-business and anti-tax interests, and in alliance with more conservative political forces, denounced financial and social reforms as a threat to property.

After about 1910, differences on social and economic policy were increasingly linked to foreign policy positions, with the adherents of reform calling for a peaceful foreign policy and cooperation with, or at least not hostility towards, Germany, while the opponents of reform were aligned with the 'national reawakening', which advocated a build-up of the French armed forces, offensive military planning and a foreign policy aiming at confrontation with the Germans. French politics swung back and forth on these two related issues, with the expansion of the army by the increase in the term of military service from two years to three in 1913, a victory for the right. The socialist triumph in the 1914 elections, though, heralded a swing to the left, and the leader of the pro-reform and anti-militarist wing of the Radical Party, Joseph Caillaux (1863–1944), was about to be named prime minister, when a sex scandal – Caillaux's wife shooting the editor of a right-wing newspaper who had published some of her husband's love letters – kept him out of office on the very eve of the outbreak of the First World War.

The development of Italian politics shows what might have been the fate of a reforming coalition in France, had Caillaux not run into personal problems. The liberal Giovanni Giolitti who had dominated Italian politics from the beginning of the twentieth century to the outbreak of the First World War, with his policy of balancing off the socialists, republicans and radicals to his left, and the nascent Christian Democratic movement to his right, found this task steadily more difficult as the introduction of universal manhood suffrage led to a decline in the number of liberal deputies and a rise in socialist and Catholic representatives. Growing labour strife and waves of strikes strengthened both the socialist party and its radical wing. Slowing economic growth after the 1907 recession, with the consequent drop in tax revenues, unbalanced the state budget and offered unpleasant choices about state finance, which Giolitti temporarily evaded by expanding government borrowing. Italy's participation in the European arms race, and its new imperialist enterprise – the seizure of Libya from the Ottoman Empire in 1911 – strained relations between Giolitti's liberals and his potential partners on the left, although it did offer his government the possibility of support from the Nationalists, the Italian version of right-wing radicalism.

Yet for all the ambivalent results of reform coalitions and reform processes in the Mediterranean world, the political situation there seemed much more workable than in either the Austro-Hungarian or the Russian Empire. In the former, the main question was how to get the political institutions of the multinational empire to function, in view of the growing militancy of the nationalist movements. The government of Austria was quite unable to get any parliamentary majorities to support it, or even, much of the time, to have a functioning parliament, in view of the disruptive tactics of nationalist deputies, so the prime minister had increasing recourse to rule by decree. By contrast, parliamentary institutions in Hungary functioned quite normally, although the liberals and Magyar nationalists who dominated the Hungarian parliament were moving increasingly in the direction of demanding complete independence from the empire while vigorously suppressing the anti-Magyar nationalist movements of the Croats, Serbs or Slovaks. The status quo in Austria, Hungary and the monarchy as a whole appeared increasingly unsupportable; the question was what alternatives remained.

One proposal came from the socialists, committed, in theory at least, to opposing nationalism. Their leader, Karl Renner (1870–1950), proposed to recast the monarchy as a federation of equal nationalities. It would have been odd for a monarchy, whose ruling dynasty traced its lineage back to Charlemagne, to look to the socialist labour movement for assistance, and just as odd for the socialists, with their democratic and republican sympathies, to help out the Habsburgs. In any event, the socialists were proving to be far from immune to nationalism. In 1911, the Czech socialists seceded from the Austrian Social Democratic Party, objecting to the domination of the Germans within it, to found their own socialist grouping. Socialists of other nationalities were heading in the same direction.

A more plausible source of salvation for the dynasty was in another ancient European institution, the Catholic Church. About 80 per cent of the Habsburgs' subjects were Roman Catholics; the episcopate was loyal to the dynasty, and kept that way by government policies ensuring that nationalists were not named to high church offices. Leaders of the growing Catholic political parties, admittedly organized on national lines, and often subject to nationalist temptations, were nonetheless willing to cooperate politically with each other.

There was a broader strategy of constitutional realignment accompanying this Catholic politics, known as trialism, whose chief proponent was the heir apparent to the throne, the Archduke Franz Ferdinand (1863–1914). Trialists wished to see the dual Austro-Hungarian Empire turned into a triple monarchy, by carving out a third, South Slav kingdom from Austria and Hungary. In doing so, it was hoped, Croat and Slovene nationalist movements – both possessing ties to the Catholic Church – would align with the monarchy. Of course, trialism would have done little for the nationalist demands of the Czechs, Serbs, Romanians or Ukrainians; most of all, it would have been unacceptable to the Magyar nationalists, who would have had to cede Hungarian territory to the proposed South Slav kingdom. Franz Ferdinand was well aware of potential Magyar opposition to his plans, and his reign – expected imminently, given that the emperor Franz Joseph had been born in 1830 – was to begin with the army marching into Budapest.

Franz Ferdinand was assassinated before he could succeed to the throne, so we can never known the fate of his plans. We can see the 1907 and 1911 general elections in Austria, held under universal manhood suffrage (Hungary retained its property franchise until 1918) as referenda on nationalism. With constituencies organized not just on regional but on national lines as well, to prevent elections from becoming a scene of clashes between national groups, the less nationalist Catholic-clericals and socialists did very well in 1907. But four years later, the nationalists regained much of their lost ground, and vote totals for the Catholic parties, the potential mass basis for Trialism, declined. There seemed to be no peaceful, legal way out of the travails of competing nationalisms in Europe's great multinational empire.

State and society were even further out of alignment in the Russian Empire. The prime minister Peter Stolypin, who came to power in the wake of the 1905 revolution, carried out a vigorous two-pronged policy of repression and reform. Special military tribunals he had set up to repress revolutionary activists handed down over one thousand death sentences – a modest number by the standards of the post-1914 world, but shockingly many to contemporaries. The hangman's noose became known in Russia as 'Stolypin's necktie'. A new, more restrictive franchise for elections to the Duma reduced representation of the liberal and socialist opposition to a tiny minority of the deputies. The major form of opposition was the terrorist campaign of assassinating high government officials, carried out by the Socialist Revolutionaries, one of the left-wing parties, although its terror apparatus was thoroughly infiltrated by operatives of the Tsar's secret police.

Stolypin's repression worked well; his proposed reforms, less so. If Witte, his predecessor, had turned his attention to industry, Stolypin concentrated on agriculture, where most of the Tsar's subjects still earned their living. Stolypin proposed to allow Russian peasants to withdraw from the communal system of landed property, by which villages distributed and redistributed land to farm families, and to gain private ownership of their land. This measure would give them an incentive to improve their farming and also, Stolypin hoped, turn them into conservative, property-owning subjects of the Tsar. In addition to the economic reforms, Stolypin proposed to place state administration in the hands of trained, full-time bureaucrats, rather than nobles doing the work on a voluntary basis, and move towards equality under the law for all the national and religious groups in the empire, including, especially, the Jews.

Stolypin's land reforms gained a certain amount of traction, with 20 per cent of eligible peasants participating in them by 1914 – although there was evidently still a long way to go. By contrast, his other reforms failed completely. The nobility vigorously opposed his administrative reforms as did the conservative majority in the Duma, elected, ironically, as a result of Stolypin's counter-revolutionary and repressive measures. The idea of equal rights for all subjects was even less successful, with the Tsar informing his prime minister that God would not permit him to end discrimination against the Jews. Towards the end of Stolypin's tenure, state policy began to turn more vigorously in the direction of promoting Russian nationalism, enforcing discriminatory policies against other nationalities, and stepping up anti-Semitic persecution. Even before Stolypin's assassination by revolutionary terrorists in August 1911 the reforming side of his combination of repression and reform, and with it, the last possibilities for legal and peaceful political change in the Tsar's realm, had been stymied.

It is against this backdrop of domestic political conflicts and political quandaries that we need to see the diplomatic confrontations occurring in the decade before the outbreak of the First World War. The initial confrontation was the first Moroccan crisis of 1905, whose origins lay in the French intent of gaining control over the nominally independent sultanate of Morocco. The French initiative was promptly opposed by Germany, not out of any real interest in Morocco – whose strategic importance was hard to see, and whose chief economic resource, besides a modest amount of iron ore, was sand – but as part of continental European Great Power politics. France's ally, Russia, was incapacitated by its East Asian war and revolution, so that the French would be unable to resist any German initiatives. Germany's leaders considered and rejected a pre-emptive war, but thought the threat of it would suffice.

The French government was shaken, foreign minister Théophile Delcassé, architect of the Anglo-French entente and a more anti-German foreign policy, was forced to resign, and his successor had to agree to an international conference about Morocco. But when the Algeçiras conference met at the beginning of 1906, France's ally Russia, Great Britain, and most of the other powers represented – even the Americans, foreshadowing US engagement in the First World War – lined up behind France, while Italy and Austria-Hungary, Germany's partners in the Triple Alliance, showed little enthusiasm for their ally's position. Germany's action demonstrated primarily its diplomatic isolation.

In 1908, the Eastern Question burst into the centre of the diplomatic stage once again, as a result of a military coup in the Ottoman Empire, led by officers with liberal sympathies, the Young Turks. The government of Austria-Hungary responded by formally annexing the province of Bosnia-Herzegovina, which it had ruled as a protectorate since 1878 although officially still under Ottoman sovereignty. Austria's action was at least as much domestic as international in nature. It was aimed at securing control over an area with a large Serb and Croat population, the better to repress their nationalist movements, since the potential dissolution of the Ottoman Empire set in train by the Young Turk revolution threatened both the legal status of the empire, and thus of its province of Bosnia-Herzegovina, but also encouraged nationalist agitation against multinational empires in the Balkans.

The Austrian move provoked a sharp response from Russia. This was part of long-term Russian preoccupations with the Balkans, and Russian interest in profiting from the disintegration of the Ottoman Empire as well as Russian defensiveness over the possibility of the disintegration of the Ottoman Empire and the subsequent prospects for control of the Straits. The Russian response also had a domestic element, an aggressive assertion of Russian national interest and Russian protection for its fellow Slavs in the Balkans, to reinforce the conservative government in power following the suppression of the 1905 revolution. Indeed, Prime Minister Stolypin overruled the initial steps of his minister of foreign affairs, Alexander Izvolsky (1856–1919), to negotiate with the Austrians for compensation in favour of a more aggressive policy.

Encouraged by the Russian attitude, the government of Serbia demanded compensation from the Austrians and backed up its demand by mobilizing its army in the autumn of 1908. The prospect of war in the Balkans appeared, one in which a clash between Austria-Hungary and Serbia would be met by a Russian military intervention that would, in turn, bring Germany into the war – and then France and Great Britain. This was how the First World War would begin in 1914, but in 1908 the Russian army was too weak to fight, still suffering the after-effects of its defeat in Japan and the revolutionary events of 1905–06. Russia's French ally showed little inclination to be dragged into a war over the Balkans. Russia ended up at the beginning of 1909 where Germany had been over Morocco three years earlier – lacking support even from allies, and forced to back down – which the Russians did, by recognizing the Austrian annexation.

The next major confrontation between the Powers was the Second Moroccan Crisis of 1911. It was largely a rerun of its predecessor of 1905, sparked by a further step in the process of turning Morocco into a French protectorate, in this case the occupation of the capital city by French troops. The German response involved a symbolic escalation over 1905, the sending of a gunboat to the Moroccan port of Agadir. Tensions mounted through the summer of 1911, when it seemed that the European continent was on the brink of a large-scale war – a much stronger and more widespread perception of the imminence of the outbreak of war than in 1914, when the war finally began. The outcome was largely the same as in 1905: the French received strong backing from Russia and Great Britain; Germany found little support, even from its allies. Ultimately, Germany recognized the French position in Morocco, in return for which the French ceded to the Germans a small amount of colonial territory in central Africa.

In contrast to the First Moroccan Crisis, though, the consequences of the Second would lead directly to war. Franco-British staff talks during the crisis brought forth British plans to send a land army to the continent in case of a war between France and Germany. The French right-of-centre government of the 'national reawakening' committed itself to expanding the French armed forces, implementing a plan for an offensive in case of war with Germany and lending money to the Russians for strategic railways to the German border. The General Staff in Germany realized that the current strength of the army would not suffice for a war with France and Russia and called for a large increase in troop strength.

Concluding the long train of pre-1914 crises were the two Balkan Wars of 1912–13. In the first war, the smaller Balkan monarchies of Serbia, Greece, Bulgaria and Montenegro declared war on the Ottoman Empire, and, in the space of two months, October and November 1912, crushingly defeated Ottoman armies already shaken by the Italian invasion of Libya the previous year. The smaller states' armies, particularly the Bulgarians, who did most of the fighting, conquered the Ottomans' entire European possessions and marched on Constantinople, finally being held up a few miles from the city by a desperate Turkish stand on the last lines of fortifications. The victorious allies soon fell out with each other, and in the Second Balkan War of June 1913, Greece, Montenegro and Serbia turned on the Bulgarians. Romania entered the war to seize territory from Bulgaria, and the Ottomans regained a portion of their European territory.

In the course of the two wars, especially the second, uniformed soldiers and insurgent irregulars, to say nothing of the civilian population, robbed, raped and murdered enemy civilians. These prosecutions became increasingly systematic, resembling what in a later conflict of the region would be called ethnic cleansing. The Balkan Wars were the showcase of a radical nationalism which saw no way to deal with other nationalities other than to murder or expel them, a distinct precursor of a genocidal twentieth century.

The wars and their outcome were a shock to the Great Powers, although the different powers felt this shock quite differently. France scored a proxy victory and Germany suffered a proxy defeat, since the victorious armies used French weapons and had been trained by French military instructors, against the German-sponsored Ottomans and Bulgarians. While the wars were a victory of countries and causes the Russian government had been supporting for decades, the outcome of the war was also a threat, as it suggested the imminent dissolution of the Ottoman Empire and some other power gaining control of the Straits.

But the biggest loser of the war was unquestionably the government of Austria-Hungary. The defeat of the Ottomans by a coalition of smaller Balkan powers raised the unpleasant prospect of a similar war against the Habsburgs' empire. The way these Balkan nation-states had sponsored and encouraged demands of their fellow nationals for the dissolution of a multinational empire would encourage nationalist movements in the Austro-Hungarian Empire, especially those that could look to a neighbouring nation-state for assistance, to redouble their efforts. Habsburg responses to this threat focused on the Kingdom of Serbia, the patron of Serb nationalists in both the Ottoman and Austro-Hungarian Empires. Yet an increased Russian assertiveness, backed up by the more aggressive policy of Russia's French ally, prevented the government of Austria-Hungary from intimidating Serbia as it had during the Bosnian annexation crisis of 1908. After complicated negotiations, the

The Balkan Wars
Source: From *THE MAKING OF THE WEST 3E* by Lynn Hunt et al., Copyright © 2009 by Bedford/
St. Martin's. Reproduced by permission of Bedford/St. Martin's.

Austro-Hungarian government was able to salvage an extremely modest diplomatic success by the end of 1913, the creation of an independent Albania from former Ottoman territories, instead of their incorporation into Serbia and Greece.

The crisis that brought about the First World War proceeded directly from the situation created by the Balkan Wars, and in fact just three-and-a-half months after

BOX 21.2

Ethnic cleansing during the Balkan Wars

Complaints about atrocities committed in the course of the Balkan Wars inspired the New York-based and recently founded Carnegie Endowment for International Peace, an early non-governmental organization, to send an international commission to investigate the situation in 1913. In spite of attempts on the part of the Balkan governments to hinder or prevent the commission's work, its report revealed not just atrocities but the nationalist attitudes and state planning behind them.

During the First Balkan War, the chief victims were the Muslim population, generally described as 'Turks', regardless of their ethnic affiliation – a good example of the transformation of religious hostilities into nationalist ones. The Muslims of Kosovo, Albania, Macedonia and Thrace suffered physical assaults, robbery, arson, rape and murder. While the perpetrators of these offences were sometimes the soldiers of the invading Bulgarian, Greek or Serbian armies, these soldiers often just created the conditions in which others – revolutionary insurgents, such as the Bulgarian *comitadji*, the Greek *andarte* or the Serbian *voyévoda* – carried out the assaults. In ethnically mixed villages, ordinary civilians often joined in the attacks on the 'Turks'. When the tide of war turned, as happened in Thrace, reoccupied by Ottoman forces during the Second Balkan War, the former victims got their revenge. Here as well, it was sometimes Ottoman soldiers responsible for the actions, and sometimes the irregularly organized Arab and Kurdish cavalry, a group responsible for the Bulgarian massacres of 1878, as well as civilian Islamic villagers.

During the Second Balkan War, the formerly allied Bulgarians on the one hand, and the Greeks and Serbs on the other, turned against each other. The major object of their conflict was control of Macedonia. It was at this point that the atrocities entered a new stage. The previous forms of assault, theft, rape and murder continued, but this time with a clearer degree of organization and control on the part of the occupying armed forces, with the purpose of systematically expelling members of enemy nationalities – Bulgarians from Greek- and Serb-controlled territories, Greeks from Bulgarian-controlled ones. Dozens of villages were burnt down to ensure that expelled populations could not return. Thousands of civilians were killed and hundreds of thousands turned into refugees. The combatant nations began to organize propaganda about these events, exaggerating the atrocities committed against their civilians, and denouncing as false atrocity stories any claims of atrocities committed by their forces.

The Balkan Wars saw the transmutation of religious into nationalist hostilities, the application of radical nationalist ideas, the use of government power to create an ethnically unitary state – all via large-scale assault, theft, rape and murder. These features of the conflict would be repeated over and again in twentieth-century Europe and the Near East – in the massacre of the Armenians of the Ottoman Empire during the First World War (some of the perpetrators were Muslim refugees from the Balkans), in the civil wars that raged in the former Russian and Ottoman Empires in the aftermath of the First World War, in the policies of the Nazis during the Second World War in German-occupied eastern Europe, in the expulsion of the ethnic Germans from eastern Europe after 1945, and in the former Yugoslavia during the 1990s.

the final treaty was signed, ending those wars. It was brought on by the assassination of Archduke Franz Ferdinand, heir to the Habsburg throne, while he was on an official visit to the Bosnian capital of Sarajevo on 28 June 1914. The assassin, Gavrilo Princip (1894–1918), and his co-conspirators, who were quickly arrested by the police, were Bosnian Serb nationalists aspiring to unite the province of Bosnia-Herzegovina with the Kingdom of Serbia. Their nationalist association, Young Bosnia, had received weapons, money and instructions from officers of the army of Serbia – although apparently not from the Serb government, which the army officers opposed as insufficiently nationalist.

These details were less important to the rulers of Austria-Hungary, who, following the shock administered by the Balkan Wars, were determined to end the nationalist menace – a menace, one should remember, that was coming at least as much from inside the monarchy as from without – once and for all. Their plan was to issue an ultimatum to the Kingdom of Serbia concerning the assassination, couching it in such strong language that it would have to be rejected, and the rejection would then be a cause for war. Planning a war against Serbia, though, required dealing with the possibility, already evident during the Balkan Wars, of a Russian intervention in support of the Serbs. Fighting both the Serbs and the Russians was more than the Habsburgs' army could accomplish; any attack on Serbia would require the permission and cooperation of Austria-Hungary's German ally.

In negotiations occurring in Berlin at the beginning of July 1914, Germany's leadership – the emperor personally, his chancellor and the top generals – were unanimous in encouraging the Austrians to go ahead. By taking such a position, the German government was demonstrating its willingness to fight the Russians, should they intervene against Austria-Hungary. Since German war plans called for a conflict with Russia to begin with an invasion of France, the consent to the Austrian plans to attack Serbia was endorsing the possibility of the escalation of a regional conflict in the Balkans into a great European war, on a scale that had not been seen since the days of Napoleon, a century previously.

The German endorsement of the Austrians' plans was the central turning point in the crisis of July 1914, the one decision more than any other that led to the First World War. It involved taking a chance on a major war, when the situation still seemed favourable, with Germany, for the moment, ahead of France and Russia in the land arms race, but the future more doubtful, both in view of the Russian plans to build strategic railways and also in view of the growing political strains of financing a further arms build-up, given the strong position of the opposition in the German parliament. Germany's leaders did not plan on a major war; they hoped that the Russians would back down, as they had in 1909, and allow Austria to defeat Serbia and so gain a major diplomatic victory from a limited war in the Balkans. But if it did come to a great European war, they thought, then the summer of 1914 was the time to fight it.

The Austro-Hungarian ultimatum to Serbia appeared on 22 July; a partial acceptance by the government of Serbia did not prevent the Austrians from going to war, with the official declaration on 28 July followed by an artillery bombardment of the Serb capital Belgrade. The ball was now in Russia's court, and the Russian government was forced to decide, largely lacking the ability to consult with its French ally. The French president and prime minister had just left St Petersburg after a state visit, and, following the ultimatum, were quite literally, at sea, unable to use the primitive wireless apparatus at their disposal to receive the news or to issue any orders. The Austrian ultimatum had been issued on that particular day precisely in order to confound the Russians and the French.

Nonetheless, the Tsar's government took the decision to support the Serbs, accepting the possibility of a war with both Austria-Hungary and Germany. Although unhappy about the idea of going to war with an only partially prepared army and a turbulent situation at home, the Russian leaders believed that allowing Serbia to be destroyed would end Russian influence in the Balkans and promote Austrian and German domination of the Straits. This outcome would, as the Russian ambassador in Constantinople put it, 'result in the total destruction of our prestige and our position in the Near East'.[28]

Once this Russian attitude became known, and the Russian armed forces were mobilized at the end of July, the German government had no choice but to attack France. Any delay would endanger its military plan of using the bulk of the German army to defeat the French while the Russians were still mobilizing their forces. The French were thus dragged into the war by the decisions of the other Great Powers – not unwillingly, it must be said, since the French government was firmly committed to its alliance with Russia, and to taking the offensive against the Germans in the event of war – but still, of all the Great Powers during the July crisis of 1914, France was the one with the least influence on the course of events.

The German declaration of war on Russia and invasion of France, both occurring on 1 August, were the beginning of a great, continental European war. It would become a world war only with the intervention of the worldwide British Empire. Unlike Austria-Hungary, Germany, Russia or France, Britain had no formal treaty commitments to come to the aid of an attacked ally. These legal matters were reinforced by some practical problems. During July, the British government was fully occupied with the domestic situation, especially the imminent civil war in northern Ireland, so its response to the growing crisis on the continent was to bombard all the parties involved with proposals for mediation and for international conferences. When it became clear both that war was going to break out and that it would involve a German invasion of France through Belgium, the British government issued an ultimatum to the Germans, stating that such an invasion would mean war.

The formal legal reason for the British action was the violation of Belgian neutrality, to which all the Powers of Europe had agreed in 1839. This was certainly a useful pretext and would prove to be an even more useful propaganda point among the neutral powers, especially the United States, once the war had broken out. But it was primarily a pretext. A British government, even a reforming Liberal one, with

Labour support and quite a few pacifists in its ranks, increasingly concerned about growing German economic and maritime strength, whose military planning had, for a decade, seen Germany as the chief rival, could hardly stand aside and let Germany conquer Belgium, defeat France and gain a dominant position in western Europe.

Germany's leaders, in taking into account the prospect of war with France and Russia, had hoped that Great Britain would remain neutral, and the British ultimatum was a shock, causing Germany's chancellor Bethmann-Hollweg to take a few half-hearted steps in the direction of trying to call off the war at the last minute. Neither the emperor nor the generals would accept this move, and German military planning for war with France required the invasion of Belgium, so the British ultimatum had no effect on Germany's military actions. Consequently, on 4 August, the British parliament voted a declaration of war, and with this commitment of the British Empire to the conflict, the First World War had begun.

BOX 21.3

Historians debate the origins of the First World War

The debate over the origins of the First World War began during the war itself, as governments of all the combatant nations published collections of diplomatic documents designed to prove that they had acted to preserve the peace and that their enemies were the aggressors responsible for the conflict. The end of hostilities only escalated this clash of views, since the 1919 peace treaty of Versailles included Article 231, the 'war guilt clause', asserting the responsibility of the Kaiser's German government for the outbreak of the war. Trying to revise the terms of the peace treaty, the republican government of Germany, emerging from the overthrow of the Kaiser in 1918, nonetheless defended the 1914 actions of the Kaiser's government, creating a special 'war guilt' desk in the foreign office to deal with the question. The German government enlisted historians in this campaign, appointing them to edit a fifty-volume collection of German diplomatic documents, which would prove their country's innocence. The British and French governments responded by assigning historians to edit their own multi-volume collection of diplomatic papers, which would reinforce the assertions of Article 231. There was a similar collection of Russian documents published by the communist government of the USSR, but this revolutionary regime emerging from the First World War, unlike its German counterpart, attacked the actions of its predecessor; its documents aimed to show the responsibility of the Tsar's government for the outbreak of the war.

Academic histories of the 1920s and 1930s followed the arguments of the different governments. Some historians placed the blame for the outbreak of the war on Germany and its ally, Austria-Hungary, while others, the 'revisionists', saw Russia and France as the aggressive parties, or blamed Great Britain for not making its position known until it was too late to deter the outbreak of the war. Mostly, these differences of opinion followed the wartime alliances, except that in the United States, a latecomer

Box 21.3 continued

to the anti-German cause, the revisionist case became increasingly influential, among academic historians and public opinion more generally. In spite of these opposing interpretations, a gradual consensus began to emerge, dominating historians' opinions from the 1930s through much of the 1950s, that all the Great Powers bore an equal share of responsibility for the outbreak of the war.

This dominant viewpoint began to change, at first gradually, with the publication in 1953 of Luigi Albertini's three-volume work on the origins of the First World War. An Italian politician opposed to Mussolini's fascist government, Albertini had had to retire from public life, and thus had ample time to study the topic. Basing his research on the many published documents, he suggested that the governments of Austria-Hungary and Germany bore the primary responsibility for the outbreak of the war. Then, the West German historian Fritz Fischer, in the course of a study of German war aims, came across many unpublished documents demonstrating the aggressive stance of the German government in the summer of 1914 and before. Fischer's views, first published in 1959, struck like the proverbial bombshell, and he was widely denounced by his fellow West German historians and in the press. The West German foreign office even revoked the funding he had received for a lecture tour in the United States to explain his theses.

In the end, the ideas of Albertini and Fischer have generally carried the day. While not denying the potentially aggressive policies of France or Russia, Serbian complicity in the terrorist plot to assassinate the Archduke Franz Ferdinand, or the ambivalent attitude of the British government during the July crisis of 1914, it now seems clear that the decisions taken by the political and military leadership of Austria-Hungary and Germany were decisive in leading to war – and to a great, worldwide war. Historians still debate the extent to which these decisions were taken from aggressive or defensive attitudes, but their central importance for the outbreak of the war seems well established.

Quite in contrast to the summer of 1911, when the threat of war in the wake of the Second Moroccan Crisis had been tangible and oppressive, the crisis of July 1914 was completely out of public view until the Austrian ultimatum to Serbia towards the end of the month, after which events moved very quickly and the public became ever more informed. Europe's socialists, as they had previously proclaimed, made an effort to stop the war in the last week of July. They called anti-war demonstrations with tens of thousands of participants in major cities; the executive bureau of the Socialist International summoned leaders of the labour movement to its headquarters in Brussels to consider joint action. Socialist leaders, though, knew that their proclaimed threat of a general strike to stop the war was a hollow one, and they were painfully aware that their governments were planning to arrest them at the outbreak of the war. Prominent union activists of the French CGT went into hiding; the leaders of the German Social Democrats sent the party treasury to Switzerland to keep it out of the authorities' hands. In the end, governments decided to gain the cooperation of the labour movement at the outbreak of war, rather than repressing it, and by the end of July the labour movement in each of the future combatant nations was increasingly aligned with its government, each perceiving its country as the victim of foreign aggression in need of defence.

The failure of the socialists to stop the war is usually told as part of a story about the wave of nationalist excitement sweeping across Europe at the end of July and the beginning of August 1914. The images of cheering crowds waving flags and singing the national anthems, throwing flowers at soldiers, and young women kissing them as they marched to the front have long been a set piece in the account of the outbreak of the First World War. In recent years, historians, digging deeper and reading more carefully contemporary journalism, police reports on public opinion and memoirs and recollections, especially those written soon after the events, have drawn a somewhat different picture. The enthusiastic demonstrations took place in business districts and affluent neighbourhoods, with students and other well-off young men playing a particularly prominent role. Similar manifestations of nationalist and pro-war sentiment in working-class areas or, especially, in the countryside were lacking. When posters were put up proclaiming the mobilization of the reserves, a sign of the imminent outbreak of war, the response was shock, fright and – particularly on the part of women – a lot of public tears. This response gave way to resignation and then, as the soldiers marched to the front, a feeling of reluctant necessity. At the beginning of August 1914 many Europeans – ironically, the less educated rather than the better educated ones – had a greater sense of foreboding about the future than most accounts might suggest.

The outbreak of the First World War was the culmination of many of the main features of political life in the age of classical modernism, although perhaps features whose expression took on contradictory form: both the rise of intransigent nationalism and the attempt to hold off the consequences of this nationalism; the creation of mass politics and a refusal to allow the masses their own political voice; the expansion of European power in the world and the beginning of a rejection of that power; the shifts in economic, political and military power among the European states, and the attempts to undo the consequences of these shifts in power. Particularly after about 1900, these developments were perceptible across all of continental Europe, the British Isles and, to some extent, just about the entire world. Their storm centre, though, was in the great realms of central, eastern and south-eastern Europe, in the German, Austro-Hungarian, Russian and Ottoman Empires, and it was from there that the tensions emanated which ultimately burst out into a global war.

NOTES TO PART 3

1 Figures from Wilfried Feldenkirchen, *Die Eisen- und Stahlindustrie des Ruhrgebiets 1879–1914* (Wiesbaden, 1982), table 125a.
2 Cited in Vera Zamagni, *The Economic History of Italy 1860–1990* (Oxford, 1993), 93.
3 Figures from ibid., 65.
4 Friedrich Lenger, *Sozialgeschichte der deutschen Handwerker seit 1800* (Frankfurt, 1988), 115.
5 Cited in ibid., 142.
6 Figures from Robert Gellately, *Politics of Economic Despair: Shopkeepers and German Politics, 1890–1914* (London, 1974), 30–1, and Christophe Charle, *Social History of France in the Nineteenth Century*, trans. Miriam Kochan (Oxford, 1994), 141.
7 Figures from Kevin H. O'Rourke and Jeffrey G. Williamson, *Globalization and History: The Evolution of a Nineteenth-Century Atlantic Economy* (Cambridge, MA, 1999), 30.
8 Figures from Gerhard A. Ritter and Klaus Tenfelde, *Arbeiter im Deutschen Kaiserreich 1871 bis 1914* (Bonn, 1992), 167.
9 Figures from Jürgen Kocka, *Industrial Culture and Bourgeois Society: Business, Labor and Bureaucracy in Modern Germany*, trans. Belinda Cooper, Luise von Floto and Jeremiah Riemer (New York, 1999), 39.
10 Figures from Lenard Berlanstein, *The Working People of Paris, 1871–1914* (Baltimore, MD, 1984).
11 Cited in Andrew Lees, *Cities Perceived: Urban Society in European and American Thought, 1820–1940* (New York, 1985), 158.
12 Cited in Michael F. Hamm, Introduction, in Hamm (ed.), *The City in Late Imperial Russia* (Bloomington, IN, 1986), 4.
13 Figures taken from Claire E. Nolte, *The Sokol in the Czech Lands to 1914: Training for the Nation* (New York, 2002), 165–9, 185.
14 Figures from Simon Cordery, *British Friendly Societies, 1750–1914* (Basingstoke, 2003), 149.
15 James Chapman, *Cinemas of the World: Film and Society from 1895 to the Present* (London, 2003), 65.
16 Cited in Susan Quinn, *Marie Curie: A Life* (New York, 1995), 198.
17 Cited in H. Stuart Hughes, *Consciousness and Society: The Reorientation of European Social Thought 1890–1930* (New York, 1958), 285.
18 Cited in Paul Wood (ed.), *The Challenge of the Avant-Garde* (New Haven, CT, 1999), 200.
19 Cited in Christopher Butler, *Early Modernism: Literature, Music and Painting in Europe, 1900–1916* (Oxford, 1994), 167.
20 Quoted in ibid., 35.
21 Cited in Pam Meecham and Julie Sheldon, *Modern Art: A Critical Introduction*, 2nd edn (London, 2005), 57.

22 Quoted in Jeffrey Weiss, *The Popular Culture of Modern Art: Picasso, Duchamp, and Avant-Gardism* (New Haven, CT, 1994), 96.

23 Cited in Martin Pugh, *The Tories and the People 1880–1935* (Oxford, 1985), 157.

24 Cited in Alexander De Grand, *The Hunchback's Tailor: Giovanni Giolitti and Liberal Italy* (Westport, CT, 2001), 116.

25 Cited in Duncan Tanner, *Political Change and the Labour Party 1900–1918* (Cambridge, 1990).

26 Cited in Paul Kennedy, *The Rise of Anglo-German Antagonism 1860–1914* (London, 1980), 227.

27 Quoted in Dirk Stegmann, *Die Erben Bismarcks* (Cologne, 1970), 280.

28 Cited in D. C. B. Lieven, *Russia and the Origins of the First World War* (New York, 1983), 147.

CONCLUSION

INTRODUCTION

Trying to draw conclusions about sixty-five years of history and an entire continent, whose countries, by *c.*1900, counted some 400 million inhabitants, living in very diverse conditions, is dubious business. Still, at the end of a text filled with details and specific arguments, it might be helpful to tease out some general lines of development and look at points of continuity and discontinuity. To do this, we will first consider main trends, in economy, society, culture, science, politics and international relations, between the mid-nineteenth century and the outbreak of the First World War, also commenting on times and places which were exceptions to these trends. This will be followed by a look at years 1850 to 1914 in comparison with their predecessor, the revolutionary epoch of 1780–1850, and their successor, the twentieth century age of total war, 1914–45, enabling us to see how intervening decades formed a distinct period of European history, and the ways that they blended in with times before and after.

ECONOMIC AND SOCIAL PROGRESS

Arguably, economic developments were crucial to all other aspects of the years 1850 to 1914. The expansion of total output of goods and services, and the broadening and diversification of this output were the key features of the era. We generally describe this development as the industrial revolution, and there is no question that the growth and spread of mechanized, powered, large-scale industrial production was ongoing throughout the period. Yet the importance of industry should not blind us to other crucial features: the increases in agricultural productivity, the mechanization of and improvement in transportation, the resulting growth of specialization in trade, or the innovations in finance and retailing. The intersection of all these changes produced a surge in output.

Consumption grew with production, if perhaps not quite so fast, so that standards of living were noticeably higher in 1914 than in 1850. Of course, noticeably higher does not mean high, and the cramped housing, long hours of arduous labour, modest possibilities for leisure, and low levels of sanitation and personal hygiene that characterized the lives of the large majority of the population in Europe before the First World War might not seem too impressive today. Yet both the quantity and quality of the diet, available clothing and home furnishings, the opportunities for recreation, or the condition of public health, were much superior in 1914 to those existing in the 1850s – all of which gives us an idea of the low levels of consumption enjoyed by the bulk of the population at the middle of the nineteenth century.

Looking at the structure of economic life, we can see a trend towards greater complexity, broader interconnections and larger units of production and consumption. Industry, wholesale commerce and finance led the way here, with agriculture, the crafts and retailing, if still following the trend, rather lagging behind, preserving smaller, simpler units of production and existing in smaller worlds of interaction. Everywhere, market relations grew in scope and became more prevalent. The efforts to limit and regulate and shape markets, apparent from the 1870s onward in the rise of protectionism and other forms of government economic intervention affirmed the ubiquity of the market.

This process of economic development was not smooth or continuous. Besides the fluctuations of the business cycle, there seem to have been longer periods (20–25 years) of faster or slower economic growth, with a mediocre stretch from some point in the first half of the 1870s to some point in the first half of the 1890s between two periods of greater vigour. Perhaps the single most important reason for these long-run changes was cycles of implementation of previous technological innovations. The earlier phase of prosperity saw the wide spread of the steam engine and associated forms of manufacturing and transportation, while the later one was associated with the new leading sectors of the second industrial revolution.

Turning from the distribution of economic growth over time, to its distribution over space, at the beginning of our period Great Britain stood alone as the 'workshop of the world', but that sobriquet, capturing its dominant position in manufacturing, ignores its lead in just about all other aspects of the economy, including agriculture, overseas trade, retail commerce, finance and services. By the 1870s, Britain remained the wealthiest nation in Europe, but its position was now part of a broader west–east and north–south gradient of economic development, as some of the economic features it possessed almost alone in 1850 had reached portions of western, central and northern Europe. By the beginning of the twentieth century, this gradient was still in place, but the growing strength of the economy of the German Empire, particularly in steel manufacturing and the newer chemical and electrical industries, as well as increasing economic growth in some of the peripheral regions of Europe, from northern Italy, to Norway to the Donets Basin in Russia, was beginning to scramble the picture.

Two of the major developments in social structure were integrally related to those in the economy. One was the steady expansion of the proportion of the population living in urban areas over the entire 1850–1914 period. Economic growth made this urbanization possible, and the increase in urban population played an important role in spurring on economic growth. The geographic patterns of urbanization over time were very similar to those of economic development, starting with a unique condition in the British Isles, going to a west–east gradient of urbanization, and ending with a continent-wide growth in cities, still basically on a west–east pattern, albeit with central European exceptions. Contemporaries were most impressed; indeed, they were both fascinated by and morbidly attracted to the giant metropolises, whose powerful hold on the public imagination, from Baron Haussmann's Paris to Jack the Ripper's London, cannot be overstated. The growth of smaller industrial cities and commercial centres, though, was equally important, whether understood in terms of the proportion of the population living in them or of their impact on people's lives.

Another main feature of social development closely related to economics was the transformation of social structure. Mid-nineteenth-century Europe was still largely a continent of small proprietors, of farmers and craftsmen, with a modestly sized professional and commercial middle class, and an elite group made up primarily of landowners. Admittedly, this situation was somewhat different at the western and eastern extremes, with a larger proportion of capitalist businessmen and industrial workers in Great Britain, which was the workshop of the world, and a substantial group of noble landlords and landless or enserfed labourers in the empires of the eastern and south-eastern reaches of the continent. By the beginning of the twentieth century, the largest group in society was the wage-earning working class, in industry, crafts and transportation, as well as in agriculture. A still somewhat larger old middle class of independent farmers, craftsmen and retailers (some of those retailers were not actually all that 'old') was set against a very dynamically expanding new middle class of salaried employees. Capitalist proprietors, whether in finance, commerce, industry or agriculture, and whether blue-blooded aristocrats or nouveaux riches parvenus, made up the bulk of the upper classes.

This development certainly does reveal the shift in the workforce away from agriculture and the crafts, towards industry and, to some extent, services, as well as the growing importance of wage or salary earners, and the declining salience of independent proprietors in the social structure. This latter trend, though, should not be exaggerated. The ostensibly independent proprietors of the mid-nineteenth century were often not so independent, under the control of money-lenders and merchants in outworking, or constrained by the guild system. At the beginning of the twentieth century, capitalist enterprises, even the largest, remained mostly individually or family owned; corporations and a class of corporate managers was still at a very early stage of development. Property ownership continued to be a central element of social structure throughout the entire 1850–1914 period.

There were two other major social trends that do not fit quite so well into the main economic ones. One was the steady increase in education and literacy across Europe from the mid-nineteenth century until the First World War. In spite of the modest increases in secondary schools and universities, this expansion was mostly about elementary education, the basic skills it provided, and, increasingly, the nationalist ideas pervading it. The second major trend was the enormous expansion of voluntary associations, which reached every corner of the continent and every aspect of social life. By the early twentieth century, these groups had become so ubiquitous that society itself appeared as a vast, complex network of associations.

It was this expansion and diversification of voluntary associations that both fuelled and reflected the changing social status of women in this period. The ability to join together, to meet publicly, to articulate a voice about the political and – especially – the social order, and women's position within it, was the largest change in women's circumstances over the period. While only taking the step from organization and activism to feminist demands for women's rights on a large scale in the British Isles, and to a lesser extent in Scandinavia, this growing ability of women to organize and to affect public life was one of the most significant results of the expansion of voluntary associations. Changes in women's position were connected to other kinds of developments, particularly the increase in women's white-collar employment and in the so-called helping professions, but the primary cause and locus of change lay in the associational world.

Population movements are an area in which economic trends, social structures and other considerations, including the position of women, intersect. Among the demographic trends, migration was most clearly affected by economics. The years 1850 to 1914 were the great age of trans-Atlantic migration, and the volume of emigration remained high throughout the period, with peaks in the 1850s, 1880s and 1900s. While emigration from the UK remained considerable down to the First World War, on the continent there was a definite shift in the locus of emigration, from west-central Europe in the mid-nineteenth century, to northern and east-central Europe in the later years of the nineteenth century, to eastern and southern Europe after 1900. Although often overshadowed by overseas emigration, migration within and between European countries was greater in extent than trans-Atlantic migrations. Such internal movements fluctuated with the business cycle, but increased over time, their rate perhaps tripling between 1850 and 1910. Always playing a crucial role in the growth of urban populations, at an earlier period such moves were usually within a 50–100 mile radius; after around 1890, population movements over longer distances became more common.

If migration patterns generally followed those of economic development and urbanization, the same cannot be said of changes in the nature of vital events. From the mid-nineteenth century until the 1880s, while birth and death rates differed considerably from country to country, within each country they remained at roughly the same levels. Then, in a Europe-wide development, both death rates and birth rates began to decline, slowly at first, but at an accelerated pace after 1900. This demographic change was linked to rising standards of living, scientific and medical advances, and progress of public hygiene, all of which brought down mortality rates, especially for infants and young children. The decline of the birth rate, though, seems less directly attributable to specific economic or technological changes, but reflects, instead, new attitudes and mentalities: a growing willingness to consider the future as something that could be planned and shaped, perhaps a growing respect and appreciation for the position of women and the difficulties in their lives.

THE ARTS AND SCIENCES TRANSFORMED

Such a substantial change occurring in a relatively short period is rather different from most of the social and economic developments discussed above, which fall into the pattern of steady – or, at least, relatively steady – growth and substantial increases over time. Yet this contrast might reflect a broader one between social and economic developments on the one hand, and intellectual and cultural ones on the other. The latter are more difficult to conceptualize in terms of steady growth, or linear increase; qualitative developments trump quantitative ones. This was certainly the case in the arts, the social sciences and the natural sciences.

There was a constant theme in the development of the arts between the mid-nineteenth century and the First World War, namely the search for new forms of artistic expression, ones that broke with past practices. Most pronounced in the visual arts and least seen in music, with literature somewhere in the middle, this search took various forms, from the realism prevalent at mid-century, to the naturalism, impressionism and musical late romanticism of the 1880s, to the many versions of modernism at the beginning of the twentieth century. The individual forms were very different – and it might be hard to view realist and cubist paintings as part of the same artistic endeavour – but the rejection of long-established models of artistic expression, some going back for centuries, was a common feature of the main artistic movements in the period.

A somewhat different intellectual process was evident in the social sciences, philosophy and other forms of academic humanistic studies, as well as in broader arenas of cultural criticism. The post-1850 era was a high point of positivism, with its commitment to empiricism, rationalism – generally of an anti-clerical variety – and ideas of progress, ideas that were only reinforced by a misunderstood version of Charles Darwin's theories. Doubts about every one of these concepts emerged on a large scale in the last quarter of the nineteenth century. The post-mid-century era of intellectual certainty succumbed to these doubts, but the doubters and critics did not ultimately have their way, either. The intellectual outcome, apparent by the 1900s, was not a victory of irrationalism, a major revival of revealed religion, or an understanding of human society as characterized by decline and decay. Rather, what emerged was a chastened positivism, one that de-linked rational analysis of human action from the assumption that human actions were rational, that took into account the emotional and psychological costs of progress, and that contained a substantial element of biologized racial thinking.

A still different pattern was apparent in the natural and physical sciences. Each went through a period of conceptual transformation – perhaps more strongly so in biology and physics than in chemistry. Both Darwin's theory of natural selection in the 1860s and the development of an understanding of the nature and action of micro-organisms in the following decade produced substantial changes in the enterprise of scientific biology – changes so substantial that scientists were still digesting them in the decades preceding the First World War. The creation of new physical theories at the beginning of the twentieth century, relativity and quantum mechanics, was an even more deep-seated conceptual transformation, whose results are still being worked out today. The conceptual development of chemistry seems more continuous, but the discoveries of the nature of chemical bonds and of Mendeleev's periodic table in the 1860s were reorienting events, if perhaps not to the extent of Darwin's or Einstein's theories.

None of these changes affected the public positions of the main branches of the sciences. Biology continued to be the science whose results had the broadest influence on intellectual life, while chemistry remained the 'big science', with the most extensive and expensive laboratories and the closest connections to industry and government. Physics continued to be a rather esoteric pursuit, although the first apprehensions of the potential influence of new developments in physics and the first ventures in seeing physicists as celebrities date to the decade before the First World War.

There was one significant change occurring over the period in scientific investigation: its increasingly close association with universities. Already very much a university enterprise in the mid-nineteenth century – particularly so for chemistry and physics, rather less in biology – scientific research developed ever closer ties to higher education over the second half of the nineteenth century, to the point that by the early twentieth century universities had become primary institutional sponsors of the practice of science, along with some government research institutes and a few large corporations, all of which maintained close ties with universities. This absorption of science into the university was also occurring in other aspects of intellectual life. One might compare, for instance, the major figures of mid-nineteenth century sociology, Comte and Spencer, both independent intellectuals who would never have considered associating themselves with higher education even if they had had the opportunity, with their early twentieth-century successors, Durkheim and Weber, both very much university-affiliated academics. In quantitative terms, the increase in the number of institutions of higher learning and the number of students enrolled in them was, at best, modest throughout the period (although accelerating after 1900); nevertheless, the ever closer connection between universities and most branches of intellectual endeavour suggests that universities had become central to the production of knowledge before they became institutions to impart this knowledge on a large scale.

THE RISE OF MASS AND (MOSTLY) LEGAL POLITICS

Turning to political life, we can point to three major trends in domestic politics: the development of constitutional government with its limitations on arbitrary political power and its creation of a legal framework for political activity and political change; the increasing perception of, support for and influence of nationalism; and the rise of institutions and activities of mass politics. Although conceptually distinct, the trends were interrelated. When two or more trends went in the same direction, their effects were multiplied, but trends could also work against each other, in mutually weakening fashion. Each of these trends came from different starting points around 1850 and developed at a different pace and a different rhythm.

Looking at Europe in 1850, an observer might well have been sceptical about the future prospects for legal and constitutional government, outside of a few countries with a longer history of it – the UK comes to mind in particular. Constitutions had reached much of Europe only via the revolutions of 1848 and the increasingly evident defeat of the revolutionary movement by 1850 left the future of constitutional government in doubt, with its eventual reinstatement dependent on new revolutionary outbreaks. Yet this scepticism would have been unjustified. Revolutions with major European impact or multi-country scope, such as those of 1789, 1820, 1830 and 1848, did not occur; even the largest revolution of the 1850–1914 period, the Russian Revolution of 1905, was limited to one country, albeit the largest in Europe. Furthermore, constitutional governments either continued to exist from 1850 onwards or were revived in the 1860s, and by the 1870s were to be found everywhere except for Russia, which did have to wait for its 1905 revolution to limit, even to a modest extent, the Tsar's autocratic power. More than that, though, constitutional governments proved to be surprisingly robust frameworks for political life, even in countries such as Spain, which had an unusually late phase of revolutionary activity (not ending until 1875) or Italy and Germany, where the constitutional framework was the result of these countries' respective wars of national unification, of one portion of the country militarily conquering another.

Gradually, such forms of constitutional government developed into bulwarks against the arbitrary exercise of executive – that is to say, monarchical – political power. Limits on monarchs did not necessarily mean that power was in the hands of the people or their elected representatives. Parliamentary government never reached the great empires of central and eastern Europe; nor did it reach a number of smaller states there, such as the kingdom of Romania. A democratic franchise for men (to say nothing of women's suffrage) was far from universal in 1914 and Europe's only two republics in 1850, France and Switzerland, were still Europe's only two republics in 1914. But a government based on the rule of law and an elected parliament with real powers seemed, by the outbreak of the First World War, well established throughout the continent.

In 1850, nationalism had just experienced its first continent-wide run, during the 1848 revolutions, with ambiguous results that showed both its power and popular appeal, as well as its many enemies and the alternative sources of loyalty and political identity they propounded. The story of nationalism from then until 1914 was an upward trajectory: co-opted by established governments for their own purposes in the 1850s and 1860s, finding a firm and increasingly widespread anchor in the world of voluntary associations, being spread via elementary education, reaching ever greater segments of the population, entering organized mass politics through the leagues. Nationalism's trajectory also moved in the direction of greater intolerance and hostility towards other nationalities – not that nationalism was ever free of such tendencies – and a pernicious interaction with racist and social Darwinist ideas. By the beginning of the twentieth century, nationalism was central to emerging mass politics, and a mortal threat to the continent's multinational realms. Nationalism did not reign supreme after 1900, and there were certainly impressive attempts to combat nationalism, coming primarily from two rather oddly juxtaposed sources: the socialist labour movement and the Catholic Church. Yet even nationalism's strongest opponents were forced to make concessions to it. In all these respects, for both good and evil, the years 1850–1914 were the age of the ascent of nationalism.

If nationalism's rise was a steady one, the growth of mass politics was more erratic. Following the enormous outburst in the revolution of 1848, political organizations and political movements activating tens or hundreds of thousands of people vanished altogether during the 1850s and made only episodic appearances in Europe during the following three decades. For most of this time, the notables, the locally most influential men, remained in control of political life. This state of affairs changed dramatically in the 1890s, with the rise of mass political parties, powerful and well-funded special-interest groups, and the leagues. On a Europe-wide basis, political participation surpassed the events of the 1848 revolution for the first time, and went on to new heights in the two decades before the outbreak of the First World War.

The emergence of mass politics greatly affected the political landscape, strengthening parties ideologically and organizationally predisposed to it, the socialist labour movement on the left, and Catholic and radical nationalist conservatives on the right. Liberals and more old-fashioned conservatives, two groups that were reluctant, on ideological grounds and due to the nature of their supporters, to appeal to a mass audience, did not do so well. Mass politics and intransigent, extremist nationalism had a profoundly symbiotic relationship, to their mutual benefit. By 1914, it was an open question in many European countries – for instance, in both the still very autocratic Russian Empire and the deeply parliamentary United Kingdom – whether the existing constitutional order could contain these new forms of political life.

THE PENTARCHY IN PEACE AND WAR

International relations changed less over the years 1850 to 1914 than did domestic politics. The same five Great Powers – Great Britain, France, Russia, Austria and Prussia – the 'Pentarchy', that had dominated Europe since the mid-eighteenth century continued to do so down to 1914. Admittedly, there were some territorial reorganizations, with Austria becoming Austria-Hungary, and Prussia conquering the other German states to create the German Empire, but the Great Powers were recognizably the same. Efforts of other states, most noticeably Italy, to claim Great Power status were unavailing. After 1890, rising non-European powers, particularly Japan and the United States, became an increasing influence on Great Power politics, but primarily in extra-European affairs. The decisions leading to war in 1914, for instance, were taken without the least concern for these countries.

Another element of stasis in international relations was the constant recurrence of the vexed Eastern Question, the potential disposition of the territories of the Ottoman

Empire, especially this empire's Balkan lands, but its Near Eastern and North African possessions as well. Never resolved, the Eastern Question emerged to crisis level about once a generation to trouble European diplomacy, the final time, after 1908, directly contributing to the outbreak of the First World War.

For all these ways in which relations between the European powers stayed the same, there were three elements of European diplomacy that clearly changed over the 1850–1914 period: the radius of military and diplomatic action, the relationship between domestic politics and foreign affairs, and the stability of the system of interaction of the Great Powers. An obvious change came with the new imperialism of the 1880s, which brought almost all the Great Powers, and a number of the not so great ones, on to the global stage. This was a sharp break with the post-1815 period, when Great Britain had been the only Great Power with an overseas empire substantial enough to shape its foreign policy. Although there were some precursor events in the 1860s, the development of the new imperialism, particularly the scramble for Africa, marked a new stage in the actions and aspirations of the European Powers.

In contrast to this fairly sharp break in the 1880s, the interaction between domestic and foreign policies developed steadily over the post-1850 decades. At first, it was statesmen taking domestic considerations into account when formulating their foreign policies, a trend taken up by Napoleon III, furthered by Cavour, employed by both Disraeli and Gladstone, and brought to perfection by Bismarck. The rise of mass politics following c.1890 changed the terms of this interaction. Previously, statesmen – the monarchs, their government ministers, diplomatic corps and General Staffs – may have taken domestic politics into account when designing their strategies for international affairs, or even designed these strategies explicitly to deal with domestic issues, but they were the ones designing the strategies and taking the initiatives. After 1890, statesmen found it much harder to remain in charge, and saw the initiative in formulating strategies for international relations passing to the new influences of mass politics: the special-interest groups, the mass parties and the leagues. Foreign policy had become distinctly more democratic – a development that was a distinctly mixed blessing.

Changes in interaction between the Great Powers followed a more cyclical pattern, alternating generally reasonably peaceful phases of the domination of one Power or group of Powers, with more belligerent periods of competition among the Powers. In 1850, it seemed that Russia was the dominant Power in continental Europe, with Britannia ruling the waves and dominating maritime relations between Europe and the extra-European world. This situation vanished almost immediately with the outbreak of the Crimean War in 1853 and was followed by almost two decades of competition for dominance in Europe, ending with the victory of the Prussian kingdom, the Great Power least expected to reach such a position.

The decades of the 1870s and 1880s were a period of relative stability, as Bismarck's alliance system kept Prussia's successor state, the German Empire, in the dominant position Prussia had acquired in 1870 through its war with France. By the

1890s, Bismarck's system had collapsed, with the creation of the Franco-Russian Alliance, and also because Bismarck's successors envisaged a greatly expanded position for Germany, creating a great overseas empire with navy to match, while simultaneously expanding Germany's hegemonic position in Europe. The new era of diplomatic instability commencing in the mid-1890s, when linked with other trends of the era – the growing influence of mass politics on international relations, the development of a popular and intransigent nationalism and its threat to multinational regimes – led, via an arms race and its economic and political consequences, and a series of diplomatic crises, to the outbreak of the First World War, and the destruction of the entire system of diplomacy in Europe as it had existed since the eighteenth century.

CONTINUITIES AND BREAKS

Historians are notorious for their qualified conclusions, an example of which is that an investigation of conditions on either side of 1850 and on either side of 1914 will yield examples of both continuity and change. Having made that point, we can be a bit more precise. The breaks in continuity around 1850, if relatively widespread, were far less drastic and far less traumatic than those occurring in 1914, even if the latter were restricted to somewhat fewer areas.

Most of the economic and social developments of the 1850–1914 era, discussed in the first part of the chapter, were largely non-existent in Europe during the previous decades. The one big exception to this statement is Great Britain, where industrialization and other forms of market expansion and economic growth, as well as the movement to an industrialized and urbanized society, were well under way before 1850. The contrast, though, between these developments occurring almost exclusively in an island off the coast of Europe and their permeating the entire continent is striking.

Considering artistic and intellectual developments, we can certainly point to pre-1850 realist writers and painters – Stendhal, Dickens and Courbet, to mention just a few big names almost at random. Important intellectuals of the post-mid-century period, such as Auguste Comte and John Stuart Mill, had begun their careers in the 1820s or 1830s. Observations about an age of progress were not a post-mid-century exclusive either. Yet, before 1850 these artistic and intellectual trends had a lot of competition – in the artistic styles of romanticism and classicism, both oriented towards idealized versions of past traditions, in romantic and Hegelian versions of philosophy and the nascent social sciences, and even in romantic, anti-empirical, anti-experimental, and anti-mathematical views of science. (The later, dramatic conceptual changes in the sciences, whether those of Darwin, Pasteur, Kekulé or Einstein, all presupposed the rejection of such conceptions of the scientific enterprise.) Widespread pessimism about social and economic developments, fuelled by the ideas of Thomas Malthus and David Ricardo, which led the literary critic Thomas Carlyle to coin his famous quip that economics was the 'dismal science', offered a downbeat view of the future. Admittedly, some of these trends were on the wane by the 1840s or even the previous decade, but their prevalence points to a change in intellectual climate during the post-1850 period.

Politically, the first half of the century saw the development of the main ideological features of nineteenth-century politics, with the basic conceptual frameworks of liberalism, conservatism, radicalism, socialism, feminism and nationalism all being formed between the first decade of the century and the 1840s. The practice of politics, as suggested in the previous section, changed quite a bit on either side of the revolution of 1848. Those revolutions brought to an end the almost seventy-year-long history of political instability, powerful or widespread revolutions, and precocious, if not always well organized, forms of mass politics, giving way to a period characterized by peaceful political life in constitutional frameworks, only occasional revolutionary outbursts, usually related to wartime defeat, and a political life largely dominated by the notables. The changes in international relations were perhaps part of a more regularly recurring alternation between periods of stability and those of contention, but the relatively quiet years begun after the defeat of Napoleon and the Congress of Vienna in 1815 came to an end in the 1850s, replaced by a contention between Great Powers for a hegemony and an almost two-decades-long round of – albeit rather limited – Great Power warfare.

The middle of the nineteenth century thus did mark a turning point in many different respects, but if so, it was a relatively gentle one. Although the many breaks in continuity may be apparent in retrospect, they were less evident to contemporaries, and it took a while – several decades in fact – before they became apparent. One reason was that the new trends were generally not disruptive of individual life courses.

Considering the other end of the 1850–1914 period, we see a number of areas in which the turning point was not in 1914 but in the preceding quarter-century. Perhaps the single most important area in which this was the case was the arts and sciences. Artistic modernism was widely practised by the First World War, and not just as an eccentric idea of eccentric artists but as styles respected and acknowledged by the artists' public. Popular culture of the period, with its pulp fiction and moving pictures, was another sign of future developments. The ideas of figures such as Weber, Freud or Durkheim would dominate intellectual life well into the century; and the post-1900 transformation of physics clearly marked a break with the past and a step towards the future.

Some aspects of economic, technological and social developments also suggest a continuity across the year 1914. The new products of the chemical and electrical industry or the beginnings of the industrial production of motor cars, were all developments of the 1890–1914 era that would powerfully influence economic development and consumer purchases for most of the twentieth century. The experience of mass combat in the First World War would, of course, be a massive discontinuity, but most of the major weapons of that war – machine guns, recoilless artillery, submarines, aircraft – had already been incorporated in the Great Powers' arsenals before the war began. The war brought a drastic temporary decline in the birth rate, but following the post-war demographic rebound the post-1880 trend towards lower birth rates continued.

The growing importance of organized associations, the pervasiveness of special-interest groups, and the organizations of mass politics were all features of the years 1914 to 1945 that were well in place before the First World War began. Political trends of those years, including the rise of the labour movement, the growth of an extremist radical right and the decline of liberalism, were already apparent before 1914. Some of the ugliest ideological features of the age of total war, including an intransigent nationalism based on racist principles or a vehement, racial anti-Semitism, were quite present in the belle époque and provide ample evidence for the assertion that the pre-1914 era was not all that beautiful. Admittedly, these were mostly extreme features of the right side of the political spectrum; the totalitarian, Stalinist future of the left, even with all the terrorist excesses of Russian revolutionaries, was much less apparent before the First World War.

All of these examples point to important continuities between the years 1890–1914 and 1914–45, or even 1914–1975. There are, however, a range of breaks directly related to the First World War, which we could categorize in three areas: the economy, the practice of both domestic politics and international relations, and individual life courses. All of them would have a dramatic and far-reaching impact.

The sheer scope of the First World War's diversion of production to the purposes of destruction weighed heavily on the future of the economy. Standards of living collapsed; starvation was widespread in central and eastern Europe during the war and in the immediate post-war era. After a brief recovery in the second half of the 1920s, a new economic crisis and a new world war brought standards of living down again to the point that in different European countries it was generally somewhere between the late 1940s and the early 1960s before standards of living reached and permanently surpassed their 1913 levels. In the interval, an entire adult lifetime had gone by.

The war and its aftermath brought deep structural changes to the economy as well. Government intervention in an age of total war reached levels way beyond even the most restrictive protective tariffs, agricultural subsidies, or labour protection and social insurance legislation of the pre-1914 era. State control of production, foreign trade and of international capital flows, government fixing of prices and wages, and contingency assignments of strategic raw materials were all features of the world wars, and many of them continued in the inter-war era as well. These drastic measures of government control, combined with runaway inflation and the appearance of a black market, destroyed the security in property ownership and market property transactions that had been a major feature of the 1850–1914 era, impoverished large strata of the population and so brought about an unprecedented upheaval in economic and social life.

The First World War was a disaster for Europe's monarchs, and the end of the war saw Europe's two long-term republics, France and Switzerland, joined by a whole series of new ones – the USSR, Germany, Austria, Hungary, Poland, Czechoslovakia, Latvia, Lithuania and Estonia – on the territory of the former German, Austro-Hungarian and Russian Empires. Unfortunately, the same circumstances that had created democratic – or at least nominally democratic – republics were not favourable to their development into peaceful regimes, characterized by the rule of law. For the First World War ended in widespread revolutions and subsequent civil wars, out of which emerged the major totalitarian movements and totalitarian regimes of the right and the left: fascism, Nazism, communism. To a great extent, the ideological principles of these movements had been developed in the quarter-century before 1914, but their actual cruel, violent and murderous practice was only possible after the wartime experience had disrupted most legal authority, lowered the level of inhibitions against violence and murder, and created a model of politics based on unrelenting warfare against an opponent who was to be defeated and annihilated. These new forms of politics were not limited to the combatant nations but spread to countries such as Spain, which had not been directly involved in the war.

The war disrupted international politics at least as much as domestic, bringing to an end the Austro-Hungarian Empire, one of the pillars of the Pentarchy, dissolving the Ottoman Empire, creating a series of new states out of the territory of these powers and from the defeated German and Russian Empires. The decisive intervention of the United States in the war meant that, quite in contrast to the pre-1914 world, it was non-European powers that would help determine European affairs. Although colonialism survived the war, and the empires of the victorious French and British actually expanded, the war brought an enormous impetus to anti-colonial movements, as well as an expansion in the power of another extra-European state, Japan.

Finally, and perhaps most importantly, the war caused enormous, disruptive changes to the life courses of all the citizens and subjects of the combatant nations. Experiences such as combat at a front dominated by unprecedented levels of firepower, with the resulting enormous casualties, queuing for rationed goods, dealing on the black market, doing unaccustomed heavy industrial labour (a typically female wartime experience), seeing one's life savings vanish to nothing because of inflation, being subject to foreign occupation, or becoming, during or after the war, a refugee – these had become typical, the fate of hundreds of millions of people, a fate that would haunt them for the rest of their lives. In this respect, particularly, the outbreak of the First World War was a gigantic break, an enormous discontinuity, one that brought the 1850–1914 era of European history to a jarring and horrifying end.

BIBLIOGRAPHY

GENERAL READINGS

Eric Hobsbawm's *The Age of Capital 1848–1875* (London, 1975) and *The Age of Empire 1875–1914* (New York, 1987) are closer to extended essays with the interesting and stimulating interpretations one associates with their author than they are to general histories. Robert Gildea, *Barricades and Borders: Europe 1800–1914*, 3rd edn (Oxford, 2003) is such a general history, and a very detailed one; Michael Rapport, *Nineteenth Century Europe* (Basingstoke, 2005) is briefer and more narrowly focused on politics. The articles in John Merriman, Jay Winter et al. (eds), *Europe 1789–1914: The Encyclopedia of Industry and Empire* (New York, 2006) are full of helpful information and bibliographical references.

Turning to general histories of individual countries, for the UK the two relevant volumes in the 'New Oxford History of England' series, K. Theodore Hoeppen, *The Mid-Victorian Generation 1846–1886* (Oxford, 1998) and G. R. Searle, *A New England? Peace and War 1886–1918* (Oxford, 2004) are both outstanding. For France, the simplest choice would be Alan Plessis, *The Rise and Fall of the Second Empire, 1852–1871*, trans. Jonathan Mandelbaum (Cambridge, 1985), and Jean-Marie Mayeur and Madeleine Reberioux, *The Third Republic from its Origins to the Great War, 1871–1914*, trans. J. R. Foster (Cambridge, 1984). For Germany, a couple of possibilities would be Jonathan Sperber (ed.), *Germany 1800–1870* (Oxford, 2004) and Volker Berghahn, *Imperial Germany, 1871–1914: Economy, Society, Culture, and Politics* (Providence, RI, 1994). Robin Okey, *The Habsburg Monarchy: From Enlightenment to Eclipse* (New York, 2001) is the most recent general history. On the Russian Empire, the volumes in the 'Longman History of Russia' series, David Saunders, *Russia in the Age of Reaction and Reform 1801–1881* (London, 1992) and Hans Rogger, *Russia in the Age of Modernisation and Revolution 1881–1917* (London, 1983) are both good works. The essays in John Davis (ed.), *Italy in the Nineteenth Century: 1796–1900* (Oxford, 2000) offer an up-to-date introduction to Italian history in the period. Some general histories of smaller countries in Europe include E. H. Kossman, *The Low Countries 1780–1940* (Oxford, 1978), Charles J. Esdaile, *Spain in the Liberal Age: From Constitution to Civil War, 1808–1939* (Oxford, 2000); T. K. Derry, *A History of Modern Norway* (Oxford, 1973); Keith Hitchins, *The Romanians 1774–1866* (Oxford, 1996) and, by the same author, *Rumania, 1866–1947* (Oxford, 1994). More broadly on eastern Europe, Ivan Berend, *History Derailed: Central and Eastern Europe in the Long Nineteenth Century* (Berkeley, CA, 2003) is full of information, makes interesting comparisons and offers vigorous interpretations. David Vital, *A People Apart: The Jews in Europe 1789–1930* (Oxford, 1999) deals with a distinct national, religious or ethnic (take your pick) group living across Europe.

Jonathan Sperber, *Revolutionary Europe 1780–1850* (Harlow, 2000), is the most recent account of the preceding period of modern European history, against which the years 1850 to 1914 can be measured. For a comparison of that period with its successor, two works particularly to be recommended are Harold James, *Europe Reborn: A History 1914–2000* (Harlow, 2003) and Mark Mazower, *Dark Continent: Europe's Twentieth Century* (New York, 1998).

READINGS ON POPULATION AND THE ECONOMY

There is no really up-to-date or outstanding economic history of any particular period of nineteenth-century Europe, or of the entire century. Most works tend to cover somewhat longer periods. Probably the best among them is Sidney Pollard, *Peaceful Conquest: The Industrialization of Europe 1760–1970* (Oxford, 1981), whose scope is wider than the title implies. There are a number of books focused on one country or region: Roger Price, *An Economic History of Modern France, 1730–1914*, 2nd edn (New York, 1981); Richard Tilly and Toni Pierenkemper, *The German Economy during the Nineteenth Century* (New York, 2004); *The Cambridge Economic History of Modern Britain*, 3 vols (Cambridge, 2004); David F. Good, *The Economic Rise of the Hapsburg Empire, 1750–1914* (Princeton, 1984); Peter Gatrell, *The Tsarist Economy 1850–1917* (London, 1986). On the major Mediterranean countries, the student can consult Vera Zamagni, *The Economic History of Italy 1860–1990* (Oxford, 1993) and Nicholás Sánchez-Albornoz, *The Economic Modernization of Spain, 1830–1930*, trans. Karen Powers and Manuel Sañudo (New York, 1987). Michael Palairet, *The Balkan Economies c.1800–1914: Evolution without Development* (Cambridge, 1997) is very informative about a region that usually does not get much attention.

Jeffrey Williamson, 'The Evolution of Global Labor Markets since 1830: Background Evidence and Hypotheses', *Explorations in Economic History*, 32 (1995): 141–96 is a good place to start exploring the development of real wages. Walter Nugent, *Crossings: The Great Transatlantic Migrations, 1870–1914* (Bloomington, IN, 1992) is an excellent introduction, but there is no general work on the earlier period. Dirk Hoerder (ed.), *Labor Migration in the Atlantic Economies: The European and North American Working Classes during the Period of Industrialization* (Westport, CT, 1985) is an excellent collection of very informative essays. Kerby Miller, *Emigrants and Exiles: Ireland and the Irish Exodus to North America* (Oxford, 1985) is an enormous, and enormously useful, study of one major centre of emigration. On internal migration within Europe, Steven Hochstadt, *Mobility and Modernity: Migration in Germany, 1820–1989* (Ann Arbor, MI, 1999) is a detailed study of central Europe that also poses continent-wide questions.

S. B. Saul, *The Myth of the Great Depression 1873–1896*, 2nd edn (London, 1985) is a classic short essay, which may indeed identify the 'Great Depression' of the nineteenth century as a myth but also shows that there was an economic slowdown occurring then. Michael Collins and Mae Baker, *Commercial Banks and Industrial Finance in England and Wales, 1860–1913* (Oxford, 2003) has a very interesting account of the crash of 1878 and its consequences. D. A. Farnie, *The English Cotton Industry and the World Market 1815–1896* (Oxford, 1979) contains a very good discussion of the difficulties of textile manufacture – and not just in England – during the late nineteenth century. A profoundly informative account of the development of electrical power is Thomas P. Hughes, *Networks of Power: Electrification in Western Society, 1880–1930* (Baltimore, MD, 1983). For chemical manufacturing there is Fred Aftalion, *A History of the International Chemical Industry*, trans. Otto Benfey (Philadelphia, 1991) and L. F. Haber, *The Chemical Industry 1900–1930: International Growth and Technological Change* (Oxford, 1971). There is surprisingly little on the broadening of mechanization in manufactures, but A. E. Musson, *The Growth of British Industry* (New York, 1978) has some interesting discussions of this point. Alison Fleig Frank, *Oil Empire: Visions of Prosperity in Austrian Galicia* (Cambridge, MA, 2005) is a fascinating work on an unexpected centre of the petroleum industry in pre-1914 Europe. James Laux, *In First Gear: The French Automobile Industry to 1914* (Montreal, 1976) is informative on motor manufacturing not just in France but in all of Europe. A balanced, detailed and thoughtful consideration of the enormous debate over the performance of the late nineteenth- and early twentieth-century British industry is Sidney Pollard, *Britain's Prime and Britain's Decline: The British Economy 1870–1914* (London, 1989). Some of the latest evaluations of this question are gathered in Jean-Pierre Dormois and Michael Dintenfass (eds), *The British Industrial Decline* (London, 1999). Kevin H. O'Rourke and Jeffrey G. Williamson, *Globalization and History: The Evolution of a Nineteenth-Century Atlantic Economy* (Cambridge, MA, 1999), offers a broad picture of the 1890–1914 era as a high point of international commerce and finance.

On agriculture, Michael Tracy, *Government and Agriculture in Western Europe, 1880–1988*, 3rd edn (New York, 1989) discusses the history of protectionism and state agricultural subsidies, while J. L. van Zanden, 'The First Green Revolution: The Growth of Production and Productivity in European Agriculture, 1870–1914', *Economic History Review*, NS 44 (1991): 215–39, explores the sources of increasing agricultural productivity. Two general works on small business are Geoffrey Crossick and Heinz Gerhard Haupt, *The Petite Bourgeoisie in Europe 1780–1914* (London, 1995) and idem (eds), *Shopkeepers and Master Artisans in Nineteenth-Century Europe* (London, 1984). Three good focused studies are Shulamit Volkov, *The Rise of Popular Antimodernism in Germany: The Urban Master Artisans 1873–1896* (Princeton, NJ, 1978); Jonathan Morris, *The Political Economy of Shopkeeping in Milan 1886–1922* (Cambridge, 1993); and Philip Nord, *Paris Shopkeepers and the Politics of Resentment* (Princeton, NJ, 1986).

The essays in John Gillis, Louise A. Tilly and David Levine (eds), *The European Experience of Declining Fertility, 1850–1970* (Cambridge, MA, 1992) sum up much of the received wisdom on changing fertility trends and their causes. Simon Szreter, *Fertility, Class and Gender in Britain, 1860–1940* (Cambridge, 1996) raises important questions about this wisdom. Posing similar questions particularly about birth control, is Hera Cook, *The Long Sexual Revolution: English Women, Sex, and Contraception 1800–1975* (Oxford, 2004).

READINGS ON SOCIAL STRUCTURES AND SOCIAL INSTITUTIONS

Adna Weber, *The Growth of Cities in the Nineteenth Century* (Ithaca, NY, 1963), reprint of the original edition of 1899, is still a mine of information about patterns of urban growth in the nineteenth century. Paul M. Hohenberg and Lynn Lees, *The Making of Urban Europe 1000–1994* (Cambridge, MA, 1995) is a very simple introduction to European urban history, with a helpful bibliography. Among the books focused on cities in one particular country are P. J. Waller, *Town, City and Nation: England 1850–1914* (Oxford, 1983); John Merriman (ed.), *French Cities in the Nineteenth Century* (New York, 1981); Daniel R. Brower, *The Russian City between Tradition and Modernity, 1850–1900* (Berkeley, CA, 1990); and, for one of the further corners of Europe, Raina Gavrilova, *Bulgarian Urban Culture in the Eighteenth and Nineteenth Centuries* (Selingsgrove, 1999). Studies of individual urban centres include Gareth Steadman Jones, *Outcast London* (Oxford, 1971) and Francis Sheppard, *London 1808–1870: The Infernal Wen* (Berkeley, CA, 1971); John Merriman, *The Red City: Limoges and the French Nineteenth Century* (Oxford, 1985); or James H. Jackson, Jr, *Migration and Urbanization in the Ruhr Valley, 1821–1914* (Atlantic Highlands, NJ, 1997). David Pinkney, *Napoleon III and the Rebuilding of Paris* (Princeton, NJ, 1958) is a classic account of Baron Haussmann's projects of urban renewal. Carl Schorske, 'The Ringstrasse and the Birth of Urban Modernism', in his *Fin-de-Siècle Vienna: Politics and Culture* (New York, 1980) describes another famous urban renewal programme. Leslie Page Moch, *Paths to the City: Regional Migration in Nineteenth-Century France* (Beverly Hills, 1983) discusses migration and relationships between rural and urban areas. On questions of public health in urban life, see W. F. Bynum and Roy Porter (eds), *Living and Dying in London* (London, 1991); Peter Baldwin, *Contagion and the State in Europe 1830–1930* (Cambridge, 1999); Richard J. Evans, *Death in Hamburg: Society and Politics in the Cholera Years, 1830–1910* (Oxford, 1987); and Frank M. Snowden, *Naples in the Time of Cholera: 1884–1911* (Cambridge, 1995).

For urban life at the beginning of the twentieth century, some useful works include Michael F. Hamm (ed.), *The City in Late Imperial Russia* (Bloomington, IN, 1986); Brian Ladd, *Urban Planning and Public Order in Germany, 1860–1914* (Cambridge, MA, 1990); Anthony Sutcliffe (ed.), *Metropolis 1890–1940* (London, 1984); and John P. McKay, *Tramways and Trolleys: The Rise of Urban Mass Transport in Europe* (Princeton, NJ, 1976). On attitudes towards urban life, and the hopes and fears generated by large cities, Andrew Lees, *Cities Perceived: Urban Society in European and American Thought, 1820–1940* (New York, 1985); idem, *Cities, Sin, and Social Reform in Imperial Germany* (Ann Arbor, MI, 2002); Peter Fritzsche, *Reading Berlin 1900* (Cambridge, MA, 1996); and Judith Walkowitz, *City of Dreadful Delight: Narratives of Sexual Danger in Late-Victorian London* (Chicago, 1992).

Michael Anderson, *Family Structure in Nineteenth Century Lancashire* (Cambridge, 1971) is a classic account of industrial work and family life. Louise Tilly and Joan Scott, *Women, Work and Family* (New York, 1978) offers a simpler introduction and general overview of the topic. Some general works on social classes and social structures include Gérard Noiriel, *Workers in French Society in the 19th and 20th Centuries*, trans. Helen McPhail

(New York, 1990); Trevor Lummis, *The Labour Aristocracy 1850–1914* (Aldershot, 1994); Jürgen Kocka and Alan Mitchell (eds), *Bourgeois Society in Nineteenth Century Europe* (Oxford, 1993); Pamela Pilbeam, *The Middle Classes in Europe 1789–1914* (Chicago, 1990); Harley D. Balzer, *Russia's Rising Middle Class: The Professions in Russian History* (Armonk, NY, 1996).

There has been a very large amount written on social classes in pre-1914 Europe. Just a very small selection from this body of literature would include Johanna Bourke, *Working-Class Cultures in Britain 1890–1960* (London, 1994), which is particularly good on gender; Ellen Ross, *Love and Toil: Motherhood in Outcast London 1870–1918* (Oxford, 1993); Dina Copelman, *London's Women Teachers: Gender, Class and Feminism* (London, 1996); David Cannadine, *The Decline and Fall of the British Aristocracy* (New Haven, CT, 1990); Lenard Berlanstein, *The Working People of Paris, 1871–1914* (Baltimore, MD, 1984); Helen Chenut, *The Fabric of Gender: Working-Class Culture in Third Republic France* (University Park, PA, 2005); Jo Burr Margadant, *Madame le professeur: Women Educators in the Third Republic* (Princeton, NJ, 1990); S. H. F. Hickey, *Workers in Imperial Germany: The Miners of the Ruhr* (Oxford, 1985); Carole Adams, *Women Clerks in Wilhelmine Germany* (Cambridge, 1988); Dolores Augustine, *Patricians and Parvenus: Wealth and High Society in Wilhelmine Germany* (Providence, RI, 1994); Donald Bell, *Sesto San Giovanni: Workers, Culture, and Politics in an Italian Town, 1880–1922* (New Brunswick, NJ, 1986); James West (ed.), *Between Tsar and People: Educated Society and the Quest for Public Identity in Late Imperial Russia* (Princeton, NJ, 1991); Charters Wynn, *Workers, Strikes, and Pogroms: The Donbass–Dnepr Bend in Late Imperial Russia, 1870–1905* (Princeton, NJ, 1992); Evel Economakis, *From Peasant to Petersburger* (Basingstoke, 1998).

On property ownership and its importance for nineteenth-century European society, see W. D. Rubinstein, *Men of Property: The Very Wealthy in Britain since the Industrial Revolution* (New Brunswick, NJ, 1981), or Jonathan Sperber, *Property and Civil Society in South-Western Germany 1820–1914* (Oxford, 2005). Mary Jo Maynes, 'Class Cultures and Images of Proper Family Life', in David Kertzer and Marzio Barbagli (eds), *The History of the European Family*, 3 vols (New Haven, CT, 2001–03), 2: 194–226, provides a good discussion of the idea of separate spheres. Bonnie G. Smith, *Ladies of the Leisure Class: The Bourgeoises of Northern France in the Nineteenth Century* (Princeton, NJ, 1981) and Marion A. Kaplan, *The Making of the Jewish Middle Class: Women, Family and Identity in Imperial Germany* (Oxford, 1991) are two very different interpretations of what bourgeois women were doing in their separate spheres.

The best place to begin a consideration of voluntary associations is with the brilliant essay of Stefan-Ludwig Hoffmann, *Civil Society, 1750–1914* (Basingstoke, 2006). On mutual benefit societies and organized sociability, some good works include P. H. J. H. Gosden, *Self-Help: Voluntary Associations in 19th Century Britain* (London, 1973); Simon Cordery, *British Friendly Societies, 1750–1914* (London, 2003); Allan Mitchell, 'The Function and Malfunction of Mutual Aid Societies in Nineteenth Century France', in Jonathan Barry and Colin Jones (eds), *Medicine and Charity before the Welfare State* (London, 1991), 172–89; Carol E. Harrison, *The Bourgeois Citizen in Nineteenth-Century*

France: Gender, Sociability and the Uses of Emulation (Oxford, 1999), with interesting cross-European comparisons; Alan R. H. Baker, *Fraternity among the Peasantry: Sociability and Voluntary Associations in the Loire Valley, 1815–1914* (Cambridge, 1999); Joseph Bradley, 'Subjects into Citizens: Societies, Civil Society and Autocracy in Tsarist Russia', *American Historical Review*, 107 (2002): 1094–123. On professional associations, see Geoffrey Cocks and Konrad H. Jaruasch (eds), *German Professions, 1800–1950* (Oxford, 1990) and Katherine Auspitz, *The Radical Bourgeoisie: The Ligue de l'enseignement and the Origins of the Third Republic, 1866–1885* (Cambridge, 1982).

For nationalist groups, Claire E. Nolte, *The Sokol in the Czech Lands to 1914: Training for the Nation* (New York, 2002) is a model study of gymnastics societies and national-ism. The student can also consult the older work of George L. Mosse, *The Nationalism of the Masses: Political Symbolism and Mass Movements in Germany from the Napoleonic Wars through the Third Reich* (New York, 1975) or the more recent Berit Dencker, 'Popular Gymnastics and the Military Spirit in Germany 1848–1871', *Central European History*, 34 (2001): 503–30.

On women's groups, see especially F. K. Prochaska, *Women and Philanthropy in Nineteenth Century England* (Oxford, 1980); Lilian Shiman, *Women and Leadership in Nineteenth-Century England* (New York, 1992); James F. McMillan, *France and Women 1789–1914: Gender, Society and Politics* (London, 2000); and Jean Quataert, *Staging Philanthropy: Patriotic Women and the National Imagination in Dynastic Germany, 1813–1916* (Ann Arbor, MI, 2001). The anti-prostitution campaigns can be followed through Judith Walkowitz, *Prostitution and Victorian Society: Women, Class and the State* (Cambridge, 1980). The transition from women's groups to explicitly feminist women's groups can be followed in Richard Evans, *The Feminists: Women's Emancipation Movements in Europe, America and Australasia 1840–1920* (London, 1977); Nancy R. Reagin, *A German Women's Movement: Class and Gender in Hanover, 1880–1933* (Chapel Hill, NC, 1995); and Steven Hause and Anne Kenney, 'The Development of the Catholic Women's Suffrage Movement in France, 1886–1922', *Catholic Historical Review*, 67 (1981): 11–30.

Trade unions have been very well studied. Dick Geary (ed.), *Labour and Social Movements in Europe before 1914* (Oxford, 1989) is a good general introduction. A few country-specific studies include W. Hamish Fraser, *A History of British Trade Unionism 1700–1998* (Basingstoke, 1998); John A. Moses, *Trade Unionism in Germany from Bismarck to Hitler 1869–1933*, 2 vols (London, 1982); Bernard H. Moss, *The Origins of the French Labor Movement 1830–1914: The Socialism of Skilled Workers* (Berkeley, CA, 1976); Maurice A. Neufeld, *Italy: School for Awakening Countries. The Italian Labor Movement in its Political, Social and Economic Setting from 1800 to 1960* (Ithaca, NY, 1961); and Benjamin Martin, *The Agony of Modernization: Labor and Industrialization in Spain* (Ithaca, NY, 1990). Cooperatives, by contrast are still relatively little explored. Two works with information are W. Hamish Fraser, *The Coming of the Mass Market* (London, 1981) and Brett Fairbairn, 'History from the Ecological Perspective: Gaia Theory and the Problem of Cooperatives in Turn-of-the-Century Germany', *American Historical Review*, 99 (1994): 1204–39.

David Vincent, *The Rise of Mass Literacy: Reading and Writing in Modern Europe* (Oxford, 2002) is a fine overview that supersedes previous accounts. A lot has been written about elementary education in France: R. D. Anderson, *Education in France 1848–1870* (Oxford, 1975); Robert Gildea, *Education in Provincial France 1800–1914: A Study of Three Departments* (Oxford, 1983); or Sarah A. Curtis, *Educating the Faithful: Religion, Schooling and Society in Nineteenth Century France* (DeKalb, IL, 2000). Special mention should be made of the very stimulating and perceptive chapters on education in Eugen Weber, *Peasants in to Frenchmen: The Modernization of Rural France 1870–1914* (Stanford, CA, 1976). Works on other European countries include Ben Eklof, *Russian Peasant Schools: Officialdom, Village Culture, and Popular Pedagogy, 1861–1914* (Berkeley, CA, 1986); Karl Schleunes, *Schooling and Society: The Politics of Education in Prussia and Bavaria 1750–1900* (Oxford, 1989); and, for the UK, J. S. Hurt, *Elementary Schooling and the Working Classes 1860–1918* (London, 1979). On nationalism, anti-clericalism and the politics of elementary education, see Phyllis Stock-Morton, *Moral Education for a Secular Society: The Development of 'Morale Laïque' in Nineteenth Century France* (Albany, NY, 1988); Vernon Mallinson, *Power and Politics in Belgian Education 1815 to 1861* (London, 1963); Stephen Heathron, '"Let Us Remember that We, Too, are English"; Constructions of Citizenship and National Identity in English Elementary School Reading Books, 1880–1914', *Victorian Studies*, 38 (1995): 395–427; Marjorie Lamberti, *State, Society and the Elementary School in Imperial Germany* (Oxford, 1989).

On secondary and university education, see Gary Cohen, *Education and Middle-Class Society in Imperial Austria, 1848–1918* (West Lafayette, IN, 1996); James Albisetti, *Secondary School Reform in Imperial Germany* (Princeton, NJ, 1983); idem, *Schooling German Girls and Women: Secondary and Higher Education in the Nineteenth Century* (Princeton, NJ, 1988); Keith Vernon, *Universities and the State in England, 1850–1939* (London, 2004); Charles McCleland, *State, Society and University in Germany 1700–1914* (Cambridge, 1980); and Terry Nichols Clark, *Prophets and Patrons: The French University and the Emergence of the Social Sciences* (Cambridge, MA, 1973). Broader overviews of the educational system include Fritz Ringer and Brian Simon (eds), *The Rise of the Modern Educational System: Structural Change and Social Reproduction 1870–1920* (Cambridge, 1987); Marzio Barbagli, *Education for Unemployment: Politics, Labor Markets, and the School System – Italy, 1859–1973*, trans. Robert Ross (New York, 1982); and W. R. Stephen, *Education in Britain, 1750–1914* (London, 1998) which is ideologically strongly charged.

Works on the changing nature of popular reading matter include Martyn Lyons, *Readers and Society in Nineteenth-Century France: Workers, Women Peasants* (Basignstoke, 2001) or Jeffrey Brooks, *When Russia Learned to Read: Literacy and Popular Literature 1861–1917* (Princeton, NJ, 1985). For the periodical press, see Lucy Brown, *Victorian News and Newspapers* (Oxford, 1985). On boulevard press, see Peter Fritzsche, *Reading Berlin 1900* (Cambridge, MA, 1998) or Alan J. Lee, *The Origins of the Popular Press in England 1855–1914* (London, 1976). On pulp fiction, particularly to be recommended is the intriguing essay of Michael Saler, '"Clap if You Believe in Sherlock Holmes": Mass Culture and the Re-enchantment of Modernity, *c.*1890–*c.*1940', *Historical Journal*, 46 (2003): 599–622. For pre-1914 cinema, see the relevant chapters of Robert Sklar, *Film:*

An International History of the Medium (New York, 1993) and John Fullerton (ed.), *Celebrating 1895: The Centenary of Cinema* (London, 1998).

More broadly, on leisure and popular culture in early twentieth century Europe, some good works are Lynn Abrams, *Workers' Culture in Imperial Germany: Leisure and Recreation in the Rhineland and Westphalia* (London, 1992); Richard Holt, *Sport and Society in Modern France* (London, 1981); Allen Guttmann, *The Olympics: A History of the Modern Games* (Urbana, IL, 1992); David C. Young, *The Modern Olympics: A Struggle for Revival* (Baltimore, MD, 1996); Bill Murray, *The World's Game: A History of Soccer* (Urbana, IL, 1996); and Christopher Thompson, *The Tour de France: A Cultural History* (Berkeley, CA, 2006). Michael Miller, *The Bon Marché: Bourgeois Culture and the Department Store 1869–1920* (Princeton, NJ, 1981) is a classic study of Europe's first major department store. Samples of the latest research are in Geoffrey Crossick and Serge Jaumain (eds), *Cathedrals of Consumption: The European Department Store 1850–1939* (Aldershot, 1999).

READINGS ON THE ARTS AND SCIENCES

The most useful history of chemistry is Trevor H. Levere, *Transforming Matter: A History of Chemistry from Alchemy to the Buckyball* (Baltimore, MD, 2001). Iwan Morus, *When Physics Became King* (Chicago, 2005) is an accessible general history of nineteenth-century physics. Christa Jungnickel and Russell McCormmach, *Intellectual Mastery of Nature: Theoretical Physics from Ohm to Einstein*, 2 vols (Chicago, 1986) is more technical. The reader should also consult Mary Jo Nye, *Before Big Science: The Pursuit of Modern Chemistry and Physics 1800–1940* (New York, 1996).

Daniel M. Siegel, *Innovation in Maxwell's Electromagnetic Theory: Molecular Vortices, Displacement Current and Light* (Cambridge, 1991) is an important monograph that demands of the reader a fairly advanced knowledge of physics and mathematics. On the development and reception of relativity theory and quantum mechanics, see Lloyd Swenson, Jr, *General Relativity: Einstein in Context* (New York, 1979); Peter Galison, Michael Gordin and David Kaiser, *Science and Society: The History of Modern Physical Science in the Twentieth Century*, Vol. 1, *Making Special Relativity* (London, 2001) and Thomas Glick (ed.), *The Comparative Reception of Relativity* (Dodrecht, 1987). Susan Quinn, *Marie Curie: A Life* (New York, 1995) is a good biography of the first celebrity physicist. Among the many biographies of Einstein, Albrecht Fölsing, *Albert Einstein: A Biography*, trans. Ewald Osers (New York, 1997) makes fewer demands on the reader's knowledge of mathematics and physics but is still very insightful. Alan Friedman and Carol Donley, *Einstein as Myth and Muse* (Cambridge, 1985) is a delightful account of some cultural understandings and misunderstandings of twentieth-century physics.

An excellent exposition of Darwin's theories in their historical context is Michael Ruse, *The Darwinian Revolution: Science Red in Tooth and Claw*, 2nd edn (Chicago, 1999). One of many biographies of Darwin is Peter J. Bowler's *Charles Darwin: The Man and His Influence* (Cambridge, 1996). Darwin's scientific work is eminently accessible and the student can consider a recent edition of *On the Origin of Species by Means of Natural Selection*, ed. Joseph Carroll (Petersborough, Ontario, 2003); Adrian Desmond, *Huxley: From Devil's Disciple to Evolution's High Priest* (Reading, MA, 1997) is an excellent biography of one of Darwin's leading supporters and popularizers. Thomas F. Glick (ed.), *The Comparative Reception of Darwinism* (Austin, TX, 1974) contains essays on responses to Darwin's theories by scientists (and others) in Europe and throughout the world. For pre-Darwinian theories of evolution, James A. Secord, *Victorian Sensation: The Extraordinary Publication, Reception and Secret Authorship of Vestiges of the Natural History of Creation* (Chicago, 2000) is intriguing. Later doubts about Darwin's theories and the development of evolutionary thought are discussed by Peter Bowler, *The Eclipse of Darwinism: Anti-Darwinian Evolution Theories in the Decades around 1900* (Baltimore, MD, 1983) and idem, *The Non-Darwinian Revolution: Reinterpreting a Historical Myth* (Baltimore, MD, 1988). On social Darwinism, see Alfred Kelly, *The Descent of Darwin: The Popularization of Darwinism in Germany, 1860–1914* (Chapel Hill, NC, 1981) and Mike Hawkins, *Social Darwinism in European and American Thought, 1860–1945* (Cambridge, 1997). Patrice Debré, *Louis Pasteur*, trans. Elborg Forster (Baltimore, MD, 1998) is an exaggerated eulogy of the biologist; Gerald Geison, *The Private Science of Louis Pasteur* (Princeton, NJ, 1995) is an equally exaggerated demonization. Paul De Kruif, *Microbe Hunters* (New York, 1954) is a charmingly written but very old-fashioned history of microbiology.

A stimulating interpretative essay on post-1850 intellectual developments is J. W. Burrow, *The Crisis of Reason: European Thought, 1848–1914* (New Haven, CT, 2000). Some helpful books about the intellectual climate of the age of progress include Peter J. Bowler, *The Invention of Progress: The Victorians and the Past* (Oxford, 1989); T. W. Heyck, *The Transformation of Intellectual Life in Victorian England* (New York, 1982) or George S. Williamson, *The Longing for Myth in Germany: Religion and Aesthetic Culture from Romanticism to Nietzsche* (Chicago, 2004). On the subsequent age of uncertainty, see two older but still useful books, Jerome Buckley, *The Triumph of Time: A Study of Victorian Concepts of Time, History, Progress and Decadence* (Cambridge, MA, 1966); Fritz Stern, *The Politics of Cultural Despair: A Study in the Rise of the Germanic Ideology*, 2nd edn (Berkeley, CA, 1974), and the more recent Daniel Pick, *Faces of Degeneration: A European Disorder, c.1848–c.1918* (Cambridge, 1989). H. Stuart Hughes, *Consciousness and Society: The Reorientation of European Social Thought 1890–1930* (New York, 1958) is a classic account of intellectual life before 1914.

Works on prominent nineteenth-century sociologists include J. D. Y. Peel, *Herbert Spencer: The Evolution of a Sociologist* (New York, 1971); Arline Reilein Standley, *Auguste Comte* (Boston, 1981); Fritz Ringer, *Max Weber: An Intellectual Biography* (Chicago, 2004); Wolfgang Mommsen, *Max Weber and German Politics 1890–1920*, trans. Michael Steinberg (Chicago, 1984); Steven Lukes, *Emile Durkheim, His Life and Work* (London, 1973) and Susan Stedman Jones, *Durkheim Reconsidered* (Cambridge, 2001). Arthur Mitzman, *Sociology and Estrangment: Three Sociologists of Imperial Germany* (New York, 1973) is a very insightful account of sociology in its pre-1914 golden age. For primary sources, the student can consult Herbert Spencer, *On Social Evolution: Selected Writings*, ed. J. D. Y. Peel (Chicago, 1972); Auguste Comte, *Auguste Comte and Positivism: The Essential Writings*, ed. Gertrud Lenzer

(Chicago, 1983) and any of the very many English-language editions of the works of Durkheim and Weber.

Three disciplinary histories of anthropology are George W. Stocking, Jr, *Victorian Anthropology* (New York, 1987); Andrew Zimmerman, *Anthropology and Antihumanism in Imperial Germany* (Chicago, 2001); and David G. Horn, *The Criminal Body: Lombroso and the Anatomy of Deviance* (London, 2003). On historians and their relationship to ideas of progress, see Jeffrey Paul Von Arx, *Progress and Pessimism: Religion, Politics and History in Late Nineteenth Century Britain* (Cambridge, MA, 1985); George Iggers, *The German Conception of History*, 2nd edn (Middletown, CT, 1983); and Alan Pitt, 'The Irrationalist Liberalism of Hippolyte Taine', *Historical Journal*, 41 (1998): 1035–53. Erik Grimmer-Solem, *The Rise of Historical Economics and Social Reform in Germany 1864–1894* (Oxford, 2003) is an outstanding study of the Historical School and its relationship to other currents of economics. There is no comparable work on the marginalists, but R. S. Howey, *The Rise of the Marginal Utility School 1870–1889*, 2nd edn (New York, 1989) or the relevant chapters of Alessandro Roncaglia, *The Wealth of Ideas: A History of Economic Thought* (Cambridge, 2005) can be consulted. Suzanne Marchand, *Down from Olympus: Archaeology and Philhellenism in Germany, 1750–1970* (Princeton, NJ, 1996) and J. W. Burrow, 'The Uses of Philology in Victorian England', in Robert Robson (ed.), *Ideas and Institutions of Victorian Britain* (New York, 1967), are both very revealing accounts of other aspects of the humanities.

On religion and the age of progress, Owen Chadwick, *The Secularization of the European Mind in the Nineteenth Century* (Cambridge, 1975) and Hugh McLeod, *Secularisation in Western Europe, 1848–1914* (New York, 2000) are two possibilities. Nicholas Atkins and Frank Tallett, *Priests, Prelates and People: A History of European Catholicism since 1750* (Oxford, 2003) is an excellent general history with a particularly good bibliography. Christopher Clark and Wolfram Kaiser (eds), *Culture Wars: Secular–Catholic Conflict in Nineteenth Century Europe* (Cambridge, 2003) offers a country-by-country overview.

Two figures for which the body of literature has reached the point of no return are Nietzsche and Freud. A good general overview of Nietzsche and his works is R. J. Hollingdale, *Nietzsche: The Man and His Philosophy*, rev. edn (Cambridge, 1999). Among the older works, Crane Brinton, *Nietzsche*, 2nd edn (New York, 1965) is sprightly, if betraying its origins in the era of the Second World War. Three studies that place Nietzsche in the context of his time are Peter Bergmann, *Nietzsche, 'the Last Antipolitical German'* (Bloomington, IN, 1987); Don Dombowsky, *Nietzsche's Machiavellian Politics* (Basingstoke, 2004); and Lewis Call, 'Anti-Darwin, Anti-Spencer: Friedrich Nietzsche's Critique of Darwin and "Darwinism"', *History of Science*, 36 (1998): 1–22. Jacob Golomb and Robert S. Wistrich (eds), *Nietzsche, Godfather of Fascism? The Uses and Abuses of a Philosophy* (Princeton, NJ, 2002) is a handy collection of essays debating the question raised in its title. For Nietzsche and his followers, see Steven Ascheim, *The Nietzsche Legacy in Germany 1890–1990* (Berkeley, CA, 1992); Bernice Rosenthal, *New Myth, New World: From Nietzsche to Stalinism* (University Park, PA, 2002); Christopher Forth, *Zarathustra in Paris: The Nietzsche Vogue in France 1891–1918* (DeKalb, IL, 2001); or Dan Stone,

Breeding Superman: Nietzsche, Race and Eugenics in Edwardian and Interwar Britain (Liverpool, 2002).

A book that places Freud firmly in the intellectual context of his time is the dense work of Frank Sulloway, *Freud, Biologist of the Mind: Beyond the Psychoanalytic Legend* (New York, 1979). Peter Gay, *Freud: A Life for Our Time* (New York, 1988) is a detailed, if very Freudian, biography. Frederick Crews (ed.), *Unauthorized Freud: Doubters Confront a Legend* (New York, 1988) is a handy introduction to the literature critical of Freud's theories and his therapies. Eli Zaretsky, *Secrets of the Soul: A Social and Cultural History of Psychoanalysis* (New York, 2004) attempts to connect the development of psychoanalysis with broader social and cultural developments.

Two books containing insightful discussions of artistic trends across the boundaries of different art forms are Linda Nochlin, *Realism* (Harmondsworth, 1971) and especially Christopher Butler, *Early Modernism: Literature, Music and Painting in Europe, 1900–1916* (Oxford, 1994). F. W. J. Hemmings (ed.), *The Age of Realism* (Hassocks, 1978) is a good introduction to realist literature in continental Europe. Gail Marshall, *Victorian Fiction* (London, 2002) offers a similar, although briefer and more focused, overview of English-language literature in the realist era. Realist writers seem particularly susceptible to the genre of the literary biography, in which biographers attempt to trace, generally at considerable length, connections between their subjects' lives and works. Examples would include Enid Starkie, *Flaubert*, 2 vols (New York, 1967–71); Joseph Frank, *Dostoevsky*, 6 vols (Princeton, NJ, 1976–2002); or Fred Kaplan, *Dickens: A Biography* (New York, 1988). On literary naturalism, Lilian Furst and Peter Skrine, *Naturalism* (London, 1971) is a handy short introduction; David Baguely, *Naturalist Fiction: The Entropic Vision* (Cambridge, 1990) is a more detailed and sophisticated work of literary criticism. Three studies of naturalist authors are William J. Berg and Laurey K. Martin, *Emile Zola Revisited* (New York, 1992); David Thomas, *Henrik Ibsen* (London, 1983); and Margery Morgan, *August Strindberg* (Basingstoke, 1985). Peter Nicholls, *Modernisms* (Berkeley, CA, 1995) is an introduction to literary modernism. Just as was the case with the great realist authors, literary biographies are one way to approach the modernists. Examples include Sander Gilman, *Frank Kafka* (London, 2005); Richard Ellmann, *James Joyce*, 2nd edn (New York, 1982); William C. Carter, *Marcel Proust* (New Haven, CT, 2000); or Donald Prater, *Thomas Mann: A Life* (Oxford, 1995).

Gerald Needham, *19th Century Realist Art* (New York, 1988) offers an overview of realism in painting, drawing and sculpture. Among the many art history monographs of the age of realism, I would mention just two: Patricia Mainardi, *Art and Politics of the Second Empire: The Universal Expositions of 1855 and 1867* (New Haven, CT, 1987) and James J. Sheehan, *Museums in the German Art World* (Oxford, 2000), which has, among its many other virtues, a number of interesting insights into the development of architecture. Two very helpful recent general histories of impressionism, with useful bibliographies, are James H. Rubin, *Impressionism* (London, 1999) and John House, *Impressionism: Paint and Politics* (New Haven, CT, 2004). Philip Nord, *Impressionists and Politics: Art and Democracy in the Nineteenth Century* (London, 2000) provides a political and social context of impressionist art.

The literature on artistic modernism is extremely extensive. Charles Harrison, Francis Frascina and Gill Perry, *Primitivism, Cubism, Abstraction: The Early Twentieth Century* (New Haven, CT, 1993) is an introduction to painting in this period. Two more specialized works are Belinda Thomson, *Post-Impressionism* (Cambridge, 1998); and Marit Werenskold, *The Concept of Expressionism: Origin and Metamorphoses*, trans. Ronald Walford (Oslo, 1984). From the enormous universe of writings about Picasso, two dealing with this period are Christine Poggi, *In Defiance of Painting: Cubism, Futurism and the Invention of Collage* (New Haven, CT, 1992) and Natasha Staller, *A Sum of Destructions: Picasso's Cultures and the Creation of Cubism* (New Haven, CT, 2001). The impact and reception of modernist painting is discussed by Jeffrey Weiss, *The Popular Culture of Modern Art: Picasso, Duchamp and Avant Gardism* (New Haven, CT, 1994) and Peter Paret, *The Berlin Secession: Modernism and its Enemies in Imperial Germany* (Cambridge, MA, 1980).

For the development of music, Jim Samson (ed.), *The Cambridge History of Nineteenth-Century Music* (Cambridge, 2002) is very erudite, with excellent bibliographies, but Carl Dahlhaus, *Nineteenth Century Music*, trans. J. Bradford Robinson (Berkeley, CA, 1989) offers a more sustained and comprehensive interpretation. Two good studies of romanticism in music are Arnold Whittall, *Romantic Music: A Concise History from Schubert to Sibelius* (London, 1987) and Leon Plantinga, *Romantic Music: A History of Musical Style in Nineteenth-Century Europe* (New York, 1984). On changes and continuities in late nineteenth century music, see Carl Dahlhaus, *Between Romanticism and Modernism: Four Studies in the Music of the Late Nineteenth Century*, trans. Mary Whittall (Berkeley, CA, 1980). A general work on modernist and atonal music is Paul Griffiths, *Modern Music: A Concise History*, 2nd edn (New York, 1984). For composers' biographies, a common way to write the history of music, see Joachim Köhler, *Richard Wagner: The Last of the Titans*, trans. Stewart Spencer (New Haven, CT, 2004); Jan Swafford, *Johannes Brahms: A Biography* (New York, 1997); Bryan Gilliam, *The Life of Richard Strauss* (Cambridge, 1999); and Dika Newlin, *Bruckner, Mahler, Schoenberg*, 2nd edn (New York, 1978).

READINGS ON THE POLITICS OF THE PEOPLE

On the classic reform movements of the 1860s, the student can consult Bruce Lincoln, *The Great Reforms: Autocracy, Bureaucracy and the Politics of Change in Imperial Russia* (DeKalb, IL, 1990); Ben Eklof, John Bushnell and Lariss Zakhavora (eds), *Russia's Great Reforms, 1855–1881* (Bloomington, IN, 1994); and Catherine Hall, Keith McClelland and Jane Rendall, *Defining the Victorian Nation: Class, Race, Gender and the Reform Act of 1867* (Cambridge, 2000), this last a good introduction with a detailed bibliography, but also a controversial interpretation. For a broader overview of the removal of religious disabilities, an important feature of reforms, see Rainer Liedtke and Stephan Wendehorst (eds), *The Emancipation of Catholics, Jews and Protestants: Minorities and the Nation State in Nineteenth Century Europe* (Manchester, 1999).

K. Theodore Hoppen, *Elections, Politics and Society in Ireland 1832–1885* (Oxford, 1984) is an excellent account of political life in Ireland and Great Britain in an age of notables' politics. Other useful works on UK politics in this period of liberal dominance and notables' politics include Jonathan Parry, *The Rise and Fall of Liberal Government in Victorian Britain* (New Haven, CT, 1993) and Miles Taylor, *The Decline of British Radicalism, 1847–1860* (Oxford, 1995). For notables' politics and the Bonapartist regime in France, there are two excellent books by Roger Price, *The French Second Empire: An Anatomy of Political* Power (Cambridge, 2001) and *People and Politics in France 1848–1870* (Cambridge, 2004). Louis Napoleon Bonaparte himself is the subject of the journalist John Bierman's *Napoleon III and His Carnival Empire* (New York, 1988) – delightfully written, very acerbic and quite hostile.

In central and southern Europe, where issues of nationalism, national identity and national unity were central, some useful books include, for Germany, Abigail Green, *Fatherlands: State-Building and Nationhood in Nineteenth Century Germany* (Cambridge, 2001) or Thedore Hamerow, *The Social Foundations of German Unification 1858–1871*, 2 vols (Princeton, NJ, 1969–72), an admittedly rather outdated work, but containing a wealth of information. For the Italian peninsula, see Raymond Grew, *A Sterner Plan for Italian Unity: The Italian National Society in the Risorgimento* (Princeton, NJ, 1963) or Roland Sarti, *Mazzini: A Life for the Religion of Politics* (Westport, CT, 1997). On the Habsburg Monarchy, there is Peter Judson, *Exclusive Revolutionaries: Liberal Politics, Social Experience, and National Identity in the Austrian Empire, 1848–1914* (Ann Arbor, MI, 1996); Keely Stauter-Halsted, *The Nation in the Village: The Genesis of Peasant National Identity in Austrian Poland, 1848–1914* (Ithaca, NY, 2001); or Jeremy King, *Budweisers into Czechs and Germans: A Local History of Bohemian Politics, 1848–1948* (Princeton, NJ, 2002).

One important feature of political life in the late nineteenth century was the rise of a radical right. Carl Schorske, 'Politics in a New Key: An Austrian Trio', in his *Fin-de-Siècle Vienna* (New York, 1980) is a classic essay. Monographic studies would include William D. Irvine, *The Boulanger Affair Reconsidered: Royalism, Boulangism and the Origins of the Radical Right in France* (New York, 1989); John Boyer, *Political Radicalism in Late Imperial Vienna: Origins of the Christian Social Movement* (Chicago, 1981); or Richard Levy, *The Downfall of the Anti-Semitic Political Parties in Imperial Germany* (New Haven, CT, 1975).

Complementing this rise was the development of racism and anti-Semitism. Two histories of racism, neither entirely satisfactory, are George Mosse, *Toward the Final Solution: A History of European Racism* (Madison, WI, 1985) and Neil McMaster, *Racism in Europe: 1870–2000* (Basingstoke, 2001). Albert Lindemann, *Esau's Tears: Modern Anti-Semitism and the Rise of the Jews* (Cambridge, 1997) is a – very controversial – general history of anti-Semitism. For a very different perspective, see Jacob Katz, *From Prejudice to Destruction: Anti-Semitism, 1700–1933* (Cambridge, MA, 1980). A biography of the man who coined the term is Moshe Zimmermann, *Wilhelm Marr, the Patriarch of Antisemitism* (New York, 1986). Some good monographic studies of anti-Semitism (often better than general histories) include Helmut Walser Smith, *The Butcher's Tale: Murder and Anti-Semitism in a German Town* (New York, 2002); John Klier and Shlomo Lambroza (eds), *Pogroms: Anti-Jewish Violence in Modern Russian History* (Cambridge, 1992); William Oldson, *A Providential Anti-Semitism: Nationalism and Polity in Nineteenth-*

Century Romania (Philadelphia, 1991); and Barnet Hartston, *Sensationalizing the Jewish Question: Anti-Semitic Trials and the Press in the Early German Empire* (Leiden, 2005). Brian Porter, *When Nationalism Began to Hate: Imagining Modern Politics in Nineteenth Century Poland* (New York, 2000) discusses the intersection of nationalism and racism. Andrew Whiteside, *The Socialism of Fools: Georg Ritter von Schönerer and Austrian Pan-Germanism* (Berkeley, CA, 1975) is good on radical nationalism and anti-Semitism; David Vital, *Zionism: The Formative Years* (Oxford, 1982) discusses Jewish nationalist reactions to the rise of intolerant nationalism.

Margaret Anderson, *Practicing Democracy: Elections and Political Culture in Imperial Germany* (Princeton, NJ, 2000) is very helpful on the development of mass politics, with good cross-national comparisons. Other works on this topic include Jon Lawrence, *Speaking for the People: Party, Language and Popular Politics in England, 1867–1914* (Cambridge, 1998); Terence Emmons, *The Formation of Political Parties and the First National Elections in Russia* (Cambridge, MA, 1983); or José Alvarez-Junco, *The Emergence of Mass Politics in Spain* (Brighton, 2002). Leopold Haimson and Charles Tilly (eds), *Strikes, Wars, and Revolutions in an International Perspective: Strike Waves in the Late Nineteenth and Early Twentieth Centuries* (Cambridge, 1989) discusses the post-1900 rise in labour militancy. On the leagues and right-wing mass politics, there is Eugen Weber, *Action française: Royalism and Reaction in Twentieth-Century France* (Stanford, CA, 1962); Geoff Eley, *Reshaping the German Right: Radical Nationalism and Political Change after Bismarck*, 2nd edn (Ann Arbor, MI, 1991) and Martin Pugh, *The Tories and the People 1880–1935* (Oxford, 1985). On the mass politics of the women's suffrage movement in Great Britain, Harold L. Smith, *The British Women's Suffrage Campaign, 1866–1928* (London, 1998) is a simple introduction. Detailed studies include Susan Kent, *Sex and Suffrage in Britain, 1860–1914* (Princeton, NJ, 1987); Laura Mayhall, *The Militant Suffrage Movement: Citizenship and Resistance in Britain, 1886–1930* (Oxford, 2003); and Elizabeth Crawford, *The Women's Suffrage Movement in Britain and Ireland: A Regional Survey* (London, 2006). The older work of Richard Evans, *The Feminists: Women's Emancipation Movements in Europe, America and Australasia 1840–1920* (London, 1977) is still useful for purposes of comparison.

Works dealing with some of the major political issues in pre-1914 Europe would include Paul Miller, *From Revolutionaries to Citizens: Antimilitarism in France, 1870–1914* (Durham, NC, 2002); Robert Stuart, *Marxism and National Identity: Socialism, Nationalism and National Socialism during the French fin de siècle* (Albany, NY, 2006); Kevin Repp, *Reformers, Critics and the Paths of German Modernity: Anti-Politics and the Search for Alternatives* (Cambridge, MA, 2000); Bruce K. Murray, *The People's Budget 1909/10: Lloyd George and Liberal Politics* (Oxford, 1980); Douglas Forsyth, *The Crisis of Liberal Italy: Monetary and Financial Policy 1914–1922* (Cambridge 1993), which, in spite of its title, has good observations on pre-1914 developments.

On mid-nineteenth century liberalism, some helpful works are Dieter Langewiesche, *Liberalism in Germany*, trans. Christiane Banerji (Princeton, NJ, 2000); Sudhir Hazareesingh, *Intellectual Founders of the Republic: Five Studies in Nineteenth-Century French Republican Political Thought* (Oxford, 2000); William Stafford, *John Stuart Mill* (Basingstoke and New York, 1998); and Eugenio Biagini, *Liberty, Retrenchment and*

Reform: Popular Politics in the Age of Gladstone 1860–1880 (Cambridge, 1992). Philip Nord, *The Republican Moment: Struggles for Democracy in Nineteenth-Century France* (Cambridge, MA, 1995); Mark Curthoys, *Governments, Labour, and the Law in Mid-Victorian Britain: The Trade Union Legislation of the 1870s* (Oxford, 2004); Susan A. Ashley, *Making Liberalism Work: The Italian Experience, 1860–1914* (Westport, CT, 2003) focus on liberalism in the final third of the nineteenth century. Biographies of major liberal figures of the period include Christopher Duggan, *Francesco Crispi 1818–1901: From Nation to Nationalism* (Oxford, 2002) and Eugenio Biagini, *Gladstone* (New York, 2000). On early twentieth-century liberal rethinking and the new liberalism, see Patricia Lynch, *The Liberal Party in Rural England 1885–1910* (Oxford, 2003); Duncan Tanner, *Political Change and the Labour Party 1900–1918* (Cambridge, 1990), which, in spite of its title, is extremely informative on the new liberalism as well as on the Labour Party; Alexander De Grand, *The Hunchback's Tailor: Giovanni Giolitti and Liberal Italy* (Westport, CT, 2001); and Alastair Thompson, *Left Liberals, the State and Popular Politics in Wilhelmine Germany* (Oxford, 2000).

For post-1850 radicalism, Margot Finn, *After Chartism: Class and Nation in English Radical Politics, 1848–1874* (Cambridge, 1993) is unusually helpful for the broader European context. See also Clara Lovett, *The Democratic Movement in Italy, 1830–1876* (Cambridge, MA, 1982) and Adam Ulam, *Prophets and Conspirators in Revolutionary Russia* (New Brunswick, NJ, 1998). The most recent international history of socialism, very good on developments of the late nineteenth century, is Geoff Eley, *Forging Democracy: The History of the Left in Europe, 1850–2000* (Oxford, 2002). James Joll, *The Second International 1889–1914* (New York, 1966) is older but insightful. A few monographic studies of socialism during the belle époque are Mary Nolan, *Social Democracy and Society: Working-Class Radicalism in Düsseldorf, 1890–1920* (Cambridge, 1981); Madeleine Hurd, *Public Spheres, Public Mores and Democracy: Hamburg and Stockholm* (Ann Arbor, MI, 2000); and Robert Stuart, *Marxism at Work: Ideology, Class and French Socialism during the Third Republic* (Cambridge, 1992). Three very helpful biographies of socialist leaders are Harvey Goldberg, *The Life of Jean Jaurès* (Madison, WI, 1962); Manfred Steger, *The Question for Evolutionary Socialism: Eduard Bernstein and Social Democracy* (Cambridge, 1997); and J. P. Nettl, *Rosa Luxemburg*, 2 vols (Oxford, 1966). A couple of works on anarchism and syndicalism are Kenneth H. Tucker, *French Revolutionary Syndicalism and the Public Sphere* (New York, 1996) and Temma Kaplan, *Anarchists of Andalusia 1868–1903* (Princeton, NJ, 1977).

On the intellectual universe of conservatives in the age of progress are Dmitry Shlapentokh, *The French Revolution in Russian Intellectual Life* (Westport, CT, 1996) and Steven D. Kale, *Legitimism and the Reconstruction of French Society 1852–1883* (Baton Rouge, FL, 1992). Two fine short biographies of innovative conservative politicians, both with extensive bibliographies, are Paul Smith, *Disraeli: A Brief Life* (Cambridge, 1996) and Katharine Anne Lerman, *Bismarck* (Harlow, 2004). On the late nineteenth century conservative resurgence, see Michael Bentley, *Lord Salisbury's World: Conservative Environments in Late-Victorian Britain* (Cambridge, 2001); Richard Shannon, *The Age of Salisbury, 1881–1902: Unionism and Empire* (London, 1996); William Jenks, *Austria under the Iron Ring 1879–1893* (Charlottesville, VA, 1965); and Heide Whelan, *Alexander III and the State Council: Bureaucracy and Counter-Reform in Late Imperial Russia* (New Brunswick, NJ, 1982). For the political and intellectual world of conservatism in the early twentieth century, see E. H. H. Green, *The Crisis of Conservatism: The Politics, Economics and Ideology of the British Conservative Party, 1880–1914* (London, 1995); John Boyer, *Culture and Political Crisis in Vienna: Christian Socialism in Power* (Chicago, 1995); and James Retallack, *Notables of the Right: The Conservative Party and Political Mobilization in Germany 1876–1918* (Boston, 1988). Brigitte Hamann, *Hitler's Vienna: A Dictator's Apprenticeship*, trans. Thomas Thornton (Oxford, 1999) is a superb introduction to proto-fascist tendencies in pre-1914 right-wing politics.

Frank J. Coppa's biographies of Pius IX, *Pope Pius IX, Crusader in a Secular Age* (Boston, 1979) and of his right-hand man, *Cardinal Giacomo Antonelli and Papal Politics in European Affairs* (Albany, NY, 1990) are good introductions to leading figures of ultramontanism. Jonathan Sperber, *Popular Catholicism in Nineteenth Century Germany* (Princeton, NJ, 1984) shows the more positive features of ultramontanism; David Kertzer, *The Kidnapping of Edgardo Mortara* (New York, 1997) reveals its less appealing side. A general history of Catholic political parties is Ellen L. Evans, *The Cross and the Ballot: Catholic Political Parties in Germany, Switzerland, Austria, Belgium and the Netherlands 1785–1985* (Boston, 1999); a wonderful and very insightful biography of one of Germany's and Europe's leading Catholic politicians is Margaret Anderson, *Windthorst: A Political Biography* (Oxford, 1981). Emmet Larkin, *The Roman Catholic Church and the Emergence of the Modern Irish Political System, 1874–1878* (Washington, DC, 1996), discusses the relationship of the church to Irish nationalist politics.

READINGS ON THE POLITICS OF THE POWERS

F. R. Bridge and Rogert Bullen, *The Great Powers and the European States System 1814–1914*, 2nd edn (Harlow, 2005) is a good introduction to nineteenth-century diplomatic history. The book's bibliography is particularly helpful for the very extensive older (say pre-1970) literature. William Echard, *Napoleon III and the Concert of Europe* (Baton Rouge, FL, 1983) offers an introduction to the complex world of the emperor's diplomatic and military planning. Paul W. Schroeder, *Austria, Great Britain and the Crimean War: The Destruction of the European Concert* (Ithaca, NY, 1972) makes the argument for the Crimean War as a revolution in diplomacy. On the international aspects of German unification, see Werner E. Mosse, *The European Powers and the German Question, 1848–71*, 2nd edn (New York, 1969) and William Carr, *The Origins of the Wars of German Unification* (London, 1991). On the trans-Atlantic aspects of European diplomacy in the 1850s and 1860s, see Michel Cunningham, *Mexico and the Foreign Policy of Napoleon III* (New York, 2001); Dean Mahin, *One War at a Time: The International Dimension of the American Civil War* (Washington, DC, 1999) and Norman Saul, *Distant Friends: The United States and Russia, 1763–1867* (Lawrence, KS, 1990). On changes in warfare, Arden Bucholz, *Moltke, Schlieffen and Prussian War Planning* (New York, 1991);

Dennis E. Showalter, *Railroads and Rifles: Soldiers, Technology and the Unification of Germany* (Hamden, CT, 1975) and, especially, Geoffrey Wawro, *The Austro-Prussian War: Austria's War with Prussia and Italy in 1866* (Cambridge, 1996), which is much more widely informative than its title indicates. English translations of some of Moltke's military writing can be found online at http://germanhistorydocs.ghidc.org/sub_doclist.cfm?sub_id=18&section_id=9.

The development of the post-1871 alliance system is best approached through the biographies of its architect, Otto von Bismarck, as mentioned in the bibliography to the previous section. On the background to the Eastern Question, the student might consult Martin Sicker, *The Islamic World in Decline: From the Treaty of Karlowitz to the Disintegration of the Ottoman Empire* (Westport, CT, 2001) and Barbara Jelavich, *Russia's Balkan Entanglements, 1806–1914* (Cambridge, 1991). Dealing with the Eastern Crisis of the 1870s are Frederick Kellogg, *The Road to Romanian Independence* (West Lafayette, IN, 1995) and Béla K. Király and Gale Stokes (eds), *Insurrections, Wars and the Eastern Crisis in the 1870s* (Boulder, CO, 1985). For the post-1900 escalation of the Eastern Question, see Richard C. Hall, *The Balkan Wars 1912–1913: Prelude to the First World War* (London, 2000); Béla K. Király and Dimitrije Djordjevic (eds), *Eastern Central European Society and the Balkan Wars* (New York, 1987) (some of the essays in this book can only be described as nationalist propaganda); and Duncan Perry, *The Politics of Terror: The Macedonian Liberation Movements, 1893–1903* (Durham, NC, 1988).

A good introduction to the history of the imperial ventures of all the European powers, also containing a helpful bibliography, is H. L. Wesseling, *The European Colonial Empires 1815–1919*, trans. Diane Webb (Harlow, 2004). For the British Empire, Bernard Porter, *The Lion's Share: A Short History of British Imperialism 1850–1995*, 3rd edn (London, 1996) is a handy introduction. P. J. Cain and A. G. Hopkins, *British Imperialism: Innovation and Expansion 1688–1914* (London, 1993) explores the empire's economics; Robert Johnson, *British Imperialism* (Basingstoke, 2003) provides an excellent discussion of the historiographical controversies about it. Histories of other colonial empires include Robert Aldrich, *Greater France: A History of French Overseas Expansion* (New York, 1996) and Woodruff Smith, *The German Colonial Empire* (Chapel Hill, NC, 1978).

For a discussion of the profitability, or lack of it, in the imperial enterprise, see Lance Davis and Robert Huttenback, *Mammon and the Pursuit of Empire: The Political Economy of British Imperialism, 1860–1912* (Cambridge, 1986); a recent account of Lenin's ideas about imperialism and their connection with other Marxist theorists is Anthony Brewer, *Marxist Theories of Imperialism: A Critical Survey*, 2nd edn (London, 1990). Adam Hochschild, *King Leopold's Ghost: A Story of Greed, Terror and Heroism in Colonial Africa* (New York, 1998) is a truly horrifying account of European colonial rule at its most nightmarish. For a recent example of the apologetic historiography of colonialism, see Barnett Singer and John Langdon, *Cultured Force: Makers and Defenders of the French Colonial Empire* (Madison, WI, 2004). Bernard Porter, *The Absent-Minded Imperialists: Empire, Society and Culture in Britain* (Oxford, 2004) is an excellent, refreshingly critical, consideration of the ideological contexts of imperialism. Two works on women, gender ideals and imperialism are Antoinette Burton, *Burdens of History: British Feminists, Indian Women and*

Imperial Culture, 1865–1915 (Chapel Hill, NC, 1994) and Lora Wildenthal, *German Women for Empire, 1884–1945* (Durham, NC, 2001).

The challenges to European imperialism around 1900 are discussed in Paul Cohen, *History in Three Keys: The Boxers as Event, Experience and Myth* (New York, 1997); Dennis Judd and Keith Surridge, *The Boer War* (Basingstoke, 2002); Keith Wilson, *The International Impact of the Boer War* (Chesham, 2001); Joseph Smith, *The Spanish–American War: Conflict in the Caribbean and the Pacific 1895–1902* (London, 1994); John W. Steinberg and David Wolff (eds), *The Russo-Japanese War in Global Perspective: World War Zero*, 2 vols (Leiden, 2005–07). Jonathan Schneer, *London 1900: The Imperial Metropolis* (New Haven, CT, 1999) is a fascinating study of imperialism at its high point and the origins of an anti-imperialist movement.

For post-1890 diplomatic realignments, the student can consult Aaron Friedberg, *The Weary Titan: Britain and the Experience of Relative Decline, 1895–1905* (Princeton, NJ, 1988); Paul Kennedy, *The Rise of the Anglo-German Antagonism 1860–1914* (London, 1980); Jonathan Steinberg, *Yesterday's Deterrent: Tirpitz and the Birth of the German Battle Fleet* (London, 1965); and Volker Berghahn, *Germany and the Approach of War in 1914* (London, 1973), as well as two books by the celebrated American diplomat George Kennan: *The Decline of Bismarck's European Order: Franco-Russian Relations, 1875*–1890 (Princeton, NJ, 1979) and *The Fateful Alliance: France, Russia and the Coming of the First World War* (New York, 1984).

On the arms races, David G. Hermann, *The Arming of Europe and the Making of the First World War* (Princeton, NJ, 1996) and David Stevenson, *Armaments and the Coming of War: Europe, 1904–1914* (Oxford, 1996) are both essential. A very good recent study of German military planning is in the biography of one of its chief protagonists, Annika Mombauer, *Helmuth von Moltke and the Origins of the First World War* (Cambridge, 2001). For a discussion of recent debates about the Schlieffen Plan, Robert T. Foley, 'The Real Schlieffen Plan', *War in History*, 13 (2006): 91–115 is to be recommended.

READINGS ON THE DYNAMICS OF POWER

On political repression in the era of reaction, Howard Payne *The Police State of Louis Napoléon Bonaparte 1851–1860* (Seattle, 1966) is informative; more generally, see Robert J. Goldstein, *Political Repression in 19th Century Europe* (London, 1983). The intersection of politics and economic development during the era of reaction is discussed by James M. Brophy, *Capitalism Politics and Railroads in Prussia 1830–1870* (Columbus, OH, 1998).

On the events of 1859–61 and the unification of Italy, see Dennis Mack Smith, *Cavour* (London, 1985) and idem, *Cavour and Garibaldi in 1860: A Study in Political Conflict* 2nd edn (Cambridge, 1985); or Lucy Riall, *Sicily and the Unification of Italy: Liberal Policy and Local Power, 1859–1866* (Oxford, 1998). R. F. Leslie, *Reform and Insurrection in Russian Poland 1856–1865* (London, 1963) is an older but very helpful work on the origins and course of the Polish uprising of 1863.

On German nationalism and movement towards German unification John Breuilly, *Austria, Prussia and Germany, 1806–1871* (London, 2002) is a good introduction. Besides the works of Dieter Langewiesche, Theodore Hamerow, Katherine Lerman and Abigail Green, noted in the readings on the politics of the people above, see also Nicholas Hope, *The Alternative to German Unification; The Anti-Prussian Party: Frankfurt, Nassau, and the Two Hessen, 1859–1867* (Wiesbaden, 1973) or George Windell, *The Catholics and German Unity, 1866–1871* (Minneapolis, MN, 1954).

Geoffrey Wawro's excellent book on the Austro-Prussian war of 1866 is noted in the bibliography on the politics of the powers above; his *The Franco-Prussian War: The German Conquest of France in 1870–1871* (Cambridge, 2003) is every bit as good. A recent work on the origins of the Franco-Prussian War is David Wetzel, *A Duel of Giants: Bismarck, Napoleon III, and the Origins of the Franco-Prussian War* (Madison, WI, 2001). Robert Tombs, *The Paris Commune, 1871* (New York, 1999) is a good, up-to-date introduction to the voluminous literature on the Paris Commune.

For the *Kulturkampf*, see Ronald J. Ross, *The Failure of Bismarck's Kulturkampf: Catholicism and State Power in Imperial Germany, 1871–1887* (Washington, DC, 1998). Good on the regime of moral order in France and its end is Robert R. Locke, *French Legitimists and the Politics of Moral Order in the Early Third Republic* (Princeton, NJ, 1974). On the development of populism and terrorism in Russia, besides the work of Adam Ulam, cited in the bibliography to the politics of the people above, see Deborah Hardy, *Land and Freedom: The Origins of Russian Terrorism, 1876–1879* (Westport, CT, 1987) and Derek Offord, *The Russian Revolutionary Movement in the 1880s* (Cambridge, 1986). Alan O'Day, *Irish Home Rule 1867–1921* (Manchester, 1998) is helpful on the demand for home rule and its place in British politics. On the Irish nationalist leader Charles Stewart Parnell, the essays in D. George Boyce and Alan O'Day (eds), *Parnell in Perspective* (London, 1991) offer some interesting comparisons between nationalist movements in Ireland and in continental Europe. On the diplomacy of the 1880s and early 1890s, and its domestic political connections, see Muriel Chamberlain, *The Scramble for Africa*, 2nd edn (London, 1999); Martin Swartz, *The Politics of British Foreign Policy in the Era of Disraeli and Gladstone* (New York, 1985); or Gerald Morgan, *Anglo-Russian Rivalry in Central Asia 1810–1895* (London, 1981).

Barbara Tuchman's *The Proud Tower: A Portrait of the World before the War, 1890–1914* (New York, 1966) is a wonderful portrait of the belle époque, heartily to be recommended. On domestic politics in the 1890s, John C. G. Röhl, *Germany without Bismarck: The Crisis of Government in the Second Reich, 1890–1900* (Berkeley, CA, 1967) or Pierre Birnbaum, *The Anti-Semitic Moment: A Tour of France in 1898*, trans. Jane Todd (New York, 2003) are possibilities. A useful introduction to the Dreyfus Affair and its consequences is Martin Johnson, *The Dreyfus Affair: Honour and Politics in the Belle Époque* (New York, 1999). On the Russian Revolution Abraham Ascher, *The Revolution of 1905*, 2 vols (Stanford, CA, 1988–92) is very substantial; important aspects of it are discussed by John Bushnell, *Mutiny Amid Repression: Russian Soldiers in the Revolution of 1905–1906* (Bloomington, IN, 1985) and Robert Blobaum, *Revolucja: Russian Poland, 1904–1907* (Ithaca,

NY, 1995). Upheavals in the UK are the subject of David Powell, *The Edwardian Crisis: Britain 1901–14* (Basingstoke, 1996).

On pre-1914 reformers and their opponents, some helpful works are Abraham Ascher, *P.A. Stolypin: The Search for Stability in Late Imperial Russia* (Stanford, CA, 2001); Ian Packer, *Liberal Government and Politics 1905–15* (Basingstoke, 2006); Katharine Anne Lerman, *The Chancellor as Courtier: Bernhard von Bülow and the Governance of Germany, 1900–1909* (Cambridge, 1990); Gary Cohen, 'Nationalist Politics and the Dynamics of State and Civil Society in the Habsburg Monarchy, 1867–1914', *Central European History*, 40 (2007): 241–78; Gerd Krumeich, *Armaments and Politics in France on the Eve of the First World War*, trans. Stephen Conn (Leamington Spa, 1984); Edward Berenson, *The Trial of Madame Caillaux* (Berkeley, CA, 1992); and Neal Blewett, *The Peers, the Parties and the People: The General Elections of 1910* (Toronto, 1972). Even if academic historians no longer agree with its main points, George Dangerfield, *The Strange Death of Liberal England* (London, 1935, but frequently reprinted since) remains a delightful and eminently readable evocation of an epoch.

For discussions of pre-1914 diplomatic crises, besides the works cited above in the bibliography to the politics of the powers, see Geoffrey Barraclough, *From Agadir to Armageddon: Anatomy of a Crisis* (London, 1982) and David Macfie, *The End of the Ottoman Empire* (London, 1998). *The Other Balkan Wars: A 1913 Carnegie Endowment Inquiry in Retrospect with a New Introduction . . . by George F. Kennan* (Washington, DC, 1993), is a reprint of the original report on ethnic cleansing during the Balkan Wars, and remains fascinating and deeply depressing reading today.

On the origins of the First World War, there are the individual country studies, Samuel Williamson, Jr, *Austria-Hungary and the Origins of the First World War* (New York, 1991); Mark Hewitson, *Germany and the Causes of the First World War* (Oxford, 2004). John Keiger, *France and the Origins of the First World War* (New York, 1983); and D. C. B. Lieven, *Russia and the Origins of the First World War* (New York, 1983). More generally, see Richard Hamilton and Holger Herwig (eds), *The Origins of World War I* (Cambridge, 2003). Historians' controversies are discussed by Annika Mombauer, *The Origins of the First World War: Controversies and Consensus* (New York, 2002). Two recent interpretations, both one-sided, if in different directions, are David Fromkin, *Europe's Last Summer: Who Started the Great War in 1914?* (New York, 2004) and Niall Ferguson, *The Pity of War* (New York, 1999). Recent research on public opinion in July and August of 1914 can be found in Jean-Jacques Becker, *The Great War and the French People*, trans. Arnold Pomerans (Dover, NH, 1993) or Jeffrey Verhey, *The Spirit of 1914: Myth, Militarism and Mobilization in Germany* (Cambridge, 2000).

INDEX

Great Powers (*continued*)
  diplomacy of, xiv, xvi, 5, 64, 75–6, 80, 84, 86–9, 106, 118, 119–20, 172, 180, 183, 185, 193, 199–200, 202, 211, 222, 303, 316–17, 320, 326, 334, 356–7
  financial conditions of, 286–7, 313
  hegemony among, 58, 63, 81, 103, 110, 117, 308, 359
  imperialist efforts of, 75–6, 119, 180, 187–9, 302, 306, 316, 320, 357
  non-European powers and, xvi, 304–8, 356, 361
  realignment of, 194, 212, 219–20, 302, 307–9, 311, 315, 317
  warfare of, xiv, xvi, 4, 6, 7, 8, 65, 75, 77–80, 86, 110, 118, 165, 182, 187, 193, 212, 222, 302, 304, 311–12, 314–15, 336, 340, 359
Great Reform Act (UK), 61
Great Reforms (Russia), 58–9, 117, 202, 206, 318
Greece, 183, 223, 232, 239, 306, 336, 337
guilds, 351
  abolition or limitation of, 3, 7, 28, 58–9, 70, 115
  restoration of, 118, 132, 170, 172, 173, 207
Gutehoffnunsgshüte, 125

Haber, Fritz, 266
Habsburg monarchy
  agriculture in, 236
  creation of Austria–Hungary, 8, 102, 116
  cultural, intellectual and religious conditions in, 117, 144, 178, 189, 292, 325
  government policies of, 69, 82–83, 206, 296
  manufacturing in, 11
  nationalist movements in, 8, 64, 172, 184–5, 222–4, 283–4, 306, 314, 334–7, 339
  political conditions in, 5, 59, 62, 66, 96–7, 103–4, 174–6, 202, 206, 208, 219, 222, 281, 284, 290–1, 293, 295–8, 315, 319, 322, 326–7, 332–3, 360
  reform movements in, 7, 58–9, 103, 110, 288
  social and economic conditions in, 28, 34, 38, 121–2, 130, 132, 134, 137, 139, 140, 239, 255
  warfare and diplomacy of, 6, 8, 72, 76–8, 80, 86, 88–9, 100–1, 103, 106, 117, 119–20, 170, 181–4, 197, 200, 202, 211, 220, 223–4, 302, 306–7, 311, 313–14, 329, 334–7, 339, 340–2
Haeckel, Ernst, 47
Hanover, 101, 103, 253, 256
Hauptmann, Gerhart, 161–2
Haussmann, Baron, 4, 109, 350
Haussmann, Georges, 25–7, 136
Helmholtz, Hermann von, 42
Henkel, Fritz, 227
Herero tribe, 191–2
Hertz, Heinrich, 149
Hessen–Darmstadt, 101
Hessen–Kassel, 101
Hitler, Adolf, 176, 297
Hobson, John Atkinson, 186, 296
Hobson-Lenin thesis, 186, 190
Holstein, 8, 100
Holstein, Friedrich von, 211
Household Words, 4
housing, 3, 19, 26–7, 60, 151, 246–7, 254, 349
Howard, Ebenezer, 254
human sciences, xv, 40, 116
  anthropology, 49, 51, 152–4, 274
  economics, 49, 50, 55, 152, 154–6, 265
  history, 50, 145–6, 152
  philology, 51
  psychoanalysis, 273–4
  rise of, 4, 42, 48, 54
  sociology, 48, 51, 152, 189, 271–2, 274–5, 354